TEACHING SOCIAL and EMOTIONAL LEARNING

in Physical Education

Applications in School and Community Settings

Paul M. Wright, PhD
Professor
Northern Illinois University
Department of Kinesiology and Physical Education
College of Education
DeKalb, Illinois

K. Andrew R. Richards, PhD
Assistant Professor
Department of Kinesiology and Community Health
College of Applied Health Sciences
University of Illinois at Urbana-Champaign
Urbana, Illinois

SHAPE America
SOCIETY OF HEALTH AND PHYSICAL EDUCATORS®

health. moves. minds.

JONES & BARTLETT
LEARNING

World Headquarters
Jones & Bartlett Learning
25 Mall Road, 6th Floor
Burlington, MA 01803
978-443-5000
info@jblearning.com
www.jblearning.com

Jones & Bartlett Learning books and products are available through most bookstores and online booksellers. To contact Jones & Bartlett Learning directly, call 800-832-0034, fax 978-443-8000, or visit our website, www.jblearning.com.

23695-8

Production Credits

Director of Product Management: Cathy Esperti
Product Manager: Whitney Fekete
Content Strategist: Carol Brewer Guerrero
Content Coordinator: Andrew Labelle
Project Manager: Jessica DeMartin
Project Specialist: Erin Bosco
Senior Digital Project Specialist: Angela Dooley
Director of Marketing: Andrea DeFronzo
VP, Manufacturing and Inventory Control: Therese Connell

Composition: Exela Technologies
Project Management: Exela Technologies
Cover Design: Briana Yates
Senior Media Development Editor: Troy Liston
Rights & Permissions Manager: John Rusk
Rights Specialist: James Fortney
Cover Image (Title Page, Section Opener, Chapter Opener):
    © Omelchenko/Shutterstock.
Printing and Binding: McNaughton & Gunn

Library of Congress Cataloging-in-Publication Data

Names: Wright, Paul M. (Professor of kinesiology and physical education), author. | Richards, K. Andrew R., author.

Title: Teaching social and emotional learning in physical education: applications in school and community settings / Paul M. Wright, Ph.D., Professor, Northern Illinois University, Department of Kinesiology and Physical Education, K. Andrew R. Richards, Ph.D., Assistant Professor, Department of Kinesiology and Community Health, College of Applied Health Sciences, University of Illinois at Urbana-Champaign.

Description: First edition. | Burlington, MA : Jones & Bartlett Learning, 2021. | Includes bibliographical references and index.

Identifiers: LCCN 2020058560 | ISBN 9781284205862 (paperback)

Subjects: LCSH: Physical education and training--Study and teaching. | Social learning. | Affective education. | Interdisciplinary approach in education.

Classification: LCC GV363. W75 2021 | DDC 796.071--dc23

LC record available at https://lccn.loc.gov/2020058560

6048

Printed in the United States of America
25 24 23 22 21   10 9 8 7 6 5 4 3 2 1

About SHAPE America

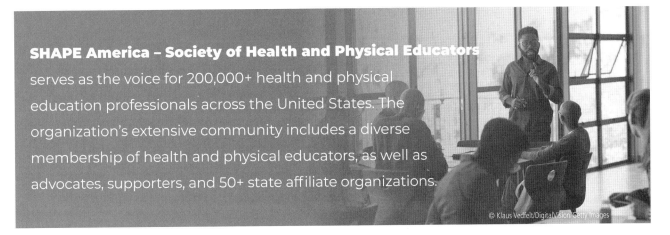

SHAPE America – Society of Health and Physical Educators serves as the voice for 200,000+ health and physical education professionals across the United States. The organization's extensive community includes a diverse membership of health and physical educators, as well as advocates, supporters, and 50+ state affiliate organizations.

© Klaus Vedfelt/DigitalVision/Getty Images

Since its founding in 1885, the organization has defined excellence in physical education. For decades, SHAPE America's National Standards for K-12 Physical Education have served as the foundation for well-designed physical education programs across the country. Additionally, the organization helped develop and owns the National Health Education Standards.

SHAPE America provides programs, resources and advocacy to support health and physical educators at every grade level as they prepare all students to lead a healthy, physically active life. The organization's newest program — health. moves. minds.® — helps teachers and schools incorporate social and emotional learning so students can thrive physically *and* emotionally.

Our Vision

A nation where all children are prepared to lead healthy, physically active lives.

Our Mission

To advance professional practice and promote research related to health and physical education, physical activity, dance and sport.

© FatCamera/E+/Getty Images

To learn more, visit
www.shapeamerica.org

SHAPE America — SOCIETY OF HEALTH AND PHYSICAL EDUCATORS®

Brief Contents

Contents

SECTION 2 **Pedagogical Models Aligned with Social and Emotional Learning in PE**   **61**

CHAPTER 5 **Connecting Skill Themes and Social-Emotional Learning in Elementary Physical Education 62**

CHAPTER 6 **Adventure-Based Learning 94**

CHAPTER 7 **Teaching Personal and Social Responsibility 117**

CHAPTER 8 Sport Education 138

CHAPTER 9 Cooperative Learning 168

SECTION 3 **Social and Emotional Learning in Specialized Programs and Contexts   187**

CHAPTER 10 Social and Emotional Development through Preschool Education 188

CHAPTER 11 Social and Emotional Learning in Adapted Physical Education 205

CHAPTER 12 Integrating Social and Emotional Learning into Whole School Approaches 222

SECTION 4 Case Examples of Social and Emotional Learning with Marginalized Communities 237

CHAPTER 13 Sport-Based Youth Development and its Relationship to the Social and Emotional Development of Youth 238

CHAPTER 14 Social Justice and SEL: Case Examples of Promising Practices 250

SECTION 5 Concluding Thoughts 287

CHAPTER 16 Concluding Thoughts and Future Directions for Social and Emotional Learning in Physical Education .288

Foreword

Wouldn't It Be Nice?

Wouldn't it be nice if all youth came to appreciate the benefits of physical education so that they would be motivated to incorporate various physical fitness and training activities into their daily routine with the possibility that the value and practice of sound physical fitness would stay with them all of their lives? Wouldn't it also be nice if all youth had the opportunity to enjoy different sport activities so they would recognize that sports are not only for those with the best or most competitive skills or talents? Finally, wouldn't it be extra nice if physical and sports education were structured so that in addition to anything youth learned about physical fitness or sports, they were also able to learn some important personal and social skills that were relevant for their current interactions with peers and adults and could enhance their later academic, social, and personal development?

Is this pie in the sky thinking? This text asserts "ABSOLUTELY NOT!" Physical and sports education has changed dramatically over the years and now there is a well-established literature that indicates that all of the above is not only possible, but it is possible for ALL youth regardless of age, physical prowess, gender, race, or ethnicity. This text illustrates how this can happen. There are at least three successful ingredients. First, we need good models for teaching physical and sports skills. These models now exist and can be used in a multitude of settings with a variety of youth. Second, this education needs to be integrated with successful approaches that help youth develop various personal and social skills (sometimes also called life skills, or 21st Century skills). This text emphasizes the integration of physical and sports education with a well-established framework for promoting social and emotional learning (SEL) developed by CASEL (casel.org).

SEL refers to a range of personal and social competencies that promote positive development in youth. These competencies include a wide range of interconnected skills related to accurate self-awareness and social awareness that influence the effective management of attitudes, thoughts, behaviors, and emotions. More specifically, some important SEL skills include the ability to understand and empathize with others, appreciate individual differences, communicate effectively, set and achieve realistic goals, and make good decisions. Other important skills involve conflict resolution skills and creating meaningful and satisfactory relationships with peers and adults.

The third ingredient in effective physical and sports education programs lies in their correct implementation, that is, conducting a program that is integrated with SEL in such a way that youth can profit as much as possible. This not only requires recognizing the key ingredients of the integrated model one is using but also delivering the program as intended. Good implementation also involves assessing accurately how youth are progressing, and determining if, when, or how to adapt the program to fit the target group, setting, and one's instructional goals.

In sum, having a good physical or sports education model, integrating this model with SEL, and implementing a program well can lead to a variety of positive benefits for participating youth. This text presents a lucid and logical game plan for how to achieve these ends. The chapters explain major principles and concepts succinctly and clearly and offer extensive examples and practical suggestions to fit a variety of contexts. Instructors at all levels, whether they are currently in training, just beginning their careers, or are very experienced in their field, will find this text to be invaluable.

Finally, there is still another dimension to applying what this text presents, and that pertains to how physical and sports education teachers or coaches will benefit. As most instructors will tell you, the ultimate joy or satisfaction in teaching comes when you see the fruits of your labors, when something works as planned. Imagine how satisfying it would be if you offered a program to youth that attracted their interest and enjoyment, that motivated them to do their best, that engendered their cooperation instead of their resistance, and that could eventually play a role in not only enhancing their physical development but also their personal, social, and academic development. Most instructors would want to know if such an opportunity exists, and if they read and follow the guidance this text offers, they will have found that opportunity.

—*Joseph A. Durlak*
Professor Emeritus of Psychology
Loyola University Chicago
Chicago, Illinois

Preface

Beginning in the early 1990s, there has been a strong push to broaden the educational agenda in the United States and to integrate social and emotional learning (SEL) competencies into the academic curriculum (Durlack, Weissberg, & Pachan, 2010). More recently, much of this work has been driven by a conceptual framework introduced by the Collaborative for Academic, Social, and Emotional Learning (CASEL; 2019), which defines SEL as "the process through which children and adults understand and manage emotions, set and achieve positive goals, feel and show empathy for others, establish and maintain positive relationships, and make responsible decisions." The CASEL framework for SEL includes five competencies focused on self-awareness, self-management, social awareness, relationship goals, and responsible decision making. Intentional focus on these five competencies is believed to help youth develop skills related to emotional regulation, goal setting, and relationship building, which are essential for success in school, home, and community life (Newman & Dusenbury, 2015).

Informed by the field of positive youth development (e.g., Catalano, Berglund, Ryan, Lonczak, & Hawkins, 2004), teachers and researchers in the field of physical education have a long history of integrating SEL into sport and physical activity (Gordon, Jacobs, & Wright, 2016). A focus on personal and social responsibility has been integrated into the national standards for physical education since their inception (National Association for Sport and Physical Education, 1995), and pedagogical models such as teaching personal and social responsibility (TPSR; Hellison, 2011), sport education (Siedentop, Hastie, & van der Mars, 2004), adventure-based learning (Dyson & Brown, 2005), and cooperative learning (Dyson & Casey, 2012) have an explicit focus on social and emotional outcomes. These models and programs seek to use sport and physical activity content as a vehicle through which to engage students in learning about SEL competencies (Richards, Ivy, Wright, & Jerris, 2019).

Despite the multiplicity of opportunities to connect physical education with SEL, the field has lacked a comprehensive resource focused on intentional integration. This text addresses this gap by providing teachers, preservice teachers, and teacher educators with a resource for learning about and integrating SEL into the structure of physical education alongside physical activity and skill development goals. It is also a key resource to guide physical education teacher education courses focused on social and emotional learning while providing supplemental readings for courses related to physical education curriculum, instruction, assessment, and models-based practice. Practicing physical education teachers who are interested in developing a stronger focus on SEL in their teaching will find that the text provides a comprehensive resource to guide their professional learning.

The text has been divided into four parts with a total of 16 chapters. As editors of the text, we wrote one-third of the chapters and invited guest authors with specific expertise to contribute the remaining chapters. This has allowed us to shape the general direction of the text while also deferring to the voices of others who have greater expertise in more specific areas.

Part 1 frames SEL both within physical education and general education more broadly. Chapter 1 provides a specific overview and describes SEL with reference to the CASEL framework. Chapter 2 connects SEL to physical education content and curriculum. Finally, Chapters 3 and 4 discuss instructional strategies and assessment practices that support the integration of SEL in practice, respectively.

Part 2 focuses on applications of SEL across selected physical education pedagogical models. While numerous models can be used to promote SEL, the chapters in this section focus specifically on the skill themes approach (Chapter 5), adventure-based learning (Chapter 6), TPSR (Chapter 7), sport education (Chapter 8), and cooperative learning (Chapter 9). Within each chapter, a brief description of the pedagogical model is provided along with specific connections to SEL competencies.

Recognizing that physical education occurs both through school-based programs as well as in adjacent settings, Part 3 highlights applications of social and emotional learning in physical activity contexts outside of standard K–12 physical education curriculum. The chapters in this part of the text focus on early childhood education (Chapter 10); adapted physical education (Chapter 11); and schoolwide SEL initiatives, including comprehensive school physical activity programs (CSPAP; Chapter 12), and provide guidelines for the explicit integration of SEL.

The chapters in Part 4 focus on case examples of physical education and activity programs that integrate social and emotional learning while working with marginalized communities. Specifically, Chapter 13 highlights examples of programs that integrate SEL to address the needs of marginalized communities, including with regard to issues of race and ethnicity. Chapter 14 takes a similar approach and specifically addresses SEL through a social justice lens with case studies bringing real-life programming to the forefront. Chapter 15 focuses on addressing issues of inequity and social injustice through the outside of school programs with case examples of practice again taking center stage.

The only chapter in Part 5, Chapter 16, concludes the text with a summary of our key take away messages across the chapters. We also discuss future directions for the integration of SEL in physical education and activity programs that we took away from editing the text.

Within each chapter throughout the text, connections are made between the practical application of SEL and supporting research. Where appropriate, explicit examples of practice are highlighted as chapter authors draw upon their own experiences integrating SEL as well as those highlighted in the literature. All chapters also include a series of discussion questions and PowerPoint slides that can be adapted to overview chapter content. Some also suggest activity ideas for integrating with coursework. Many of the chapters in Section 2 also provide example lesson plans for integrating SEL with the relevant pedagogical models that are overviewed.

Through editing this text, which has become a labor of love for both us and the contributing authors, we have come to understand social and emotional learning, as well as its place in the physical education curriculum, quite differently. We hope that you will find it similarly useful and thought provoking as you continue your mission to make physical education and activity environments safe, inviting, and meaningful spaces for young people.

—*Paul M. Wright*
—*K. Andrew R. Richards*

References

Catalano, R. F., Berglund, M. L., Ryan, J. A. M., Lonczak, H. S., & Hawkins, J. D. (2004). Positive youth development in the United States: Research findings on evaluations of positive development programs. *The Annals of the American Academy of Political and Social Science, 591*(1), 98–124.

Collaborative for Academic, Social, and Emotional Learning. (2019). *What is social and emotional learning?* Retrieved from https://casel.org/what-is-sel/

Durlack, J. A., Weissberg, R. P., & Pachan, M. (2010). A meta-analysis of after-school programs that seek to promote personal and social skills in children and adolescents. *American Journal of Community Psychology, 45*, 294–309.

Dyson, B., & Brown, M. (2005). Adventure education in your physical education program. In J. Lund & D. Tannehill (Eds.), *Standards-based physical education curriculum development* (pp. 154–175). Boston, MA: Jones and Bartlett.

Dyson, B., & Casey, A. (Eds.). (2012). *Cooperative learning in physical education.* New York, NY: Taylor & Francis.

Gordon, B., Jacobs, J. M., & Wright, P. M. (2016). Social and emotional learning through a teaching personal and social responsibility-based after school program for disengaged middle school boys. *Journal of Teaching in Physical Education, 35*(4), 358–369.

Hellison, D. (2011). *Teaching responsibility through physical activity.* Champaign, IL: Human Kinetics.

National Association for Sport and Physical Education. (1995). *Moving into the future: National standards for physical education, a guide to content and assessment.* Reston, VA.

Newman, J., & Dusenbury, L. (2015). Social and emotional learning (SEL): A framework for academic, social, and emotional success. In K. Bosworth (Ed.), *Prevention science in school settings* (pp. 287–306). New York, NY: Springer.

Richards, K. A. R., Ivy, V. N., Wright, P. M., & Jerris, E. (2019). Combining the skill themes approach with teaching personal and social responsibility to teach social and emotional learning in elementary physical education. *Journal of Physical Education, Recreation & Dance, 90*(3), 35–44.

Siedentop, D., Hastie, P. A., & van der Mars, H. (2004). *Complete guide to sport education.* Champaign, IL: Human Kinetics.

Walkthrough

The field of physical education has lacked a comprehensive resource focused on intentional integration of social emotional learning (SEL). This book addresses this gap by providing current teachers, preservice teachers, and teacher educators with a resource for learning about and integrating SEL into the structure of physical education programming alongside physical activity and skill development goals.

Chapter Overview

This book's content provides key resources to guide physical education teacher education courses specifically focused on SEL.

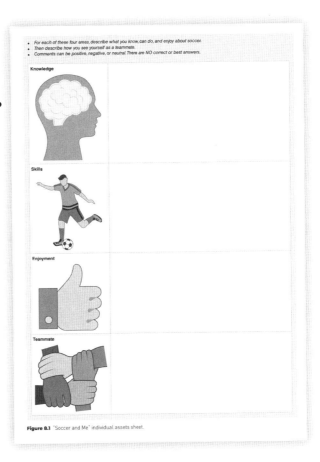

Figure 8.1 "Soccer and Me" individual assets sheet.

Table 5.4 Instructional Strategies in Relation to Goals and Social Emotional Learning Dimensions

	Instructional Strategy	Goal	Strategy in Action	Social-Emotional Learning Dimension(s)
Direct	Interactive Teaching (Direct)	Efficient skill learning	Teacher guides the students' responses by telling them what to do, showing them how to practice, and then managing their practice.	■ Self-management ■ Responsible decision making
	Task teaching	Skill learning and independence	Students practice different, specified tasks, often at their own pace (i.e., station teaching or the use of task sheets/cards)	■ Self-management ■ Responsible decision making
	Peer teaching	Skill learning and cooperation	Children work independently from the teacher to actively teach each other in pairs or small groups	■ Social awareness ■ Relationship skills
	Guided discovery	Skill learning and transfer; problem solving	Children solve problems rather than copy the teacher's or another student's correct performance	■ Responsible decision making
	Cooperative learning	Skill learning and group interdependence; individual responsibility	Process of breaking students into small groups so they can discover a new concept together and help each other learn (i.e., pairs-check, jigsaw, or co-op)	■ Social awareness ■ Relationship skills
Indirect	Child-designed instruction	Skill learning and self-responsibility	Students are the center of the learning activity while applying learned skills.	■ Self-management ■ Responsible decision making ■ Social awareness ■ Relationship skills

Data from: Graham, G., Holt/Hale, S. A., Parker, M., Hall, T., & Patton, K. (2020). *Children moving: A reflective approach to teaching physical education* (10th ed.). New York: McGraw-Hill.

Ideas for Incorporating Skills Themes and SEL into PETE

1. **Teacher Observation and Interview**: For this assignment, teacher candidates (individually or in small groups) complete a structured observation of a model SEL lesson by a local elementary physical education teacher. The structured observation can focus on: lesson objectives, instructional methods and strategies used, student engagement, assessment of learning, etc. Teacher candidates then follow up on the observation with an interview with the teacher. Questions could include: 1) in what ways do you teach to SEL competencies, 2) describe your progression for particular SEL concepts, 3) which is the most difficult and why?

2. **Student Interview**: For this learning experience, have teacher candidates interview a K–5 student focusing on their physical education experiences. Interview questions could include: enjoyable aspects of physical education; purpose of physical education; their own definitions of SEL competencies; what they learn in physical education, etc.

3. **Lesson Plan**: Have teacher candidates design a skill themes lesson with a particular SEL

Questions for Discussion

Discussion questions provide rich opportunity for synthesis and critical thinking. ———

Questions for Discussion

1. Describe the difference between assessment for learning and assessment of learning. Why is it important to include both in the overall assessment scheme for a course?
2. What are some of the characteristics of typical assessment strategies in physical education? What are some of their challenges or shortcomings?
3. What is the relationship between assessment and instruction and how can teachers use both to promote student learning?
4. If you were planning a unit of instruction focused on volleyball and you want to ensure that you integrated leadership skills as an important SEL outcome, how would you plan to assess throughout the unit?
5. How can rubrics be created to effectively measure and monitor students' SEL? What are some of the key components that should be included in a rubric?

References

Fully referenced to current literature, this book provides supplemental readings for courses related to physical education curriculum, instruction, assessment, and/or models-based practice. ———

References

Ashdown, D. M., & Bernard, M. E. (2012). Can explicit instruction in social and emotional learning skills benefit the social-emotional development, well-being, and academic achievement of young children? *Early Childhood Education Journal, 39*, 397–405.

Casey, A. (2014). Models-based practice: Great white hope or white elephant? *Physical Education and Sport Pedagogy, 19*(1), 18–34.

Catalano, R. F., Berglund, M. L., Ryan, J. A. M., Lonczak, H. S., & Hawkins, J. D. (2004). Positive youth development in the United States: Research findings on evaluations of positive development programs. *The Annals of the American Academy of Political and Social Science, 591*(1), 98–124.

Coakley, J. (2011). Youth sports: What counts as "positive youth development?" *Journal of Sport and Social Issues, 35*(3), 306–324.

Collaborative for Academic, Social, and Emotional Learning. (2019). *What is social and emotional learning?* https://casel.org/what-is-sel/

Corbin, C. B. (1993). The field of physical education: Common goals, not common roles. *Journal of Physical Education, Recreation & Dance, 64*(1), 79–87.

Cosgriff, M. (2000). Walking our talk: Adventure-based learning and physical education. *Journal of Physical Education New Zealand, 33*(2), 89–98.

Covey, S. R. (1989). *The 7 habits of highly effective people: Powerful lessons in personal change.* Freer Press.

Deci, E. L., & Ryan, R. M. (2008). Self-determination theory: A macrotheory of human motivation, development, and health. *Canadian Psychology, 49*(3), 182–185.

Durlack, J. A., Weissberg, R. P., Dymnicki, A. B., Taylor, R. D., & Schellinger, K. B. (2011). The impact of enhancing students' social and emotional learning: A meta-analysis of school-based universal interventions. *Child Development, 82*(1), 405–432.

Dyson, B., & Casey, A. (Eds.). (2012). *Cooperative learning in physical education.* Taylor & Francis.

Ennis, C. D., Solmon, M. A., Satina, B., Loftus, S. J., Mensch, J., & McCauley, M. T. (1999). Creating a sense of family inn urban schools using the "Sport for Peace" curriculum. *Research Quarterly for Exercise & Sport, 70*(3), 273–285.

Gordon, B., & Doyle, S. (2015). Teaching personal and social responsibility and transfer of learning: Opportunities and challenges for teachers and coaches. *Journal of Teaching in Physical Education, 34*(1), 152–161.

Gordon, B., Jacobs, J. M., & Wright, P. M. (2016). Social and emotional learning through a teaching personal and social responsibility based after-school program for disengaged middle school boys. *Journal of Teaching in Physical Education, 35*(4), 358–369.

Resources

- eBook
- Slides in PowerPoint format
- Test Bank
  - The Test Bank is available in LMS-compatible formats
- Sample Lesson Plans
  - Provided digitally for instructor use
- Sample Syllabus

Instructor resources are available to qualified instructors.

Acknowledgments

SHAPE America Acknowledgments

Thomas Lawson, SHAPE America Vice President of Marketing, Membership and Publications

SHAPE America Publications Advisory Committee

Holly Alperin, University of New Hampshire

Jayne Greenburg, US Department of Health and Human Services

Louis Harrison, The University of Texas at Austin

Brent Heidorn, University of West Georgia

Minsoo Kang, The University of Mississippi

Pamela Kulinna, Arizona State University

K. Andrew R. Richards, University of Illinois at Urbana-Champaign

Kristi Roth, University of Wisconsin-Stevens Point

Author Acknowledgments

First, we both wish to dedicate this book to Don Hellison (1938–2018). To us, Don was a teacher, a mentor, and a friend. Across the globe, he is recognized as a trail-blazer for promoting social and emotional development through physical education and sport. His engaged scholarship in this area continues to inspire us and others working in this field. Let us all have the humility to remember we are standing on the shoulders of giants, and among them, none loom larger than Don. This book would not have been possible without the hard work he did to pave the way.

—*Paul M. Wright*
—*K. Andrew R. Richards*

Additionally, I would like to dedicate this work to my incredible wife Amanda and our three amazing children—Virginia, Victor, and Frank. They are my greatest source of love, joy, and belonging. They help me live and experience life more deeply with each passing year. They teach me, challenge me, and inspire me to keep striving to be the best version of myself.

—*Paul M. Wright*

I dedicate this book to my partner, Alicia Richards, and our two pups, Lexi and Auggie. Alicia constantly challenges me to be a better person and to reflect on my own social and emotional development. Lexi and Auggie have been with us since graduate school and sat with me often as I worked on the book. The joy they bring me is undoubtedly infused in my writing. *Semper constans et fidelis.*

—*K. Andrew R. Richards*

About the Editors

Paul M. Wright

Paul M. Wright is the EC Lane and MN Zimmerman Endowed Professor and a Presidential Engagement Professor at Northern Illinois University with a faculty appointment in the Department of Kinesiology and Physical Education. Wright's research has specialized in topics related to social and emotional development (e.g., the Teaching Personal and Social Responsibility model, sport-based youth development).

K. Andrew R. Richards

K. Andrew R. Richards is an assistant professor of physical education at the University of Illinois at Urbana-Champaign. Richards' scholarship focuses on the recruitment, education, and ongoing socialization of physical education teachers. He also coordinates and conducts research on physical activity programs that seek to promote social and emotional learning, primarily through the teaching personal and social responsibility model.

Contributors

Jeff Bainbridge

Jeff Bainbridge is the World Language Department Chair at Sycamore High School in Sycamore, Illinois, where he teaches Spanish I and IV. In pursuit of a more communicative, active, and civil world, his graduate studies at Northern Illinois University in physical education focus on social and emotional learning. He is an active cyclist and yogi.

Ashley Casey

Ashley Casey is Senior Lecturer in Pedagogy at Loughborough University, UK, co-author of Models-based Practice in Physical Education, and Series Editor of the Routledge Focus on Sport Pedagogy.

Brian Culp

Brian Culp is a Professor of Physical Education at Kennesaw State University. Recognized as a Fulbright Scholar and Fellow of the National Association for Kinesiology in Higher Education, Culp's research examines inequity and reasons for participation in physical activity, play, and sport in communities. In his spare time, he enjoys being outdoors.

Ben Dyson

Ben Dyson is an internationally recognized researcher in Physical Education in two related areas of scholarship: research on innovative curriculum and pedagogy and Cooperative Learning as a pedagogical practice. His school-based research has an emerging area of scholarship in Social and Emotional Learning. Ben has carried out research and taught at McGill University; the University of New Hampshire; University of Memphis; University of Auckland, New Zealand; and The University of North Carolina at Greensboro (UNCG), North Carolina. In his spare time, he likes to kayak, mountain bike, downhill ski, and garden.

Judy Fowler

Judy Fowler is an Associate Professor at the University of North Carolina at UNCG, USA. Judy serves as the Physical Education Health Teacher Education (PEHTE) Program Director at UNCG. Judy is a veteran teacher and is National Board certified. She has worked in K–12 education and higher education for 25 years.

Justin A. Haegele

Justin A. Haegele is an associate professor in the Department of Human Movement Sciences at Old Dominion University, USA. His research focuses on the interdisciplinary field of adapted physical activity, with a primary interest in examining how individuals with disabilities experience physical activity participation. Haegele is a Research Fellow with the Research Council of SHAPE and Associate Editor for Adapted Physical Activity Quarterly and Quest.

Peter Hastie

Peter Hastie is a professor of physical education at Auburn University. Hastie's scholarship focuses on the use of various curriculum models on student learning within physical education. He also coordinates and conducts research on physical activity programs that seek to promote social and emotional learning, primarily through the teaching personal and social responsibility model.

Michael A. Hemphill

Michael A. Hemphill is an assistant professor of Kinesiology at the University of North Carolina at Greensboro. Dr. Hemphill's research focuses on teaching personal and social responsibility through sport, physical activity, and physical education with specific applications to urban communities and professional development programs for physical activity providers. His research is grounded in community-engaged scholarship, which features reciprocal community partnerships and interdisciplinary collaborations to address community-identified needs. This research has been situated in local contexts in Charleston, SC, and Greensboro, NC, as well as international applications in New Zealand and Sri Lanka. He has published several research articles in refereed journals including the Journal of Youth Development, Journal of Teaching in Physical Education, European Physical Education Review, Physical Education & Sport Pedagogy, and Sport, Education, and Society. Additionally, he has delivered research presentations to international, national, and regional conferences including the American Educational Research Association, SHAPE America, the International Association for Physical Education in Higher Education, and the International Association for Research on Service Learning and Community Engagement. He is a recipient of the community-engaged scholar award from the School of Health and Human Sciences and of the Charles D. Henry Award, honoring significant contributions to ethnic minorities in SHAPE America.

Cassandra Iannucci

Cassandra Iannucci is a Lecturer in health and physical education teacher education at Deakin University in Melbourne, Australia. As an early career researcher, Cassandra's main teaching and research interests revolve around (physical education) teacher education pedagogies, assessment, and student voice in primary physical education. More recently, she has been drawn to exploring what learning is privileged and valued in physical education with a particular emphasis on increasing capacity for social and emotional learning.

Jenn M. Jacobs

Jenn M. Jacobs is an assistant professor of sport psychology in the Department of Kinesiology and Physical Education at Northern Illinois University. Her research interests include studying sport as a tool for social change in a variety of settings including schools, juvenile detention centers, and community-based programs.

Karisa L. Kuipers

Karisa L. Kuipers is a doctoral student of kinesiology and instructor in the Department of Kinesiology and Physical Education at Northern Illinois University. Her research interests include using sport to teach personal and social responsibility in community programs, college classrooms, and international contexts.

Dillon Landi

Dillon Landi is an Assistant Professor at Towson University (Maryland). He conducts research on equity in health, physical activity, and education. He received his PhD in Education from the University of Auckland (New Zealand) as well as two postgraduate degrees from Columbia University (New York). Dillon previously taught K–12 health and physical education and served as the supervisor of health, physical education, and athletics in urban school districts.

Jessica Mangione

Jessica Mangione is a Physical Education and School Sport Lecturer in the Department of Sport and Physical Activity at Edge Hill University, England. She teaches undergraduate courses in physical education curriculum models and instruction. Her main research interest is physical education external provision in primary schools with particular attention on privatisation and neoliberalism.

Tom Martinek

Tom Martinek is a professor in the Department of Kinesiology at the University of North Carolina at Greensboro (UNCG). During his 44-year tenure at UNCG, Tom's research has focused on the social and psychological dynamics of teaching and youth development programming. For the past 27 years, Tom has directed and taught in Project Effort and Youth Leader Corps programs, which consist of values-based after-school sport and leadership experiences for underserved

children and youth. Most recently, he has established an alternative high school (called a middle college) for at-risk students on UNCG's campus. The school is an integral part of his "wrap around" approach to develop the assets of each individual youth. He has published four books and over 120 articles. Recognition for his work with youth has been acknowledged by receiving the Salvation Army Boys and Girls Club Youth Development Award; the University Bullard Award for Service; North Carolina Alliance for Health, Physical Education, and Recreation Presidential Citation Award; and the Community-Engaged Scholar Award given by the School of Health and Human Science. His most recent recognition was being nominated for the prestigious Max Gardner Award—the highest award given in the UNC system.

Daekyun Oh

Daekyun Oh is a Doctoral candidate in the Department of Human Sciences at Ohio State University. He has nine years of teaching experience in K–12 physical education focused on affective development. As a teaching assistant, he teaches, assists, or supervises a variety of courses in higher education. His research interests are positive youth development, social and emotional learning, and adventure-based learning in K–12 physical education and physical education teacher education.

Melissa Parker

Melissa Parker is an Emeritus Senior Lecturer in the Department of Physical Education and Sport Sciences at the University of Limerick, Ireland, and a Professor Emeritus in Sport and Exercise Science at the University of Northern Colorado. She taught undergraduate and post-graduate courses in physical education teaching and learning, and outdoor education. Her scholarly interest areas include accessing teacher and student voice and the professional learning of teachers and teacher educators. Teaching children in physical education remains her passion.

Kevin Patton

Kevin Patton is a Professor in the Department of Kinesiology at California State University Chico. He teaches undergraduate and graduate courses in physical education teaching methods, assessment, trends and issues, and reading/understanding research. Stemming from his commitment and concern for quality physical education, his scholarly interests include initial teacher education, accessing teacher and student voice, teacher educators' professional learning, and teachers' continuing professional development.

James D. Ressler

James D. Ressler is an Associate Professor of Physical Education Teacher Education and Senior Faculty Fellow in the College of Education at Northern Illinois University. Ressler's scholarship focuses on methods of teacher preparation, adventure-based learning, and youth development through physical activity and sport.

Alicia L. Richards

Alicia L. Richards is an instructor in the Department of Kinesiology and Community Health at the University of Illinois at Urbana-Champaign. In addition to her teaching responsibilities, she also serves as the Director of the Illinois Physical Activity and Life Skills (iPALS) Wellness Program, the Physical Activity Course (PAC) Program Coordinator, and the Undergraduate Kinesiology Minor Advisor.

Fernando Santos

Fernando Santos is an assistant professor at the School of Higher Education in the Polytechnic Institute of Porto and Viana do Castelo responsible for providing formal training to preschool teachers and youth sport coaches. He is also a researcher at the Centre for Research and Innovation in Education (inED) and has investigated how to foster social and emotional learning through the teaching personal and social responsibility model within preschool settings.

Oleg Sinelnikov

Oleg Sinelnikov is the Paul W. Bryant Professor of Education (Teaching) and Associate Professor in Sport Pedagogy at the University of Alabama with a faculty appointment in the Department of Kinesiology. Sinelnikov's main research areas focus on teaching and learning in physical education and sport, specifically within pedagogical models such as Sport Education, motivational climate, and the integration of technology.

Jenna R. Starck

Jenna R. Starck is an assistant professor of physical education at the University of Wisconsin-La Crosse. Starck's research focuses on topics related to assessment in physical education and assessment literacy in Physical Education Teacher Education (PETE) programs primarily through the lens of occupational socialization.

Paul T. Stuhr

Paul Stuhr is a Professor in the Department of Kinesiology at California State University San Marcos. He has over 20 years of experience working in the field of sport pedagogy. He teaches courses related to social-emotional health and physical education teacher education. His research focuses on K–16 student learning associated with social and emotional health.

Sue Sutherland

Sue Sutherland is a Professor in the Department of Human Sciences at Ohio State University. She teaches undergraduate and graduate courses in adventure-based learning, social justice, disability sport, elementary physical education methods, qualitative research, and teaching in higher education. Sue's research focuses on the use of adventure-based learning in K–12/higher education, social and emotional learning, social justice education in physical education, and physical education teacher education.

Alyssa Trad

Alyssa Trad is a doctoral student and graduate research assistant in the Department of Kinesiology and Community Health at the University of Illinois at Urbana-Champaign. Her research focuses on the socialization of adapted physical educators and how to effectively support marginalized teachers.

Zachary Wahl-Alexander

Zachary Wahl-Alexander is an associate professor of sport pedagogy in the Department of Kinesiology and Physical Education at Northern Illinois University. His research interests include studying the sport education pedagogical model and exploring its impact on physical activity and fitness markers.

Tristan L. Wallhead

Tristan L. Wallhead is a professor with a faculty appointment in the Department of Kinesiology and Health at the University of Wyoming. Wallhead's research specializes in topics related to sport-based curricular models and their influence on student learning and physical literacy. (e.g., Sport Education).

David S. Walsh

David S. Walsh is a professor in the Department of Kinesiology at San Francisco State University. Walsh specializes in physical activity-based youth development programs in underserved urban communities. He has 25 years of experience with the development, implementation, and research of Hellison's Teaching Personal and Social Responsibility Model.

Collin A. Webster

Collin A. Webster is a professor of physical education at the University of South Carolina whose scholarship focuses on the promotion of physical education and physical activity through comprehensive school physical activity programs. Webster is a former department chair and associate dean for research in the University of South Carolina College of Education and was an invited research fellow in Japan and Australia.

Wesley J. Wilson

Wesley J. Wilson is an assistant professor in the Department of Special Education at the University of Utah. Wilson completed his PhD at the University of Virginia. Wilson's research focuses on the socialization of adapted physical educators and how teachers understand and implement special education legislation in the physical education setting.

Lauriece L. Zittel

Lauriece L. Zittel is a professor in the Department of Kinesiology and Physical Education at Northern Illinois University. Her primary teaching and research disciplines are adapted physical education/activity. Her research and writing have focused on early childhood curriculum development, instruction, and assessment for children with diagnosed disabilities, developmental delays, and those at risk for developmental delay.

Reviewer

Joseph A. Durlak
Professor Emeritus of Psychology
 Loyola University Chicago
 Chicago, Illinois

SECTION 1

Introduction to Social and Emotional Learning in Physical Education

CHAPTER 1

Social and Emotional Learning in the American Educational System

Paul M. Wright
K. Andrew R. Richards

CHAPTER SUMMARY

Social and emotional skills, dispositions, and behaviors are crucial to the healthy development of children and youth. However, such learning outcomes in the American educational system have only recently been emphasized. This chapter lays a foundation for the rest of the book by defining and framing social and emotional learning (SEL) against the backdrop of American educational policy. Approaches to promoting SEL, benefits for children and youth, and connections to physical education are explored. The chapter concludes with an overview of the structure, contents, and anticipated contributions of this book.

Social and Emotional Learning in the American Educational System

Schools are meant to provide students with the knowledge, skills, and experiences they will need to succeed in life and to contribute to society. However, exactly what knowledge, skills, and experiences are those? What is most important for students to know, do, and experience? These are fundamental questions in education and the answers vary greatly based on personal values, educational philosophy, societal needs, and more (Dewey, 1938; Schubert, 1986). This text examines the intersection of two content areas: physical education and social and emotional learning (SEL). Both content areas have been defined very broadly and have often been placed on the margins of the curriculum in the United States and in other countries (Wright, Gordon & Gray, 2020; Wright & Walsh, 2015). To set the stage for our discussion, this chapter provides a brief overview of the educational policy context in the United States related to physical education and SEL. It also provides a framework for SEL and highlights the opportunity for integration with physical education.

Evolving Educational Policy

Over the past several decades, there have been substantial shifts in American educational policy. For example, reflecting the concerns of the Cold War, a landmark document called *A Nation at Risk* (National Commission on Excellence in Education, 1983) sparked concern that the United States was losing a competitive edge in areas related to mathematics, science, and technology—areas considered crucial in military development, space exploration, and in other technologically driven fields. This began an era of heightened emphasis on standardized testing, which reached a crescendo under the *No Child Left Behind Act* of 2001 (NCLB; Public Law 107-110, 20 U.S.C.A., section 6301). NCLB mandated standardized testing to assess individual students, subgroups (e.g., gender and race), and school performance. This legislation explicitly designated some subjects, such as language arts, math, and science, as "core academic subjects." Federal funding was often tied to performance in these subjects, resulting in increased pressure for principals, teachers, and students (Darling-Hammond, 2007; Ravitch, 2010). Furthermore, while the commitment to identifying and closing attainment gaps between subgroups is commendable (e.g., increasing educational attainment among youth from communities affected by poverty), the implementation of NCLB had numerous challenges. For example, critics argued that it narrowed the curriculum, forced educators to "teach to the test," and reduced time devoted to creative thinking, problem solving, and holistic development (Darling-Hammond, 2006, 2007; Ravitch, 2010). In this policy context, subject areas such as physical education, arts, and music became increasingly marginalized in the school curriculum (Amis, Wright, Dyson, Vardaman, & Ferry, 2012).

After several years of backlash, NCLB was eventually replaced with the *Every Student Succeeds Act* of 2015 (ESSA; Public Law 114-95). This new federal education legislation replaced the notion of "core academic subjects" used in NCLB with the idea of a "well-rounded education." This shift in philosophy highlights the importance of all subject areas by opening federal funding streams that had previously been restricted to "core academic" subjects. With this shift, subjects such as physical education, music, and art are on more equal footing, and there is space to pursue more holistic approaches to education (Wright, Gordon & Gray, 2020). The pressures related to standardized testing under NCLB were also somewhat relaxed because individual states and school districts are now empowered to set their own priorities for funding and accountability. These shifts have been embraced by professional associations such as Society for Health and Physical Education (SHAPE) America, which advocated for previously marginalized subject areas to play a more central role in the well-rounded, holistic education of students (SHAPE America, 2016).

With its emphasis on a well-rounded education, ESSA has created more responsiveness in the American educational system to address nonacademic outcomes that are known to be important for students' overall development as well as their succeeding in school and later in life. Learning outcomes related to attitudes, emotions and motivations, as well as the dispositions and behaviors that reflect them, have been associated with the affective learning domain (Bloom, 1956; Krathwohl, Bloom, & Masia, 1965). Such results and related personal and social skills were often neglected or dismissed in the era of standardized testing (Tough, 2012). However, the interest in developing noncognitive skills through formal education has proliferated in popular culture and research with concepts such as "grit" (Duckworth, 2016) and "growth mindset" (Dweck, 2007). Considering the expectation that schooling should prepare students to join the workforce and function well in society, competencies such as communication, cultural competence, leadership, self-direction, and initiative have been labeled 21st century skills (Trilling & Fadel, 2009).

In this book, we broadly categorize many nonacademic or noncognitive outcomes as SEL, which will be examined more fully in the next section. For now, it is important to note that this content, in physical education and across the curriculum, aligns with the guiding principles and funding structures of ESSA. According to the RAND Corporation:

Although much of the policy discussion surrounding ESSA and school improvement has focused on academic skills, the legislation addresses a broad range of school-improvement efforts and student outcomes. One particular set of outcomes that has been of increasing interest to education stakeholders in recent years is the broader range of intrapersonal and interpersonal competencies that help students succeed both in and out of school. These competencies are sometimes described as "social and emotional" competencies or skills, and the development of these competencies is often described using the phrase SEL (Grant et al., 2017, p. 1-2).

The next section of this chapter describes SEL in general terms before overviewing a specific framework that will be a frequent reference point throughout this text.

What Is Social and Emotional Learning?

When discussing SEL, one challenge is that it is defined and interpreted in many different ways. According to McKown (2017), "neither researchers nor practitioners nor policymakers have come to a consensus about what SEL is" (p. 160). Some proponents suggest that all learning is social and emotional learning, arguing that what teachers say, the values they model, their choices regarding materials and activities, and the skills they prioritize all have an impact on students' social and emotional development (Frey, Fisher, & Smith, 2019). We do not dispute these myriad influences and their importance; however, for the purposes of this text, we gravitate toward SEL approaches that use specific learning outcomes as their frame of reference. While this approach does not capture all aspects of the educational experience, it makes SEL tangible by treating it as content that can be taught, learned, practiced, and assessed as opposed to something ephemeral that students may or may not pick up by osmosis.

Because the topics are connected in practice, it is worth explaining the relationship between SEL and the affective learning domain (Bloom, 1956) in more detail. The affective learning domain relates to the feelings, attitudes, emotions, and motivations that students experience and develop in the learning process. While such affective outcomes are not behavioral in nature, they are often reflected in observable behaviors and a range of personal and social skills. First, let us consider the range of affective responses. According to Krathwohl, Bloom, and Masia (1973), there are five progressively complex stages in the affective domain: (a) receiving, (b) responding, (c) valuing, (d) organization, and (e) characterization. In the first stage, receiving, students are simply aware of and taking in information. This is reflected in behaviors such as paying attention and listening respectfully. After receiving information, the next stage is responding to the information. This might involve answering questions or participating in a discussion—activities that require communication skills. The next stage, valuing, has to do with assigning worth or value to the learning content. This could be reflected in one's level of enthusiasm, focus, and desire to engage with the

content. The stage after valuing is organization. At this stage, students' affective response is strong enough that they would choose to engage with the content over other options, look for ways to apply it, and integrate it into their sense-making. Characterization is the highest stage affective engagement. It involves sufficient value and commitment to the content that these affective responses are consistently evidenced in the students' outward behavior. Therefore, even though students' affective responses are internal processes rooted in attitude and emotion, they strongly contribute to and are often reflected in their behaviors. For these reasons, learning objectives focused on the affective domain are often tethered to observable behaviors and SEL skills, e.g., respecting the feelings of others, staying on task, cooperation.

Several systematic approaches to addressing affective learning outcomes and associated SEL skills (Bloom, 1956; Krathwohl, Bloom, & Masia, 1965) have emerged in the last few decades. For example, *Character Education* (Lickona, 1991), which focuses on developing respect and responsibility, is an approach that became popular in classrooms and school-wide approaches to positive behavior management. Another example that continues to gain momentum is Goleman's (1995) concept of emotional intelligence. Emotional intelligence provides a framework for helping students develop self-awareness, empathy, self-motivation, and relationships. As interest in nonacademic learning has developed in our educational system, such frameworks have become operationalized and promoted with concrete strategies and guidelines for educators and policymakers. For example, the Yale Center for Emotional Intelligence conducts research and produces evidence-based materials to support emotional intelligence in classrooms and schools. The acronym for their approach is **RULER**, which is defined as: *R*ecognizing, *U*nderstanding, *L*abeling, *E*xpressing, and then *R*egulating emotions (Brackett, 2019). This is one of many frameworks supported by a strong base of evidence that now produces lesson plans, teacher resource guides, and student materials as interest, policy support, and funding for such programming grows.

There has been a parallel evolution in the approach to SEL outside of the school context. Positive youth development (PYD), for example, is a term used to describe an extensive list of programs and approaches to working with youth in community settings (Catalano, Berglund, Ryan, Lonczak, & Hawkins, 2004). PYD programs are characterized as an alternative to prevention and intervention programs that focus on deficits or risk factors (e.g., violence prevention, drop-out prevention). PYD programs tend to focus on identifying and building upon youths' assets and strengths. They frequently focus on developing personal and social skills as well as providing empowering, youth-centered experiences (Catalano et al., 2004). One PYD approach that has become widely disseminated and supported by research is Lerner's (2007) 5 Cs. This model focuses on building confidence, connection, competence, caring, and character in order to help youth flourish and become positive contributors to society (Lerner, 2007). Another prominent PYD approach focuses on understanding and building developmental assets (Scales & Leffert, 1999). Malleable internal assets related to attitudes about learning, social competencies, positive identity, and positive values have been the focus of this approach. Many of the best practices and outcomes associated with such PYD programs in out-of-school-time settings are comparable to those of SEL programs delivered within the school setting (Taylor, Oberle, Durlak, & Weissberg, 2017).

With a growing consensus that noncognitive skills are important in life and are strong predictors of academic success (Tough, 2012), one might ask if we need yet another buzz-word or model to advance this idea (i.e., SEL). It could be argued that this is like putting old wine in a new bottle (Weiss, 2016). However, we believe that to enable progress, a thorough examination of relevant skills, attitudes, and behaviors in physical education requires well-defined learning outcomes as part of a coherent conceptual framework that rests upon careful empirical research regarding their importance.

The CASEL Framework for Social and Emotional Learning

We acknowledge that there are many interpretations and iterations of SEL that have been well-articulated, tested in practice, and supported by centers at reputable institutions. These include the Yale Center for Emotional Intelligence, the Search Institute, the Ecological Approaches to Social Emotional Learning (EASEL) Laboratory at Harvard, and the National Commission on Social, Emotional, and Academic Development at the Aspen Institute, to name a few. In this text, we have chosen to focus on the Collaborative for Academic, Social, and Emotional Learning (CASEL) framework because of its strong research base as well as its prominence in educational policy and practice in many schools, school districts, and states. Moreover, many other SEL resources and best

practices align with this framework even if they were not developed specifically by CASEL. For example, the RULER framework (Brackett, 2019) promoted by the Yale Center for Emotional Intelligence fits within the broader CASEL framework and complements it by providing a more targeted resource to develop self-awareness and self-management competencies. In short, we see the CASEL framework as relevant, comprehensive, and flexible enough to pull together and bridge a wide range of specific programs, approaches, and outcomes that fall under the wide umbrella of SEL.

CASEL defines SEL as "the process through which children and adults understand and manage emotions, set and achieve positive goals, feel and show empathy for others, establish and maintain positive relationships, and make responsible decisions" (see www.casel.org). Below, we outline the SEL competencies of this framework as well as approaches to implementation. We also review evidence of the impact of such programming and support from various stakeholders.

SEL Competencies

As displayed in **Figure 1.1**, the CASEL framework comprises five interrelated social and emotional learning competencies. These are self-awareness, self-management, social awareness, relationship skills, and responsible decision making. These competencies overlap and are dependent on each other in many ways; therefore, their presentation does not depend on any particular order or progression. It is also important to note that these competencies can be cultivated and applied across contexts such as the classroom, school, home, and community. The competencies are also adaptable. They can be developed among students from different backgrounds and with different learning needs through strategic initiatives and differentiated instruction. Each of these general competencies is explained in more detail in this section and illuminated with concrete personal and social behaviors that characterize them.

According to CASEL, **self-awareness** involves accurately recognizing one's own emotions, thoughts, and values and how they influence behavior (CASEL, 2020). Specific skills that fall under this competency include identifying emotions, accurate self-perception, and the ability to reflect on strengths and weaknesses. Such skills are an important part of developing self-confidence and self-efficacy. Self-awareness is foundational to personal growth and healthy relationships with others.

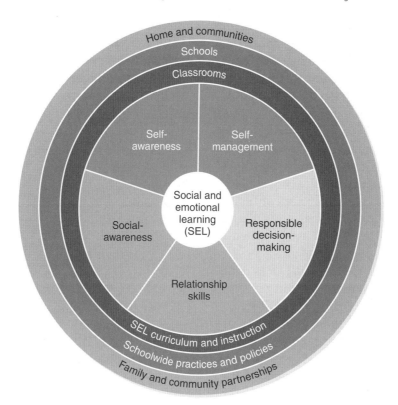

Figure 1.1 CASEL framework for SEL competencies.

Self-management involves successfully regulating one's emotions, thoughts, and behaviors in different situations. This includes effectively managing stress, controlling impulses, and motivating oneself to set and work toward personal and academic goals (CASEL, 2020). This competency is also connected with characteristics such as self-discipline and self-motivation. Informed by awareness of self and others, self-management involves acting in ways that align with our thoughts, values, and desires.

Social awareness involves taking the perspective of and empathizing with others, including those from diverse backgrounds and cultures. This requires a person to understand social and ethical norms for behavior (CASEL, 2020). This competency is characterized by perspective-taking, empathy, appreciating diversity, and respecting others. It also includes recognizing family, school, and community resources and supports.

Relationship skills relate to establishing and maintaining healthy and rewarding relationships with diverse individuals and groups. These skills include the ability to communicate clearly, listen well, cooperate with others, resist inappropriate social pressure, negotiate conflict constructively, and seek or offer help when needed (CASEL, 2020). Relationship skills are important in social engagement, relationship-building, leadership, and working as part of a team.

Responsible decision making involves making constructive choices about personal behavior and social interactions based on ethical standards, safety concerns, and social norms (CASEL, 2020). This requires skills such as identifying and solving problems, analyzing and evaluating situations, reflecting on consequences, and taking ethical responsibility into account. Therefore, responsible decision making not only addresses the choices we make but also how and why we make them.

Approaches to Addressing Social and Emotional Learning

One strength we see in the CASEL framework is that their evidence-based model of competencies has been implemented effectively across a range of grade levels, ranging from preschool through high school. As noted above, the CASEL framework addresses varied educational contexts (e.g., classroom, school, school district) as well as the home and community settings (CASEL, 2020). CASEL has published guides presenting dozens of evidence-based programs aligned with their framework for the preschool through elementary grades (CASEL, 2013) as well as the middle and high school grades (CASEL, 2015). These and other resources include the following approaches: explicit SEL skills instruction, SEL-aligned teacher instructional practices, integration of SEL with academic curriculum areas, and strategies to create an SEL-fostering culture and climate within the classroom and larger school community (see www .casel.org).

Across programs and settings, CASEL (2020) asserts that effective SEL programs share the following characteristics, which are represented in the acronym *SAFE* (*S*equenced, *A*ctive, *F*ocused, and *E*xplicit). To illustrate these characteristics, we discuss how they are applied in Second Step, a popular evidence-based SEL program for teaching students in elementary grade classroom settings (Upshur, Heyman & Wenz-Gross, 2017). *Sequenced* refers to activities being coordinated over time to develop specific skills and learning as opposed to random or disconnected activities or lessons. Depending on the grade level, the Second Step program includes 22 to 28 sequential lessons that build upon each other and can be implemented across the school year. *Active* refers to a learning environment in which students are actively engaged participants as opposed to passive recipients of information, in other words, students are asked to practice different skills, receive feedback on their performance, and continue to refine their behavior over time. In the case of Second Step, teachers are provided with active learning strategies, discussion prompts, and home links. *Focused* alludes to a focus on SEL competencies (i.e., personal and social skills). Second Step lessons are organized into units that focus on specific skills such as learning, empathy, friendship skills, and problem solving. *Explicit* means directly addressing and giving feedback on specific SEL skills as opposed to assuming that such skills are being developed/learned in a given activity. In the case of Second Step, the lessons and units identify, define, and reinforce discrete SEL skills. Teachers are encouraged to deliver these lessons with the same intentionality that they would any other content.

Impact of SEL Programming

Another strength of the CASEL framework is its research base. Extensive research has shown that the five core competencies in this framework are connected to both academic and nonacademic outcomes. In a meta-analysis of 213 studies involving more than 270,000 K-12 students, researchers found that students who participated directly in effective SEL programs were more likely than control groups to show improved academic performance and classroom behavior; to manage stress and depression; and to have better attitudes about themselves, others, and school (Durlak, Weissberg, Dymnicki, Taylor &

Schellinger, 2011). These findings were extended by another meta-analysis of 82 studies including 100,000 students (Taylor et al., 2017). This second review determined that students participating in quality SEL programs not only had immediate benefits but that many benefits were long-term and global in nature (e.g., improved academics, fewer conduct problems, less emotional distress, and lower rates of drug abuse compared with control groups). Moreover, these researchers found that the best predictor of future or later outcomes was the extent to which students learned different SEL skills during the initial program. The findings from the meta-analyses noted above have been associated with targeted programs and classroom interventions. However, benefits have also been associated with schoolwide SEL approaches. Specifically, a recent analysis indicates that students who attend schools that have integrated SEL into the overall curriculum tend to have more favorable academic outcomes than students who attend schools that have not (Mahoney, Durlak & Weissberg, 2018).

Other research has connected SEL development to improved economic mobility (American Enterprise Institute for Public Policy Research and the Brookings Institution, 2015) and improved outcomes in domains such as employment, criminal activity, substance abuse, and mental health (Jones, Greenberg & Crowley, 2015). For reasons such as these, the Center for Benefit-Cost Studies in Education at Columbia University examined the economic value of SEL and determined that the return on investment (ROI) of high-quality SEL interventions is 11 to one (Belfield, Bowden, Klapp, Levin, Shand, & Zander, 2015). In light of this body of evidence related to both academic and nonacademic outcomes, it is easy to understand why many states and districts are adopting SEL standards (often based on the CASEL framework) and/or programs into their curriculum (CASEL, 2020). As noted previously, the ESSA opens the door at the federal level for such initiatives and federal legislation to integrate SEL standards nationwide is under review.

The Purpose of This Book

The purpose of this book is to explore the intersection of SEL with physical education. As much as this connection appears strong and natural to us, we are surprised that despite the groundswell of support for integrating SEL into the American educational system, there is an obvious omission in literature related to physical education and activity. Most of the leading researchers and centers driving the SEL field forward do not capitalize on (or even acknowledge, in some cases) physical activity settings. For example, according to Jones and Kahn (2017), "major domains of human development—social, emotional, cognitive, linguistic, academic—are deeply intertwined in the brain and in behavior, and all are central to learning" (p. 4). The noticeable absence of physical and/or psychomotor development in this reference to human development is not the exception. Special issues of *Educational Leadership* (in 2018) and *The Future of Children* (in 2017) focused on SEL and advocated a commitment to holistic development; however, across these two special issues, not a single contribution focused on physical education, physical activity, or the psychomotor domain.

We see a similar pattern in reviews of SEL best practice programs. The previously mentioned guidebooks for school-based programs published by CASEL do not include any approaches or best practices from physical education or activity settings although classroom-based programs are numerous (CASEL, 2013, 2015). Similarly, a study published by the RAND Corporation (2017) reviewed in-school and out-of-school SEL programs that represent promising practice. Of 60 programs reviewed, only three involve physical activity (i.e., Tae Kwon Do, yoga, and a play-based program), and none are rooted in physical education.

To those familiar with best practice and innovation in fields such as physical education and sport-based youth development, there is a long history and rich opportunity for connection with SEL (Jacobs & Wright, 2014). However, it is apparent that this connection and the potential for integration into the larger SEL movement goes largely unnoticed by the public. We believe that those working in the field of physical education have much to offer and much to gain from alignment with the current SEL movement. Therein lies the purpose of this book. We wish to demonstrate what a rich and ideal setting physical activity can be for the authentic development of SEL competencies. This is done in part by reviewing existing best practices that can be aligned with and counted among effective approaches for promoting SEL within the general curriculum. We also highlight the emergence of innovative programs and ideas that represent intentional and robust integration of SEL with in-school physical education as well as out-of-school physical activity programs.

Book Overview and Organization

This book is divided into five sections. Section One is composed of four chapters that we (Paul and Kevin) have co-authored. This first chapter provides an introduction and background information on the topic of SEL in the American educational system. Chapter 2 highlights the deep roots of SEL in the physical education curriculum. From a historical and international perspective, Chapter 2 also makes the point that SEL can be integrated into the formal K–12 physical education curriculum as well as other educational and developmental physical activity programs outside of the formal school curriculum. Next, Chapter 3 overviews teaching practices in physical education that effectively promote SEL. Concrete examples of teaching approaches and styles that connect with specific SEL competencies are highlighted. Chapter 4 is written with Jenna Starck and is the last chapter in Section One. This chapter discusses assessment strategies that teachers can use to understand and support student performance relative to SEL objectives. Student-centered practices that actively engage students in the assessment process to promote growth and reflection are highlighted.

Section Two of this book focuses on established pedagogical models aligned with SEL in physical education and activity settings. Chapter 5, written by Missy Parker, Kevin Patton, Cassandra Iannucci, and Jessica Mangione, describes the skill themes approach in elementary physical education. Sue Sutherland, Paul Stuhr, Jim Ressler, and Daekyun Oh have written Chapter 6 on adventure-based learning. Chapter 7, written by Dave Walsh, presents the teaching personal and social responsibility model. Peter Hastie, Oleg Sinelnikov, and Tristan Wallhead have contributed Chapter 8, which focuses on sport education. Chapter 9 is written by Ben Dyson, Judy Fowler, and Ashley Casey with a focus on cooperative learning. In each of these chapters, authors illustrate the alignment of their respective pedagogical models with SEL objectives. Research support as well as concrete examples of teaching strategies, learning activities, and assessment strategies are provided in each case.

Section Three of the book is composed of three chapters that examine SEL promotion in specialized physical activity programs and contexts that are adjacent to K–12 physical education. Chapter 10, written by Fernando Santos and Laurie Zittel, examines developmentally appropriate ways to integrate SEL with physical activity for preschool age children.

Chapter 11, written by Wes Wilson, Justin Haegele, and Alyssa Trad, explores the integration of SEL in adapted physical education. Chapter 12 is written by Collin Webster, who examines the integration of SEL into whole school approaches such as the Comprehensive School Physical Activity Program (CSPAP) promoted by the Society of Health and Physical Educators (SHAPE) America (see https://shapeamerica.org).

Section Four is composed of three chapters that provide case examples of programs and concepts that use physical activity as a vehicle to meet the needs of learners from marginalized communities. Chapter 13 is written by Tom Martinek and Michael Hemphill. This chapter illustrates how extracurricular sport and physical activity programs with developmental objectives (e.g., sport-based youth development programs) are effective settings to promote SEL. In Chapter 14, Jim Ressler, Brian Culp, Dillon Landi, and Jeff Bainbridge discuss SEL promotion in physical education through the lens of social justice and equity. They profile programs and approaches that create inclusive, culturally competent, and empowering experiences. In Chapter 15, Jenn Jacobs, Karisa Kuipers, Zach Wahl-Alexander, and Alicia Richards present additional case examples framed around social issues; however, their focus is on programs operating in alternative settings (e.g., after-school, summer camp, and juvenile detention). To conclude, we have written Chapter 16 in the fifth and final section of the book. In this chapter, we consider commonalities across the practices and perspectives shared by the authors as we reflect on the past, present, and future of SEL in physical education. Strengths, gaps, and opportunities that we see in terms of policy, practice, and research are discussed.

Conclusion

In this chapter, we have introduced the notion of SEL and highlighted a leading framework (i.e., CASEL) that will serve as an important reference point in subsequent chapters. We began by explaining how the educational policy climate in America, currently characterized by the ESSA, has become more supportive of a well-rounded education that includes noncognitive (i.e., SEL) content as well as health and physical education. Given the long history and expertise of physical educators in promoting SEL, we see this as an important moment for the intentional integration of SEL within physical education and other physical activity settings.

In this chapter, we have previewed the contents of this book and hope readers gain additional insight as they progress through the chapters. Within each chapter, connections are made between the practical application of SEL and supporting research. Where appropriate, explicit examples of practice are highlighted as chapter authors draw on their own experiences integrating SEL as well as those highlighted in the literature. Although the size and scope of any edited volume is limited, we have tried to present a diverse range of perspectives and topics in this book. Although it is impossible to present all perspectives and teaching approaches in a single text, we hope representation is strong enough to make the contents informative, relevant, and widely applicable. All chapters include a series of discussion questions and several include practical resources such as lesson plans and sample activities that can be used to promote active learning of these concepts. In these ways, we hope this book can encourage meaningful dialogue, interaction, reflection, and application among its readership.

Regarding our readership, we hope this book is accessible to anyone interested in topics such as SEL, physical education, sport-based youth development, and their intersections. However, the book has also been shaped with certain audiences in mind. Despite the multiplicity of opportunities to connect physical education with SEL, the field has lacked a comprehensive resource focused on intentional integration. This book addresses this gap by providing teachers (as well as coaches and youth workers), preservice teachers, and teacher educators with a resource for learning about and integrating SEL into the structure of physical education programming alongside physical activity and skill development goals. We anticipate that this book will be a significant resource to guide physical education teacher education courses specifically focused on SEL while also providing supplemental readings for courses related to physical education curriculum, instruction, assessment, and/or model-based practice. Similarly, practicing physical education teachers who are interested in developing a stronger focus on SEL in their teaching will find that the book provides a comprehensive resource to guide their professional learning and practice.

In closing, physical education and SEL are both essential to a well-rounded education and we argue there is great synergy to be found at the intersection of these content areas. Fortunately, we have come to a point in the evolution of the American educational system where strong support is building for this idea. To capitalize on this opportunity, we believe the ideas and examples shared in this book can shape best practice and inform conversations among educational stakeholders as they consider what knowledge, skills, and experiences will most benefit our students the most.

Questions for Discussion

1. What is SEL? Define the concept broadly and provide some specific examples of relevant learning outcomes.
2. Should SEL be taught in schools? Explain your reasoning.
3. What have been some obstacles to effectively addressing SEL in American schools?
4. What are some of the arguments for explicitly teaching SEL concepts and skills to K–12 students?
5. Looking at the contents of this book as they have been previewed here, are there any approaches, perspectives, or voices you think might have been left out? Identify potential omissions and explain why that may be problematic.

References

American Enterprise Institute for Public Policy Research and the Brookings Institution. (2015). *Opportunity, responsibility, and security: A consensus plan for reducing poverty and restoring the American dream*. Washington, DC: Author.

Amis, J. M., Wright, P. M., Dyson, B., Vardaman, J. M., & Ferry, H. (2012). Implementing childhood obesity policy in a new educational environment: The cases of Mississippi and Tennessee. *American Journal of Public Health, 102*(7), 1406–1413.

Belfield, C., Bowden, A. B., Klapp, A., Levin, H., Shand, R., & Zander, S. (2015). *The economic value of social and emotional learning*. New York: Center for Benefit-Cost Studies in Education, Teachers College, Columbia University.

Bloom, B. S. (1956). *Taxonomy of Educational Objectives, Handbook I: The Cognitive Domain*. New York: David McKay Co Inc.

Brackett, M. (2019). *Permission to feel: Unlocking the power of emotions to help our kids, ourselves, and our society thrive*. New York: Celadon Books.

Catalano, R. F., Berglund, M. L., Ryan, J. A. M., Lonczak, H. S., & Hawkins, J. D. (2004). Positive youth development in the United States: Research findings on evaluations of positive development programs. *The Annals of the American Academy of Political and Social Science, 591*(1), 98–124.

Collaborative for Academic, Social, and Emotional Learning. (2013). *2013 CASEL Guide: Effective social and emotional learning programs – preschool and elementary school edition*. Chicago, IL: Author.

Collaborative for Academic, Social, and Emotional Learning. (2015). *2015 CASEL Guide: Effective social and emotional learning programs – middle and high school edition*. Chicago, IL: Author.

Collaborative for Academic, Social, and Emotional Learning. (2020). *What is social and emotional learning?* https://casel.org/what-is-sel/

Darling-Hammond, L. (2007). Race, inequality and educational accountability: The irony of "No Child Left Behind." *Race, Ethnicity and Education, 10*(3), 245–260.

Darling-Hammond, L. (2006). No child left behind and high school reform. *Harvard Educational Review, 76*(4), 642–667.

Dewey, J. (1938). *Experience and education*. New York: Touchstone.

Duckworth, A. (2016). *Grit: Passion, perseverance, and the science of success*. New York: Scribner.

Durlak, J. A., Weissberg, R. P., Dymnicki, A. B., Taylor, R. D., & Schellinger, K. B. (2011). The impact of enhancing students' social and emotional learning: A meta-analysis of school-based universal interventions. *Child Development, 82*(1), 405–432.

Dweck, C. S. (2007). *Mindset: The new psychology of success*. New York: Balantine Books.

Frey, N., Fisher, D., & Smith, D. (2019). *All learning is social and emotional: Helping students develop essential skills for the classroom and beyond*. Alexandria, VA: ASCD.

Goleman, D. (1995). *Emotional intelligence: Why it can matter more than IQ*. New York: Bantam Books.

Grant, S., Hamilton, L. S., Wrabel, S. L., Gomez, C. J., Whitaker, A., Leschitz, J. T., Unlu, F., Chavez-Herrerias, E. R., Baker, G., Barrett, M., Harris, M., & Ramos, A. (2017). Social and emotional learning interventions under the Every Student Succeeds Act: Evidence review. Santa Monica, CA: RAND Corporation.

Jacobs, J. M., & Wright, P. M. (2014). Social and emotional learning policies and physical education. *Strategies, 27*(6), 42–44.

Jones, D. E., Greenberg, M., & Crowley, M. (2015). Early social-emotional functioning and public health: The relationship between kindergarten social competence and future wellness. *American Journal of Public Health, 105*(11), 2283–2290.

Jones, S. M., & Kahn, J. (2017). *The evidence base for how we learn: Supporting students' social, emotional, and academic development*. Consensus statements of evidence from the National Commission on Social, Emotional, and Academic Development. Aspen, CO: The Aspen Institute.

Krathwohl, D. R., Bloom, B. S., & Masia, B. B. (1965). *Taxonomy of Educational Objectives, Handbook II: Affective Domain*. New York: David McKay Co Inc.

Lerner, R. M. (2007). *The good teen: Rescuing adolescence from the myths of the storm and stress years*. New York: Random House.

Lickona, T. (1991). *Educating for character: How our schools can teach respect and responsibility*. New York: Bantam.

Mahoney, J. L., Durlak, J. A., & Weissberg, R. P. (2018). An update on social and emotional learning outcome research. *Phi Delta Kappan, 100*(4), 18–23.

McKown, C. (2017). Social-emotional assessment, performance, and standards. *The Future of Children, 27*(1), 157–178.

National Commission on Excellence in Education. (1983). *A nation at risk: The imperative for educational reform*. Secretary of Education. Washington, DC: Author.

RAND Corporation. (2017). *Social and emotional learning interventions under the Every Student Succeeds Act: Evidence review – intervention summaries*. Santa Monica, CA: Author.

Ravitch, D. (2010). *The death and life of the great American school system*. New York: Basic Books.

Scales, P. C., Leffert, N., & Lerner, R. M. (1999). Developmental assets: A synthesis of the scientific research on adolescent development. Minneapolis, MN: Search Institute Press.

Schubert, W. (1986). *Curriculum: Perspectives, paradigm, and possibility*. Upper Saddle River, NJ: Prentice Hall.

Society for Health and Physical Educators (SHAPE) America. (2016). *Getting started with ESSA: A guide for health and physical educators*. Reston, VA: Society for Health and Physical Educators (SHAPE) America.

Taylor, R. D., Oberle, E., Durlak, J. A., & Weissberg, R. P. (2017). Promoting positive youth development through school-based social and emotional learning interventions: A meta-analysis of follow-up effects. *Child Development, 88*(4), 1156–1171.

Tough, P. (2012). *How children succeed: Grit, curiosity, and the hidden power of character.* New York, NY: Houghton Mifflin Harcourt.

Trilling, B. & Fadel, C. (2009). *21st century skills: Learning for life in our times.* San Francisco, CA: Jossey-Bass/Wiley.

Upshur, C. C., Heyman, M., & Wenz-Gross, M. (2017). Efficacy trial of the Second Step Early Learning (SSEL) curriculum: Preliminary outcomes. *Journal of Applied Psychology, 50*, 15–25.

Weiss, M. R. (2016). Old wine in a new bottle: Historical reflections on sport as a context for youth development. In N. Holt (Ed.), *Positive youth development through sport, (2nd edition)*. New York: Routledge.

Wright, P. M., Gordon, B. & Gray, S. (2020). Social and emotional learning in the physical education curriculum. In W. H. Schubert and M. Fang (Eds.), *Oxford Encyclopedia of Curriculum Studies*. Oxford, UK: Oxford University Press. doi: https://doi.org/10.1093/acrefore/9780190264093.013.1061

Wright, P. M. & Walsh, D. S. (2015). Subject matters of physical education. In M. F. He, B. D. Schultz, and W. H. Schubert (Eds.). *Guide to Curriculum in Education* (pp. 70–77). Thousand Oaks, CA: Sage.

CHAPTER 2

Connecting Social and Emotional Learning to the Physical Education Curriculum

K. Andrew R. Richards
Paul M. Wright

CHAPTER SUMMARY

Whereas Chapter 1 sets the stage by presenting an overview social and emotional learning (SEL) in the American educational system, this chapter highlights connections between SEL and sport and physical activity programming. School-based physical education programs are given particular attention. These relationships are discussed within a historical context and specific connections between the Society for Health and Physical Educators (SHAPE) America, (2014) national standards and the Collaborative for Academic, Social, and Emotional Learning (CASEL) (2019) SEL framework are explored. The chapter concludes with a discussion of pedagogical models that have been used to teach SEL in physical education and activity environments.

Connecting Social and Emotional Learning to the Physical Education Curriculum

Chapter 1 provided a general overview of social and emotional learning (SEL), its emergence as an important focus within the American educational system, and a description of CASEL (CASEL, 2019) framework as one approach to promoting SEL in schools. In this chapter, the SEL and CASEL frameworks are linked to the physical education curriculum. Specifically, in the first part of the chapter, the reasons why sport and physical activity are viewed as developmental sites for SEL are discussed, some of the historical connections between sport and life skill development are highlighted in more general terms, and an overview the history of social and emotional learning in the physical education curriculum is presented. In the second part of the chapter, CASEL SEL competencies are linked to (SHAPE) America (2014) national standards, the need to intentionally design SEL-focused learning experiences in physical education is addressed, and an overview of examples of physical education and activity programs and curricula focused on SEL is presented. Several of these programs and curricula will be discussed in greater detail later in the book, but we also focus here on highlighting the diversity of approaches that can be used to teach SEL in physical education and activity environments.

Why Is There a Connection Between Sport and Character Development?

As discussed in Chapter 1, there are a variety of reasons why schools are increasingly being considered places where social and emotional learning skills can be taught, developed, and practiced. From a big-picture perspective, focusing on social and emotional learning is important in its own right as these programs help to enhance nonacademic outcomes related to children's health (e.g., drug prevention), safety (e.g., violence prevention), citizenship behaviors (e.g., service-learning and engagement in local communities), and the ability to take responsibility for themselves (e.g., self-direction and goal setting) and those around them (e.g., leadership; Zins et al., 2004). Fostering social and emotional learning, however, has also been linked to the promotion of children's academic performance and lifelong learning, as well as improved classroom behavior; an increased ability to manage stress and depression; and better attitudes about themselves, others, and school in more general terms (Durlack et al., 2011). These effects can be long lasting with some programs showing continued influence on youth participants up to 18 years after implementation (Taylor et al., 2017), including increased social mobility for youths who grow up in communities affected by poverty (D. E. Jones et al., 2015). To summarize, there is a compelling argument for the inclusion of social and emotional learning in the school curriculum—from elementary school through high school graduation—in relation to (a) social and emotional learning outcomes, (b) academic development, and (c) future success.

Beyond the connections between social and emotional learning and the school curriculum, the extent to which sport and physical activity can be used as incubators of personal and social skills should also be considered. This connection has important implications for the school physical education curriculum where sport and physical activity provide the primary content foci. Many of us have likely heard the old adage at some point in our lives that "sport builds

character." This relationship is often prompted on the basis that sport includes some inherent qualities that help participants develop nonphysical skills, developmental outcomes (e.g., self-esteem) that are transferable to other areas of their lives (G. J. Jones et al., 2017). On the surface, the primary content that is taught through sport, physical activity, and physical education—throwing, kicking, running, jumping, etc.—does not have much to offer in terms of character development, so why are sports viewed as a space for social and emotional learning? What, for example, does learning how to throw a ball overhand have to do with becoming a more personally and socially responsible individual in our society? In short, they do not have much to do with these outcomes directly. In fact, when youth sport and physical activity programs are not designed to include positive, developmental outcomes, youths may learn less-adaptive skills such as cheating, cutting corners, and a winning-at-all-costs mentality (Coakley, 2011). In other words, sports can either have a positive or negative influence on personal development, depending how it is introduced, developed, and taught.

Taken together, the connection between sport and social and emotional learning is not as direct and automatic as the "sports build character" mantra may suggest (Lyras & Welty Peachey, 2011). With that said, however, sport and physical activity programs that take an intentional approach to developing social and emotional learning skills can be successful. Specifically, physical activity has been used as a medium through which to teach youths lessons related to a range of outcomes such as goal setting, perseverance, relationship development, cooperation, emotional regulation, and leadership (Holt et al., 2017). Children benefit from learning about these competencies from an early age, so the integration of social and emotional learning can begin as early as preschool (see Chapter 10) and carry through the high school experience (Ashdown & Bernard, 2012). Successful programs tend to view movement, physical activity, and sport as a hook to draw youth in and open lines of communication related to social and emotional learning through purposefully structured learning experiences (Gordon et al., 2016). In describing the integration of social and emotional learning into physical education and activity programs, Richards, Ivy, Wright, and Jacobs (2019) highlight four key facilitators that can help programming run more smoothly and work toward relevant goals:

- Develop a student-centered learning environment that empowers students to take positive risks, make their own decisions and understand the consequences of their actions, demonstrate competence in the activities being learned, and develop meaningful relationships with other students and the instructional leaders (Deci & Ryan, 2008).

- Create progressions for personal and social responsibility learning that lead students through a sequence of activities, gradually building their comfort and competence. For example, young children may be asked to practice discrete leadership tasks, such as leading a class line into or out of the gym, before they advance to more intensive tasks such as leading a small group through a new game.

- Social and emotional learning skills should be taught explicitly and as part of the content in physical education and activity programs. Accordingly, when games and activities are introduced and practiced, students should have the opportunity to practice and demonstrate competence related to selected social and emotional learning skills.

- Students should be provided developmentally appropriate and relevant examples to promote the transfer of learning from the physical activity program to other aspects of their lives. The ultimate goal of integrating social and emotional learning into physical activity programming is to help students develop skills that will transfer beyond the gymnasium and make them better people in a more holistic sense (Gordon et al., 2016).

In summary, if physical education and sport-related activities are presented and developed strategically, intentionally, and carefully, they serve an additional purpose of strengthening children's personal and social competencies in several ways.

Prioritizing social and emotional learning outcomes may feel difficult and uncomfortable for physical activity professionals, including physical education teachers, who believe in the importance of developing physical skills. With practice; however, individuals can become more comfortable integrating these competencies into their teaching and note any array of positive outcomes including classroom management, on-task behavior, and personal and social responsibility (Hemphill et al., 2015; Richards & Gordon, 2017). Physical education and activity leaders may also find that, as students learn these developmental skills, lessons go more smoothly with fewer instances of off-task behavior, which, in turn, increases the available time for physical activity and skill learning (Graham et al., 2013). That is, children will become more attentive, engaged, and interested in various activities.

As a result, investing in the pursuit of youth development goals through physical education and activity programs does not require program leaders to choose between SEL and psychomotor goals. However, it may take some additional time when first introducing social and emotional learning goals because it may be new to both the instructional leader and the students (Gordon et al., 2016). Take your time and stick with it. Instructional leaders who commit to the idea that physical activity presents a meaningful context to teach social and emotional learning will likely be successful with time and patience.

There is an added benefit of linking SEL with physical education. Many physical education teachers feel marginalized in their work contexts, meaning that they do not always feel like they teach a subject that is viewed as important to the overall mission of schooling (Laureano et al., 2014). Marginalization can appear in a variety of ways, including larger class sizes, limited facilities and equipment, and a lack of respect from colleagues and administrators. One key advantage of integrating social and emotional learning into physical education and activity programs is that it often aligns with larger school missions focused on encouraging positive developmental outcomes. Physical education instructors should look for connections regarding how their goals and activities fit in with the local school's general goals and aims. For example, some schools with which we have worked, have adopted *The 7 Habits of Highly Effective People* (Covey, 1989) as a guiding framework for student development and strive toward status as a *Leader in Me* Lighthouse School. Others embrace the CASEL (2019) framework more directly and have a school-wide mission focused specifically on developing social and emotional learning. Integrating social and emotional learning into school-based physical activity programs, therefore, may increase the relevance of physical education programming by helping children work toward broader school goals. While it is important that physical education be viewed as an important standalone subject, contributing to the broader mission of schooling may reduce physical educators' feelings of marginalization and help them to feel as if they are more important (Richards & Gordon, 2017).

Related to connecting physical education to larger school missions, it is also important to consider the target environment when teaching social and emotional learning in physical education. While it is important to strive toward increasing students' personal and social responsibility *within* physical education (SHAPE America, 2014), the ultimate goal of pursuing developmental outcomes often relates to the *transfer* of the associated behaviors and skills to other areas of youth's lives (Hellison, 2011). Ideally, for example, youth would learn about competencies such as goal setting within physical education and those lessons would help them to set better goals at school and in their personal lives. Transfer can be difficult, however, particularly when the environment in which a skill is learned is very different from the one into which it is being transferred (Gordon & Doyle, 2015). It may be easier for youth to transfer skills from physical education to a youth sport context than it would for them to apply skills in their mathematics class. Therefore, it is important for physical educators to specifically teach for transfer and provide relevant, developmentally appropriate examples (Richards et al., 2019).

While transfer can be challenging, youth, along with their parents and teachers, are able to identify how skills learned in well-designed programs are being used in other environments (Gordon & Doyle, 2015; Hemphill & Richards, 2016). It is also important to consider what counts as evidence of transfer. Although many practitioners and researchers have narrowly defined transfer only in relation to behavioral outcomes (e.g., actually showing the behavior), others have noted that transfer also includes cognitive and emotional dimensions (Jacobs & Wright, 2018). Drawing from the notion of a transformative experience (Pugh, 2004), Wright, Richards, Jacobs, and Hemphill (2019) proposed a three-pronged approach to understanding transfer that goes beyond observed behavior. *Expansion of perception* highlights the cognitive learning that takes place where youth learn about social and emotional skills and begin to understand their relevance beyond the immediacy of sports and physical activity. *Experiential value* indicates that youth see the value or worth of the skills they are learning relative to other contexts. Finally, *motivated use* relates to the motivation to apply skills outside of physical education in other areas of life. This expanded understanding of transfer highlights the role of cognitive learning, perceived value, and motivation in the transfer process and allows for transfer to be recognized outside of just behavior. A student may, for example, understand the importance of helping others, value the importance of this skill, and be motivated to help an elderly person take groceries out to the car, but other factors may prevent the student from actually helping. In this instance, while the behavior did not manifest, some of the cognitive and emotional processes have.

Historical Connections Between Social and Emotional Learning and Physical Activity

Connections between sport and the ability to build character or teach life skills goes back further than we might think. The Latin phrase, *mens sana in corpore sano*, which translates to "a sound mind in a sound body," is believed to have originated with the pre-Socratic Greek philosopher, Thales (624-546 BCE). While some debate exists relative to what was initially meant by this phrase, it was later adopted by educational theorists and philosophers, including John Locke in *Some Thoughts Concerning Education*, to emphasize connections between physical and mental health. Ancient Greek philosophers, including Socrates and Plato, discussed the relationship between physical body and mind, and Plato felt as if the primary goal in education should be to strive toward balance and harmony between the body and soul. In Eastern traditions, the connections between the body, mind, and soul can similarly be seen in religious practices, such as Yoga, that use physical exercise as a way to reach greater enlightenment. More recently, yoga has been adopted as a way to develop mindfulness practices and reduce stress (Smith et al., 2020). Many martial arts practices have in their roots a focus on mental and physical discipline and virtues such as humility, persistence, and respect (Maliszewski, 1996).

While connections between SEL and physical activity are evident in the ancient world, concrete associations are also found in more contemporary times. The specific virtues claimed for sport in relation to character development vary, however, depending on the specific time and place in history. In England during the 19th century, for example, sports were a fixture in many elite boarding schools because it was believed that the lessons taught through sport would help to develop qualities associated with leadership, strategic thinking, loyalty, and courage. This was linked to the Muscular Christianity movement that was initiated in England and eventually spread to the United States and other countries in which followers pursued physical strength and health alongside Christian ideals (Putney, 2003). It was this view of sports as a vehicle through which to develop character that led to the Duke of Wellington to say that "the battle of Waterloo was won on the playing fields of Eaton." The Duke, who was a graduate of Eaton and commander of the British forces at the Battle of Waterloo against the French and Napoleon Bonaparte, was attributing the military success to the qualities of character learned through sport and physical activity.

In the early 20th century in the United States, the character-building focus of sport was still recognized, but with different virtues in mind. Sport was viewed as a vehicle to socialize U.S. immigrants into the American values system while preparing the workforce with dispositions related to obedience, discipline, patriotism, and self-sacrifice. Eventually, discussions of physical education and activity recognized differences between the education of the physical and education through the physical (Williams, 1930). Education *of* the physical referred to the development of the physical body (e.g., stronger muscles, greater cardiorespiratory endurance), whereas education *through* the physical referred to learning cognitive and SEL-aligned lessons while being physically active. In the latter case, physical education and activity are viewed as the medium through which lessons are learned, including those related to social and emotional skills.

The continued commitment to education both *of* and *through* the physical is reflected in the SHAPE America (2014) national standards, which emphasize the physical domain (e.g., skill development, fitness) as well as cognitive understanding and value for movement and the associated health benefits. Personal and social responsibility is also emphasized in these standards. The emphasis on education of and through the physical is also reflected in the theory and practice of sports-based youth development (Holt et al., 2017). As an application of the broader focus on positive youth development (Catalano et al., 2004), these programs seek to use sport to teach social and emotional learning competencies. Defined as "programs that use a particular sport…to facilitate learning and life skill development in youth" (Perkins & Noam, 2007, p. 75), sport-based youth development reflects the education *through* the physical tradition of using sport as a vehicle to teach SEL goals. According to Perkins and Noam (2007), sport-based youth development programs include the following elements that have been adapted from larger positive youth development frameworks to focus on sport:

- **Physical and psychological safety**: The program provides a safe physical environment for activity and a positive and nurturing emotional climate characterized by support, mutual respect, and inclusivity.
- **Appropriate structure**: The program environment includes clear communication, developmentally appropriate activities and instructions,

and clear rules and expectations. Consequences for breaking rules are clear, fair, and accepted by all in the environment.

- **Supportive relationships**: Caring adults, who are invested in developing positive, supportive relationships with youth, are involved in leading the programs.
- **Opportunities to belong**: The culture of the program provides opportunities for students to connect with one another, develop positive interpersonal relationships, and feel a sense of belonging so that the experience becomes collective rather than just individual.
- **Positive social norms**: Programs promote positive social norms and good sporting behavior. A positive peer group culture helps to support the development of sportspersonship while reducing feelings of isolation and alienation.
- **Support for efficacy and mattering**: In relation to efficacy, programs focus on self-improvement relative to physical skill development rather than social comparisons based on athletic ability. Programs also help youth feel as if they matter and are able to make a positive difference in the lives of others in the group by encouraging helping behaviors.
- **Opportunities for skill building**: Program participants are able to develop both physical skills related to the activity focus (e.g., basketball, tennis) as well as life skills such as leadership, decision making, and problem-solving.
- **Opportunities to foster cultural competence**: Programs are sensitive to the cultural surroundings of the communities in which they are imbedded. Accordingly, the program structure, rules, and expectations are sensitive to and respectful of the values of the larger community. Furthermore, they provide youth with opportunities to develop cultural competence by working with peers who are different from them.
- **Active learning**: Programs provide learning experiences that engage multiple learning styles. Learning opportunities are experiential in nature and encourage participants to take positive risks and then learn from and through their experiences. Youths are given many opportunities to reflect on their experiences and grow through their mistakes.
- **Opportunities for recognition**: Youth participants are genuinely recognized for their contributions to the program that goes beyond winning physical competitions. Effort, improvement, and sportspersonship are also recognized and praised.

- **Strength-based focus**: Programs are structured in a way that draws on individual assets to develop new and refine existing skills. While programs may also decrease negative outcomes, the primary target is on developing strengths to help individuals thrive within their social environment to promote youth resiliency.
- **Ecological and holistic programs**: Effective programs are holistic in the sense that they address the whole child by targeting multiple facets of the physical and social environment. Accordingly, these programs use multiple methods that address the multiple roles that children play within their lives.
- **Integration of family, school, and community efforts**: Program coordinators work to coordinate their efforts and communicate regularly with families and schools to develop and enforce similar norms and expectations for youth. In an effort to build shared expectations, parents are invited to become involved in select program activities. Relationships developed with schoolteachers help to coordinate efforts, such as integrating academic foci into the program.

History of Social and Emotional Learning in Physical Education

Beyond the historical connections between sport and social and emotional learning in general developing life skills has been a focus in the physical education literature for decades. Without a doubt, the more historical discussions, such as those surrounding education *through* and *of* the physical, influenced the perspectives of early physical educators. For example, in the early 1900s, physical education pioneer Clark Hetherington promoted four goals for physical education that related to psychomotor, intellectual, organic, and character development outcomes (Siedentop, 2009). The work of Hetherington and other early physical educators led to the conceptualization of physical education as education for the whole child in body, mind, and spirit (Lund, 2010). While a focus beyond the "physical" part of physical education has been present for some time, the discipline has historically been very focused on physical skill development and delivered using teacher-centered instructional approaches (Corbin, 1993; Siedentop, 1980).

Hellison (1973) presented what may be among the first accounts of teaching social and emotional learning in physical education using what he called a humanistic approach. Humanistic physical education was presented as a values-based approach that contrasted with the prevailing models of physical education at the time. Rather than taking a detached view that focused primarily on physical skill development, the humanistic approach "means a concern for [people] above all else behaviorally and a concern for [people's] social and emotional wellbeing" (Hellison, 1973, p. 3). Later iterations of Hellison's (1978, 1995) work continued to elaborate what it meant for physical education to be humanistic and values-based, which led to the identification of SEL goals related to personal and social responsibility. This humanistic model for physical education would go on to become the teaching personal and social responsibility (TPSR) approach (Hellison, 2011), which is a now viewed as a best practice model for teaching social and emotional learning in physical education (see Chapter 7).

While Hellison's (1973) early work laid the foundation for physical education programs focused on social and emotional learning, the road was not always easy. Through the 1980s and 1990s, much of the mainstream physical education community continued to take a narrow view of the discipline focused primarily on physical skill and fitness development. This led those who prioritized SEL outcomes to feel like outsiders or as if they were on the margins of the discipline (Hellison & Martinek, 2009). A shift occurred, however, through the 1990s and into the early 2000s. During this time, TPSR and other developmental and holistic approaches, such as sport for peace (Ennis et al., 1999), and specific curricula designed to address the needs and interests of teenage girls (Oliver, 1999), was introduced, developed, field-tested, and garnered popularity. This movement from marginal to more central within the physical education community was punctuated with the publication of the first national standards for physical education (National Association for Sport and Physical Education, 1995), which included an explicit focus on personal and social responsibility, and valuing the benefits of physical activity.

Building from the work of early pioneers and more contemporary physical educators, social and emotional learning continued to gain a foothold within the physical education community into the 2000s and beyond. Two of the five current SHAPE America (2014) national standards include a focus on personal and social responsibility (Standard 4) and learning to value the many benefits of being physically active (Standard 5). Given the imprint of social and emotional learning in the national standards (see **Table 2.1** for a complete list of the SHAPE America

Table 2.1 National Standards for Physical Education

Standard	Descriptor
Standard 1	The physically literate individual demonstrates competency in a variety of motor skills and movement patterns.
Standard 2	The physically literate individual applies knowledge of concepts, principles, strategies, and tactics related to movement and performance.
Standard 3	The physically literate individual demonstrates the knowledge and skills to achieve and maintain a health-enhancing level of physical activity and fitness.
Standard 4	The physically literate individual exhibits responsible personal and social behavior that respects self and others.
Standard 5	The physically literate individual recognizes the value of physical activity for health, enjoyment, challenge, self-expression, and/or social interaction.

Modified from Society of Health and Physical Educators America. (2014). *National standards and grade-level outcomes for K-12 physical education.* Human Kinetics. Copyright © 2022 by the Society of Health and Physical Educators (SHAPE America), a 501(c)(3) corporation.

national standards), it can be considered part of the content that is intended to be taught in physical education (Gordon et al., 2016). As a result, many physical education programs and curricula also attend to SEL, even if that is not the primary domain priority. At the elementary level, for example, the skill themes approach is primarily concerned with learning fundamental movement skills (Metzler, 2011), but references strategies from the TPSR model for developing personal and social responsibility as well (Graham et al., 2013). In sum, the major standards of the discipline focus on the importance of developing SEL competencies as an intrinsic part of physical education. In other words, to be effective in meeting the national standards, physical educators must include a clear and coordinated emphasis on the development of various related SEL competencies.

More recently, physical educators have taken strides to align with the broader push toward social and emotional learning in education generally (Gordon et al., 2016). SHAPE America (2014), for example, notes that social and emotional learning can improve student behavioral and academic outcomes and they support the integration of social and emotional learning in the school curriculum. One key milestone in this process was the announcement and implementation of SHAPE America's *Health. Moves. Minds.* initiative (www.shapeamerica.org/events /healthmovesminds/), which seeks to "inspire healthy habits, fuel active minds, and teach kids to thrive physically and emotionally." The program seeks to address both the fact that children in contemporary schools do not get enough physical activity and may have social, emotional, and mental health challenges by promoting lessons focused on both physical

activity and social and emotional competencies. By addressing these challenges, *Health. Moves. Minds.* seeks to promote an active school environment that helps children to better cope with the stress, bullying, and social pressures they encounter both inside and outside of the school environment. Furthermore, teachers committing to *Health. Moves. Minds.* can organize events to raise awareness as well as funds for their programs and local community charities.

Connections Between Physical Education Goals and the CASEL Framework

The CASEL (2019) framework has emerged as one prominent model for conceptualizing social and emotional learning across education. As elaborated in Chapter 1, CASEL (2019) conceptualizes social and emotional learning as the process through which youth develop both understandings and skills related to emotional self-regulation, relationship development, social skills, goal setting, and the ability to make healthy choices. This is done through the development of competencies across five interrelated domains: self-management, self-awareness, social awareness, relationship skills, and positive decision making. Given the prominence of the CASEL framework, it provides one standard against which we can evaluate the relationship between physical education and social and emotional learning. The SHAPE America (2014) national standards, which represent the knowledge, skills, and dispositions that individuals should

Table 2.2 Connections Between the SHAPE America (2014) Standards and CASEL (2019) Competencies

SA Standards	Primary Components	Secondary Components	Associated CASEL Competencies
Standard 1	Skill development	----	N/A
Standard 2	Knowledge of movement	----	Self-management, positive decision making,
Standard 3	Life-enhancing activity	----	Self-management, positive decision making
Standard 4	Personal responsibility	Participation and effort	Positive decision making, self-awareness
		Self-direction	Self-management, self-direction
	Social responsibility	Respect	Self-awareness, social awareness
		Caring and leadership	Relationship skills, self-awareness
	Transfer	----	Positive decision making, self-awareness, social awareness
Standard 5	Valuing physical activity	----	Self-awareness, self-management, positive decision making

SA = SHAPE America

Data from Gordon, B., Jacobs, J. M., & Wright, P. M. (2016). Social and emotional learning through a teaching personal and social responsibility-based after school program for disengaged middle school boys. *Journal of Teaching in Physical Education, 35,* 358–369; and Society of Health and Physical Educators America. (2014). *National standards and grade-level outcomes for K–12 physical education.* Human Kinetics.

develop through physical education to be considered physically literate, and thus reflect a consensus statement on the overarching goals of physical education. By comparing the SHAPE America national standards with the CASEL framework, we can get a sense of alignment between social and emotional learning and physical education (see **Table 2.2**).

In an effort to connect social and emotional learning via CASEL (2019) with the SHAPE America (2014) national standards, SHAPE America (2019) released a crosswalk document to illustrate connections across the two frameworks. Therein, it is argued that "the knowledge, skills and confidence learned in a physical education classroom not only allow students to enjoy a lifetime of physical activity, but also allow students to learn and refine social and emotional skills" (Society of Health and Physical Eductors America, 2019, p. 1). Given that first SHAPE America (2014) national standard emphasizes psychomotor outcomes, we can focus the discussion on the remaining four standards. Standard 2 focused on cognitive development, stating that "the physically literate individual applies knowledge of concepts, principles, strategies and tactics related to movement and performance." Activities such as creating workout or practice plans, analyzing game situations, and selecting and using appropriate skills given the

contextual demands of the game can relate to social and emotional skills such as self-management and responsible decision making if they are taught intentionally. They provide students with time to practice taking care of themselves through planning and problem solving.

Standard 3 suggests that "the physically literate individual demonstrates the knowledge and skills to achieve and maintain a health-enhancing level of physical activity and fitness." Given that physical activity is connected to self-management, students working toward Standard 3 can also practice better understanding and managing themselves and their bodies, and making responsible decisions as they analyze and reflect upon physical activity and health information. They can also work toward goal setting as they seek to identify and improve upon areas of fitness that they find personally meaningful, and perhaps in relation to data obtained through physical fitness and health screenings or evaluations. Again, the key opportunity here relates to taking personal responsibility for one's own health and well-being.

Standard 4 suggests that "the physically literate individual exhibits responsible personal and social behavior that respects self and others." This objective relates primarily to the development of personal and social responsibility, which can be interpreted further through the TPSR approach, which includes five responsibility-based goals (Hellison, 2011). The participation and effort and self-direction goals relate to personal responsibility, whereas the respect and caring and leadership goals are focused on social responsibility. The fifth goal, transfer, highlights the value and relevance of the first four goals outside of the physical education or activity program. Gordon and colleagues (2016) showed the connection between these goals and CASEL framework. Specifically, the TPSR *respect* goal connects to self-awareness and social awareness, whereas *participation and effort* relate to the CASEL competencies of positive decision making and self-awareness. The *self-direction* TPSR goal connects to self-management and self-awareness, whereas *caring and leadership* relate to relationship skills and social awareness. Finally, the *transfer* goal within TPSR connects to the positive decision making, self-awareness, and social awareness CASEL competencies.

The fifth SHAPE America (2014) standard indicates that "the physically literate individual recognizes the value of physical activity for health, enjoyment, challenge, self-expression and/or social interaction." This focus on valuing or appreciating the role of physical education in one's life similarly maps to several of the CASEL (2019) framework competencies. Becoming more aware of what we value and how what we value influences our lives relates to self-awareness. Learning to value physical activity also promotes self-management, particularly given that a physically active lifestyle has been associated with stress management and often involves setting and working toward goals for physical development. Through physical education, students can also learn important lessons about perseverance in the face of obstacles or stress (e.g., when they have a difficult time learning a new skill), which helps them learn to cope with setbacks, slow progress, and emotional responses such as frustration. There are also elements of responsible decision making within SHAPE America Standard 4 as valuing and participating in physical activity is a responsible decision in relation to physical, mental, and emotional health. Collectively, therefore, it can be concluded that the SHAPE America (2014) national standards and the social and emotional learning competencies stressed by CASEL (2019) overlap and have a lot in common (SHAPE America, 2019). This further substantiates the argument that social and emotional learning is an essential part of physical education, making it something that we should be teaching rather than something that is added to the curriculum or viewed as supplemental.

Physical Education Pedagogical Models That Connect with Social and Emotional Learning

Pedagogical models provide specific guidelines for the role of the teacher and students and include unique features to differentiate them from one another and to allow for an interplay between the subject matter taught and the learning context (Sinelnikov & Hastie, 2017). The physical education community has increasingly embraced model-based instruction over the last several decades (Casey, 2014), in part because it allows teachers to highlight different goals or priorities within the physical education context (Metzler, 2011). While pedagogical models emphasize multiple domains for learning (e.g., psychomotor, cognitive, SEL), and those such as sport education do so pretty equally (Siedentop et al., 2004), most have different domain priorities (see **Table 2.3**). Models such as the skill themes approach (Graham et al., 2013) prioritize the psychomotor domain through skill development, whereas the tactical games approach (Mitchell et al., 2006) is more concerned with cognitive understanding of skills and strategies. Others, such as TPSR (Hellison, 2011) and cooperative learning (Dyson & Casey, 2012), are better suited to addressing the SEL. Teachers, therefore, have the ability to select a pedagogical model that aligns best with the needs of their students, the context of their school, and the content they are planning to teach.

Since most pedagogical models emphasize SEL to varying degrees, many can be used to teach social and emotional learning competencies. There are, however, some models that tend to emphasize SEL more than others. In Section 2 of this book, authors highlight five different pedagogical models that have been used to emphasize SEL. We acknowledge that this list is not all inclusive; models such as sport for peace (Ennis et al., 1999), and other curricular approaches, such as Oliver's (1999) work with adolescent girls, reflect just a few of the approaches for emphasizing social and emotional learning that are not covered in this text. The foundation provided herein will, however, be a good start for learning many of the basics and to see the variety of ways through which social and emotional learning can be integrated into the physical education curriculum.

The common thread across all of these pedagogical models is that SEL skills are built into their

Table 2.3 Common Pedagogical Models in Physical Education with Domain Priorities

Model Name	Description	Domain Priorities
Skill themes approach	Focus on the development of fundamental motor skills (i.e., skill themes) and associated movement concepts that are later in a variety of applications related to sports, dance, and gymnastics activities.	Typically, the psychomotor domain is most prominent but can be adapted to include elements of more of an SEL focus, such as is the case when combined with TPSR.
Adventure-based learning	Takes students through an intentional sequence of adventure activities that promote trust, problem-solving, and positive risk taking in order to help students develop personally (e.g., increased confidence) as well as socially (e.g., group processing skills).	Given that the focus is more on interpersonal and intrapersonal development, the psychomotor domain is less of a focus. The domain priorities typically prioritize SEL followed by cognitive and psychomotor.
TPSR	Youth work toward the pursuit of SEL goals related to personal (i.e., participation and effort, self-direction) and social (i.e., respect, helping others and leadership) goals with the ultimate goal being to transfer learning beyond the gym to other settings.	Addresses all learning domains, and the emphasis may shift, but priorities tend to be in the following order: SEL, cognitive, and psychomotor
Sport education	Seeks to help youth develop into competent, literate, and enthusiastic sportspeople through the creation of an authentic sporting culture in physical education or activity settings. Key elements include: prolonged units of instruction (i.e., seasons), continuous team affiliation throughout the season, formal competition, a culminating event or ceremony, team, and individual record keeping, and festivity.	Addresses all three domains, but specific priorities shift depending on the particular activity in which students are engaged. During the preseason, for example, team coaches are engaged in activities that prioritize cognitive, then SEL and psychomotor goals.
Cooperative learning	Students work in teams toward tasks that require interdependence. Key elements include: intentional group formation, continuity of group interaction, interdependence among group members, individual accountability, explicit development of social skills, and instructor as a facilitator	SEL always shares the main priority with either cognitive or psychomotor learning depending on the focus of the task. For example, if working on a project related to the history of soccer, SEL and cognitive would be primary followed by psychomotor.

TPSR = teaching personal and social responsibility
Data from Pedagogical model domain priorities adapted from: Metzler, M. W. (2011). *Instructional models in physical education* (3rd ed.). Holcomb Hathaway.

framework highlighting the opportunity to bring these outcomes to the surface. As mentioned previously, it cannot be assumed that students will learn life skills just by participating in sport and physical activity—sport does not naturally build character (Lyras & Welty Peachey, 2011)—however, when programs are intentionally created to promote character development, certain elements occurring naturally in sport (e.g., teamwork) can be brought to the surface (Holt et al., 2017). These pedagogical models can help develop learning experiences that facilitate this process.

At the elementary level, Parker, Patton, Iannucci, and Mangione highlight the skill themes approach, which is among the most widely used approaches for the development of physical education curricula for young children (Metzler, 2011). It has also been used in conjunction with the TPSR model as a way to teach social and emotional learning in elementary school contexts (Richards et al., 2019). Beyond the skill themes approach, we have recruited area specialists to draft four chapters to describe pedagogical models that have some application in elementary environments but tend to be more widely implemented in secondary school settings. These include adventure-based learning (Chapter 6), TPSR (Chapter 7), sport education (Chapter 8), and cooperative learning (Chapter 9).

Conclusion and Final Thoughts

The purpose of this chapter was to overview the history of and strong connections between social and emotional learning and the physical education curriculum. Building upon Chapter 1, which described social and emotional learning in general and in relation to the CASEL framework, we began with an overview of the connections between sport and physical activity and social and emotional learning. The history of this intersection was then explored in greater detail, beginning with ancient Western and Eastern philosophers and leading up to the development of sport-based youth development programs (Holt et al., 2017). The discussion then turned to the historical connections specific to school physical education,

beginning with the ideals of early physical education pioneers, through the development of national standards that promote social and emotional learning and SHAPE America's recent *Health.Moves.Minds.* initiative. The emphasis was then placed on the connection between the SHAPE America (2014) national standards and the CASEL (2019) framework, with the case being made that physical education is well-aligned with social and emotional learning and well positioned to address it through intentionally developed curricula. The chapter then concluded with examples of pedagogical models that are particularly well suited to address social and emotional learning. These will be elaborated in Section 2 of the book. Moving on from curriculum, Chapter 3 and Chapter 4 of this text will now turn to teaching practices and assessment techniques that align with social and emotional learning in physical education, respectively.

Questions for Discussion

1. Describe the historical relationship between physical activity and SEL. How has this relationship developed and influenced the movement toward sport-based youth development?
2. Why are sport and physical activity spaces often viewed as places for addressing SEL?
3. How would you describe the relationship between the SHAPE America (2014) national standards for physical education and the CASEL (2019) framework for SEL?
4. What are pedagogical models and how can they be used to address SEL in physical education environments?

References

Ashdown, D. M., & Bernard, M. E. (2012). Can explicit instruction in social and emotional learning skills benefit the social-emotional development, well-being, and academic achievement of young children? *Early Childhood Education Journal, 39*, 397–405.

Casey, A. (2014). Models-based practice: Great white hope or white elephant? *Physical Education and Sport Pedagogy, 19*(1), 18–34.

Catalano, R. F., Berglund, M. L., Ryan, J. A. M., Lonczak, H. S., & Hawkins, J. D. (2004). Positive youth development in the United States: Research findings on evaluations of positive development programs. *The Annals of the American Academy of Political and Social Science, 591*(1), 98–124.

Coakley, J. (2011). Youth sports: What counts as "positive youth development?" *Journal of Sport and Social Issues, 35*(3), 306–324.

Collaborative for Academic, Social, and Emotional Learning. (2019). *What is social and emotional learning?* https://casel.org/what-is-sel/

Corbin, C. B. (1993). The field of physical education: Common goals, not common roles. *Journal of Physical Education, Recreation & Dance, 64*(1), 79–87.

Cosgriff, M. (2000). Walking our talk: Adventure-based learning and physical education. *Journal of Physical Education New Zealand, 33*(2), 89–98.

Covey, S. R. (1989). *The 7 habits of highly effective people: Powerful lessons in personal change.* Freer Press.

Deci, E. L., & Ryan, R. M. (2008). Self-determination theory: A macrotheory of human motivation, development, and health. *Canadian Psychology, 49*(3), 182–185.

Durlack, J. A., Weissberg, R. P., Dymnicki, A. B., Taylor, R. D., & Schellinger, K. B. (2011). The impact of enhancing students' social and emotional learning: A meta-analysis of school-based universal interventions. *Child Development, 82*(1), 405–432.

Dyson, B., & Casey, A. (Eds.). (2012). *Cooperative learning in physical education.* Taylor & Francis.

Ennis, C. D., Solmon, M. A., Satina, B., Loftus, S. J., Mensch, J., & McCauley, M. T. (1999). Creating a sense of family inn urban schools using the "Sport for Peace" curriculum. *Research Quarterly for Exercise & Sport, 70*(3), 273–285.

Gordon, B., & Doyle, S. (2015). Teaching personal and social responsibility and transfer of learning: Opportunities and challenges for teachers and coaches. *Journal of Teaching in Physical Education, 34*(1), 152–161.

Gordon, B., Jacobs, J. M., & Wright, P. M. (2016). Social and emotional learning through a teaching personal and social responsibility based after-school program for disengaged middle school boys. *Journal of Teaching in Physical Education, 35*(4), 358–369.

Graham, G., Holt-Hale, S. A., & Parker, M. (2013). *Children moving: A reflective approach to physical education* (9th ed.). McGraw-Hill.

Hellison, D. (1973). *Humanistic physical education*. Prentice-Hall.

Hellison, D. (1978). *Beyond balls and bats: Alienated (and other) youth in the gym*. AAHPER.

Hellison, D. (1995). *Teaching responsibility through physical activity*. Human Kinetics.

Hellison, D. (2011). *Teaching personal and social responsibility through physical activity* (3rd ed.). Human Kinetics.

Hellison, D., & Martinek, T. (2009). Living in the margins of our field. In L. D. Housner, M. W. Metzler, P. G. Schempp, & T. J. Templin (Eds.), *Historic traditions and future directions of research on teaching and teacher education in physical education* (pp. 267–270). Fitness Information Technology.

Hemphill, M. A., & Richards, K. A. R. (2016). "Without the academic part, it wouldn't be squash": Youth development in an urban squash program. *Journal of Teaching in Physical Education, 35*(3), 263–276.

Hemphill, M. A., Templin, T. J., & Wright, P. M. (2015). Implementation and outcomes of a responsibility-based continuing professional development protocol in physical education. *Sport, Education and Society, 20*(3), 398–419.

Holt, N. L., Neely, K. C., Slater, L. G., Camiré, M., Côté, J., Fraser-Thomas, J., . . . Tamminen, K. A. (2017). A grounded theory of positive youth development through sport based on results from a qualitative meta-study. *International Review of Sport and Exercise Psychology, 10*(1), 1–49.

Jacobs, J. M., & Wright, P. M. (2018). Transfer of life skills in sport-based youth development programs: A conceptual framework bridging learning to application. *Quest, 70*(1), 81–99.

Jones, D. E., Greenberg, M., & Crowley, M. (2015). Early social-emotional functioning and public health: The relationship between kindergarten competence and future wellness. *American Journal of Public Health, 105*(11), 2283–2290.

Jones, G. J., Edwards, M. B., Bocarro, J. N., Bunds, K. S., & Smith, J. W. (2017). An integrative review of sport-based youth development literature. *Sport in Society, 20*(1), 161–179.

Laureano, J., Konukman, F., Gümüşdağ, H., Erdoğan, S., Yu, J. H., & Çekin, R. (2014). Effects of marginalization on school physical education programs: A literature review. *Physical Culture and Sport: Studies and Research, 64*(1), 29–40.

Lund, J. (2010). Educating the whole child. *Journal of Physical Education, Recreation & Dance, 81*(5), 3–10.

Lyras, A., & Welty Peachey, J. (2011). Integrating sport-for-development theory and praxis. *Sport Management Review, 14*(4), 311–326.

Maliszewski, M. (1996). *Spiritual dimesions of the martial arts*. Tuttle.

Metzler, M. W. (2011). *Instructional models in physical education* (3rd ed.). Holcomb Hathaway.

Mitchell, S. A., Oslin, J. L., & Griffin, L. (2006). *Teaching sport concepts and skills: A tactical games approach* (2nd ed.). Human Kinetics.

National Association for Sport and Physical Education. (1995). *Moving into the future: National standards for physical education—a guide to content and assessment*. Mosby.

Oliver, K. L. (1999). Adolescent girls' body-narratives: Learning to desire and create a "fashionable" image. *Teachers College Record, 101*(2), 220–246.

Perkins, D. F., & Noam, G. G. (2007). Characteristics of sport-based youth development programs. *New Directions for Youth Development, 115*, 75–84.

Pugh, K. J. (2004). Newton's laws beyond the classroom walls. *Science Education, 88*(2), 182–196.

Putney, C. (2003). *Muscular Christianity: Manhood and sports in Protestant America, 1880–1920*. Harvard University Press.

Richards, K. A. R., & Gordon, B. (2017). Socialisation and learning to teach using the teaching personal and social responsibility approach. *Asia-Pacific Journal of Health, Sport and Physical Education, 8*(1), 19–38.

Richards, K. A. R., Ivy, V. N., Wright, P. M., & Jerris, E. (2019). Combining the skill themes approach with teaching personal and social responsibility to teach social and emotional learning in elementary physical education. *Journal of Physical Education, Recreation & Dance, 90*(3), 35–44.

Siedentop, D. (1980). *Physical education introductory analysis*. Wm. C. Brown.

Siedentop, D. (2002). Content knowledge for physical education. *Journal of Teaching in Physical Education, 21*(4), 368–377.

Siedentop, D. (2009). *Introduction to physical education, fitness and sport* (7th ed.). McGraw-Hill.

Siedentop, D., Hastie, P. A., & van der Mars, H. (2004). *Complete guide to sport education*. Human Kinetics.

Sinelnikov, O. A., & Hastie, P. (2017). The learning of pedagogical models in physical education: The socialization perspective. In K. A. R. Richards & K. L. Gaudreault (Eds.), *Teacher socialization in physical education: New perspectives* (pp. 130–143). Routledge.

Smith, B. H., Esat, G., & Kanojia, A. (2020). School-based yoga for managing stress and anxiety. In C. Maykel & M. A. Bray (Eds.), *Applying psychology in the schools. Promoting mind–body health in schools: Interventions for mental health professionals* (pp. 201–216). American Psychological Association.

Society of Health and Physical Educators America. (2014). *National standards and grade-level outcomes for K-12 physical education*. Human Kinetics.

Society of Health and Physical Eductors America. (2019). *Crosswalk for SHAPE America National Standards & Grade-Level Outcomes for K-12 Physical Education and CASEL Social and Emotional Learning Core Competencies*. Author.

Taylor, R. D., Oberle, E., Durlack, J. A., & Weissberg, R. P. (2017). Promoting positive youth development through school-based social and emotional learning interventions: A meta-analysis of follow-up effects. *Child Development, 88*(4), 1156–1171.

Williams, J. F. (1930). Education through the physical. *The Journal of Higher Education, 1*(5), 279–282.

Wright, P. M., Richards, K. A. R., Jacobs, J. M., & Hemphill, M. A. (2019). Measuring perceived transfer of responsibility learning from physical education: Initial validation of the Transfer of Responsibility Questionnaire. *Journal of Teaching in Physical Education. 38*(4), 316–327. doi.org/10.1123/jtpe.2018-0246

Zins, J. E., Weissberg, R. P., Wang, M. C., & Walberg, H. J. (Eds.). (2004). *Building academic success on social and emotional learning: What does the research say?* Teachers College Press.

CHAPTER 3

Teaching Practices That Align with Social and Emotional Learning

Paul M. Wright

K. Andrew R. Richards

CHAPTER SUMMARY

Having introduced social and emotional learning (SEL) and discussed its place in the physical education curriculum in Chapters 1 and 2, respectively, we now turn our focus to teaching practices. A range of perspectives is discussed on teaching as well as approaches and strategies commonly used in physical education. The range of decisions that teachers make in shaping their practice and the continuum of teaching styles that result is also examined. The extensive analysis is focused on identifying practices that align most strongly with the promotion of SEL.

Teaching Practices That Align with Social and Emotional Learning

In the preceding chapters, social and emotional learning (SEL) was introduced and framed within the physical education curriculum. Flowing from Chapter 2, which provided a framework for promoting SEL through the selection of content, this chapter addresses the delivery of that content (i.e., teaching practices). A range of teaching practices is employed by physical education teachers and several that align strongly with SEL are highlighted. We also address common notions and practices that sometimes get in the way of good SEL teaching. Finally, framed largely through the work of Mosston and Ashworth (2017), we introduce and orient readers to the range of decisions that teachers make and the variation in teaching styles that can result from those decisions. Against this backdrop, we highlight strategies that can be readily applied to teach SEL competencies. Subsequent chapters provide more detail on specific model-based practices as well as case examples of programs that have applied such strategies in school-based physical education and other physical-activity settings.

Definition of Terms

Before proceeding, we believe it is important to clarify our use of certain terms and concepts that are relevant to this discussion but are often used interchangeably and/or defined in many different ways. For example, *teaching practices*, *instruction*, and *pedagogy* are highly related terms with overlapping definitions. The same can be said of terms such as *instructional model*, *curriculum model*, *pedagogical model*, and *models-based practice*. In fact, the nuances among such terms and concepts are actively debated in the current physical education literature (Casey, 2017; Kirk, 2013; Sinelnikov & Hastie, 2017). It is beyond our scope to examine the semantic and etymological differences among these terms; rather, our approach has been to select terms that are commonly used and that we believe convey our meaning effectively. As needed, we provide our working definitions for such terms. However, when we quote or refer to the ideas of others, we frequently adopt their preferred terminology.

In this chapter, we refer to *teaching practice* as an intentional activity in which one party (i.e., the teacher) interacts with another (i.e., the learner or student) with the goal of helping the latter attain a learning objective (Dewey, 1938). According to educational theorist Joseph Schwab (1973, 1983), teaching–learning exchanges occur at the intersection of four essential factors including the (a) teacher, (b) student, (c) subject matter, and (d) the context in which the exchange occurs. The notion of context as used here is layered and includes the immediate physical and social environment as well as the broader political and socio-historical context that influences social justice issues related to education (Schubert, 1986). Our primary focus in this chapter is the *subject matter* of SEL competencies embedded in physical education as it is delivered in the context of the school curriculum. However, the fundamental decisions, teaching practices, and strategies we discuss are universal and can be used to teach other skills and other subject matter. Toward this end, most examples here, and in subsequent chapters, reference general physical education teachers working in K–12 schools. However, examples of work in a variety of other settings are also addressed, including preschool (Chapter 10) and adapted physical education (Chapter 11) settings as well as community-based programs (e.g., afterschool sport and juvenile detention centers; Chapter 15).

While we write primarily from the U.S. context, the integration of SEL in physical education is an international phenomenon (Dyson, Howley & Wright, 2020; Wright, Gordon & Gray, 2020). The concepts and teaching approaches we share are based on practice and research conducted in several countries around the world in a wide array of settings as reflected in multiple reviews of the literature (e.g., Baptista et al., 2020; Dyson et al., 2020; Pozo et al., 2018). Therefore, we ask the reader, to keep in mind the general nature of this discussion and not to be restricted by the details of any specific example. With this said, for consistency, the terms "teacher" and "student" will be used frequently in the discussion. We also acknowledge that most of our discussion revolves around teaching-learning exchanges involving multiple students coming together face-to-face with a teacher in the same physical space. These dynamics do not characterize all educational exchanges, but they are the most relevant to the objectives of this text. Especially in light of the recent COVID-19 pandemic, we encourage the reader to be flexible and apply their own situational insight into considering how these fundamental practices could generalize to other contexts, subject matters, and circumstances (e.g., virtual instruction).

Influences That Shape Teaching Practices

Teaching practices (e.g., styles, strategies, and techniques) do not exist in a vacuum. They are brought to life by teachers who select and deliver them. There are a range of curriculum perspectives and value orientations that inform teaching decisions, shape a teacher's practice, and manifest in their interactions with students (Jewett, Bain & Ennis, 1995; Schubert, 1986). The styles and strategies a teacher uses are shaped by many influences, including their own personal values and beliefs, philosophy of teaching, prior educational experiences and socialization, and initial teacher education (Chen et al., 1997; Richards et al., 2019). Teachers are often encouraged to reflect on their teaching philosophy to clarify and articulate their core beliefs, values, assumptions, and motivation for teaching (Schön, 1987). These issues are the basis for the decisions that shape a teachers' style, the teaching–learning experience, and ultimately their students' development (Hellison & Templin, 1991). In the following section, we highlight the role of reflection, teaching philosophy, and value orientations in shaping teaching practices. We also describe and contrast teacher- versus student-centered approaches, which will set the stage for further discussion.

Reflection

Despite the strong case for teacher reflection (Hellison & Templin, 1991; Schon, 1987), teaching practices are often reduced to a technical or mechanical level (e.g., techniques and tactics; Wright & Craig, 2011). We are not opposed to a concrete, practical, and operational approach; however, we believe techniques and tactics are most effective when they are selected intentionally as part of a coordinated approach that is informed by reflective thought. For example, think-pair-share is a cooperative learning technique that is fairly easy to explain and implement (Johnson & Johnson, 1994). A simplistic overview of the technique is that students are asked to first think of their response to a question or topic, pair up with a partner to discuss, and then share with the larger class (Dyson & Casey, 2016). While many such techniques are identified and offered as examples of promising practice in this book, we do not want them to appear random or isolated. Rather, we encourage teachers to consider the underlying assumptions and commitments reflected in certain strategies.

Regarding the think-pair-share example, this reflective approach to decision making could be driven by questions such as: (a) what is the value in a think-pair-share activity over direct instruction? (b) what assumptions about the learning process would lead a teacher to use this strategy? (c) what SEL skills are students practicing in this particular cooperative learning experience? and (d) where do those skills fit within the learning objectives for this lesson? The teacher's responses and thoughts on questions like these are reflective of their teaching philosophy. A high level of agreement between teaching philosophy and teaching practice results in a more intentional and coherent approach to promoting certain learning experiences and outcomes (i.e., a teaching style; Byra, 2006). Both reflection-in-action (i.e., while teaching) and reflection-on-action (i.e., before and after teaching) are important in helping a teacher to refine and clarify their teaching philosophy and to increase alignment between their philosophy and their practice (Jung, 2012; McCollum, 2002; Standal & Moe, 2013; Tsangaridou & O'Sullivan, 1997). In the next section, we explore the notion of teaching philosophy in more depth, including the various curricular value orientations commonly associated with physical education.

Teaching Philosophies and Value Orientations

Teaching philosophies are personal and idiosyncratic but address the fundamental purposes of education (i.e., beliefs about what is most important for students to know, experience, and be able to do; Schubert, 1986). They also reflect on the teacher's beliefs about the roles of the teacher and the students, appropriate teacher–student interactions, and the nature of learning (Schubert, 1996). For example, some teachers are primarily concerned with the transmission of subject matter knowledge they consider inherently valuable, whereas others are more concerned with the process of learning itself as a way of teaching students how to learn and think critically about social injustice (Schubert, 1986, 1996). In the physical education literature, five distinct value orientations have been associated with the kind of curricular and instructional decisions a teacher makes. These include disciplinary mastery, learning process, self-actualization, social responsibility, and ecological integration (Jewett, Bain & Ennis, 1995).

Disciplinary mastery is primarily concerned with the student developing competence in the subject matter whereas *learning process* emphasizes helping students to become better learners by solving problems and developing critical thinking skills. *Self-actualization* is an individualized and holistic approach emphasizing the development of psychological well-being, autonomy, growth, and self-concept, whereas *social responsibility* is focused on the potential of education to address broader issues (e.g., equity and social justice) that shape society. Finally, *ecological integration* is strongly related to self-actualization but balances this with an ecological perspective (i.e., different spheres of influence such as family, peer group, and broader community that shape and reinforce learning). In practice, many teachers' personal philosophies reflect a combination of such value orientations. Chen and colleagues' (1997) value orientations inventory provides a series of question blocks, with one question in each block corresponding to one of the five value orientations. Individuals are asked to rank order the questions in each block based on priority relative to the other questions in the block. This represents one activity that preservice and inservice teachers can take on to better understand their own value orientations. Greater clarity in this regard can help teachers to set instructional priorities and make curricular decisions.

Teacher- versus Student-Centered Practice

Despite the range of educational perspectives, value orientations, and socialization experiences that feed into individual teaching philosophies, they generally manifest in one of two broad categories of teaching practice based on their relative focus on the role of the teacher and the student (Byra, 2006). Teacher-centered practices tend to focus on the delivery and mastery of disciplinary content that is organized and presented by the teacher. Information flows primarily in one direction with the teacher in the role of the expert who holds and imparts knowledge on the student who is largely a passive recipient (Levesque-Bristol et al., 2006). Student-centered teaching practices, on the other hand, are focused more on the learning process and development of the student (Richards & Levesque-Bristol, 2014). Those who subscribe to this approach tend to believe students actively create their understanding through experience, reflection, and interaction with others (Dewey, 1938; Deci et al., 1996). Therefore, students have more active and interactive roles (appropriate to their developmental abilities) in student-centered teaching with the teacher serving as a learning facilitator. As we explain in a later section, both teacher-centered and student-centered styles can be effective in promoting certain learning outcomes when applied appropriately. However, best practices in SEL and physical education generally gravitate toward the student-centered approach (Dyson et al., 2020).

Common Notions That Can Obscure SEL Teaching Practice

In the preceding sections, we identified a range of factors that shape and characterize teaching practice. In this section, we examine some common perspectives and practices that can indirectly limit SEL teaching in physical education. Whether they result from socialization processes, a lack of reflection, or incompatible recommendations, some widespread perspectives and practices hinder best practice with regard to SEL. In this section, we challenge some prevailing assumptions and distinctions that appear widely accepted in physical education practice and discourse. These include the artificial distinctions made between instructional, managerial, and assessment activities. We also address a common understanding of behavior management that can be combined with and/or get in the way of teaching SEL. Our experience and research (e.g., Richards & Gordon, 2016; Wright & Irwin, 2018; Wright, Richards & Gray, 2020) indicates that imprecise understandings of such topics can mask or dilute promising practices. Through dispelling some of the notions that obscure important practices for promoting SEL as content, we propose a fresh way of conceptualizing SEL teaching practices.

Management as Part of Teaching Practice

Many influential scholars in physical education make a clear distinction between instruction and management tasks (e.g., McKenzie, Marshall, Sallis & Conway, 2000; Metzler, 2011). This orientation may reflect an assumption that the primary and most valuable subject matter and learning objectives in physical education relate to the psychomotor domain (Amis et al., 2012; Byra, 2006; Wright & Walsh, 2015). From this perspective, time dedicated to organization, grouping, and setting up equipment is viewed as a means to an end (i.e., things we have to do in order to work on our learning objectives). We believe that, when SEL competencies are intentional outcomes in physical education, tasks that are sometimes dismissed as being "managerial" can be an integrated part of our teaching. For example, both the teaching personal and social responsibility (TPSR; Hellison, 2011; see Chapter 7) model and the sport education (SE; Siedentop et al., 2011; see Chapter 8) prominently feature management roles and responsibilities for students. Both models promote this as a way for teachers to share power with students, foster ownership in the program, and provide authentic opportunities for students to practice personal and social skills (e.g., responsible decision making, self-management, relationship skills).

Numerous studies indicate student involvement in management tasks has been an important aspect of TPSR and SE implementation and associated affective outcomes (e.g., enjoyment and motivation) as well as personal and social skills (e.g., communication, cooperation, self-management) (see reviews by Baptista et al., 2020; Bessa et al., 2019; Dyson et al., 2020; Pozo et al., 2018). For example, when students are given roles such as organizing equipment, keeping records, and other tasks that facilitate the delivery of a lesson, they are taking on real responsibility for supporting their own learning as well as that of their peers. Students often work independently and make decisions when they take on such roles and are, therefore, exercising self-management and responsible decision making. Management may require communication skills and sensitivity to others (e.g., time keeper, referee) and, therefore, provide opportunities to develop social awareness and relationship skills. Student engagement with these roles often reflects the extent to which they value, enjoy, and feel motivated by the learning experience. We argue that rather than being viewed as a means to an end, management tasks should be viewed as important opportunities to engage students with SEL competencies related to physical education content standards (see Chapter 2; Jacobs & Wright, 2014; Society for Health and Physical Education [SHAPE] America, 2014; Wright, Gordon & Gray, 2020).

Assessment as Part of Teaching Practice

The following chapter, which we have written with Jenna R. Starck, is devoted to the topic of assessment practices that promote SEL competencies. Assessment in physical education has also traditionally been viewed as an activity that is separate from or added onto instruction (Starck et al., 2018). This view is generally outdated and incompatible with quality education practices. We assume that when teachers neglect assessment or view it as separate from instruction, they tend to miss out on rich opportunities to engage students in the learning process and to use SEL competencies. For example, self- and peer-assessments offer students opportunities to practice skills related to self-awareness, self-management, social awareness, and communication.

It is also important to note that assessment in physical education is most often focused on psychomotor learning, followed by cognitive learning (Hastie, 2017). In Chapter 1, we discussed the connection between the affective learning domain (Bloom, 1956) and SEL skills. It is important to explore this more precisely here as it informs the topic of assessment in physical education. While affective outcomes relate to internal processes and phenomena (e.g., attitudes, emotions), they often correspond with student behaviors and their enactment of certain personal and social skills (Krathwohl, Bloom & Masia, 1973). Recently, a systematic literature review (Teraoka, Ferreira, Kirk & Bardid, 2020) revealed that affective outcomes in physical education can be organized around the following four themes: (a) motivation, (b) emotional responses, (c) self-concept, and (d) resilience. Based on the intervention studies reviewed, findings indicated that a number of student-centered teaching practices appear to support affective responses.

These teaching practices include offering choice, encouraging peer feedback, asking deductive questions, focusing on personal improvement, and differentiating. Teaching practices like these clearly provide students with opportunities to practice and develop SEL skills (e.g., communication, responsible decision making, goal-setting). Therefore, in the field of physical education, as in general education, we see that students' affective engagement can be supported by intentional teaching practices and reflected in a range of student behaviors and SEL skills that can be the focus of concrete learning objectives. These learning objectives, in turn, can be important focal points for performance-based assessments that relate to the affective domain even if they are not affective outcomes in and of themselves.

The integration of authentic and performance-based assessment strategies into physical education has proven effective in supporting student learning even in schools with high levels of student disengagement (e.g., DeBusk & Hellison, 1989; Wright & Burton, 2008). Readers will find a more detailed treatment of this topic in the following chapter, which should strengthen our case that viewing assessment as separate from instruction restricts effectiveness. Moreover, viewing assessment as an integrated part of teaching practice provides a wealth of opportunity to let students apply and develop SEL competencies.

SEL Is More Than Behavior Management

The last notion that we challenge in this section relates to behavior management in physical education (Lavay, French & Henderson, 2016). In our research and extensive interactions with physical education teachers, we perceive that SEL is often conceptualized and used as a way to manage student behavior rather than as a meaningful learning outcome (e.g., Wright, Gray & Richards, 2020). As with other aspects of management, this perspective on SEL seems to reflect the prioritization of physical activity and psychomotor outcomes (e.g., Amis et al., 2012; McKenzie, Marshall, Sallis & Conway, 2000), and the need to address and control student behavior in service of maximizing physical activity time. Although a range of positive behavior management strategies exist in physical education (French et al., 2016), teachers' approaches are often reactive, inconsistent, and focused on the correction or remediation of perceived negative behaviors (Hellison, 2011). We believe that in many cases this reflects an insufficient understanding of the place of personal and social development in physical education. Students' attitudes and feelings (i.e., affective development) as well as personal and social behaviors that reflect them are part of the curriculum—every bit as much as the psychomotor and cognitive content we address (see Chapter 2; SHAPE America, 2014).

The psychomotor aspects of the physical education curriculum are the most likely to be addressed intentionally with an eye on helping all students reach their highest possible level of performance (Hastie, 2017). Unfortunately, some teachers view time devoted to the affective domain and related SEL competencies as time they are taking out of physical education (Richards & Gordon, 2017). However, this represents the inaccurate assumption that physical education and physical activity are one and the same. Many teachers who initially report that they are already addressing personal and social development realize upon reflection that they may have set the bar too low (Coulson, Irwin & Wright, 2012; Gray et al., 2019; Pascual et al., 2011). If, for example, a teacher aims for and is satisfied with her students being "busy, happy, and good" (Placek, 1983), they may have addressed student behavior to the extent that they do not present a problem, but not necessarily taught their students any skills, differentiated instruction, or challenged them to demonstrate competencies related to SEL.

In short, we recommend that teachers look at SEL competencies in a fresh light and position them as skills that can be taught, practiced, and assessed (Richards et al., 2019). This approach is in line with humanistic and proactive approaches to behavior management (Lavay et al., 2016), but this shift in mindset might help teachers (a) view SEL as part of physical education content, (b) set appropriate learning objectives that apply to all students in a class, and (c) plan for differentiated instruction and modes of practice so all students can develop from their individual starting point. Of course, there will always be a need to react to specific situations and teachers need to have plans and protocols in place for clarifying expectations and managing extreme behavior transgressions (Lavay et al., 2016). However, if the mindset toward SEL as skill and content has been disentangled from these more traditional behavior management views, we believe teachers might be more effective on both fronts (for more on this topic, see Chapter 11).

Section Summary

This section has addressed misconceptions, habits of thinking, and practices that are common in physical education but may present obstacles to effective SEL teaching practice. As socialization experiences (e.g.,

acculturation, teacher preparation, organizational norms) heavily influence practice, teachers' ability to fully understand and deliver SEL may be limited without them realizing it. We encourage teachers to reflect on their own experience and other factors that frame their use of SEL instruction to become more self-aware of their assumptions and decisions. Without doing this, it may be hard for teachers to truly look at SEL teaching practices with fresh eyes and develop their own coherent, effective approach.

Teaching Practices That Can Promote SEL

Having unpacked some limiting perspectives on the role of instruction, management, and assessment, we now take a fresh look at teaching practices that can promote SEL in physical education. We take a holistic view of teaching practice that is composed of the teacher's formal instruction and other activities such as management, assessment, and behavior management. We also interpret practices in light of general features for good SEL implementation described in Chapter 1 that are represented in the SAFE acronym (i.e., *Sequenced*, *Active*, *Focused*, and *Explicit*; CASEL, 2020). If SEL instruction is *Sequenced*, it has been planned and is presented in a structured and developmentally appropriate way over time. A great benefit of physical education is its *Active* nature, wherein students interact socially and learn experientially. These should be characteristics of SEL instruction as well. The more *Focused* SEL instruction is, the better. This focus must be provided by the teacher and reflected in learning objectives and planned activities that intentionally target SEL skills. Finally, *Explicit* instruction involves the teacher speaking directly with students about the SEL skills, their value, as well as their application in physical education (and beyond). See **Table 3.1** for descriptions and examples of how the criteria associated with SAFE can be implemented in physical education. Of these criteria, the greatest challenges in many programs relate to increasing the *Focus* on SEL and promoting it *Explicitly* with students.

The opportunity to increase the focus and explicit promotion of SEL is great as many best practices in physical education can be aligned with quality SEL teaching (Dyson et al., 2020; Jacobs & Wright, 2014). However, developing best practice should be an intentional and active process undertaken by individual teachers to make sure SEL is realized as part of the living curriculum. This process should be reflective of and supported by a clear definition of SEL content,

Table 3.1 Criteria for a SAFE Approach to Teaching Social and Emotional Learning in Physical Education

SAFE Criteria	Description	Example in Physical Education
Sequenced	SEL is addressed in planning and delivered in structured and developmentally appropriate ways over time.	An elementary school (grades K-5) aligns SEL competencies with SHAPE America (2014) standards to effectively integrate SEL learning objectives throughout their curriculum.
Active	SEL lessons are rooted in dynamic, interactive, and experiential learning.	A high school (grades 9–12) team sport classes capitalize on authentic sport experiences to help students enact and reflect on SEL learning objectives related to social awareness and relationship skills.
Focused	SEL lessons are designed to highlight specific SEL learning objectives.	A middle school (grades 6–8) teacher first facilitates and then leads a debrief on an ice-breaker challenge in which students' success hinges on utilizing nonverbal communication skills.
Explicit	SEL skills are named and discussed directly by the teacher who promotes their value and application in physical education (and beyond).	A middle school teacher promotes responsibility in a Sport Education unit by introducing roles (e.g., equipment manager) in terms of responsibilities (e.g., what equipment manager must do), explaining those responsibilities to all students, and administers self- and peer-assessments of how well students met assigned responsibilities.

an understanding of the SAFE guidelines, and a comprehensive approach to helping students attain the highest level of performance that they can.

To support reflection, analysis, and planning in this regard, we present several approaches that are not mutually exclusive, but rather complement one another. **Figure 3.1** graphically displays how we see these various approaches coming together to support

Figure 3.1 Conceptual framework for teaching SEL in physical education.

quality SEL in physical education. Built on the foundation of a positive learning environment, teachers can support SEL in physical education through implicit, reactive, explicit, and empowering approaches (note that the empowering approach is represented by the far right pillar in Figure 3.1 labeled "Empower"). **Table 3.2** describes these approaches and provides examples of how they can be utilized to promote SEL. This best practice framework is consistent with the SAFE guidelines, has been developed through our research in secondary physical education (Wright, Gray & Richards, 2020), and rings true with our experience in other settings as well as in the current literature (Baptista et al., 2020; Dyson et al., 2020; Pozo et al., 2018; Wright et al., 2020).

Creating a Positive Learning Environment

Creating a positive learning environment is foundational to good teaching and, especially to promoting SEL, therefore, it represents the base in Figure 3.1. Teachers and researchers understand the importance of creating a safe, organized, social, and motivating environment to support teaching and learning in physical education (Dyson et al., 2020; Hellison, 2011; Richards & Levesque-Bristol, 2014). While many of the actions a teacher takes to create such an environment might be directly related to SEL competencies, others

Table 3.2 A Comprehensive Approach to Teaching SEL Based in Physical Education

Component	Description	Example in Practice
Positive learning environment	Physically, emotionally, and psychologically safe learning environment that is motivating and characterized by respectful social interaction.	A 9th grade teacher plans basketball lessons in a way that allows all of her students to participate and feel successful by balancing teams based on skill level, instituting an "all touch before shooting" rule, and emphasizing teamwork and improvement over winning.
Implicit approach	Teacher's words, actions, and demeanor reflect SEL even when that content is not being taught explicitly.	An 11th grade teacher models SEL competencies such as self-management and relationship skills by remaining calm and communicating respectfully when a student is challenging his authority and being disrespectful about being marked tardy for class.
Reactive approach	Teacher capitalizes on situations, surprises, and changes in ways that align with and reinforce their commitment to SEL, i.e., teachable moments.	A 3rd grade teacher reinforces the importance of encouraging peers when clarifying behavioral expectations in a tumbling unit (e.g., one student laughing at another's mistake) as well as praising exceptional performance (e.g., one student is always the first to applaud and give a compliment after their peers perform).
Explicit approach	Teacher plans for, articulates, and debriefs on specific SEL concepts and skills that are integrated into a lesson or activity.	A 7th grade teacher includes "giving constructive feedback" in the objectives for a volleyball lesson, includes a peer assessment activity so student can practice this skill, and addresses this topic in a check for understanding debrief at the end of the lesson.
Empowering approach	Teacher recognizes students' capacity for taking responsibility and enacting continually higher levels of SEL engagement, including the transfer of these skills in other contexts.	A 1st grade teacher who routinely assigns leadership and helping roles to students sets aside time for a group discussion in which he asks students to explain why it is important to help others and to provide examples of how they can help people in other places (e.g., classroom, recess, home).

may not. However, if these actions contribute to an environment where students feel physically and psychologically safe, engaged with the learning experience, and motivated to achieve, they have helped lay a foundation for subsequent SEL processes (Hellison, 2011).

Implicit Approach

Starting at the left side of Figure 3.1, we see pillars that represent fairly common practice. These approaches do not represent a robust treatment of SEL on their own but are influential and can make important contributions to an overall SEL agenda in physical education. The Implicit approach, by definition, involves teacher actions that are not directly or explicitly connected to an SEL topic. This is frequently manifest in role modeling as well as the ways teachers address

personal and social development more generally (Wright, Gray & Richards, 2020; Wright & Irwin, 2018). Students are sharp observers of their teacher's actions and reactions. Regardless of what teachers say or share in other ways (e.g., posters on the wall, the written curriculum), students' impressions of how teachers conduct themselves and treat others carries a much stronger message. The ways teachers respond to individuals and stressful situations as well as the student behaviors they allow, encourage, or ignore send implicit, but important messages that will influence how students make sense of SEL topics.

Reactive Approach

The Reactive approach is another avenue that may be common in practice, but alone is insufficient to promote SEL (Wright, et al., 2020). As acknowledged earlier, teachers must always be prepared to respond to unplanned situations such as disruptive student behavior (e.g., loud outbursts) or student-student conflict (e.g., heated arguments over a foul during a soccer game). However, if the only way teachers address SEL involves isolated incidents with students perceived as "misbehaving," they may be neglecting to (a) treat SEL as content, (b) set SEL objectives for the whole class, (c) actively teach SEL skills, and (d) assess or support the SEL needs of all students. We suggest that teacher reactions to challenging situations be framed as "teachable moments" and as just one aspect of promoting SEL. If SEL objectives and related norms are explained, practiced, and reinforced with the whole class, when positive or negative situations and surprises arise, the teacher can respond accordingly. For example, if a fourth grade teacher has been clear and explicit about expecting students to encourage one another, that teacher has laid a foundation to respond to students' reactions to a peer who stumbles and falls when playing a game of tag. The teacher is now in a position to use this teachable moment to clarify expectations (e.g., with students who laugh or tease) as well as praise exemplary performance (e.g., with students who offer help or show support). In more serious and/or ongoing situations (e.g., bullying), the teacher may develop individual contracts or employ restorative practice strategies. Hopefully, these responses will be more impactful because they do not come across as random, isolated, inconsistent, or (at worst) desperate. To be clear, we commonly see the Reactive approach used, but not to its full potential. Within a comprehensive and coordinated approach to promoting SEL, the "teachable moment" version of the Reactive approach has much to offer.

Explicit Approach

In any given lesson or unit of instruction, the Explicit approach involves the teacher introducing a skill or learning objective, making sure students understand the desired performance, allowing students to practice and demonstrate their ability, and providing feedback to support learning and further development (Wright, et al., 2020). For example, during a volleyball unit, a teacher may explicitly include communication as a learning objective. The teacher could introduce this objective at the beginning of a lesson, clarify exactly what the desired performance would include (e.g., calling shots, encouraging teammates), remind students to communicate during scrimmages, and give appropriate feedback. As described in more detail in the next chapter (Chapter 4), such an approach

seamlessly blends with authentic assessment practice because clear expectations and criteria for evaluating performance have been presented.

Teachers using the Explicit approach may also have overarching behavioral norms and expectations that span instructional units (or even grade levels). Such guidelines are generally easy to align with state and national standards related to affective development as well as school-level initiatives (e.g., restorative practice, school values; Jacobs & Wright, 2014; Richards & Gordon, 2017). The key in this case would be making those ideas explicit, clear, and consistent. For example, Hellison (2011), in his TPSR model, placed great emphasis on respecting the rights and feelings of others. A teacher (or faculty team) who wanted to make this a consistent theme throughout their program could generalize it across grade levels and activities (for more on TPSR, see Chapter 7). The same approach could be used to emphasize teamwork in a sport education season (see Chapter 8) or positive communication in a cooperative learning unit (see Chapter 9). In these examples, reference points are established up front that support alignment of individual learning objectives as well as teachable moments.

Empowering Approach

If we view SEL skills as a developmental progression, we should provide students with opportunities to challenge and increase their skills to the best of their ability over time. Some teachers are satisfied with compliance and participation, which sets a fairly low bar (Hellison, 2011; Placek, 1983). Even some student-centered practices foster active learning but within fairly tight parameters. For example, cooperative learning activities involve accomplishment of a discrete task to achieve a specific learning objective (see Chapter 9). Students engage in positive interdependence to achieve their goal, but the task, objective, and process are generally prescribed for them by the teacher. The Empowering approach in our framework pushes the boundaries of typical teacher-student roles. This approach is characterized by teachers not only becoming facilitators of student learning but also becoming advocates for students taking ownership of and directing their own learning. This approach, championed by Hellison (2011) in his TPSR model, often takes the form of managing and organizing activities, engaging in self-directed and peer learning, making decisions about content, and even having an active role in assessment (Wright & Craig, 2011). These are just some ways teachers can help students progressively develop SEL skills.

For example, becoming a peer-coach requires a student to develop self-awareness (i.e., how are they coming across to others?), social awareness (i.e., what does their partner need?), and relationship skills (i.e., how to understand others' feelings and behaviors and how to offer feedback so their partner will be receptive to it). Recent reviews of TPSR literature strongly indicate that this empowerment-based orientation can contribute to a positive learning environment in which students develop a range of skills related to SEL (e.g., self-management, self-awareness, social awareness, relationship skills) as well as affective outcomes such as a sense of belonging and confidence (Baptista et al., 2020; Dyson et al., 2020; Pozo et al., 2018).

As students are ready to expand and take greater ownership of their SEL, teachers can facilitate reflection and discussion of transfer (i.e., how can students apply these skills in other settings? Hellison, 2011; Jacobs & Wright, 2018). Examples with young children will likely be more concrete (e.g., getting along well with siblings and helping out at home; Wright et al., 2020), whereas older students may be ready to discuss how these skills could be applied to critical issues that may manifest in but go far beyond physical education settings (e.g., romantic relationships, gender and racial stereotypes, homophobia, equity; Jacobs & Wright, 2019). The chapters led by Ressler (Chapter 14), Jacobs (Chapter 15), Walsh (Chapter 7), and Martinek (Chapter 13) in this text highlight the potential of the Empowering approach in terms of addressing transfer as well as equity and social justice issues with students.

Moving Toward Explicit and Empowering Approaches

While the structure depicted in Figure 3.1 is composed of several components, we find that effective physical education teachers have often already created a positive learning environment and naturally implemented some aspects of the implicit, reactive, and explicit approaches described above (Pascual et al., 2011; Richards & Gordon, 2017; Wright, Gray & Richards, 2020; Wright & Irwin, 2018). However, in line with the SAFE framework (CASEL, 2020), we find that with increasing their focus and being more explicit about SEL content, effective teachers can quickly raise the bar. For example, when teachers strengthen their use of the Explicit approach, they cross an important threshold that shows they view SEL and the associated competencies as legitimate content. Only when teachers view and promote SEL in this way does it begin to take its rightful place in the lived curriculum

(Schubert, 1986). While this can be achieved through many best practices, we challenge teachers to push the envelope by inviting students to take on as much ownership in their learning as possible and to find ways to apply these SEL skills in other contexts. By addressing this final pillar, the Empowering approach, teachers set their expectations higher than simply organizing, managing, and securing compliance from students (Placek, 1983). Rather, they invite students to take responsibility for their own learning, contribute to the learning of others, and apply SEL in authentic and individualized ways (Hellison, 2011).

Having examined and reframed teaching practice as it relates to SEL in physical education, a more granular framework for analyzing, reflecting on, and planning teaching is needed. Therefore, in the following section, we examine the decision-making process and the prototypical teaching styles described by Mosston and Ashworth (2017) in order to demonstrate how SEL teaching practice can be operationalized in specific physical education lessons and activities.

Spectrum of Teaching Styles

The spectrum of teaching styles (Mosston & Ashworth, 2017) is familiar to many physical education teachers and researchers (Byra, 2006) and is useful to our discussion in several ways. First, the spectrum provides an approach to analyzing teaching styles and the decisions that give rise to them. Second, the range of prototypical styles presented in the spectrum resonates with and shows opportunities for integration with many of the teaching practices already discussed in this chapter. Third, the spectrum sets a horizon and framework for interpreting other practices described in later chapters. Across these functions, we employ the spectrum here to show how SEL can be highlighted in a wide range of teaching styles through active decision making on the part of the teacher.

Decision Making

As discussed earlier in this chapter, teaching practice is influenced by myriad factors including a teacher's personal philosophy, value orientations, context, and socialization experiences. The mechanism by which these influences translate into practice is the teacher's decision making. According to Mosston and Ashworth (2017), teaching behavior is guided by and composed of a chain of decisions. This axiom is essential to the conceptual framework undergirding the spectrum of teaching styles, as explained here:

Every act of deliberate teaching is a consequence of a prior decision. Decision making is the central or primary behavior that governs all behaviors that follow: how we organize students; how we organize the subject matter; how we manage time, space, and equipment; how we interact with students; how we choose our verbal behavior; how we construct the social-affective climate in the classroom; and how we create and conduct all cognitive connections with the learners. All these concerns are secondary behaviors that emanate from, and are governed by, prior decisions. (Mosston & Ashworth, 2017, p. 8).

We agree with this perspective and find it relevant to a discussion of how we teach SEL competencies. Consistent with our view of teaching practices that foster SEL, especially regarding the Explicit and Empowering approaches (see Figure 3.1), Mosston and Ashworth (2017) recognize that deliberate decisions reflect intention and shape quality teaching.

In the spectrum (Mosston & Ashworth, 2017), decisions are considered so essential that various categories of decisions are actually used to describe the anatomy of a style. The three main decision-making categories proposed in the spectrum are (a) preimpact, (b) impact, and (c) postimpact. *Preimpact decisions* primarily relate to planning. It is at this stage that teachers define the intent of the teaching–learning exchange and consider its organization and the necessary preparations. Preimpact decisions include everything from learning objectives to grouping, equipment, organization, and student roles. *Impact decisions* are made during the teaching–learning exchange as the preimpact decisions are being implemented. These decisions can involve factors such as the order of tasks, start time, pace/rhythm, stop time, interval, location, posture, attire/appearance, and behavioral expectations. Finally, *postimpact decisions* relate to assessment and feedback of the learner's performance, the learning experience, and/or attainment of the learning objectives after the teaching–learning exchange.

Teaching Styles with SEL Connections

A key feature in differentiating between the teaching styles in the spectrum is the extent to which decisions (i.e., preimpact, impact, postimpact) are made by the teacher or the learner (Mosston & Ashworth, 2017). The more traditional, teacher-centered styles have the teacher making all of these decisionçs. The more decision-making power shifts to the student, the more

student-centered the style becomes (Byra, 2006). This sharing of decision-making power with students offers a concrete way to think about the Empowering approach to promoting SEL presented previously in our framework (Figure 3.1).

The spectrum includes 11 prototypical or landmark styles. These range from Command Style – A, in which all decisions are made by the teacher, through Self-Teaching Style – K, in which the learner has become fully self-directed and is making all decisions related to their learning (Mosston & Ashworth, 2017). Across this continuum, the styles are divided into two broad clusters. The first five styles, and arguably the most common in practice (Byra, 2006), are about reproducing knowledge provided by the teacher (e.g., focused on memory, practice, refinement). The remaining seven styles increasingly focus on the production of knowledge by the student (e.g., focused on problem-solving, creativity, critical thinking). While the majority of research and practice related to the spectrum of teaching styles in physical education has focused on teaching for physical skill development (Byra, 2006), it is important to note that the spectrum is intended to addresses the full range of human development, including physical, social, emotional, cognitive, and moral learning (Mosston & Ashworth, 2017). In the following sections, we highlight SEL connections that can be made explicit for students within each style. In fact, in most of our examples, we describe ways that teachers could select and apply specific styles with the intention of explicitly promoting a particular SEL skill or competency.

Reproduction Styles

The reproduction styles are the most commonly used in practice (Byra, 2006). It is important to understand that multiple styles could be applied in the same lesson and the appropriateness of any given style must be determined by the teacher based on the intersection of factors such as the students' developmental level and the subject matter. Reproduction styles, for example, may be more appropriate when introducing new material to younger students and introducing activities that have a higher level of inherent risk such as archery. The reproduction styles are routinely applied within a physical education lesson and represent a fairly traditional approach to teacher and student roles (Byra, 2006). However, the amount of decision-making power shifted to students generally increases across the styles. Opportunities for student empowerment and concrete SEL connections are highlighted in **Table 3.3**.

Table 3.3 Reproduction Teaching Styles with Connections to SEL

Teaching Style	Typical Pedagogical Focus	Sample Activities with Explicit SEL Objectives	Corresponding CASEL Competencies
Command — Style A (Direct instruction)	Precision and uniformity in performance Appropriate response to a stimulus	A 1st grade teacher directs a parachute activity and highlights the importance of knowing self-space versus other-space, and moving together.	Self-awareness Social-awareness
Practice — Style B (Individual practice with private feedback)	Refining accuracy or quality of reproduction through repetition	A 4th grade teacher gives students task cards to practice jump rope skills and highlights the importance of working independently and staying on task.	Self-management Responsible decision making
Reciprocal — Style C (Students take turns practicing and giving feedback)	Refining accuracy or quality of reproduction by taking turns in practice mode and observer mode	An 8th grade teacher asks students to engage in peer-assessment of basketball lay-ups. She highlights the importance of paying attention to their partner's strengths and weaknesses and providing constructive feedback.	Social awareness Relationship skills
Self-check — Style D (Independent practice with self-assessment)	Refining accuracy or quality of reproduction through self-assessment using teacher provided criteria	A 10th grade teacher asks students to self-assess their ability to perform a sequence of trampoline skills. He highlights the importance of honest self-assessment to identify areas of improvement.	Self-awareness Self-management
Inclusion — Style E (Learners with varying skill levels participate in same task choosing level of difficulty)	Refining ability and reproduction by individuals but in a group practice format that accommodates differences	A 2nd grade teacher invites students to run and jump over a string attached to floor on one end and a height of two feet at the other end. He highlights the importance of students choosing the right level of challenge (i.e., height of jump) for themselves and encouraging their peers regardless of their level of challenge.	Self-awareness Responsible decision making Social awareness Relationship skills

Command style (A). In command style, which is also referred to as direct teaching and direct instruction, the teacher is responsible for all decisions preimpact, impact, and postimpact. This style may be appropriate when introducing skills that require a high level of precision (e.g., gymnastics) or a strong emphasis on safety (e.g., weight-lifting). This style is also helpful when students are being introduced to new material that must be performed in a specific manner (e.g., dance movements) and in tasks that must be performed in synchronization (e.g., parachute games). While the teacher is in control of all decisions in this style, students do have opportunities to work on SEL-related skills such as self-regulation, focus, and respect for others (e.g., space, safety, rules, procedures). Group performance (e.g., dance) and the practice leading up to it can contribute to building a sense of group identity, pride, and a sense of belonging. Performing and practicing individual routines (e.g., trampoline) can help students develop self-confidence and perseverance. As explained previously, however, the extent to which the teacher is aware, intentional, and explicit about making these SEL connections varies tremendously. We encourage teachers to be explicit in introducing and giving feedback on student enactment of specific SEL skills that are brought out by the combination of teaching style and the activity.

Practice style (B). Practice style is focused on individual practice by the student with private feedback coming from the teacher. In this style, the teacher has shared some decision-making power with the student in the impact phase (e.g., the student may choose the mode of practice, pace, intermediate performance goals). The use of this style may follow up on the command style in which students were introduced to a skill. The use of this style allows them time to refine their accuracy or quality of reproduction through repetition. Teachers often use task cards to help students engage in this self-directed practice. Regarding SEL development, this style allows students to practice self-management and responsible decision making as they take increased responsibility for their learning and experience independence. Of course, while students are engaged in independent practice, they should also be respectful of others and ensure their practices does not encroach on others. If teachers deal with this explicitly, they can make connections to social awareness even while students are engaged in individual practice.

Reciprocal style (C). The reciprocal style involves students (generally in pairs) taking turns in two different modes (i.e., practice and observation). As one student is in practice mode, refining their reproduction of a given skill, their partner is observing the performance and evaluating it against the given criteria (i.e., critical elements or learning cues). After a round of practice is complete, the observers provide feedback to their partners and the two swap roles. In this style, the teacher has still made all pre-impact decisions but allows students significant power over the impact decisions (e.g., pace, timing, when to switch). Another shift in this style is that some postimpact decision-making power is shared as students now have a role in providing feedback to one another on skill performance (i.e., peer assessment). New SEL skills that are highlighted in this style involve social awareness (e.g., paying attention to a partner's strengths and limitations) and relationship skills (e.g., communication skills such as giving and receiving feedback in a positive manner). Variations of this style can be used to introduce basic social skills like turn taking to young students as well as subtle skills such as empathy, patience, and trust. We encourage teachers to be explicit about how and when students have opportunities to demonstrate SEL skills to make sure these lessons are not assumed or "lost" on the students.

Self-check (D). The focus in the self-check style is the student's self-assessment based on their own independent practice. This is another style in which the teacher makes preimpact stage decisions but students have some control over impact-stage decisions. Students practice independently with the goal of consistent and accurate reproduction of a skill. Students also have some personal decision-making power regarding the postimpact stage. The assessment criteria have generally been provided by the teacher, but the student is charged with applying these criteria and using their analysis to guide continued practice and improvement. In terms of SEL, this style presents students with opportunities for self-awareness by making an honest and realistic assessment of their strengths, limitations, and opportunity for improvement. The teacher can also make explicit links to self-management skills as this style requires independent

practice and self-directed, goal-oriented learning. Ideally, students' self-assessment would address their performance relative to some of these SEL skills as well as the psychomotor skill.

Inclusion style (E). Whereas the previous styles involved different combinations of individual and partner practice, the inclusion style has a greater focus on the whole group and accommodating the full range of differences in performance ability. In this style, learners of different skill levels can practice together to refine their ability to accurately reproduce the same skill or task. The task or activity in this case is designed with enough inherent flexibility that students can be engaged and working socially while individuals are selecting the personal level of challenge. The key is that options are presented in the impact stage that allows learners to adjust the level of difficulty so that each student can be challenged at the appropriate level. For example, in a physical fitness unit, students may rotate through a series of exercise stations and at each one they can control factors such as weight (e.g., dumbbells), pace (e.g., running), form (e.g., push-ups), and number (e.g., jumping jacks). Because individual students make impact decisions, they are developing self-awareness and self-management skills. They also need SEL skills related to social awareness and relationship skills because making everyone feel included and successful requires empathy, compassion, and respect for differences. In fact, to maximize higher-level SEL skills, the teacher can involve students in the design of the inclusive activities so they actively develop their awareness of others' needs and abilities as well as the value of including everyone.

Discovery Styles

The discovery styles continue down a path of increasing student empowerment in terms of decision making and ownership of the learning process. Students are no longer simply reproducing knowledge and skills imparted by the teacher but taking more control over the learning process by discovering and creating their own knowledge. As the traditional roles of "teacher" and "student" blur, even the identification of problems and the assessment of the result or endpoint resides with the student. Opportunities for student empowerment and explicit connections to SEL in the Discovery Styles are discussed in the following style descriptions and summarized in **Table 3.4**.

Guided discovery (F) and convergent discovery (G). For the purposes of this text, the Guided and Convergent Discovery styles are presented together

Table 3.4 Discovery Teaching Styles with Connections to SEL

Teaching Style	Typical Pedagogical Focus	Sample Activity with Explicit SEL Objectives	Corresponding CASEL Competencies
Guided discovery — Style F (Logical design of questions to help student come to predetermined response)	Engage learner in discovery process with teacher guidance throughout	A 5th grade teacher guides a student though a series of questions to discover the use of the toe-kick in long and high-flying soccer kicks. He highlights the importance of logic in thinking through a problem to "make a good choice."	Responsible decision making
Convergent discovery — Style G (Teacher poses problem and learner develops questions and logic to reach predetermined response)	Discover a correct, predetermined response with convergent process	A 7th grade teacher challenges a student to discover the relationship between center of mass and base of support during balance positions. She highlights the need be patient and focused even if the problem-solving process is frustrating and stressful.	Self-awareness Self-management Responsible decision making
Divergent discovery — Style H (Teacher poses question or challenge with multiple appropriate responses)	Multiple correct or appropriate responses are possible within and across learners	A 3rd grade teacher places students in cooperative learning groups to develop design posters to promote physically active lifestyles for members of their school community. He highlights the importance of cooperating effectively within their groups and respecting the fact that other groups will take different approaches to the same task.	Social-awareness Relationship skills
Learner designed individual program — Style I (Learner identifies problem or issue as well as the steps to address it)	Teacher provides prompt, impetus, and subject focus but student carries out in largely self-directed manner.	A 6th grade teacher assigns a project in which students must select a favorite sport and research its origins. She highlights the importance of planning and managing time well to successfully complete the project by the deadline.	Self-awareness Self-management Responsible decision making
Learner initiated — Style J (Learner initiates and guides learning experience with teacher available for support)	Learning experience is individual and based on learner's initiative; timeline, outcomes, and location do not necessarily connect to school.	A high school teacher follows up and expresses interest in a former student who she knows to be an avid runner. The learner appreciates the interest and support. The learner often provides updates on his race times and training regime. He is open to input and suggestions from the teacher about motivation, good nutrition, and other topics.	Self-awareness Self-management Responsible decision making Relationship skills
Self-teaching — Style K (Learning is completely self-directed. All decisions are made by the learner)	Lifelong learning approach that is self-directed. Teacher may have had an impact but does not necessarily have knowledge of or role in learner's progress at this point.	A young professional becomes interested in yoga for stress reduction and relaxation. He becomes fascinated by the history and broader philosophy as well. He makes the practice and study of yoga a lifelong passion, ultimately becoming a certified yoga teacher because of a desire to share this practice with others who may also find it meaningful and helpful.	Self-awareness Self-management Responsible decision making Relationship skills Social awareness

because they share so much in common and we wish to avoid redundancy. These styles are especially useful when the teacher has a predetermined response in mind but wants to guide their students through the process of discovering that response on their own. In Guided Discovery, the teacher has planned a series of steps or questions to guide the student to the response, whereas in Convergent Discovery, an initial question is posed and students determine the logical steps or processes required to arrive at the one predetermined response. Therefore, Convergent Discovery shifts more decision-making power to the student throughout, especially in preimpact and impact phases. With either of these styles, teachers who apply these styles must successfully establish a positive learning environment and positive pedagogical relationships so that students are comfortable and feel safe sharing their thoughts and responses.

The skillful teacher will also have a good sense of their students' cognitive abilities and a logical series of questions prepared to guide them to the predetermined response. The tactical games approach (Mitchell et al., 2006) effectively puts these styles into practice. For example, students may be put into a gameplay scenario with minimal instruction to experience what does and does not work well at a tactical level. Then, when pulled back into a discussion with the teacher, they are asked guiding questions that will help them discover through their own reasoning what tactic or rule would enhance their performance. In addition to understanding "what" is called for, the aim with this approach is that students will have a deeper understanding of "why" certain decisions are made in sport and physical activity contexts.

Regarding SEL connections, the cognitive dimension and problem-solving focus in Guided Discovery and Convergent Discovery enhance students' decision-making abilities. Their confidence can also be challenged and built as they answer questions and share their thoughts. Social skills and other aspects of communication can be integrated if students are engaged in the discovery process together, e.g., group-level deliberation and discussion. SEL connections can be enhanced by making the topic of discovery an SEL concept or principle. Icebreakers and team-building activities can be great vehicles for achieving this. For example, when students are given a team-building challenge such as lining up in order of birth dates without speaking, the teacher can be guiding them to a debriefing session that would result in discovery related to different modes of communication, (e.g., verbal, nonverbal).

Divergent discovery (H). The Divergent Discovery style also hinges on a specific question or

challenge introduced by the teacher. However, in this style, there is not only one correct, predetermined response. There can be multiple correct answers or solutions generated by students. This includes many of the same processes and skills as the previous discovery styles but allows for more creativity and flexibility. This allows for some student decision making in all phases of the learning process: preimpact, impact, and postimpact. For example, after teaching several discrete dance skills to her students, a teacher might ask them to choreograph their own dance sequence by making use of those elements. Whether this is done alone or in a group, such a task involves SEL skills such as decision making, focus, creativity, and self-expression. Especially in a group activity, a wide range of social skills such as communication are required. An example of using Divergent Discovery with SEL content could look like having students work together to develop a "Bill of Rights" (i.e., social norms and behavioral expectations), for themselves. Of course, the teacher would facilitate this process, but the examples and priorities would be set by the students. This type of activity would highlight empowerment and an explicit treatment of SEL in any physical education class.

Learner designed individual program (I). In the Learner Designed Individual Program style, and those that follow it, the student becomes increasingly independent and empowered. While the teacher might provide a prompt or the impetus to address a certain problem or issue at the preimpact stage, the student discovers the structure and steps needed to resolve the problem on their own. This process is no longer tied to a specific class activity or lesson. In fact, the "where," "when," and "how" of addressing the issue is determined by the student. Clearly, the Learner Designed Individual Program approach shifts much decision-making power to the student and provides ample opportunity to focus on SEL skills related to self-awareness, self-management, and responsible decision making as the learning process becomes very self-directed. An example of using this style with a psychomotor focus could be challenging students to assess their physical fitness and determine what they believe they should be doing to improve it. With only general guidance and structure from the teacher, students are empowered to assess their own strengths and limitations, set goals, design a plan to achieve those goals, monitor their own progress, etc. Hence, through impact and postimpact phases, students are taking the primary responsibility for decision making. An example of using this style with an SEL focus might involve challenging students to find ways to apply SEL skills that have been taught in class (e.g., leadership, helping others) in other settings. In this example, one student may decide they need to be a better role model for younger siblings at home, while another may decide to run for class president, and yet another may decide to volunteer at a community garden. This approach to promoting transfer can be effective because students are allowed to find or create opportunities to apply life skills in ways that are relevant and personally meaningful to them (Hellison, 2011; Jacobs & Wright, 2018).

Learner initiated style (J). The next step toward student empowerment and ownership is the Learner Initiated style. In this style, the student initiates the learning experience. Therefore, control over preimpact and subsequent decision making now resides with the student. It is up to them to identify, find the motivation for, and develop a plan to address the topic of learning. Because learning of this type is no longer under the teachers' control, it is less frequently applied or discussed in physical education discourse (Byra, 2006). The teacher ideally remains available as a resource and support but exerts no control over this process. For example, a student may independently be studying Tae Kwon Do in their community and connecting many of the concepts and principles from their physical education class (e.g., the components of physical fitness or the importance of tactical thinking in sparring competitions). The role of the physical education teacher in this case would be to support, serve as a sounding board, and perhaps point the student to relevant concepts or resources for this journey. An SEL example along these lines might relate to a student coming to their teacher for advice as they grapple with notions of fair play and ethics. Such topics can be promoted in games and sports as early as elementary physical education. From this foundation, as students mature, teachers can support their questioning of how core principles like fair play and ethics apply to broader social structures that students may see featured daily in the news (e.g., systemic racism).

Self-teaching style (K). The Self-Teaching style represents the apex of student empowerment and self-directed learning. At this end of the continuum, all decision making has shifted to the student. The "teacher" has no set role and the learning process is not necessarily tethered in any way to a physical education class or even a school. Because the "teacher" does not control, have a set role, or even necessarily know about this learning experience, this style is rarely mentioned in the physical education discourse (Byra, 2006). Ironically, in some ways, this represents the highest aims of education (i.e., providing "students"

with the knowledge, skills, and dispositions to become independent and lifelong learners). It is a rare, but generally very happy, teacher who finds out later in life that they were influential in their students' lives and that their influence led to lifelong hobbies, habits, and avocations. Certainly, this can be said of some of the sports and physical activities introduced in physical education over the years. However, considering SEL skills, it is equally (or perhaps more) likely that knowledge, skills, and dispositions promoted in physical education could apply throughout life. For example, few could argue that success in the workplace is not enhanced by good communication, confidence, leadership, respect for differences, and a plethora of other SEL skills that can be explicitly taught in physical education.

Conclusion

Throughout this chapter, we have examined ideas about what constitutes teaching practice as well as what influences it. To be effective in teaching SEL, we assume that teachers should be clear in their understanding of SEL as content and its role in the physical education curriculum. In some cases, this requires reflection on and even disruption of some artificial distinctions between instruction and activities such as management, behavior management, and assessment. Looking at SEL teaching practice with fresh eyes, we encourage teachers to continue but perhaps be more intentional about the ways they create a positive learning environment, send implicit messages to students, and respond to teachable moments that have implications for SEL. If these fundamental but important practices are in place, the enhancement of SEL through explicit teaching and student empowerment can be truly potent. Making the shift to a comprehensive approach to teaching SEL, characterized by explicit and empowering approaches, requires intentionality. To provide concrete opportunities to make a shift, we encourage practitioners to consider the decision-making processes and range of styles proposed by Mosston and Ashworth (2017) in their spectrum of teaching styles. Many of the teaching practices, including models-based practice, that are introduced in subsequent chapters make use of the landmark styles from the spectrum that were introduced in this chapter.

Table 3.5 illustrates how many of the topics addressed throughout this chapter can be pulled together. We present a series of questions and prompts for reflection that may be useful for preservice or inservice teachers who want to develop their teaching practice in ways that fully support and integrate SEL.

Table 3.5 Putting it Together: Questions to Guide Teachers' Reflection on SEL Integration

Regarding your approach to integrating SEL with your physical education teaching practice...	Prompts for reflection — What role might these factors play?
What influences shape your understanding and approach to teaching SEL?	■ Socialization ■ Value orientations ■ Context
Are there any assumptions or habits that may present obstacles to improving your practice?	■ Behavior management ■ Management versus instruction ■ Assessment versus instruction
What ideas or resources can you seek from outside of physical education to develop in this area?	■ CASEL or other SEL frameworks ■ State/national guidelines and standards ■ Local (school/district) initiatives
What approaches commonly found in physical education can you build upon and extend in your own practice?	■ Positive learning environment ■ Combination of implicit, reactive, explicit, and empowering approaches ■ Models-based practice
How can you be more intentional and concrete about integrating SEL into specific lessons and activities?	■ Involve students in decision making ■ Set explicit SEL objectives ■ Tailor activity and teaching style to maximize SEL focus

Tracing through the major topics of this chapter, these questions address influences and assumptions that shape teaching practice as well as resources from outside of physical education and approaches within physical education that can be integrated to create best practice for teaching SEL. While good examples of teaching SEL in practice are unlimited, we hope this chapter has been useful in providing some guidelines and examples of promising practice. We encourage teachers to develop an approach that works best for them and their students. However, we do hope that by the end of this chapter, it is clear to readers that any effective approach to promoting SEL should be thoughtful, comprehensive, and integrated—it does not happen automatically! The next chapter will continue this discussion with a primary focus on assessment practices that are especially relevant to the development of SEL.

Questions for Discussion

1. How would you describe your own teaching philosophy, specifically as it relates to the affective learning domain?
2. Think of one of your own favorite coaches or physical education teachers—how would you describe their approach to fostering SEL?
3. What concerns do you think a middle school physical education teacher might have about using the Empowering Approach to teaching SEL?
4. Compare and contrast reproduction versus discovery teaching styles including examples of when each one might be appropriate for promoting an SEL learning objective.

References

Amis, J. M., Wright, P. M., Dyson, B., Vardaman, J. M., & Ferry, H. (2012). Implementing childhood obesity policy in a new educational environment: The cases of Mississippi and Tennessee. *American Journal of Public Health, 102*(7), 1406–1413.

Baptista, C., Corte-Real, N., Regueiras, L., Seo, G., Hemphill, M., Pereira, A., . . . Fonseca, A. (2020). Teaching personal and social responsibility after school: A systematic review. *Cuadernos de Psicología del Deporte, 20*(2), 1–25.

Bessa, C., Hastie, P., Araújo, R., & Mesquita, I. (2019). What do we know about the development of personal and social skills within the sport education model: A systematic review. *Journal of Sports Science & Medicine 18*(4), 812–829.

Byra, M. (2006). Teaching styles and inclusive pedagogies. In D. Kirk, M., O'Sullivan, & D. Macdonald, *Handbook of physical education* (pp. 449–466). London: Sage.

Casey, A. (2017). Models based practices. In C. D. Ennis (Ed.), *Routledge Handbook of Physical Education Pedagogies* (pp. 54–67). Routledge.

Chen, A., Ennis, C. D., & Loftus, S. (1997). Refining the value orientation inventory. *Research Quarterly for Exercise and Sport, 68*(4), 352–356.

Collaborative for Academic, Social, and Emotional Learning. (2020). *What is social and emotional learning?* https://casel.org/what-is-sel/

Coulson, C. L., Irwin, C. C., & Wright, P. M. (2012). Applying Hellison's responsibility model in a youth residential treatment facility: A practical inquiry project. *Agora for Physical Education and Sport, 14*(1), 38–54.

DeBusk, M., & Hellison, D. (1989). Implementing a physical education Self-Responsibility Model for delinquency-prone youth. *Journal of Teaching in Physical Education, 8*(2), 104–112.

Deci, E. L., Ryan, R. M., & Williams, G. C. (1996). Need satisfaction and the self-regulation of learning. *Learning and Individual Differences, 8*(3), 165–183.

Dewey, J. (1938). *Experience and education.* New York: Touchstone.

Dyson, B., & Casey, A. (2016). *Cooperative learning in physical education and physical activity: A practical introduction.* Routledge.

Dyson, B. P., Howley, D. F., & Wright, P. M. (2020). A scoping review critically examining research connecting social and emotional learning with three model-based practices in physical education: Have we been doing this all along? *European Physical Education Review.* Online first at: https://doi.org/10.1177/1356336X20923710

Gray, S., Wright, P. M., Sievwright, R., & Robertson, S. (2019). Learning to use teaching for personal and social responsibility through action research. *Journal of Teaching in Physical Education, 38*(4), 347–356.

Hastie, P. A. (2017). Revisiting the national physical education content standards: What do we really know about our achievement of the physically educated/literate person? *Journal of Teaching in Physical Education, 36*(1), 3–19.

Hellison, D. (2011). *Teaching personal and social responsibility through physical activity* (3rd ed.). Human Kinetics.

Hellison, D., & Templin, T. J. (1991). *A Reflective Approach to Teaching Physical Education.* Champaign, IL: Human Kinetics.

Jacobs, J., & Wright, P. (2014). Social and emotional learning policies and physical education. *Strategies: A Journal for Physical and Sport Educators, 27*(6), 42–44.

Jacobs, J. M., & Wright, P. M. (2018). Transfer of life skills in sport-based youth development programs: A conceptual framework bridging learning to application. *Quest, 70*(1), 81–99.

Jacobs, J., & Wright, P. M. (2019). Thinking about the transfer of life skills: Reflections from youth in a community-based sport programme in an underserved urban setting. *International Journal of Sport and Exercise Psychology.* Online first at: https://doi.org/10.1080/1612197X.2019.1655776

Jewett, A. E., Bain, L. L., & Ennis, C. D. (1995). The curriculum process in physical education. Dubuque, IA: Brown & Benchmark.

Johnson, D. W. & Johnson, R. (1994). *Learning together and alone.* Needham Heights, MA: Allyn and Bacon.

Jung, J. (2012). The focus, role, and meaning of experienced teachers' reflection in physical education. *Physical Education and Sport Pedagogy, 17*(2), 157–175.

Kirk, D. (2013). Educational value and models-based instruction. *Educational Philosophy and Theory, 45*(9), 973–986.

Lavay, B. W., French, R., & Henderson, H. L. (2015). *Positive behavior management in physical activity settings* (3rd ed.). Human Kinetics.

Levesque-Bristol, C., Sell, G. R., & Zimmerman, J. A. (2006). A theory-based integrative model for learning and motivation in higher education. In S. Chadwick-Blossey & D. R. Robertson (Eds.), *To Improve the Academy* (Vol. 24, pp. 86–103). Anker.

McCollum, S. (2002). The reflective framework for teaching in physical education: A pedagogical tool. *Journal of Physical Education, Recreation & Dance, 73*(6), 39–42.

McKenzie, T. L., Marshall, S. J., Sallis, J. F., & Conway, T. L. (2000). Student activity levels, lesson context, and teacher behavior during middle school physical education. *Research Quarterly for Exercise and Sport, 71*(3), 249–259.

Metzler, M. W. (2011). *Instructional models in physical education* (3rd ed.). Scottsdale, AZ: Holcomb Hathaway.

Mitchell, S. A., Oslin, J. L., & Griffin, L. (2006). *Teaching sport concepts and skills: A tactical games approach* (2nd ed.). Champaign, IL: Human Kinetics.

Mosston, M., & Ashworth, S. (2017). *Teaching physical education* (1st online). Spectrum of Teaching Styles. http://www.spectrumofteachingstyles.org/

Pascual, C. B., Escartí, A., Guiterrez, M., Llopis, R., Marin, D., & Wright, P. M. (2011). Exploring the implementation fidelity of a program designed to promote personal and social responsibility through physical education: A comparative case study. *Research Quarterly in Exercise and Sport, 82*, 499–511.

Placek, J. H. (1983). Conceptions of success in teaching: Busy, happy and good? In T. J. Templin & J. L. Oslin (Eds.), *Teaching in physical education* (pp. 46–56). Champaign, IL: Human Kinetics.

Pozo, P., Grao-Cruces, A., & Pérez-Ordás, R. (2018). Teaching personal and social responsibility model-based programmes in physical education: A systematic review. *European Physical Education Review, 24*(1), 56–75.

Richards, K. A. R., & Gordon, B. (2017). Socialisation and learning to teach using the teaching personal and social responsibility approach. *Asia-Pacific Journal of Health, Sport and Physical Education, 8*(1), 19–38.

Richards, K. A. R., & Levesque-Bristol, C. (2014). Student learning and motivation in physical education. *Strategies: A Journal for Physical and Sport Educators, 27*(2), 43–46.

Richards, K. A. R., Ivy, V. N., Wright, P. M., & Jerris, E. (2019). Combining the skill themes approach with teaching personal and social responsibility to teach social and emotional learning in elementary physical education. *Journal of Physical Education, Recreation & Dance, 90*(3), 35–44.

Richards, K. A. R., Pennington, C. G., & Sinelnikov, O. A. (2019). Teacher socialization in physical education: A scoping review of literature. *Kinesiology Review, 8*(2), 86–99.

Schön, D. A. (1987). *Educating the reflective practitioner.* San Francisco, CA: Jossey-Bass.

Schubert, W. H. (1986). *Curriculum: Perspective, paradigm, and possibility.* McMillian.

Schubert, W. H. (1996). Perspectives on four curriculum traditions. *Educational Horizons, 74*(4), 169–176.

Schwab, J. J. (1971). The practical: Arts of eclectic. *School Review, 29*, 493–542.

Schwab, J. J. (1973). The practical 3: Translation into curriculum. *School Review, 81*(4), 501–522.

Schwab, J. J. (1983). The practical 4: Something for curriculum professors to do. *Curriculum Inquiry, 13*(3), 239–265.

SHAPE America. (2014). *National standards & grade-level outcomes for K-12 physical education.* Human Kinetics.

Siedentop, D., Hastie, P. A., & van der Mars, H. (2011). *Complete guide to sport education* (2nd ed.). Human Kinetics.

Sinelnikov, O. A., & Hastie, P. (2017). The learning of pedagogical models in physical education: The socialization perspective. In K. A. R. Richards & K. L. Gaudreault (Eds.), *Teacher socialization in physical education: New perspectives* (pp. 130–143). Routledge.

Standal, O. F. & Moe, V. F. (2013). Reflective practice in physical education and physical education teacher education: A review of literature since 1995. *Quest, 65*(2), 220–240.

Starck, J. R., Richards, K. A. R., & O'Neil, K. (2018). A conceptual framework for assessment literacy: Opportunities for physical education teacher education. *Quest, 70*(4), 519–535. https://doi.org/10.1080/00336297.2018.1465830

Teraoka, E., Ferreira, H. J., Kirk, D., & Bardid, F. (2020). Affective learning in physical education: A systematic review. *Journal of Teaching in Physical Education.* https://doi.org/10.1123/jtpe.2019-0164

Tsangaridou, N., & O'Sullivan, M. (1997). The role of reflection in shaping physical education teachers' educational values and practices. *Journal of Teaching in Physical Education, 17*(1), 2–25.

Wright, P. M., & Burton, S. (2008). Implementation and outcomes of a responsibility-based physical activity program integrated into an intact high school physical education class. *Journal of Teaching in Physical Education, 27*(2), 138–154.

Wright, P. M., & Craig, M. W. (2011). Tool for assessing responsibility-based education (TARE): Instrument development, content validity, and inter-rater reliability. *Measurement in Physical Education and Exercise Science, 15*(3), 204–219.

Wright, P. M., & Irwin, C. (2018). Using systematic observation to assess teacher effectiveness in promoting personally and socially responsible behavior in physical education. *Measurement in Physical Education and Exercise Science, 22*(3), 250–262.

Wright, P. M., Gordon, B., & Gray, S. (2020). Social and emotional learning in the physical education curriculum. In W. H. Schubert and M. Fang (Eds.), *Oxford Encyclopedia of Curriculum Studies.* Oxford, UK: Oxford University Press. https://doi.org/10.1093/acrefore/9780190264093.013.1061

Wright, P. M., Howell, S., Jacobs, J. M., & McLoughlin, G. (2020). Implementation and perceived benefits of an after-school soccer program designed to promote social and emotional learning. *Journal of Amateur Sport, 6*(1), 125–145.

Wright, P. M., Richards, K. A. R., & Gray, S. (2020). Understanding the interpretation and implementation of social and emotional learning in physical education. *The Curriculum Journal.* http://dx.doi.org/10.1002/curj.85

Wright, P. M., & Walsh, D. S. (2015). Subject matters of physical education. In M. F. He, B. D. Schultz, and W. H. Schubert (Eds.). *Guide to Curriculum in Education* (pp. 70–77). Thousand Oaks, CA: Sage.

CHAPTER 4

Assessment Strategies That Align with Social and Emotional Learning

K. Andrew R. Richards
Jenna R. Starck
Paul M. Wright

CHAPTER SUMMARY

Whereas Chapter 3 introduced the reader to instructional strategies aligned with social and emotional learning (SEL) in physical education, in this chapter, we turn to consider assessment strategies that support students' SEL. We begin with a review of assessment terminology before considering the relevance and importance of assessment both generally and specifically to physical education. We then address common assessment strategies in physical education before pushing for a move toward assessment literacy. The chapter then turns toward important considerations and relevant strategies for assessing students' SEL in physical education.

Assessment Strategies That Align with Social and Emotional Learning

Chapter 3 provided an overview of teaching practices that align with social and emotional learning (SEL) in physical education and activity spaces, including the need to reconceptualize the division between instructional and managerial tasks. Many tasks traditionally conceptualized as managerial can actually be aligned with SEL goals and outcomes, which makes them an important part of the instructional process. Similar to other instructional targets in physical education, the use of fluid assessments is needed to understand and evaluate both student- and program-level outcomes as well as inform students and teachers of their learning relative to SEL. In this chapter, we discuss contemporary assessment approaches in physical education with an explicit focus on the use of assessment strategies that align with SEL competencies. Through this process, and similar to Chapter 3, we will challenge the traditional separation of instructional and managerial tasks in the framing of assessments. We also advocate that teachers develop assessment literacy (DinanThompson & Penney, 2015) that fully integrates assessment into the teaching-learning processes. We begin with a review of some assessment terminology to help frame the rest of the chapter.

Review of Assessment Terminology

From our perspective, one of the challenges related to starting a conversation about SEL-aligned assessment strategies in physical education and activity settings is the multitude of different terminology used to explain and define various approaches and purposes of assessment. Our approach, therefore, is to provide an overview and definition of different terms to set the stage for a deeper discussion. Defining these terms

initially will also allow us to use them later in the chapter without having to define them as we go. Generally, we understand assessment to be a combination of observable student behaviors and performances as well as perceptions and options that require an evaluative judgment relative to some standard of quality (Hay, 2006) with the ultimate goal of supporting the student learning experience (DinanThompson & Penney, 2015). Additional assessment terminology is summarized in **Table 4.1**. If you are interested in learning more about assessment, there are numerous books and journal articles that delve more deeply into the topic with specific reference to physical education and activity spaces (e.g., Collier, 2011; DinanThompson & Penney, 2015; Lund & Kirk, 2020; Starck et al., 2018). We have drawn upon many of these sources in developing our arguments within this chapter.

Table 4.1 Definitions for Key Assessment Terms

Category	Assessment Term	Definition
Formality	Formal Assessment	Preplanned, intentional assessments that involve the collection of student data related to learning
	Informal Assessment	In the moment, often spontaneous activities that involve providing feedback and checking for understanding without the collection of data
Focus	Assessment *for* Learning	Formative assessment that is integrated into and intended to inform the learning process
	Assessment *of* Learning	Summative assessment included at the end of a unit of instruction and intended to evaluate what students have learned
Person Responsible	Self-Assessment	Assessments conducted by the students as an evaluation of their own performance
	Peer Assessment	Assessments in which students evaluate and provide feedback on one another's performance
	Teacher Assessment	Assessments conducted by the teacher with the goal of evaluating student learning
Timing	Formative	Ongoing assessment that is integrated with the teaching-learning process to provide both students' and teachers' feedback on learning in real time to allow changes to instruction
	Summative	Assessment positioned at the end of a period of learning that is typically formal and serves as a final evaluation of student learning
Type	Traditional Assessment	Teacher-driven, formal assessment that prioritizes objective and forced-choice responses
	Performance-based Assessment	Assessments that allow for more holistic approaches to understanding student learning. Examples include group projects, portfolios, and written work. Includes activities that ask students to complete tasks in environments that mirror real-world application of the skills being learned
	Standards-based Assessment	An approach to assessment that is aligned with educational standards guiding instruction and evaluates student mastery of those standards

Traditionally, assessment has been conceptualized as an evaluation *of* the learning process or something that was done at the end of an instructional period (DinanThompson & Penney, 2015; Earl, 2013). This *summative* form of assessment is typically formal (e.g., skills test, written quiz) and is intended to understand what students learned through a unit of instruction. This approach is limited, however, in that it prevents teachers and students from receiving feedback through the process of learning to inform continued growth. Assessment *for* learning, on the other hand, is a *formative* process that is integrated into the learning experience to inform student learning and provide feedback to encourage continued growth (Black & Wiliam, 1998). Students could, for example, conduct peer assessments during a learning task and then use the feedback provided to continue to improve. Viewing assessment as a formative process positions it as an integral part of the teaching–learning process—on par with planning and instruction. **Figure 4.1** provides an overview of the teaching and learning process, which includes planning, instruction, and assessment. This illustrates how, through formative assessment, three main components of the teaching/learning process can more fluidly influence one another as what teachers learn through assessment influences their planning and instructional activities in real time rather than waiting until the end of a unit (Starck et al., 2018).

One important distinction in how assessment is implemented relates to whether it is implemented informally or formally (Lund & Kirk, 2020). *Formal assessment* is preplanned and involves the intentional collection of data related to student learning. Examples include skill tests, cognitive examinations, group

projects, and written essays. By contrast, *informal assessments* are either preplanned or spontaneous and implemented regularly through a lesson to gauge learning from a group. Teacher observation accompanied by feedback, check-for-understanding questions, and asking students to share their opinions and perspectives during a class conversation are all examples of informal assessment strategies. Generally, these help teachers make decisions in the act of teaching but do not involve the collection of data or documentation of student learning. Although teachers conduct informal assessment regularly, it should not be the only way they assess student learning (Collier, 2011).

Beyond the formal nature of assessment, a third distinction relates to who is conducting the assessment. *Self-assessments* ask students to evaluate their own learning, understanding, or performance. For example, students could be asked to self-report their engagement in learning activities in a class or their contributions to a group project. They could also be asked to watch videos of themselves demonstrating a skill and evaluate performance using a rubric. *Peer assessment* occurs when students are involved in evaluating one another's learning. Such would be the case when a student is asked to observe and evaluate a partner's skill performance using a rubric or to evaluate team members' contributions to a group project. Finally, *teacher assessments* are those in which the teacher controls the collection of information and evaluation of student learning. Such would be the case when the teacher evaluates student skill performance using a rubric or checklist, or knowledge using a quiz or writing assignment.

There are further distinctions related to the type of assessment conducted and the information gathered (DinanThompson, 2013). *Traditional assessments* are those that adopt standardized approaches using questions that provide a limited number of response categories (e.g., true/false and multiple-choice questions). Skill and fitness assessments require students to perform skills and activities in decontextualized, contrived environments (e.g., a volleyball skills test). By contrast, *performance-based assessments* ask students to demonstrate knowledge in divergent ways and in real-world environments. Generally, students are provided with the opportunity to (a) demonstrate their ability, (b) perform a meaningful task, and (c) receive feedback from a qualified person using predefined criteria (Mintah, 2003).

Performance-based assessments can be further understood as being alternative or authentic (López-Pastor et al., 2013). Alternative assessments provide students with opportunities to demonstrate

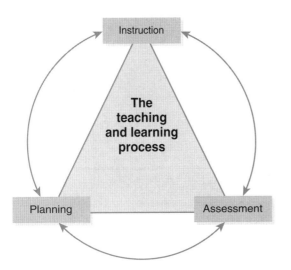

Figure 4.1 Overview of the teaching–learning process emphasizing the relationships among planning, instruction, and assessment.

knowledge in a variety of different ways beyond standardized tests, including writing assignments, portfolios, group projects, and performance tasks. These typically require evaluation using a rubric rather than an answer key given the diverse range of acceptable responses. These forms of assessment allow students to apply learned information to illustrate what they know and are able to do rather than what they can remember from instruction. Authentic assessments are a specialized form of alternative assessment in which learners are asked to perform skills in contexts that mirror the real world. Evaluating students' use of skills and tactics during a game of tennis using the game performance assessment instrument (GPAI; Oslin et al., 1998) is one example of an authentic assessment in physical education that when combined with instruction, can enhance student learning (Lund & Kirk, 2020).

Finally, *standards-based assessment* is a movement in contemporary education that prioritizes the linkages among educational standards, student learning objectives, instructional activities, and assessment (Lund & Tannehill, 2015). In the field of physical education, the Society of Health and Physical Educators (SHAPE) America (2014) provides overarching national standards to guide instruction that provide the foundation for most standards and learning benchmarks developed at the state level. Aligning assessment with standards lends itself to backward curriculum design (see **Figure 4.2**). This approach to curricular planning begins with the intended outcomes (i.e., standards), which are linked to learning objectives. Instructional activities are then designed to help students progress toward objectives and meet the standards. Assessment strategies are then used to understand student learning that resulted from instruction and in relation to the objectives and standards (Wiggins & McTighe, 2011). The success of these instructional activities in bringing about the desired student learning outcomes in reference to objectives and educational standards is then evaluated using assessments that link to the standards. However, the collection and tracking of assessment data should be used to make "decisions about instruction and to measure student learning continually throughout learning sequence" not just at the end (SHAPE America 2014, pp. 90–91). In physical education, SHAPE America (2019) has developed as a battery of assessment instruments as part of *PE Metrics* that aligned with the national standards.

Importance of Assessment in the Teaching-Learning Process

As mentioned in the last section, the teaching–learning process occurs as educators and students work together in learning spaces to evaluate learner needs, set learning objectives, design and implement instructional tasks, and evaluate learner growth (Ololube et al., 2015). Assessment is an integral component of this process in terms of understanding learners' needs at the beginning of an instructional

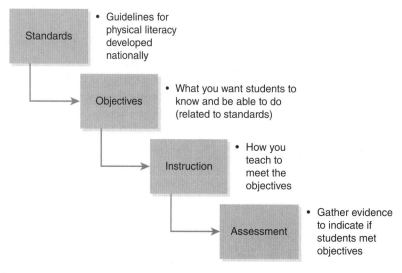

Figure 4.2 Overview of the backward design process whereby teachers begin with the guiding standards to determine relevant outcomes and objectives. Instruction is designed to lead students toward the objectives and assessment planned and implemented to evaluate progress. Although assessment is positioned at the end of this process, there is actually interplay among the elements as assessment drives future instructional activities, evaluates progress toward learning objectives, and can lead to the modifications of activities or objectives that do not meet students' learning needs.

unit (i.e., preassessment), monitoring student progress through instruction (i.e., assessment for learning) and evaluating overall growth at the end (i.e., assessment of learning; DinanThompson & Penney, 2015; Lund & Kirk, 2020). Accordingly, without appropriate assessment strategies, it becomes difficult for educators to understand learner's needs, make adjustments to accommodate those needs, and understand student learning in relation to instructional goals. Promoting student learning in relation to instructional objectives and educational standards is, therefore, one goal of assessment.

Linked to, but distinct from, assessment is grading, which is the process through which instructors assign a numerical and/or letter grade to evaluate student learning and performance (McMillan et al., 2002). From elementary school through postsecondary education, grading is a central component of the course experience in the United States and abroad and is often considered an indicator of what students learned within a course. Challenges have been noted, however, given that teachers' grading practices are often not valid or reliable measures and include a "hodgepodge…of attitude, effort, and achievement" (Brookhart, 1991, p. 31) that are not linked to identified standards or learning outcomes (Starck et al., 2018). In many cases, however, grades in physical education are assigned for student dress, attitude, and behavior without evaluating aligned instructional goals that link to learning standards. In these situations, grades are assigned for criteria that are not aligned with learning outcomes.

A further distinction between assessment and grading is that, while assessments are often used in the grading process, not all assessments need to be graded. Many formative, either formal or informal, assessments conducted on a daily basis to provide immediate feedback are not included in students course grades, for example (D'Angelo & Cross, 1993). Self- and peer-assessments are also important tools in the assessment *for* learning process that do not have to be graded but provide valuable feedback to help students understand and improve their performance. It may actually be undesirable to grade students' reflective evaluations of their own work and their evaluations of peers because the students may focus too much on the graded outcome, which could negatively impact their willingness to provide honest evaluations. Students may be so concerned with getting a good grade on the assignment that they focus on that grade rather than the associated learning activity and opportunity to be self-critical or provide meaningful feedback to their peers.

A fourth important goal of assessment that aligns with SEL relates to helping youth practice and develop the ability to receive feedback and provide self- and peer-feedback that requires them to engage in evaluative and reflective skills (Andrade & Valtcheva, 2009; Topping, 2009). This reinforces the fact that assessment is a learning activity in and of itself where students can critically reflect on their own experiences. Receiving feedback can, however, be difficult for students, particularly when it indicates that they are not making appropriate progress toward desired outcomes. However, when designed intentionally and debriefed appropriately, assessment activities can help students contextualize feedback and understand that evaluations of their performance do not necessarily have implications for them as people. When students conduct appropriately designed self-assessments, such as being asked to identify and explain the level of effort they gave in class on a particular day, they are asked to reflect on their own performance and provide an honest evaluation, which is an important skill not only in school but also in everyday life. Similarly, peer-assessments provide students with the opportunities to both give feedback to and receive it from classmates; however, they are not meant for evaluative purposes but instead to promote thinking critically toward the intended outcomes. These can be challenging skills for youth and require practice but are nevertheless critical for self-improvement and development. When used in this way, assessment shifts from evaluating students to enhancing learning (Lund & Kirk, 2020). Collectively, self- and peer-assessment can help students learn skills related to managing their own learning and providing feedback to others that can equip students to be more capable, self-directed learners in their everyday lives.

Beyond the importance of assessment for student-level outcomes, there are associated program-level implications that should be considered. Teachers who conduct a wide variety of assessments, including those that capture student attitudes and perceptions of the program, can learn important information about what students learn and how they feel about their physical education experiences. This information can be used to adjust the program in ways that better address student needs and can help to identify culturally relevant content and approaches to teaching that may not be apparent otherwise. By asking for student input, for example, a teacher may learn that certain forms of dance are highly valued within a particular community and take steps to integrate them into a dance unit. Similarly, considering assessment data indicating that most students are not meeting grade-level benchmarks related to the performance of a certain skill, adjustments can be made at the program level through common assessments (e.g., focusing on this skill longer, integrating different learning activities) to further address students' learning needs. Furthermore, being able to provide such feedback is important in terms of engaging students and providing them with a voice in the physical education program, which is essential to implementing SEL (Hellison, 2011). Engaging in this process may not be natural for students, however, and may represent an important learning experience in physical education.

Assessment Strategies in Physical Education

While the physical education community generally agrees that assessment is an important element of the teaching–learning process and foundational to effective teaching practice (DinanThompson & Penney, 2015; Hay, 2006; Lund & Kirk, 2020), it is also one area of teachers' practice that is often absent or underdeveloped (López-Pastor et al., 2013; Lund & Kirk, 2020). While it may be tempting to blame teachers for limited and ineffective implementation of assessment, Starck and colleagues (2018) argued that the challenges are larger, more systematic, and reflective of how teachers are recruited, socialized, and taught. When prospective recruits experience physical education that does not include a focus on assessment, they may not see it as an important part of practice. This view of assessment may be solidified in teacher education programs where assessment is not integrated meaningfully into course content and through field experiences in schools (Hay & Penney, 2013; Veal, 1988). Accordingly, preservice teachers may leave their program experiences feeling as if assessment is not important or practical as they begin their teaching careers in schools (Starck et al., 2018).

Once newly qualified teachers transition into school environments and begin their teaching careers, school contexts can have a large influence on teachers' perspectives on and ability to effectively utilize assessments (Starck et al., 2020). In some cases, schools may issue students a grade for physical education, or grade on a pass/fail basis, which has implications for how teachers use and conceptualize assessments. While assessment and grading are not synonymous, they often become conflated and teachers may feel that assessment is not worth their time if it does not contribute to students' grades (Collier, 2011). Furthermore, physical educators are often asked to teach classes that are much larger than those taught by classroom teachers, which can make student assessment feel overwhelming (Lynn & Woods, 2010). Particularly at the elementary level, physical educators may only see their students a few times a week for 30 minutes at a time, which can make assessment feel impractical.

Limitations related to class size and meeting frequency may be particularly challenging for teachers who conceptualize assessment as being teacher-driven and separate from rather than an integral part of the learning process (Starck et al., 2020). Given that they do not see assessment as an instructional activity itself, and rather as a process that occurs at the end of learning (i.e., assessment *of* learning) which is driven by the teacher and closely aligned with grading, assessment may not be valued as an appropriate used of limited class time. Furthermore, while assessment instruments, including *PE Metrics* (SHAPE America, 2019) are available, teachers may not feel well prepared to use them. Lund and Kirk (2020) suggest that the use of assessment may be a difficult task for teachers who do not comprehend it as an essential part of the teaching–learning process. Given the culture surrounding assessment, assessment strategies may not change until there is evidence that the use of assessment does improve learning for students. Additionally, outside of states such as South Carolina where statewide, comprehensive physical education assessment was implemented for a period of time (Rink & Mitchell, 2003) and is no longer in practice, most state policies emphasize fitness testing and do not include assessments aligned with the cognitive domain or SEL. Collectively, teachers' current and prior socialization experiences may leave them feeling as if assessment is important in terms of student and school accountability but less important for students' educational experience (i.e., improving student learning; Starck et al., 2020).

Narrow and limited conceptualizations of assessment are most likely found in environments where physical education is not valued and teachers work under conditions (e.g., large classes, limited meeting time) that do not promote quality educational practices (Laureano et al., 2014; O'Sullivan, 1989). In these contexts, teachers tend to rely most heavily on teacher-driven assessment strategies rather than those that engage students in the assessment process (López-Pastor et al., 2013). Based in part on their socialization, teachers may also have a narrow conceptualization of assessment that prioritizes the psychomotor domain and neglects the opportunity for and importance of teaching toward and assessing SEL

(Richards & Gordon, 2017). Where assessment strategies are used, they tend to include criteria related to dress, participation, and effort that are not well connected to stated learning objectives or curricular outcomes (Hay & Penney, 2013; Veal, 1988). Physical educators may also integrate fitness testing, particularly when required by state law, but concerns have been raised about how these assessments are used, particularly when they are not discussed or debriefed with students in meaningful ways and are instead used to body shame those students who are overweight or struggle with obesity (DinanThompson & Penney, 2015). Scholars have suggested that for teachers to be able to critically engage with inappropriate assessment strategies, their assessment literacy must improve (Hay & Penney, 2013; SHAPE America, 2014).

Movement Toward Assessment Literacy

Assessment communicates criteria that are of importance for students for student learning; however, it is often separate from the curriculum and is only utilized to gather data (i.e., fitness testing not embedded into a unit). Often not realized is the potential damage assessment can inflict upon students when they receive negative or critical information without follow up or feedback to aid in interpretation. All too often, assessment is completely separate from the teaching process and used for evaluation and documentation purposes only. Hay and Penney (2013) suggested that teachers need to understand how assessment, as a part of the overarching teaching–learning process, makes information visible to both the teacher and the student. However, this requires, that teachers develop a greater sense of assessment literacy (Dinan Thompson & Penney, 2015). Assessment literacy includes comprehending, applying, interpreting, and critically engaging with assessment while also helping students grow in their own assessment literacy (Hay & Penney, 2013). Although these four elements will be discussed separately and they do build on one another, they do not represent a linear progression and individuals often draw from multiple elements simultaneously in making assessment decisions.

Comprehension of assessment includes teachers' knowledge of the purposes of assessment, its place in the teaching–learning process, and the technical and sociopolitical capacities that impact adoption and use (Starck et al., 2018). This includes helping students understand what is expected when assessment is used and how to implement a given assessment instrument. It also relates to understanding how to create rubrics, provide justification to students for the grade they earned, and deliver constructive feedback to inform future learning. For example, grading on effort and participation do not provide identifiable criteria in advance to allow students to work toward a desired outcome. Instead, a teacher might identify outcomes of a unit, provide formative assessment opportunities for students to learn the material throughout the unit, and finally provide a summative assessment opportunity at the end of the unit. This process of using assessment allows teachers to promote learning through the use of assessment (assessment *for* learning) and demonstrate outcomes of the unit while providing a grade to students based on their learning (assessment *of* learning).

Even when teachers understand and value the role of assessment, given the dearth of appropriate assessment strategies in many physical education programs, students may not value what assessment affords them and see it as a waste of time. This relates to the marginalized nature of physical education and highlights that students may not expect to be evaluated in the same ways as in other subjects (O'Sullivan, 1989). There is, therefore, a concurrent need for assessment to better substantiate the outcomes claimed for the discipline so as to overcome marginality. For this to be effective, however, teachers must understand assessment as central components of the instruction process and on par with curriculum (i.e., planning) and pedagogy (i.e., instruction; Starck et al., 2018). Taken together, how teachers comprehend and value assessment is based on their own beliefs as well as barriers and facilitators to implementation in schools. If teachers do not comprehend assessment as a meaningful part of the teaching–learning process, and/or do not feel supported in implementing appropriate practices, they may believe assessment is either not valuable or impractical in their given environment (Starck et al., 2020).

The second component of assessment literacy, *application*, refers to the use of appropriate assessment in a teaching practice. If teachers understand assessment as a part of the teaching–learning process, they may embed assessment as a task during the lesson, such as using self- and/or peer-assessment strategies (Lund & Kirk, 2020). On the other hand, teachers may not fully comprehend or value assessment, which can limit engagement in formative and continual assessments that are embedded in the lessons (Starck et al., 2018). Sociocultural and technical conditions can play a large role in the fluidity and embeddedness of assessment tasks. While assessment can be difficult with large classes, for example, teachers who develop well-constructed protocols and procedures for managing the technical nature of implementation such as managing assessment instruments (e.g., paper, pencils, iPads), providing demonstrations of assessment tasks (e.g., how the task should be facilitated for accountability), and demonstrating acceptable criteria (e.g., show what is an acceptable performance), assessment can be more manageable. Furthermore, with technological advances, assessment strategies that involve video reflections, Google forms, Plickers, Chromebooks, and activity monitors, assessment may better meet the learning needs of students and take some burden off of the teacher. Such technologically driven approaches have become even more relevant during the recent COVID-19 pandemic as schools were forced to move instructional activities into online spaces.

Assessment *interpretation* describes how teachers understand and make sense of the information they collect from assessment in relation to framing future learning (Dinan Thompson & Penney, 2015). This includes using the data to reflect on what the assessment says about their teaching, students learning, and how the resulting information can be leveraged toward developing more realistic personalized learning experiences for students. Hay and Penney (2013) explain that, depending on how teachers understand the purpose of assessment, they may either interpret assessment in relation to promoting student learning (i.e., assessment for learning) and/or toward evaluation of achievement outcomes (i.e., assessment of learning). In addition, interpretation includes how teachers help their students understand what information is being communicated to them, and what it means for their future learning. For example, if a teacher embedded a peer assessment to help teach game play behaviors, students will have the opportunity to learn the desired behavior (i.e., criteria), interpret what is of importance during gameplay, and evaluate levels of achievement toward the desired outcome. This opportunity is lost if interpretations are narrowly conceptualized in relation to what students have learned rather than how they can continue learning (Hay & Penney, 2013).

Finally, *critical engagement* with assessment encourages teachers to consider the position of power they hold over students, be reflective about what assessment information means to both the teacher and the student, and consider how to best communicate the results of assessment. In teaching, there is an inherent power dynamic that occurs between the teacher and the student; therefore, it is important to assess students in ways that are valid and promote equitable outcomes (Starck et al., 2018). It is also important to consider how the use of assessment may impact students' perceptions of themselves (Hay & Penney, 2013). For example, teachers should consider what the assessment tells students about themselves and how they can continue to improve. Teachers with high assessment literacy should be able to select appropriate criteria, use assessment tools to promote learning, provide constructive feedback to students, make changes to their teaching, and evaluate achievement outcomes. In doing so, teachers may avoid potential consequences to students' learning as well as their ability and desire to learn in the future. When considering SEL, critically engaging in assessment may provide students the opportunities to be self-reflective and gain the necessary feedback to continue working toward desired outcomes.

Considerations for Social and Emotional Learning in Physical Education

Evaluating social and emotional learning requires an understanding of appropriate criteria that can be developed into learning objectives. When writing an objective, an educator must consider who the students are, and what they already know. Further, the objective should identify a verb that is developmentally appropriate and select specific criteria that will be used to evaluate student learning (Lund & Tannehill, 2015). Often; however, objectives are written vaguely without specific criteria and with verbs such as "learn," "appreciate," and "think," which do not describe the level of learning complexity and cannot be measured. Alternatively, Bloom's Taxonomy is a hierarchical classification system that describes performance indicators to help differentiate levels of human cognition in learning and assessment (Bloom, 1956; Krathwohl, 2002). These indicators include six levels of learning arranged in a hierarchy that require students to engage in content by remembering, understanding, applying, analyzing, evaluating, or creating. By recognizing which level of thinking must come first (i.e. remembering before you can understand; analyze before you can evaluate), teachers can develop objectives, lesson tasks, and assessments that hold students accountable and place them at the center of their learning.

Importantly, sometimes it is assumed that students will progress toward SEL outcomes naturally as a consequence of being in physical education. This reflects the sports-build-character misnomer (Lyras & Welty Peachey, 2011) discussed in Chapter 2 and also connects to the artificial division between instructional and managerial tasks noted in Chapter 3. Teachers who take this position may not see the value in developing objectives aligned with SEL, perhaps because they believe time spent teaching SEL interferes with their ability to maximize other learning activities such as physical skill development (Richards & Gordon, 2017). These positions are challenged in Chapter 2 and elsewhere throughout this text as the core connections between SEL and physical education are described and SEL is positioned as part of the content that should be taught in physical education (Gordon et al., 2016). Similar to psychomotor and cognitive outcomes, therefore, SEL-focused objectives should be planned, explicit, discussed with students in advance, and evaluated appropriately so as to fully integrate them within the teaching–learning process. This will help students to focus on learning in this area and identify ways they can improve and develop the desired skills.

Consider an objective written to increase social awareness where students are tasked with identifying positive ways to express their understanding of differing perspectives. Because the verb asks students to *identify*, the assessment utilized should be developed to evaluate accordingly. For example, using teacher observation would not be an appropriate assessment as this approach would not help determine if students can identify positive expressions. The assessment in this case would not align with the intended outcome.

However, using a self-assessment that requires students to identify moments during the class period when they either viewed differing perspectives being worked out among classmates or when they positively expressed a different perspective, and in doing so showed respect for others. To extend this and promote transfer of learning, students might be asked to identify instances of positive expression outside of class. **Figure 4.3** provides a rubric for gaining social awareness where students are evaluated on their ability to identify and use positive expression toward differing perspectives with performance specified across four rubric levels. This process reflects the backwards design approach discussed earlier in this chapter as the teacher selects an assessment strategy that aligns with the level of learning described in the objective.

As another example, consider an objective written for students to articulate their *self-awareness* of physical activity enjoyment. A common grading error would be to evaluate students' level of enjoyment, perhaps by asking them to rate their enjoyment from 1–7 on a self-report survey. Alternatively, a first step would be to identify criteria that represent having self-awareness of ones' enjoyment. Aligned with CASEL's (2019) conceptualization of SEL, the teacher writing the objective in this scenario may integrate the components of self-awareness into a rubric that will be used to assess student learning. **Figure 4.4** provides a rubric for students to be evaluated on their ability to gain self-awareness of enjoyment of physical activity. Specifically, this rubric includes three associated

Social Awareness of Differing Perspectives				
	1	**2**	**3**	**4**
Identifies differing perspective-taking	Students are able to identify their own perspective	Students are able to identify one instance in which they shared the same perspective as someone in class	Students are able to identify instances in which they or someone else used a differing perspective positively	Students are able to identify instances in which they or someone else used a differing perspective and connects this observation to a time outside of class
Uses a positive expression to show respect to others	Student discusses possible instances of positive expression in general	Student identifies positive expression being used	Student identifies positive expression being used and discusses how those actions respected others	Student identifies positive expression being used and discusses the connection to respect for others and connections to outside of class

Figure 4.3 Example rubric to evaluate SEL related to social-awareness of differing perspectives. The rubric includes two elements that define social-awareness and four evaluation levels to identify students' progress related to each element.

Self-Awareness of Physical Activity Enjoyment				
	1	**2**	**3**	**4**
Articulates emotions	Students are able to accurately identify emotions	Students are able to accurately identify and understand the cause of those emotions	Students are able to accurately identify, understand the cause of emotions about physical activity, but lack specificity	Students are able to accurately identify, understand the cause of emotions, and articulate feelings toward specific types of physical activity
Identifies unique strengths	Student identifies an activity they could potentially enjoy	Student identifies an activity they enjoy	Student identifies an activity they enjoy and discusses their own unique strengths	Student identifies an activity they enjoy, discusses their own unique strengths, and identifies how to continue building on them
Justifies based on accurate self-perception	Student reflects on enjoyment by providing a broad explanation	Student reflects on enjoyment of specific physical activity	Student reflects on enjoyment of physical activity based on their own specific strengths	Student reflects and justifies enjoyment of physical activity based on own specific strengths

Figure 4.4 Example rubric to evaluate SEL related to self-awareness of physical activity enjoyment. The rubric includes three elements that define self-awareness and four evaluation levels to identify students' progress related to each element.

criteria: (a) articulates emotions, (b) identifies unique strengths, and (c) justifies based on accurate self-perception. Four levels of performance associated with the identified criteria are also included to provide consistency in assessment and feedback. For example, the assessment activity aligned with this rubric could be asking students to journal and articulate their own self-awareness of physical activity enjoyment at the end of each lesson, once per week, or even as homework. Teachers would then evaluate students' journal entries using the rubric.

When using rubrics such as the one depicted here, it is critical that students are provided with access to the rubric in advance, the criteria for performance are discussed with illustrative examples, and the levels of achievement align with appropriate expectations for what students should know and be able to do as a result of learning. Relative to the rubric scores, Lund and Kirk (2020) note that the lowest level should not be written as the student simply "not doing something," but instead with criteria that describes what the student could do in order to improve future performance. In this case, a score at the lowest level (1) may be given if the student does provide thought but does not reflect or express emotion through essay. Similarly, the highest level (4) should be the criteria provided to students as the target criteria for learning and be used regularly to cue students toward the learning goals. When evaluating student

performance, teachers should also provide qualitative comments related to each of the performance criteria in order to help students understand the score they received and how they can improve in the future. While time consuming, failure to provide such feedback may make it difficult for students to understand why they earned the score they did and how they can improve in the future.

Assessment for learning has been identified as essential for integrating assessment strategies intentionally into the teaching–learning process with the goal of engaging students in their own learning (Hay, 2006). Important in pursuing SEL outcomes, this form of assessment helps teachers formatively evaluate where students are in their learning to provide feedback and make future curricular decisions without the pressures of being graded (Starck et al., 2020). Peer assessments are one common assessment for learning activity, which allows students to enhance learning a concept by reviewing criteria, making decisions with reference to other students' performance, and providing feedback based on observations. Closely aligned with goals of SEL, Noonan and Duncan (2005) suggested that both self- and peer-assessments can enhance learning by: (a) increasing student involvement in the learning process (e.g., students taking on teaching roles), (b) increasing social interactions and trust in others, (c) facilitating individual feedback, and (d) focusing on the process rather than the product. As the intended function of peer assessment is to emphasize the process rather than the product of learning, it should not be used for evaluation and grading purposes. Additionally, due to the subjective nature of peer evaluation (i.e., liking or disliking a peer, knowledge and application of content), it would not be considered a valid or reliable tool. However, this does not undermine the formative benefits of peer assessment both in terms of giving and receiving feedback.

As discussed in Chapter 3, the reciprocal style of teaching (Mosston & Ashworth, 2017) is one strategy that encourages peers to work together (i.e., peer-assisted learning; Rosenshine, 1979) and has been shown to develop positive SEL outcomes (Byra & Marks, 1993). Within this teaching study, the instructor interacts with the student by asking them questions and providing feedback about their observation as opposed to directing their feedback to the doer. However, for the observer to provide quality feedback, they need to understand the language and criteria on the assessment. This means that the teacher needs to identify and make the criteria known, the students need to be taught how to use the assessment tool, and accountability of the task needs to be provided just as in any other learning experience. When done effectively, this style of teaching takes the weight of management off of the teacher and alternatively provides students with more autonomy and control of their own learning. Furthermore, using this teaching style sets up many opportunities to emphasize SEL outcomes such as establishing and maintaining positive relationships, making responsible decisions, managing emotions, setting and achieving positive goals, and feeling and showing empathy for others in a peer-assessment exchange (CASEL, 2019). Finally, when using reciprocal teaching, the learning process is for both peers and brings together the cognitive, psychomotor, and SEL focus of the task.

While physical education represents one place in which SEL outcomes can be integrated and addressed, it should not be the only place. Rather, SEL is best addressed across classrooms, the whole school, at home in their daily lives, and in the community (Collie et al., 2012; Gordon et al., 2016). If embedded in a cross curricular format, students have more opportunities to learn SEL competences in authentic ways. Based on the CASEL (2019) model for conceptualizing SEL, broader initiatives can focus on self- and social-awareness, self-management, building positive relationships, and making healthy decisions, all of which were mapped to the SHAPE America (2019) national physical education standards in Chapter 2. Although SEL frameworks have the potential to be very powerful and impact students in positive ways, when not intentionally integrated into the full teaching–learning cycle, teachers may experience notable challenges driven by misalignment of planning, instruction, and assessment. In other words, teachers must go beyond referencing schoolwide SEL initiatives (e.g., The 7 Habits of Highly Effective People; Covey, 1989) by hanging a poster on the gymnasium wall and more authentically aligning their instruction and assessment strategies to promote SEL development that connects meaningfully with these larger initiatives.

Evaluating Social and Emotional Learning Using Formal and Informal Assessments

With some general considerations for effective SEL instruction in place, we now turn to a more concrete discussion of how students' SEL can be assessed both formally and informally in physical education environments. Within the broader education literature, strategies for evaluating SEL typically include self-assessments, observation protocols and rating scales, performance-based assessments (Durlak et al., 2016). Self-assessments can be given on paper, electronically, or through an interview by asking students to evaluate their own SEL, and aligning with the self-check teaching style described in Chapter 3 (Mosston & Ashworth, 2017). Doing so assumes that they already have the necessary perspective taking and self-awareness skills but are helpful in terms of empowering students to critically and honestly reflect on their learning. Observation protocols and rating scales are viewed as being more objective measures and provide teachers with the ability to observe and make informed evaluations of students' SEL based on stated criteria. Typically, teachers will either observe students in real time or on video recordings and then make judgments to evaluate performance based on stated criteria. The social skills improvement system SEL version (Gresham et al., 2020) reflects one such direct observation protocol that has been shown to align with the CASEL (2019) framework. Finally, performance-based assessments provide structured opportunities for students to engage in real-world or simulated tasks including discipline-embedded projects (e.g., developing SEL-informed guidelines for positive behavior in youth sport contexts) and game-based simulations that ask students to work through scenarios that reflect real-world applications. These performance-based assessments are typically evaluated using a rubric to score students' work against predetermined criteria and performance expectations.

In physical education, both formal and informal assessment tools can be used to monitor learning in relation to SEL outcomes. As noted earlier in the chapter, formal assessments should be preplanned and involve the intentional collection of data related to student learning. Types of formal assessment to assess SEL outcomes could include self- and peer-assessments, checklist and rubrics, reflective writing and journaling, and role playing. Similar to the broader education context, self-assessments are intended for students to evaluate their application of a skill. This places them at the center of their own learning toward becoming independent learners (Lund & Kirk, 2020). The intended focus of this formative assessment is for students to judge their process based on the criteria provided and to gain feedback toward the desired outcome. Furthermore, it provides an opportunity for students to learn the intended criteria prior to being evaluated by the course instructor through a summative assessment. An example of a self-assessment might be to ask students to evaluate their performance in nonplaying roles intended to facilitate formal competitions (e.g., referee, score keeper) during a sport education season (see; Siedentop et al., 2011). The intended SEL outcome may focus on the CASEL (2019) responsible decision making competency. Therefore, students identify criteria that need

improvement, and consider the application of their role to a time outside of physical education, such as coordinating pick-up basketball games at a local park.

Peer-assessments are also useful tools when embedded formatively as they encourage students to work together and evaluate one another's learning (Lund & Tannehill, 2015). Students could, for example, be asked to observe and evaluate their partner's skill performance using a rubric or to evaluate other team members' contributions to a group project. Peer assessments allow students to think critically about SEL criteria when assessing each other and also provide the opportunity to recognize others' feelings to make decisions about how to give helpful feedback to their peers, which is an important competency in relation to SEL. For example, students may learn about the SEL concept of empathy by considering how their peers feel when receiving their feedback. **Figure 4.5** provides a rubric for empathy and giving feedback in which students are evaluated on their ability to recognize feelings and provide feedback with performance specified across four rubric levels. Moreover, planning a unit in which empathy is a major focus in addition to psychomotor and cognitive outcomes makes the integration of SEL competencies into the learning process more authentic.

Exit/entrance slips can be used as a quick way to collect a snapshot of student learning. While there are many formats for students to respond on an exit slip (e.g., drawing a picture, matching words to definitions or photos, multiple choice, true/false), it is important to match the student output with the objective based on Bloom's (1956) taxonomy. For example, if

Using empathy During Feedback				
	1	**2**	**3**	**4**
Recognizes feelings	Student recognizes own feelings	Student recognize own feelings and with help may recognize others' feelings	Students are able to recognize both verbal and nonverbal feelings of others	Students recognize both verbal and nonverbal feelings and can predict how their response will affect others
Provides feedback	Student provides feedback	With help, student may be able to provide feedback and respond with empathy	Based on both verbal and nonverbal cues, student provides appropriate feedback	Based on both verbal and nonverbal cues, student provides empathy by responding with positive, process-orientated, and constructive feedback and makes connections outside of class

Figure 4.5 Example rubric to evaluate student's reflection of showing empathy for others while providing feedback while using a peer assessment. The rubric includes three elements that define social-awareness and four evaluation levels to identify students' progress related to each element.

students were asked to *identify* their level of engagement during a teaching personal and responsibility (TPSR; Hellison, 2011; also see Chapter 7) unit, they could simply write down the goal they worked on that day or circle from among multiple choices. However, if you were expecting students to *reflect* on their engagement, having them circle a number would not match the intended objective. Instead, students could be asked to identify TPSR goals and then reflect on how they worked toward those goals. For alternatives to writing, teachers could ask students to take a photo that best represents their level of engagement or draw a photo and reflect on their decision making with a caption. These approaches provide greater latitude for students who express themselves best using media other than the written word.

As suggested previously, performance-based assessments can be developed to provide students with opportunities to demonstrate SEL growth. For example, this could involve role playing simulated scenarios that pose SEL challenges, through projects that ask students to apply SEL information either inside or outside of class, and by writing essays to critique and connect SEL to other areas of their life or broader sport and physical activity contexts (e.g., violence in youth sport). Regardless of the specific activity developed, performance-based assessments tend to use rubrics that identify criteria to help an assessor make judgments about the quality of student work and also let students know what kind of work is expected of them (Stiggins, 2001). Given the SEL goal for students to take more responsibility for their learning, rubrics provide students with the tools toward which they can strive to achieve. Specifically, when using performance-based assessment, a rubric that defines SEL criteria is helpful when students are required to use higher ordered thinking and apply the material (Lund & Kirk, 2020) as opposed to traditional assessments that tend to prioritize memorization and recitation. Generally, it is important to first identify criteria (e.g., relationship skills—teamwork and communication) and levels (e.g., 1–4) along with a description that allows for differentiation in the quality of the work (e.g., break down what teamwork and communication are at each level). Teacher rubrics may be used to evaluate students' understanding and application of their non-playing roles (i.e., duty role) within a team in sport education (see Chapter 7; Siedentop et al., 2011). Checklists can also be an effective tool to measure whether criteria are present. Although checklists do not identify the quality of the criteria, they still remain a useful formative assessment to engage students in

their own learning as well as provide teachers with data on student progress within the unit.

Reflective writing and journaling are also effective ways to formally utilize assessment to teach and evaluate a desired objective. Although commonly used for students to express their feelings and perceptions, it is important that when used for assessment, journaling is intentionality aligned and focused on the intended objective for two major reasons. First, it would be difficult to assess the objective without identifiable criteria and, second, students should know how to critically engage with the material in order to meet instructor expectations. For example, if students were required to compare and contrast communication styles during the lesson, a rubric could be developed to identify criteria that require students to provide examples of communication, compare and contrast different styles, and connect them to a real-life example outside of class. Finally, it is imperative that if students are asked to reflect honestly, the teacher needs to develop an environment in which students feel safe responding honestly to questions that may involve expressing opinions that do not align with those of the teacher.

In addition to more formal approaches to evaluating SEL, teachers can informally assess on a regular basis to gauge student learning and also to help students evaluate their own learning (Lund & Kirk, 2020). Although often thought of as spontaneous and unplanned in response to "teachable moments," informal assessments can be used intentionally and planned throughout a unit in alignment with objectives in addition to more unplanned and spontaneous opportunities to connect with SEL. While a variety of different SEL-aligned informal assessments can be developed, we focus on common forms of informal assessment including checking for understanding tasks, task challenges, informal teacher observation, and partner and group discussion. We discuss these strategies below to illustrate how they can be integrated into regular teaching and be used to give regular feedback to students.

First, checking for understanding is used as a mechanism to see what students understand immediately during a class at a specific moment in time. For example, a teacher may ask students questions throughout the lesson to engage them in thinking about the lesson focus or SEL objective. Students' responses to these questions provide insight into their understanding of the content, which may lead to instructional modifications in real time. Another example of checking for comprehension might be to use a "thumb-o-meter" (i.e., thumb up, thumb sideways, thumb down) to gauge students' enjoyment if the intended objective is to work toward self-awareness. In addition, students could be asked to "tap in or out" on a wall using a stoplight metaphor (i.e., green, yellow, and red lights) to indicate their responsible decision making during the class period while the teacher observes and gives feedback. Importantly, checks-for-understanding are not random, should be aligned with the intended outcomes, with students being provided with opportunities to practice and reflect throughout the lesson. For example, a teacher may ask students to apply a specific SEL skill, such as empathy, in the next task or activity. The teacher then follows up by asking students to consider how they could use it in their own lives and discuss with a partner. Both of these strategies align with the TPSR model discussed in Chapter 7.

Finally, before, during, or after activities, a teacher may ask students to sit in a circle and share what did and did not work throughout the class. This group reflection draws upon circle processes common in restorative justice practices that provide students' with voice and the ability to hear and be heard by others (Amstutz & Mullet, 2015). For example, when teaching toward relationship-building skills and identifying good communication skills, a teacher may probe students to discuss how well they communicated and what they could do more effectively next time. In the adventure education model (see Chapter 6), group reflection is coordinated as part of debriefing processes, which helps the student make sense of intra- and inter-personal relationships (Dyson & Brown, 2005). Finally, the use of group discussions as an informal check for understanding is critical when using teaching styles such as guided discovery so as to help students work toward producing the intended outcome (Mosston & Ashworth, 2017).

Considerations for Assessment Implementation

Woven throughout this discussion, we continue to provide considerations for using both process and product assessments for continuous assessment and the use of assessment for grading. As previously mentioned in this chapter, teachers may consider implementing a balance of process and product assessments as sometimes growth in SEL occurs while processing in group environments. Accordingly, a

focus on process-based, assessment *for* learning, and performance-based assessment may be valuable. When planning a unit of instruction, identifying opportunities for continuous, performance-based assessment can be embedded intentionally to help teachers plan for an interplay between instruction and assessment.

Lund and Kirk (2020) suggest that formative assessments should be built in throughout the unit in direct alignment with a desired objective so as to measure student learning and progress. For example, a teacher who wants students to recognize social differences among students (i.e., social awareness; CASEL, 2019) may choose to use an exit slip at the end of the lesson (i.e., formal assessment), which asks students to discuss a time they recognized differences either with themselves or other students during class. This assessment would allow the teacher to gather information that could be used to adjust and guide future lessons as the class explores social difference through movement. As another example, at the beginning of a unit when teaching to self-awareness, the teacher may choose to build in a preassessment to gauge how students feel about a particular unit. Finally, summative assessments should include a direct measure of student learning that aligns with the stated outcomes and is ideally performance based. This means that students will have to apply the material in authentic ways or in a context outside of the gym to help students draw connections and value in the curriculum based on self.

As discussed earlier, assessment can be used with the purpose of engaging students in their learning (formative; assessment for learning) and also for the purpose of evaluation (summative; assessment of learning). Given that we are largely focused on the process and students improving their SEL competencies, our dialogue has not included grading. However, teachers need to grade, and there must be opportunities for assessment to demonstrate student achievement in alignment with the intended outcomes. While there is no universal agreement on the appropriateness of assigning grades based on SEL assessments (see Chapter 16 for a broader discussion), we do believe that teachers' grading structures can include SEL evaluations. However, many traditional grading structures have included managerial concerns such as dressing out, behavior, and participation—none of which can be objectively measured or aligned with student achievement outcomes. Although student behavior may fall into SEL outcomes and align with SHAPE America Standards 4 and 5, student behavior should only be graded if it is an intended outcome for the unit, written into objectives, have identifiable criteria, content and criteria embedded in tasks, and assessment (Lund & Kirk, 2020).

Although many arguments have been couched for the elimination of grading, when used appropriately, it can motivate students and hold them accountable for their learning. In addition, the use of assessment for grading allows physical educators to provide various stakeholders (e.g., administrators, parents) evidence that students are meeting desired outcomes and working toward national standards. Although many administrators may value effective management over quality instruction due to experiencing traditional forms of physical education and grading themselves in K–12 school, there is a need to advocate for the profession by providing and sharing evidence of student learning. Furthermore, using the SEL framework presented by CASEL (2019) while collecting assessment data as evidence may help to improve the status and value of physical education in our schools as others begin to realize the many varied benefits that can be derived from physical education.

Validated Instruments for Evaluating Social and Emotional Learning

In addition to teacher-designed instruments that can be used to evaluate and assess students' social and emotional learning, we want to acknowledge the multiple valid and reliable instruments developed to evaluate SEL for both teaching and research purposes. These instruments include both self-report questionnaires as well as systematic observation methods. Related to self-report instruments, the Personal and Social Responsibility Questionnaire (PSRQ; Li et al., 2008), which was developed to reflect the TPSR goals (see Chapter 7), can be used to evaluate students' self-reported SEL learning within physical education. Some researchers have also used relevant subscales from the Youth Experience Survey 2.0 (Hansen & Larson, 2005) that map to SEL competencies (e.g., leadership, identity reflection, goal setting) when asking students to self-report learning. The transfer of responsibility questionnaire (TORQ; Wright et al., 2019), which is based on the notion of a transformative experience as including the elements of motivated use, expansion of perception, and experiential value (Pugh, 2004), can then be used to evaluate the transfer of responsibility beyond the classroom. Importantly, this instrument conceptualizes transfer as more than a behavioral outcome and includes changes to the way students think and feel about SEL

competencies in relation to their lives outside of physical education (Jacobs & Wright, 2018).

Importantly, if selecting from among these previously validated self-report instruments, we suggest avoiding evaluations of how students rate themselves. If students feel as if their grade or standing in physical education is reflective of the rating they provide, social desirability bias may lead them to inflate their ratings to coincide with what they think the teacher wants. Instead, students could be asked to complete the survey and then reflect on their responses. This reflection could include providing examples to illustrate their ratings, or setting goals to work on areas in which they scored themselves low. For example, students who rate themselves highly on leadership behaviors could then provide examples of how they lead inside and/or outside of the gymnasium. Alternatively, students who give themselves low ratings on their ability to work effectively with others could set goals for how they could improve in the future.

In addition to previously validated self-report instruments, teachers may consider using the Tool for Assessing Responsibility-Based Education 2.0 (Escarti et al., 2015), which represents a classroom observation system designed specifically to evaluate SEL integration in physical activity spaces. As explained in more detail in Chapter 2, the TARE 2.0 includes both teacher- and student-behaviors that are indicative of an environment that effectively integrates SEL. While the TARE 2.0 is often used by researchers to evaluate the implementation fidelity of pedagogical models such as TPSR, Hemphill and colleagues (2015) illustrate how it can also be used as a teacher reflection tool. Teachers can either observe and code a videotaped lesson using the TARE 2.0 and then reflect on the outcomes or ask a colleague to observe them teach. When working with a colleague, a postobservation meeting can provide time to discuss findings and identify areas of strength and those in need of improvement. Regardless of whether the process is completed individually or with peers, using the TARE 2.0 can provide teachers with important information that can help them to evaluate the extent to which SEL is being implemented as intended and where improvements can be made.

Conclusions and Final Thoughts

Whereas Chapter 3 provided an overview of instructional approaches that align with SEL, this chapter introduces the reader to high-quality assessment strategies that connect to social and emotional learning. While we present instruction and assessment separately, we also acknowledge that these two areas of teachers' practice should be interwoven and reciprocal. When using the assessment tool for learning strategies, assessment *is* instruction as students practice and learn about their competencies while receiving feedback from their peers and/or the teacher. Throughout the chapter we discuss and distinguish between different types of assessments (e.g., formative versus summative; process versus product), propose

important considerations for assessing SEL, and provide practical strategies and recommendations. This chapter also concludes the introductory section of the book, which has sought to introduce the reader to SEL generally (Chapter 1), applications specifically in the physical education curriculum (Chapter 2), instructional strategies (Chapter 3), and assessment considerations (Chapter 4). In the next section of the book, we turn to invited chapter authors who discuss pedagogical models common in physical education that are particularly well suited for addressing SEL.

Questions for Discussion

1. Describe the difference between assessment for learning and assessment of learning. Why is it important to include both in the overall assessment scheme for a course?
2. What are some of the characteristics of typical assessment strategies in physical education? What are some of their challenges or shortcomings?
3. What is the relationship between assessment and instruction and how can teachers use both to promote student learning?

4. If you were planning a unit of instruction focused on volleyball and you want to ensure that you integrated leadership skills as an important SEL outcome, how would you plan to assess throughout the unit?
5. How can rubrics be created to effectively measure and monitor students' SEL? What are some of the key components that should be included in a rubric?

References

Amstutz, L. S., & Mullet, J. H. (2015). *The little book of restorative discipline for schools*. Good Books.

Andrade, H., & Valtcheva, A. (2009). Promoting learning and achievemennnt through self-assessment. *Theory into Practice, 48*(1), 12–19.

Black, P., & Wiliam, D. (1998). Assessment and classroom learning. *Assessment in Education: Principles, Policy & Practice, 5*(1), 7–74.

Bloom, B. S. (1956). *Taxonomy of educational objectives, handbook: The cognitive domain*. David McKay.

Brookhart, S. M. (1991). Grading practices and validity. *Educational Measurement: Issues and Practice, 10*(1), 35–36.

Byra, M., & Marks, M. C. (1993). The effect of two pairing techniques on specific feedback and comfort levels of learners in the reciprocal style of teaching. *Journal of Teaching in Physical Education, 12*(3), 286–300.

Collaborative for Academic, Social, and Emotional Learning. (2019). *What is social and emotional learning?* https://casel.org/what-is-sel/

Collie, R. J., Shapka, J. D., & Perry, N. E. (2012). School climate and social–emotional learning: Predicting teacher stress, job satisfaction, and teaching efficacy. *Journal of Educational Psychology, 104*(4), 1189–1204.

Collier, D. (2011). Increasing the value of physical education: The role of assessment. *Journal of Physical Education, Recreation & Dance, 82*(7), 38–41.

Covey, S. R. (1989). *The 7 habits of highly effective people: Powerful lessons in personal change*. Freer Press.

D'Angelo, T. A., & Cross, K. P. (1993). *Classroom assessment techniques: A handbook for college teachers*. Jossey Bass.

DinanThompson, M. (2013). Claiming 'educative outcomes' in HPE: The potential for 'pedagogical action.' *Asia-Pacific Journal of Health, Sport and Physical Education, 4*(2), 127–142.

DinanThompson, M., & Penney, D. (2015). Assessment literacy in primary physical education. *European Physical Education Review, 21*(4), 485–503.

Durlak, J. A., Domitrovich, C. E., Weissberg, R. P., & Gullotta, T. P. (2016). *Handbook of social and emotional learning research and practice*. Guilford Press.

Dyson, B., & Brown, M. (2005). Adventure education in your physical education program. In J. Lund & D. Tannehill (Eds.), *Standards-based physical education curriculum development* (pp. 154–175). Jones and Bartlett.

Earl, L. M. (2013). Assessment of learning, for learning, as learning. In *Assessment as Learning: Using Classroom Assessment to Maximize Student Learning* (pp. 25–33). Corwin.

Escarti, A., Wright, P. M., Pascual, C., & Gutiérrez, M. (2015). Tool for Assessing Responsibility-based Education (TARE) 2.0: Instrument revisions, inter-rater reliability, and correlations between observed teaching strategies and student behaviors. *Universal Journal of Psychology, 3*(2), 55–63.

Gordon, B., Jacobs, J. M., & Wright, P. M. (2016). Social and emotional learning through a teaching personal and social responsibility-based after-school program for disengaged middle-school boys. *Journal of Teaching in Physical Education, 35*(4), 358–369.

Gresham, F., Elliott, S., Metallo, S., Byrd, S., Wilson, E., Erickson, M., . . . Altman, R. (2020). Psychometrics foundations of the social skills improvement system: Social–emotional learning edition rating forms. *Assessment for Effective Intervention, 45*(3), 194–209.

Hansen, D. M., & Larson, R. (2005). *The youth experience survey 2.0: Instrument revisions and validity testing.* The University of Illinois.

Hay, P. (2006). Assessment for learning in physical education. In D. Kirk, D. Macdonald, & M. O'Sullivan (Eds.), *The handbook of physical education* (pp. 326–346). SAGE Publications.

Hay, P., & Penney, D. (2013). *Assessment in physical education: A sociocultural perspective.* Routledge.

Hellison, D. (2011). *Teaching personal and social responsibility through physical activity* (3rd ed.). Human Kinetics.

Hemphill, M. A., Templin, T. J., & Wright, P. M. (2015). Implementation and outcomes of a responsibility-based continuing professional development protocol in physical education. *Sport, Education and Society, 20*(3), 398–419.

Jacobs, J. M., & Wright, P. M. (2018). Transfer of life skills in sport-based youth development programs: A conceptual framework bridging learning to application. *Quest, 70*(1), 81–99.

Krathwohl, D. R. (2002). A revision of Bloom's taxonomy: An overview. *Theory into Practice, 41*(4), 212–218.

Laureano, J., Konukman, F., Gümüşdağ, H., Erdoğan, S., Yu, J. H., & Çekin, R. (2014). Effects of marginalization on school physical education programs: A literature review. *Physical Culture and Sport: Studies and Research, 64*(1), 29–40.

Li, W., Wright, P. M., Rukavina, P. B., & Pickering, M. (2008). Measuring students' perceptions of personal and social responsibility and the relationship to intrinsic motivation in urban physical education. *Journal of Teaching in Physical Education, 27*(2), 167–178.

López-Pastor, V. M., Kirk, D., Lorente-Catalán, E., MacPhail, A., & Macdonald, D. (2013). Alternative assessment in physical education: A review of international literature. *Sport, Education and Society, 18*(1), 57–76.

Lund, J., & Kirk, M. F. (2020). *Performance-based assessment for middle and high school physical education* (3rd ed.). Human Kinetics.

Lund, J., & Tannehill, D. (2015). *Standards-based physical education curriculum development* (3rd ed.). Jones & Bartlett Learning.

Lynn, S. K., & Woods, A. M. (2010). Following the yellow brick road: A teacher's journey along the proverbial career path. *Journal of Teaching in Physical Education, 29*(1), 54–71.

Lyras, A., & Welty Peachey, J. (2011). Integrating sport-for-development theory and praxis. *Sport Management Review, 14*(4), 311–326.

McMillan, J. H., Myran, S., & Workman, D. (2002). Elementary teachers' classroom assessment and grading practices. *The Journal of Educational Research, 95*(4), 203–213.

Mintah, J. K. (2003). Authentic assessment in physical education: Prevalence of use and perceived impact on students' self-concept, motivation, and skill achievement. *Measurement in Physical Education and Exercise Science, 7*(3), 161–174. https://doi.org/10.1207/S15327841MPEE0703_03

Mosston, M., & Ashworth, S. (2017). *Teaching physical education* (1st online). Spectrum of Teaching Styles. https://spectrumofteachingstyles.org/

Noonan, B., & Duncan, C. R. (2005). Peer and self-assessment in high schools. *Practical Assessment, Research & Evaluation, 10*(17), 1–8.

Ololube, N. P., Kpolovie, P. J., & Makewa, L. N. (Eds.). (2015). *Handbook of research on enhancing teacher education with advanced instructional technologies.* IGI Global.

Oslin, J. L., Mitchell, S. A., & Griffin, L. L. (1998). The Game Performance Assessment Instrument (GPAI): Development and preliminary validation. *Journal of Teaching in Physical Education, 17*(2), 231–243.

O'Sullivan, M. (1989). Failing gym is like failing lunch or recess: Two beginning teachers' struggle for legitimacy. *Journal of Teaching in Physical Education, 8*(3), 227–242.

Pugh, K. J. (2004). Newton's laws beyond the classroom walls. *Science Education, 88*(2), 182–196.

Richards, K. A. R., & Gordon, B. (2017). Socialisation and learning to teach using the teaching personal and social responsibility approach. *Asia-Pacific Journal of Health, Sport and Physical Education, 8*(1), 19–38.

Rink, J. E., & Mitchell, M. F. (2003). State level assessment in physical education: The South Carolina experience. *Journal of Teaching in Physical Education, 22*(5), 471–472.

Rosenshine, B. (1979). Content time and direct instruction. In *Research on teaching: Concepts, findings, and applications* (pp. 28–53). McCutchan.

SHAPE America. (2014). *National standards and grade-level outcomes for K-12 physical education.* Human Kinetics.

SHAPE America. (2019). *PE metrics* (3rd ed.). Human Kinetics.

Siedentop, D., Hastie, P. A., & van der Mars, H. (2011). *Complete guide to sport education* (2nd ed.). Human Kinetics.

Society of Health and Physical Eductors America. (2019). *Crosswalk for SHAPE America National Standards & Grade-Level Outcomes for K-12 Physical Education and CASEL Social and Emotional Learning Core Competencies.* Author.

Starck, J. R., Richards, K. A. R., Lawson, M. A., & Sinelnikov, O. A. (2020). The influence of socialization factors on physical educators' conceptions of assessment and perceived quality of assessment. *Journal of Teaching in Physical Education, 40*(1), 66–75. https://doi.org/10.1123/jtpe.2019-0096

Starck, J. R., Richards, K. A. R., & O'Neil, K. (2018). A conceptual framework for assessment literacy: Opportunities for physical education teacher education. *Quest, 70*(4), 519–535. https://doi.org/10.1080/00336297.2018.1465830

Stiggins, R. J. (2001). *Student-involved classroom assessments.* Merrill/Prentice-Hall.

Topping, K. J. (2009). Peer assessment. *Theory into Practice, 48,* 20–27.

Veal, M. L. (1988). Pupil assessment perceptions and practices of secondary teachers. *Journal of Teaching in Physical Education, 7*(4), 327–342.

Wiggins, G., & McTighe, J. (2011). *The Understanding by Design guide to creating high-quality units.* ACSD.

Wright, P. M., Richards, K. A. R., Jacobs, J. M., & Hemphill, M. A. (2019). Measuring perceived transfer of responsibility learning from physical education: Initial validation of the Transfer of Responsibility Questionnaire. *Journal of Teaching in Physical Education, 38*(4), 316–327. https://doi.org/10.1123/jtpe.2018-0246

SECTION 2

Pedagogical Models Aligned with Social and Emotional Learning in PE

© Omelchenko/Shutterstock.

CHAPTER 5

Connecting Skill Themes and Social-Emotional Learning in Elementary Physical Education

Melissa Parker

Kevin Patton

Cassandra Iannucci

Jessica Mangione

CHAPTER SUMMARY

The skill themes approach is a widely adopted model emphasizing the importance of children learning to move. Within the model, both the content and pedagogy for elementary physical education are described. This chapter provides an overview of the skill themes approach and its alignment with social and emotional learning (SEL) objectives. We first summarize research supporting the integration of SEL, and then describe the characteristics of the skill themes approach, presenting examples of teaching strategies, learning activities, and assessment techniques. Finally, we present several progressions including sample lesson plans, of how SEL can be integrated into teaching practice framed by skill themes.

Introduction

The purpose of this chapter is to provide an overview of the skill themes approach and its alignment with social and emotional learning (SEL) objectives for elementary physical education. In doing so, we provide concrete examples of teaching strategies, learning activities, and assessment techniques that might be used. Research supporting the integration of SEL will also be summarized, and specific examples related to how SEL can be integrated into teaching practice are framed by the skill themes provided.

Skill themes are initially the fundamental movements that form the foundation for success in physical activities and sports in later years (Graham, Holt/Hale, Parker, Hall, & Patton, 2020). With its focus on introducing children to fundamental motor skills, the skill themes approach is recognized as a best-practice model in elementary physical education (Lund & Tannehill, 2014) and is viewed as a robust method to teach SEL because it focuses on developing a student-centered learning environment (Richards, Ivy,

Wright, & Jerris, 2019). Being physically active for a lifetime requires a variety of skills, knowledge, and dispositions. The goal of the skill themes approach, as outlined in *Children Moving* (Graham, et al., 2020), is to describe both a curriculum and the companion teaching skills designed to guide youngsters in the process of becoming physically active for a lifetime.

Skill Themes in the Literature

Despite the widespread adoption of the skill themes approach, few empirical studies have examined skill themes and even fewer have reported on the use of skill themes to teach SEL. Despite limited research; however, scholarship across a variety of learning domains and educational levels has consistently indicated that students learn best when teachers create supportive environments in which students feel physically and emotionally safe and supported (Zins, Bloodworth, Weissberg, & Walberg, 2007). Students thrive when they are empowered to make decisions and provided with opportunities to build relationships and demonstrate competence (Deci & Ryan, 2000, 2008). Relatedly, within the skill themes approach, students are given a choice in terms of the equipment they use and develop competence through the numerous extension and refining tasks (Rink, 2020) in which they engage. Additionally, teachers encourage students to suggest and make modifications to instructional tasks based on the movement concepts of relationships, effort, and spatial awareness. These modifications can be made by whole classes, small groups, or individual students.

The supportive environment provided within the skill themes approach helps students feel that they are important to the learning process and that their voices are valued. By honoring student's voices, teachers focus on what students know, believe, can do, and bring to the learning situation, and on how children understand, interpret, think, and feel about the content presented (Graham et al., 2020). Students' perspectives should inform your choices as a teacher because they are not only important for how curricula are managed and taught but also for understanding broader questions in relation to movement choice and children's health (Macdonald, et al., 2005).

Due to its focus on student voice and a supportive learning environment, students taught using skill themes tend to enjoy physical education, demonstrate positive attitudes toward physical education, and, when asked, express that it is an important subject (Gossett & Silverman, 2019). Additionally, the learning environment created within a skill themes approach is conducive to the development of SEL. For example, one study indicated that when children were given the choice to decide on the order in which they engaged in the learning tasks and the amount of time spent at each learning station, children took advantage of the opportunity and improved their performance further (Chatoupis & Vagenas, 2017). These results indicate that children can be given decision-making responsibility and maintain a level of achievement greater than that of a learning environment in which the teacher makes most of the decisions for students. Additionally, when learners were paired with friends in peer-teaching situations, they felt more comfortable in giving and receiving feedback than learners paired with non-friends. Coincidently, motor skill development was also greater in children who were paired with their friends (Chatoupis, 2015). (See Chapter 3 regarding a more complete discussion about sharing decisions with children as part of the empowerment process.)

Despite the widespread acceptance of the skill themes approach and a growing evidence base, learning to teach using skill themes can be complex for beginning teachers. This is, in part, because a skill themes approach is not scripted. Rather, the approach requires teachers to adapt the skill themes to match the ability level of the students. Initially, the teacher focuses on one skill at a time; in later grades as children become more accomplished, skills are combined and used in more complex settings. The intent is to help children develop a variety of locomotor, nonmanipulative, and manipulative fundamental movement skills that provide the foundation to become healthy and physically active for a lifetime (Graham et al., 2020). To successfully accomplish this within a skill themes approach, teachers must:

- Possess a high level of content knowledge (Wahl-Alexander & Curtner-Smith, 2019). Teachers who know their content well are able to successfully modify their lessons based on student engagement and learning.
- Use positive negotiation (i.e., choice) in their lesson as a pedagogical skill. Initiated by themselves or their students, choice decreases task ambiguity and risk (Wahl-Alexander & Curtner-Smith, 2019). Students are motivated by choice and most often will choose a task appropriate for their own skills and experience.
- Demonstrate flexibility by changing/modifying learning tasks based on student success, not time indicated on a lesson plan (Hall, 2003).

Despite the potential of the skill themes approach to positively impact student learning while teaching SEL skills, when researchers studied preservice teachers learning to teach using skill themes they discovered that the structure of the approach created potential difficulties in terms of management (Wahl-Alexander & Curtner-Smith, 2019). While the preservice teachers valued the skill themes approach, they also had problems associated with responding to students' inappropriate and limited movement responses (Chen, 2004). The relationship of management, instruction, and SEL skills is addressed in detail in Chapter 3. It is an important concept and we urge you to read about the implications of prioritizing one over the other.

Based on our own experience, SEL competencies are among the most difficult to teach. The reality is that as teachers, we cannot simply ask students to engage in an activity and automatically learn SEL skills. That is, children placed on a team do not automatically learn how to work together or how to respect others (Coakley, 2011). Instead, teachers must be intentional in their presentation of SEL competencies. If this sounds like hard work, it is! Just like most anything worthwhile, learning SEL competencies takes practice and so does the process of teaching these skills to an entire class of students. To assist you, the remainder of this chapter will introduce the skill themes approach as well as the dimensions of SEL and provide some concrete examples of what this looks and sounds like in a physical education setting.

What Are Skill Themes?

Skills themes (Graham et. al, 2020) can be considered a developmental approach to teaching elementary physical education. A developmental approach means that content, instruction, and assessment are designed based on the developmental needs of children. Instead of determining content and instruction by grade, pedagogical decisions are made with respect to children's abilities in combination with fundamental movement skill principles. Therefore, skill themes are a combination of content (or what is taught), instruction (how it is taught), and assessment (how it is measured).

The Content of the Skill Themes Approach

The content of skill themes is initially fundamental psychomotor movements that serve as the foundation for physical activity over a life span. These movements are categorized as being locomotor, nonmanipulative,

or manipulative. *Locomotor* movements refer to those where a person travels from one place to another. Walking and running would be examples of locomotor movements. *Nonmanipulative* movements are generally those movements of certain body parts or the whole body performed in a limited space without the intention to travel from one point to another. Examples would be bending, stretching, jumping and landing, and transferring weight to different body parts. Finally, *manipulative* skills are those movements that involve the hands, feet, or other body parts to move or manipulate an object. Throwing, catching, dribbling, and striking are examples of manipulative skills. See **Table 5.1** for a more comprehensive list of the different fundamental movements.

Within the skill themes approach, these fundamental movements are called skill themes. These fundamental movements are then enhanced and

Table 5.1 Fundamental Movements

Category	Movement
Locomotor	Walking
	Running
	Hopping
	Leaping
	Sliding
	Galloping
	Skipping
Non-manipulative	Bending
	Stretching
	Twisting
	Curling
	Jumping and Landing
	Balancing
	Transferring Weight and
	Rolling
Manipulative	Kicking
	Punting
	Throwing
	Catching
	Volleying
	Dribbling
	Striking with Implements—horizontal plane
	Striking with Implements—vertical plane

Modified from Graham, G., Holt/Hale, S. A., Parker, M., Hall, T., & Patton, K. (2020). *Children moving: A reflective approach to teaching physical education* (10th ed.). New York: McGraw-Hill.

described by movement concepts, which serve to modify the skill themes to make them more or less complex by expanding the range of the movement and enriching the quality (Graham et al., 2020). Movement concepts include the aspects of space, effort, and relationships. *Space* signifies the place where the action is taking place or where the body moves. This can refer to movement at different levels, in different pathway, or in different directions, for example. The movement concept of *effort* addresses how the body moves. For instance, what is the time of the movement, fast or slow; or what force is used in the movement, strong or light? Relationship movement concepts focus on with whom or what is the movement performed. For example, is the skill performed alone or within a group of people? Or, is it performed over or on a piece of equipment? An easy way to remember this classification is that skill themes are verbs—they always reflect an action; while movement concepts are adjectives or adverbs because they describe the movement. See **Table 5.2** for a listing of all movement concepts and skills. Themes perform three functions. First, they link skills to concepts, for example running fast or throwing low. Second, they link one skill to another, such as running while throwing. Finally, they are all linked to dance, games, and gymnastics. For example, the skill theme of traveling, when used as a form of expression, could be developed in a dance

context coupled with movement concepts of effort and relationships. Alternatively, balance and weight transfer can be combined into sequences performed on the floor or equipment in a gymnastics environment or dribbling while traveling could be expanded though a games perspective.

How is the content developed? Basic to understanding skill themes is not just to know the content but to understand how the aspects of the content interact with each other to allow for developmentally appropriate progressions. This is where "the wheel" comes in! (See **Figure 5.1**). The "wheel" is a movement analysis framework that allows for a visual representation of how movement concepts and skill themes work with each other. One cannot teach a movement concept without a skill theme or a skill theme without a movement concept.

The wheel is composed of five concentric circles. The two innermost circles describe the skill themes. The center circle lists the three broad categories of skill themes: manipulative, non-manipulative, and locomotor, then the second circle lists the skill themes within each category. For instance, in conjunction with the manipulative category, skills such as dribbling, throwing, kicking, and striking are listed in the second circle. The outermost circle describes the three movement concept categories of space, effort, and relationships. Each of these movement concept

Table 5.2 Movement Concepts and Skill Themes

Skill Themes	Movement Concepts
Locomotor ■ Traveling ■ Chasing, fleeing, dodging Non-manipulative ■ Bending, stretching, twisting, and curling ■ Jumping and landing ■ Balancing ■ Transferring weight and rolling Manipulative ■ Kicking and punting ■ Throwing and catching ■ Volleying and dribbling ■ Striking with rackets and paddles ■ Striking with long-handled implements	Space Awareness (where the body moves) ■ Location: self-space and general space ■ Directions: forward, backward, right, left, up, down, clockwise, counterclockwise ■ Levels: low, medium, high ■ Pathways: straight, curved, zigzag ■ Extensions: near, far, large, small Effort (how the body moves) ■ Time: fast, slow, sudden, sustained ■ Force: light, heavy ■ Flow: bound, free Relationships (of body parts, with objects, with people) ■ Of body parts: round, narrow, wide, and twisted; symmetrical and non-symmetrical ■ With objects and/or people: Over/under; on/off; near/far; in front/behind, alongside; along, through; meeting/parting, surrounding, around ■ With people: leading/following; mirroring/matching; unison/contrast; alone in a mass, solo, partners, groups, between groups

Modified from Graham, G., Holt/Hale, S. A., Parker, M., Hall, T., & Patton, K. (2020). *Children moving: A reflective approach to teaching physical education* (10th ed.). New York: McGraw-Hill.

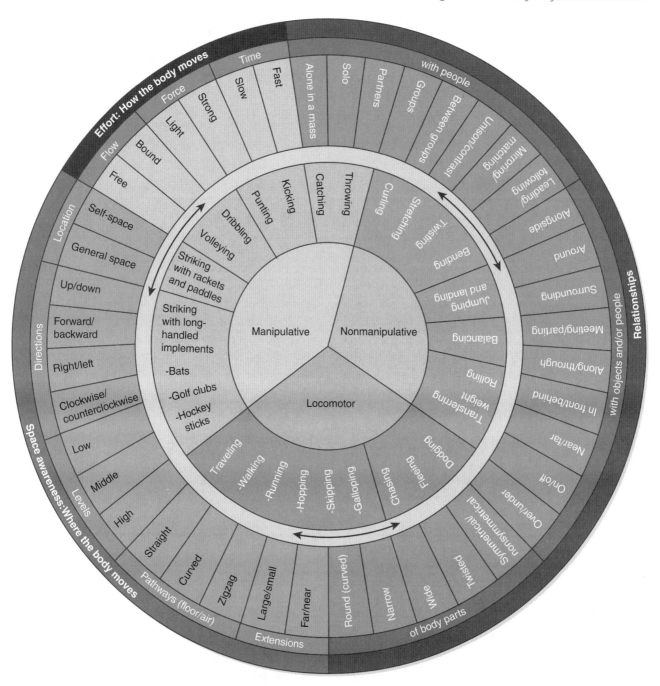

Figure 5.1 The Wheel: Movement analysis framework.

Reproduced from Graham, G., Holt/Hale, S. A., Parker, M., Hall, T., & Patton, K. (2020). *Children moving: A reflective approach to teaching physical education* (10th ed.). New York: McGraw-Hill. Reprinted with permission from McGraw-Hill, New York, NY.

categories consists of several movement concepts. For example, space awareness includes location, directions, levels, pathways, and extensions. These are listed on the second circle from the outside. The third circle contains the components of the movement concepts that would be taught in lessons to children. For example, if focusing on the space concept of pathways, the focus would be on straight, curved, and zigzag pathways. The circle with the double arrows allows the two inner circles to spin against the outer three to mix and match combinations of movement concepts and skill themes. Thus, a teacher could spin the wheel and teach throwing

and catching at different levels and move it again to teach balancing at different levels.

The progression spiral represents the development of a skill theme from simple to more complex and is designed to be read from bottom to top. The spiral is organized according to generic levels of skill proficiency of precontrol, control, utilization, and proficiency rather than grade levels. Each of these levels identifies children's developmental levels with respect to a skill theme. At the *precontrol* level, a child's movement is erratic and unpredictable. It appears as if a child cannot intentionally replicate a movement or they are not able to control the movement. For example, when trying to throw a ball, sometimes it goes forward to the ground and sometimes it is dropped behind the head. The *control* level is characterized by less haphazard movements. A child's movements do, however, require intense concentration as the movements are not yet automatic. At the *utilization* level, children's movements are increasingly automatic and a child is able to use the movement in a variety of ways and combine movements into sequences. The last level, *proficiency*, is characterized by somewhat automatic and effortless movements. At this point, the movement can be used in a variety of changing environments. **Figure 5.2** represents the progression spiral for punting. While there is no time allocation assigned to any task, the progression suggests possible combinations of how skill themes and movement concepts may be combined, revisited, and developed. Depending on the characteristics of your class, we would suggest you start lower down on a progression spiral and work your way up, all the while changing and adapting the sequence based on your teaching situation.

While skill themes may have a primary focus on fundamental movement skills, we believe that physical education should educate the whole child. Thus, the skill themes approach also highlights the cognitive and affective domains in important ways that lay the building blocks for more advanced learning later in school and life. For this chapter, our attention is on the affective domain. We teach so that children learn the skills needed to become increasingly responsible for their own learning, behavior, and attitudes while also exhibiting responsible personal and social behavior that respects the self and others (SHAPE America, 2014). These concepts are developed in a learning environment that seeks student voice and helps students to make decisions about learning and managerial situations that purposefully teach to larger SEL goals (i.e., self-management and decision making).

Social emotional learning is specifically referenced in the *Crosswalk for SHAPE America National Standards & Grade-Level Outcomes for K–12 Physical Education and CASEL Social and Emotional Learning Core Competencies* (SHAPE, 2019). Sample grade-level outcomes for student learning and their alignment to SEL competencies that are particularly applicable to skill themes are presented in **Table 5.3**. While this table identifies some realistic examples, it is not intended to be exhaustive and additional alignments may be made with other National Standards and Grade-level Outcomes for K–12 Physical Education. For example, some connections are obvious such as a variety of possibilities when connecting the SEL competencies of self-management, social awareness, and responsible decision making with Standard 4 (Personal and Social Behavior) grade-level outcomes. Perhaps more loosely connected is the responsible decision making required to apply movement concepts to strategy in game situations (Standard 2) or the self-awareness required to identify physical activities that are enjoyable or challenging/difficult (Standard 5).

Instructional Approaches Aligned with the Skill Themes Approach

As stated previously, skill themes are about both the content (what is taught) and the pedagogy (how it is taught). The pedagogy provides critical links to SEL. Two pedagogical aspects are important: the creation of a positive environment and self-directed instructional strategies. The learning environment is foundational to everything else that occurs. A developmentally appropriate, student-centered learning environment is one where physical education is for everyone and

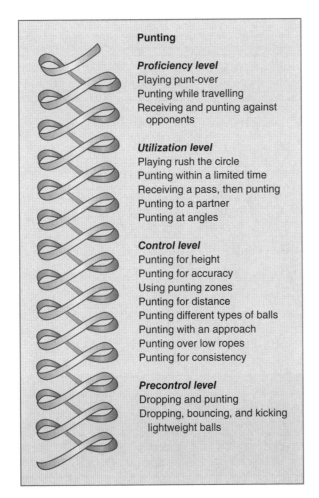

Figure 5.2 Punting progression spiral.

Table 5.3 Sample Grade-level Outcomes and Corresponding SEL Competencies that Address Skill Themes

SHAPE America National Standards and Grade-level Outcomes for K–12 Physical Education (grade)	Grade-level Outcomes Sub-Category	CASEL Core Competencies and Related Skills
Standard 2—*The physically literate individual applies knowledge of concepts, principles, strategies and tactics related to movement and performance*		
■ Applies movement concepts to strategy in game situations (5)	Movement concepts (speed, direction, force)	Responsible decision making ■ Analyzing situations
■ Recognizes the type of throw, volley, or striking action needed for different games and sports situations (5)	Movement concepts (strategies and tactics)	Responsible decision making ■ Solving problems
Standard 3—*The physically literate individual demonstrates the knowledge and skills to achieve and maintain a health-enhancing level of physical activity and fitness*		
■ Engages actively in the activities of physical education class without teacher prompting (3)	Engages in physical activity	Self-Management ■ Self-motivation
■ Analyzes results of fitness assessment (pre and post), comparing results to fitness components for good health (5)	Assessment and program planning	Responsible decision making ■ Analyzing situations
Standard 4—*The physically literate individual exhibits responsible personal and social behavior that respects self and others*		
■ Works independently for extended periods of time (3) ■ Exhibits respect for self with appropriate behavior while engaging in physical activity (5)	Personal responsibility	Self-Management ■ Self-discipline
■ Accepts players of all skill levels into the physical activity (4) ■ Accepts, recognizes, and actively involves others with both higher and lower skill abilities into physical activities and group projects (5)	Working with others	Social Awareness ■ Empathy
■ Reflects on personal social behavior in physical activity (4)	Personal responsibility	Responsible decision making ■ Reflecting
■ Recognizes the role of rules and etiquette in physical activity with peers (3) ■ Exhibits etiquette and adherence to rules in a variety of physical activities (4) ■ Critiques the etiquette involved in rules of various game activities (5)	Rules and etiquette	Responsible decision making ■ Ethical responsibility
Standard 5—*The physically literate individual recognizes the value of physical activity for health, enjoyment, challenge, self-expression, and/or social interaction.*		
■ Identifies physical activities that are enjoyable (K)	Self-expression and enjoyment	Self-awareness ■ Identifying emotions
■ Acknowledges that some physical activities are challenging/difficult (K)	Challenge	Self-awareness ■ Accurate self-perception

Modified from SHAPE America. (2014). *Crosswalk for SHAPE America National Standards & Grade-Level Outcomes for K-12 Physical Education and CASEL Social and Emotional Learning Core Competencies.* Reston, VA: Author. Copyright © 2022 by the Society of Health and Physical Educators (SHAPE America), a 501(c)(3) corporation.

characterized by seeking and acknowledging student voice. From the outset, children are "caught being good" rather than reprimanded for inconsequential misbehavior. You will most often hear comments such as, "Jesse is really listening well" rather than "Laura, we are waiting for you to listen." This change alone creates a positive, rather than subtly negative environment.

The actions within the classroom also adhere to the principles of change, challenge, and choice (Stiehl, Morris, & Sinclair, 2008) as a way to differentiate instruction so that all learners feel competent, useful, optimistic, and empowered. Teaching by invitation and intra-task variation (Graham et al., 2020) are ways that change, challenge, and choice might be implemented. When teaching by invitation, the teacher invites all students to decide on certain aspects of the task such as how far from a target they want to stand. Alternatively, when using intratask variation, the teacher suggests to individuals or small groups of children that they may want to increase or decrease the difficulty of a task when they feel ready. For example, a pair of students may be asked if they want to combine their balance and rolling skills into a routine while others practice the individual skills. The use of both teaching by invitation and intra-task variation promote the SEL competency of responsible decision making. Catching children being good while using teaching by invitation and intratask variation are the first steps in creating a physical education environment that is both physically and psychologically safe.

Second, the instructional approaches used increasingly move toward more child-centered learning (see **Table 5.4**). Instructional approaches refer to planned interactions between the teacher and the

Table 5.4 Instructional Strategies in Relation to Goals and SEL Dimensions

	Instructional Strategy	Goal	Strategy in Action	SEL Dimension(s)
Direct	Interactive teaching (Direct)	Efficient skill learning	Teacher guides the students' responses by telling them what to do, showing them how to practice, and then managing their practice.	▪ Self-management ▪ Responsible decision making
	Task teaching	Skill learning and independence	Students practice different, specified tasks, often at their own pace (i.e., station teaching or the use of task sheets/cards)	▪ Self-management ▪ Responsible decision making
	Peer teaching	Skill learning and cooperation	Children work independently from the teacher to actively teach each other in pairs or small groups	▪ Social awareness ▪ Relationship skills
	Guided discovery	Skill learning and transfer; problem solving	Children solve problems rather than copy the teacher's or another student's correct performance	▪ Responsible decision making
	Cooperative learning	Skill learning and group interdependence; individual responsibility	Process of breaking students into small groups so they can discover a new concept together and help each other learn (i.e., pairs-check, jigsaw, or co-op)	▪ Social awareness ▪ Relationship skills
Indirect	Child-designed instruction	Skill learning and self-responsibility	Students are the center of the learning activity while applying learned skills.	▪ Self-management ▪ Responsible decision making ▪ Social awareness ▪ Relationship skills

Data from Graham, G., Holt/Hale, S. A., Parker, M., Hall, T., & Patton, K. (2020). *Children moving: A reflective approach to teaching physical education* (10th ed.). New York: McGraw-Hill.

students designed to accomplish chosen learning outcomes (Byra, 2006). Several aspects distinguish one approach from another in terms of the actions and decisions the teacher and students make and the objectives that the student-teacher relationship accomplishes (Mosston & Ashworth, 2008). These approaches range from teacher directed at one end of the continuum to student directed at the other end (see Chapter 3 for a more complete discussion of this concept.) While there is place and need for teacher-directed learning for the achievement of specific skills and control-level learners, even with the use of direct instruction, incorporating teaching by invitation and intra-task variation can be used. Within these strategies, children are given small choices regarding the content of the task they are to practice. Increasingly, the goal is to gradually move toward more indirect styles of learning that foster personal and social responsibility. Therefore, we use task teaching, peer teaching, guided discovery, cooperative learning, and child-designed instructional approaches. *Task teaching* allows different students to practice different tasks at the same time. This could be either through station teaching or the use of task sheets/cards. From a SEL perspective, depending on how it is structured, task teaching provides for practice in self-management and responsible decision making. In a *peer teaching* format, children work independently from the teacher to actively teach each other in pairs or in small groups. This strategy supports the SEL constructs of social awareness and relationship skills. *Guided discovery*, on the other hand, is designed to enhance children's critical thinking and let them solve their own problems, enhancing the SEL constructs of responsible decision making. *Cooperative learning* instructional approaches are designed to promote group interdependence and individual responsibility. (Please see Chapter 9 by Dyson and colleagues for a more detailed discussion of *cooperative learning*). The principles underlying cooperative learning support social awareness and relationship skills. Finally, *child-designed instruction* allows children to take major responsibility for their own learning. Thus, children practice the skills of self-management, responsible decision making, or social awareness and relationship skills depending on whether the child-designed activity is individually based or group based. For example, students could be asked to combine a variety of skills they have practiced by making up a game that involves striking with a racket. After creating and playing their game, students describe its rules, write down how to play, and then share with others.

The Skill Themes Approach and Assessment

Like instruction, assessment should be child-centered. At this point, as discussed in Chapter 4, the focus is on assessment for learning. This type of assessment is ongoing and positions assessment as an integral part of the teaching and learning process (Black & Wiliam, 2018). It allows teachers to make inferences about what children have learned and children to understand what they have learned.

In the skill themes approach, assessment, whether informal or formal, adheres to five criteria (Graham et al., 2020). First, it is linked to instruction. The teacher devises instructional tasks "disguised" as assessment that allow children to demonstrate what they are able to do. Second, assessment is student centered, meaning that first and foremost, it provides feedback to students that they can use to enhance their learning. Third, assessment is ongoing. It occurs in small steps instead of a one-shot global deal at the end of a unit or grading period. Fourth, it is meaningful and relevant. It should take place in situations that mimic the skill being assessed as closely as possible. Finally, the criteria are known in advance. Children are very aware of what it is they are expected to learn. Some teachers convey this aspect as WALT and WILF or telling children and posting on the wall "what we are learning" (WALT) and "what I am looking for" (WILF) at the beginning of every lesson.

We are so accustomed to traditional assessment measures that an example may help. The context is a series of lessons on balancing combined with the movement concept of relationships of body parts (wide, narrow, twisted, curled). At the beginning of one lesson, the teacher shares the WALT as "we are learning about balancing in different body shapes" (psychomotor) and "the ability to identify strengths" (affective), as well as the WILT of "I am looking for your choice of wide, narrow, twisted, curled balances that you can hold still for three seconds." During the lesson, children are asked to draw their favorite wide, narrow, twisted, and curled balance. (See **Figure 5.3**). A peer then observes as each balance is performed and rates the balance based on stillness using the criteria of still for three seconds, a few wiggles, or loss of balance. After both children have performed their balances, they brainstorm one suggestion of what they did well and one idea that would help each of them improve (thus identifying strengths). The task is linked to instruction as it is part of a lesson on balance and focuses on what has been taught; the children get immediate feedback that can be used to improve their

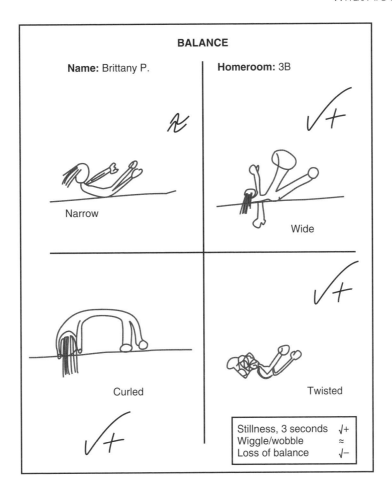

Figure 5.3 Formative assessment example.

balancing skills; the assessment happens in the middle of a lesson and possibly in the middle of a unit; the assessment is exactly and precisely what has been taught, and children were told ahead of time what it is that they were learning and what they are learning should look like. The bottom line is, if cognitive, psychomotor, and SEL (affective) skills are being taught, all three should also be assessed.

There is an important point here. Skill themes provide a conceptualization of psychomotor content and instructional strategies that *allow* for the development of SEL competencies, but this does not ensure that SEL skills will actually be learned. It is much like the false assumption that sportspersonship is acquired just by playing sport, when in many instances sport may lead to maladaptive outcomes (e.g., cheating, cutting corners) (Coakley, 2011). If students are to truly learn SEL skills, they must be purposefully taught. To be purposefully taught, they must be defined in "child friendly" terms, demonstrated, and practiced. It is a bit like skill themes provides the potential environment or medium for the development of SEL skills, but the teaching must be *purposeful.* SEL

skills must be overt, not covert; they must be taught, not hoped to be caught. (See Chapter 3 for further discussion of explicit versus implicit approaches to promoting SEL in physical education.) SEL skills must be taught with structured progressions, multiple learning experiences, clear feedback, and assessment just as a psychomotor skill would be. As explained in Chapter 2, this is a SAFE environment; one that is Sequenced, Active, Focused, and Explicit (CASEL 2019). So, what does this look like in combination with skill themes? An illustration may help. Take, for example, the peer teaching task of practicing the psychomotor skill of the overhand throw:

"For this next task, you will get to teach another classmate how to throw. Each of you will get to be the player and the coach. When you are the player, you will throw five times against the wall. Your partner, the coach, will have a card with a picture of someone throwing and all the cues labeled (see **Figure 5.4***). The coach will call out one cue at a time to you. Then you will practice and they will watch to see if you bring your arm way back, step forward on the opposite foot, and follow through. If you do it correctly, your coach will give you a "thumbs-up"; if you*

Help your partner learn to throw!!!
The three cues on which we are focusing today are:

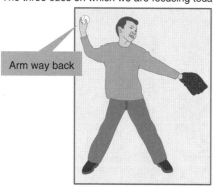  

You should "coach" your partner using one cue at a time. For example, have your partner use the first five throws making sure their arm is way back. Then when they throw the second five throws make sure that they step with the opposite foot. On the last five throws focus on the follow-through. When you are done help each other decide what you need to practice more.

Figure 5.4 Example of a coaches' card for the overhand throw.

still need some practice, your coach will tell you what to correct for the next throw. Then you get to practice again. After every five throws, change roles. This is how it will look and sound." (Graham et al., 2020, pg. 146)

At this point, the teacher would demonstrate the entire task including what it would sound like to give appropriate feedback to the partner statement using the "one glow and one grow" statement (one positive and one improvement comment) and having the partner say thank you and repeat back what they thought was said. Thus, the SEL competency of relationship building is taught by explicitly focusing on the skills of communication and listening. The teacher would then circulate around the room, checking in with groups and asking the children what they said to their partner for feedback and/or what feedback their partner gave them. The teacher would then give feedback about the feedback. Any feedback about the throw would be to the "coach," not the player. If the teacher decided to give feedback to the player, the SEL learning would be undermined as the children would not be practicing those skills.

Likewise, assessment for learning with the above task might ask children to indicate on an exit slip one thing they said to their partner to aid their learning and one thing their partner said to them that was helpful. Thus content—psychomotor, cognitive, and affective (i.e., SEL)—instruction and assessment are aligned and taught purposefully in a synergistic manner and the environment is SAFE (CASEL, 2019). Simultaneously, the SEL competency of relationships would be scaffolded in a step-by-step manner. Initially, it would be practiced in a structured, supported, and limited environment, e.g.,

specific cues, task card for assistance, guidance on how to provide the feedback; later, tasks might ask children to provide feedback without the same support mechanisms. At this point, however, children are actively practicing both throwing and communicating; they are focused on a single task that is quite explicit to feedback (and three cues of throwing).

Skill Themes and SEL in Action

In skill themes, content is developed in a spiral progression using the wheel to combine movement concepts and skills; it is fairly clear—we can see these skills. What is not as clear is the development of SEL skills, which may not be as obvious because these skills tend to be vague and abstract. For example, what does respecting others really look and sound like to a child? Or how do you reflect on consequences? Or how does one listen well? In **Tables 5.5** to **5.9**, we have provided the SEL concepts as identified by CASEL with an abbreviated definition and then explicitly defined SEL constructs in terms of child-friendly language. These child-friendly descriptors operationalize what the abstract SEL concept represents to children and thus allows for the teaching of each concept. The third and fourth columns provide a snippet of a skill theme learning experience designed to also "teach" the SEL construct while the last column represents the instructional strategy being used. In Table 5.8, you will notice a spiral in the right-hand column. This is to indicate the sequencing or progression of the skill of listening well within the relationship construct.

Table 5.5 Self-Awareness

SEL Concept (CASEL Definition)	Child Friendly Descriptors	Skill Theme Learning Experience Combined with SEL[1]	Instructional Strategy
Accurately recognizing one's own emotions, thoughts, and values and how they influence behavior. Skills involved: ■ Ability to reflect on strengths and limitations ■ Possessing a well-grounded sense of confidence and optimism. ■ Identifying emotions			
	Ability to reflect on strengths and limitations means: Identify what you are good at and not	Maintaining transfer from feet to hands. Practice transferring weight from feet to hands until you can balance for three seconds. Record in your journal the date you successfully took their weight on their hands for three seconds and describe the feeling of "weight on hands." What is one balance you did well and what is one you still need to work on?	Interactive teaching—direct instruction
	Ability to identify emotions means: Being perceptive	From all of the balances you have practiced, choose your three favorites, each showing a different combination of body parts as bases of support. Practice until you can hold each balance for three seconds without moving or falling over. When you are ready, show your balances to a partner, who will give you a thumbs up if you hold the balance stationary for three seconds. Then tell your partner why these were your favorite balances.	Peer teaching

[1]Please note that all learning tasks used as examples in the chapter are taken or adapted from Graham et al. 2020, *Children Moving: A Reflective Approach to Teaching Physical Education.*

Much like the progression spiral used with the skill of punting earlier, it moves from teacher-directed to child-directed instruction and represents the small and sequential steps that are consistently revisited if the skill of listening is to truly be learned.

While these tables are just small examples of tasks that might be used with children, two things are important. First, the SEL concept is explained through instruction and students practice it in the task. Thus, it is taught, not hoped to be caught. Second, the instructional strategies range from direct instruction to more student-centered approaches,

much like the progression spiral skill themes uses with psychomotor skills. This progression helps children gradually take more responsibility for their own learning with one skill building on the next. The lesson here is that when teaching SEL skills, you must start small and develop them incrementally. Take a look at the tasks: can you see how the SEL concepts are taught?

At this point, we have explained skill themes and given you some examples of ideas that might use skill themes to teach SEL. Now, let's take this a step further. What would a lesson look and sound like that

Table 5.6 Self-Management

SEL Concept (CASEL Definition)	Child-Friendly Descriptors	Skill Theme Learning Experience Combined with SEL	Instructional Strategy
Ability to successfully regulate one's emotions, thoughts, and behaviors in different situations Skills involved: ■ Effectively managing stress ■ Controlling impulses ■ Self-discipline ■ Motivating oneself set and work toward personal and academic goals			
	Setting a goal means: Keep going and just keep trying	Play the game of soccer golf by combining the skills of dribbling in pathways, kicking for a goal, and kicking over a low height. The playground is arranged as a golf course. The task is to complete the course with the fewest number of kicks. There are boxes to dribble around, zones to zigzag through, hoops to kick into, and poles to kick over. Each child has a score card and records the number of kicks it takes to make each hole as they proceed through the course. When they finish the course, they begin again, trying to lower their score. Remind them to keep going and keep trying to lower their score by choosing one thing to focus on doing better in the second round. Have a place on the score card for the first round; a place for the second round goal; and then a place for the second round score.	Interactive teaching – Direct Instruction
	Self-discipline means: When your will is stronger than the temptation Doing the right thing even if people aren't looking	Children are given cards with four body actions listed. They are asked to make up a sequence of jumps that shows those body actions in the air. To do this, they'll first travel a bit and then jump, showing the first body action; then they'll travel again and jump and show the second body action listed; they'll travel again and jump using the third body action; they will then travel one more time and jump showing the last body action. The sequence should be like this: Travel, jump; travel, jump; travel, jump; travel, jump, freeze. They should repeat the sequence enough times so that they can do it the same way each time. When giving instructions, the teacher will be sure to emphasize that children will need to practice over and over again until they have memorized the sequence. In others words, they should keep practicing even when the teacher is not looking or they are tempted to quit.	Interactive teaching—direct instruction and guided discovery

Table 5.7 Social Awareness

SEL Concept (CASEL Definition)	Child Friendly Descriptors	Skill Theme Learning Experience Combined with SEL	Instructional Strategy
Ability to take the perspective of and empathize with others and ability to understand social and ethical norms for behavior Skills involved: ■ Perspective-taking ■ Empathy ■ Appreciating diversity ■ Respect for others			
	Respect for others and perspective taking means: Do to others like you would like to be treated Treat others like they are better than you	Children stand three to four feet from a partner. Partner 1 tosses the ball to the partner at high level/above the partner's head. Partner 2 volleys the ball back to tossing partner. Partner 1 catches the ball and repeats the task. After three attempts, switch positions for tossing and volleying. When you are tossing, remember to give your partner "sympathetic" or good tosses so that they are able to volley the ball back. You want to give tosses like the ones you would like to receive. A teacher demonstration of sympathetic tosses (and not) would be appropriate.	Interactive teaching—direct instruction
	Appreciating diversity means: Accepting others who may not be like you	Children in groups develop a neighborhood friendship dance using the skills of skipping, galloping, hopping, and the concepts of level, directions, and pathways. Class is divided into four groups and each group has different color streamers (e.g., red for one group; blue for another, etc.) to represent their neighborhood. Each group works in one quadrant of the room and develops a unique turn and travel pattern. On the signal, one group at a time travels to the center of the space performing their movements and waving their streamers. Groups then decide to visit each other's neighborhoods and learn their movements. As children are developing their movements, have them decide what is unique about their neighborhood and have the movements reflect that; when teaching the movements to another group, make sure children share what the movements represent. (This task is loosely adapted from Cone, T.P. and Cone, S.L. 2012. *Teaching Children Dance*; a full version of it can be found there or in Graham et al. *Children Moving*).	Child-designed

Table 5.8 Relationship Skills

SEL Concept (CASEL Definition)	Child Friendly Descriptors	Skill Theme Learning Experience Combined with SEL	Instructional Strategy
Ability to establish and maintain healthy and rewarding relationships with diverse individuals and groups. Skills involved: ■ Communicate clearly ■ Listen well ■ Cooperate with others ■ Resist inappropriate social pressure ■ Negotiate conflict constructively ■ Seek and offer help when needed			
	Listen well and cooperate with others means: Being open to new ideas Let them speak Do not control everything	In the task of creating a self-designed game involving striking with paddles; the instructions include everyone in the group sharing one idea for the game and all listen without interrupting. When children are later asked to reflect on their game making, they are asked to also reflect on whether they listened to everyone's ideas	Child-designed
	Listen well and cooperate with others means: Let them speak Do not control everything	When using the cooperative task of developing a dance routine, each group member brings their movement to group to teach. The group decides an order in which to teach and lets the designated person teach before moving on. In explaining the task, the teacher would demonstrate what this would look and sound like.	Cooperative Learning
	Lesson well and communicate clearly mean: Repeat back what you thought was being said	When given the peer teaching task of providing feedback to a partner after having been given feedback from the partner, the first thing the receiver does is repeat back what he or she thought was said. When explaining the task the teacher demonstrates what this would sound like.	Peer Teaching
	Lesson well and communicate clearly mean: Repeat back what you thought was being said	After the teacher explains the station procedures, the children in partners explain to each other what will happen and then ask questions. The teacher first monitors the discussion and then asks a group to explain	Task Teaching—Stations
	Lesson well and communicate clearly mean: Look at others when they are talking; look at others when you are talking	With any task, develop a "freeze" or "stop" mnemonic such as: Teacher: Freeze, please Children respond: Hands on knees; Teacher; 1,2,3, Eyes on me As a teacher, you then give positive feedback to students who do it correctly; not scolding those who may be slower at it.	Interactive Teaching—direct instruction

(continues)

Table 5.8 Relationship Skills (continued)

SEL Concept (CASEL Definition)	Child Friendly Descriptors	Skill Theme Learning Experience Combined with SEL	Instructional Strategy
	Seek and offer help means: Help other people and do it with a kind heart. Don't complain.	Children are in partners; each partner group has a paddle and a variety of objects to strike. Three hoops serve as targets. Children are instructed to place the three hoops on the floor, one about three feet away, one six feet away, and one 10 feet away. One partner will try to strike so the object lands in each hoop; the other partner will collect the object after the hits. Then the partners switch places. They can make up any other rules they wish, but they both need to practice striking into all three hoops. After children have completed three rounds, they should decide which distance was best for them. When giving instructions, remind children when they collect the objects to do so pleasantly without complaining and to return the equipment to the proper place by putting it there and not throwing. The striker should then say, "thank you" before becoming the collector. A demonstration would be useful.	Interactive teaching and guided discovery

Table 5.9 Responsible Decision Making

SEL Concept (CASEL Definition)	Child Friendly Descriptors	Skill Theme Learning Experience Combined with SEL	Instructional Strategy
Ability to make constructive choices about personal behavior and social interactions based on ethical standards, safety concerns, and social norms. Skills involved: ■ realistic evaluation of consequences of various actions ■ consideration of the well-being of oneself and others ■ identifying problems ■ analyzing situations ■ solving problems			
	Realistic evaluation of consequences of various actions means: Make good judgments Taking precautions; having foresight.	When inappropriate behavior occurs, use a four strike plan. Strike 1 = a prompt toward appropriate behavior Strike 2 = asking the child if they need a timeout Strike 3 = Telling the child to take a timeout but he or she may re-enter whenever they feel they are ready Strike 4 = Take a timeout, complete a reflection form, and wait for the teacher.	Guided Discovery
	Identifying and solving problems means: Think about and fix things	When deciding which partner will lead first in a follow-the-leader activity involving traveling while changing directions, use rock, paper, scissors to determine which partner goes first.	Interactive teaching—direct instruction

(continues)

Table 5.9 Responsible Decision Making   *(continued)*

SEL Concept (CASEL Definition)	Child Friendly Descriptors	Skill Theme Learning Experience Combined with SEL	Instructional Strategy
	Reflecting on consequences means: Think about what you did wrong and why	When having to sit out of an activity for inappropriate behavior a child completes a form indicating what they were doing, what they did that was wrong, how it impacted others, how their behavior needs to change, and a plan of action.	Interactive teaching—Direct instruction
	Analyzing situation means: Breaking it down and inspecting it Thinking before doing Deciding what is right for you	For a warm-up activity using different skills, a variety of "stations" are scattered in general space. At each "station" is a set of three laminated cards: one green, one blue, and one purple containing different related versions of the same skill. For example: dribble a basketball in self-space; dribble a rubber ball at different places around the body; and dribble a basketball at different levels. At each station, the child chooses which activity they do based on their needs or skills. When giving instructions, the teacher will want to add ways that the children can break the choices down and think about which one is right for them. Switch stations every 60 seconds. Children choose which station to do next—they just eventually have to do them all.	Task teaching—stations

taught both skill themes and SEL concepts? We have provided two "scripted" lesson plans that combine skill themes with SEL concepts. The first lesson is a games lesson designed to teach the skills of chasing, fleeing, and dodging and the SEL construct of relationship skills, specifically cooperation, in a self-designed game (see **Table 5.10**). In this lesson, students are taught to practice respectful listening when provided corrective feedback as well as to work cooperatively with others by listening to and trying everyone's ideas and taking turns when talking. As an assessment, students are asked to rate (thumbs up/side/down) how well they cooperated. You will notice that cooperation is defined in child-friendly terms and taught and assessed throughout. This would be the final lesson in a series of lessons.

The second lesson is a gymnastics lesson and focuses on the skills of balance, responsible decision making, and self-management (see **Table 5.11**). In this lesson, self-management and responsible decision making have been operationalized in terms of safety and how to make safe decisions about balancing. You may notice that children are also asked to identify their favorite balance; while not the focus of this lesson, the idea of choosing their favorite reinforces the SEL concept of self-awareness and the skill of identifying emotions. Throughout the lesson, students are taught to exhibit responsible personal and social behavior

that respects self and others. They get to apply these traits when providing feedback to a peer, relative to the quality of balance.

Conclusions and Final Thoughts

As we conclude this chapter, there are four points that we would like to reinforce. First, SEL skills must be explicitly taught if they are to be learned, and they must be practiced, just as a motor skill would be. Several opportunities for quality practice are needed. Remember, teaching does not equate to telling. Asking a child to "be a good sport" does not mean he or she knows what "being a good sport" means. Second, students must be given helpful feedback and must not be punished for making mistakes. Think of it this way—if a child was practicing throwing and made the mistake of stepping forward on the same foot as the throwing arm, he would be given feedback to improve. Therefore, if a child is learning to listen well and talks while someone else is talking; they need feedback about how to listen well; they don't need to be punished. It is far better to focus on the positive and avoid the negative as much as possible. Third, start small and start smart. SEL skills, like

Table 5.10 Child-Designed Games—Chasing, Fleeing, and Dodging

Class: 4th–5th grade (Control/Utilization)

Lesson Length: 40 min   **No. of Students:** 20–25

Pupil's previous knowledge/experience: This would be about the 5th or 6th lesson children would have experienced with chasing, fleeing, and dodging. Students would have previous experiences working in small groups and designing their own games. Yet, it is assumed they will still need some guided introduction. Most students dodging skills will not yet be at a control to utilization level.

Lesson Focus:
1. Motor skill–The focus is on dodging to avoid a chaser.
2. SEL–The focus is on students developing their ability to establish and maintain healthy and rewarding relationships with diverse individuals and groups. Specifically, cooperating with others.

Learning Outcomes: students will be able to...
1. Work <u>cooperatively</u> in small groups to create an original tag game.
   - Today, working cooperatively means listening to and trying everyone's ideas and taking turns when talking.

> Standard 4. The physically literate individual exhibits responsible personal and social behavior that respects self and others.
> Grade Level Indicator(s): Listens respectfully to corrective feedback from others (e.g., peers, adults). (S4.E3.4) and works cooperatively with others. (S4.E4.3a)
> SEL: Relationships

   - Success Criteria: Cocreate success criteria with students (what does it look like, sound like, feel like, etc.?)
   - Assessment: Peer and self-assessment; thumbs up/side/down, peer oral feedback.
2. Successfully dodge a chaser during a game-like situation.

> Standard 1. The physically literate individual demonstrates competency in a variety of motor skills and movement patterns.
> Grade Level Indicator(s): Applies simple strategies and tactics in chasing activities. (S2.E5.3a) and applies simple strategies in fleeing activities. (S2.E5.3b)

   - Success Criteria: Students will avoid being "tagged" or avoid making contact with opponents and other players by moving their body to be in the open space. Eyes are focused in direction of travel, body lowered during change of direction, and move "quicker than the speed of light."
   - Assessment: Self-assessment (thumbs up/side/down), teacher observation.

Resources/Equipment: Activity space, learning outcomes, and success criteria signs

Safety Considerations: Check for appropriate active wear, shoe laces tied, no gum, no equipment or obstacles in the movement space. Avoid slippery surfaces. Also, be sure that students have their game creation area marked and separate from others to avoid collision.

Time	Content & Activity Development Set, Task Development, Progressions, Learning Experiences, and Closure	Organization Diagram Showing Organization of Students and Equipment	Teaching Cues Behavior Prompts, Teaching Cues, Diagram, or Pictures	Adaptations How to Adapt for All Participants
Instant Activity/ Warm-up Three minutes	**Instant Activity:** Students are instructed to enter the activity space, moving in their own space while listening for the "stop signal." After about 30 seconds, signal students to stop and tell students that, "we are going to play a game called **I see...**" When I say, "I see," you say,	Students and teacher will be moving around in open space. Use boundaries as necessary for safety.	Use positive pinpointing and feedback to enforce routines and positive responses to managerial and instructional signals.	When giving instructions and calling out cues, be sure to stand near students who might have visual or auditory impairments.

(continues)

Table 5.10 Child-Designed Games—Chasing, Fleeing, and Dodging *(continued)*

Time	Content & Activity Development Set, Task Development, Progressions, Learning Experiences, and Closure	Organization Diagram Showing Organization of Students and Equipment	Teaching Cues Behavior Prompts, Teaching Cues, Diagram, or Pictures	Adaptations How to Adapt for All Participants
	"what do you see?" Let's try, "I see..." (students respond). "Now, whatever I tell you I see, I want you to do. The actions continue until I say "I see..." again." Let's try, "I see..." (students respond, "what do you see?") – "I see all the students tiptoeing around being very sneaky." (students do it, until your stop signal) – "I see all the students hopping around like a bunny rabbit" (students do it, until your stop signal) – "I see all the students walking around like their feet are stuck in mud" (students do it, until your stop signal) – "I see all the students jumping as high as they can" (students do it, until your stop signal) – "I see all the students jogging around giving each other a high five" (students do it, until your stop signal) – "I see all the students sitting in a circle in front of me being as silent as they can" (students do it, until your stop signal)			
Introduction Four minutes	Explain to students what the learning goals are and discuss/determine success criteria.			– Have learning goals printed or written on a visual so that students can read it, and refer back to it throughout the lesson. (This will also appeal to the visual learner)
Dodging 15 min	**Dodging in response to a signal/no signal:** **T1** Have students walk along the lines on the floor. When they get to a new line, quickly change directions to follow the new line.	Setting: Children scattered in general space.	Throughout the learning experience, highlight the following skills for dodging (avoiding being tagged or trying to tag others). Note that this list is not exhaustive and further learning opportunities may arise during the task.	More advanced dodgers might need to following cues. – Change direction by pushing off outside foot; push off – Change direction both ways; go left, go right

Table 5.10 Child-Designed Games—Chasing, Fleeing, and Dodging *(continued)*

Time	Content & Activity Development Set, Task Development, Progressions, Learning Experiences, and Closure	Organization Diagram Showing Organization of Students and Equipment	Teaching Cues Behavior Prompts, Teaching Cues, Diagram, or Pictures	Adaptations How to Adapt for All Participants
	T2 "Now you are going to have to become really sneaky. As you travel throughout the general space, when you hear the signal (a clap/"go," etc.) pretend you are going in one direction and then quickly change and go in a different direction." – Stop students after about one minute. Ask the following questions. **Q**: What might happen if you are not looking where you are going? – Listen to responses. "Good! I think you are right. So do we agree that it is really important to look where you are going when you change direction quickly, we call that dodging?" – Add "look where you are going" to cue list/success criteria. **Q**: "If you are trying to trick somebody and surprise them with which way you travel, do you think we should move really quick, or slow?" – listen to students' responses. "Good! I think so too! A good dodge happens really fast, quicker than the speed of light! – Add "quicker than the speed of light" to cues list/ success criteria **T3 (refinement)**: "Let's try the activity again. This time, I want you to think about moving quicker than the speed of light when you change directions and always look where you are going." – Check for understanding: "what two things are we thinking about?" "who can show me what that looks like?" **Assessment**: – Ask students what two things they were thinking about. – Do a thumbs up/side/down self-assessment – Celebrate success.	Safety: Inspect the activity area and eliminate potential hazards. Check that the activity surface provides sufficient traction. Set boundaries for the activity a safe distance from walls and obstacles. Students are moving in pairs in their own space.	Dodging Action; Cues – Eyes focused in the direction of travel; look where you are going – Body lowered during change of direction; get low – Change direction quickly; quicker than the speed of light "Look where you are going!" "Get low!" "Quicker than the speed of light!" "Remember the teaching cues!" "Remember everyone is moving around the space. Keep your head up, and look where you are going." It is easy to get caught up in the excitement and lose sight of the quality of movement. – Emphasize that a tag is a touch, not a push or a grab. – Keep your eyes up, everyone will be dodging around you; you don't want to collide with anyone. – If players are complaining about tagging each other at the same time, you can either have them both out, or have them do rock paper scissors to see who remains standing.	If students are having difficulty judging the distance to stationary or moving objects, give the children more opportunities to vary the distance to the object and vary the angle of approach and exit. Start with stationary objects and progress to an increase in unpredictability. If students are crossing their feet, ensure that they understand the footwork sequence. Use colored tape on the ground to indicate when to step with the left foot and when to step with the right foot. If students are taking several small steps to change direction of travel, then encourage children to push off and change direction in one step. The children will need to plant their outside foot next to a cone or line and take the next step on another path. To maximize the challenge and the enjoyment, students could identify their own ways to make the game more challenging.

(continues)

Table 5.10 Child-Designed Games—Chasing, Fleeing, and Dodging *(continued)*

Time	Content & Activity Development Set, Task Development, Progressions, Learning Experiences, and Closure	Organization Diagram Showing Organization of Students and Equipment	Teaching Cues Behavior Prompts, Teaching Cues, Diagram, or Pictures	Adaptations How to Adapt for All Participants
	T4: "Now, instead of me giving you the signal, you'll fake on your own. Whenever you come to another person, pretend you're going to go one way, but go the other. Really try to confuse the other person so he or she doesn't know where you'll be going." (2 min) – Stop students after about two minutes, or when needed. **Q**: "Is it easier to change directions quicker than the speed of light if you are standing up really tall, or bending your knees to get nice and low? When I say go, give both a try." Have students explore, give stop signal, and have them answer. "Good! You are absolutely right, it is much more effective to dodge when you are nice and low. So, let's remember to bend our knees and get low." – Add "get low" to the dodge cues/ success criteria list **T5 (application)**: See if you can travel and dodge for 20 seconds without colliding with anyone. Application task 2/Tag game intro: **Knee Tag —> Everybody's It Tag.** **G1**: "When I go, you are going to find a partner with whom you work well. I will know you are ready when you are touching your head. GO" "We are going to play a game called, knee tag. This is a tag game with two people who are both it at the same time. Your goal is to tag your partner on their knee, but not let them tag you." "If one of you gets tagged, play again until my stop signal" Play for two minutes. Stop students to ask them what they need to remember about dodging (refer back to dodging cues/success criteria list)			**Tail Tag** *This can be an adaptation from "knee tag & everybody's it tag." This requires equipment (one flag/scarf/penny etc., per student. Students place the material like a tail coming off their lower spine. – In pairs, students try to remove their partner's tail (but not touching their body).

(continues)

Table 5.10 Child-Designed Games—Chasing, Fleeing, and Dodging   *(continued)*

Time	Content & Activity Development Set, Task Development, Progressions, Learning Experiences, and Closure	Organization Diagram Showing Organization of Students and Equipment	Teaching Cues Behavior Prompts, Teaching Cues, Diagram, or Pictures	Adaptations How to Adapt for All Participants
Child-Designed Games 15 min	Have students get into groups of three to six, depending on the number of students you have in class. To support the development of SEL skills, this could be done by: – Having students find someone they work well with and then join with another pair – Students choose their own groups of three to six with the criteria of working well together by staying on task and listening to all in the group. – Tell students you will know they are ready when they are sitting with their group facing you. **Q**: Who can tell me what all games have? (you may need to prompt students to think of the answers) Listen for – A name – Rules – Boundaries – An objective – Are fun! (etc.) "If your groups, you are going to work co-operatively to make up your own game that has all of those parts. Who can remind us what working cooperatively means today?" **T1**: "In small groups (of 3-6) you are going to work cooperatively as a group to make up your own tag game. All of you must play at once. Your game must be played inside your square (quarter of the space as identified with pylons/floor markers)." Explain to the students that on the go signal, the group will all go to their space and work to come up with their game. They will come up with a name, object, rules, and boundaries. Remind them that everyone should share an idea and everyone's ideas should be tried out and only one person speaks at a time. When the group thinks they are ready, they can try playing their game. To check for understanding, ask students what they need to do. "Go"	*How will you get your students into groups?	*Remind students to think about dodging cues. This can be done through questioning or direct teaching. – Avoid as many decisions as possible about their game (except in the case of safety; even then, use questioning to guide students to a safer option). Cooperation cues: – Let everyone have a chance to speak – No interrupting when others are speaking – Try everyone's idea/s – Only one person speaks at a time; everyone else listens Provide prompts and feedback related to the cues of working cooperatively. For example: "I noticed you just stopped yourself from speaking over your teammate; that's a really good job making sure you're not interrupting your teammates." "Blue team is showing good cooperation by taking turns when talking so that everyone's ideas are heard."	

(continues)

Table 5.10 Child-Designed Games—Chasing, Fleeing, and Dodging *(continued)*

Time	Content & Activity Development Set, Task Development, Progressions, Learning Experiences, and Closure	Organization Diagram Showing Organization of Students and Equipment	Teaching Cues Behavior Prompts, Teaching Cues, Diagram, or Pictures	Adaptations How to Adapt for All Participants
	Stop students; **A**: Provide feedback on students' cooperation. Have students do a self-assessment (thumbs up/side/down) on their cooperation in general, or depending on the students' cooperation observed, you may decide to break the self-assessment down into specific success criteria. Remind them of the success criteria (cooperation cues). **T2**: Have students refine their game. Ask students to think if there are any ways to make their game better. Do they need to change any rules? Add any new rules? When ready, have students play their revised game. Ask students for examples of how they might use good cooperation with their teammates during the refinement task. Give students a transition time warning, "you still have 2 min... etc.", then stop students. Gather them in for closure.		"I heard someone on your team give an idea, but then someone else talked before you tried the idea. How can we show better cooperation when working as part of a team in this situation?"	
Closure Three minutes	**Assessment**: **Q**: Ask students how their game creation went? What was it like working cooperatively? What is something they did that showed good cooperation? What is something they can improve for next time? – Have students do a self-assessment (thumbs up/side/down) on their cooperation. **Q**: Did you use your dodging skills when playing your game? When? Who remembered to think about the teaching cues? What were they? Who can show me what they look like?	Gather students at a "home base" zone near the displayed learning intentions, success criteria, and vocabulary wall, etc.		

Table 5.11 Educational Gymnastics—Stationary Balances

Class: 3rd–4th grade (Control level)

Lesson Length: 40 min   **No. of Students:** 20–25

Pupil's previous knowledge/experience: Students would have experienced a variety of locomotive skills and progressions of educational gymnastics including: exploring shapes, weight-transfer actions, and exploring balances in stillness on the floor/mats using a variety of body parts/bases of support. Safety has been a major focus throughout the gymnastics unit. "Safety check" is a well-developed safety protocol in this class. There is a wide variety of skill proficiency and movement control within the class.

Lesson Focus:
1. Motor skill: The focus is on doing stationary balances on a variety of objects/apparatus
2. SEL: The focus is on students developing their responsible decision making skills for personal safety.

Learning Outcomes: Students will be able to...
1. Make responsible decisions for personal safety

> SHAPE Standard 4. The physically literate individual exhibits responsible personal and social behavior that respects self and others.
>
> Grade Level Indicator(s): Works safely with peers and equipment in physical activity settings. (S4.E6.4)
>
> SEL Constructs: Responsible decision making and self-management

- Today, making responsible decisions means that before we do a balance on an apparatus, we stop and think if it's a safe idea using our stoplight guide. If it's a green, we do the balance, if it's yellow we try another apparatus first or ask the teacher for supervision. If it's red, we don't do the balance because it is not safe.
  a) Green = mostly easy = give it a go
  b) Yellow = a little bit hard/some wobbles and wiggles = try a different apparatus first; ask for teacher supervision
  c) Red = really hard/no stillness = not safe, choose a different balance

- Success Criteria: Cocreate specific success criteria with students (what does it look like, sound like, feel like, etc.?) ...
- Assessment for learning: Teacher observation, questioning, and self-assessment
2. Successfully balance in stillness on a variety of apparatus

> SHAPE Standard 1. The physically literate individual demonstrates competency in a variety of motor skills and movement patterns.
>
> Grade Level Indicator(s): Balances on different bases of support, demonstrating muscular tension and extensions of free body parts. (S1. E7.3) and balances on different bases of support on apparatus, demonstrating levels and shapes. (S1.E7.4)

- Success Criteria: You will know you are successful when ... cocreate with students (what does it look like, sound like, feel like, etc.?) For example, you are 'frozen like a statue' for three to five seconds (no wiggles or wobbles) and "squeezing all of your muscles" AND balance on more than one apparatus.
- Assessment for learning: Peer assessment, teacher observation

Resources/Equipment: Activity space, mats, a variety of low apparatus (boxes, crates, benches), stop light system posters, learning outcomes and success criteria signs.

Safety Considerations: Check for appropriate active wear, shoe laces tied, no gum, no equipment or obstacles in the movement space. No slippery surfaces. Mats are surrounding and flush against apparatus. Apparatus is sturdy and of good quality/condition. Appropriate footwear.

(continues)

Table 5.11 Educational Gymnastics—Stationary Balances *(continued)*

Time	Content & Activity Development Set, Task Development, Progressions, Learning Experiences and Closure	Organization (diagram of) Organization of Students & Equipment	Teaching Cues Behavior Prompts, Teaching Cues, Diagram, or Pictures	Adaptations How to Adapt for All Participants
Instant Activity/ Warm-up Five minutes	**Instant Activity:** Students are instructed to enter the activity space and find an empty mat (an established and practiced routine). Students begin on their individual mat by using as many different body shapes as they can to spell the word "BALANCE." Once all of the students have safely found a mat and began exploring body shapes, use your stop signal to have students come to stillness. For example, "when it is safe to do so, come to sitting, eyes and ears on me." (This might be a different stop signal than non-gymnastics classes to consider the safety risks of students "freezing" in the middle of a gymnastics action, roll, inverted balance, etc.)	Various pieces of gymnastics apparatus arranged throughout general space: individual mats (varying sizes?), low tables, boxes, benches, climbing frames, low balance beams, etc. All apparatus is surrounded with mats flush against equipment. Safely secure a "stop light system" sign at each apparatus.' Have learning intentions, success criteria, and the vocabulary wall displayed.	Reinforce start/ stop signals as necessary.	When giving instructions and calling out cues, be sure to stand near to students who might have visual or auditory impairments.
Introduction Five minutes	"Earlier in our gymnastics unit, we explored balancing in stillness on the floor/mats using all different bases and body parts. What do we need to remember when we are balancing in stillness? ... That's right! We are thinking about being frozen like a statue with no wiggle or wobbles and squeezing all of our muscles really tight. How long do we need to be frozen to have a still balance...? Right, three "gymnastics." When I say go, where you are in your own space, everyone show me your very best balance from last week. Go! "one-gymnastics, two-gymnastics, three-gymnastics" good! I saw some really still and strong balances. I also saw some wiggles. What do we have to remember when doing a balance? Today, we have two learning intentions. By the end of this lesson, **you will be able to successfully balance in stillness on a variety of apparatus**. You have already told me that a really good balance is	The organization does not change throughout the lesson unless you are working in a large space where you need to use a "home base" zone to gather and talk with students between tasks.		Have learning goals printed or written on a visual so that students can read it and refer back to it throughout the lesson. (This will also appeal to the visual learner)

Table 5.11 Educational Gymnastics—Stationary Balances *(continued)*

Time	Content & Activity Development Set, Task Development, Progressions, Learning Experiences and Closure	Organization (diagram of) Organization of Students & Equipment	Teaching Cues Behavior Prompts, Teaching Cues, Diagram, or Pictures	Adaptations How to Adapt for All Participants
	"frozen like a statue," "squeezing all your muscles," and "held for three 'gymnastics'". So, you will know that you are successful today when you can do a really good balance, doing those three things, on more than one apparatus. Our second learning intentions is that **you will be able to make responsible decisions for personal safety**. We've been talking a lot about safety in gymnastics; what do you think it means to make responsible decisions for personal safety? That's right. Today, making responsible decisions (good choices) to keep you safe means that you stop before you do a balance on an apparatus to think if it is safe using the stop light system and you finish the lesson just as you are now, with no new bumps or bruises. [go through stoplight system with students referring to the stoplight system visual. For example, green light is if you can do the balance really well holding it like a statue on the floor or lower apparatus. Green means go.]			
Content Development 35 min	**T1:** "When I say go, on your mat, you have two minutes to explore some of your favorite balances from last week using different bases and body parts on the mat. Remember our success criteria for a good balance" Let's remember when we were learning about bases of support. Was it easier to balance with a big base of support or a small base of support? ... That's right. It's usually harder to balance on a small base of support. Let's look around at all the apparatus we have today. What apparatus has the smallest surface? What apparatus has the biggest surface? ... Do you think it would be more challenging to balance on a big surface or a little surface? ... That's right. Sometimes, we can do a really tricky balance on a big surface, like holding a handstand on a mat. Just like what we learned about balancing with different bases, usually, as the surface gets smaller, it becomes more and more challenging to hold a balance.		**T1**—Cue/feedback on success criteria related to quality of balance. "Bobby, I see your muscles are squeezed really strong! You are very frozen" "Remember to count to three 'gymnastics' in your balance!" **T2**—Safety prompts and cues to change apparatus, as necessary	Students with more advanced balancing skills might need cues to differentiate what is an appropriate movement response (balance on apparatus) in physical education class compared with their artistic gymnastics clubs. What does this look like when making responsible decisions in a physical education class, etc.

(continues)

Table 5.11 Educational Gymnastics—Stationary Balances (continued)

Time	Content & Activity Development Set, Task Development, Progressions, Learning Experiences and Closure	Organization (diagram of) Organization of Students & Equipment	Teaching Cues Behavior Prompts, Teaching Cues, Diagram, or Pictures	Adaptations How to Adapt for All Participants
	The sizes of the space for us to balance on are all different, what else is different that might make it harder or easier to balance? ... Yes, that's right, height. We have lots of options from mats on the ground all the way up to a horse that's pretty high. **T2:** "Last week we explored traveling on the apparatus and getting on and off safety. What are the important things we need to remember about using the apparatus safely? ... That's right. When I say go, you have five minutes to explore some of the apparatus that you might like to use today to remember how it feels. You might travel forward and backwards. Go" "Remember we have two learning intentions for today. We are going to be able to do really good balances on more than one apparatus. And we are going to choose which balances we are doing on which apparatus by making responsible decisions for our safety." "Let's try one together. If we were all thinking of trying a handstand on the box, do we just go ahead and try? .. No! That's right, good! What do we do first? .. A "safety check," yes that's right, and then what? Good! Let's use the stop light system. Let's think, can we hold a handstand with no wiggles or wobble for three "gymnastics" every time? It is really easy for us? Nope, okay, so not green. Let's think about yellow light. Can we hold a handstand in stillness *most* of the time on the floor? Nope! Is a handstand hard for us to hold in stillness for three 'gymnastics'? ...Yeah, so what would be the responsible decision for our safety? ... That's right! We would think of a balance that is a green light or yellow light and start again." **T3:** "When I say go, you are going to try some balances you did on the floor/mat surface on the apparatus. Go"		"Remember one of our learning intentions requires us to balance on more than one apparatus. This is a good opportunity to explore some different apparatus that you might want to use for your balancing later." **T3**—Highlight the following skills for balancing and balancing on apparatus. Note that this list is not exhaustive and further learning opportunities may arise during the task. – "Frozen like a statue": no wobbles or wiggles – "Squeezing all your muscles": strong muscular tension – "3 gymnastics": balances need to be held for at least three seconds Also highlight/ feedback the following cues for making responsible decisions.	If students are having difficulty, you might provide more guided practice by walking/ talking through the decision-making process. Depending on the age/abilities of students, you might consider having students draw their two favorite balances on a handout. You might include a check list for peer observation and have students check for the success criteria of a quality balance.

(continues)

Table 5.11 Educational Gymnastics—Stationary Balances
(continued)

Time	Content & Activity Development Set, Task Development, Progressions, Learning Experiences and Closure	Organization (diagram of) Organization of Students & Equipment	Teaching Cues Behavior Prompts, Teaching Cues, Diagram, or Pictures	Adaptations How to Adapt for All Participants
	T4: "Well done, I really like that I am seeing you stop, do a safety check of the apparatus, and go through the stoplight system before getting on the apparatus to do your balance. But I am also seeing some of us forget to hold our balances in stillness for a full '3 gymnastics.' This time, when I say go, make sure you are counting your gymnastics all the way to three before you stop your balance. Go"		– Stop and think "is this a safe decision?" before you attempt the balance – Use the stop light system to help make the responsible choice for your safety	
	T5: "How many different balances can you *safely* create on this apparatus?" Assessment: Let's do a self-check. Are you making a responsible decision for your safety when balancing on apparatus? If you have been every time, thumb up; if so-so, thumb to the side; if not really and you could make better decisions, thumb down. If your thumb is up, what are you doing that makes you a responsible decision maker? Thumb side or down, what can you do to make more responsible decisions? Good.		"I see you are about to try to do your balance on the high beam, but I noticed you were having lots of wobbles when you were practicing on the mat first. Do you think this is a responsible decision for your safety? What might be a safer option to try first? Let's use the stoplight system together to make a good choice."	
	T6: "This time, when I say go, you are going to continue to do some balances on the apparatus and really think about making responsible decisions for your safety. Go" **T7:** "Remember our learning intention for today is to be able to balance on more than one apparatus. If you haven't changed apparatus yet, I'd like you to think about selecting a new apparatus now." Assessment: If I try this balance three times on my mat, and it looks like this [model], and I want to try it on the bench. What would be a responsible decision for my safety? Everyone touch the color on the stoplight at your apparatus... That's right. Why is it a responsible decision?		"That was a really good decision. I like how you went through the stoplight and decided to try your balance on the box instead of the beam first. Well done." "Sally, I noticed you put your thumb up, but I just saw you walk up to the box and try your	

(continues)

Table 5.11 Educational Gymnastics—Stationary Balances   (continued)

Time	Content & Activity Development Set, Task Development, Progressions, Learning Experiences and Closure	Organization (diagram of) Organization of Students & Equipment	Teaching Cues Behavior Prompts, Teaching Cues, Diagram, or Pictures	Adaptations How to Adapt for All Participants
	T8: "I'd like you to think to pick your favorite two balances that you did on two different apparatus. [pause] Now, when I say go, you are going to find a partner who is at the same (or similar) apparatus as you. I will know you are ready to proceed when you are sitting next to each other beside the apparatus. Go. Now, you are going to show your partner your two favorite balances. [include peer feedback relative to the quality of balance]		balance straight away but fell off, how might we show more responsible decision making?" **T3–T8**—Provide Feedback/Cues on quality of balances "Remember to squeeze all your muscles really tight!" "That was a really good balance; you had no wiggles at all for more than '3 gymnastics'!" **T3–T8**—Use questioning to have students explain their use of the stoplight system out loud "Luke, I noticed you using the stoplight system before you did your really still one-foot balance on the horse. Good job. Can you tell me what your thinking was?" **T3–T8**—Provide feedback/cues on making a responsible decision (as discussed above)	

(continues)

Table 5.11 Educational Gymnastics—Stationary Balances　(continued)

Time	Content & Activity Development Set, Task Development, Progressions, Learning Experiences and Closure	Organization (diagram of) Organization of Students & Equipment	Teaching Cues Behavior Prompts, Teaching Cues, Diagram, or Pictures	Adaptations How to Adapt for All Participants
Closure 5 min	Review learning intentions and success criteria. Include closing questions, as necessary. For example, what did your partner do that showed they could do a really good balance on apparatus? What does it mean to make responsible decisions for your safety? Where can we use the stoplight system to make a good safety decision when in recess? Etc	Gather students at a "home base" zone near the displayed learning intentions, success criteria, vocabulary wall, and stoplight system visual.		

psychomotor skills, are learned in small, progressive steps; not all at once. This notion of progression is important for students to be able to apply SEL competencies later in life. This is similar to sports skills, for example, if you have not learned throwing (skill theme), it will be difficult to play softball (sport) in middle school. Likewise, if you have not learned to develop relationships by cooperating with peers, you will find it difficult to work with others as a member of a staff or team in a work setting. Finally, the combination of skill themes and SEL is not an either/or concept. Both can and should be taught, taught well, and taught simultaneously. Neither skill themes nor SEL concepts need to be compromised.

Acknowledgement

We would like to sincerely thank Dillon and Brian Patton for persisting with the constant bombardment of questions about "what does this mean?" that allowed us to more fully understand social and emotional concepts through the eyes of children.

Questions for Discussion

1. Why is the skill themes approach considered a robust method to teach SEL?
2. What is meant by the phrase "skill themes are about both the content (what is taught) and the pedagogy (how it is taught)"?
3. What are the two pedagogical aspects of skill themes that are used to promote SEL learning?
4. Using the sample lesson plan in Figure 5.5, identify all of the assessment for learning instances in the lesson.
5. Following the example provided in Figure 5.3, develop a similar assessment for another movement and SEL construct.
6. What does the acronym SAFE mean? Develop a learning task that represents SAFE in terms of SEL and skill themes.
7. What instructional approaches can be used within skill themes and SEL? Give an example of a task that represents each approach.
8. Using Table 5.8 as a guide, develop a progression from simple to complex for another SEL.

Ideas for Incorporating Skills Themes and SEL into PETE

1. **Teacher Observation and Interview**: For this assignment, teacher candidates (individually or in small groups) complete a structured observation of a model SEL lesson by a local elementary physical education teacher. The structured observation can focus on: lesson objectives, instructional methods and strategies used, student engagement, assessment of

learning, etc. Teacher candidates then follow up on the observation with an interview with the teacher. Questions could include: 1) in what ways do you teach to SEL competencies, 2) describe your progression for particular SEL concepts, 3) which is the most difficult and why?

2. **Student Interview**: For this learning experience, have teacher candidates interview a K–5 student focusing on their physical education experiences. Interview questions could include: enjoyable aspects of physical education; purpose of physical education; their own definitions of SEL competencies; what they learn in physical education, etc.

3. **Lesson Plan**: Have teacher candidates design a skill themes lesson with a particular SEL focus (i.e., throwing/catching and relationship skills). Lessons should be developmentally and instructionally appropriate, informed by state and/or national standards, and should address specific grade level indicators.

Other Possible Learning Experiences

1. **Modeling:** PETE faculty model skill themes/SEL lessons with K–5 students or where teacher candidates serve are participants. After the lesson, have a focused discussion on how SEL aspects were introduced and taught.

2. **Peer Teaching:** Prospective teachers create and deliver skill themes/SEL focused lessons in a peer-teaching format. The peer-teaching lesson plan should indicate an SEL teaching progression and identify alignment with state/national physical education standards.

3. **Lived Experience:** Embed teaching of SEL in a major's activity course and/or elementary content course.

4. **Field based Elementary Methods Course:** Requires ongoing collaboration with a local elementary school, spending considerable time teaching physical education in a university supervised environment where elements of SEL are embedded in every lesson taught (through affective objectives).

References

Black, P., & Wiliam, D. (2018). Classroom assessment and pedagogy. *Assessment in Education: Principles, Policy & Practice, 25*(6), 551–575.

Byra, M. (2006). Teaching styles and inclusive pedagogies. In *The handbook of physical education*, D. Kirk, D. Macdonald, and M. O'Sullivan (Eds.) 449–466. Thousand Oaks, CA: Sage.

Chatoupis, C. (2015). Pairing learners by companionship: Effects on motor skill performance and comfort levels in the reciprocal style of teaching. *The Physical Educator, 72*(5), 307–323.

Chatoupis, C. C., & Vagenas, G. (2017). Effects of two practice style formats on fifth grade students' motor skill performance and task engagement. *The Physical Educator, 74*, 220–238.

Chen, W. (2004). Learning the skill theme approach: Salient and problematic aspects of pedagogical content knowledge. *Education, 125*(2), 194–212.

Coakley, J. (2011). Youth sports: What counts as "positive youth development?" *Journal of Sport and Social Issues, 35*(3), 306–324.

Collaborative for Academic, Social, and Emotional Learning. (2019). Core SEL Competencies. Retrieved from https://casel.org/core-competencies/

Cone, T. P., & Cone, S. L. (2012). *Teaching children dance* (3rd ed.). Champaign, IL: Human Kinetics.

Deci, E. L., & Ryan, R. M. (2000). The "what" and "why" of goal pursuits: Human needs and the self-determination of behavior. *Psychological Inquiry, 11*(4), 227–268.

Deci, E. L., & Ryan, R. M. (2008). Self-determination theory: A macrotheory of human motivation, development, and health. *Canadian Psychology, 49*(3), 182–185.

Gosset, M. E., & Silverman, S. (2019). Upper elementary school students' attitudes toward physical education in skill-themes and multiactivity approaches. *The Physical Educator, 76*(5), 1225–1246.

Graham, G., Holt/Hale, S. A., Parker, M., Hall, T., & Patton, K. (2020). *Children moving: A reflective approach to teaching physical education* (10th ed.). New York: McGraw-Hill.

Hall, T. (2003). *Content development decision-making of elementary physical education teachers.* [Dissertation University of Georgia].

Lund, J., & Tannehill, D. (2014). *Standards-based physical education curriculum development* (3rd ed.). Burlington, MA: Jones and Bartlett.

Macdonald, D., Rodger, S., Abbott, R., Ziviani, J., & Jones, J. (2005). I could do with a pair of wings: Perspectives on physical activity, bodies and health from young Australian children. *Sport, Education, and Society, 10*(2), 195–209.

Mosston, M., & Ashworth, S. (2008) *Teaching physical education: First online edition.* Spectrum Institute for Teaching and Learning. (United States). [E-Book Download]

Richards, A., Ivy, V. N., Wright, P. M., & Jerris, E. (2019). Combining the skill themes approach with teaching personal and social responsibility to teach social and emotional learning in elementary physical education. *Journal of Physical Education, Recreation & Dance, 90*(3), 35–44.

Rink, J. E. (2020). *Teaching physical education for learning* (8th ed.). New York, NY: McGraw-Hill.

SHAPE America. (2013). *Grade-level outcomes for K-12 physical education.* Reston, VA: Author.

SHAPE America. (2014). *Crosswalk for SHAPE America National Standards & Grade-Level Outcomes for K-12 Physical Education and CASEL Social and Emotional Learning Core Competencies.* Reston, VA: Author.

SHAPE America. (2014). *National Standards & Grade-Level Outcomes for K-12 Physical Education.* Reston, VA: Author.

Wahl-Alexander & Curtner-Smith, M. D. (2019). Influence of negotiations on preservice teachers' instruction within the skill themes approach unit. *Journal of Teaching in Physical Education*, ahead of print.

Zins, J. E., Bloodworth, M. R., Weissberg, R. P., & Walberg, H. J. (2007). The scientific base linking social and emotional learning to school success. *Journal of Educational and Psychological Consultation, 17*(2–3), 191–210.

CHAPTER 6

Adventure-Based Learning

Sue Sutherland

Paul T. Stuhr

James D. Ressler

Daekyun Oh

CHAPTER SUMMARY

The adventure-based learning model is a student-centered, strength-based approach through which intrapersonal and interpersonal relationship skills can be developed. This chapter provides an overview of the model, the theoretical foundation and support for the model, the alignment between adventure-based learning (ABL) and social and emotional learning (SEL), and specific ways that adventure-based learning can promote life skills development. We have included a detailed discussion of five specific activities that promote SEL and a 10-day ABL unit plan that aligns with specific life skills. We conclude the chapter with our teaching tips and additional resources to provide a deeper understanding of adventure-based learning.

This chapter highlights the ways in which the adventure-based learning (ABL) model aligns with and promotes social and emotional learning (SEL). We begin by providing a brief historical overview of the development of ABL. We then discuss the theoretical foundations for and the SEL outcomes aligned with the ABL model. We end the chapter with a discussion of ABL in practice and how it aligns with and promotes SEL. The goal of this chapter is to illustrate the essential purpose and intrinsic nature of ABL with regard to guiding individuals toward cultivating SEL in physical education and activity settings. Educational settings play an important role in cultivating social

and emotional development for students. The use of ABL holds tremendous promise to create further space and opportunity for students to develop social and emotional skills through physical and experiential activities.

What Is Adventure-Based Learning?

The ABL model embodies "a student-centered approach, encompassing a form of adventure, where the educative purpose of the experience is emphasized, and students reflect on their personal and social developments through a debrief process" (Sutherland & Legge, 2016, p.308). Furthermore, ABL involves a purposeful sequence of activities that foster the development of intrapersonal and interpersonal skills (Cosgriff, 2000). The activities used in ABL can be wide ranging from more traditional outdoor endeavors such as rock climbing or white water rafting to group activities with low equipment needs that can occur within a gymnasium, classroom, or outdoor space. Whichever activities are used, the focus of ABL is on interpersonal and intrapersonal development. Accordingly, within ABL, a student-centered, strength-based approach to engaging in activity is accentuated in lieu of a win-at-all-costs, competitive mentality. The ABL model has an assortment of features that make it an appropriate and standard-based model for physical education (Stuhr, Sutherland, Ressler, & Ortiz-Stuhr, 2016), especially in relation to promoting social and emotional learning (SEL). A brief overview of the historical foundation of ABL in outdoor and/or adventure education will help to situate its current use in fostering SEL.

Outdoor and/or adventure education (OAE) within the United States has a rich history that can be traced back to the 1800s, when the focus was on the use of healthy, supervised activities for children via recreational camping. Growing out of the camping movement, OAE developed in both school and community settings beginning in the 1890s. Two main developments were the establishment of the scouting movement (1910 for boys and 1912 for girls) and the incorporation of overnight camping programs in public schools in the 1920s (Raiola & O'Keefe, 1999). The use of outdoor residential centers allowed for teaching OAE as part of the educational experience of young people from the 1950s onward. In 1961, the first Outward Bound program in the United States occurred and influenced the use of OAE within the school curriculum. Using many elements of Outward Bound, Project Adventure was developed in the 1970s specifically for use in school physical education (Prouty, Panicucci, & Collinson, 2007). Project Adventure is grounded in adventure education, which is defined as "structured learning experiences that create the opportunity for increased human performance and capacity. There is conscious reflection on the experience and application that carries it beyond the present moment" (Bailey, 1999, p.39). The Project Adventure curriculum has been a successful addition to K–12 physical education within the United States and abroad, and is the basis of the ABL model presented in this chapter.

ABL is viewed as a model that has the potential to help students develop and transfer social and emotional skills aligned with the Collaborative for Academic, Social, and Emotional Learning (CASEL, 2019) core competencies of self-awareness, self-management, social awareness, relationship skills, and responsible decision making. A well designed and facilitated ABL unit provides a strong foundation in developing many of the skills associated with the five SEL competencies. Knowledge of the ABL model is vital to understanding the alignment between ABL and SEL and how the model fosters the development of specific SEL skills, which is discussed later in this chapter.

Adventure-Based Learning Model

ABL has its theoretical roots in experiential education and experiential learning. Experiential education espouses the use of experience and critical guided reflection to increase participants' knowledge, skills, and values (Gass, Gillis, & Russel, 2012). Experiential learning is the vehicle through which learning occurs in experiential education, and in this case, within ABL. Broadly framed, experiential learning is a sequential process with components or steps that promote change and transferability of skills presented to the learner (Stuhr, De La Rosa, Samalot-Rivera, & Sutherland, 2018). Specifically, it reflects a hands-on approach in which the act of doing creates the conditions through which knowledge is constructed.

The ABL model focuses on the development of SEL through experiential learning. The student-centered ABL activities, when coupled with the reflective process, are the medium through which SEL is fostered and for potential student growth to occur. Student growth in the affective domain is the main focus of ABL and is firmly grounded in Kolb's (1984) experiential learning cycle (ELC). The affective domain refers to internal processes such as attitudes and emotions, which are often demonstrated through external behaviors. The premise of the ELC is acquiring abstract concepts through experience that can be applied in different situations. The cycle is comprised of a four-stage learning process:

- Concrete Experience: Engaging in an experience.
- Reflective Observation: Reflecting on the experience and asking the "What happened" question.
- Abstract Conceptualization: Learning from the experience; prompting a new idea or modification of an existing concept.
- Active Experimentation: Applying or transferring the learning to a new situation and reflecting on the process.

Kolb's cycle is the most widely cited model for experiential learning in the adventure education field (Priest & Gass, 2005). The importance of the ELC lies in the guided reflection process, with a primary focus on making meaning of learning in the affective domain and how that can be transferred to life beyond the activity in which it was learned.

Essential Components of the ABL Model

With the understanding that the ELC provides the overarching framework, the following five essential components comprise the model in ABL: Sequence and flow of activities, processing, facilitation and content knowledge, emotional and physical safety, and assessment (**Table 6.1**).

Sequence and flow of activities. The sequence in which the activities are presented is important in fostering SEL through the ABL model. Building on the work of Sutherland and Stuhr (2014) and Sutherland, Stuhr, and Ayvazo (2016), who in turn drew

on the work of Bisson (1999) and Prouty (1999), the sequence of activities for the proposed model is as follows: Deinhibitizers (i.e., icebreakers), communication, cooperation, emotional trust, physical trust, problem solving, and challenge. Tuckman's (1965) theory of small group development, which comprises four stages (i.e., forming, storming, norming, and performing), is helpful when designing the sequence of activities with the intent of nurturing SEL as certain group behaviors are prevalent in the different stages. *Forming* is the first stage that occurs when the members of a group first come together and begin getting to know one another. The *storming* stage occurs once the group has developed some relationships and

Table 6.1 Characteristics of the Essential Components of ABL

Essential Components	Characteristics
Sequence & Flow	*Sequence for ABL*: Deinhibitizers (or icebreakers), communication, cooperation, emotional trust, physical trust, problem solving, and challenge. Questions used to guide the sequence may include: ■ How much time do I have? ■ Who are these participants? ■ What are their prior experiences? ■ What are the goals for the unit? ■ What space or equipment do I have? *Flow*: How the sequence is chosen and experienced by each group or class.
Processing	*Brief*: Frontloading the lesson to highlight the SEL focus for the activities. A brief may include a quote, short story, YouTube clip, cartoon, photo, diagram, song, etc., that provides a focus for the lesson. *Debrief*: Where group members understand and can transfer the learning through the activities. Using a debrief strategy and/or model can help novice facilitators. The *Sunday Afternoon Drive* debrief model has been shown to be effective as a strategy in ABL.
Facilitation and Content Knowledge	*Facilitation*: Guide the group through the experiential learning process. Set the stage for the lesson through the brief, explain the boundaries of the activity, and let the group work through the process while ensuring emotional and physical safety. Conclude the lesson with a student-centered debrief. *Content Knowledge*: In addition to understanding the activities, the content knowledge needed for ABL is: ■ Understanding the importance of the sequence and flow of ABL ■ Processing ■ Facilitation ■ Challenge by Choice ■ Full Value Contract ■ Experiential Learning Theory ■ Social and Emotional Learning ■ Group Dynamics
Emotional and Physical Safety	*Emotional and Physical Safety*: Creating an environment where all students feel safe, valued, respected, and supported. Achieving this environment will allow students to fully engage in ABL and develop their SEL. Using *Challenge by Choice* and a *Full Value Contract* is important, along with a carefully chosen sequence and flow of activities for each group.
Assessment of Student Learning	*Assessment Focus*: Student understanding and development of SEL and the transfer of these skills beyond the ABL class.

members feel comfortable taking risks, which may then lead to conflict within the group. When the group develops norms for group behavior and begins to function more effectively, they have entered the *norming* stage. The *performing* stage occurs when the group begins to act as a cohesive unit and can work together on a variety of tasks. Stanfield (2016) recommends that sequencing ABL activities for groups should be set to a bar of relative scale and informed by the frequency and duration of sessions, individual and group goals, and prior experiences of the facilitator under similar circumstances. Complementing the sequence of activities with the needs and skills of the group is important. Stanchfield (2016) further compares effective sequencing to the skillset of a chef, equipped with recipes, ingredients, seasoning, materials, and space to create an entrée specific to the tastes and preferences of patrons. A facilitator, recognizing that a group is in the storming stage, creates a sequence of activities that allows the group to build communication and cooperation skills.

The flow of the activities refers to how the sequence plays out in practice with each group of participants based on their level of group development. Although the same sequence of activities could be designed for a unit of instruction with two sixth grade classes, the flow of the activities (i.e., the rate at which they move through the activities) could be different for both classes as they move at different paces through the stages of group development. A unit of instruction that does not follow the proposed sequence of activities or is not aligned with the appropriate stage of group cohesion could actually have a detrimental effect on SEL, as the experience could be miseducative and hinder the desired growth from future activities. For example, if a group is engaging in more difficult cooperation activities but has not demonstrated active listening skills, it may lead to one or two group members dominating the decision making and inhibiting other group members from contributing their ideas because they were being ignored. In turn, this may lead to disengagement from group members in future activities. **Table 6.2** outlines common issues that may arise (Frank, 2013) and for which the teacher can better prepare to address in practice.

Processing. Processing consists of frontloading the experience, otherwise known as the brief and the reflective process, otherwise known as the debrief. Frontloading the experience with a brief helps to set the stage for students to begin to think about the SEL focus of the lesson (Stuhr & Sutherland, 2013). The structure of the brief can include: a short

quote, watching a short video, listening to a short story, or looking at pictures. The debrief occurs after the experience and involves the teacher guiding the students through a student-centered reflection. The power of the ABL model ultimately lies in the debrief as it is here that the participants derive meaning of their experience and begin to understand how they can use this learning in other areas of their life beyond the activity. Under the guidance of the facilitator, it is during the debrief process that participants begin to make sense of the SEL skills (Stuhr, Sutherland, Ressler, & Ortiz-Stuhr, 2015; Sutherland, Ressler & Stuhr, 2011). Over the last 20 years, more has become known about leading an effective ABL debrief, through industry-accepted standards (Frank, 2013; Panicucci, 2007; Rohnke, 2010; Stanchfield, 2016), empirical studies (Stuhr et al., 2015; Stuhr et al, 2018), and professional papers (Schwamberger, Wahl-Alexander, & Ressler, 2017; Stuhr et al., 2016) outlining effective strategies developed and practiced in schools.

The debrief process should be student-centered and focus on the transfer of learning beyond the experience. However, learning to facilitate an effective student-centered debrief is not easy for novice facilitators or teachers (Stuhr & Sutherland, 2013; Stuhr et al., 2018; Sutherland et al, 2011; Sutherland & Stuhr, 2014; Sutherland et al, 2016). In light of these difficulties, the *Sunday Afternoon Drive* debrief model (Stuhr & Sutherland, 2013; Sutherland, Stuhr, & Ressler, 2012) was developed to provide a framework and strategies for conducting a student-centered reflection within the time constraints of a physical education setting. Our recent work has concentrated on making the model more meaningful to teachers (Stuhr et al., 2015; Stuhr et al., 2018; Sutherland et al., 2011; Sutherland, Stuhr, & Ressler, 2014). While this is certainly not the only means by which a student-centered reflection session can be conducted, we have found in our work with preservice and in-service teachers that the model is easy to use and resonates with those new to the ABL model.

The *Sunday Afternoon Drive* (**Figure 6.1**) uses the metaphor of driving a car where the facilitator has an idea of the final destination (i.e., learning outcomes) but without a set route to get there. The drive (i.e., discussion) can take many different roads but "the facilitator follows the various rhythms, feelings, power, and aesthetics of the road (i.e., the group) as they negotiate the journey" (Sutherland et al, 2012, p.6). **Table 6.3** outlines the nine components to the *Sunday Afternoon Drive* model that provide the tools and

Table 6.2 Issues within the ABL Sequence

Stage of ABL Sequence	Main Issues and Possible Solution
Communication	*Active Listening*: Not listening to all members of the group but are more interested in putting their ideas forward. Have the group decide on a process to allow each person's ideas to be heard. *Perspective Taking*: Not considering the perspective of others in their communication or engagement in the activities. Engage the group in active listening strategies.
Cooperation	*Put Up/Put Down*: Put downs are used instead of put ups and represent a form of teasing that can inhibit the full engagement of group members. Highlight examples of appropriate put ups and inappropriate put downs. *Mixing*: Group members just want to work with their own group of friends. Use strategies to mix groups to allow for working with all members. *Hidden Agendas*: Group members acting out or sabotaging an activity because they may feel they don't belong in the group, feel powerless, feel a lack of control, or feel they aren't engaged in the decision making. Finding out the root of the hidden agenda is important and then working to alleviate the cause.
Trust	*Emotional and Physical Trust*: Trust is easily broken and can result in disengagement of group members. Understanding the interplay of both emotional and physical trust is important and engaging the group in activities that focus on both. *Making Mistakes*: Placing blame and making fun when mistakes are made will quickly erode trust. Use activities where all group members will make a mistake and discuss the implications in the debrief, focusing on how to support group members when mistakes are made. *Empathy*: A lack of care for others' feelings. Highlighting the difference between a verbal message and how it is conveyed (body language). Helping group members to understand that body language speaks volumes. *Trustworthiness*: Inconsistent behavior, or consistently inappropriate behavior, toward others can lead to a lack of trustworthiness in group members. Including discussions on the debrief on the effects of untrustworthy behaviors on both individuals and group dynamics. *Risk Taking*: A lack of trust between group members inhibits risk taking and potential personal and social development. Establishing a level of trust between group members and building on this through additional activities.
Problem Solving	*Decision Making*: 'Rule of the loud' is used to make decisions resulting in only one or two group members' involvement in the process. Introduce the group to the *Five Finger Consensus* (Frank, 2013) as a decision-making tool. Each group member 'votes' on the different solutions by holding a hand in the air, demonstrating the following: ■ Five Fingers = Best thing since sliced bread ■ Four Fingers = Great ■ Three fingers = OK ■ Two Fingers = I'll go along with it ■ One Finger = I won't block it ■ Fist = Block The group can then determine which decision has the most support. If a block is given, an alternative decision must be used unless the block is deemed to be self-serving (e.g., my idea is better!) *Taking Turns*: The important, or glory, roles are always taken by the same people without considering the needs of the group. Engage the group in a strategy to ensure roles are switched when appropriate or to meet the needs of the group. *Leadership*: Certain group members always take leadership roles in every activity. Help the group to understand that there is a time to take the initiative and a time to support another group member based on the activity and the need of the group. *Conflict Resolution*: A lack of conflict resolution skills can lead to a break down in group cohesiveness. Provide win/win strategies for group members to decide conflict.

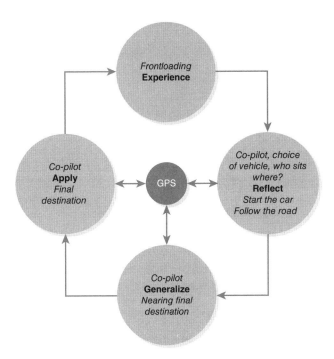

Figure 6.1 Sunday Afternoon Drive Debrief Model.

Data from Sutherland, S., Stuhr, P. T., & Ressler, J. (2012). The Sunday afternoon drive debrief model. *International Sport Studies,* *34*(2), 5-12; and Stuhr, P. T., & Sutherland, S. (2013). Undergraduate perceptions regarding the debrief process in adventure-based learning: Exploring the credibility of the Sunday Afternoon Drive debrief model. *Journal of Outdoor Recreation, Education, and* *Leadership, 5*(1), 18–36.

strategies for facilitators to lead a student-centered reflection. For a more detailed description of the model in practice, please see Sutherland et al. (2014) and Dyson and Sutherland (2014).

Facilitation and Content Knowledge. The role of the teacher within the ABL model is that of guiding the group through the experiential learning process (Dyson & Sutherland, 2014) rather than teaching them how to complete the activities. Effective facilitation is an art and includes the practice of keen observation, knowledge of and quick application of theory, as well as a growing spirit of creativity. An effective facilitator can help the process of leading groups to slow down, acutely manage the learning environment, and support students more effectively.

Once the sequence of activities has been determined for a class, the teacher begins each lesson by frontloading the focus of the day's activities and explains the objectives and boundaries of the activities The teacher then steps back and lets the students work through the activities while ensuring emotional and physical safety, stepping in to prompt or refocus the group as necessary. To wrap up the lesson, the teacher leads a student-centered debrief to help students to make meaning of the SEL skills used during the activities and how this learning can be applied to other areas of their lives. Building facilitation skills takes time to develop with plenty of repetition in framing

activity sessions, sequencing and stacking these over multiple days or leading extended excursions or training sessions.

The content knowledge needed to effectively implement the ABL model is above and beyond knowledge of the actual activities and focuses on the importance of sequence and flow of activities, processing, facilitation, challenge by choice, full value contract, experiential learning theory, SEL, and group dynamics. The ABL model does not prescribe a specific set of activities but rather a sequence to be followed that may include any of the numerous ABL activities available. The content knowledge required for the successful implementation of the ABL model may be beyond what is typically needed or indeed utilized within a physical education context. As such, some additional work may be required for those seeking to use the model within physical education or physical education teacher education (PETE; Backman, 2011; Stuhr et al., 2015; Stuhr et al., 2018; Sutherland & Legge, 2016; Sutherland et al, 2016).

Emotional and Physical Safety. To offer the best chance for SEL to develop, it is imperative to create an emotionally and physically safe environment. Stanchfield (2016) outlined skills for facilitators in leading effective ABL programming grounded in emotional safety and supports, values, and mutual respect. Strong facilitators create community in the learning environment and are quick to connect experiences to relevance and significance. To ensure emotional safety in the learning environment, Stanchfield (2016) suggests that facilitators consider the following questions: (a) "what does this group need now?" (b) "what is the sequence at this point for the group?" and (c) "what options are provided to maximize engagement and participation?" (p. 63). These questions guide the facilitator to consider if the sequence of activities helps to foster an emotionally safe environment.

In addition, using *challenge by choice* and creating a *full value contract* are two strategies to foster an emotionally and physically safe environment in ABL. Challenge by choice is one of the cornerstones of the adventure education curriculum of Project Adventure (Panicucci, 2007) as well as the ABL model as it helps to promote a caring and emotionally safe environment for students (Sutherland et al, 2016). In essence, challenge by choice means that students can choose their level of participation within an activity to support their own learning based on a variety of factors such as their own intrapersonal or interpersonal development, group

Table 6.3 Components of the *Sunday Afternoon Drive Debrief Model*

Component	Function
Frontloading	A brief or hook that provides the SEL focus of the ABL lesson.
Co-Pilot	The facilitator's role in guiding the students along the drive by offering initial questions for the debrief, helping steer the car where necessary in the following strategies, and taking more of a back seat when appropriate.
Choice of Vehicle	Refers to the grouping strategy for the debrief session from individual (motorcycle), pairs or small group (car), and large group (bus). The *choice of vehicle* is important as it can influence the level of student comfort and participation in the debrief. We recommend using a car to generate conversation before moving to a bus to enable sharing with the large group.
Who Sits Where	We prefer to use a circle format as it allows for both small- and large-group discussion and promotes student-to-student engagement rather than funneling through the facilitator.
Start the Car	The strategy used to begin the conversation or get the engine running. The quality and relevance of this strategy is important in setting the tone of the debrief. It allows the group to begin the reflection process. Please see Cain, Cummings, and Stanchfield (2005) and Stanchfield (2007) for more examples.
Follow the Road	The facilitator chooses an initial road for the discussion based on the students' responses to the start the car activity. We recommend that facilitators initially focus on the lesson outcomes or a critical incident from the lesson to guide the discussion. Honing in on roads (comments) that will lead to a powerful discussion is important and will develop with more practice. Please see Stuhr et al., (2018) for more *Follow the Road* strategies.
GPS Recalculating	There are times where it becomes obvious that the group hits a roadblock in their journey and the discussion stops. This could be because the group no longer wants to talk about the issue for whatever reason, or they have nothing else to say. When this occurs, the facilitator recalculates the route based on student responses in the *Start the Car* activity. It is better to recalculate than continue to head down a road that is going nowhere.
Nearing Final Destination	Generalization of key topics of the conversation and what strategies helped and/or hindered the groups success in the ABL activities.
Final Destination	Provides space for the group to reflect on the main take-home messages from the Nearing the Final Destination stage and engage in conversation about applying these to their lives beyond the ABL lesson.

Data from Sutherland, S, Stuhr, P. T., Ressler, J., Smith, C., & Wiggin, A. (2019). A model for group processing in cooperative learning. *Journal of Physical Education Recreation and Dance, 90*(3), 22–26, https://doi.org/10.1080/07303084.2019.1559676

dynamics, and personality traits. It is important to note that challenge by choice is not a "get-out-of-jail-free" card where no participation is required (Sutherland et al, 2016). The three main considerations for challenge by choice are that students choose when to participate and in what way, students must add value to the experience at all times, and students must respect and value the decisions of their group (Panicucci, 2007). For example, a student may decide that they do not want to participate in a blindfold activity, but they can help to ensure the physical safety of those in the activity by taking the role of a spotter.

The *full value contract* is developed collaboratively and is a social contract that provides a framework for guiding personal behaviors and interactions within the group (Dyson & Sutherland, 2014). The use of the full value contract aids in creating an emotionally safe environment for students that allows them to further explore their intrapersonal and interpersonal development through ABL. Different methods can be used to create a full value contract, but two powerful methods that we use are the *five-finger contract* (Frank, 2013) and *the body* (Sutherland, 2019). The *five-finger contract* (**Figure 6.2**) uses a visual of the hand to show a

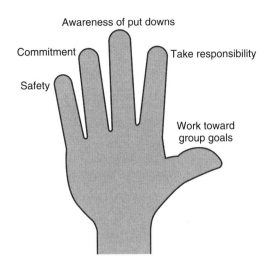

Figure 6.2 Five finger contract.

© Jones & Bartlett Learning.

behavior that is acceptable for the group during the ABL unit as follows:

- Index (Pointer) finger represents the behavior of not placing blame on others, but rather *taking responsibility* for our own actions.
- Middle finger represents being aware of the negative impact of using *put downs* rather than *put ups* with group members.
- Ring finger represents the behavior of *commitment* to work with the group and move on and not hold grudges against group members.
- Little (Pinky) finger represents a commitment to ensuring the *emotional and physical safety* of all group members.
- Thumb represents the behavior of *working toward group goals*.

The body is a way to allow students to consider and share what behaviors, actions, or words either help create or detract from an emotionally and physically safe environment. It can also be used to challenge bullying in classes. If large sheets of paper are available, students can draw around the outline of a group member for this activity. If not, gender neutral outlines are available for download on the Internet through a simple search for body outlines, or can be hand drawn if you have artistic talent. Once a body outline has been created, small groups of students discuss what they need to feel emotionally and physically safe in a class and what threatens their emotional and physical safety. After the discussion, students write what they need to feel safe inside the body, and what causes them to feel unsafe outside the body. These bodies can then be discussed as a whole class to agree upon the behaviors that are acceptable or unacceptable for the ABL unit.

Assessment of student learning. The nature of the ABL model clearly locates the emphasis on learning in the affective and cognitive domains. The focus of assessment in ABL should, therefore, be on student understanding and development of SEL skills and how they derive meaning from the skills beyond the ABL activities. Dyson and Sutherland (2014) outlined a number of assessments such as Y-charts, reflective journals, the Sunday Afternoon Drive reflection rubric, a cognitive test for the Hand of Fair Play, photo journals, and The Body project, which can provide meaningful ways of demonstrating affective and cognitive learning of SEL skills.

Photo journals can be used to help students express themselves and become self-aware through reflection of visual imagery. This type of qualitative assessment can be used to capture authentic social and emotional learning within the classroom and provide students with the opportunity to develop social and emotional skills that can be applied to other areas of their life. The goal behind the use of a photo journal is to allow students to visually capture, through photos or drawings, representations of SEL concepts that have been introduced and/or practiced in the physical education setting. Once the photos (or drawings) have been created, students can reflect on these images in an effort to develop and strengthen social and emotional skills. From a procedural standpoint, the following steps are taken in creating a photo journal: students select a SEL topic covered in class, such as empathy; find or take a personal photo (or drawing) that represents their selected SEL topic; reflect on and analyze the visual image in a way that demonstrates the individual's perspective of the SEL topic in relation to the student's lived-experience in or outside of the classroom. **Table 6.4** is an example guideline sheet that can be used at the middle-school level to help students understand how to create a photo journal.

Support for Adventure-Based Learning

ABL has become well established within K–12 physical education and PETE programs worldwide. While there have been some studies with primary or elementary school/populations, the majority of the studies have taken place with secondary school-aged populations and have highlighted outcomes associated with the CASEL core competencies of (a) *self-awareness* (intrapersonal outcomes), and (b) *relationship skills* (interpersonal outcomes).

Table 6.4 Photo Journal Assignment and Guidelines

A photo journal is a means to visually capture your thoughts and feelings as they relate to the social and emotional topics covered and experienced during your ABL unit. The goal of this project is for you to select a visual image (a photo or drawing) that represents your selected SEL topic, and then reflect on (through writing) how this image represents your selection. In this photo journal, you will write about how your image represents or is connected to your selected SEL topic. In addition, you will be asked to write 2–3 sentences about how you use (or envision using) this SEL topic in your life outside the classroom.

Process	Explanation
Step 1	Write your name at the top of your journal entry.
Step 2	Give your journal entry a title and include the chosen SEL topic. Be creative!
Step 3	Find an image or take/draw a picture that represents how you have experienced, used, or will use this SEL topic in class.
Step 4	Write a description for your image. The description should include the following: (a) describe the scenario in which the SEL topic was experienced, used, or will be used, (b) how or why this experience or SEL topic is important to you? (c) what have you learned about this SEL topic in relationship to your life? (d) describe one way you can apply this skill to your life or in a similar situation outside of class.
Step 5	Handwriting should be legible and please check for spelling and grammar.

More specifically, the findings of several studies have indicated an increase in middle school students' perceptions of social acceptance, physical appearance, athletic ability, behavioral conduct, and global self-worth after participating in a team building through a physical challenge program and an adventure curriculum for physical education (Ebbeck & Gibbons, 1998; Gibbons & Ebbeck, 2011, Gibbons, Ebbeck, Gruno, & Battey, 2018). ABL has also been found to have a significant, positive outcome on several components related to SEL, such as enjoyment, body image and self-esteem, and perceived competence (Baena-Extremera, Granero-Gallegos, & Ortiz-Camacho, 2012). The ABL model was also perceived by high school students as (a) unique and a different way to be physically active that was more motivating than traditional physical education fitness activities, and (b) a relevant curriculum to enhance components of physical self-concept such as fitness, flexibility, strength, and overall physical activity (Gehris, Kress, & Swalm, 2010). Using ABL led to a positive impact on changing the boys' perception of what it means to be physically active in physical education, specifically what it means to be competitive, take risks, and persevere (Tischler & McCaughtry, 2014).

Focusing on relationship skills using ABL has demonstrated that middle-school students found the activities to be fun and engaging, perceived the relationship skills as a valuable learning outcome, and demonstrated the positive effects that relationship skills had both inside and outside of the classroom (Stuhr et al., 2015). With upper elementary school students, ABL was effective in producing perceived social and emotional growth (i.e., commitment, helping others, leadership, and responsibility) and a catalyst in teaching, connecting to, developing, and transferring SEL skills (Stuhr et al., 2018).

Learning to teach ABL is not always smooth sailing, as highlighted in a number of studies working with preservice physical education teachers. In particular, while an undergraduate ABL course was helpful in understanding ABL and planning units of instruction, preservice teachers found a contrast between their experience of the ABL activities and the experiences of the middle school age students, and were "limited in their ability to see beyond their own experiences" (Dillon, Tannehill, & O'Sullivan, 2017, p. 452). Additionally, although preservice teachers believed in using ABL as part of a quality K–12 physical education program, it was met with resistance when taught to urban middle school students leading to the preservice teachers' belief that teaching ABL was more difficult than their own experience of ABL (Sutherland & Stuhr, 2014). The importance of incorporating a student-centered debrief (i.e., group processing) as part of the successful delivery of ABL and promoting the transfer of learning beyond the ABL activities has also been demonstrated (Stuhr & Sutherland, 2013; Sutherland et al., 2011; Sutherland et al, 2016).

Beyond the K–12 school environment, ABL and OAE have been related to Positive Youth Development (PYD), which is a strength-based approach to child and adolescent development based on the premise that all people have strengths and potential for positive change

(Damon, 2004). The enhancement of life skills, such as goal setting, emotional control, self-esteem, and hard work ethic, is a central feature of PYD settings because many studies utilize life skills as fundamental frameworks of PYD (Gould & Carson, 2008). Participating in adventure-based activities and programs has become an increasingly popular strategy to work with youth on the development of life skills such as self-esteem, self-concept, communication, group problem-solving, interpersonal skills, and group cooperation (Moote & Wodarski, 1997). Second, the developmental assets approach is also acknowledged as one of the most widespread and influential frameworks for understanding and strengthening PYD (Damon, 2004). There is compelling evidence that wilderness and adventure programs, if they are based on the developmental assets framework, can foster both internal and external developmental assets, specifically in youth who are facing obstacles that are considered risks to positive development (Norton & Watt, 2014). Third, building resilience is an important element of PYD. Youth development researchers view the field of adventure education as a promising venue for resilience enhancement, and empirical studies have supported the notion that outdoor adventure-based programs have a positive influence on strong indicators of resilience such as goal setting, aspiration, self-concept, and self-efficacy (Beightol, Jevertson, Carter, Gray, & Gass, 2012). In short, all of these findings support the notion that ABL and OAE programs play a role in promoting learning associated with PYD and aligned with SEL.

Alignment between ABL and SEL

ABL and SEL can complement one another in physical education to accentuate themes and behaviors associated with the affective domain. The sequence in ABL is clearly aligned with all five SEL competencies, and particularly with specific skills under each competency. More generally, we have found that the SEL competencies align with the ABL sequence in the following ways. First, self-awareness relates to skills developed through deinhibitizer, communication, and cooperation activities in ABL. Individuals can enhance their abilities to (a) deal with frustration through deinhibitizer activities, (b) appreciate different experiences of one another through communication activities, and (c) set their own goals and take risks through cooperation activities. These abilities are closely connected to sub-skills of self-awareness,

such as labeling one's feelings, relating feelings and thoughts to behavior, and assessing their own strengths and challenges accurately.

Second, self-management can be reinforced by communication, cooperation, trust, and problem-solving activities in ABL. For instance, communication activities highlight active listening and nonverbal communication skills. Cooperation activities help students facilitate setting a goal, putting forth effort, and taking responsibility. Trust activities emphasize positive attitudes and self-discipline skills. Problem-solving activities focus on developing participants' perseverance and patience. ABL activities can foster the development of the specific self-management skills of (a) successfully regulating one's emotions, thoughts, and behaviors, and (b) setting and working toward personal and academic goals.

Third, social awareness is closely associated with communication and cooperation activities in ABL. For example, communication activities can be used to reinforce perspective taking, which is one of the specific skills in the social awareness competency. Moreover, ABL facilitators typically encourage participants to support each other with respect in cooperation activities. The attitudes and behaviors promoted by communication and cooperation activities in ABL are aligned with the sub-skills of social awareness to (a) take the perspective of and empathize with others and (b) understand social and ethical norms for behavior.

Fourth, relationship skills are associated with all stages of the ABL sequence. Specifically, for the large majority of activities in each stage of the sequence, students are involved in group work rather than individual tasks. Thus, during the ABL activities, participants are engaging in and developing skills such as active listening, caring, supporting peers, putting forth effort, showing trustworthy behaviors, and/or taking turns. These behaviors play an important role in relationship skills, especially clear communication; active cooperation; and the willingness to resolve conflict.

Last, responsible decision making relates to cooperation, trust, and problem-solving activities in ABL. Students demonstrate appropriate risk-taking behaviors through cooperation and trust activities. They also understand the importance of safety for others, leadership, and conflict resolution through problem-solving activities. These skills have a strong connection to the sub-skills of responsible decision making such as identifying and solving problems, constructive and safe choice, and ethical responsibility. **Table 6.5** provides the alignment between the ABL sequence and the skills for each SEL competency.

Table 6.5 Alignment between the ABL Sequence and SEL Competencies

SEL Competency and Skills	ABL Sequence
Self-Awareness ■ Labeling one's feelings ■ Relating feelings and thoughts to behavior ■ Accurate self-assessment of strengths and challenges	Deinhibitizer ■ Specific skills: Dealing with frustration, sense of humor, and flexibility ■ An example activity: Morphing Communication ■ Specific skills: Appreciating different experiences ■ An example activity: Have you ever? Cooperation ■ Specific skills: Goal setting and risk taking ■ An example activity: Turnstile
Self-Management ■ Regulating one's emotions ■ Self-control ■ Setting and achieving goals	Communication ■ Specific skills: Active listening and nonverbal communication ■ An example activity: Marketplace relay Cooperation ■ Specific skills: Goal setting, effort, and responsibility ■ An example activity: Fill the basket Trust ■ Specific skills: Positive attitude and self-discipline ■ An example activity: Goal Toss Problem Solving ■ Specific skills: Perseverance and patience ■ An example activity: Knots
Social Awareness ■ Perspective taking ■ Empathy ■ Understanding social and ethical norms of behavior	Communication ■ Specific skills: Active listening and perspective taking ■ An example activity: Growth circle Cooperation ■ Specific skills: Risk taking, support peers, and goal setting ■ An example activity: Warp speed
Relationship Skills ■ Communicating clearly ■ Working cooperatively ■ Resolving conflict	Deinhibitizer ■ Specific skills: Effective listening, caring, and interpersonal interactions ■ An example activity: The big question Communication ■ Specific skills: Active listening, perspective taking, and honesty ■ An example activity: Group interview Cooperation ■ Specific skills: Support peers, effort, and risk taking ■ An example activity: Group juggle Trust ■ Specific skills: Support peers and trustworthy behaviors ■ An example activity: I trust you but... Problem Solving ■ Specific skills: Taking turns, conflict resolution, and initiative ■ An example activity: Stepping stones
Responsible Decision Making ■ Identifying and solving problems ■ Constructive and safe choice ■ Ethical responsibility	Cooperation ■ Specific skills: Risk taking and honesty ■ An example activity: Asteroids Trust ■ Specific skills: Risk taking and support peers ■ An example activity: Ready aim Problem Solving ■ Specific skills: Responsible for safety for others, leadership, and conflict resolution ■ An example activity: All aboard

ABL and SEL in Action

Over the years of leading ABL in different physical education environments, we have our go-to activities that are used to reinforce key themes. These favorites can serve different outcomes based on framing the activity and the readiness of the group. Five of our favorite activities are presented below and on the following pages to show how ABL can be used to develop SEL.

The Big Question

The Big Question (Frank, 2013) is an icebreaker activity we like to use with groups to establish a foundation for group interactions and norms for a single-day event or at the start of a university class. The activity involves participants with an index card and pen and each participant writes down a question that they would be comfortable asking anyone in the group. Once the questions are prepared, students are expected to meet one at a time and chat for about one minute. The conversation may or may not include the question on the cards. If participants have difficulty chatting for that one-minute interval, the questions are in hand as a starting point or a security to have at least one to two items to discuss. It is, however, possible and acceptable that a conversation develops unrelated to the questions on the card and they never get asked.

When we facilitate *The Big Question* for the first time, we seek to keep the environment light to emphasize a goal of meeting a person each minute and starting a conversation. After a few minutes, the facilitator may pause the activity and reinforce other goals of the task (i.e., to meet and learn more about others, as well as form a stronger connection with a new group). The facilitator circulates during the activity to monitor the communication between the participants and may restate effective communication skills such as active listening and asking follow-up questions to gain information. After five or more minutes, participants may be asked to introduce someone they just met to the larger group as a way to further connect individuals to others they may not have met one-on-one in the activity. This activity has been used to reinforce interpersonal interactions and communication. At times, other themes that have been prioritized include mixing with others, active listening, recall, and gaining perspective. A sense of belonging, fit, and connectedness are also commonly shared as positive outcomes when discussing in debrief sessions. *The Big Question* has been very well received in most every learning environment. First, it is meant to be quick paced, light-hearted, and can be reduced to simply meeting a new person per minute for six to seven minutes. Most often, we refine the activity after a few minutes to remind the group that the focus is the interaction and quick conversations, not a competition to see how many people they can meet.

When reflecting on the different ways we have organized *The Big Question*, the most common note is its effectiveness to help a new group gain comfort. This sense of ease is established through a realization that an entire group is in the same, awkward position to mix and interact with others immediately. While gaining comfort does not mean that individuals are comfortable, it serves a purpose to recognize the value of social interaction to improve a shared sense of belonging in a learning environment. In addition, we have used *The Big Question* later in a sequence when groups may be experiencing some challenges related to personal and social interactions, or if observed group behaviors may be at risk of being distant, fragmented, or hollow. We have also framed the activity differently to promote asking of higher-order questions to provoke deeper conversations and more sharing of thoughts around personal and social issues that emerge in a class or are visible in local and global communities.

Relationship skills is one CASEL (2019) competency that aligns with *The Big Question*. This is a mixing activity that promotes many interactions in a quick time frame. A residual effect is the establishment of norms around building relationships with new members of the community and improving one's understanding of diversity with a new group. Participants invariably practice their social interactions and one-on-one communication skills during the quick meetings. Effective listening and asking thoughtful questions help individuals understand the skills and other assets, which improves the *fluency* of individuals with their community and establishing humility across the group.

Growth Circles

We have also used *Growth Circles* (Frank, 2013) early in a sequence with groups to reinforce others' perspectives, and recognizing differences between themes presented in the activity such as *comfort*, *growth*, and *panic*. There are three distinct circular zones marked off by tape or cones similar in shape to a bullseye, where a smaller circle is in the center (*panic zone*), then a medium-sized circle (*growth zone*), and larger-sized outside circle (*comfort zone*). The facilitator presents individual scenarios or questions, and individuals move into the circled zones they feel are most appropriate for them. For example, "sleeping late on the weekend" may cause many participants to move toward the comfort zone while others (e.g., "taking an important test"; "driving in the middle of a large city") may have participants move toward areas of growth or panic. In each scenario, we have deliberately taken pause to coach participants to respectfully observe and support others who move into the circle they feel is most suitable for them, as well as offer time to share why they moved into a specific zone. In these moments, some students have been open to share unique stories that inform their movement into a particular zone that may have initially come as a surprise to others until gaining this additional context.

The activity has most often served as a good anchor in a given lesson for further processing, both in and after the activity and at the end of the session or later days/weeks in the scope of the ABL experience. We have used it to address the themes and zones of the activity but also other related concepts, such as risk, confidence, poise, fear, failure, and self-esteem. There are times when Growth Circles are presented lightly to help groups warm up and move into different zones based on preferences, comforts, and experiences. However, this activity has served us well when revisited during an ABL sequence to discuss when and how learning takes place. We name *comfort* as a zone in which learning does not take place, *growth* as the place where learning takes place, and *panic* as another zone where learning does not take place. On both sides of comfort and panic is an attempt to move into a competent range of growth. Comfort is safe, but stepping out of this zone to growth suggests an openness of all participants to new ideas and experiences. In these moments, individuals are breaking new ground (Frank, 2013). However, going too far in the growth zone leads to panic, and at that, individuals are experiencing a great threat and are not learning. They want to get back to the comfort zone as soon as possible.

Our facilitation of Growth Circles has ranged in time from 10-minutes to more than one hour. When participants are given the space to share their perspectives in an activity like this, others have joined in both agreement and consensus as well as offering different perspectives that arrive at the same or different zone. It has become an effective lesson for experiential learning early in an ABL sequence for groups to understand the value of experiences that influences the choices we make, which Frank (2013) refers to as personal wisdom.

Social awareness is a CASEL competency that relates well to the ways in which we have integrated Growth Circles in ABL lessons. It implies empathy, respecting differences, understanding individual and group norms, and recognizing available supports in all forms of community. There is risk involved with individuals self-selecting a zone to stand in that opposes the norms of the group. Scenarios prepared and presented by the facilitator should balance an expectation of participants gaining comfort in the activity as well as its purpose to help individuals better relate to scenarios in this public forum. For that reason, there is more risk and a greater responsibility of the facilitator to carefully present scenarios that offer the right amount of challenge as it pertains to students' movements in different zones and individuals' behaviors or responses to observing others who may be in the same or different zones. When debriefing the activity in the moment, questions are posed related to the ways we can support others as well as our own preferences for being encouraged when trying something new and less comfortable.

Ready Aim

Ready Aim (Panicucci et al., 2002) is a game that reinforces the interpersonal relationship between two participants and their communication to direct one player to toss an object to hit identified targets. Players use soft throwable objects (e.g., soft yarn or foam balls) and targets in the playing space such as bowling pins, light vertical cones, or wall markings. Participants should get into pairs and designate one person as the *launcher* and one as the *controller*. The launcher is equipped with two soft objects. The launcher is also blindfolded or has their eyes closed. On the signal, the controller guidance directs their launcher into position to throw to one of the targets. Once the launcher has been positioned and aimed, the guidance announces "fire!" and the object is thrown. Once the launcher has thrown both objects, the controller must direct their launcher to retrieve any discarded objects and continue to throw. Among the common rules include restricting the speed of moving while blindfolded, the different types of throws (i.e., underhand, with an arc), and importance of guiding the launcher in the playing space using only verbal cues and no physical contact.

When facilitating *Ready Aim* to different groups, we differentiate the playing conditions and movement patterns of the controller and the launcher. In some experiences, the launcher is walking from a starting point to a throwing area, preparing to throw, and completes the throw toward a bowling pin, taped target on a wall, basketball backboard, or some other target. In other instances, we have asked the launcher to stand blindfolded or with their eyes closed in open space in the playing area to seek targets that have been scattered throughout the playing space. Another extension that has worked well in reinforcing outcomes of the activity is the opportunity to make the playing space feel very large and open, or the ability to close off space to make it feel more restricted and cramped.

During our facilitations of *Ready Aim*, we make the time for participants to experience both controller and launcher roles. A key conversation piece and regular theme during a debrief is recognizing individual preferences in being in the role of controller or launcher and explaining one's perspective. Participants have shared their comfort level as the launcher is related to the support from their controller using clear cue words while they move across the space. Their sighted partner would continue to check in and regularly reaffirm their proximity to the launcher and praise the launcher's effort (e.g., "good job," "almost there," "you got this," "nice and easy"). Some of our observations over the years have included participants' demonstrating a sense of freedom and flexibility in the task when blindfolded, throwing objects loosely and without reservation to targets they cannot see. Others have shared their preference in being the controller and seeing success of their launcher based on their cues and feeling valued.

There have also been times when the launcher expressed reservations in completing the task because of the lack of communication or miscommunication from the controller. The launcher expressed feelings of being hurried or anxious because of noises from other groups, a tighter playing space, and uncertainty regarding targets, distance, and other obstacles. We have also observed throws and interactions from blindfolded players that are more rigid and reserved. Throwing mechanics may appear tense and tight due to nerves or discomfort in the task as presented as well as guidance from their controller. Similar feelings have been mentioned from those new to the experience of directing someone else. A fear of letting down their launcher, keeping them safe, and pressure to move faster are some barriers for comfort during the activity.

Responsible decision making is a CASEL competency that aligns appropriately with the facilitation of *Ready Aim* discussed above. Concepts such as caring, choices about personal behaviors, and examining actions show relevance in both the roles of controller

and launcher throughout the activity. In *Ready Aim*, the activity can help unpack perspectives and attitudes related to choosing to be more assertive or passive in different roles, measuring issues of safety, and checking the norms of the surrounding environment. While the differences and preferences for both roles have been mentioned earlier, the role of the facilitator is vital to initiate this reflection and conversation during the debrief session. For example, we have often heard feelings of isolation or vulnerability from the launcher when not supported by their controller. Debriefing these feelings provides an opportunity to emphasize the consequences of our actions on others, choices made outside of ABL experiences, and what responsible decision making looks like. The practical application or transfer of these themes include leadership, trust, and confidence.

Group Juggle

Group Juggle (Frank, 2013) is an activity that is commonly used for teambuilding and cooperation. There are numerous approaches to the activity that can address other themes and, even though it is known as a group activity, it can also help address individual preferences, challenges, and goals. Simple rules of the activity are for participants to "juggle" or toss an object (e.g., yarn ball, bean bag, stuffed animal, rubber chicken) to their peers who are standing in a circle. Each object juggled is meant to represent a theme or idea that the entire group values as being important and necessary to the success and productivity of the group. Once the object has been tossed and caught by everyone, the group may be asked to toss the object around the circle but in a specific pattern. For example, each person should pass the object to someone not directly to their right or left, everyone should throw and catch the object once, and it begins and ends with the same person. If the object is ever dropped, a player picks it up and continues to toss the object in the same pattern.

One of our favorite approaches to introducing *Group Juggle* early to participants in an intact group (e.g., class, club, team) is scaffolding the themes most important for the vitality and productivity of the given group. For example, the introduction of a theme such as "empathy" on the first day may help address circumstances later with the same group where empathy may not be fully present or positive. Other common themes "juggled" include honesty (with each other), joy, and being yourself around the group. Throughout the activity, extensions are added to promote norms expected by the facilitator when working as a group, including eye contact, expressing gratitude, showing care, and delegitimizing failure or frustration. It is a common practice among our team to discuss the importance of being good jugglers in this activity where the objects truly represent the assigned theme.

As described above, *Group Juggle* could be observed as a very deliberate exercise of throwing an object around a circle in a specific pattern to participants. However, we have regularly led sessions with groups that integrate extensions to the activity such as adding multiple objects (themes) to juggle at the same time, reversing the pattern of the juggle, and either tightening or expanding the circle to make it more difficult for the group to juggle. Another strategy commonly used by our team is to say the name of the person to whom you are throwing, or thank the person to whom you threw an object, or both. At that moment, with multiple objects being juggled in a pattern and the audible volume of every participant recognizing others in the group when an object is thrown, the activity may seem hectic. It is often at this time when there is so much activity that the facilitator recognizes group progress of keeping objects in a pattern, or if the objects were true representations of the valued themes (e.g., caring, honesty, hard work), it may afford the facilitator a chance to ask participants to describe what a caring, honest, and hardworking group would look like a couple of weeks from now.

Group Juggle is a unique activity that allows facilitators to scaffold a range of ABL themes most important for a given group and a given time, and to come back to the activity later to revisit the same themes. Additionally, the activity may be used to pause or reset a group, to remind participants of their group norms, or to adjust the pace of the juggling because it may be a metaphor for unrealistic individual goal setting or based on the speed and number of objects being juggled (e.g., the perfect child, the best student, the greatest athlete, the most successful entrepreneur, etc.). There are instances when the facilitator may intervene to ask if the juggling is realistic for you and/ or the group. Other common themes recalled from *Group Juggle* include commitment, positivity, multitasking, selflessness, and personal management.

Self-awareness is one CASEL competency that closely relates to *Group Juggle*. Concepts such as feelings, self-assessment, challenges, self-efficacy, and optimism have strong links particularly as conversations unfold during debrief sessions related to the themes juggled and generated at a personal level. When examples are asked to be self-created or thought about when engaged in *Group Juggle*, there is a dependence on others and of you to be a reliable

participant in the juggling of themes or concepts that you may not have fully considered before. The activity has helped our team push forward with issues of equity, inclusivity, social justice, and individualism. *Group Juggle* highlights the notion of being connected through the sharing of objects in a pattern and reliance on others to achieve goals.

Goal Toss

Goal Toss (Frank, 2013) may be used to reinforce personal behaviors and actions in an activity that is largely dependent on individuals' collective, simultaneous success. The entire group of participants complete each step at the same time. The purpose of the activity is to count from 1 to 10 and perform a particular motion with the objects (yarn ball, tennis ball, bean bag) used for each number. For example, step 1 is to throw an object in the air; step 2 is to throw the object in the air, clap once, and catch it; step 3 is to clap twice, etc., all the way to step 9 (throw object in the air, do a little dance, and catch it) and step 10 (throw, say a celebratory phrase, and catch). To advance from step 1 to step 2, every participant must complete step 1 successfully at the same time. If that does not happen, the entire group stays at step 1. If the entire group completes steps 1–6 successfully and in unison but makes an error on step 7, the entire group returns to step 1.

Planning and using *Goal Toss* in an ABL program can work well at different stages of a group's development. At the beginning of an experience when a group will work together for an extended time, it can work as a way to build in failure and reinforce the notion of the acceptability of making mistakes in the learning environment. Recently, a group of graduate students who participated in *Goal Toss* shrugged their shoulders and chanted the phrase, "No big deal!" when someone in the group made a throwing, catching, or timing error. The regular practice of this verbal cue and shoulder shrug became a fun reminder of not taking all experiences so seriously, and to reset and keep trying.

Two other prominent themes regularly emphasized in *Goal Toss* is goal setting, especially at the very beginning of the activity or after 1–2 trials, as well as cooperation and completing each step in sync. Goal setting could take the form of individuals' estimating the number that the group could achieve and sharing it with someone else or the entire group coming up with a target number/step to complete successfully during an allotted time. As for cooperation in *Goal Toss*, our most vivid examples are related to all participants adjusting their pace and care as a group progresses through steps 6, 7, and all the way until 10. It's also more easily detected when one of the participants serves as the vocal leader and calls out the rhythm to begin and complete each step. When a group is working well until an error is made late in the 1–10 step sequence, the encouraging chant of "No big deal!" carries more importance and should be recognized for its place in the activity, or if the positive norm of built-in failure is compromised.

Among the CASEL competencies, *Goal Toss* carries a strong connection to self-management. It is a regular theme addressed during the debrief, particularly when participants share the unexpected feeling of stress, pressure, and tension in the moment and throughout the activity when the entire group continues to advance beyond the first few steps of the activity. When debriefing *Goal Toss*, participants regularly comment about the feeling of potentially letting the group down. Some share their feelings of nervous energy of approaching the goal and the real pressure to achieve all 10 steps. Other ways in which *Goal Toss* has been integrated includes a more cooperative, lighthearted game that overtly reinforces trial and error and enjoyment of the process while scaffolding and adapting each step for all 10 to be achieved. In ABL programming, self-management emerges through collaboration and perspective taking of others—especially when participating in a large group where errors are made early and often. Embracing trial and error through individual goal setting allows for a shift toward an achievement perspective and valuing the collective success of being able to strive toward a target "step" with coordinated leadership, communication, understanding, and perseverance.

The five activities shared above are regularly used by us to reinforce specific personal and social interactions and highlight key themes for an ABL lesson, unit of instruction, or program. They were also presented in a sequence aligned to the ABL model with most attention given to early themes of the sequence such as SEL skills. The activities presented were selected because they are versatile and can be implemented earlier or later in an ABL sequence, depending on the needs of the group. While each activity has its own expected outcomes, the activities themselves do not fully represent ABL. This section is just a snapshot of activities that could be implemented as part of the ABL sequence. When activities are planned for specific groups in a specific context, the ABL model may elicit expected outcomes as well as unique, shared experiences for a group informed by the early and careful planning of activities.

ABL Unit Plan

In addition to the five activities stated above, **Table 6.6** presents an example of a 10-day ABL unit plan that provides the structure for teaching ABL in middle school physical education. Each lesson in this plan addresses specific SEL competencies, so that it highlights how the ABL unit is connected to SEL. A variety of brief strategies are included to set the stage for each lesson in a way that gets students to think about SEL competencies and specific skills that will be addressed through the physical activities. We provide a total of 30 activities, which are aligned with SEL competencies. Detailed descriptions and procedures of the activities are available in the following books:

- Panicucci et al., (2002). *Adventure Curriculum for Physical Education Middle School.*
- Frank (2013). *Journey Toward the Caring Classroom: Using Adventure to Create Community*

The debrief strategies and questions are also included as examples of what can be used each day. Physical education teachers can switch these strategies around based on how the group is working and their comfort level with the debrief strategy. The debrief strategy provides the "*Start the Car*" stage of the *Sunday Afternoon Drive* model. The questions listed for each day are provided as possible questions the teachers can ask as they progress through each phase of the *Sunday Afternoon Drive* model. It is important to understand that these questions are provided as a guide and that the conversation should be driven by the students. Groups of students may move through the ABL sequence differently (e.g., some groups will move through stages more quickly than other groups) depending on how well they work together. Thus, teachers can adjust the unit plan accordingly based on how each class functions and works together.

Final Thoughts

Through this chapter, we have provided an overview of the ABL model and how it can be used to promote SEL. Below, we offer six points that we believe will enhance your teaching of ABL.

- *Flow is important—no artificial timeline.* ABL cannot and should not be taught on an artificial timeline. Every class or group is different and they will determine how quickly they move through the sequence of activities. As a facilitator, you will need to adjust the plan based on how each

Table 6.6 ABL 10-day Unit Plan with SEL Alignment

Lesson 1 — De-Inhibitizer	Lesson 2 — De-Inhibitizer	Lesson 3 — Communication	Lesson 4 — Communication
Focused SEL competencies ■ Self-awareness ■ Relationship skills	**Focused SEL competencies** ■ Self-awareness ■ Relationship skills	**Focused SEL competencies** ■ Self-awareness ■ Self-management ■ Social awareness ■ Relationship skills	**Focused SEL competencies** ■ Self-awareness ■ Self-management ■ Social awareness ■ Relationship skills
Brief "All human beings are born with unique gifts. The healthy functioning of our community depends on its capacity to develop each gift." — Peter Senge 'The Learning School'"	**Brief** "A mind is like a parachute. It does not work if it is not open." — Frank Zappa, Multi-instrumentalist	**Brief** "A clever arrangement of bad eggs will never make a good omelet." — C S Lewis, Writer	**Brief** "Wise people talk because they have something to say; fools because they have to say something." — Plato
Activities ■ Name tag ■ Categories and line ups ■ The big question See Frank (2013) for detailed descriptions of the three activities.	**Activities** ■ Morphing ■ Screaming Toes ■ People to people See Frank (2013) for detailed descriptions of the three activities.	**Activities** ■ Growth circles ■ Group interview ■ Everybody's it See Frank (2013) book for detailed descriptions of the three activities.	**Activities** ■ Marketplace relay ■ Blob tag ■ FFEACH See Panicucci et al (2002) book for detailed descriptions of the three activities.
Debrief ■ Follow the Sunday Afternoon Drive model. ■ A debrief strategy and possible processing questions are listed below.	**Debrief** ■ Follow the Sunday Afternoon Drive model. ■ A debrief strategy and possible processing questions are listed below.	**Debrief** ■ Follow the Sunday Afternoon Drive model. ■ A debrief strategy and possible processing questions are listed below.	**Debrief** ■ Follow the Sunday Afternoon Drive model. ■ A debrief strategy and possible processing questions are listed below.
Think, pair, share. Have students choose a partner to discuss the following questions with. Remind the students that they will share their discussion with the whole class. ■ What did you learn about your peers? ■ Why is it important to know people's names? ■ Were these competitive activities? ■ What are some of our similarities and differences? ■ What are some of the other things that make each one of us unique?	*Draw a face (Emotion Cards)* Provide students with a pen/pencil and paper. Ask students to draw a face that demonstrates how they felt when participating in the activities. Each student will then share their pictures and provide a brief explanation. Alternatively, you can preprint emotion cards using clip art or emoticons and ask students to choose a face that best represents how they felt during the activities. ■ Did you think these games were fun? Why or why not?	*Crumpled paper* Ask students to write something on the piece of paper that they would not normally share with people they don't know well. Then ask them to crumple the paper and put it in the middle of the circle. Students will take a piece of paper from the middle and read it to the group. Use the following questions as a guide if needed. ■ What does your paper tell us about the group? ■ What types of things do we share with one another upon first meeting them? ■ What does this tell us about first impressions?	*Thumbs up, thumbs to the side, and thumbs down* Guide a discussion that focuses on building community in physical education. Rate how we (or you) did during the activities, and say why you rated it that way. ■ How was communication important in these activities? ■ Could you have been successful if you weren't communicating with each other? ■ Did you see instances where the communication broke down? What was the result of this breakdown?

(continues)

Table 6.6 ABL 10-day Unit Plan with SEL Alignment *(continued)*

Lesson 1 — De-Inhibitizer	Lesson 2 — De-Inhibitizer	Lesson 3 — Communication	Lesson 4 — Communication
■ What were you able to learn about people in this class? ■ How did it feel when you were in the middle in the name tag activity? ■ How did your group help you to feel comfortable in these activities?	■ Was this hard for you? How? ■ What made this game fun/not fun for you? ■ Did it matter who you were partners with? ■ What are ways for people to connect so they have an opportunity to become friends?	■ Why shouldn't we rush to judgment when getting to know someone? ■ Why should we give someone a second chance at making that first impression? ■ How can we make those around us feel more comfortable with sharing their feelings? ■ How can we avoid rushing to judgment with our peers?	■ What are some strategies that you can use to enhance your communication within the group? How can you further develop your communication skills? ■ Are there areas in your life where you could improve in your communication? ■ Is there someone in your life who you could help to improve communication?

Lesson 5 — Cooperation	Lesson 6 — Cooperation	Lesson 7 — Emotional Trust	Lesson 8 — Physical Trust
Focused SEL competencies ■ Self-awareness ■ Self-management ■ Social awareness ■ Relationship skills ■ Responsible decision making **Brief** http://www.youtube.com/watch?v=1qzzYrCTKuk	**Focused SEL competencies** ■ Self-awareness ■ Self-management ■ Social awareness ■ Relationship skills ■ Responsible decision making **Brief** Look at the following picture and keep it in mind while we go through the activities today © Jones & Bartlett Learning.	**Focused SEL competencies** ■ Self-management ■ Relationship skills ■ Responsible decision making **Brief** A little girl and her father were crossing a bridge. The father was kind of scared so he asked his little daughter, *"Sweetheart, please hold my hand so that you don't fall into the river"* The little girl said: *"No, Dad. You hold my hand."* *"What's the difference?"* Asked the puzzled father. *"There's a big difference,"* replied the little girl. *"If I hold your hand and something happens to me, chances are that I may let go of your hand. But if you hold my hand, I know for sure that no matter what happens, you will never let my hand go."*	**Focused SEL competencies** ■ Self-management ■ Relationship skills ■ Responsible decision making **Brief** **Trust!** Trust takes years to build, seconds to break, and forever to repair. – *Author Unknown* © Jones & Bartlett Learning.

(continues)

Table 6.6 ABL 10-day Unit Plan with SEL Alignment *(continued)*

Lesson 5 — Cooperation	Lesson 6 — Cooperation	Lesson 7 — Emotional Trust	Lesson 8 — Physical Trust
Activities ■ Warp speed ■ Asteroids ■ Fill the basket See Panicucci et al (2002) for detailed descriptions of the three activities.	**Activities** ■ Circle clap ■ Group juggle ■ Turnstile See Panicucci et al (2002) for detailed descriptions of the three activities.	**Activities** ■ Goal Toss ■ Ready aim ■ I trust you but... See Panicucci et al (2002) and Frank (2013) for detailed descriptions of the three activities.	**Activities** ■ Trust lean ■ Quantum leap ■ Velcro circle See Panicucci et al (2002) and Frank (2013) for detailed descriptions of the three activities.
Debrief ■ Follow the Sunday Afternoon Drive model. ■ A debrief strategy and possible processing questions are listed below.	**Debrief** ■ Follow the Sunday Afternoon Drive model. ■ A debrief strategy and possible processing questions are listed below.	**Debrief** ■ Follow the Sunday Afternoon Drive model. ■ A debrief strategy and possible processing questions are listed below.	**Debrief** ■ Follow the Sunday Afternoon Drive model. ■ A debrief strategy and possible processing questions are listed below.
Bumper sticker With a partner design, a bumper sticker on a piece of paper that depicts something that happened in the activities. Each pair shares their bumper sticker with the group ■ How does it feel to be excluded from the class? ■ How does it feel to have to rely on someone else to keep you in the game? ■ Are you more comfortable working with people or by yourself? And why? ■ What are things you thought the class did poorly as a group? ■ What are things you think the class did well today in class? ■ If you received help from your classmates, how did that make you feel? ■ If you didn't receive help from your classmates, how did that make you feel? ■ What is the importance of having strong bonds with your classmates and teams? ■ What happens if these bonds are broken during the class? ■ How does getting "put-down" affect the whole team?	*Miniature metaphors* In a small group of three, pick a miniature metaphor that depicts something that happened or they felt during the activities. Share the metaphor with the group. ■ How did you have to work together? ■ What happened if you didn't work together? ■ Did everyone contribute the best they could? ■ Why is it important to play by the rules? ■ How can you ensure that all play by the rules? ■ How can you ensure that you play by the rules outside of this class? ■ Give some examples from your life of needing to play by the rules	*Pairs poem* In groups of 2–3, give students time to create a haiku poem that relates to the day's experiences. Groups will share their poems with the class ■ Did you feel at risk during this activity? ■ What did you do to keep yourself and others safe? ■ What did your partner do to keep you safe? ■ How do we encourage other students to continue to take risks? ■ Why is emotional trust so important? ■ Did you feel self-conscious when you made a mistake? ■ What helped you to keep trying? What kept you from trying? ■ How did the group help or hinder the success of these activities? ■ How will this affect your trust of others in future activities?	*Statue* In groups of three students will strike a pose related to something that happened during the activities and others will view each of the poses for a period of 15 seconds. The teacher will ask students to explain their poses if necessary. ■ What does it take to trust others with your physical safety? ■ What did you do as a spotter to help the other person? ■ How did your group engender trust? ■ Did you find that it was easy or hard to trust your partner? Why? ■ What could your partner have done to help you trust him or her better? ■ How do you build trust? ■ Once the trust has been built, how do you keep it? ■ If you break the trust among other people, how can you rebuild it? ■ How can trust help you to cooperate better with others? ■ In real life, how can the amount of trust we have with an individual affect us?

Table 6.6 ABL 10-day Unit Plan with SEL Alignment *(continued)*

Lesson 9 — Problem Solving	Lesson 10 — Problem Solving
Focused SEL competencies ■ Self-management ■ Relationship skills ■ Responsible decision making	**Focused SEL competencies** ■ Self-management ■ Relationship skills ■ Responsible decision making
Brief https://www.youtube.com/watch?v=cbSu2PXOTOc	**Brief** "For every failure there is an alternative course of action. You just have to find it. When you come to a roadblock, take a detour." — Mary Kay Ash, Businesswoman
Activities ■ Mass Pass ■ Welded Ankles ■ Stepping Stones See Panicucci et al (2002) for detailed descriptions of the three activities.	**Activities** ■ All Aboard ■ Knots ■ Balloon Trolleys See Panicucci et al (2002) and Frank (2013) for detailed descriptions of the three activities.
Debrief ■ Follow the Sunday Afternoon Drive model. ■ A debrief strategy and possible processing questions are listed below.	**Debrief** ■ Follow the Sunday Afternoon Drive model. ■ A debrief strategy and possible processing questions are listed below.
Snapshots Everyone needs to close their eyes and silently reflect back on the previous activities. Now by yourself, you'll need to take a mental snapshot of a key moment, frame it in a picture frame, and then verbally present this snapshot to the class. ■ What feelings were you experiencing in your snapshot? ■ What was the strategy that you used and did it work? ■ What allowed you to be successful? ■ What hindered your success? ■ Did you just go with the first strategy or did you look for alternative ideas and then select the best one? ■ Did anyone have an idea that was not used or maybe not heard and how did that make you feel? ■ Can anyone think of how strategies can be used outside of our class?	*Song title* With a partner, students should choose a song title that represents how the group worked together to complete the activities. Each pair will then share and explain their song title to the group. ■ What happened when the group began to be frustrated? ■ What strategies did you use to overcome the frustration? ■ Did anyone have an idea that was ignored? ■ How did you feel if your strategy was ignored? ■ How did being negative or positive about the activities make you feel? ■ How did you feel about the leadership? ■ How did the leadership benefit you and your group? ■ How can we learn from the activities we fail at both within and beyond this class?

class/group works together. This may mean adding more activities in a particular stage in the sequence to allow the class/group time to develop the necessary SEL skills.

- *Emotional and physical safety.* Developing SEL is very difficult if a student doesn't feel safe in the class or environment. Using the concepts of *Challenge by Choice* and the *Full Value Contract* can help to create an environment in which all students feel safe, valued, and respected. As the facilitator, ensuring students' safety is a high priority and one that cannot be overstated.
- *Facilitate.* For some, facilitating rather than giving direct instruction may be a new teaching strategy, but it is of vital importance in an ABL unit. The goal is to allow the group time to work through the activities as these are the vehicle to develop SEL skills. Teaching a class/group how to solve an activity undermines the experiential learning process.
- *Overprepare.* As stated above, classes/groups will move through the sequence and indeed through each lesson at a different rate. Therefore, it is important to prepare more activities than you may actually need to allow for flexibility. Having more activities will also allow you to change activities based on how well a class/group is working on that particular day.

- *Leave time to debrief.* The debrief is where the students derive meaning from their learning in terms SEL. This is where the "magic" happens. Allowing adequate time for the debrief is essential for developing SEL. If you are not accustomed to using part of a class session to hold reflective discussions, this may be an adjustment but it is nonnegotiable in our view. The debrief is also where planning for the transfer of learning beyond ABL occurs.
- *Debrief tips.* The debrief has been recognized as the most difficult segment of leading an ABL lesson. Some suggestions for gaining comfort in leading a debrief include preparing and asking open-ended questions, visualizing outcomes of participants in certain activities, notating turning points with a group during activity time or debrief, making notes of importance in each activity, paraphrasing powerful student comments, asking follow-up questions to obtain clarification or go deeper into specific concepts or ideas, acknowledging student comments with positive praise, adding the instructor's perspective when appropriate, and promoting more participant engagement through self-reflection, paired groupings, and small-group instruction.

As can be expected, it is difficult to provide an in-depth discussion of the intricacies of the ABL model within one chapter. In addition to the information provided in this chapter, we point you to the following resources to further enhance your understanding of the ABL model.

- Dyson, B., & Sutherland, S. (2014). Adventure Education in Your Physical Education Program. In *Standards-based physical education curriculum development* (3rd Edition). Edited by Jacalyn Lund & Deborah Tannehill. Burlington, MA: Jones & Bartlett.
- Frank, L. (2013). *Journey toward the caring classroom: Using adventure to create community* (2nd ed.). Bethany, OK: Wood 'N' Barnes.
- Sutherland, S. (2012). Borrowing strategies from adventure-based learning to enhance group processing in cooperative learning. In *Cooperative learning in physical education: An international perspective.* Edited by Ben Dyson & Ashley Casey. London: Routledge Publishing.
- Sutherland, S., Stuhr, P. T., Ressler, J., Smith, C., & Wiggin, A. (2019). A model for group processing in cooperative learning. *Journal of Physical Education, Recreation and Dance 90*(3), 22–26.
- Stuhr, P. T., Ressler, J., Sutherland, S., & Ortiz-Stuhr, E. M. (2016). The nuts and bolts of adventure-based learning: From brief to debrief and beyond. *Journal for the California Association for Health, Physical Education, Recreation and Dance, 2*(2), 6–12.
- Stuhr, P. T., Sutherland, S., Ressler, J., & Ortiz-Stuhr, E. M. (2016). The ABCs of adventure-based learning. *Strategies: A Journal for Physical and Sport Educators, 29*(1), 3–9.

Questions for Discussion

1. In general, how can ABL promote SEL in physical education?
2. What specific features are embedded in ABL that promote social and emotional growth?
3. What historical movements and organizations helped pave the way for ABL?
4. What are some of the nonnegotiables for teaching ABL in physical education?
5. Why is the sequence and flow of the activities in ABL foundational?
6. What are some assessment examples to demonstrate student learning from ABL?
7. Why is group processing or use of a debrief critical in helping to promote SEL in ABL?
8. What is the Sunday Afternoon Drive Debrief Model? How is this model used during delivery of an ABL lesson?
9. What strategies can educators use to promote student-centered debrief sessions?
10. What are the advantages and disadvantages of using ABL as a model in physical education?

Example of Small-Group Activities

This small group activity is ideal at the start of the term to help preservice teachers begin to understand some of the more prominent features and best practices of teaching ABL in physical education. The jigsaw activity requires the preservice teachers to form groups of five or six. Using the resource from Stuhr et al., (2016), titled the ABC's of ABL, the instructor will hand out four to six features/best practices from the article. Each preservice teacher will read their features and take notes on the importance of each. Once everyone has finished taking notes, one at a time, each group member will share aloud their four to six features/best practices while the other members of the group listen. This small group jigsaw activity allows all preservice teachers to be exposed to over 25 ABL features. If time permits, the instructor can extend the activity by having each group choose their top three features in terms of importance in promoting SEL in an ABL unit. Then, each group can share their top three with the rest of the class aloud.

Another small-group activity that the PETE instructor may use in teaching ABL is the compass points activity—an exercise for understanding preferences in group work. The gym is set up with four signs, one in each corner. Each direction has its own characteristics (i.e., North—likes to act first, South—likes to consider others' feelings and voices before acting, East—likes to look at the big picture before acting, and West—likes to pay attention to detail before acting). Students are invited to choose one of the signs based on the description and move to that area in the gym. Within each group (north, south, east, west), students are asked to answer questions such as "What are the strengths and/or limitations of your style?" "What style do you find most difficult to work with and why?" or "What do you value about the other three styles?" When complete, they report back to the whole group. Through this activity, students have a chance to think about the individual differences and how these differences might influence group work (i.e., cooperation) in ABL.

References

Backman, E. (2011). What controls the teaching of *friluftsliv*? Analysing a pedagogic discourse within Swedish physical education. *Journal of Adventure Education and Outdoor Learning, 11*(1), 51–65.

Baena-Extremera, A., Granero-Gallegos, A., & Ortiz-Camacho, M. (2012). Quasi-experimental study of the effect of an adventure education programme on classroom satisfaction, physical self-concept and social goals in physical education. *Psychologica Belgica, 52*(4), 369–386.

Bailey, J. (1999). A world of adventure education. In J. Miles & S. Priest (Eds.), *Adventure programming* (pp. 39–42). State College, PA: Venture.

Beightol, J., Jevertson, J., Carter, S., Gray, S., & Gass, M. (2012). Adventure education and resilience enhancement. *Journal of Experiential Education, 35*(2), 307–325.

Bisson, C. (1999). Sequencing the adventure experience. In J. Miles & S. Priest (Eds), *Adventure programming* (pp. 205–214). State College, Venture Publishing.

Collaborative for Academic, Social, and Emotional Learning (CASEL). (2019). *Core SEL competencies.* Retrieved from https://casel.org/core-competencies/

Cosgriff, M. (2000). Walking our talk: Adventure based learning and physical education. *Journal of Physical Education New Zealand, 33*(2), 89–98.

Damon, W. (2004). What is positive youth development? *The Annals of the American Academy of Political and Social Science, 591*(1), 13–24.

Dillon, M., Tannehill, D., & O'Sullivan, M. (2017) "I know when I did it, I got frustrated": The influence of 'living' a curriculum for preservice teachers. *Journal of Teaching in Physical Education, 36*(4), 445–454.

Dyson, B., & Sutherland, S. (2014). Adventure education in your physical education program. In J. Lund, & D. Tannehill (Eds.), *Standards-based physical education curriculum development* (3rd ed.; pp. 229–254). Burlington, MA: Jones & Bartlett.

Ebbeck, V., & Gibbons, S. L. (1998). The effect of a team building program on the self-conceptions of grade 6 and grade 7 physical education students. *Journal of Sport and Exercise Psychology, 20*(3), 300–310.

Frank, L. (2013). *Journey toward the caring classroom: Using adventure to create community* (2nd ed.). Bethany, OK: Wood 'N' Barnes.

Gass, M. A., Gillis, H. L., Russell, K. C. (2012). *Adventure therapy: Theory, research, and practice.* New York, NY: Routledge.

Gehris, J., Kress, J., & Swalm, R. (2010). Students' views on physical development and physical self-concept in adventure-physical education. *Journal of Teaching in Physical Education, 29*(2), 146–166.

Gibbons, S. L., & Ebbeck, V. (2011). Team building through physical challenges in gender-segregated classes and student self-conceptions. *Journal of Experiential Education, 34*(1), 71–86.

Gibbons, S., Ebbeck, V., Gruno, J., & Battey, G. (2018). Impact of adventure-based approaches on the self-conceptions of middle school physical education students. *Journal of Experiential Education, 41*(2), 220–232.

Gould, D., & Carson, S. (2008). Life skills development through sport: Current status and future directions. *International Review of Sport and Exercise Psychology, 1*(1), 58–78.

Kolb, D. (1984). *Experiential learning.* Englewood Cliffs, NJ: Prentice Hall.

Moote, G. T., & Wodarski, J. S. (1997). The acquisition of life skills through adventure-based activities and programs: A review of the literature. *Adolescence, 32*(125), 143–167.

Norton, C. L., & Watt, T. T. (2014). Exploring the impact of a wilderness-based positive youth development program for urban youth. *Journal of Experiential Education, 37*(4), 335–350.

Panicucci, J. (2007). Cornerstones of adventure education. In D. Prouty, J. Panicucci, & R. Collinson (Eds.), *Adventure education: Theory and applications* (pp. 33–48). Champaign, IL: Human Kinetics.

Panicucci, J., Faulkingham Hunt, L., Kohut, A., Rheingold, A., & Stratton, N (2002). *Adventure Curriculum for Physical Education Middle School*. Berverly, MA: Project Adventure Inc.

Priest, S., & Gass, M. (2005). *Effective Leadership in Adventure Programming*. Champaign, IL: Human Kinetics.

Prouty, D. (1999). Project adventure: A brief history. In J. Miles & S. Priest (Eds.), *Adventure programming* (pp. 93-101). State College, PA: Venture Publishing.

Prouty, D., Panicucci, J., & Collinson, R. (2007). *Adventure education: Theory and practice*. Champaign, IL: Human Kinetics.

Raiola, E., & O'Keefe, M. (1999). Philosophy in practice: A history of adventure programming. In J. C. Miles & S. Priest (Eds.), *Adventure programming* (pp. 45–53). State College, PA: Venture Publishing.

Rohnke, K. (2010). *Silver bullets: A guide to initiative problems, adventure games and trust activities* (2nd ed.). Dubuque, IA: Kendall Hunt.

Schwamberger, B., Wahl-Alexander, Z., & Ressler, J. (2017). Ensuring moral development in physical education. *Strategies: A Journal for Physical and Sport Educators, 30*(2), 33–37.

Stanchfield, J. (2016). *Tips & tools for the art of experiential group facilitation* (2nd ed.). Bethany, OK: Wood 'N' Barnes.

Stuhr, P. T, De La Rosa, T., Samalot-Rivera, A., & Sutherland, S. (2018). The road less traveled in elementary physical education: Exploring human relationship skills in adventure-based learning. *Education Research International*. doi.org /10.1155/2018/3947046

Stuhr, P. T. & Sutherland, S., (2013). Undergraduate perceptions regarding the debrief process in adventure-based learning: Exploring the credibility of the Sunday Afternoon Drive debrief model. *Journal of Outdoor Recreation, Education, and Leadership, 5*(1), 18–36.

Stuhr, P. T., Sutherland, S., Ressler, J., & Ortiz-Stuhr, E. M. (2015). Students' perception of relationship skills during an adventure-based learning unit within physical education. *Journal of Outdoor and Environmental Education, 18*(1), 27–38.

Stuhr, P. T., Ressler, J., Sutherland, S., & Ortiz-Stuhr, E. M. (2016). The nuts and bolts of adventure-based learning: From brief to debrief and beyond. *Journal for the California Association for Health, Physical Education, Recreation & Dance, 2*(2), 6–12.

Stuhr, P. T., Sutherland, S., Ressler, J., & Ortiz-Stuhr, E. M. (2016). The ABC's of adventure-based learning. *Strategies: A Journal for Physical and Sport Educators, 29*(1), 3–9.

Sutherland, S. (2019). Challenging bullying: Lessons from Adventure-based learning. In J. Walton-Fisette, S. Sutherland, & J. Hill (Eds), *Teaching about social justice issues in physical education* (pp. 43-52). Charlotte, NC: Information Age Publishing.

Sutherland, S., & Legge, M. (2016). The possibilities of 'doing' outdoor and/or adventure education in physical education/ teacher education. *Journal of Teaching in Physical Education, 35*(4), 299–312.

Sutherland, S., Ressler, J., Stuhr, P. T. (2011). Adventure-based learning and reflection: The journey of one cohort of teacher candidates. *International Journal of Human Movement Science, 5*(2), 5–24.

Sutherland, S., & Stuhr, P. T. (2014). Reactions to implementing adventure-based learning in physical education. *Sport, Education and Society, 19*(4), 489–506.

Sutherland, S., Stuhr, P. T., & Ayvazo, S. (2016). Learning to teach: Pedagogical content knowledge in adventure-based learning. *Physical Education and Sport Pedagogy, 21*(3), 233–248.

Sutherland, S, Stuhr, P. T., Ressler, J., Smith, C., & Wiggin, A. (2019). A model for group processing in cooperative learning. *Journal of Physical Education Recreation & Dance, 90*(3), 22–26. doi: 10.1080/07303084.2019.1559676

Sutherland, S., Stuhr, P. T., & Ressler, J. (2012). The Sunday afternoon drive debrief model. *International Sport Studies. 34*(2), 5–12.

Sutherland. S., Stuhr, P.T., & Ressler, J. (2014). Group processing in cooperative learning: Using the Sunday afternoon drive debrief model. *Active & Healthy: Australian Council for Health, Physical Education, and Recreation. 21*(2), 12–14.

Tischler, A., & McCaughtry, N. (2014). Shifting and narrowing masculinity hierarchies in adventure physical education: Status matters. *Journal of Teaching in Physical Education, 33*(3), 342–362.

Tuckman, B. W. (1965). Developmental sequence in small groups. *Psychological Bulletin, 63*(6), 384–399.

CHAPTER 7

Teaching Personal and Social Responsibility

David S. Walsh

CHAPTER SUMMARY

The purpose of this chapter is to introduce the Teaching Personal and Social Responsibility (TPSR) model (Hellison, 2011) as a supporting approach for the integration of the social and emotional learning (SEL) framework. While there is a difference in the language used for TPSR and SEL, there is also a strong degree of overlap. The chapter highlights how the TPSR model is a well-developed pedagogical model that represents best practices for developing SEL competencies. A full description of TPSR ideas, goals, and strategies for implementation are provided.

Teaching Personal and Social Responsibility

The Social and Emotional Learning (SEL) framework includes a range of social and emotional competencies organized into five broad categories: self-awareness, self-management, social awareness, relationship skills, and responsible decision making (Collaborative for Academic, Social, and Emotional Learning (CASEL), 2019). The purpose of this chapter is to introduce the TPSR model (Hellison, 2011) as a supporting approach for the integration of SEL in physical education. The TPSR model is a well-developed pedagogical model that represents best practices for developing SEL competencies. In recent years, colleagues of mine in the TPSR community have been bridging the similarities between SEL and the model (Jacobs & Wright, 2014; Gordon, Jacobs, & Wright, 2016). They describe a difference in the language used for TPSR and SEL but have concluded that there is a strong degree of conceptual and practical overlap. Richards, Ivy, Wright, and Jerris (2019) also provide a progression of SEL learning competencies in elementary physical education through the TPSR model goals (TPSR Levels), further justifying this alignment.

What Is TPSR

The TPSR model was developed by Don Hellison through a process of trial and error over several decades. In his first book, *Humanistic Physical Education* (Hellison, 1973), he explained the philosophical approach and values that eventually shaped the model. As he developed these ideas through his direct experience working with troubled or "at risk" youth, he added more concrete goals and strategies, such as described in *Beyond Balls and Bats* (Hellison, 1978). Since that time, TPSR has continued to evolve through other books written by Hellison (1985, 1995, 2003) as well as a large number of chapters and articles written by him and his colleagues. The goals and structure of the model as it is today are fully explained in the third edition of Hellison's (2011) book, *Teaching Responsibility through Physical Activity*. TPSR is applied by physical education teachers, coaches, and youth workers throughout the United States and many other countries such as Australia, Brazil, Canada, New Zealand and Spain. It has been field tested in school-based physical education as well as in after-school and community-based programs. The practical effectiveness of the model and its unique approach to empowering students makes it appealing to practitioners and also align with the SEL competencies. Moreover, the base of empirical and theoretical literature supporting the model has expanded over a period of almost 50 years.

The Big Picture of the TPSR Model

The TPSR model promotes student learning in the cognitive, psychomotor, and affective learning domains, but it places a primary emphasis on the affective domain (Metzler, 2005; Parker & Stiehl, 2010). Another point that distinguishes TPSR from traditional instruction in physical education is that physical activity and motor development are not viewed as an end in and of themselves, but rather as a means to an end. The ultimate aim of this model is to help students develop themselves as people, learning to be responsible for how they conduct themselves and treat others (Hellison, 2011).

Before getting into more of the details of the model, Hellison (2011) describes TPSR program leader responsibilities that are more in line with the true essence of the model. First is the idea of *being relational with students*. None of the ideas and strategies in the TPSR model will matter or work if the teacher does not have a certain kind of relationship with students. This is a challenging concept to write about because the way we talk to students, get to know them, and share parts of ourselves with them are unique and personal to each of us. Being relational with students must be genuine and real; however, a few key concepts to help describe being relational is to recognize that every student has strengths, is an individual and needs to be recognized that way, has a voice that needs to be heard and valued, and has the capacity to make good decisions. Second is the idea of *empowerment*. To be considered a TPSR model program, teachers need to believe in facilitating an empowerment process, gradually shifting responsibility—"the power"—to their students. The idea is that as students become more responsible, they assume more of a role in the decisions and direction of the program. Third is the idea of *reflection*, both *self-reflection* and *group reflection*. To be considered a TPSR model program, teachers need to focus on helping students reflect on their own actions and performance, which is also a form of empowerment. The model has reflection strategies built into the daily format that I address later on in this chapter. Fourth is the idea of *embedding certain life skills* into the physical activity. These life skills are often referred to as TPSR goals, personal and social responsibilities, or levels that can be practiced in the gym or on the playing field. Fifth is the idea of helping students *transfer* the life skills to other areas of their life beyond the physical activity setting. These life skills are described in the next section.

The TPSR Levels of Responsibility

The primary goals of the TPSR model are often referred to as *Levels of Responsibility* (Hellison, 2011). As indicated in the name of the model, the framework Hellison developed came to focus on two aspects of responsibility, personal (how we conduct ourselves) and social (how we treat others). The levels of the model are organized into a loose progression and address both of these. Level 2 (participation and effort) and Level 3 (self-direction) relate to personal responsibility with the former addressing more fundamental objectives and the latter addressing more empowerment-based and autonomous objectives. Level 1 (respecting the rights and feelings of others) and Level 4 (leadership) relate more to social responsibility with the former representing the least we can do for others and the latter representing the ideal. Level 5 (transfer "outside the gym") was incorporated into the model to operationalize Hellison's intention to impact the lives of students beyond the sport or physical activity setting. Next, the Levels are described along with examples of objectives, or life skills, which are connected to them.

Level 1: Respect for the Rights and Feelings of Others

In TPSR, respecting the rights and feelings of others is a fundamental aspect of social responsibility. At a minimum, this level calls for students to do no harm to others. However, the ideal is that they demonstrate this proactively by recognizing the inherent value in others and treating them accordingly. Behaviors often used to operationalize this level include controlling one's temper and impulses to avoid doing harm to others verbally or physically. Examples of more proactive behaviors are including others, recognizing and appreciating individual differences, developing empathy and understanding of others viewpoints, and resolving conflicts peacefully. According to Gordon, Jacobs, & Wright (2016), the two SEL competencies that strongly align with TPSR Level 1 and are integrated into its teaching practice are self-awareness and self-management.

Level 2: Participation and Effort

In TPSR, participation and effort are fundamental aspects of personal responsibility. At a minimum, this level calls for students to partake in the activities and educational tasks. Beyond this, it is hoped that students will fully engage in these activities and try to give their personal best. Behaviors often used to operationalize this level include self-motivation, staying on task, trying your best, and persisting in difficult tasks. Ideally, we want to see students take responsibility for motivating themselves so that they can approach tasks in this manner without requiring constant supervision and prodding from the teacher. According to Gordon, Jacobs, & Wright (2016), the two SEL competencies that best align with TPSR Level 2 and are integrated into its teaching practice are positive decision making and self-awareness.

Level 3: Self-Direction

In the TPSR model, self-direction is an aspect of personal responsibility. It is more advanced than participation and effort in that it involves the student in taking greater responsibility for their learning. The behavioral objectives and life skills commonly related to self-direction include working independently,

setting and working toward goals, and making good decisions. However, this list can be expanded to include acting with autonomy, planning and/or directing one's own progress, being a self-regulated learner, expressing one's voice in program decisions, and resisting peer-pressure. According to Gordon, Jacobs, & Wright (2016), the two SEL competencies that best align with TPSR Level 3 and are integrated into its teaching practice are self-management and self-awareness.

Level 4: Leadership

In TPSR, leadership is an aspect of social responsibility. It builds on the basic expectation of respecting the rights and feelings of others. When students have genuine concern for the welfare of others and find ways to show it, they can contribute to creating a caring environment in which their own learning experience and that of their classmates is more positive (Newton, et al., 2007). The behavioral objectives and life skills commonly related to leadership can be as simple as encouraging classmates, to taking on more advanced roles like leading a group or peer-coaching. Students in TPSR programs are also challenged to reflect on and enact an ethic of caring. Noddings (1992) has been a leading proponent of the importance of caring in educational environments. According to Gordon, Jacobs, & Wright (2016), the two SEL competencies that align strongly with TPSR Level 4 and are integrated into its teaching practice are relationship skills and social awareness.

Level 5: Transfer "Outside the Gym"

Level Five could be considered the ultimate goal of the TPSR model. It represents the enactment, in other settings, of the personal and social responsibilities contained in the first four levels. The assumption is that once students have learned and practiced the various TPSR levels and life skills in the physical activity setting, they should be able to "transfer" this knowledge and behavior to other settings. The first step in this process is cognitive, for example, seeing and understanding opportunities for transfer. The second step is more behavioral, for example, actual application of the TPSR levels and life skills outside of the gym. According to Gordon, Jacobs, & Wright (2016), the three SEL competencies that align most directly with TPSR Level 5 and are integrated into its teaching practice are positive decision making, self-awareness, and social awareness. The SEL literature also describes a need for its principles to be applied across academic areas and in different learning contexts. This notion is also compatible with Level 5 and the goal of transfer.

The TPSR Daily Format

Hellison (2011) developed a daily lesson plan format to organize lessons in a way that would effectively promote these goals and objectives. It consists of five components that are also intended to address parts of the big picture and true essence of the model. The format gives structure to the model and a way to help effectively and systematically implement the model.

Relational Time

The first component of the TPSR lesson format is *Relational Time*. This refers to the informal one-on-one interactions the teacher has with students that help to create a welcoming environment and establish personal relationships. It is an opportunity to chat, ask students how their day is going, and discuss things that may be going on in their lives. Unlike the other components that occur in a specific order, *Relational Time* can happen whenever an opportunity arises (i.e., before or after the lesson, or even during the lesson while the students are in transitions).

Awareness Talk

The next component of the lesson format is the *Awareness Talk*. Having clearly defined goals is essential for effectively facilitating SEL. The *Awareness Talk* is consistent with this SEL concept by helping students connect the program goals (TPSR Levels) to the physical activity content. This is a brief, structured meeting that officially begins the lesson. During this talk, usually just a few minutes, the teacher can go over the plan for the day, invite input from students, and most importantly, remind them of the goals and objectives of the program. Depending on the stage (explained more fully later) of the program, a teacher might be focusing on a particular aspect of responsibility or just reminding students of the overall emphasis in the program, for example, how they conduct themselves and how they treat others (see Appendix D for Awareness Talk questions to consider using).

The Physical Activity

Next begins the third component of the lesson format, the *Physical Activity*. A way to promote SEL competencies is to create active forms of learning. With the TPSR model, the program goals (TPSR levels) are integrated into the physical activity content. This constitutes the majority of the lesson and could involve any age-appropriate physical activity, exercise, or sport content that would normally be taught to a given group in their physical education program. The key difference is that the teaching strategies employed during this activity time shift power to the students and provide them with responsible roles. The idea here is to integrate the teaching of responsibility with the teaching of the physical activity. In a later section, a number of specific strategies for how to achieve this will be described.

Group Meeting

Part of the SEL framework is for students to build self-awareness through recognizing their emotions, strengths, and weaknesses. A part of the TPSR Model daily format that strongly aligns with this SEL concept is the fourth component of the lesson plan format called the *Group Meeting*. A *Group Meeting* takes place after the physical activity is completed. The teacher gathers students together to discuss the lesson. This provides students with an opportunity to share their opinion about the lesson, make suggestions, as well as comment on the group's performance and cohesion. If the day's activities had involved student leadership, this *Group Meeting* could provide a safe and structured opportunity for students to provide feedback to their peer-leaders and vice versa. About five minutes are necessary for this meeting and it can transition smoothly into the fifth and final component of the lesson format, *Reflection Time*.

Reflection Time

Whereas the Group Meeting focuses on group reflection, *Reflection Time* provides the opportunity for individual reflection, which is also part of the SEL framework of building self-awareness through recognizing their emotions, strengths, and weaknesses. For the last few minutes of the lesson, students are asked to reflect on their own attitudes and behaviors during the lesson. Using the responsibility levels as reference points, the teacher prompts the students to think about their performance that day. Depending on the number of students and the climate of the program, the teacher may have students share their self-reflections verbally, with a hand signal (e.g., thumb up for "great," sideways for "okay," or down for "needs work"), or writing in a reflective journal.

A Day in the Life of the TSPR Model Implementation

If you were to observe a 7th grade basketball lesson in a class where the physical education teacher had been progressively implementing TPSR for the past 15 lessons, it might look something like this (Wright & Walsh, 2018):

> Students enter the gym having informal conversations with both the teacher and peers. The teacher, Ms. Thomas, talks to various students about their day, their previous experiences in class, and other life adventures since the last class session. After a few minutes, Ms. Thomas brings the class together for an Awareness Talk. As the students have grown accustomed to these talks, Ms. Thomas has advanced to asking a general question to prompt her students to talk about TPSR Levels 1–4 in their own way, "Who has some words of wisdom to get us focused for the day?" Following several student comments, the teacher discusses how to transfer the TPSR Levels to other areas of their lives such as in school, at home, and in the community (Level 5). Next, the Physical Activity Lesson begins with Ms. Thomas signaling students to begin working on their individualized basketball goals (Level 3). She scans the class to make sure students are independently on-task, asking many of them to describe their goals. Checking in on students individually further develops effective teacher-student relationships. During goal-setting time, she then gathers four students who have taken on major leadership roles, asking if they are each ready to organize the class into fair teams—without choosing in front of the class—and run a team practice (Level 4). These leaders are told their practice should include a few drills, offensive and defensive strategies, and any other preparation needed to get ready for the game. She helps make any needed adjustments to their plan based on the rest of the students' skill levels and needs. Ms. Thomas then makes suggestions for each of four major leaders to recruit an assistant coach to take on minor leader roles, another form of leadership (Level 4). At this point the rest of the class has been working on individual goals for about 10 minutes. The teacher then signals both major leaders and minor leaders to gather their four teams and begin the practice. All other students are reminded to focus on being respectful to all classmates (Level 1) and participate in the leaders' activities (Level 2). Ms. Thomas helps the teams that either ask for it or seem to need it, providing both general and specific basketball feedback in addition to TPSR Levels comments. When the student leaders are ready, the teams play five versus five games. During earlier stages in the program, students have learned to referee their own games, solve their own conflicts, and make sure everyone is included in the game. With about 10 minutes left in the class period, Ms. Thomas calls the class together for a Group Meeting. She asks the major leaders to talk about the day, followed by minor leaders, and then the rest of the students. This group reflection and group empowerment has evolved over several class sessions in which students have learned how to constructively talk about likes, dislikes, problems, and changes to future class sessions. Ms. Thomas then provides feedback on the session and makes thoughtful and inspirational connections to the transfer of the TPSR Levels to other areas of their lives (Level 5). Finally, she moves on to individual empowerment through Reflection Time. Students are asked to individually reflect on each of the five TPSR Levels one at a time, indicating their self-rating with a hand gesture: a thumb pointing up for "great job," sideways for "okay," down for "needs work." Finally, Ms. Thomas closes with some positive comments about the students' performance, an indication of what will be covered in the next lesson, and a challenge for the students to experiment with transfer before the next class so they can come in with one concrete example of how they applied one of the TPSR Levels in another setting.

Characteristics of TPSR

The TPSR goals/levels and lesson format described above are two of the most well-known features of the model. Even though Hellison (2011) has laid out the goals and objectives for a TPSR program as well as a framework to organize instruction, teachers still need more detailed approaches to implementing the model and concrete ways of knowing if they are, "doing it right." There can be difficulty in the implementation of the model because the model is, by its very nature, flexible and adaptable (Richards & Gordon, 2017). It is an approach to working with students based on a particular teaching philosophy rather than a scripted or formulaic curriculum. Next, I provide two strategies for effective implementation of the model. First, I address the idea of fidelity to the model, which includes certain student interactions and behaviors that serve as good indicators that they are experiencing and enacting the model as it was intended (Wright & Craig, 2011; Escarti, Wright, Gutierrez & Pascual, 2015). Second, I address the idea of implementing the model through three "Developmental Stages," which were created to provide a systematic progression to implementing the various components of the model, slowly shifting more responsibility and empowerment from the teacher to the students (Walsh, 2016; Walsh 2008).

Fidelity to TPSR Implementation

The teaching strategies proposed for assessing the fidelity of TPSR implementation were articulated by Wright and Craig (2011) as the core content of an observational instrument, the Tool for Assessing Responsibility-based Education (TARE). These nine strategies are not meant to be exhaustive; others could certainly be identified. However, they provide a manageable list of concrete strategies that are consistent with the TPSR teaching philosophy and frequently used by experienced practitioners. The TARE strategies include the following:

- *Modeling Respect:* The teacher models respectful behavior in interactions with the students and others.
- *Setting Expectations:* The teacher organizes all aspects of the lessons and clearly communicates directions and behavioral expectations to students.
- *Providing Opportunities for Success:* The teacher structures all activities so that no students are excluded or unable to successfully participate due to individual differences.
- *Fostering Social Interaction:* The teacher creates structures that allow students to have interactions with one another that are not directly controlled by the teacher.
- *Assigning Management Tasks:* The teacher asks students to contribute to the management and organization of the lesson by taking on specific tasks or jobs.
- *Promoting Leadership:* The teacher shares some instructional responsibility with students by giving them the opportunity to instruct or lead some of their peers.

- *Giving Choices and Voices:* The teacher creates opportunities for students to voice their opinions, offer suggestions, and make decisions.
- *Involving Students in Assessment:* The teacher lets students engage in self- and/or peer-assessment.
- *Addressing Transfer of Life Skills:* The teacher directly addresses the life skills taught in the program and their application outside of the program.

These are framed as strategies because they represent certain pedagogical approaches to move students toward the desired TPSR goals and objectives. Under each, there are numerous specific tactics that a teacher might use depending on the content and the nature of the group. For example, promoting leadership is a general strategy that could be implemented with various tactics such as (a) having one student lead the whole class in warm up exercises, (b) assigning team captains for a soccer game, (c) having the class work through fitness stations, each with a student leader, and (d) having students pair up and take turns being peer-coaches.

Appendix A: TPSR Implementation Checklist, which is provided at the end of the chapter, includes the nine TARE strategies. In the end, the teaching strategies from the TARE are not prescriptive but provide guidelines for assessing implementation. For more complete descriptions and examples of these TARE strategies, refer to the article describing the original instrument (Wright & Craig, 2011). A post-teaching reflection version of the instrument has also been published in Hellison's (2011) last textbook. Also, a number of responsible behaviors are often observed among students in high functioning TPSR programs, which are articulated in a second version of the TARE (TARE 2.0; Escarti, Wright, Gutierrez & Pascual, 2015). It has been developed to include a set of student behaviors that can be observed in group interactions throughout a lesson. Appendix A also includes these nine concepts to consider reviewing for a checklist:

- *Participating:* Students are following directions and taking part in the activity at hand.
- *Engaging:* Students are demonstrating high degrees of attention, interest and/or effort in the task at hand.
- *Showing Respect:* Students are interacting with others in respectful ways and abstaining from disrespectful behaviors.
- *Cooperating:* Students are collaborating effectively on a shared task.
- *Encouraging Others:* Students are conveying support for others verbally or nonverbally.

- *Helping Others*: Students are assisting others to accomplish a task.
- *Leading*: Students are taking responsibility for directing their peers.
- *Expressing Voice*: Students are expressing their views and opinions.
- *Asking for Help*: Students are asking for assistance from the teacher and/or their peers.

Like the TARE teaching strategies, these categories of student behavior are broad and serve as reasonable indicators that students are receiving and enacting the core lessons of the TPSR model. Certainly, other examples can be found in practice and in the literature, but if you frame your program around the TPSR Levels, organized lessons around the TPSR lesson format, and consistently implemented the TARE strategies noted above, you would gradually see increases in many of these student behaviors. Taken together, these factors constitute the pedagogical infrastructure of the TPSR model.

The TPSR Model through Developmental Stages

I have spent the past 17 years teaching a year-long progression of the TPSR model to physical education teacher education (PETE) students at San Francisco State University. When I initially began teaching a course on the model, they struggled with the concept associated with empowerment such as how to give students a voice in their class, and how to help students learn independence and leadership skills. They also struggled with having a different lesson plan format and overall purpose of physical education. Based on these struggles, I created "TPSR Developmental Stages" to provide PETE students with a systematic progression to implementing the various components of the model, slowly shifting more responsibility and empowerment from the teacher to the students (Walsh, 2016; Walsh 2008). An exact time frame for advancement to the next developmental stage requires teachers to be reflective and intuitive about when a given class is ready for more advanced responsibilities.

Advancement may take several months and even years for the final developmental stage, all of which depends on the students' ability to take on the advanced stages and the teacher's ability and comfort in empowering their students. In the following paragraphs, a description of each developmental stage is provided within the context of the TPSR lesson format described earlier. Of course, any given lesson

should have appropriate cognitive and psychomotor objectives. My focus here is on the affective objectives, which are framed around the TPSR levels. It should be noted that *Relational Time* is similar across all developmental stages; however, the depth and connection with students intensifies in later stages.

My most recent students have a question of the day to create dialogue and a lighthearted feel before getting into their lessons. A few examples are, "Does pineapple belong on pizza?" and "Who is your favorite superhero and why?" It seems to take away inhabitations, helps students laugh, blurt out their thoughts in a light-hearted way, and connect with their teacher and peers on a topic they surely know about. The main point of *Relational Time* is to develop relationships by conveying that they are unique individuals, have strengths and a voice that matters, and the ability to make good decisions. Therefore, in the following paragraphs I illustrate the progression of a program through the developmental stages in terms of what occurs in the *Awareness Talk, Physical Activity, Group Meeting*, and *Reflection Time* components. In each case, I give approximate proportions of time devoted to various topics. The percentages provided are only estimations and also vary depending on both the teacher and students (see Appendix B & C for lesson plan development).

Developmental Stage 1

In this stage, the focus is generally on TPSR Levels 1 and 2. In the *Awareness Talk*, the teacher would focus on Levels 1 and 2 and this talk would be 100% teacher led. The teacher could ask specific questions regarding respect, self-control, and positive attitude (Level 1) as well as effort and teamwork (Level 2). The teacher might then provide specific examples following student comments. Be sure to ask engaging questions to keep students' interest and allow them to address these two basic personal TPSR Levels. Common mistakes I have seen are asking questions with little acknowledgment of students' responses. Or talking about the TPSR levels without students voicing their thoughts about what they mean and what they could look like during the physical activity. Empowerment begins in Developmental Stage 1 with students being able to voice their thoughts. Students should have the opportunity to talk and teachers should recognize and elaborate on student comments (see Appendix D for Awareness Talk questions).

During the *Physical Activity*, the teacher should integrate Levels 1 and 2 during 100% of the class time. In other words, teach the physical activities providing demonstrations, cues, drills, tactics, game sense, feedback, etc. The physical activity taught in Developmental Stage 1 resembles a traditional physical education setting. The teacher might stop the lesson two to three times (or as needed) for brief check-ins, for example, to ask students how they are doing with Levels 1 and 2. After hearing student responses, the teacher might then provide his or her perceptions very briefly without disrupting the momentum of the physical activity.

With about five to seven minutes left in a class session, stop the physical activity and gather the students for the final two TPSR components, *Group Meeting* and *Reflection Time*. The *Group Meeting* involves group reflection when students can express their likes, dislikes, and overall perception of the day's physical activities including Levels 1 and 2. This is a beginning form of empowerment that increases in the future stages. Students should first be asked to provide their own thoughts and perceptions followed by the teacher so you do not influence their reflections. The teacher then provides his or her own overall perceptions of the class session including Levels 1 and 2 thoughts and insight into what is to come in the next class sessions. A common mistake I have seen is that teachers allow students to voice their thoughts, but do not acknowledge what the students are saying. I suggest simply reiterating what a student says, maybe say, "Thanks for the great comment," or "I also thought the class put in great effort today." If an idea is proposed for future lessons, let the students know that you will take note of their idea and try to integrate it into a future lesson.

Lastly, during *Reflection Time*, students individually reflect on Levels 1 and 2 using a thumb scale (i.e., up, sideways, or down), which is also a beginning form of empowerment. The teacher might ask, "how respectful were you toward others (Level 1)?" "how was your self-control (Level 1)?" "how was your attitude (Level 1)?," "how hard did you try today (Level 2)?," or "how well did you work as a team (Level 2)?"

Developmental Stage 2

Once students are, for the most part, being respectful to each other and are putting a good effort into the physical activities taught, it is time to introduce the more advanced TPSR model Levels. In this stage, the affective objectives would broaden to include TPSR Levels 1–4. In the *Awareness Talk,* the teacher would (a) facilitate a reminder of Levels 1 and 2 (80% student led/20% teacher led), and (b) introduce and focus on Levels 3 and 4 (100% teacher led). Students should be able to talk about Levels 1 and 2 with

minimal help from the teacher. The teacher should then talk about examples of the new responsibilities offered including helping and leadership roles, considering welfare of others (Level 4), and working independently and making good personal choices (Level 3). The teacher should make sure to provide specific examples of what these levels look like in practice (see Appendix D for Awareness Talk questions).

During the *Physical Activity*, the teacher should integrate activities that highlight Levels 1 & 2 approximately 30% of the time. This could include some teacher-directed activities for students to demonstrate Levels 1 and 2 and advance the physical activity content. Roughly 70% of the time should be devoted to activities that highlight Levels 3 and 4. The teacher should provide time for students to work independently (Level 3) by describing what quality self-direction time looks like, and the idea of making good decisions for themselves. I suggest beginning by offering three specific choices for students to choose to work on for a designated period of time. It is useful to start with five minutes, which should be extended as students learn how to be more self-directed. A common mistake I see teachers make is that they do not walk around and check in on what students are working on during Level 3 time. It is a great time to extend relational time, to connect with students individually, give specific feedback to help students improve on a skill, and help reiterate the idea of self-direction time.

The teacher also needs to provide opportunities for the most responsible students to take on leadership roles (Level 4). The first student leaders set the stage for others to follow in future class sessions. Begin by having student leaders run previously taught drills or activities. The teacher does not simply take a break while students run these activities, but rather helps the student leader be successful running the activities. In other words, it could give the teacher time to give more specific feedback to students who need extra help or even expand on what the student leaders are teaching. When student leaders become capable enough, they can run activities completely on their own while the teacher works with a smaller group that needs or wants the extra help. A common mistake I see teachers make is that they allow students to demonstrate an activity or help the teacher run the activity but do not let them take ownership of the drill or game. Students need to talk about the activity being taught and run as much of it as possible on their own. When giving feedback to my teachers after a lesson, I often ask, "Did the student leaders provide "leadership" or were they just "demonstrators?" It takes a few lessons of feedback from both me and their peers before they understand the difference and properly prepare and implement student leadership.

As in Stage 1, *Group Meetings* involve group reflection. In this stage; however, students who provided leadership talk about their experience with being a leader. They could be asked how well they led the group and how students responded to their leadership. Next, the rest of the students talk about how well the leaders led in addition to other likes, dislikes, and overall perception of the day including Levels 1–4. The teacher then talks about the leaders' performance, the rest of the student performance, overall perceptions of the group's implementation of Levels 1–4, and what is to come in future class sessions. A common mistake I see teachers make is that they praise a student for their leadership before allowing them to describe their own reflections on their leadership performance. Another common mistake I see teachers make is they ask student leaders to talk about their leadership experience but do not allow the rest of the class to reflect on the day, which sends a message that only a leader's voice is valued and is important. During Developmental Stage 2, I have a general "1, 2, 3 strategy": (1) leaders talk first, (2) the rest of the class talks second, and, finally, (3) the teacher talks last.

During *Reflection Time*, students individually reflect on Levels 1–4 using a thumb scale (i.e., up, sideways, or down). The teacher might prompt them with questions such as, "how respectful were you toward others (Level 1)?" "how was your self-control and attitude (Level 1)?" "how hard did you try today (Level 2)?" "how well did you work as a team (Level 2)?" "how well did you work independently (Level 3)?" and "did you provide any leadership today (Level 4)?"

Developmental Stage 3

By this stage, the students should have enough understanding and experience with the first four TPSR Levels to address the fifth and final, Transfer. During *Awareness Talks* in this stage, the teacher may prompt a reminder of Levels 1 and 2 but allow the discussion to be 100% student led. The teacher might also facilitate a review of Levels 3 and 4, with the discussion being 80% student led to 20% teacher led. Finally, the teacher can make connections between these earlier levels and Level 5; this would be 100 % teacher led. In this discussion, the teacher should provide specific "outside the gym" examples and also ask students to provide examples. A profound comment, short story, or personal experience related to transfer is strongly suggested. It needs to

be inspiring! A common mistake I see with the additional "Level 5" is a lack of teacher preparation on their delivery to the students. They seem to "wing it" and their transfer talk is either flat, too short, really long, or lacks passion and meaning. I commonly say to teachers, "your students just ran a fantastic Awareness Talk. What are you bringing to the talk?" I have found that when learning how to give an effective transfer talk, teachers should write out and practice it like any well-delivered speech. In time, they can be done more impromptu (see Appendix D for Awareness Talk questions).

During the *Physical Activity*, the teacher might provide activities that highlight Levels 1 and 2 only 5% of the time and Levels 3 and 4 about 95% of the time. In this stage, the teacher extends working independently to setting and working on goals (Level 3). Also, the best student leaders can take on more advanced leadership roles such as rather than just teaching a drill they organize and run a full lesson (Level 4). The new idea for leadership in developmental stage 3 is introducing "Major Leaders" and "Minor Leaders." Major Leaders are the students who have already been leaders in developmental stage 2. They help other students, "Minor Leaders," develop their leadership skills (Level 4). Major Leaders can help the average and even timid students become Minor Leaders to learn to provide leadership to the class. A typical approach is for a Minor Leader to simply help a Major Leader run a drill. In time, Minor Leaders can become Major Leaders and teach activities and run a full lesson on their own.

Group Meetings in Developmental Stage 3 would involve my general "1, 2, 3, 4 strategy": (1) major leaders talk first, (2) minor leaders then talk, (3) the rest of the class talks, and (4) teacher talks last. Major Leaders could also support and comment on Minor Leaders' performance. All students need to have the chance to share their likes, dislikes, and overall perception of the day including Levels 1–4. The *Group Meeting* would end with the teacher sharing overall perceptions related to Levels 1–4 and connecting these back to a statement about Level 5, transfer. An example could be, "respect, effort, setting-goals and leadership are all powerful life skills that can benefit your life. They have been guiding forces in my own life. Consider trying them out beyond physical education in your life."

During *Reflection Time*, the students would individually reflect on Levels 1–5 using a thumb scale (i.e., up, sideways, or down). The teacher might prompt them with questions such as , "how was your self-control, respect, and attitude (Level 1)?"

"how hard did you try today (Level 2)?" "how well did you work as a team (Level 2)?" "how well did you set and work on goals independently (Level 3)?" "did you provide any leadership (Level 4)?" and "have you been trying out these responsibilities outside of this class (Level 5)?"

Once again, these are general descriptions of the TPSR Developmental Stages. The actual flow and evolution of each program will vary. I encourage practitioners to use a reflective process and common sense to make adjustments as needed. For practical reference, see Appendix B & C for general lesson plans representative of each stage.

Teaching Tips on the Use of TPSR

Changing teaching styles, experimenting with new pedagogical strategies, and trying to change the culture of a physical activity program are a lot of work. Over the years I have worked with many in-service and preservice physical education teachers and youth workers who have taken on this challenge, some with more success than others. I also have almost 25 years of my own experience trying to use the TPSR model in various youth programs. I would like to end this chapter with some additional suggestions that might help you through the process. The following section includes specific strategies to foster each of the five levels in the TPSR model. The final section will include some general advice on how to approach the implementation of the model.

Strategies for Fostering Implementing the TPSR Levels

Strategies to Foster Level 1

To teach students about respect, teachers must discuss the topic directly and explicitly. Age-appropriate definitions, explanations, and examples should be provided. Basic social skills such as making eye contact, using peoples' names when speaking to them, and sharing equipment can be offered as ways to show respect. Also, it is important that the teacher looks for teachable moments to highlight respect. This might include praising a student who models respectful behavior, for example, maintaining self-control after being accidentally kicked in a soccer game. It could also include referring back to the core issue of respect when addressing a student who has failed to meet expectations, for example making fun of a classmate for being the last to finish a race.

Conflict resolution skills can be taught by first explaining the principles and desired process to students and then giving them authentic opportunities to apply them. For instance, in game situations, students can be given responsibility for calling their own fouls and making determinations about penalties on their own (Hellison, 2011). Initially, students may be stubborn and waste time arguing. However, as time passes and they realize no adults are going to intervene, they may realize they would all be better off by being honest and fair with each other so they can return to play. Other strategies for handling conflicts between individuals could involve teacher mediation and/or having the two students go off to the side to discuss their conflict until they have reached a mutual understanding—at which point they can rejoin the class. Escarti et al. (2006) refer to this strategy as the "peace bench."

A final but crucial strategy for teaching respect is modeling respect. A teacher exerts great influence over students by the example they set. One might speak about respect with students and hold them accountable, but if the teacher does not act accordingly, they are sending a mixed message. Teachers who wish to teach respect must be sure to show it to others, including to their students. They must avoid behaviors such as being intimidating, embarrassing students, and losing their temper with students. They must find ways to set expectations and to express frustration or disappointment in student behaviors without treating students disrespectfully. They must also be aware of the more subtle messages that they send. For example, if a teacher does not intervene when some students are bullying or excluding others, they are failing in their responsibility to provide a safe and inclusive environment for all their students. Beyond missing an opportunity to teach lessons about respect, they are, in these instances, condoning disrespectful behavior.

Strategies to Foster Level 2

In TPSR programs, students are challenged to participate in all activities, even those that might not appeal to them. Beyond this, they are asked to give their best effort in every task and to persist even in those that prove most difficult. To promote such behavior, the teacher should encourage students to focus on the controllable aspects of the process rather than outcomes that are not necessarily within their control. Providing instruction and feedback that highlights internal (e.g., effort, improvement, personal best) as opposed to external (e.g., final score, absolute performance, social comparison) factors are important. The teacher should create an environment in which these messages are consistently reinforced. For example, if a teacher tells students that effort is highly valued but always assigns leadership roles to the most athletic students regardless of their effort, they send a mixed message.

To promote self-motivation, it is important to provide an effective balance between challenge and success. If tasks are consistently too difficult for students, they are likely to disengage as they become discouraged and frustrated. On the other hand, if tasks are too easy and present no real challenge, students may disengage due to bordom. Therefore, in planning and organizing activities the teacher must consider the developmental stage and ability of individuals and the group overall. Well-designed activities with opportunties for differentiation will maximize the chance that each student can experience an effective balance between challenge and success.

In delivering instruction, the teacher must also remember to clearly set expectations and communicate directions. It is difficult to assess whether students are "on task" when no clear task has been assigned. Along the same lines, it is hard for students and others to know what constitutes "success" in the absense of clear objectives and expectations. It is also the teacher's responsibility to structure activities in such a way that all students have a reasonable chance to experience success. This can be achieved by allowing for appropriate modifications of the task, framing objectives around personal best, and letting students choose their level of difficulty or challenge. The most important point is to avoid creating situations in which some students will be excluded or experience failure because of their ability level.

Strategies to Foster Level 3

Like any other skill, if teachers want students to become better at directing themselves, they need to give them chances to practice. Provided that students have demonstrated sufficient levels of responsibility (i.e., Levels 1 and 2), teachers can integrate short bouts of self-direction time into their lessons. At first, this may be a period as short as five minutes. During self-direction time, the teacher can let students choose from a range of acceptable options such as practicing a skill independently, practicing a skill with a partner, or doing physical fitness exercises independently. The students must make it clear which mode of practice they have chosen and take responsibility for working on the chosen task without direct supervision for the allotted time.

Self-direction can also be promoted by giving students choices in the program. Any time students can make individual decisions, for example, which three out of four fitness stations they will visit or group decisions, for example when voting on which game to play next, they are taking more responsibility for their own learning. The same is true when students have the opportunity to provide feedback and input on the program itself. For instance, in group meetings and other structures that give students a voice in the program they have the power to evaluate and influence their learning experience.

Finally, goal-setting activities are a good way to promote self-direction. By teaching students about the value and process of setting goals, teachers are training them in a highly transferable life skill. For example, a teacher can introduce personal goal-setting activities into a physical fitness unit. The teacher can facilitate this process but it is important that the student has a sense of ownership and is given the opportunity to come up with a personal goal that is meaningful to them as opposed to being given a goal by the teacher.

Strategies to Foster Level 4

Peer coaching and leadership strategies create opportunities for students to develop qualities that convey a sense of caring such as patience, support, empathy, and sensitivity to the needs of others. In addition, TPSR teachers can promote an ethic of caring in more subtle ways. By asking for volunteers to assist with organizational tasks such as setting up equipment, teachers can provide other opportunities for students to help. They can address the importance of helping and caring for others in group discussions. They can stress the importance of empathy for others as well as the importance of considering the needs of individuals and group welfare. It is also important to stress how meaningful it is to offer supportive comments and encouragement to others. Hopefully, TPSR teachers not only model these behaviors but also praise and highlight them when they see their students engaging in them.

Strategies to Foster Level 5

In most TPSR programs, transfer is addressed in group discussions during *Awareness Talks, Group Meetings,* and *Reflection Times.* Of course, the topic can be broached with individual students during *Relational Time.* In discussions, an instructor may introduce the idea of transfer by highlighting very concrete examples in familiar contexts such as the classroom or home environment. For example, a teacher could highlight the importance of students controlling their temper (Level 1) when a classmate accidentally bumps into them in the hall, concentrating (Level 2) in math class even if they are feeling bored, doing extra music practice (Level 3) at home even if no adults have required it, and helping (Level 4) to clean the house with a positive attitude. With time, the teacher can ask students to provide their own examples to check their understanding of transfer for each of the levels.

Beyond demonstrating their knowledge by discussing hypothetical examples, students can be assigned or given the challenge to actually apply the levels and report back to the teacher in follow-up discussions or a written reflection. Some advanced ways to accomplish this could be organizing service learning or volunteer experiences for the students to participate in, discussing the aspects of transfer in these experiences explicitly, and having students process and reflect on them to solidify the connections to lessons from the TPSR program.

General Advice for Getting Started

As I stated at the beginning of this chapter, the TPSR model goals and strategies are very different from traditional approaches to teaching physical education. The thought of the primary goal of physical education as helping students developing themselves as people, and learning to be responsible for themselves and others, is surely novel to most physical education teachers. Where to begin can be seen as a daunting task. In the following section, I describe three strategies for getting started (Wright & Walsh, 2018).

Start Small

One potential mistake is to try and change everything at once. If the strategies and structures of TPSR are new to you, it may be wise to add one piece at a time and experiment with it until you build your confidence and feel ready to add the next piece. You might go through a few rounds like this before you feel ready to introduce an entire unit framed around the model. When you get to that stage, you may want to just try out a mini-unit, again, to build your experience and confidence with the aspects that are new to you. Keeping the developmental stages in mind could take a lot of pressure off of getting started. In Developmental Stage 1, you don't need to address all five levels, just the first two! Also, bear in mind

that when starting out, you don't need to implement TPSR in all of your classes. At first, you may want to select one class to try it with. How to choose that class is up to you. You may pick one of your easiest classes to minimize the risk of problems, or, on the other hand, you may pick one of your most challenging groups because you think they need it the most. In the end, I simply encourage you to take small steps in developing your skills, and building your confidence to avoid feeling overwhelmed and unsuccessful from the beginning.

Assess Your Implementation

Appendix A is a simple form that would allow you or a colleague (provided they also understand TPSR) to quickly assess which aspects of the model were clearly implemented in any given lesson. After some basic documentation for recordkeeping purposes, you would circle which TPSR Developmental Stage best describes your program at that point. Next, you would go on to check the TPSR Levels you had addressed, the components of the TPSR Lesson Format you used, the TARE Teaching Strategies you employed, and the Student Behaviors from the TARE 2.0 that you observed. This checklist could be completed after each lesson or at the end of each week. Even a simple approach like this will help you stay focused on the key elements of the model and help you to document the progression of your program. It is also useful in prompting reflection on your strengths and areas for improvement. Of course, if you like, you can adapt this basic form and make it more detailed by adding more room for contextual information and expanding the rating scales.

Assess Your Students

Personal and social responsibility is part of the content (see Chapter 4 on Assessment by Richards, Starck & Wright). Just as you would want to assess student performance relative to your cognitive and psychomotor objectives, so should you assess their performance on these objectives. This can be achieved through teacher observation, but we also encourage you to use more authentic and structured assessments. You could create rubrics aligned with TPSR objectives that could be self-, peer-, or teacher-administered (or all three). Students could also complete a reflective journal or log documenting their performance in this area. For example, as well as more involved assessment approaches to authentic assessment, I encourage you to read the chapter on assessment in Hellison's (2011) latest book.

Be Flexible

Finally, it is important to remember that TPSR is a flexible approach that was developed through trial and error (Hellison, 2011). While you want to be aware of the essential aspects of the model, feel free to adapt it to fit your own style, your students' needs, and your teaching context. The structure and examples provided here and in the TPSR literature should be enough to get you started, but no one knows your program better than you do. No rigid curriculum or formula can adapt to the day-to-day flow of your program in a responsive way. That is the art of teaching. You should feel confident and empowered to play with this approach in your practice, reflect on the experience, and be creative in your own implementation of TPSR for the betterment of your students.

Conclusion

The purpose of this chapter was to introduce TPSR as a well-developed pedagogical model that supports and represents best practices for developing SEL competencies in physical education. While there is a difference in the language used for the TPSR model and SEL, there is a strong degree of overlap and alignment. The SEL movement is rather new; however, the TPSR model has an almost 50-year span of trial and error, refinement, and various applications

to make it practical, flexible, and effective. The SEL competencies of self-awareness and self-management are best addressed with TPSR Level 1 and Level 3, positive decision making and self-awareness strongly align with TPSR Level 2, and relationship skills and social awareness are supported by TPSR Level 4. Three SEL competencies that align most directly with the TPSR Level 5 are positive decision making, self-awareness, and social awareness, along with the SEL principle of applying the application across academic areas and in different learning contexts. Additionally, the TPSR Awareness Talk is consistent with the SEL concept of helping students connect program goals to program content. For our field, and for the TPSR model, the content is physical activity, which also addresses the SEL competencies of active forms of learning. Finally, the TPSR Group Meeting and Reflection Time best align with the SEL framework of building awareness through recognizing emotions, strengths, and weaknesses (Gordon, Jacobs, & Wright, 2016).

Acknowledgments

I would like to thank Bobby Chen for his help in creating Appendix D: TPSR Questions for Awareness Talks. I would also like to thank Michael Wright and Kesia Williams for their help in creating Appendix C: TPSR Developmental Stages Fully Developed Lessons.
—David S. Walsh

Questions for Discussion

1. What are the five "Big Picture" leader responsibilities that are in line with the true essence of the TPSR model? Briefly describe each of them and the potential impact they could have on teaching physical education.
2. What are the five TPSR life skills/program goals, which are often referred to as "Levels of Responsibility"? Describe why Levels 1 & 2 are considered basic life skills/goals. Describe why Levels 3 & 4 are considered advanced life skills/goals. Also describe your understanding of Level 5, the ultimate TPSR advanced life skill/goal.
3. Some of the Levels are described as "personal responsibilities" and others as "social

responsibilities." Describe your understanding of what is meant by "personal" and what is meant by "social".
4. List and describe the five components of the TPSR model Daily Format. How could these be used in your own physical education classes?
5. What are the TPSR Levels used in Developmental Stage 1? What are the TPSR Levels added to Developmental Stage 2, and how do these added Levels impact the way physical activity content is delivered? Level 5 is the TPSR Level is added to Developmental Stage 3. Provide a 50 word Level 5 transfer talk that you could give in a physical education class.

References

Collaborative for Academic, Social, and Emotional Learning (2019). What is social and emotional learning? Retrieved from https://casel.org/what-is-sel/

Escarti, E., Gutierrez, M., Pascual, C., Marin, D., Martinez, C., & Chacon, Y. (2006). Ensenando responsabilidad personal y social a un grupo de adolescentes de riesgo: Un estudio observacional [Teaching personal and social responsibility to a group of 'at-risk' adolescents: An observational study]. *Revista de Educacion, 341*, 373—396.

Escartí, A., Wright, P. M., Pascual, C., & Gutiérrez, M. (2015). Tool for assessing responsibility-based education (TARE) 2.0: Instrument revisions, inter-rater reliability, and correlations between observed teaching strategies and student behaviors. *Universal Journal of Psychology, 3*(55), –63.

Gordon, B., Jacobs, J. M., & Wright, P. M. (2016). Social and emotional learning through a teaching personal and social responsibility based after school program for disengaged middle-school boys. *Journal of Teaching in Physical Education, 35*(4), 358–369.

Hellison, D. (1973). *Humanistic Physical Education.* Cliffs, NJ: Prentice-Hall.

Hellison, D. (1978). *Beyond balls and bats: Alienated (and other) youth in the gym.* Washington, DC: AAHPER.

Hellison, D (1985). *Goals and strategies for teaching physical education.* Champaign, IL: Human Kinetics.

Hellison, D. (1995). *Teaching responsibility through physical activity.* Champaign, IL: Human Kinetics.

Hellison, D. (2003). *Teaching responsibility through physical activity* (2nd ed.). Champaign, IL: Human Kinetics.

Hellison, D. (2011). *Teaching responsibility through physical activity* (3rd ed.). Champaign, IL: Human Kinetics.

Jacobs, J., Wright, P. M. (2014). Social and emotional learning policies and physical education. *Strategies, 27*(6), 42–44.

Metzler, M. (2005). *Instructional models for physical education.* Boston, MA: Allyn & Bacon.

Newton, M., Fry, M., Watson, D., Gano-Overway, L., Kim, M. S., Magyar, M., & Guivernau, M. (2007). Psychometric properties of the caring climate scale in a physical activity setting. *Revista de Psicologia del Deporte, 16*(1), 67–84.

Noddings, N. (1992). *The challenge to care in schools.* New York: Teachers College Press.

Parker, M., & Stiehl, J. (2010). Personal and social responsibility. In J. Lund, & D. Tannehill (Eds.), *Standards-Based Physical Education Curriculum Development* (pp. 163–191). Sudbury, MA: Jones and Bartlett Publishers.

Richards, K. A. R., & Gordon, B. (2017). Socialization and learning to teach using the teaching personal and social responsibility approach. *Asia-Pacific Journal of Health, Sport and Physical Education, 8*(1), 19–38.

Richards, K. A. R., Ivy, V. N., Wright, P. M., Jerris, E. (2019). Combining the skills themes approach with teaching personal and social responsibility to teach social and emotional learning in elementary physical education. *Journal of Teaching Physical Education, Recreation & Dance, 90*(3), 35–44.

Walsh, D. (2008). Strangers in a strange land: Using an activity course to teach an alternative curriculum model. *Journal of Physical Education, Recreation & Dance, 79*(2), 40–44.

Walsh, D.S. (2016). Teaching the teaching personal and social responsibility model through developmental stages. *Active and Healthy Magazine 23*(2/3), 8–11.

Wright, P. M., & Craig, M. W. (2011). Tool for assessing responsibility-based education (TARE): Instrument development, content validity, and inter-rater and reliability. *Measurement in Physical Education and Exercise Science, 15*(3), 204–219.

Wright, P.M., & Walsh, D.S. (2018). Teaching personal and social responsibility. In P. Ward & S. Sutherland (Eds). *Curricular Models of Physical Education* (pp. 140–160).

Appendix A: TPSR Implementation Checklist

Teacher _____   Date _____

Class period/time _____   School _____

Person completing this form _____

What TPSR developmental stage is this program in overall? (circle one)   Stage 1   Stage 2   Stage 3

Which of the Levels (goals) was directly addressed in this lesson? (mark all that apply)	*Which components of the Lesson Format were used in this lesson? (mark all that apply)*
_____ Level One (respect)	_____ Relational time
_____ Level Two (self-motivation)	_____ Awareness talk
_____ Level Three (self-direction)	_____ Physical activity with responsibility
_____ Level Four (caring)	_____ Group meeting
_____ Level Five (transfer)	_____ Reflection time
_____ Modeling respect	_____ Participating
_____ Setting expectations	_____ Engaging
_____ Providing opportunities for success	_____ Showing respect
_____ Fostering social interaction	_____ Cooperating

_____ Assigning management tasks	_____ Encouraging others
_____ Promoting leadership	_____ Helping others
_____ Giving choices and voices	_____ Leading
_____ Involving students in assessment	_____ Expressing voice
_____ Addressing transfer of life skills	_____ Asking for help

Additional Comments _____

_____

_____

_____

Appendix B: TPSR Developmental Stages Lesson Plan Templates

Developmental Stage 1 Lesson Plan

Objective:

Cognitive: (Know Outcomes)

Psychomotor: (Do Outcomes)

Affective: (Focus on TPSR Levels 1 & 2)

1. **Relational Time (before and after class)**
   - Develop relationships with students.
     - Convey to students that they are unique, have strengths, a voice that matters, and the ability to make good personal and social decisions.

2. **Awareness Talk**
   - Teach Levels 1 & 2 (100% teacher led)
     - Ask specific questions regarding respect, self-control, and positive attitude (Level 1), and effort and teamwork (Level 2). Provide specific examples following student comments.

3. **The Lesson**
   - Integrate Levels 1 & 2 into the physical activity (100%)

   - Stop lesson 2–3 times for brief check in. Ask students how they are doing with Levels 1 & 2. Teacher then provides perceptions.

4. **Group Meeting**
   - Group Reflection
     - Students talk first. Teacher asks likes, dislikes, and overall perception of the day including Levels 1 & 2.
     - Teacher then talks. Provides overall perceptions including Levels 1 & 2.

5. **Reflection Time**
   - Individual reflection on Levels 1 & 2
     - How respectful were you toward others (Level 1)?
     - How was your self-control (Level 1)?
     - How was your attitude (Level 1)?
     - How hard did you try today (Level 2)?
     - How well did you work as a team member (Level 2)?

Developmental Stage 2 Lesson Plan

Objective:

Cognitive: (Know Outcomes)

Psychomotor: (Do Outcomes)

Affective: (Focus on TPSR Levels 1–4)

1. **Relational Time (before and after class)**
   - Develop relationships with students
     - Convey to students that they are unique, have strengths, a voice that matters, and the ability to make good personal and social decisions.

2. **Awareness Talk**
   - Reminder of Levels 1 & 2 (80% student led/20% teacher led)
   - Introduce and focus on Levels 3 & 4 (100% teacher led). Provide specific examples.

3. **The Lesson**
   - Integrate Levels 1 & 2 into physical activity (30%)
     - o Provide some teacher directed activities for students to demonstrate Levels 1 & 2.
   - Integrate Levels 3 & 4 into the physical activity (70%)
     - o Provide time for students to work independently (Level 3).
     - o Provide time for best students to provide leadership roles (Level 4). They provide the foundation for others to follow.
4. **Group Meeting**
   - Group Reflection
     - o Students who provided leadership talk first followed by the rest of the students. They discuss likes, dislikes, and

overall perception of the day including Levels 1–4.
     - o Teacher then talks. Provides overall perceptions including Levels 1–4.
5. **Reflection Time**
   - Individual Reflection on Levels 1–4
     - o How respectful were you toward others (Level 1)?
     - o How was your self-control and attitude (Level 1)?
     - o How hard did you try today (Level 2)?
     - o How well did you work as a team (Level 2)?
     - o How well did you work independently (Level 3)?
     - o Did you provide any leadership (Level 4)?

Developmental Stage 3 Lesson Plan
Objective:

Cognitive: (Know Outcomes)

Psychomotor: (Do Outcomes)

Affective: (Focus on TPSR Levels 1–5)

1. **Relational Time (before and after class)**
   - Develop relationships with students
     - o Convey to students that they are unique, have strengths, a voice that matters, and the ability to make good personal and social decisions.
2. **Awareness Talk**
   - Reminder of Levels 1 & 2 (100% student led)
   - Reintroduce Levels 3 & 4 (80% student led/20% teacher led)
   - Make the connection to Level 5 (100% teacher led). Provide specific examples outside of the gym.
3. **The Lesson**
   - Integrate Levels 1 & 2 into physical activity (5%)
   - Integrate Levels 3 & 4 into the physical activity (95%)
     - o Extend working independently to setting and working on goals (Level 3).
     - o Best leaders take on more leadership roles (e.g., rather than just teaching a drill they organize and run a full practice).
     - o Best leaders become mentor leaders who help others develop leadership skills (Level 4). They will help the average and

even timid students provide leadership to the class (e.g., assist mentor leaders in running a drill).
     - o In time, average or even timid students may teach activities and run a full practice on their own.
4. **Group Meeting**
   - Group Reflection
     - o Mentor leaders talk first followed by assistant leaders and then the rest of the class. Mentor leaders also support and comment on assistant leaders' performance. They all provide likes, dislikes, and overall perception of the day including Levels 1–4.
     - o Teacher then talks. Provides overall perceptions including Levels 1–4.
     - o Teacher also creates discussions on Level 5.
5. **Reflection Time**
   - Individual Reflection on Levels 1–5
     - o How was your self-control, respect, and attitude (Level 1)?
     - o How hard did you try today (Level 2)?
     - o How well did you work as a team (Level 2)?
     - o How well did you set and work on goals independently (Level 3)?
     - o Did you provide any leadership (Level 4)?
     - o Are you trying these responsibilities outside of PE (Level 5)?

Appendix C: TPSR Developmental Stages Fully Developed Lessons

TPSR Developmental Stage 1 Lesson Plan
Balance and Quickness & Passing & Catching

Cognitive: Students will be able to verbally recall two cues on offensive and defensive stances.

Psychomotor: Students will be able to perform the chest, bounce, and overhead passes.

Affective: Students will be able to demonstrate <u>respect</u> toward other classmates and <u>effort</u> throughout the lesson plan. Students will show <u>teamwork</u> by working with their classmates.

1. **Relational Time**
Teachers will speak with the students before and after class to create a deeper connection with them. During this time, students will be given the opportunity to either warm up or stretch. This will give the teachers time to speak with the students.

2. **Awareness Talk**
Teachers will introduce TPSR Developmental Stage 1 responsibilities, <u>respect,</u> and <u>effort</u>. Teachers will lead the discussion by talking about and asking questions about these responsibilities.

3. **The Lesson**
Activity 1: Offensive and Defensive Stances
Teachers will go over the proper form for offensive and defensive stances. Students will get into two or three lines and be provided cues for each stance. This will lead to the next drill.

Cues: Offensive: 1) Head over waist, eyes up 2) Back Straight 3) Knees bent, weight on balls of feet. 4) Feet shoulder width apart 5) Hands open, ready to catch the ball.

Defensive: 1, 2 & 3 the same 4) Feet shoulder-width apart or wider 5) Arms out ready to knock down a pass.

Activity 2: Defensive Slides, and Catching a Pass
There will be one line of students to start, and once we get started, most of the students will be moving quite a bit in a large square. The first student in line will run forward toward the first teacher and stop in a solid offensive position. The teacher will pass them the ball, and the student will pass it back any way they want. Student will then work on defensive slides to their left until they get to the next corner of the square. Then,

student will turn and run forward to the other teacher where they will again catch a pass and pass it back. They will then pivot around and work on defensive slides to the right until they get to the place they started. They will then go to the back of the line.

Cues: 1) When using offensive stance, come to a jump stop 2) Turn and run 3) When using defensive slides, don't cross feet 4) Make a pivot on one foot, and swing around to run to the next place.

Activity 3: Partner Passing and Partner Passing while Moving
Students will get into partners, and spread out 10–12 feet practicing passing the ball to each other. We will work on the chest pass, the bounce pass, and the overhead pass for about 40 seconds each. We will then move onto partner passing while moving. Students will line up across from their partners in two lines at one end of the court. They will chest pass the ball back and forth down the court twice, and come back around the outside.

Cues: 1) Ball in both hands 2) Locate Target 3) Elbows in 4) Follow though "open the door" 5) For bounce pass, bounce the ball to your partner.

Activity 4: Three-Person Weave
Students will get into three lines at one end of the court. There will be four lines. Each person in the middle line will hold a ball. The first person will start with passing the ball to the second person, who is on their right, and the first person will follow their pass and run behind the second person. The second person will then pass to the third person who will be cutting toward them. After they pass it to them, they will follow their pass as well and run behind the third person. The third person will then do the same, passing to the first person, and follow their pass behind the first person. The group will continue this all the way down the court. All passes will be chest passes. When each group is done, they will wait at the other end. Once all the groups have gone, they will come back the other way.

Cues: 1) Use a chest pass 2) Follow your pass 3) Run behind the person you pass to

4) Catch the pass coming to you 5) Chest pass again.

Activity 5: Game

Offer three choices: 1) Play a competitive game, 2) Play a recreational game, or 3) No game and practice skills.

Students playing a game get into groups of three and will play against another group of three, in a three-on-three matchup of basketball. They will work on their offensive and defensive stances, as well as passing.

Rules for the game: 1) Soft defense (don't steal the ball from anyone). 2) At least three passes before shooting (the focus is on teamwork and working together).

Cues: 1) Students will work on offensive and defensive stances. 2) Students will work on

all passes. 3) Students will work together as teammates to score points.

4. **Group Meeting**

End class by having class meet for group reflection time. Teachers will ask students questions, encouraging them to discuss their likes, dislikes, and overall perception of the lesson including responsibilities of respect and effort. Teachers will then provide their overall perceptions of the class session including respect and effort.

5. **Reflection Time**
   Individual Reflection on Developmental Stage 1 TPSR Responsibilities
   - How respectful were you toward others?
   - How was your self-control?
   - How was your attitude?
   - How hard did you try today?
   - How well did you work as a team member?

TPSR Developmental Stage 2 Lesson Plan
Dribbling and Shooting
Objectives:

Psychomotor: Students will be able to successfully demonstrate dribbling and shooting techniques during drills and game play.

Cognitive: Students will be able to describe at least three learning cues associated with dribbling and shooting techniques.

Affective: Students will be able to demonstrate respect and effort as well as the responsibilities of self-direction and leadership skills. Students will be given time during the lesson to demonstrate these responsibilities.

1. **Relational Time:**
   Teachers will take time to interact with students before and after class in order to establish meaningful connections. For example, "Hey Markham, how did your wrestling season end? Did you do as well as you had hoped?" Students will also have the opportunity to stretch and warm up if they choose to do so.

2. **Awareness Talk:**
   Teachers ask students to begin running the awareness talk, giving words of encouragement on Developmental Stage 1 TPSR responsibilities, respect and effort. Teachers then introduce Developmental Stage 2 responsibilities of self-direction time and leadership.

3. **The Lesson:**
   Activity 1: Self-Direction
   Students will have about 5 minutes to work on any previous skills covered during past lessons.

Students should stay on task and stay focused. This is also time for students to warm up and stretch before the drills begin. Teachers will check in on what the students are working on, reinforcing the purpose of self-direction time.

Activity 2: Zigzag Dribbling

Players will dribble with their right hand to the sideline, perform various crossover techniques, then dribble to the free-throw lane line with their left hand and perform various crossover techniques. They will perform this sequence up the court and repeat it on the way back.

Cues: 1) Keep your head up when you dribble 2) Plant your outside foot 3) Push off in the opposite direction while you are performing a crossover technique.

Activity 3: Goal Dribbling and Layup Drill

Student Leader 1 will help run this activity

Students will line up under main basket facing right-side hoop. The first player will dribble hard to the side basket and perform a lay-up. Next, the same player will dribble to mid-court with their left hand and perform a crossover (left to right) and perform another layup at the next side basket. Students will all follow the same procedure and perform layups at all six baskets and perform crossover at mid-court.

Cues: 1) Explode to the basket on the lay-up 2) Dribble with your left hand to the middle, try to make every shot 3) Keep your head up.

Activity 4: Dribbling and Spot Up Shooting

Student Leader 2 will help run this activity

Students will break into groups of two and be working on dribbling and shooting skills. Each group will have one ball. The first person in line will dribble to a designated spot and pull up to shoot the ball. They will then get their own rebound and pass the ball to their partner, who will then do the same thing. They will shoot at each spot at least three times, then move to the next spot. The spots will be short corner on the left, right sides of the hoop, a free-throw line extended, and shooting from the free-throw line. Each new shot will incorporate a different dribble to initiate the spot up.

> Cues: 1) Dribble head up 2) Stay on balance 3) Jump straight up 4) Follow your shot 5) Pass to you partner.

Activity 5: Game:

Offer three choices: 1) Play a competitive game 2) Play a recreational game or 3) No game and practice skills.

Ask student leaders to help set up both competitive and recreational games.

Students playing a game of either three-on-three or four-on-four matchup of basketball.

Encourage students to focus on the dribbling and shooting skills learned during today's lesson.

Suggested rules for the game: 1) Soft defense (don't steal the ball from anyone). 2) At least three passes before shooting (the focus is on teamwork and working together).

However, let student leaders determine the rule that will foster successful, positive, and fun experiences for all student.

> Cues: 1) Break into teams of three 2) Work on skills 3) Work on teamwork.

4. **Group Meeting:**

The teacher will ask the Student Leaders to talk first. They will be asked how they performed as leaders, and what they liked and disliked about the lesson. The rest of the students will then be asked to talk about their thoughts of the lesson, including feedback for the student leaders. This gives students time to share their opinions about their feelings and the instruction of the teacher. Teachers will then give their feedback about how the students performed along with their own performance during the lesson.

5. **Reflection Time**
Individual Reflection on Developmental Stage 2 TPSR Responsibilities
- How respectful were you toward others?
- How was your self-control and attitude?
- How hard did you try today?
- How well did you work as a team?
- How well did you work on your own during self-direction time?
- Did you provide any leadership?

TPSR Developmental Stage 3 Lesson Plan
Basketball: Moving without the Ball
Objectives:

Psychomotor: Students will be able to successfully demonstrate the V-Cut and Back cuts.

Cognitive: Students will be able to describe the cues of the V-Cut and Back Cut. They will also be able to describe the importance of moving without the ball.

Affective: Students will be able to demonstrate respect and effort as well as responsibilities such as goal-setting time and leadership skills. Goal-setting will be longer than Developmental Stage 2 self-direction time. As a Developmental Stage 3 lesson, both Minor and Major Leaders will be selected. Students will be given time during the lesson to demonstrate these responsibilities to the teachers and their classmates. Teachers will make the connection to "transfer of responsibilities" by providing specific outside of the gym examples.

1. **Relational Time**
Teachers will communicate with the students before and after class to create a deeper connection between student and teacher. Teachers might address ideas about goal-setting and leadership outside of the gym.

2. **Awareness Talk (done by Student Leader 1)**
Teachers will ask students to begin the awareness talk, giving words of encouragement on Developmental Stage 2 TPSR responsibilities, respect, effort, self-direction, and leadership. As a Developmental Stage 3 lesson, the teachers will extend self-direction time to ongoing goals-setting, and also introduce the idea of both Minor and Major Leaders. The teachers will then discuss examples of using these responsibilities outside of the gym

in addition to suggestions, encouragement, and ideas for the students to explore them in their own lives.

3. **The Lesson**
Activity 1: Goal-Setting Time (Led by Student Leader 1).
Students will have about 10 minutes for Goal-Setting Time. Have the <u>Student Leader</u> ask students to set a goal or two (volleyball related or stretching) and try to accomplish those goals. The idea is to lead to <u>ongoing goals</u> over several class sessions.

Activity 2: "V-Cut and Back Cut"
<u>Student Leader 2</u> will run this activity with the help of a <u>Minor Leader</u>. The class will split up into two groups, and will go to each side of the court. First, we will work on V-cuts. We will have each teacher be a passer, one student be a defender, and one student an offensive player. Two students will stand down on the block. The offensive player will perform a V-cut, taking a jab step toward the basket, and then turn and run out. The teacher will then pass the ball to the cutter where they will catch and shoot the ball. We will then move onto the Back Cut, which is similar to the V-Cut, but the offensive player will jab away from the basket and run to the basket for a layup. During this time, the defender will play soft defense to give the offensive player a feel for getting open. We will rotate every pass, going from defense to offense and to the back of the line.

> Cues: 1) Three-Quarter step in first direction 2) Turn on ball of foot 3) Push hard off to the inside 4) Take a big step with other foot 5) Call for ball 6) Catch and shoot.

Activity 3: "3 on 0 Offense: Down Screen"
<u>Student Leader 3</u> will run this activity with the help of a <u>Minor Leader</u>. The class will split into groups of three and go to a basket. We will be working on the down screen with no defenders. The first few times through we will have one person on the block and the other two up top. The first student will pass the ball, run down and screen for the player on the block, run up to an open spot, and the screen will cut to the basket. The person with the ball will pass to the person who came up, and run down to the person who is on the block on their side, and screen for them. This will be a continuous drill.

> Cues: 1) Sprint to set screen 2) Solid base 3) Feet shoulder width apart 4) Hands down or crossing chest 5) Sprint around screen

Activity 4: "Screen and roll"
We will have one more <u>Student Leader</u> who will start by breaking up the class into partners. They will work on the screen and roll with no defenders. The screener will start away and come up and set a screen. The student with the ball will go around the screen, either pass the ball, or dribble it to the basket. They will rotate after each screen and roll. After a short time of practicing, the groups will be matched together to practice with the defense. Each group will have both students play offense and defense, and then switch. The defense will only go about 50% intensity to let the offense really practice the screen and roll.

> Cues: 1) Screener screens 2) Dribbler goes around screen 3) Screener rolls opening chest to dribbler 4) Dribbler looks to pass or shoot 5) Defenders switch

Activity 5: Game:
<u>Student Leaders</u> will break up their groups into teams and each court decides on three-on-three half court games to full five-on-five games. They will offer the three choices: 1) Play a competitive game, 2) Play a recreational game, or 3) No game and practice skills.
<u>Student leaders</u> determine rule that will foster successful, positive, and fun experiences for all students.
Encourage the idea of practicing the V-cut, back cut, and the other screens.

4. **Group Meeting**
<u>Major and Minor Student Leaders</u> will be asked about their experiences and how the lesson went. The other students will then be asked how they thought the lesson went with their likes and dislikes (3–4 students). Both teachers will then provide feedback on the lesson and explain again why it's important to use these responsibilities in other areas of life <u>(outside the gym)</u>.

5. **Reflection Time**
Individual Reflection on Developmental Stage 3 TPSR Responsibilities
- How was your self-control, respect, and attitude?
- How hard did you try today?
- How well did you work as a team?
- How well did you set and work on goals independently?
- Did you provide any major or minor leadership?
- Are you trying out these responsibilities outside the gym?

Appendix D: TPSR Questions for Awareness Talks

Applicable to TPSR 1-4

1. How has your views of [insert TPSR level 1–4] changed from [insert time period] to right now?
2. Do you have a special quote or saying that a friend, family member, or someone important to you said about [insert TPSR level 1–4]?
3. [Name] displayed [insert TPSR level 1-4] really well last class. [Specific student or to the class] what was your mindset for it?
4. [Specific student or to the class] do you have a role model or someone you look up to in terms of [insert TPSR level 1–4]?
5. [Specific student or to the class], what is an important quality to have for [insert TPSR level 1–4]?
6. Give a student a hypothetical situation with regard to a TPSR 1-4 level and ask how they would respond.
7. [Specific student or to the class], what is the most important TPSR level to you and why?
8. [Specific student or to the class], what TPSR levels available would you like to focus on today and why?

Respect Questions

1. The three main ways of respect that we usually talk about is respect toward: yourself, others, and the equipment. Which one is the most important to you and why?
2. Which type of respect (yourself, others, equipment) would you like to focus on today and why?
3. [Specific student or to the class], can you describe how you will respect [yourself/others/equipment] today?

Effort Questions

1. [Specific student or to the class], has there been anything that you initially weren't good at but got better through effort and perseverance?
2. What are your thoughts when a person says "effort requires no talent"?
3. [Specific student or to the class], can you give us a rewarding moment when you benefited from applying effort?

Self-Direction Questions

1. [Specific student or to the class], are you close to completing any of your goals since the start of the [insert time period]?
2. [Specific student or to the class] would you like to tell the group one of your short-term and one long-term goals?
3. [Specific student or to the class], what have you been working on during the past self-direction times? Has it helped you?

Leadership Questions

1. [Name] was recently a student leader who is very knowledgeable in the sport; do you have any advice for any students who want to be leaders?
2. [Specific student or to the class], do you think you have to be really good at the sport/skill to be a leader?
3. [Specific student or to the class], what is the difference between "telling people what to do" and being a "true leader"?

Transfer Questions

1. [Specific student or to the class], how can the TPSR responsibilities be used in the classroom?
2. [Specific student or to the class], in what ways can the TPSR responsibilities help you become a better person in life?
3. [Specific student or to the class], how have you improved on [one of the levels] in an area of your life?

CHAPTER 8

Sport Education

Peter A. Hastie

Oleg A. Sinelnikov

Tristan L. Wallhead

CHAPTER SUMMARY

This chapter is presented in three parts. First, the idea of the Sport Education model is presented, following which an outline is provided explaining where social and emotional learning (SEL) competencies fit within the structure and pedagogy of the model. The second and third parts of chapter are the outlines of two Sport Education seasons. The first is a 15-lesson soccer season focusing on self-awareness and self-management for upper elementary school students. This is followed by a secondary level team fitness season in which the SEL competencies of social-awareness and relationship skills are placed at the forefront.

Sport Education and Social Emotional Learning

The Sport Education pedagogical model is a well-established, thoroughly researched, and evidenced-based practice of teaching that provides authentic and developmentally appropriate sporting experiences to participants across a variety of settings, including in-school physical education programs. First published as a small paperback by Daryl Siedentop (1994), there have been three editions of the more expansive *Complete Guide to Sport Education* (Siedentop, Hastie, & van der Mars, 2004; 2011; 2020), numerous books and book chapters (e.g., Kinchin, 2006; Hastie, 2012) written to explain the model and provide guidance to those who use it in their teaching. Numerous theoretical and evidence-based research papers have also been presented in the literature, including several research summaries and reviews (e.g., Araujo, Mesquita, Hastie, 2014; Bessa, Hastie, Araujo, Mesquita, 2019; Hastie, Martínez de Ojeda, & Calderón, 2011; Wallhead & O'Sullivan, 2005).

The notion of a *pedagogical model* in this chapter is based on the understanding offered by Haerens, Kirk, Cardon, & De Bourdeaudhuij (2011) and Kirk (2013). Kirk (2013) defines a pedagogical model as one that "identifies distinctive learning outcomes and shows how these might be best achieved through their tight alignment with teaching strategies and curriculum or subject matter" (p. 979). Pedagogical models have been identified as integral to providing quality physical education and are becoming essential to the core practice of the discipline (Casey, 2014; Kirk, 2013). Using pedagogical models in teaching practice allows for several benefits to be realized by the learner and the teacher and, while initially envisaged as an alternative to ineffective teacher-directed traditional practices, Sport Education has become a significant contributor in providing better sporting experiences for children in their physical education (Siedentop, 2002).

Although many pedagogical models, including Sport Education, use a set of nonnegotiable features within a certain design specification to allow the interplay of learning, teaching, subject matter, and context in its development (Rovegno, 2006), the Sport Education model is very flexible in its design and implementation. Teachers can easily tailor the structure of the model to emphasize different aspects of learning according to the learning needs of students and a variety of outcomes, some of which may not be readily achieved during traditional teaching. As such, it becomes a highly suited model in which to develop social and emotional learning (SEL) competencies. Whereas the three-pronged goal of Sport Education drives the process of creation, implementation, and reflection for each season, it is its requirements and structural features that allow for SEL competencies to be attained. The following sections provide an overview of Sport Education's goals and unique features before delving into how some notions of SEL are already embedded in the model, and how we can add further SEL competencies to expand the reach of the model.

Goal of Sport Education

While interpretations of Sport Education goals have been substantially expanded since the model's origin, its central goal remains "to educate students to be players in the fullest sense and to help them develop as competent, literate and enthusiastic sportspersons" (Siedentop et al., 2020, p. 9). It is important to note here the expanded definition of a team "sport" in the name of the model and the way it is intended to encompass any and all types of activities that are appropriate in the educational setting and is not limited to traditional sports such as basketball or football. In fact, the authors of this chapter have been involved in a number of successful, nontraditional "seasons" including bicycle safety, fishing, and obstacle course fitness. Nevertheless, the tenets

of *competence*, *literacy*, and *enthusiasm* continue to be at the forefront of Sport Education and must be included when developing and implementing Sport Education season.

Competency relates to participants developing sufficient skills, strategies, and tactical understanding in order to satisfactorily participate in games and activities. A competent sportsperson is not only able to understand complexities, tactical and/or technical, of a game, activity, or dance but also is able to execute and perform required skills and movements If one is familiar with the Society of Health and Physical Education (SHAPE) America's *National Standards and Grade-Level Outcomes for K–12 Physical Education* (2013), competency tenet of Sport Education can be thought of as mainly referring to Standard 1 (The physically literate individual demonstrates competency in a variety of motor skills and movement patterns), Standard 2 (The physically literate individual applies knowledge of concepts, principles, strategies, and tactics related to movement and performance), and Standard 3 (The physically literate individual demonstrates the knowledge and skills to achieve and maintain a health-enhancing level of physical activity and fitness).

Literacy refers to learners' understanding and valuing the rules, traditions, and rituals of sport, games, and activities. Additionally, literate sportspersons can distinguish between good and bad sporting practices and behaviors. Moreover, literate sportspersons value prosocial behaviors when participating in activities and work to eliminate inappropriate behaviors. Literacy also expresses itself off the playing field as students become more discerning sport consumers as spectators or fans. Most of the literacy tenet can be attributed to Standard 5 (The physically literate individual recognizes the value of physical activity for health, enjoyment, challenge, self-expression, and/or social interaction).

Enthusiasm signifies how participants behave to preserve, protect, and enhance sport culture, regardless of the context. An enthusiastic sportsperson seeks to participate in sport and physical activity because of self-determined factors of experiencing elevated levels of enjoyment, competence, and relatedness when engaging in activity. Further, enthusiastic sportspersons exhibit prosocial behaviors because the structure of Sport Education affords deliberate practice of positive sporting behavior (Pennington & Sinelnikov, 2018). This tenet can mostly be attributed to SHAPE America's Standard 4 (The physically literate individual exhibits responsible personal and social behavior that respects self and others).

Sport Education Requirements and Distinctions

While the goals of Sport Education are ambitious and lofty, if achieved, they certainly contribute to the advancement of a more educationally sound and appropriate sporting culture. However, the development of learners cannot be achieved unless we recognize the distinctions between typical sporting practices prevalent in our society and those espoused by Sport Education, which are educationally sound and developmentally appropriate. In fact, when using the Sport Education model, the teacher and students should strive to create and facilitate a healthier culture, better climate, and educational experience than that of a typical sporting experience where the highly skilled are prioritized as is winning at all costs. Given these requirements, there are typically three distinctions made between Sport Education in schools and others sporting pursuits (e.g., youth, interscholastic, professional sports) which include: (a) participation requirements, (b) developmentally appropriate involvement, and (c) inclusion of diverse roles (Siedentop et al., 2020).

Participation for all, by all, and at all times. In short, Sport Education requires the meaningful participation of ALL learners at ALL times. This means that at any given moment of the season or lesson all students are engaged in a meaningful contribution to achieving one of the goals of Sport Education. Good Sport Education seasons used small-sided and modified games in order to reduce as much as possible the need for substitutions or waiting for turns. Some seasons also incorporate "graded competitions" in which students are matched according to their skill levels for competition and there is research evidence suggesting that graded competition in Sport Education improves game performance and motivation to persist during play (Hastie, Ward, & Brock, 2017). Additionally, all students are tasked with individual and group responsibilities that promote their own learning, the learning of others, and contribute to the administration and management of all aspects of a competition for small or large groups. For example, students, in a span of one lesson, may be responsible for officiating when other teams compete against each other and then collecting and posting individual and team statistics after playing for their own teams. Similarly, students may be responsible for coaching and providing motivational and performance feedback to their team and then working on organizing a culminating event for the entire class.

Developmentally appropriate involvement. It is critical for teachers to create and foster developmentally appropriate involvement of students in Sport Education. The idea of developmentally appropriate involvement should concern all aspects of a season, not just those issues related to modified team size and playing conditions. Examples also include the selection of a sport or physical activity for a season, team selection processes, competition formats, rule modification, and creation of mastery instead of performance climates among others. Student learning and student success should serve as guiding principles for such decision making. To ensure developmentally appropriate involvement, the games or activities to be played in a season of Sport Education are most often small-sided, modified, and involve graded competition. For example, in addition to following appropriate instructional practice guidelines (SHAPE America, 2009), adult game forms of competition (where winning is the sole goal) need to be avoided since they may benefit only higher-skilled students in favor of a small-sided game format that will benefit all, including those who are lower-skilled and marginalized (Hastie & Sinelnikov, 2006). Thus, instead of an 11 vs. 11 game of adult-like soccer, a Sport Education season may feature games of 2 vs. 2, 3 vs. 3 and 5 vs. 5. An example of an even more complex soccer season will be described later in this chapter. Rules, equipment, and field/court size should also be modified while preserving the nature of competition (e.g., nets are lowered, a slower and lighter ball is used, the size of the court is reduced for volleyball Sport Education season).

Inclusion of diverse roles. The final distinction between Sport Education and other competitive sport and activities such as club, competitive, and interscholastic sports is the requirement of learners participating in a variety of playing and nonplaying roles during the season. There are three types of roles in a Sport Education season: (a) player role, (b) duty team role, and (c) team role. The most important role is that of a player or performer and it is crucial that all students have that role. This means that each student plays on their team and contributes to its success through playing. In addition to playing, students also help with organization and administration of competition by officiating, keeping scores and statistics, umpiring, or being line judges. These are examples of duty team roles that help to facilitate and teach students about game function. A team role is one that has critical responsibilities to the functions of each individual team. Examples of such roles include coach, manager, warm-up leader, journalist, reporter, choreographer, web designer, and others. These roles are critical to team management and function. Additionally, diverse roles allow for peer learning to take place within the season and enhance social interactions within small and large groups of students.

Having diverse roles not only helps in class management, team organization, functions, and competition administration but it also allows students to be responsible for their learning, structure, and organization. Additionally, while engagement in playing roles during Sport Education leads to significant improvements in skills, decision making, tactical understanding, and cognitive development (Bessa, Hastie, Araujo, Mesquita, 2019; Hastie, Martínez de Ojeda, & Calderón, 2011), participation in nonplaying roles enhances students' understanding of a sport or activity and contributes to literacy and enthusiasm goals of Sport Education (Araujo, Mesquita, Hastie, 2014; Hastie & Sinelnikov, 2006).

Structural Features of Sport Education

The structure of Sport Education includes several unique features that distinguish it from other pedagogical models. These structural elements include seasons, affiliation, formal competition, festivity, recordkeeping, and culminating events (Siedentop et al., 2020). These structural features are intentionally designed to resemble a sporting season. It is within these six pedagogical structures that the core competencies of SEL can be implemented. First, we will present a brief overview of each feature and then describe how to seamlessly integrate SEL competencies with Sport Education.

Seasons. A Sport Education unit is organized as *a season,* which mirrors a flow of a regular season for a team sport. One can think of the following sequential phases of a season to help with season organization: training camp, preseason, regular season, and postseason. During training camp, students are organized in teams and train skills and gameplay within their team. During preseason, teams engage in nonconsequence competitions against other teams. Nonconsequence competition means that teams participate in competition to learn how to compete and officiate, but results do not count toward season standings. It is during the regular season when teams compete and duty team officiate games, that such results count and are publicized. Based on the regular season, teams advance to competing in a championship round or a festival type event.

Team affiliation. Team affiliation is maintained by students being a part of the same team for the duration of the entire season, and in some cases, for multiple seasons. The structural feature of team affiliation

presents valuable opportunities for meaningful student interactions and engagement with others during Sport Education. Being a part of a consistent small group (i.e., a team), for an extended period of time allows for construction and maintenance of personal identity, social support, and the development of friendships and relationship skills.

Formal competition. The regular season provides students with an opportunity to engage in formal competition. There are several different formats of formal competition to suit the game or performance (e.g., round-robin format for a soccer season, event format for a tennis season, dual competition for a dance season). It is important to note that season champions are typically determined by a system that can include points for items beyond just a team's win–loss record. These can include factors such as fair play, quality of officiating, or the performance of other team roles. Often, these elements are weighted more heavily than mere winning. This is also an area where SEL competencies can be emphasized.

Festivity. Sport Education is also characterized by festivity, which allows students and teachers to create a festive environment that celebrates improvement, fair play, and competencies. Examples of festivity include team and league posters on the wall, team jerseys, game reports, and team introductions before games. The atmosphere of festivity created in Sport Education seasons helps create meaningful and impactful memories that have personal significance to participants and last well beyond initial exposure to the model (Sinelnikov & Hastie, 2010).

Recordkeeping. All Sport Education seasons should have a form or multiple forms of recordkeeping. Public recordkeeping allows teams and individuals to assess their performances and improvements, provides standards of performance, and holds individuals and teams accountable for their learning. Recordkeeping can be accomplished in a variety of forms starting from posters on the wall to writing blogs and creating league websites.

Culminating event. A Sport Education season ends with a culminating event, which is designed to celebrate individual and team accomplishments. These events come in a variety of different forms depending in part on the type of sport or physical activity involved. For example, for a season of Sport Education synchronized juggling or dance in a middle school, a culminating event may be a half-time performance during a high school sporting event. A track and field Sport Education season may culminate with an Olympic style final event, held over several days, for which parents, other classes, and administration may be invited to attend. This feature also provides ample opportunities for the teacher to intentionally create a learning environment in which SEL competencies can be learned.

Where SEL Competencies Are Relevant to Sport Education

The unique features of Sport Education provide a framework for both curriculum and instructional design. The model also includes specific guidelines for the role of the teacher and students such as to allow for an interplay between the subject matter being taught and the learning context (Sinelnikov & Hastie, 2017). Research conducted on the model over the past 20 years has shown that if these guidelines are followed, student learning can occur across the psychomotor, cognitive, and affective domains of learning (Wallhead & O'Sullivan, 2005). Given that there is no one best way to do Sport Education, teachers can prioritize student learning in one or more of these learning domains. Within this section of the chapter, we focus on how affective learning outcomes, and specifically SEL, can be built into Sport Education's structural framework, thus highlighting the opportunity to bring the Collaborative for Academic, Social, and Emotional Learning (CASEL; 2019) competencies to the forefront of students' learning experiences. These competencies include developing student self-awareness, self-management, social awareness, relationship goals, and responsible decision making. The six features of Sport Education are used as an organizational framework to connect how teachers can employ pedagogical strategies within the model to elicit specific SEL competencies.

Seasons

Sport Education's seasonal structure and extended duration provide an opportunity for students to experience repeated and sequenced SEL opportunities. As the teacher and students move through the different phases associated with a Sport Education season, a progressive series of tasks are developed. These include an organizational phase, teacher-directed phase, preseason role development phase, and finally, the formal competition and culminating event (Sinelnikov, Hastie, & Prusak, 2007). Each of these phases presents a shift in the pedagogical foci of teachers. Rather than being center stage and taking

a teacher-directed approach, they move off-stage and adopt a more facilitative role within a student-centered learning environment that includes student roles and responsibilities. The pedagogical shift associated with the model presents an opportunity for the teacher to build situations for sequenced SEL development. This idea of a sequenced model connects to one of the key components of effective SEL programs that they should be **SAFE** (**S**equenced, **A**ctive, **F**ocused, and **E**xplicit; CASEL, 2019). These progressive phases and the season's extended duration not only provides the potential for the delivery of "sequenced" learning activities but also the opportunity for multiple attempts at refining SEL competencies. As with variance in motoric competence, students inevitably come into Sport Education with different SEL competencies. Having repeated opportunities to develop these competencies gives students opportunities to learn different competencies at different paces. As the season begins, it is important that the teacher explain the progressive nature of the tasks across the season and that students will have multiple opportunities to develop their SEL skills as they work with their team. The Sport Education seasonal structure thus connects to the Richards et al. (2019) proposition that creating opportunities for progression is important for personal and social responsibility learning. The model leads students through a sequence of activities that gradually builds their comfort and competence in working toward relevant SEL goals.

Affiliation

The affiliation feature of Sport Education is a key contributor to students' SEL development (Harvey, Kirk & O'Donovan, 2014). As students are placed in persisting teams for the duration of the season, they are provided with a platform to plan, practice, and compete together. This collaborative work toward a shared group goal has the potential to foster a sense of belonging and relatedness to the other members of the team. For this potential to be realized, the teacher needs to be explicit in educating students on the key SEL competencies of *social awareness* and *relationship skills*. A number of examples of these possibilities are included in the seasons described in this chapter. Explicit in the context of teaching SEL means directly addressing and giving feedback on these skills as opposed to assuming such skills are being developed/learned automatically in a given activity (Richards et al., 2019). The SEL competency of *social awareness* can be developed within the persistent team structure and associated team affiliation. Social awareness involves students taking the perspective of and empathizing with others, including those from diverse backgrounds and cultures (CASEL, 2019).

For the team to evolve across the season, students need to learn and develop social and ethical norms of behavior. Within Sport Education, these norms are characterized by taking the perspective of others, demonstrating empathy to the diverse skills of the group, and respecting the work and efforts of others. Ciotto & Gagnon (2018) suggested that *social awareness* can be taught in physical education by providing opportunities to problem solve through movement in ways that allow for the use of self-expression and cooperation. Within Sport Education, this self-expression and collaboration often manifests when teams reflect together on tasks and then problem-solve to plan how to use their strengths in subsequent tasks. For example, during games, teachers can use the pedagogy of "coaches' time-outs" to give teams a short time to reflect on how effectively their team is working together to maximize their strengths to achieve their chosen strategy.

Effective collaborative planning and building team affiliation not only requires the development of *social awareness* but also *relational skills*. Relationship skills are a key SEL competency and relate to establishing and maintaining healthy and rewarding relationships with diverse individuals and groups (CASEL, 2019). These skills include the ability to communicate clearly, listen well, cooperate with others, resist inappropriate social pressure, negotiate conflict constructively, and seek and offer help when needed (Ciotto & Gagnon, 2018). As teams progress through the Sport Education season, students collaborate to plan, practice, and compete together and need to infuse their skills to build strong relationships within the team. To facilitate this process, the teacher needs to be explicit in encouraging students to be active listeners and seek to offer and receive help. Ang and colleagues (2011) found that *relationship skills* became most evident when team coaches/captains motivated their teammates during games and helped to resolve conflicts among players, specifically concerning instances of conflicts with official calls.

Formal Competition

The feature of formal competition within the structure of Sport Education provides inherent accountability for group and individual performance. This accountability provides an overarching contingency for performance where tasks have an authentic meaning as the outcome of the tasks matter. Engaging in progressive formal competition environments provides students with opportunities to deal with these accountabilities

and the win and loss situations that inevitably arise. For students to learn and grow through these experiences requires a focus on the development of the key SEL competency of *self-awareness*. According to CASEL (2019), *self-awareness* involves accurately recognizing one's own emotions, thoughts, and values and how they influence behavior. Specific skills that are critical to the development of this SEL competency include students identifying emotions and self-reflecting on these experiences. As students engage in competitive tasks, they are given the opportunity to experience a range of emotions. Following these competitive events, students can self-reflect on these emotional responses and how they may influence behavior. For example, a student can reflect on what frustrates them during sports or what is most enjoyable or satisfying. The teacher can use these moments to verify that student self-perceptions are accurate and guide them on how best to deal with them. At the end of a game, teachers can explain to students that the result of any meaningful game elicits an emotional response. For example, it is okay to feel happy when they win, or disappointed if they lose a contest as long as they played the game by the rules and with full effort.

Connected to this development of self-awareness is the potential for growth in students' *self-management* as they progress through the formal competition phase of the Sport Education season. Self-management involves students successfully regulating their emotions, thoughts, and behaviors in different situations and includes effectively managing stress, controlling impulses, and motivating oneself to set and work toward personal and academic goals (CASEL, 2019). Informed by their *self-awareness, student self-management* relates to how the student acts as a function of their self-perceptions. Within the formal competition feature of Sport Education, this may include the teacher reminding students before the event that they need to remain calm during games when they are losing, or being able to maintain focus on a specific strategy during close games. The development of *self-management* competency has the potential not only for personal growth but also for the development of positive relationships with others.

Growth in *self-management* is more likely to manifest in Sport Education when teachers explicitly discuss with students how to respond to the emotions associated with winning and losing. For example, after a formal competition event within the preseason phase of a season, the teacher could gather the students to give them feedback based on their observations of how they dealt with their emotions during and after the game. Failure to control their emotions through over-celebration or excessive negative reactions should be emphasized as not appropriate. By discussing the feelings and emotions involved in meaningful competition, students are provided an opportunity to control their impulses and regulate their own behaviors during subsequent tasks. This capacity for self-management leads into another important SEL competency within the formal competitive aspects of Sport Education, namely *responsible decision making.*

Responsible decision making involves students making constructive choices about personal behavior and social interactions based on ethical standards, safety concerns, and social norms (CASEL, 2019). Responsible decision making not only includes the choices that students make as they work with their team through the season but how and why they make them. This SEL skill requires the students to analyze and evaluate situations and then look to make decisions and set goals that attempt to solve the problem with some level of ethical responsibility. Having students reflect on outcomes of games and events within the formal competition phase of a season is important; however, this may be insufficient to effectively teach *responsible decision making.* To develop this skill requires teachers to provide opportunities for students to become self-motivated, self-reliant, and to take responsibility for their decisions (Ciotto & Gagnon, 2018). One example is for the teacher to take time before learning tasks for students to work with their team to set individual and team goals. Examples of goal-directed student behaviors during the formal competition phase of the season include: students giving unprompted high fives to opponents at the end of each game, developing team strategies for gameplay that includes the skills and abilities of all team members, or taking time during recess to practice as a team (Ang et al., 2011).

Recordkeeping

Recordkeeping is a key structural feature of Sport Education that provides teachers and students with an ongoing assessment of how teams and individuals are performing as they progress through the season. Records can come in multiple formats, either from the teacher or from students, and can relate to student performance in practices and games, roles, organizational effectiveness, or adopting fair play behaviors. These records help serve to clarify the teachers' definitions and standards for success and achievement within the model and as such provide a cultural norm or tradition of expectation for student behavior. The records also serve to provide students with ongoing

feedback on their progress toward these standards and can be used to guide goal setting aligned with their learning trajectory. These records should be explicitly connected to the students' ongoing SEL development.

As the teacher or student duty teams maintain records of student performance in the ongoing tasks associated with the model, points or records can be used as reflective prompts for the development of the SEL skills of *self-awareness, self-management,* and *responsible decision making.* For students to develop accurate self-perception and the ability to reflect on strengths and weaknesses, they need an overt reference for their current performance. Records provided by the teacher or peers, such as assigned team fair play points for behaviors during gameplay that include not arguing with the official, providing supportive comments to teammates and giving high fives to the opponents after the game provide individuals with a clear reference for how their current competencies are meeting teacher expectations. From these records, students are provided with the opportunity to make responsible decisions about future efforts within games and to attempt to self-manage their fair play behaviors within these events. Previous research that tailored 'measures of performance' toward fair play and fulfilling team duty responsibilities was found to be effective in developing SEL competencies during a Sport Education season (Ang et al., 2011).

Festivity and Culminating Event

The structural feature of festivity is intertwined with the process of recordkeeping, but with the important caveat that as improvements in SEL competencies are made by individuals or teams, a concerted effort is made to celebrate this growth. This festivity or celebration is generally initiated by the teacher and is contingent on prioritized learning outcomes and specified criteria for success. Teachers who use Sport Education regularly are often purposeful in connecting the celebration of success with a mastery orientation such that it is aligned to individual or team improvement. This growth can coalesce with SEL learning goals such as the celebration of an increased team effort or fortitude during coach-led practice tasks or the display or more positive fair play behaviors within competitive game contexts. The notion of celebrating individual and team improvement in SEL behaviors connects to elements of effective sport-based youth development programs. Perkins & Noam (2007) suggested that programs should focus on self-improvement rather than social comparisons if they are to support students' ongoing efficacy and perceived mattering within the learning environment. The celebration of SEL successes such as effort, improvement, and fair play provides an opportunity to recognize individuals for their contributions to the season that goes beyond winning competitions (Perkins & Noam, 2007).

The culminating event represents a summative celebration of both the students' own accomplishments and the accomplishments of others. As students move toward the end of the Sport Education season, they have the opportunity to problem solve regarding what makes a winning team and how multiple outcomes can be valued in the celebration. A well-designed culminating event is designed by students and for students and can easily be connected to SEL. When designing the culminating event and the associated team and individual awards, the teacher guides students to appreciate the diversity of skills and knowledge of the group and to respect the differential learning trajectories that individuals have experienced throughout the season. These recognitions can include individual rewards for significant growth in one of more of the SEL competencies or team progress in achieving the wider goals of the season. Culminating events provide a platform for the teacher to celebrate the accomplishments of the class and thus should be aligned with the learning focus and be sufficiently inclusive to be empathetic to all students who have grown in their SEL competencies as the season progressed.

Responsibility

A final, but critical, feature of the Sport Education experience in developing a student-centered learning environment and addressing SEL goals is the infusion of student roles and responsibilities within the season structure. Student roles are integral to team functioning and provide a platform for students to develop

interpersonal and social skills and encourage critical awareness of social issues and responsibilities (Ang et al., 2011). The accomplishment of several of these roles, such as coach or captain, includes the pedagogy of peer teaching. To effectively peer teach, students need to develop the *relationship skills* of communication, persuasion, collaboration, and conflict management. Coaches need to learn to embrace the notion that their role is to help others to learn such that their team can grow to meet the challenges of the ongoing season. This latter competency requires both leadership in *responsible decision making* and a willingness to listen to others in formulating goals for the group. The teacher is a critical pedagogue in the development of these roles and the associated SEL skills and competencies. In choosing roles, students should be encouraged to reflect on their own strengths and how they apply to other team members' interests, values, and strengths. Teachers should also model the pedagogies required to effectively communicate content within peer-teaching contexts and the type of feedback that demonstrates empathy and values peers' efforts in meeting the demands of the task (Wallhead & O'Sullivan, 2007).

Summary

The first two sections of this chapter have provided an outline of the key characteristics of Sport Education, together with a description of how the SEC competencies promoted by CASEL fit comfortably within the educative agenda of the model. **Table 8.1** provides a summary of how we believe the various SEL competencies might best be addressed within the features of Sport Education. The remaining two sections of this chapter present two Sport Education seasons that have been designed to explicitly foreground selected SEL competencies. First, an

Table 8.1 Alignment of SEL Competencies within the Features of Sport Education

Seasons	SEL competencies	
Longer than usual Greater depth	Allows for an extended experience and repeated experiences with different elements of SEL competencies	
Affiliation	**SEL elements**	
Plan, practice, and compete as a team Sense of belongingness and relatedness	3. Social awareness Empathy Perspective taking Respecting others	4. Relationship skills Communication Listening Cooperation Seek/offer help

(continues)

Table 8.1 **Alignment of SEL Competencies within the Features of Sport Education**   *(continued)*

Formal competition	SEL elements	
Allows for planning and goal setting Outcomes with real meanings Dealing with wins and losses	1. Self-awareness Reflect on strengths and weaknesses Recognizing emotions/thoughts Self-management Regulating emotions/behaviors Controlling impulses	5. Responsible decision making Identify/solve problems Take ethical responsibilities

Culminating event	SEL elements	
Celebration of own and others' accomplishments Finding out what it takes to make a winning "team" beyond just winning games Multiple outcomes valued	3. Social awareness Respecting others	

Recording keeping	SEL elements	
Feedback for individuals and groups Records define standards Help in defining goals Provide tradition	Same as formal competition	

Festivity	SEL elements	
Celebrate improvement Celebrate effort Fair play	1. Self-awareness Recognizing emotions and thoughts	2. Self-management Self-motivation Goal setting

Managerial routines	SEL elements	
Class entry Team practice Games/officiating	2. Self-management Self-discipline	

Duty teams	SEL elements	
Officials Pre- and post-match responsibilities	3. Social awareness Perspective taking Respecting others Understanding ethical norms	

Team roles	SEL elements	
Individual tasks for team functioning Role of the coach	2. Self-management Self-discipline	4. Relationship skills Communication Listening Cooperation Seek/offer help

Peer teaching	SEL elements	
Helping others learn Working as a team	3. Social awareness Perspective taking Respecting others Understanding ethical norms	4. Relationship skills Communication Listening Cooperation Seek/offer help

outline of an upper elementary/middle school soccer season is provided in which the focus is placed on *self-awareness* and *self-management*. This is followed by a secondary level fitness season in which *social-awareness* and *relationship skills* are imbedded in 20 lessons. Both of these seasons have been designed to include those same **SAFE** (**S**equenced, **A**ctive, **F**ocused, and **E**xplicit) characteristics that are evident in effective SEL programs.

"I CAN PLAY .... Overload Soccer"

A Sport Education Season for Upper Elementary/Middle School Students

This season of soccer Sport Education is designed for students in upper elementary or middle school grade levels. The skill focus is on dribbling, passing, and shooting, with the primary game form being a 4 versus 4 overload game. That is, when a team is on offense, it has four players on the field, but immediately when they lose possession, one player must retreat to a sideline, creating the overload or imbalance in terms of team strength. Of course, on regaining possession or after a score, that team regains its player.

The season is grounded on two specific SEL competencies: self-awareness, and self-management. While acknowledged in the introductory chapter of this book as inter-related and overlapping, we believe that these individual competencies are prerequisites for successful participation in a team-based sport season. An outline of the season plan is presented in **Table 8.2**, which is followed by a detailed description of each lesson. Necessary resources such as forms, handouts, sample charts, and record forms are included.

Lesson 1

Introduction. In lesson 1, we introduce students to the three key features of the unit. The first of these is that they will be doing skills and games related to soccer, with a focus on dribbling, passing, and shooting. For some students, this will be new, as manipulating objects with the feet is not part of the everyday experience of a lot of young people. However, for others,

Table 8.2 Soccer Season Outline

Lesson	Class Events	Sport Education Features	SEL Incorporation
1. First class	Overview of the unit—which will be called a season Soccer dribbling challenges	Introduction to the key ideas of Sport Education. Students are not in teams during this lesson	Students complete "Soccer and Me"—Individual Assets sheet
2. Team formation	Teachers announces teams and role requirements Students play small sided passing games within teams	Students work together to determine (i) team name, (ii) colors, (iii) mascot, (iv) team cohesion slogan Students allocate roles and receive contracts	Introduction of "action words"
3. Skill instruction	Teacher directed soccer skill instruction Focus on dribble, pass, score	Teacher directed practice within teams	Teacher presents and class discusses "growth mindset" poster
4. Skill instruction	Teacher introduces "Overload soccer" game and rules	Officiating responsibilities outlined Teams have internal practice games	
5. Pre-season games	Officiating responsibilities and protocols Practice games (short ~ 5–6 minutes)	Teacher directed practice of officiating roles (i) pregame responsibilities, (ii) officiating roles, (iii) postgame responsibilities Introduce the score sheets and fair play assessment	"Turtle" technique of anger management

(continues)

Table 8.2 Soccer Season Outline   (continued)

Lesson	Class Events	Sport Education Features	SEL Incorporation
6–7. Preseason games	Practice games (short ~ 5–6 minutes) 3 teams per set, rotate playing and officiating	Nonconsequence games Focus on learning and developing skills and strategies	Introduce the anonymous compliment board
8–11. Competition	Competition games (~10 minutes) 3 teams per set, rotate playing and officiating Multiple games per day	Formal competition	During team warm-up, "word" and "action" managers present terms for the day. Word and action managers ensure terms are included on the fair play assessment.
12–13. Playoffs	Competition games to rank teams for finals	Formal competition	
14. Finals	Ranking and consolation matches Championship game	Culminating event	
15. Festival	Celebration of season outcome	Presentation of awards	Word and action managers present their final posters All students re-do their "Soccer and Me"—Individual Assets sheets

soccer is their sport of choice and they have extensive experience playing either locally or in more competitive club and team situations. By consequence, soccer is one of those activities where we could expect to have a wide variety of skills present among students in the class. However, it is important to remind students that in this particular unit there are plenty of opportunities for success, and that the unit has been designed so that everyone should have an enjoyable experience and feel they are more competent at the sport and know it a little bit better than when they began. That same sentiment applies to those students who are highly skilled and have significant experience.

The second aspect of the unit is that everyone will become a member of a team. These teams will develop an identity with names, colors, and mascots. They'll have a home space, and they will have their own team poster board to which everybody can contribute. Students will stay on these teams for the entire 15 lessons with the goal of improving individually and as a group. It should be mentioned briefly here that many factors will contribute to the success of the team and teams can earn points on the league table for aspects other than just the scores they get in competitions. That is, winning isn't the only thing that contributes to the season champion. These features will be outlined in more detail as we progress through

the unit. Students should also be introduced to the idea that within each team they will have a responsibility, which is called a "role." Some will be captains, some will be dealing with equipment, while others will be the warm-up leader. Other students will have responsibilities for helping their team to develop its identity as well as deciding on a daily focus in terms of individual responsibility.

The third unique aspect of this unit that needs to be introduced is the idea that it will include various aspects of SEL. The tasks, strategies, and challenges included throughout the unit are designed to help students to become more self-aware and self-responsible, as they will have responsibilities to themselves as well as helping others to enjoy the unit and improve their skills.

Dribbling skills challenges. Following this introduction, the class will then progress through several skill tasks relating to dribbling and trapping a soccer ball. At this point, students are not in teams. They are free to work in pairs or individually in cases or in pairs, select their own partners, or follow a protocol typically used by the teacher. Three sample tasks are included in **Table 8.3**, which can be used, modified, or replaced based on the teacher's content knowledge of soccer and their appreciation for student's current skill and experience levels.

Table 8.3 Sample Dribbling Tasks

Dribbling challenge 1—dribbling in general space.

Dribbling in general space using the inside and outside of the foot. Move on different pathways (straight and zigzag).

Dribbling challenge 2—dribble with turn.

Dribbling with turns (sole trap and pullback, or cut with inside or outside of the foot).

Dribbling challenge 3—dribble across the square.

Groups of four students set up a square using four cones.

Each student begins on a different side, and must dribble to the other, turn, and return to their origin. Each turn counts as one point.

The goal is to get to 6 points as quickly as possible.

Groups can determine the size of their square.

Add players to squares to promote congestion, or change the shape to a rectangle with the more skillful dribblers having to dribble across the longer distance.

"Soccer and Me" assets sheet. After the period of practice, and as the culminating activity for the class, the teacher will distribute the "Soccer and Me" assets sheet (**Figure 8.1**). The students' task is to outline their self-perceptions according to the four characteristic items listed on the sheet. They can be done in notes or written in sentences. Those students who wish to take extra time should be advised to return the completed form before the next class meeting.

Lesson 2

Placement of students on teams. In lesson 2, the major focus is on the creation of teams. Teams should consist of eight students where possible. While there are several different ways to create teams in Sport Education (e.g., drafts, selection panels, teacher-created) in this unit, it is recommended that the teacher take note of the students' responses to the "Soccer and Me" forms to ensure that teams are as balanced as possible in terms of skill and perceived enjoyment of the sport.

Upon the announcement of teams, each group will be responsible for creating its identity (i.e., team name, colors, and chant). In selecting team names, it is useful to require an adjective-noun couple (the "something somebodies"), with the terms being related to the vocabulary of the sport. Examples are the "Straight Shooters," "Goal Seekers," or "Super Strikers."

The teacher should briefly explain that the competition format will see these teams of eight dividing

into two mini teams of four. That is, if the "Headers" play the "Dribblers," they will be one Headers team of four playing the Dribblers four, and then a second game using the same organization. As the teacher, you can decide how you want to organize the competition. In one option, teams create two equal teams each day (e.g., a Blue squad and a Green squad), or if you prefer to have a form of graded competition, which means each team will have an A squad and a B squad. The value of this graded competition is that it allows the higher-skilled students to all play with each other and the lower-skilled students to play with each other against another group of equal ability levels. It is important to inform students that the results of both games count equally toward the team total. As a consequence, in graded competitions, we find that the high-level players become particularly invested in the performance of the lower-skill players and become proactive in helping them improve their soccer skills and understanding.

Introduction of team roles. Within each team, all students have a role. The captain's main responsibility is to coordinate with the teacher and understand where their team is expected to be playing or their particular responsibility. Two equipment managers will be responsible for the collection of soccer balls for practice or games, as well as any cones or goals that will be used. The warm-up leader's responsibility will include leading the team in its physical activity preparation at the beginning of lessons.

In this season, we introduce two new roles that serve to promote SEL competencies and will be named the "word managers" and "action managers." The task of these word and action managers is to identify terms such as "respect" or "helping" that represent attributes that the players on the team will focus on during the particular day or particular match. The word managers are responsible for selecting the word and sharing it with the action managers. The action managers are then responsible for identifying two examples of how that particular attribute would be enacted by students. **Textbox 8.1** gives further examples of these types of words.

Skill practice. The lesson will then proceed with whole-group instruction with the idea of creating space and making lead passes. Students work in groups of two or three. The focus is on the notion of a "receivable pass"; one that is made with enough force to get to the partner without being intercepted but not so strong that the partner cannot trap it. The distance that students can make these passes will vary depending on the skills of the students in the class, their ability to make the pass, and their ability to receive

- *For each of these four areas, describe what you know, can do, and enjoy about soccer.*
- *Then describe how you see yourself as a teammate.*
- *Comments can be positive, negative, or neutral. There are NO correct or best answers.*

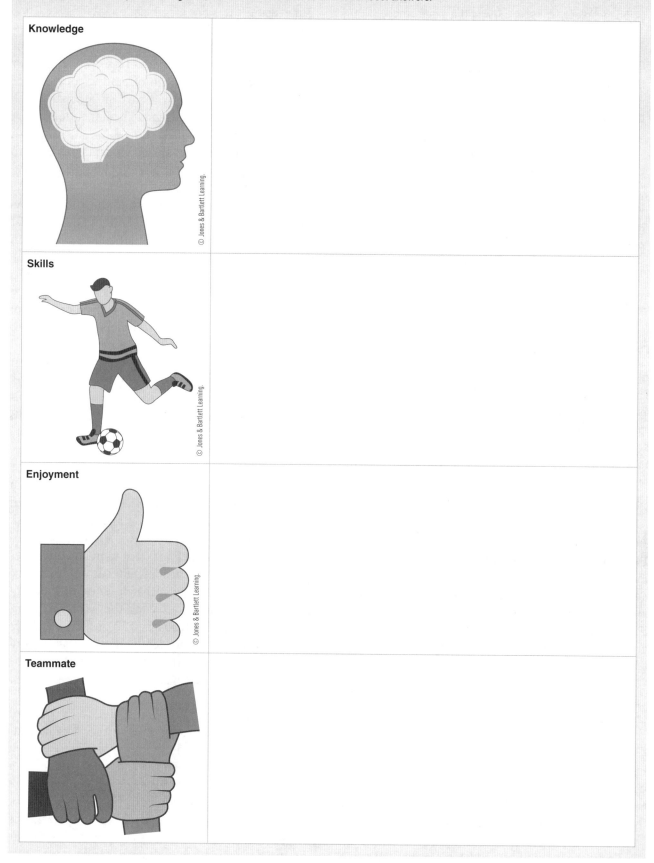

Figure 8.1 "Soccer and Me" individual assets sheet.

TEXTBOX 8.1

Sample Terms for Word and Action Managers

Respect	Helping	Kindness	Cooperation
Effort	Trying	Encouragement	Sharing

the pass. As teams work in their groups, encourage the higher-skilled players to practice with someone with less experience, focusing on the idea of *helping* and *encouraging*. Following this practice, students will participate in a mini-game of "5 consecutive passes." Here, the focus is on making passing a receivable pass to an open player and then moving into space to be a receiver. The organization for this game is presented in **Figure 8.2**.

Lesson 3

In lesson 3, we see the beginning of team activities and the initiation of some of the routines that are required for a proficient season. Teams should arrive at class and go to their designated team areas. The warm-up leaders should go to the teacher to receive a "mission possible" card, which they will then lead their team through a series of activities. A sample mission impossible card is included in **Textbox 8.2**.

Skill practice. Following warm-ups, teams will engage in small practices. Activities should focus on dribbling (including stopping and turning) and

passing into space. Captains can either lead practices or receive a task card from the teacher with suggested drills to introduce. This will depend on the experience of the student coaches and/or the teacher's readiness to hand over some instructional responsibilities to students.

One highly suitable mini game that can be played within teams is a "2 vs. 1+1" passing game. This game focuses on dribbling and passing to score, while supporting the player in possession. This is shown in **Figure 8.3**.

TEXTBOX 8.2

Your mission: Complete the following

10 jumping jacks – 5 mountain climbers – Plank exercise for 15 secs – Wall sit for 15 secs – V V-sit stretch for 10 secs – Your Mission Is Complete!

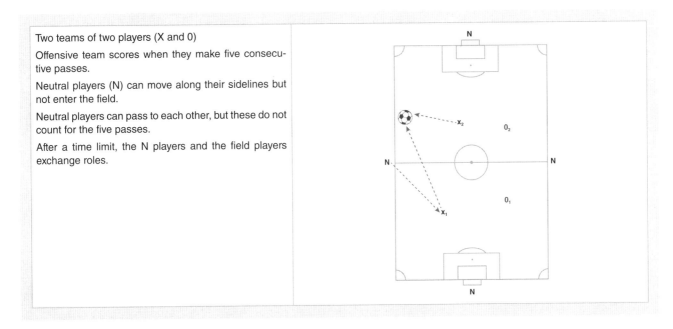

Two teams of two players (X and 0)

Offensive team scores when they make five consecutive passes.

Neutral players (N) can move along their sidelines but not enter the field.

Neutral players can pass to each other, but these do not count for the five passes.

After a time limit, the N players and the field players exchange roles.

Figure 8.2 Five consecutive passes game.

Data from Ward, P. C., & Lehwald, H. (2018). *Effective physical education content and instruction: An evidence-based and teacher-tested approach.* Champaign, IL: Human Kinetics.

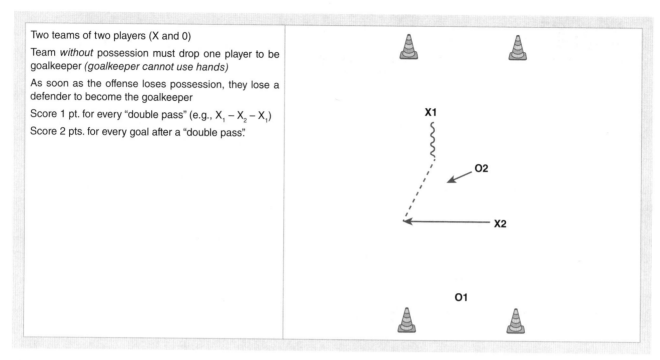

Two teams of two players (X and 0)

Team *without* possession must drop one player to be goalkeeper *(goalkeeper cannot use hands)*

As soon as the offense loses possession, they lose a defender to become the goalkeeper

Score 1 pt. for every "double pass" (e.g., $X_1 - X_2 - X_1$)

Score 2 pts. for every goal after a "double pass."

Figure 8.3 2 vs. 4 1+1 passing game.

Data from Ward, P. C., & Lehwald, H. (2018). *Effective physical education content and instruction: An evidence-based and teacher-tested approach.* Champaign, IL: Human Kinetics.

Growth mindset. After this skills practice and mini-games section, the teacher will present the idea of a "growth mindset." According to Dweck (2016), there are two main types of mindsets: growth and fixed. When a student has a fixed mindset, they believe that their basic abilities, intelligence, and talents are fixed traits and are essentially unchangeable. They may also believe that external factors are mainly responsible for their success. In a growth mindset, however, students believe their abilities and intelligence can be developed with effort, learning, and persistence—brains and talent are just the starting point. This growth mindset gives them the room to grow and takes the opportunities at hand to do just that, whereas someone with a fixed mindset closes them off from the learning experience, causing their progress to stagnate (**Figure 8.4**).

By discussing the two mindsets, we can help students to "unlock their willingness to learn" during the coming soccer season. That is, they probably will not win every game or score every goal, but it is the effort to keep getting better and trying hard that will result in

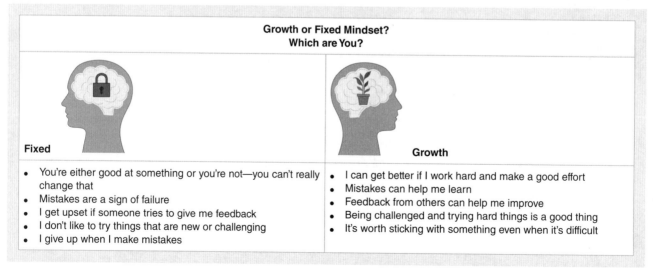

Figure 8.4 What is your mindset?

Data from Dweck, C. S. (2016). *Mindset: The new psychology of success.* New York, NY: Random House.

a better outcome. Likewise, seeing teammates as people who can help you get better is another positive way to improve as a soccer player.

Lesson 4

In lesson 4, the teacher's main goal is to introduce the game form that will be played during the competition phase of the season. The game is a "4 vs. 4" game, but in essence, it is 4 vs. 3. That is, as soon as a team loses possession either by the ball going out of bounds, by an interception, or after a goal, one player from that team must immediately run to the sideline and remain there until the team gains possession of the ball. As a result, the team in possession now has an overload of players so that someone should always be unguarded. The defensive team will then have to decide whether to drop a player to act as a goalkeeper, (which then creates a 4 vs. 2 situation for the offense), or bring all of their players into defensive roles with the goal of regaining possession.

In explaining the game, the teacher will gather the whole class and present a demonstration game of two groups of four players from different teams. These students then participate in a mock game with the teacher starting and stopping to reinforce the rules about out of bounds, what happens after a score, and legal ways to gain possession. Gaining possession in this game can consist of a player taking the ball from another player who is dribbling, or by intercepting a pass. **Figure 8.5** shows the setup of the game.

After a short period of play, the teacher will rotate in eight new players until all students have developed a solid understanding of how the game is played. Games need to be long enough that there are sufficient examples of quick turnovers so that players have practiced running to the sideline quickly. Students should be reminded that in an instant, their team may regain possession, but they still need to cross the sideline before rejoining the team.

The teacher also needs to explain to students that they need to develop tactics regarding which player will leave the field. While some teams may decide to rotate their players in order as they transition on and off, they will soon realize that following this pre-planned system is quite counterproductive. Rather, the player best suited to leave the field will depend on many factors. These can include (i) the position of the ball relative to the defensive players, (ii) how close the team gaining possession is to making a shot on goal, or (iii) whether the team that gains possession is deep in their backfield. Nevertheless, the teacher must reinforce to everybody that the best players cannot be the ones on the field all the time, and time

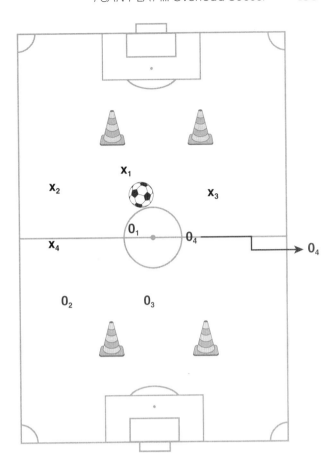

Figure 8.5 4 vs. 4 4 game set up.

spent on the sideline should be distributed in a fair way among the players.

Team practice. Depending on the time available, the teacher can send teams to their home areas to get up fields where they can practice this 4 vs. 4 game for the remainder of the lesson. Teams can self-officiate and explore player combinations, as during the formal competition the performance of both mini teams counts equally to the league table.

Lesson 5

In lesson 5, we mimic the organization of lesson four where students are gathered with the teacher who presents a single game to the whole class. The difference in this case, however, is that the focus is on the officials rather than on the rules of the game. The teacher will be responsible for taking the students through three key aspects of game day, those being the pregame responsibilities of each team, officiating roles and duties, and postgame responsibilities.

Pregame responsibilities. In terms of pregame responsibilities, students need to know whether they will be playing or officiating. Second, they also need to know to which field or area they should report. There are two ways to do this. First, the teacher can call the captains at the beginning of each lesson and overview the teams involved in competitions (playing and officiating) as well as the field on which games are to be played. Alternately, this schedule can be listed on a whiteboard or notice board either immediately as the students enter the gym, or outside the locker rooms if students are required to change. It is helpful to instruct students that the first named team would be wearing a specific jersey color, with the second team wearing another. In some cases, teachers will have black and white striped jerseys for the officiating team.

After identifying their playing/officiating role and game area, students will go to their team areas and do their mission possible warm-up and get into their two groups of four for their upcoming games. This is a protocol that needs to be formally taught and needs significant practice. Teams should be held accountable for following this routine to maximize the time spent playing games.

Introducing the officials. The next segment of the lesson will involve the teacher going over the responsibilities of the officiating team in preparation for a game. There will be four officials responsible for each game (see **Figure 8.6**). Two players will be standing behind the two goals, each with a ball. Their responsibility is to signal whether a goal has been scored and then also to give a ball to the playing teams

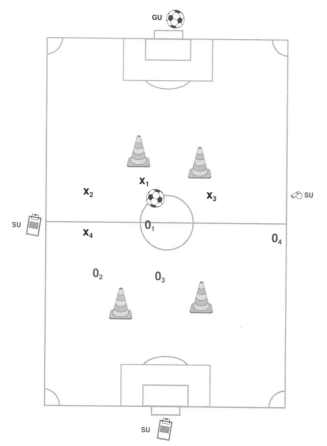

Figure 8.6 4 vs. 4 4 game with officials.

if it was kicked over the end line. This "goal umpire" will then chase the loose ball so that play can continue.

On the two long sidelines, there will be two "side umpires." One of these will be the chief scorekeeper and the other will be the referee. The scorekeeper is responsible for keeping account for which players score goals and the direction of play should the ball cross their sideline. They will also be responsible for ensuring that the players who need to go to that sideline cross the field of play. The nonscoring side umpire is responsible for stopping play after a goal, ensuring that the scorekeeper has recorded the result of the play, and gathering the other officials to evaluate fair play at the end of a match. These officials will not be part of the practice games during day four, but it is worthwhile for the teacher to explain this system as it will come into the games that follow in lessons five onward.

When it is their turn to officiate, a team needs to first identify which field to go to, and then collect a box that includes all of the materials they need for the game. This will consist of clipboards, scoresheets, and pencils at a bare minimum. Each student will also take a ball used in their team practice to use during games. Before each game, the captains from the two teams need to meet with the scorekeeper, tell them their team name, team color, and the word and action managers will also tell the scorekeeper the "action word" for the day and an example of what the scorekeeper should be looking for.

A practice game can then take place with the rest of the class observing. It is the teacher's prerogative to stop play and ask the offensive team about rules or scoring. The teacher can also ask those students who are observing what the off team should be doing at this point. This involves all students in the class. A series of example games can be played with the whole class observing so that at least half of the students get an opportunity to participate.

Post-game responsibilities. At the end of each game, there is another set of protocols that students need to learn. First, both teams will line up and shake hands in the center of the field (also with the officials). The two captains will complete the two-item referee report, answering yes or no for each question. At the same time, the officiating team will get together to answer the three fair play questions listed on the officiating report. The officiating team will also indicate if they saw an example of the action word chosen by each team before the game. The scoresheet will then be put on the bottom of the clipboard and returned to the box. Teams will then change jerseys as required and the second match can begin. A sample of a complete scoresheet is shown in **Figure 8.7**.

Team Name Super Strikers	Score		Team Name Devilish Dribblers	Score	
	YES	NO		YES	NO
Did this team play by the rules and not argue with the officials?	✓		Did this team play by the rules and not argue with the officials?	✓	
Did the players on this team encourage each other?	✓		Did the players on this team encourage each other?		✓
Did the players on this team not get angry when a teammate made a mistake?	✓		Did the players on this team not get angry when a team mate made a mistake?	✓	
Team action word "Effort—not giving up even if losing"	✓		Team action word "Cooperation—not arguing about who goes to the side"	✓	
They really tried hard. They never stopped running after the ball.			No one ever argued about whose turn it was to go to the side.		

Figure 8.7 Sample completed fair play report.

Data from Siedentop, D., Hastie, P., & Van der Mars, H. (2019). *Complete guide to sport education*. Champaign, IL: Human Kinetics.

Introducing the "turtle." In the first set of competitive matches, it is likely that there will be cases of students getting angry, arguing with officials, or being critical of teammates. These provide opportune teachable moments for the introduction of the "turtle technique of anger management" (Robin, Schneider, & Dolnick, 1976). **Figure 8.8** provides a graphic of the four steps that a student can take for their frustration to dissipate and to prevent it from escalating into some form of conflict. As demonstrated in this figure, the first step is perhaps the most important in that students must recognize they are frustrated or angry. Once they can do this, they can progress to "stop and think," "take deep breaths and become calm," and then "reemerge when thinking of a solution." Of course, when teaching this technique, the teacher needs to help students identify some potential solutions. At this point, it is more than worthwhile to make the class come up with scenarios when students might become angry and possible solutions to those scenarios.

Lessons 6 and 7

In lessons 6 and 7, we see all teams engaging in practice games. These will be short, 5 to 6-minute games with three teams occupying two fields, if possible. Two teams will be playing with their subgroups of four, while the third group sends four officials to each field. The focus of these games is learning skills and strategies and helping the officiating team practice all the pre- and postgame protocols. Having teams in groups of three means that after each five-minute

game, teams rotate one space with one of the playing teams taking the place of the officiating team. It is for this reason that at the beginning of the season it is very helpful to have the total number of teams in the class divisible by three.

Each lesson will start with a quick gathering in team areas and a warm-up with a mission possible card. Team captains will have checked the notice board and teams will divide into their two groups of four and on the teacher's signal, go to their field and start games. It is helpful to have all games start and stop at the same time so the entire class is on the same timeline in terms of filling out game forms, either before or after completion of the game.

It is important to remind students that these games do not count toward the regular season standings, allowing them to experiment with their line ups, practice efficient ways of substituting the lost player, and not demonstrate *self*-awareness by not getting frustrated with the officials who are also learning the skills. The teacher can stop a particular game to clarify a rule with the players, to interject with an official to make sure they are doing their job, or to make sure they understand their responsibility. It is also important for the teacher that the forms that are submitted after the game are done correctly so that when the class moves into formal competition in lesson 8, these practices are automatic for students and their scores can be used for the class league table.

Anonymous Compliment Board. At the end of lesson 6, the teacher will introduce the "anonymous compliment board." Each time a student sees

Step 1. Recognize your feelings.

Step 2. Stop your body.

Step 3. Tuck inside your shell and take three deep breaths.

Step 4. Come out when you are calm and think of a solution.

Figure 8.8 Turtle technique.

Created by and available from the National Center for Pyramid Model Innovations (NCPMI) at ChallengingBehavior.org

a classmate engage in a positive behavior (e.g., kind, thoughtful, generous, sympathetic), they should feel free to write what they saw and/or heard on a board created by the teacher and displayed where it is easily seen **without** using any names (including their own or the other person's). All that should be given is a brief description of the positive act they observed or words they heard. To encourage participation, the teacher might provide a small poster that includes removable "post-it" notes that students can use, as well as a larger "compliments board" for posting. Every second or third lesson, the teacher can celebrate the class's positive acts by reading aloud some of the contributions. During the introduction of the board in lesson 6, the teacher can encourage students to consider "what's it like to look for positive acts and words in others?" "what's it like for others to notice when you are doing or saying positive things?" and "how may this activity help us to feel more respected or valued?"

Lessons 8 to 11

In lessons 8–11, the formal competition takes place. It is in these games that points for fair play, points for win/loss, and points allocated to the officiating team by the players count toward the league table. Competition games in these lessons are 10 minutes long with teams set in groups of three who rotate through placing and officiating responsibilities. The teacher should aim for a transition time between games of less than four minutes, with the reminder for students being that the more efficient and quicker they are in terms of getting pre- and postgame paperwork completed, the longer time can be allocated toward games. It will be a teaching decision at this time as to whether to allow teams to change up the composition of their players from game to game or day to day.

Word and action managers. It is during the formal competition that the word and action managers present their terms for the day onto the score sheet. The word manager will write the term word for their team on the scoresheet while the action manager will provide the scorekeeper and the goal umpires examples of actions that would represent that particular positive word. During games, it is the responsibility of the officiating team to identify, where possible, at least one example where each team has put its positive action into place and record this on the sheet. It should be noted that these do not count toward league standings but rather as an awareness exercise. In some cases, teachers allocate time at the end of each lesson for officiating teams to present the results of games and explain the fair point allocation, and it would be during this time that each officiating team gives one example of a successful positive action put in play by one of their teams.

Lessons 12 and 13

In lessons 12 and 13, the teacher will schedule matches that form a type of playoff. The results of these games determine the final ranking games in lesson 14. It is important to remember that the inclusive nature of Sport Education sees *all* teams making the playoffs and engaged in the postseason. Rather than having one overall champion, some teachers divide their class into bronze, silver, and gold divisions based on their rankings to date. These teams will then participate in a further set of competitions over these two days. If teams are level on points and a teacher is interested in separating them across divisions, the normal protocol is to use the accumulated fair play points as the first divider or tiebreaker.

Lesson 14

In lesson 14, we see the finals of the division championships being played. These can be run simultaneously or one after the other leading to the gold division final. Depending on the time available, third-place playoff games can be included. The officiating teams for these championship games can be those with the highest refereeing grades if they are not engaged in the games themselves, thereby acting as an acknowledgment of their achievement during the season. Classroom teachers, administrators, or parents can be invited to attend these matches.

Lesson 15

In lesson 15, we celebrate the outcomes of the season from a multitude of perspectives. It should be remembered that the focus should be on the *festive* nature of the event. As Scheibler (1999) notes, "in the festival, the focus is not directed to the individual but to their participation in something [an event]…the festival celebration is shared; participation is a sharing in an event" (p. 151–152). As Siedentop, Hastie, & van der Mars (2020) note, a wonderful way to promote this sharing is to involve those from outside the regular physical education classes. At a minimum, classroom teachers, school administrators, and parents and friends can be formally invited. Furthermore, some teachers and classes have invited the local press to their celebrations and have garnered newspaper coverage of the final day's activities. Others have produced a highlights video and shown these together with a special guest speaker at a special "players' breakfast." Given the focus on the SEL competencies of self-awareness and self-direction, part of the program for this final day could include the word and action managers making a presentation of their team's poster, which lists the attributes they have developed over the season. Each term could be responsible for selecting two or three words they found particularly powerful in directing their actions across the season.

A key part of a culminating event lies in honoring those who have achieved high levels concerning the goals of the season. It is important, however, to remember that as the goals of the Sport Education go beyond skillful play, the awards given should reflect those goals. In this season, teachers might choose from the following: championship team in each division, most improved individuals (nominated by their teammates), best fair play teams (those with the highest fair play points), and best officiating teams, as well as quality coaching awards. While not part of the formal celebration, we believe it would be particularly worthwhile for teachers to ask students to revisit the "Soccer and Me" Individual assets sheet, and to make any comments with respect to any changes they have in their perceptions of the sport, their skill, or their enjoyment of the game. Students could also be asked to identify one single case from the season that seems pivotal in changing their beliefs about their assets.

"Together Everyone Achieves More" TEAM Fitness

A Sport Education Season for Secondary School Students

This fitness Sport Education season is designed for students in secondary physical education classes and is based on the unit described by Hastie et al. (2020). It is different from the elementary example in the format of the season, as well as the specific SEL competencies promoted. The season follows the event model format of Sport Education (Siedentop, Hastie, & van der Mars, 2020) in which lessons focusing on teacher instruction and team practice are interspersed by a series of competitions. Within this season, all competitions are team-based, but with each student making an individual contribution toward a team score.

The season is grounded on two specific SEL competencies: social-awareness and relationship skills. These competencies are important features where a

team's success depends on the active engagement of all members in planning, training, and competition performance. Nonetheless, there are additional connections to SEL that are threaded throughout the season.

Season Outline

There are three types of lessons within the season, with their labels representing the emphasis of instruction: instruction days, team practice days, and competition days. On *instruction days* (I), students participate in fitness circuits with either an aerobic or muscular strength/endurance emphasis or are introduced to upcoming challenges. *Team practice days* (TP) are designated for teams to spend class time training for or designing upcoming challenges. Teams have control over how they choose to spend their time and are encouraged to prepare individually by focusing on exercises they believe will prepare them for success.

Three *competitions* (C) are held during the season. Each competition takes two lessons, with the first being a practice day where students learn the organization of the competition and how to officiate. These competitions are given the following titles: *Everyone across the Gym, Head-to-Head Challenge*, and the *Until Challenge*. An outline of the season plan is presented in **Table 8.4**.

Lesson 1

The first lesson introduces students to the idea of a season based on three specific challenges. Following the announcement of teams, the teacher will remind students that even though everyone will participate in the challenges as individuals, all competitions are team-based, in which the performance of individuals are combined to create a team score. At this point, the teacher will introduce students to the TEAM (**T**ogether **E**veryone **A**chieves **M**ore) moniker, which is central to the season. Given that the format of the

Table 8.4 Fitness Season Outline

Lesson	Class Events	Sport Education Features	SEL Incorporation
1. First class (I)	Introduction to the season Concept of challenges Announcement of teams (based on earlier fitness test scores) Complete team sheets	Announcement of teams Team affiliation tasks	Strategies to promote productive group discussions
2. MSE (I)	Aerobic circuit Focus on the aerobic concept of "rhythmical, repetitive activities using large muscle groups over prolonged periods"	Teacher directed instruction	Self-awareness, self-management, and responsible decision making during tasks

(continues)

Table 8.4 Fitness Season Outline *(continued)*

Lesson	Class Events	Sport Education Features	SEL Incorporation
3. Aerobic lesson (I)	Muscular strength and endurance (MSE) circuit Focus on MSE concept of "resistance"	Teacher-directed instruction	Self-awareness, self-management, and responsible decision making during tasks
4 (I)	Introduce Challenge 1 *(Across the Gym)* Team practice and training	Teacher directed instruction	Defining teamwork poster
5-6 (TP)	Team practice and training Refine challenge course	Individual and team training	Self-awareness, self-management, and responsible decision making during tasks Exploring "Grit" and "Resilience"
7 (C)	Challenge 1 practice run Encourage quick set up and explanation Focus on scorekeeping	Officiating responsibilities and scorekeeping outlined Practice competitions	Responsible decision making
8 (C)	Across the Gym competition	Formal competition	Responsible decision making
9 (I/TP)	Introduce Challenge 2 *(The "Until" Challenge)* Team practice and training	Teams discuss strategies and design training tasks	Team SWOT analysis
10-11 (TP)	Team practice and training	Individual and team training	Self-awareness, self-management, and responsible decision making during tasks Exploring "Openness" and "Leadership"
12 (C)	Challenge 2 practice run The "Until" Challenge	Officiating responsibilities and scorekeeping outlined Practice competitions	Responsible decision making
13 (C)	The "Until" challenge competition	Formal competition	Responsible decision making
14 (I/TP)	Introduce challenge 3 *(Head to Head)* Team practice and training	Teams discuss exercise options for challenge	Share, Co-Create and Trust
15-16 (TP)	Team practice and training	Teams finalize their challenge Individual and team training	
17 (C)	Challenge 3 practice run Head to Head	Officiating responsibilities and scorekeeping outlined Practice competitions	
18-19 (C)	Head to Head Competitions Multiple rounds depending upon class time	Formal competitions	
20 (I)	Present awards and final festivity	Presentation of awards	Teams present their Teamwork poster

I .. teacher instruction days
TP .. team practice days
C .. competition days

competitions requires teams to make decisions about training and planning for competitions, this first lesson includes an activity designed to help students identify strategies that promote productive group discussions. Working on communication skills provides opportunity for explicit connection to SEL *relationship skills* and *social awareness* competencies.

The activity included in this lesson introduces students to four personality types of different individuals who have the potential to derail quality group discussions. We call these "the organizer," "the quiet kid," "the system bucker," and "the uncommitted." The activity is presented in **Table 8.5** and should not take long as it is designed as an awareness exercise. Rather than coming up with definitive solutions, students are asked to first think inwardly about how they would contribute positively to group discussions, and then collectively in terms of how they could successfully incorporate the students represented.

Table 8.5 Threats to Productive Group Discussions Task

---

1. Distribute four cards to one student with the cards in this order:

THE ORGANIZER

- Always the first to come up with an idea
- Needs to organize everything and everyone
- Has an answer for every situation

THE QUIET KID

- Rarely if ever speaks
- Answers questions only briefly
- Never bothers the other group members

THE SYSTEM BUCKER

- Consistently disagrees or opposes ideas
- Doesn't take the tasks seriously
- Often acts as a comedian

THE UNCOMMITTED

- Doesn't participate
- Tells the group, "just let me know what to do when you decide"
- Performs other work or is distracted (e.g., on their phone, etc.)

2. One student reads the first card
3. All students silently score themselves on a "that's so me" to "that's not like me at all" scale
4. Students identify the risk to productive group discussions
5. All students brainstorm a solution strategy
6. Repeat with the next card, until all four are discussed
7. Teacher then gives a Wild Card, wherein each team can identify any other sport personality that could be counterproductive

---

Lessons 2 and 3

During lessons 2 and 3, students participate in fitness circuits with either an aerobic or muscular strength/endurance emphasis. As students progress through each station of a circuit, they are challenged with modifying the base exercise to either increase its intensity (aerobic lessons) or to change the resistance (muscular strength/endurance). For example, at a jump rope station, options that increase intensity may include single leg hops, squat jumps, or lunge jumps. Likewise, students at a push-up station are encouraged to "change angles" to either increase or decrease the difficulty (i.e., resistance). Answers may include doing push-ups against a wall as an easier option or by elevating the legs on a bench as one that creates more resistance.

The arrangement of these circuits, with in-built opportunities for modification, connect to SEL competencies including *self-awareness* (i.e., understanding and honestly assessing strengths and needs), *self-management* (i.e., individual focus and discipline required to develop and stick to a plan, goals, etc.), and *responsible decision making* (i.e., making choices and decisions throughout that must be guided by considerations for safety and health enhancement).

Lesson 4

In lesson 4, the "Across the Gym" challenge is introduced exclusively as a team competition. That is, while different team members will produce different performance levels, it is only the team's score that will be used in the ranking system. In simple terms, the teams will have to use teamwork to help them maximize their performance in the challenge. The concept of "teamwork" will be developed through the season rather than something expected to be achieved from all groups from day one.

The SEL task in lesson 4 is the presentation of a better teamwork template. Students will be asked to make additions to this template as the season progresses to get examples that they saw from either their own group or another group during training or competitions. In the final lesson of the season, each team will present their "Teamwork" poster, which represents the five elements of effective teamwork. **Figure 8.9** represents the skeleton of this poster and students are expected to develop it throughout the unit. In this lesson, students are only asked to discuss potential or tentative definitions of these terms. Through the season, teams will begin to formalize those definitions and will provide other artifacts such

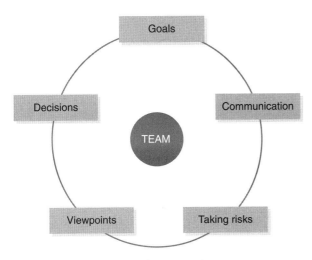

Figure 8.9 The concept of teamwork.

as photos of students engaged in practice or competition, quotes from students, or images from magazines or online media.

Across the Gym Challenge. The *"Across the Gym"* challenge follows a traditional Cross Fit-like format where students advance from one side of the activity area to the other by completing specific exercises. However, in this season, while all students will perform the same exercises, the number of reps of each exercise is reduced for each successive team member. In this challenge, the goal is to get one's whole team "across the gym" in the fastest time possible. Typically,

there are two heats so that half of the teams are competing while the other half are officiating. If lessons are of sufficient length, a finals series can be held matching the positions from the semifinals.

This challenge involves, in order, jump ropes; sitting leg extensions; bench push-ups; medicine ball squats; and finally, a core exercise involving pushing a scooter using only the legs. The first team member will complete 40, 30, 20, 15, and 10 reps of the respective exercises, with the remaining members completing successively fewer reps. **Figure 8.10**, provides details of each challenge, and the number of reps for each participant. Each team member can begin a station only when the player before them has completed the appropriate number of reps. This rule requires teams to strategize about the order of their team members and connected to *social awareness* and *relationship skills*. Remind earlier finishers to support and encourage their teammates who are still competing.

Note for teachers. Place one member from the officiating team at each station. Their responsibility is to count the reps (only those completed appropriately) and indicate to the competitor when they have completed the task. They then motion to the next competitor that the station is "open." Ensure that these judges have a card with the progressive rep count. The jump rope judge will also be responsible for recording the time taken for the entire competing team to finish the

	Jump Rope		Leg extensions		Bench push-ups		Med Ball Squat		Scooter Swim		
START	40 35 30 25 20	→	30 25 20 15 10	→	20 17 14 11 8	→	15 12 10 8 5	→	5 4 3 2 1	→	FINISH

Jump rope
- Jump ropes in place

Sitting leg extensions
- Sit in a hoop, with hands on the floor, and a foam ball between the feet
- Player extends legs straight and then brings knees to chest
- Ball must pass across the edge of the hoop

Bench Push-ups
- Begin with feet placed on a low aerobics bench
- Hands are on the floor
- Player must complete the set number of push-ups for their round

Medicine Ball Squat
- Holding the medicine ball, squat to touch a box or a milk crate

Scooter Swim
- Lie on a scooter and using only arms, complete one circuit around a cone

Figure 8.10 Across the gym organization and rules.

Data from Hastie, P., Boyd, K., Ward, J. K., & Stringfellow, A. (2020). Promoting the 50 million strong agenda through sport education. *Journal of Physical Education, Recreation, & Dance, 91*(8), 8–14.

challenge. This person is best suited as their station is completed first.

Lessons 5 and 6

Lessons 5 and 6 are allocated to team practice as they prepare for the first competition. Individual differences and preferences can be accommodated here, and students are encouraged to spend this time developing their strengths and weaknesses (an example of *self-awareness*). For example, some students may run to develop aerobic fitness, while other students may focus on muscular strength or endurance activities by doing bodyweight squats with a weighted ball. In essence, team practice days provide students with autonomy to select physical activities that they find personally enjoyable. As such, they provide significant opportunities for *self-management, self-awareness,* and *responsible decision making.*

In order to help students identify behavioral examples of these constructs, we turn to the ACT Tessera conception of the "Big 5" social emotional skills they believe attributes contribute to academic skills and academic achievement, career success, and lifelong well-being. These have been aligned with the CASEL competencies by Walton et al. (2019) and are listed as "grit" (*self-management* and *responsible decision making*), teamwork (*social awareness, relationship skills,* and *responsible decision making*), openness (social awareness), resilience (*self-awareness* and *self-management*) and leadership (*self-awareness* and *relationship skills*). **Table 8.6** provides behavioral examples of four of

these skills, with teamwork being omitted because it is a central part of team posters.

In lesson 5, the teacher will introduce two of these skills to students (grit and resilience), and challenge them to not only show them during team practices but also to identify examples of them through photos or "call-outs" with descriptive examples. The teacher will have a "Big 5" notice board associated with these skills where students can add artifacts in various forms.

Lessons 7 and 8

Lesson 7 is allocated to a practice run of the Across the Gym challenge. The focus during this lesson is on scorekeeping and officiating responsibilities. As such, teachers will remind students of the need for *responsible decision making*, as officials have ethical and moral obligations to help the competition be a fair contest. In lesson 8, the formal competition takes place. It is in these lessons that teams have the opportunities to collect photos or written callouts highlighting "Grit" and "Resilience." Furthermore, these don't have to be limited to members of the students' own team but of any examples they deem worthy.

Lesson 9

In lesson 9, the "Until" challenge is introduced. Following the presentation of the challenge, teams are given the opportunities to discuss strategies and design training tasks for the next three lessons.

Table 8.6 Behavioral Examples of ACT Tessera Skills

Grit	
	■ Attempts challenging things ■ Keeps trying even when things get difficult ■ Checks to see if he/she is meeting goals ■ Seeks out and responds to feedback (from peer or teacher)
Resilience	
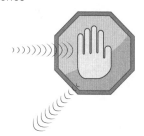	■ Doesn't worry much about things that have happened in the past ■ Doesn't worry much about upcoming events that are out of his/her control

(continues)

Table 8.6 Behavioral Examples of ACT Tessera Skills *(continued)*

Openness 	■ Attempts to be creative on team challenges ■ Tries to think of new or different ways to solve problems ■ Is willing to consider others' points of view
Leadership 	■ Volunteers to be leader even when not asked to do so ■ Expresses positive ideas and opinions ■ Offers encouragement to others

Data from Walton, K. E., Burrus, J., Anguiano-Carrasco, C., Way, J., & Murano, D. (2019). Aligning ACT Tessera to the Collaborative for Academic, Social, and Emotional Learning (CASEL) framework. Technical brief. ACT, Inc.

To help teams become more systematic in terms of planning, training, and competition, and strategies, we introduce the concept of a SWOT (**S**trengths, **W**eaknesses, **O**pportunities, **T**hreats) analysis in this lesson. **Table 8.7** provides a sample task sheet that could be given to teams.

'Until" challenge. In this challenge, each team must complete a specific number of set exercises, but with only a limited amount of equipment (see **Figure 8.11**). All team members must do at least one rep of each exercise, but not all team members have to do equal numbers of repetitions, *until* the entire challenge is completed. A sample challenge may

consist of 300 jump ropes, 200 mountain climbers, 200 bench step-ups, 100 burpees, and 15 crab walks (around two cones 10 feet apart).

During the challenge, team members can move from one activity to another at any time allowing for significant group strategic planning, particularly given that the equipment is limited. This arrangement of exercise choice highlights *self- and social-awareness* as it provides individual students as well as the teams with the opportunity to evaluate their fitness strengths and weakness, thereby encouraging them to implement strategies that would allow the team to maximize each player's potential as they strive to complete the

Table 8.7 SWOT Analysis

SWOT Analysis

■ As a group, discuss and identify your:
■ **STRENGTHS—WEAKNESSES** (internal) and **OPPORTUNITIES—THREATS** (external)
■ This will generate information about your situation and provide a platform to air everybody's assumptions and opinions. Remember that weaknesses can be viewed as opportunities and serious weaknesses can be small threats.

STRENGTHS	WEAKNESSES
OPPORTUNITIES	THREATS

300 jump ropes	200 mountain climbers	100 bench step ups	100 burpees (1 available)	15 crab walks
2 ropes	2 stations	2 benches	1 mat	1 circuit

Figure 8.11 Equipment used during the Until Challenge.

Data from Hastie, P., Boyd, K., Ward, J. K., & Stringfellow, A. (2020). Promoting the 50 million strong agenda through sport education. *Journal of Physical Education, Recreation, & Dance, 91*(8), 8–14.

challenge the fastest. It also allows for diversity during training days, where students can select to maximize their strengths or work on their weaknesses.

Notes for teachers. During the competition, one team completes the challenge while the other keeps score and time (then teams reverse roles). We gave the scoring teams pieces of equipment, such as bean bags or yarn balls with which to score. For jump rope as an example, the two scorekeepers have 10 yarn balls. They drop a yarn ball each time the student/s they watch complete 30 jump ropes. This means that a station becomes CLOSED when all of the scoring equipment has been dropped. When all teams have completed the challenge, the teacher ranks the times of all the teams. An example of an eight-team league might see the fastest scoring 10 pts, 2nd = 8, 3rd = 6, 4th = 5, 5th = 4, 7th = 3, and 8th = 2. As per the first competition, teachers should remind those in charge of roles such as time management and judging of the value of practicing *responsible decision making* as their choices and actions set the tone for fairness, structure, and safety.

Lessons 10 and 11

Similar to lessons 5 and 6, these lessons are allocated to team practice as they prepare for the second competition. However, the competencies of *self-awareness, self-management,* and *responsible decision making* are highlighted here in that teams are relying on each individual to contribute in a unique way, as they will have a specialty role. In these lessons, and during the subsequent trail run and competition in lessons 12 and 13, the teacher will encourage students to again look for behavioral examples of "openness" and "leadership." Again, any artifacts can be added to the "Big 5" notice board through voluntary contributions from students.

Lessons 12 and 13

Lesson 12 is allocated to a practice run of the 'Until' challenge. As per the first competition, the focus during this lesson is on scorekeeping and officiating responsibilities. As before, teachers will revisit with students that their choices and actions

during these roles set the tone for fairness, structure, and safety. In lesson 13, the formal competition takes place.

Lesson 14

In lesson 14, the "Head to Head" challenge is introduced. This is the challenge where teams can decide or create their own fitness obstacle course understanding that they will compete against other teams in a head-to-head format. In the presentation of the challenge, teams will be encouraged to construct a course that maximizes the fitness strengths present within their team. That is, some courses will focus more on aerobic fitness, while others might favor muscular strength and endurance.

To help focus students on this task, the concept of "three foundational collaboration behaviors" will be introduced. These are presented in **Figure 8.12**. At the center is the concept of "vision," teams will be asked to create their "vision of success" for the upcoming competitions. This vision is ringed by the concepts of "share," "trust," and "co-create." Teams will also be asked to briefly identify and discuss what these concepts mean to them with the idea of using

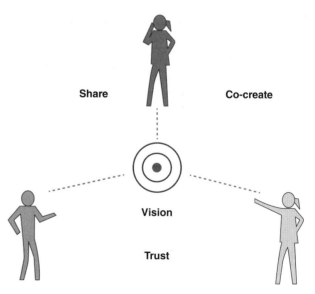

Figure 8.12 Three foundational collaboration behaviors.

these collaborative behaviors to maximize their performance as they design their challenge and engage in competitions.

Head to Head Challenge. The Head-to-Head Challenges can be organized in either of two formats. In the first format, teams design their own "Across the Gym" challenge as per the first competition. In the second format, teams design an exercise obstacle course in the form of a relay. In both cases, there should be elements of both aerobic endurance and muscular strength/endurance, but the ratio of each should reflect each team's fitness strengths. That is, teams should create challenges they believe will maximize their fitness strengths, a process requiring *self- and social-awareness*, as well as *responsible (strategic) decision making*. On the two competition days, each team will compete against one other team. First, one representative from each team will explain their team's rules and demonstrate the challenge to their opponents. This team then officiates that challenge and records the visiting team's time and/or score. The teams then exchange roles. The team that scores the faster time/higher score on each challenge is awarded five points, a total of 10 possible points if a team wins both challenges. Multiple challenges can take place with newly matched teams depending on the length of the lesson. Complete instructions to students are provided in **Figure 8.13**.

Note for teachers. In relay events, teams might choose to include penalty points, by adding five seconds if an opponent knocks over a hurdle or touches a jump rope when crawling under or jumping over an object. Teams are encouraged to design circuits that will maximize their abilities and fitness profiles while potentially exploiting their opponents' weaknesses. They are also encouraged to "look around" and see what other teams are designing.

Lessons 15 and 16

By the end of lesson 15, the team should have finalized their challenge and started training, which continues through lesson 16. The teams will also be required to submit a master sheet of their challenge, as well as any materials they will need to officiate the challenge. Time can also be allocated at the end of each lesson for the teams to work on their "Teamwork" posters.

Lesson 17

As per the first two challenges, this lesson is allocated to practicing the administrative responsibilities that are necessary for the efficient running of the competitions. However, since these challenges are individualized by team, teams will present their challenge to the whole class. These could either be done as a demonstration, or through a video presentation (made during lessons 15–16), or a PowerPoint presentation set as a homework task. A quick question-and-answer sessions may follow each presentation to ensure that everyone is familiar with the rules/activities/intricacies of the challenge.

1. Your team is to design your own special fitness challenge.
2. The challenge will need to match the outline provided below (a) or (b)
   a. You need to design a five-station "Across the Gym" challenge.
   b. An obstacle course relay with multiple elements.
3. On competition day, you will compete against one other team.
4. You will present your challenge and then time your opponent on how long they take to complete it. You will then do your own challenge to attempt to beat that time.
5. You will then repeat this, by completing the other team's challenge.
6. The team that scores the fastest time on each challenge gets 5 points.

Describe the challenge here	Drawing of your challenge	What equipment do you need?
(for across the gym) ... *How many reps does each player complete of each exercise?*		

Figure 8.13 Instructions for designing secret fitness challenges.

Data from Hastie, P., Boyd, K., Ward, J. K., & Stringfellow, A. (2020). Promoting the 50 million strong agenda through sport education. *Journal of Physical Education, Recreation, & Dance, 91*(8), 8–14.

Lesson 18 and 19

Lessons 18 and 19 see multiple rounds of Head-to-Head challenges. As noted, the home team (the team that designed and presents the challenge) officiates first, and then attempts to better the performance of the visiting team. The roles are then reversed.

From our experience with this format, challenges usually take less than five to ten minutes to complete. This allows for multiple contests to take place across the two lessons. It is the responsibility of the teacher to ensure that all match results are reported so that an ongoing scoreboard can be kept during these lessons.

Lesson 20

In lesson 20, the winning teams of each of the three challenges as well as the overall class champions are presented with their awards. Following this festive time, each team will present its "Teamwork" poster, where they provide their interpretations (with associated evidence) of the five elements as they shaped the team's conception of teamwork. The teacher may also present a summary of the Big 5 notice board and highlight students' accomplishments during the season.

Conclusion and Final Thoughts

The goal of this chapter was to demonstrate how the Sport Education model is a particularly amenable vehicle through which to present students with an authentic team-based sporting experience and foregrounding specific SEL competencies without doing a disservice to either. Indeed, there seems to be a natural coalition between the two. Both SEL and Sport Education focus on the notion of "competency," whether it is becoming more competent in a particular physical activity or through increases in the competencies of self- and social-awareness, teamwork, and responsible decision making. As mentioned, the two seasons presented in this chapter are designed to include those same **SAFE** (**S**equenced, **A**ctive, **F**ocused, and **E**xplicit) characteristics that are evident in effective SEL programs. While "sport" often conjures up negative reactions from many within the field of physical education, we believe that the season plans included in this chapter provide ample opportunities through which sport and physical activity can indeed be used as high-quality incubators for the development of personal and social skills.

Questions for Discussion

1. What other physical education content areas might provide a rich context for a Sport Education season incorporating various SEL competencies?
2. Which SEL strategies that have been presented elsewhere in this book might be suitable for including in a season of Sport Education?
3. SEL competencies need to be deliberately taught and practiced, but Sport Education is a strongly student-centered model. How do you think you can manage this balance?
4. What might be the benefits or drawbacks of counting students' performance on the SEL tasks toward the class league table?
5. Discuss how various technologies might be used to promote the learning of SEL competencies during Sport Education.

References

Ang, S. C., Penney, D., & Swabey, K. (2011). Pursuing social and emotional learning outcomes through sport education: An Australian case study. In P. Hastie (Ed.), *Sport education: International perspectives* (pp. 116–132). London: Routledge.

Araújo, R., Mesquita, I., & Hastie, P. A. (2014). Review of the status of learning in research on sport education: Future research and practice. *Journal of Sports Science & Medicine, 13*(4), 846–858.

Bessa, C., Hastie, P., Araújo, R., & Mesquita, I. (2019). What do we know about the development of personal and social skills within the Sport Education model: A systematic review. *Journal of Sports Science and Medicine, 18*(4), 812–829.

Casey, A. (2014) Models-based practice: Great white hope or white elephant? *Physical Education and Sport Pedagogy, 19*(1), 18–34.

Collaborative for Academic, Social, and Emotional Learning. (2019). *What is social and emotional learning?* Retrieved from https://casel.org/what-is-sel/

Ciotto, C. M., & Gagnon, A. G. (2018). Promoting social and emotional learning in physical education. *Journal of Physical Education, Recreation & Dance, 89*(4), 27–33.

Dweck, C. S. (2016). Mindset: The new psychology of success. New York, NY: Random House.

Haerens, L., Kirk, D., Cardon, G. & De Bourdeaudhuij, I. (2011). Toward the development of a pedagogical model for health-based physical education. *Quest, 63*(3), 321–338.

Harvey, S., Kirk, D., & O'Donovan, T. M. (2014). Sport Education as a pedagogical application for ethical development in physical education and youth sport. *Sport, Education and Society, 19*(1), 41–62.

Hastie, P. (2012). *Sport education: International perspectives*. London: Routledge.

Hastie, P., Boyd, K., Ward, J. K., & Stringfellow, A. (2020). Promoting the 50 million strong agenda through sport education. *Journal of Physical Education, Recreation, & Dance, 91*(8), 8–14.

Hastie, P. A., & Sinelnikov, O. A. (2006). Russian students' participation in and perceptions of a season of sport education. *European Physical Education Review, 12*(2), 131–150.

Hastie, P. A., Martinez de Ojeda, D., & Luquin, A. C. (2011). A review of research on sport education: 2004 to the present. *Physical Education and Sport Pedagogy, 16*(2), 103–132.

Hastie, P. A., Ward, J. K., & Brock, S. J. (2017). Effect of graded competition on student opportunities for participation and success rates during a season of Sport Education. *Physical Education and Sport Pedagogy, 22*(3), 316–327.

Kinchin, G. D. (2006). Sport education: A view of the research. In D. Kirk, D. Macdonald & M. O'Sullivan (Eds.), *Handbook of physical education* (pp. 596-609). London; London: SAGE Publications Ltd.

Kirk, D. (2013). Education value and models-based practice in physical education. *Educational Philosophy and Theory, 45*(9), 973–986.

Pennington, C. G., & Sinelnikov, O. A. (2018). Using sport education to promote social development in physical education. *Strategies, 31*(6), 50–52.

Perkins, D. F., & Noam, G. G. (2007). Characteristics of sport-based youth development programs. *New Directions for Youth Development, 2007*(115), 75–84.

Richards, K. A. R., Ivy, V. N., Wright, P. M., & Jerris, E. (2019). Combining the skill themes approach with teaching personal and social responsibility to teach social and emotional learning in elementary physical education. *Journal of Physical Education, Recreation & Dance, 90*(3), 35–44.

Robin, A., Schneider, M., & Dolnick, M. (1976). The turtle technique: An extended case study of self-control in the classroom. *Psychology in the Schools, 13*(4), 449–453.

Rovegno, I. (2006). Situated perspectives on learning. In D. Kirk, D. Macdonald, & M. O'Sullivan (Eds.), *The handbook of physical education.* (pp. 262–274). London: Sage, UK.

Scheibler, I. (2001). Art as festival in Heidegger and Gadamer. *International Journal of Philosophical Studies, 9*(2), 151–175.

SHAPE America – Society of Health and Physical Educators. (2009). *Appropriate instructional practice guidelines, K–12: A side-by-side comparison* (Position statement). Reston, VA: Author.

SHAPE America – Society of Health and Physical Educators. (2013). *National Standards for K-12 Physical Education.* Reston, VA: Author.

Siedentop, D. (1994). *Sport Education: Quality physical education through positive sport experiences.* Champaign, IL: Human Kinetics.

Siedentop, D. (2002). Sport Education: A retrospective. *Journal of Teaching in Physical Education, 21*(4), 409–418.

Siedentop, D., Hastie, P. A., & van der Mars, H. (2004). *Complete guide to Sport Education.* Champaign, IL: Human Kinetics.

Siedentop, D., Hastie, P. A., & van der Mars, H. (2011). *Complete guide to Sport Education* (2nd ed.). Champaign, IL: Human Kinetics.

Siedentop, D., Hastie, P. A., & van der Mars, H. (2020). *Complete guide to Sport Education* (3rd ed.). Champaign, IL: Human Kinetics.

Sinelnikov, O. A., & Hastie, P. A. (2010). Students' autobiographical memory of participation in multiple Sport Education seasons. *Journal of Teaching Physical Education, 29*(2), 167–183.

Sinelnikov, O. A., & Hastie, P. (2017). The learning of pedagogical models in physical education: The socialization perspective. In K.A.R. Richards & K.L. Gaudreault (Eds.), *Teacher socialization in physical education: New perspectives* (pp. 130–143). New York, NY: Routledge.

Sinelnikov, O. A., Hastie, P. A., & Prusak, K. A. (2007). Situational motivation during seasons of Sport Education. *ICHPER-SD Research Journal, 2*(1), 43–47.

Wallhead, T., & O'Sullivan, M. (2005). Sport Education: Physical education for the new millennium? *Physical Education and Sport Pedagogy, 10*(2), 181–210.

Wallhead, T. L., & O'Sullivan, M. (2007). A didactic analysis of content development during the peer teaching tasks of a Sport Education season. *Physical Education and Sport Pedagogy, 12*(3), 225–243.

Walton, K. E., Burrus, J., Anguiano-Carrasco, C., Way, J., & Murano, D. (2019). Aligning ACT Tessera to the Collaborative for Academic, Social, and Emotional Learning (CASEL) Framework. Technical Brief. Iowa City, IA: ACT

Ward, P. C., & Lehwald, H. (2018). *Effective physical education content and instruction: An evidence-based and teacher-tested approach.* Champaign, IL: Human Kinetics.

CHAPTER 9

Cooperative Learning

Ben Dyson
Judy Fowler
Ashley Casey

CHAPTER SUMMARY

Social and emotional skills are foundational for children's health and well-being. These are particularly significant as students' physical and mental well-being become increasingly important in the COVID-19 era. Creative pedagogies are increasingly relevant to foster well-being as they help students benefit from meaningful interactions and learning experiences. In this chapter, we highlight the potential development of social and emotional learning (SEL) using Cooperative Learning. Practical examples include (a) *Team Building Block Plan*, (b) *Learning Teams*, and (c) *Jigsaw*. We also highlight the need and value of an "ethic of care" as it supports the inclusive care of our students and of our teachers.

The Case for Social and Emotional Learning in Physical Education

Social and emotional skills are a foundation for children's healthy growth, development, and lifelong wellness (Durlak et al., 2011; Dyson et al., 2019). There are a large number of frameworks describing and defining social and emotional learning (SEL), leading to different research questions, different intervention approaches, and different choices for assessment (Garcia & Weiss 2016). We present the Jones and Bouffard (2012) framework for SEL as an alternative to the Collaborative for Academic, Social, and Emotional Learning (CASEL, 2019) competencies (i.e., self-awareness, self-management, social awareness, relationship skills, and responsible decision making) introduced in Chapter 1 and referenced throughout many of the other chapters in this text. In addition to the Jones and Bouffard (2012) SEL framework, our work in this chapter is grounded in the learning theory of social constructivism (Rovegno & Dolly, 2006) in an effort to position and understand cooperative learning (CL) as a pedagogical model within the practice of Physical Education (Dyson & Casey, 2012, 2016).

The characteristics of Cooperative Learning (CL) are grounded in a focus on student-centered learning. The student is the main driver of the pedagogical work done by the teacher. Tasks include physical, social, emotional, and cognitive goals. The students work in small heterogeneous groups to enable equity and inclusion. All students contribute to interdependent group work, which establishes a learning environment where students rely on each other to complete the task: "We sink or swim together." The teacher is seen as the facilitator of learning and is in the role of active supervision, that is, the teacher continually monitors and interacts with students. The teacher creates tasks that shift responsibility to the students and students are encouraged to take ownership for their work. In addition, the tasks are designed to hold students accountable. To scaffold CL, we start with reciprocal partner activities and progressively work toward more complicated CL structures like *Jigsaw* and *Think, Pair, Share*. CL Structures are organizational mechanisms (e.g., Jigsaw or Think, Pair, Share) that purposely provide a well-designed strategy for a task that tries to facilitate the student experience so that they *want* to participate and they *want* to learn more about the specified content (Dyson & Casey, 2012; 2016). To encourage positive interdependence, Dyson and Casey (2012) suggested assigning each member complementary and interconnected roles such as manager, reader, recorder, checker, and coach.

While the CASEL (2019) competencies appear commonsense to most teachers, they were developed from reported research that relied on teachers' self-reports, checklists, and surveys of both SEL activities and students' outcomes. Since this research was all quantitative (i.e., driven by statistics), it makes it difficult to establish a relationship between SEL activities and student development (Corcoran, et al., 2018; Zhai, et al., 2015). That is, this work lacks teacher and/or student perspectives that could be obtained through qualitative observations or interviews. In contrast, Jones and Bouffard's framework (2012), which is made up of three domains: social and interpersonal skills, emotional processes, and cognitive regulation (see **Figure 9.1**), draws on such perspectives, observations, and interviews. Cognitive skills are not frequently emphasized or recognized in physical education. With the use of CL structures, teachers can generate an imaginative and creative classroom. For example, in CL structure of group processing, students are encouraged to be creative and think critically. Educators have referred to this process as meta-cognition or self-reflection. Group processing as a form of meta-cognition has been found to be one of the most fundamental skills for lifelong learning, along with the ability to adjust to changing requirements and settings (Dyson, Howley, & Shen, 2020).

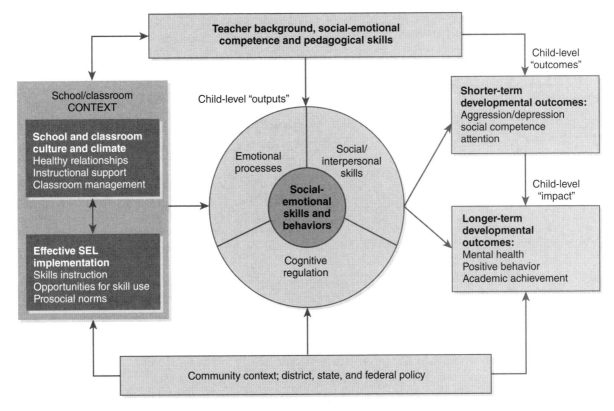

Figure 9.1 A framework for SEL.

These domains provide the basis for positive behavior in school (Barbarasch & Elias, 2009), social and interpersonal skills (Boyd et al., 2005), emotional processes (Denham, 2006), and cognitive regulation (Jones, et al., 2017; Raver, 2002). This chapter will explore how SEL has been represented in the CL literature in physical education (PE) and presents its potential contribution to the development of SEL in schools.

The area of SEL has grown into a substantial body of theory, research, and practice in education (Barbarasch & Elias, 2009; Garcia & Weiss, 2016), with interest continuing to expand (Humphrey, 2013; Martin et al., 2017). Jones et al., (2017) definition, of SEL refers to "the process through which individuals learn and apply a set of social, emotional, behavioral, and character skills required to succeed in schooling, the workplace, relationships, and citizenship" (p.12). The Jones and Bouffard (2012) SEL framework provides a broader definition of SEL, using levels from the micro to the macro across the personal, cultural, institutional, and political levels. This frames the construct of SEL from a broader perspective where transactions among people; within their social and physical settings; over time; and across personal, cultural, institutional, and political levels are examined. Jones and Bouffard's (2012) framework, which is connected to the social ecological model (Bronfrenbrenner, 1979), views child development as taking place in a broad, nested, and interactive set of contexts, ranging from immediate classroom environment (micro) to more distal school administration (macro), allowing students in the school community to feel socially, emotionally, and physically safe (Jones, et al, 2017). The social-ecological model recognizes that the development of SEL skills is influenced by multicomponent environmental factors and systems, including culture and climate in the school and effectiveness of SEL instruction (Jones & Doolittle, 2017). An example of a multilevel analysis of physical education using the social-ecological model explored the different levels of influence on the amount of physical activity offered to high school students in Tennessee and Mississippi (Dyson et al., 2011). Dyson et al., (2011) explored the views of students and teachers within eight school contexts, ranging from the classroom environment at the micro level to more distal school administration at the macro level (Bronfrenbrenner, 1979).

The social-ecological model is the theoretical foundation for some health and PE curricula in countries around the world, including the Aotearoa New Zealand Curriculum (NZC; Ministry of Education, 2007). The NZC views child development as taking place in a broad and interactive set of contexts, ranging from immediate to more distal, allowing students in the school community to feel socially, emotionally, and physically safe (Jones et al., 2017). It recognizes that the development of SEL through CL structures (see Dyson, et al., 2020) is influenced by multicomponent environmental systems and political factors, including culture and climate in the school and social and policy initiatives outside of the school (Dyson et al. 2011; Jones & Doolittle 2017). The center of the SEL framework (Figure 9.1) highlights the core components of SEL (i.e., social and interpersonal skills, cognitive regulation, and emotional processes). The teacher's pedagogical skills help guide the child-level outcomes, leading to potentially improved child-level impacts (e.g., social and interpersonal skills, emotional process, and cognitive regulation). Connected to these behaviors are the school and classroom culture, climate, and effective SEL implementation. As the social-cultural model extends out from the school, we consider the wider community context to policy initiatives (Jones & Doolittle 2017). From the perspective of a teacher, social constructivist theory is a common element to the structures and dynamics of any classroom. The following section presents Social Constructivism as a potential teaching and learning theory for SEL and PE.

Social Constructivism in Teaching and Learning SEL and PE

The basic tenet of social constructivism is that students "learn by doing" rather than observing. Students bring prior knowledge into a learning situation in which they must critique and re-evaluate their understanding of what is being learned. So, when using CL, we are challenging students to complete work in heterogenous teams and this "learn by doing" is an example of using social constructivism. The CL Structures or teaching strategies (e.g., *Jigsaw* or *Think, Pair, and Share*) provide specific methods to facilitate the student experience (Dyson & Casey, 2012; 2016). Our applications of CL in this chapter are closely aligned with Perkins' (1999) understanding of social constructivism as including the active learner, the social learner, and the creative learner. As *active learners*, Perkins (1999) argues that students are not passive recipients of knowledge but are involved in tasks that stimulate decision making, critical thinking, and problem-solving. Students are *social learners* in that they construct knowledge through social interaction with their peers and facilitated by their teachers. As *creative learners*, students are guided to discover knowledge themselves and to create their own understanding of the subject matter. Individuals draw on prior knowledge and experiences to construct knowledge. This is socially interactive by design and emphasizes the interdependent role of the individuals within a CL environment and connects to the wider community. Cooperative learning naturally incorporates social constructivism and the development of social-emotional learning through the student's social interactions and contributions to the class community. In practical terms, the teacher as social constructivist will plan specific CL activities that emphasize an authentic way to learn through socially situating students to participate in activities where they must interact to problem solve. As the old adage states, "you can lead a horse to water, but you can't make him drink." You can provide the opportunity to the student for learning, and a positive climate in which that learning can occur, but you can't make them actively participate in the activity or learn the content. In this example, whether you know it or not, you are approaching your teaching from a social constructivism perspective.

Through the use of Jones and Bouffard's (2012) SEL framework, and the adoption of a complimenting social constructivism learning theory, we propose CL as a pedagogical model for enhancing students' SEL development. In PE, we argue that we have the fundamental tools to investigate and promote SEL through Models-based Practice (MbP): "where multiple models become the organizing centers for individual teachers, in and across school programs and, as guidance at least, at school, district, regional and national levels" (Casey and Kirk, 2021, p. 18). For example, SEL can be developed through the tasks that teachers use while teaching through MbP. For our purposes, we will focus on CL as a pedagogical model that can develop students' SEL competencies (Casey & Fernandez-Rio, 2019; Casey & Goodyear, 2015; Dyson & Casey, 2012). Other chapters in this text address other pedagogical models that show promise for addressing SEL in PE, including the skills themes approach (Chapter 5), adventure-based learning (Chapter 6), teaching personal and social responsibility (Chapter 7), and sport education (Chapter 8).

Common Characteristics and Elements of Cooperative Learning

PE has a history of not being welcoming and not creating a place of belonging for all students (Carlson, 1995). In contrast, CL is a pedagogical approach that sees students working in small, structured, heterogenous groups with two to four of their peers to support one another, master subject matter content, and/or complete a task (Cohen, 1994; Slavin, 2010). Heterogeneous grouping provides the opportunity for CL to be an *equitable* and *inclusive* pedagogy for all students. However, in the real world of your classroom, it is not easy to develop "true" heterogeneous groups. You can start with mixing based on gender, ethnicity, and/or ability. But, the only way to develop *real heterogeneous groups* is for you to know your students well enough to understand their differences and similarities. In addition, if you want to enhance every individual student's education, you have to decide what your planned *learning intentions* are for each student. Is it your learning intention to focus on physical, or cognitive, or social and emotional, and/or spiritual growth? Or is it a combination of physical and social and emotional growth? Answers to these questions depend on your goals as well as your students and the context in which you teach. Later in this chapter, we do provide specific learning tasks that you can scaffold into your teaching in a progressive manner. To assist you with a focus on CL, here is a list of characteristics to help you with this innovative pedagogy. There is a robust body of literature on the pedagogical approach of CL presented in the research papers listed earlier (for example, Casey & Goodyear, 2015; Dyson, et al., 2010; Dyson & Casey, 2012; Dyson, et al., 2020).

In PE, five elements have been often used to help teachers and students learn about CL as a pedagogical practice: (a) Positive interdependence, (b) Individual accountability, (c) Promotive face-to-face interaction, (d) Interpersonal and small group skills, and (e) Group processing (Dyson & Casey, 2012, 2016). *Positive interdependence* exists when students perceive that they are linked to group members in such a way that they cannot succeed unless other group members do. That is, students rely on each other to complete the predesigned task; "we sink or swim together" (Dyson & Casey, 2016, p. 22). In PE, sport and different physical activities, we are familiar with many examples of positive interdependence. Every team sport requires interdependence to be successful. For example, in volleyball, we rely on a pass from the backcourt to the frontcourt to set up the attack. In basketball, we rely on the point guard to take the ball up the court, and in rowing, each rower must row in time to move the boat forward. In your PE program, whenever students rely on each other to complete the task, they are positively interdependent.

Individual accountability refers to students taking responsibility for completing their part of the task for their group. Accountability mechanisms, such as task sheets, hold students individually accountable and create a situation where assigned tasks are more explicit for students (see example task sheet in **Figure 9.2**; Lund, 1992). This task sheet presents the motor, cognitive skills, and affective (SEL) objectives, and provides an example of group processing and assessment. However, individual accountability is broader than just assessment. It is about the student taking personal and social responsibility for their individual contribution to the purposeful and meaningful work of the group or class activity.

Dribbling with a Soccer Ball Task Sheet

Team Name: _____

Coach's name: _____
- Reads the activities to the group
- Helps the group to learn skill

Recorder's name: _____
- Writes down information on task sheet
- Responsible for folder and pencil

Equipment Manager's name: _____
- Gets equipment ready for group
- Makes sure equipment is cleaned up at the end of class

Encourager's name: _____
- Watches for good form
- Provides the group with positive feedback

Objectives:

Motor: Students will be able to dribble the ball using three of the four learning cues.
Cognitive: Students will be able to recall three of the four learning cues.
Affective/SEL: Students will be able to work with their group to achieve the task.

Dribbling Activities:

Learning Cues:

1. Crouched position—bent knees
2. Keeps the ball close to the body
3. Keeps eyes forward
4. Taps the ball with the inside, outside, and laces

Tasks: You may choose any of the tasks after the entire group has completed the task and signed the task sheet. You may complete as many as time will allow. But I'm looking for "good form" = learning cues.

Note: **Remember, after each task, ask the teacher to check your form to make sure your group is ready to move on to the next task.

_____ a. As a group, set up some domes or cones to dribble around

_____ b. With a partner, dribble the ball around the outside of your square

_____ c. Dribble the ball to goal, pass to partner, and shoot

_____ d. Create your own dribbling task (Please describe/draw)

Group processing and assessment:

How well did each group member do their job today?

Coach:	Awesome	Good	Ok	Needs Improvement
Recorder:	Awesome	Good	Ok	Needs Improvement
Equipment Manager:	Awesome	Good	Ok	Needs Improvement
Encourager:	Awesome	Good	Ok	Needs Improvement

What went well today?

What do you need to work on?

Figure 9.2 Dribbling with a soccer ball task sheet.

These individual accountability strategies attempt to reduce the number of *competent bystanders* (Tousignant & Siedentop, 1983). Competent bystander is a term that refers to students in PE who behave well but avoid participation. For example, a child who is third or fourth in the order to bat in a baseball game will slowly move to the back of the line, or will maintain their position in the queue, so they can avoid batting at all. The teacher is usually too busy to notice this well-behaved child who avoids activities because they become adept at fading into the background and not drawing attention to themselves.

Promotive face-to-face interaction refers to a positive discussion within the group while group members are in close proximity to each other. The term "promotive face-to-face interaction" was coined by Johnson and Johnson (1989) and it is crucial for the appropriate functioning of the group. If the students are not physically close to each other, it is easier for them to be "free riders" or be "officially" a member of the team or group but not contribute anything to completing the task (Slavin, 1996). Have you ever been on a team when a teammate did not contribute to the team's efforts but received the same mark or praise as everyone else for the group completing the task? We all have; it's a common occurrence in group activities if there is no appropriate individual accountability because social loafing can then occur.

Interpersonal and small group skills are a key element of CL. Teachers present tasks that help students develop strong social skills that they can socially interact and communicate with each other. Over time, teachers progressively design student behaviors that allow free and easy communication between groupmates. Interpersonal and small group skills naturally incorporate many SEL skills. In a CL classroom, social and relational skills are developed through the tasks students participate in and may include such skills as listening, shared decision making, taking responsibility, giving and receiving feedback, solving problems with the group, and encouraging each other.

Group processing is usually in the form of an open dialogue or group discussion related to the content focus that can occur at any time during the lesson. Group processing is based on a task or activity that is followed by a reflective dialogue. If we are implementing adventure-based learning (see Chapter 10), the process of the debrief is a well-developed and extended example of group processing. Here, we refer to group processing as a cognitive task often represented during the PE lesson as "strategizing." For example, the students in their team may create and discuss an offensive or defensive strategy (Dyson,

et al., 2010). More comprehensive group processing often occurs at the end of a lesson (Dyson, et al., 2010) or in a student or teacher's reflective journal. Many teachers base group processing on the Experiential Education Reflective Cycle (Kolb, 1984). You can develop a number of SEL skills, such as listening, empathy, relationship skills, and/or conflict resolution, using group processing (see Chapter 10). In CL, you can start developing your group processing by using the Experiential Education Reflective Cycle with four useful questions: (a) What was the task and/or activity, (b) What happened? (c) So what? and (d) Now what? Teachers and teacher educators with experience of outdoor education or adventure-based learning will be familiar with this teaching strategy of debriefing after a physical task or problem-solving activity (see Chapter 10 for examples of debriefing or group processing from adventure-based learning).

CL and SEL

CL has emerged as a pedagogical model capable of developing SEL competencies and motivation in PE (Dyson et al., 2020). More specifically, PE content can be taught effectively and learned in a supportive and cooperative environment. Despite over 2,000 research studies conducted in general education (Johnson & Johnson, 2009), the impact of CL in Health Education and PE is limited (Casey & Goodyear, 2015). One such gap in the current literature is school-based research on SEL in PE using CL (Dyson, 2019; Dyson et al., 2020). With that said, there have been a number of studies using CL in PE that have shown evidence of enhancing students' social learning outcomes (Casey & Dyson, 2009; André et al., 2011; Darnis & Lafont, 2015). Studies have shown effective outcomes related to social learning, most notably students demonstrating care, concern, helping, empathy, and inclusion.

Through CL, it is possible to develop helping behavior (Casey & Dyson, 2009; Polvi & Telama, 2000), tolerance, empathy, and compassion (Yoder, 1993). Noddings (2005) describes a *caring relation* as "a connection or encounter between two human beings—a career and a recipient of care, or cared-for" (p. 15). As *carers*, teachers contribute to the growth of their students by constructing a classroom climate where care can flourish. The caring classroom climate can be attributed to a teacher modeling how to care and allowing for students to practice, dialogue and confirm caring practices within specific learning activities (Noddings, 2005). The CL elements, collectively and independently, provide opportunities for students to exhibit and experience care on different levels.

For example, consider when students work in small groups and an action by one person assists a peer in accomplishing a task. The students are focusing on a relational activity (Noddings, 2007) where care is not a virtue but an action that is based on individuals contributing to cooperation and success for the entire group during the task. When teachers consider the "ethic of care" as pedagogy, they prepare their students for experiences outside of their classrooms where students can transfer their understanding of care.

Notably, CL has been effective in building social and emotional development among mainstream students and students with disabilities where students' interactions and acceptance of each other were observed alongside prosocial behavior, which promoted inclusion (Grenier & Yeaton, 2012; Klavina et al., 2014; André et al., 2013). More importantly, recent studies involving CL in PE have demonstrated how social learning can encourage shifts in social relations tied into gendered attitudes, sexism, and equality (Sánchez-Hernández et al., 2018). All students can yield positive experiences in PE activities that focus and integrate CL elements that allow all students to exhibit individual strengths. Small adaptations to official game rules can create inclusive experiences that provide all students with a space to contribute to group goals. For example, in a group activity, a teacher can intentionally incorporate purposeful breaks in activity to allow students to reflect or strategize to develop a plan for all members of the group to contribute to the group's successes in activities. By implementing CL elements, teachers are presented with opportunities to reimagine the purpose and outcomes of an activity. The shift in instructional approaches may help teachers to create an emotionally and physically safe environment by providing activities that encourage inclusivity; SEL competencies are developed (Sapon-Shevin, 2010). CL structures that develop students' SEL need to be taught purposefully.

While it is possible to say that SEL outcomes are accomplished through the use of CL, it would be more appropriate to suggest that there is evidence of some affective aspiration being reported in the CL literature (Casey & Goodyear, 2015). The results of much of the current research challenges future research to examine characteristics of the affective domain through CL methods to help develop a deeper understanding of affective learning. Calls for further inquiry to examine characteristics of the affective domain through CL methods persists (Casey & Goodyear, 2015; Goudas & Magotsiou, 2009). Casey and Goodyear's (2015) review of literature of CL's ability to achieve the four learning outcomes of PE (physical, cognitive, social,

and affective) confirms the lack of evidence of affective learning. More recently, Goodyear's (2017) study on the impact of a sustained school-based continuing professional development program on teachers' practices and students' learning through implementing CL only reported physical and social learning. In a positive response to the lack of research, there is now a small but steadily growing number of school-based research studies, which indicate that CL can promote affective outcomes and SEL (Dyson et al., 2020).

Practical Examples of CL in Health and Physical Education

The following section provides examples of SEL in CL and connects to real-world tasks for your gymnasium or classroom. These practical tasks provide different perspectives on how SEL in CL can be contextualized and connected to real-world applications in the classroom.

There are many opportunities to integrate the elements of CL across school settings. Often, teachers play a variety of roles at their school to accompany their official assignment as an elementary, middle, or high school physical education specialist. Depending on the official assignment, health education could also be a portion of the assigned teaching responsibility. Additionally, teachers may have other, less-formal opportunities to interact with students during passing time, at lunch, and through their involvement in roles such as monitoring recess. These are all opportunities for reinforcing SEL lessons. To align with the theories of social constructivism, CL, and the Jones and Bouffard (2012) SEL framework, the following section offers readers a variety of ideas to consider as you teach K–12 students in a PE setting or if you are preparing preservice teachers for their student teaching experiences and beyond. Next, we provide specific Health Education and PE examples that represent the different CL elements: positive interdependence, individual accountability, promotive face-to-face interaction, interpersonal and/or small group skills, and group processing.

Connections to K–12 Health Education

Many physical educators and preservice teachers are required to teach Health Education, so in the next section, we provide you with connections between the National Health Standards, CL, and SEL competencies. CL elements and SEL components can integrate with skills-based health education for

Table 9.1 A Connection of the National Health Standards, CL, and SEL Competencies

NHES Health Standards	CL Elements	SEL Components
Standard 4: Communication skills	■ Face-to-Face Interactions ■ Interpersonal/Small Group Skills ■ Group Processing ■ Positive Interdependence	■ Social/Interpersonal Skills
Standard 5: Decision-making skills	■ Interpersonal/Small Group Skills ■ Positive Interdependence	■ Emotional Processes
Standard 6: Goal setting	■ Group Processing ■ Positive Interdependence ■ Individual Accountability	■ Cognitive Regulation

K–12 students. The eight National Health Education Standards (NHES) are a foundation to guide students to obtain, maintain, and promote healthy behaviors (American Cancer Society, 2020). Standard one addresses the content associated with health promotion and disease prevention. Standards two through eight contain the skills that students should be able to apply to promote healthy behaviors (**Table 9.1**).

The NHES focus on important skills that are used across many curricula and content areas. This is important to note as Health and Physical Education (HPE) standards directly connect to SEL competencies and should be highlighted as one of the many benefits and reasons to move toward daily PE (see Table 9.1). Table 9.1 provides a connection between the National Health Standards, Cooperative Learning, and SEL competencies. There are many opportunities for PE teachers to integrate Health Education into PE lessons, in fact, many PE teachers already do this naturally. Table 9.1 provides an overview of the many communication sub-skills taught by teachers such as active listening, expressing care and concern, nonverbal communication, refusal skills, negotiation, and conflict resolution. These skills are critical for students to develop so they can have the ability to have healthy and productive exchanges during school time and other challenges in life. As we consider CL, teachers can purposefully preplan learning activities that present students with opportunities to develop a variety of communication sub-skills. For example, as students work in group processing to determine if a strategy was effective, students can be reminded to frame all comments as "I" Messages instead of pointing the finger to blame a group member.

Educators would agree that emotions play a part in decision-making skills. Decision-making tasks help students in identifying choices, identifying alternatives, and assessing short-term and long-term consequences to self-select and make a healthy choice of action. The student-centered nature of CL provides students with the autonomy and ownership to make decisions in a variety of activities. For example, students can learn about putting by designing their own 9-hole putt-putt course. Child-designed games (Grenier & Yeaton, 2019) allow teachers to facilitate learning opportunities that encourage students to take responsibility for their own learning. Teachers can guide students by setting the basic parameters of each hole (e.g., students should plan specific obstacles, like a ramp or a hazard; or a hole can be completed in three putts). Students are provided with the time to plan, test, present their ideas, and actually play the entire putt-putt course.

Goal-setting is also critical for students to identify an aim and develop a plan of action to include steps and strategies to achieve the desired purpose. Goal-setting is a life skill that is easily developed in HPE settings through a plethora of opportunities. Teachers can guide students through a variety of strategies to identify or develop SMART goals in CL activities in the PE setting. S refers to goals being *Specific*, M requires that the goal is *Measurable*, A indicates that the goal is *Achievable*, R recommends that the goal is *Realistic*, and T refers to goals being completed in a *Timely* fashion.

Furthermore, CL includes a reflection session that is necessary in goal setting to allow students to evaluate if the plan to achieve the goal worked. In health education, students can identify personal goals for increasing physical activity or eating five servings of fruits and vegetables each day.

Team Building 101

The following Block Plan for CL for PE represents an example of six lessons/*learning activities* for an instructional unit that teachers can use at the beginning of your work on CL (**Figure 9.3**). The intention is that the students will learn many SEL skills and want to

Cooperative Learning Team Building
Overall Plan

Learning activity 1:	Learning activity 4:
Intro to Team Building Activities	**Problem-solving activity**
Task 1- Introduction: What is team building? Create a class definition.	Task 1- Life raft
Task 2- Guidelines for Student's and Teacher's Journals: Based on the Reflective Cycle. This is the basis of the CL element Group Processing.	Task 2- Group processing
	Assessment: Daily journal after class
a) Task/ activity, b) What happened? c) So what? d) Now What?	
Task 3- Two-minute teach	
Task 4- Pattern ball	
Task 5- Group processing	
Assessment: Daily journal after class	
Learning activity 2:	Learning activity 5:
Communication activities	Team Work activities
Task 1- Team jump roping. Students practice a number of team jump rope activities.	Task 1- Capture the Flag
Task 2- Minefield	Task 2- Group processing
Task 3- Group Processing	Assessment: Daily journal after class
Assessment: Daily journal after class	
Learning activity 3:	Learning activity 6:
Critical Thinking Activities	**Application/Transfer activities**
Task 1- Create your own Obstacle Course, based on Minefield. Then share it with the class. Class chooses best three obstacle courses to trial for the whole class.	Task 1- Create your own team building activity
	Task 2- Take time to write in your daily journal
Task 2- Group processing	Task 3- Assessment: Group processing and share journal comments
Assessment- Journal	

Note: Flexibility in planning is important for the teacher when developing Team Building Activities. The teacher will have more activities planned that they can use in a single lesson. The teachers also need to provide sufficient structure to ensure a supportive positive learning environment, but the teacher must also learn to be more "student-centered" as the students are encouraged to make their own choices and discoveries.

Learning activity 1:

Intro to Team Building Activities

Task 1-

Introduction: What is team building? Create a class definition.

Task 2-

Guidelines for Student's and Teacher's Journals: Based on the Reflective Cycle:

a) Task/ activity, b) What happened? c) So What? d) Now What?

When beginning to integrate Team Building Activities into a physical education program, use group processing: *What happened? So What? Now What?* This is based on adventure education and the Experiential Reflective Cycle (Dyson, 1994; Kolb, 1984). These questions and specific concepts can be used as an initial step into group processing, although to "truly access" the students' perspectives you will need to ask more in-depth and contextually relevant questions.

1. The first stage of the Team Building Activities is '*The Activity.*'
   The teacher asks the group to perform the activity or task.
2. The second stage: '*The observation and reflection on that experience.*'
   The teacher/facilitator asks the group to reflect on the activity and speak about the experience as a group. The teacher/facilitator asks the group to describe "What happened?" The teacher can begin with descriptive questions: "What happened in the pattern ball activity?" "Describe what your group did" "Was it enjoyable?" "What were the main skills involved?" "What did you see or notice in the Pattern Ball activity?"
3. The third stage: '*The formation of generalized principles based on these reflections.*'
   The teacher/facilitator asks the group to openly discuss the success or failure of the activity. This step can be thought of as asking, "So what?" The facilitator may start by saying "So what happened when you were learning the Pattern Ball task?" "How did it work as an activity for your group?" "How did it make you feel?" "What were you thinking during the Pattern Ball activity?" "Was this a successful activity for you and why?" "What would make it more successful?" "What would make it more enjoyable?" "What didn't work well in the Pattern Ball activity?"

Figure 9.3 Block plan for CL. *(Continued)*

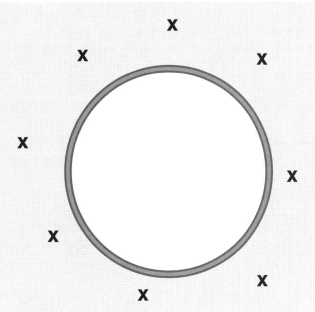

Figure 1 Pattern ball.

© Jones & Bartlett Learning.

4. The fourth stage: '*The reapplication of these generalized understandings in new situations*'.
   The teacher/ facilitator asks, "Now what?" Applying or transferring new concepts in different situations is the most difficult part of the Experiential Learning Cycle. The facilitator could ask questions like: "In the Pattern Ball activity, what would you change the next time you play it?" "Can you think of other adaptations or modifications to the pattern ball activity?" "What other balls or objects could you use with pattern ball?" Can you think of other places in your life where people have to work together? "How did your group adjust to suit individual needs? "Could you play this activity on the weekend with your friends?"

   For a teacher beginning to use Team Building Activities, an immediate concern will be that there is not enough time for group processing. There will be conflict between allocating time for activity compared with allocating time for verbally reflecting or discussing the experience. The recommendation is to start with a short 5-minute group processing session at the end of the lesson, trying to ask students about their issues or concerns (What happened? So What? Now What?)

Task 3- Two-minute teach

Ask group members to choose a partner whom they do not know well. Each group member has two minutes to teach your partner something they do not know. Then your partner will take two minutes to teach you something. When students are finished, select a couple of students to show the group what they have learned from their partner. Students can teach each other any physical or cognitive skill (For example, a word or phrase in a foreign language, a rhyme, a stretch, etc.).

Task 4- Pattern ball

Pattern ball organization: The teacher/ group facilitator organizes a group of 8–12 students in a circle (**Figure 1**).

Task: Eight students are in a circle facing each other. The first student starts a pattern of throwing the ball to another student who throws to a different student. All students begin with one hand in the air to begin the pattern. When you have passed, you drop you hand. The pattern continues with each student throwing to the same person each time. When the students are able to throw one ball in this way, another ball is added and so on until several balls are being thrown simultaneously around the circle in a pattern. During the activity, students are encouraged to use other students' names, use appropriate throwing and catching skills, and give and receive appropriate feedback to each other.

Modification: The teacher can then modify the task to challenge the group by asking them to throw faster, reverse the order of passing, or use different passes like a chest pass and a bounce pass. The equipment should be in a bucket beside the first student who starts the pattern.

Equipment: Many different objects to be thrown (Frisbees, balls, bats, cones, etc.).

Learning activity 2:

Communication activities

Task 2- Minefield

Minefield

Task: Minefield is an activity for groups of 8–12 people. The goal of this activity is to get each team member across a "minefield" without touching any objects as fast as possible while the participant is blindfolded. The "minefield" is an area covered with randomly arranged objects that must be avoided.

Equipment: Four cones as the markers for the grid area. Many different objects (that act as mines) arranged in randomly on the floor (cones, Frisbees, balls, bats, etc.….).

The group will break into pairs, choosing a partner whom they have not worked with before. One person will call out directions first and the other partner wears a blindfold. The person without the blindfold will navigate their teammate through the minefield by helping them

Figure 9.3 Block plan for CL. *(Continued)*

avoid any objects (mines) on the floor. Verbal directions can only come from the sidelines. The partners stand on opposite sides of the minefield. For each object touched, they lose five seconds of their time.

Verbal communication is an important skill for students in physical education and life. The Minefield activity helps students tune into the value of listening and speaking in a clear and concise manner.

Modification: Can be done by one student at a time or several students at a time. Students can move one way or have to return to the original starting point.

Learning activity 3:

Critical Thinking Activities

Task 1- Students create their own obstacle course, based on Minefield. Then share it with the class. Class chooses best three obstacle courses to trial for the whole class.

Learning activity 4:

Problem-solving activity

Task 1- Life raft

The task is to turn two "rafts" over so that both teams can be saved from the shark-infested waters.

Equipment: Two tarps (2m × 3m) to act as rafts. Each raft (tarp) will have a big blue X on the bottom so the team knows when they have turned the raft over.

Ask students to find a partner and then determine which one of the partners is older. The older partner is on team B and the younger partner is on team A. Place the two tarps close to one another on the gymnasium floor. Ask team A to get on one raft (tarp) and team B to get on the other raft (tarp). "Each team is on a lifeboat in the middle of the ocean. Unfortunately, the underside of the lifeboats has been chewed by sharks and after 15 minutes, the raft will no longer be afloat and the entire group will drown. Each team must turn their raft over completely in the next 15 minutes without stepping off the raft and into the shark-infested waters or their teammates will die. The team must keep the raft stationary (that is, the raft cannot be moved across the floor).

Solution: Hopefully, the two groups will cooperate and they will all get onto one raft and flip the other raft over.

This is a problem-solving task that requires that both teams cooperate for both teams to be able to complete the task. If the two teams are in competition with each other they will not be able to complete the task.

Modification: Have the rafts farther apart. Have three rafts.

Learning activity 5:

Task 1- Capture the Flag

Task: To get students to work together as a team to capture the flag of the opposing team. Students will start in their own territory or side of the field. Members of a team invade territory of the other team to capture the flag. Group members try not to get tagged and try to get back to their own territory without getting tagged. The teacher will first explain that students will form groups of eight on each team. Two teams play against each other. Players try to capture the flag of the other team and bring it back to their territory without getting tagged. Players may get tagged once they enter the opponents' territory. Once a player gets tagged, they must go to jail where an untagged teammate can free them. They both get a free walk back to their territory. They must go back. There is a free zone where the flag is on each team's side where opponents may not tag them. A person has a choice of either freeing up a jailed teammate or getting the flag. They cannot do both. If a player, who has possession of the flag, gets tagged, the flag must be placed back in its original location.

Modification: Have more than one flag on each side. Use Safety Zones where players cannot be tagged.

To improve students success Refining task could be: a) Have students focus on chasing, fleeing, and dodging skills. b) Have students focus on being on the offensive or being on the defensive.

Learning Activity 6:

Application/Transfer activities

Task 1: The group must create your own team building/problem-solving task

Equipment: Different kinds of equipment will be available. This equipment would be typical for a physical education program. Different sizes and shapes of mats, balls, bats, cones, rope, elastic fabric, flexible rope, or bungee cord (same cord as they use in bungee jumping), etc....

The intention is for students to be creative and based on their experiences, create a team building/problem-solving task that emphasize one of the concepts of team building.

There are five elements of Cooperative Learning that are used here: i) Promotive face-to-face interaction, ii) Interpersonal skills and small-group skills, iii), Group processing, iv) Individual accountability, and v) Positive interdependence. In small groups, they are placed in a **face-to-face promotive interaction**. Consequently, **interpersonal skills and small group skills** are developed through the building and **group processing** is used to solve possible issues that arise or behavior problems. The challenge of the task is designed to demonstrate **individual accountability**, because each student has a role (creator, presenter, facilitator, equipment manager, and/or assessor). Each student must be part of the group, to play in the group, and importantly without their specific contribution, the task will not be completed appropriately. This task helps develop **positive interdependence** among group members as they rely on each other to complete the task. Once the team building/problem solving task is created, it can be integrated in the physical education sessions. The teacher will take on the role as an overall facilitator—guiding and assisting students to be successful. That is, each group creating their own initiative/problem-solving task.

Modification: After students present their team-building tasks, modification and adaptations can be suggested by group members or other students in the class.

Figure 9.3 Block plan for CL.

work as a team. Relevant SEL skills developed would be inter-personal and communication skills, team-building skills, and working together. The assumption is that if students can develop team-building skills, they learn to work together and can advance to a small group of 3–5 students working on a CL Structure such as Learning Teams and Jigsaw (presented later as Figure 9.5 and Figure 9.6). CL has a progressive focus on scaffolding the different tasks for students. In the past, we have talked about "Lesson Zero" (Dyson & Casey, 2012; 2016). Here, we are presenting a mini unit of six "Lesson Zeros" for the preservice or in-service teachers to experiment with in their exploration and start to scaffold CL into your pedagogical practice. The mini six-lesson unit contains learning activities, such as team building, communication, critical thinking, problem-solving, team work, and application/transfer activities.

Moving Toward More Specific Cooperative Learning Structures

CL Structures are presented here to provide the preservice teacher, in-service teacher, and/or teacher educator with specific strategies to develop CL tasks in their teaching. We introduced CL Structures earlier in the chapter as organizational mechanisms (e.g., *Jigsaw* or *Think, Pair, and Share*) that purposely provide a well-designed strategy for activities that engages students in the experience so that they are encouraged to participate and learn more about the content in the activity (Dyson & Casey, 2012; 2016).

In this practice-based session, we initially present *Numbered Heads Together* in **Figure 9.4** as a way for learners to work in a small group while ensuring that all students know an answer to the posed problem. Put differently, this approach encourages each student to be individually accountable by knowing an answer developed by their group while also being positively interdependent when coming to that conclusion. The learning intention encourages the students to work together to solve the problem presented by the teacher and teach the answer to all members of the group. Remember, the old proverb *many heads are better than one*.

This is followed by creating your own game in **Figure 9.5** where students create their own game with guidance from the teacher. We have found that students like to create their own games and often kids will do this in their own time, in the school playground or their backyard with their friends. In addition, students start to learn to take on a role, for example, equipment person or coach.

In the more complicated CL Learning Structures, we provide more advanced and more complex examples of CL. We present two learning activities that provide examples of CL Structures

---

Teammates put their heads together to reach a consensus.

Teacher poses problems, students have own time (teacher choose as to how long) to think about/answer questions, students stand up and put heads together to create shared group answers, discussing, and teaching. Students sit down when everyone knows the answer. The teacher calls a number, students' answer could take the form of writing on task sheet; answer board; finger responses; response cards; manipulative demonstrations and/or explanations.

For example, this CL structure could be used to develop strategies in a game or activity.

The teacher notices a common error related to skills or tactics and poses the question.

For example:

"What is your role as a back-row player in your team?"

"What can teams do to vary their tactics when setting up the attack?"

Figure 9.4 CL numbered heads together structure.

Task: In a group of 3–5 students, "Create your own game."

Create a game using all of the correct forms for passing a soccer ball. The game must include all members of your group.

_____ 1. Create a name for our game.

_____ 2. What equipment will you need for the game?

_____ 3. What are the rules of your game?

_____ 4. In this game, you score by

_____ 5. Draw a diagram of the game.

Start with one or two roles for your students. For example, you could start with the role of coach and the role of organizer:

The coach: _____

While participating, the coach provides feedback—against the learning cues/success criterion—to the group members to improve their performance.

Reader: _____

The reader reads the task and makes sure all group members understand it—gets clip board.

The organizer/equipment person: _____

While participating, the organizer arranges equipment for the next group—puts equipment away at the end of class.

Team Contract:

As a team, we agree to:

1. Be nice to one another
2. Work together
3. Help one another to solve problems on our own

Note: All team members sign their names below:

Group Processing: Discuss with your group:

1. What went well?
2. What do you need to work on?

Figure 9.5 Creating your own game.

aimed at developing SEL skills for students: (a) *Learning Teams* for elementary students (e.g., Triangle Ball; TB) (see **Figure 9.6**) and (b) *Jigsaw* (J) for high school students (see **Figure 9.7**). More specifically, we suggest that both TB and J can purposefully and meaningfully

---

In *Learning Teams,* the groups (teams) work to play the game or complete the task.

The roles are designed to facilitate the activity or help the students be more successful.

Suggestion for roles:

The coach: _____

While participating, the coach provides feedback—against the learning cues/success criterion—to the group members to improve their performance.

The recorder: _____

While participating, the recorder records each student's performance—totals the group score

The reader: _____

While participating, the reader reads the task and ensures that all group members understand it—gets clip board

The organizer/equipment person: _____

While participating, the organizer organizes equipment for next group—puts equipment away at the end of class

The manager/The facilitator:

While participating, the manager keeps group members on task. Leads by example.

The encourager: _____

While participating, the encourager encourages group members to be involved and provides positive comments to all group members.

Note to students: Remember, in Cooperative Learning, everyone participates in the activities and everyone has a role to play. Everyone actively participates and holds fellow student's individually accountable. You can have each team member checked off on the task sheet to show that they completed the activity.

The learning activity "Triangle Ball" as an example of "CL Structure Learning Teams"

Triangle Ball

Physical task: Accurate passes and support
Cognitive learning intention: Understand support play
SEL learning intention: Give feedback and receive feedback appropriately

Triangle Ball Task Sheet

1. Four players in a square, 3 v 1; three players work on the corners and sides of the square.
2. One of the four players works in the middle area and tries to intercept the ball as the other three pass it around.
3. Players with the ball can only pass and run along the perimeter lines of the square.
4. No diagonal passes. Passive defender first—focus on offense = good accurate pass.
5. When a player has possession of the ball, they cannot move.

Λ O1 o ——→ Λ O2   —— ball movement
                        —— movement of support player
D 4

Λ O3 ——→ Λ

Task 1:

Play triangle ball and support the ball carrier on both sides with accurate passes.

1. Passive defender first—focus on offense = good accurate pass.

Task 2:

What went well? What do you need to work on? (Rally Team CL Structure).

Task 3:

Choose a modification to task:

- Success criteria = support play, i.e., moving to ball
- Triangle ball—no defender
- Students come up with a modification (Rally Team CL Structure = strategizing).

Learning Cues/success criteria:

1. Call names and make eye contact
2. Reach for the ball—show a target
3. Move into a supporting position
4. Give appropriate feedback
5. Accept feedback appropriately
6. Accurate pass/catch

When you all feel ready, complete the form below, rating each player's performance with each skill.

Figure 9.6 The cooperative learning structure of *Learning Teams.* *(Continued)*

To assist the assessment of the student's participation, embedded in this *Learning Teams* CL Structure we present the CL Structure *Pair Check Perform:*

1. A assesses B, while C assesses D.
2. B assesses A, while D assesses C.
3. Pairs of students now move to assess other students. The teacher can randomly assess any pair.

> **Awesome**—uses the cues every time
>
> **Good**—uses the cues most of the time
>
> **Needs Work**—rarely uses the cues

Names	Call Names	Reaches for Ball	Support— Move to Ball	Give Feedback	Receive Feedback	Accurate Pass/Catch

Figure 9.6 The cooperative learning structure of *Learning Teams.*

A jigsaw classroom has two key components (in addition to heterogenous teams) 1. Home groups and 2. Expert groups. The first is the team that students play for and work for and the second is the ideas factor. Using Jigsaw requires you to divide the class twice (see below):

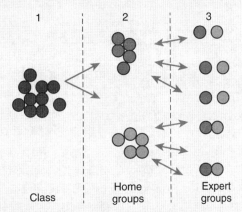

You start with the class and divide it into home groups (1 to 2 above). Then you divide the groups into expert groups (2 to 3 above). The expert groups will be tasked with learning something specific (this might be a parkour move or part of a dance or gymnastic routine). Once all members of the expert groups become 'expert,' they return to their home groups and take it in turns to teach their peers about their specialism.

In our example and drawing in the work of Casey and Quennerstedt (2020), we use invasion games as a vehicle for teaching SEL components such as helping behaviors, tolerance, empathy, compassion, social awareness, and relationship skills. These are the things we will value above skill development and performance.

Expert Group Tasks

1. Group 1 – develop a small-sided game that focuses on *restarts*
2. Group 2 – develop a small-sided game that focuses on *possession*
3. Group 3 – develop a small-sided game that focuses on *progression*
4. Group 4 – develop a small-sided game that focuses on *scoring*

As the expert groups work, the teacher recognizes incidences where students help one another, to show tolerance, etc. These things are rewarded implicitly through praise and explicitly through points or prizes. Time is allowed for each individual to make suggestions and the skills of interaction and relationship building are important. Small-sided games that encourage everyone to be involved and which represent the whole group's ideas should also be rewarded.

Once games are developed, the experts then, in turn, teach these to their home group. Again, reward the SEL behaviors you value. You would be mindful of gendered attitudes, sexism, racism, and equality but look to see how students deal with these. The hope is that as they learn about SEL, they will start to see problems and voice concerns that perhaps they hadn't previously noticed. These could be raised by the whole group and collective solutions found.

Figure 9.7 A jigsaw classroom for the CL structure *Jigsaw* for the middle school and the high schools level.

develop recognizable SEL skills, for example: Call names and make eye contact (TB); move into a supporting position (TB), give appropriate feedback (TB, J), accept feedback appropriately (TB, J), and feel good when you accurately pass or catch the ball (TB).

To help teachers to use CL Structures—based on different CL Structures that Spencer Kagan (1992) originally designed, such as, *Rally Robin, Peer Check,* and *Numbered Heads Together*—can be used. An example of a CL Structure, 'Numbered Heads Together' appears in Figure 9.4.

Students like to take ownership of some of the tasks that they are asked to complete in PE. Using CL with colleagues from a number of different countries, we have found that students are interested and excited to create their own games (Dyson & Casey, 2012). Of course, like any high-quality CL task, you need to prepare students with progressive tasks to take over and create their own game. An obvious way to scaffold toward students creating their own game is to allow them to modify games that you typically play with your students. This could be a rule change (e.g., allowing for more than one try at serving the ball), change the scoring (e.g., more points for good defense or good offense), change the equipment (e.g., use a larger or softer ball), change the size of the field (e.g., reduce the size of a soccer pitch to reduce cardiorespiratory requirements), and/or change the number of players on a team (e.g., reduce player numbers to get individual teammates more opportunities to respond). Figure 9.5 presents a task sheet that could be used for preservice or K–12 students. Students are encouraged to start to learn a specific role, in this example, coach or equipment person.

Michelle Grenier, at the University of New Hampshire, and Pat Yeaton, at North Hampton Elementary School, have formed a strong collaborative partnership to present and write about how to *truly integrate* persons with disabilities into PE in an inclusive and equity manner (Grenier & Yeaton, 2019). This example of creating your own game comes from their school-based work.

The Structure of Learning Teams at the Elementary Level

In the CL Structure *Learning Teams*, teachers should imagine that they are teaching a team sport. The idea is to develop team cohesion through positive interdependence. To encourage individual contribution to

the team effort, each individual should be assigned a role. For example: point guard, defender, mid-field, wing, attack, and/or goalkeeper. When students rely on each other to play well or be successful, they are being *positively interdependent!*

In a PE lesson, the roles could be coach, equipment person, motivator, and manager/recorder. What are the best roles for each student? Each learning team decides on a name with the teacher's guidance. Teachers can foster student responsibility in learning teams through the implementation of roles within CL activities. The teacher explains and demonstrates the skill. They divide their students into groups, describe group learning intentions or objectives, and/or student goals. The intention is that the students learn and then carry out their assigned roles (coach, encourager, and/or recorder) but the students also perform. The roles are designed to facilitate the activity or help the students be more successful. The student-centered teaching strategy of learning teams provides students with opportunities to take leadership and responsibility roles and work together as a team. Learning Teams can be similar to teams organized in the Sport Education curriculum model (Siedentop et al., 2011). However, often in Sport Education, there is *team accountability* but in CL, there should be *individual accountability* built into the task as well.

The Structure of *Jigsaw*

Think of jigsaw as the puzzle of the same name, but with two pictures. The first picture depicts a number and the second picture is a collection of different letters (A through D). The first picture represents the heterogeneous group each student has been assigned to. This is the home group. The home group is defined as the collection of students who will work together for the duration of the unit. They will come to rely on one another (positive interdependence), interact, problem solve, and communicate with each other (face-to-face interaction and small-group skills), and go on a reflective learning experience (group processing). But before they do this, they need to learn something that is unique to them so they can then teach it to the rest of their group. In other words, they need to become individually accountable.

To do this, we turn over the picture to see the letters (see Figure 9.7), and we break up the jigsaw. Each student, in each group, takes a letter and goes to find the other people from the other groups with the same letter as them. Then they make a new jigsaw made just of As, Bs, Cs, or Ds. These new completed puzzles represent the expert groups and they will be responsible for developing and learning a piece of key content. In our example below, this is part of a student-made game, but it could be a type of defense, a type of exercise, or a form of yoga. The key is that they develop something that only that group of experts knows and then they (individually) take it back to their home group. When students return and remake their number as part of their jigsaw groups, students will realize that only student A has knowledge about what the As develop and likewise with students Bs, Cs, and Ds, respectively. They must then teach the others (be individually accountable) so their group can complete the task. In short, they must sink or swim together. Jigsaw is a great way of scaffolding the five elements and ensuring that everyone has a part to play in the learning experience.

Conclusion

Social and emotional skills are a foundation for children's healthy growth, development, and lifelong physical and mental well-being (Dyson et al., 2019; Dyson et al., 2020). SEL is particularly significant as the COVID-19 pandemic highlighted at the time of this writing students' physical and mental well-being becomes increasingly fragile but still is fundamental for our students. The need for creative pedagogies such as CL is now even more relevant for preservice and in-service teachers to implement in classes for their students so they will benefit from meaningful interactions and learning experiences that aid in the development of student well-being. In this chapter, we have highlighted the potential development of SEL using CL in PE. Practical examples are included as cooperative learning structures: (a) *Team Building Block Plan*, (b) Cooperative Learning Structure *Learning Teams*, and (c) Cooperative Learning Structure *Jigsaw (d) Creating your own game*. We also emphasize the need and value of a fundamental concept in SEL, that of the "ethic of care," which includes care for our students and care for our teachers. In addition, many preservice and in-service PE teachers are required to teach Health Education, so we provide connections between the National Health Standards, Cooperative Learning, and SEL competencies.

CL is a pedagogical approach that sees students working in small groups; it is a *student-centered* and *equity-based pedagogy* that highlights *inclusive*

practices through strategies such as heterogeneous groupings to complete tasks in a positive and interdependent process. CL has emerged as a pedagogical model capable of developing SEL competency and student motivation to actively contribute in PE (Dyson et al., 2020; Dyson et al., 2021). PE content can be taught effectively and learned in a supportive, caring, and cooperative environment. We present how many CL elements CL structures, and SEL components can be integrated with skills-based health education for K–12 students. We suggest that as well as the PE Standards; the eight National Health Education Standards (NHES) have the potential to be a foundation to guiding students to obtain and maintain a healthy lifestyle and also achieve healthy and developmentally appropriate physical education PE (SHAPE America Standards, 2013).

There is, however, still very limited school-based research evidence of SEL or the affective domain of learning in PE (Bailey et al., 2009; Casey 2014; Dyson et al., 2020; 2021; Kirk, 2013). It would appear that while CL can deliver SEL outcomes, specific competencies, and social skills (e.g. relationships, relating to others, and self-management) have been prioritized over others. Consequently, we have a long way to go in our understanding and implementation of SEL in PE: "where are the emotions and social interactions and interpersonal skills that are part of PE?" (Dyson, 2014, p. 146). Appropriate and positive school and classroom climates are germane to the promotion and development of SEL in our gymnasiums, classrooms, on our sports fields, and in the outdoor education experiences. Historically, we all know that too many students are alienated in PE (Carlson, 1995; Cothran & Ennis, 1999). While we acknowledge that a large body of work already exists, we have a great deal more work to do with CL and other pedagogical models presented in this text (teaching personal and social responsibility, sport education, adventure-based learning, teaching games for understanding, etc.), to develop SEL skills in the K–12 classroom.

We hope you agree that PE is a great place to teach, emphasize, and practice social and emotional development for our K–12 students (Ciotto & Gagnon, 2018; Jacobs & Wright, 2014). In closing, we believe it is time for this field to *step up to the plate* and provide more encouragement and support for preservice, in-service, and teacher educators to use CL and other pedagogical models to enable and enhance SEL in K–12 PE settings.

Questions for Discussion

1. Why is SEL an important part of any Physical Education program?
2. How would you define SEL?
3. What is one SEL activity that you think works well in a K–12 setting?
4. What parts of CL do you think will work well in your educational setting or context?
5. What parts of CL do you think will not work in your educational setting or context?
6. How do we assess SEL skills like empathy?

References

American Cancer Society. (2020). *American Cancer Society Guideline for Diet and Physical Activity*. https://www.cancer.org/healthy/eat-healthy-get-active/acs-guidelines-nutrition-physical-activity-cancer-prevention/guidelines.html

André, A., Deneuve, P., & Louvet, B. (2011). Cooperative learning in physical education and acceptance of students with learning disabilities. *Journal of Applied Sport Psychology, 23*(4), 474–485.

André, A., Louvet, B., & Deneuve, P. (2013). Cooperative group, risk-taking and inclusion of pupils with learning disabilities in physical education. *British Educational Research Journal, 39*(4), 677–693.

Bailey, R., Armour, K., Kirk, D., Jess, M., Pickup, I., Sandford, R., & BERA Physical Education and Sport Pedagogy Special Interest Group. (2009). The educational benefits claimed for physical education and school sport: An academic review. *Research Papers in Education, 24*(1), 1–27.

Barbarasch, B., & Elias, M. J. (2009). Fostering social competence in schools. *School-based mental health. A practitioner's guide to comparative practices*, 125–148.

Boyd, J., Barnett, W. S., Bodrova, E., Leong, D. J., & Gomby, D. (2005). Promoting children's social and emotional development through preschool education. *National Institute for Early Education Research*, 1–21.

Bronfenbrenner, U. (1979). *The ecology of human development: Experiments by nature and design*. Harvard University Press.

Carlson, T. B. (1995). We hate gym: Student alienation from physical education. *Journal of Teaching in Physical Education, 14*, 467–477.

Casey, A. (2014). Models-based practice: Great white hope or white elephant? *Physical Education and Sport Pedagogy, 19*(1), 18–34. doi: 10.1080/17408989.2012.726977

Casey, A., & Dyson, B. (2009). The implementation of models-based practice in physical education through action research. *European Physical Education Review, 15*(2), 175–199. https://doi.org/10.1177/1356336X09345222

Casey, A., & Fernandez-Rio, J. (2019). Cooperative learning and the affective domain. *Journal of Physical Education, Recreation & Dance, 90*(3), 12–17.

Casey, A., & Goodyear, V. A. (2015). Can cooperative learning achieve the four learning outcomes of physical education? A review of literature. *Quest, 67*(1), 56–72.

Casey, A., & Kirk, D. (2021). *Models-based practice in physical education*. London: Routledge.

Casey, A., & Quennerstedt M. (2020). Cooperative learning in physical education encountering Dewey's Educational theory. *European Physical Education Review, 26*(4), 1023–1037. doi:10.1177/1356336X20904075

Ciotto, C. M., & Gagnon, A. G. (2018). Promoting social and emotional learning in physical education. *Journal of Physical Education, Recreation & Dance, 89*(4), 27–33. https://doi.org/10.1080/07303084.2018.1430625

Cohen, E. G. (1994). Restructuring the classroom: Conditions for productive small groups. *Review of Educational Research, 64*(1), 1–35. https://doi.org/10.3102/00346543064001001

Collaborative for Academic Social and Emotional Learning. (CASEL). (2019). *Core SEL competencies, available at:* https://casel.org/core-competencies/

Corcoran, R. P., Cheung, A. C. K., Kim, E., & Xie, C. (2018). Effective universal school-based social and emotional learning programs for improving academic achievement: A systematic review and meta-analysis of 50 years of research. *Educational Research Review, 25*, 56–72. https://doi.org/10.1016/j.edurev.2017.12.001

Cothran, D. J., & Ennis, C. D. (1999). Alone in a crowd: Meeting students' needs for relevance and connection in urban high school physical education. *Journal of Teaching in Physical Education, 18*(2), 234–247.

Darnis, F., & Lafont, L. (2015). Cooperative learning and dyadic interactions: Two modes of knowledge construction in socio-constructivist settings for team-sport teaching. *Physical Education and Sport Pedagogy, 20*(5), 459–473. https://doi.org/10.1080/17408989.2013.803528

Denham, S. A. (2006). Social-emotional competence as support for school readiness: What is it and how do we assess it? *Early Education and Development, 17*(1), 57–89.

Durlak, J. A., Weissberg, R. P., Dymnicki, A. B., Taylor, R. D., & Schellinger, K. B. (2011). The impact of enhancing students' social and emotional learning: A meta-analysis of school-based universal interventions. *Child Development, 82*(1), 405–432. https://doi.org/10.1111/j.1467-8624.2010.01564.x

Dyson, B. (2014). Quality physical education: A commentary on effective physical education teaching. *Research Quarterly for Exercise and Sport, 85*(2), 144–152.

Dyson, B. (2019). Cooperative Learning: A model-based practice in physical education. Guest Editor. *Journal of Physical Education, Recreation, and Dance, 90*(3), 10–133.

Dyson, B., & Casey, A. (2012). Cooperative learning in physical education. Taylor & Francis.

Dyson, B., & Casey, A. (2016). Cooperative learning in physical education and physical activity: A practical introduction. Routledge.

Dyson, B., Howley, D., & Shen, Y. (2019). Teachers' perspectives of social and emotional learning in Aotearoa New Zealand primary schools. *Journal of Research in Innovative Teaching & Learning, 12*(1), 68–84. https://doi.org/10.1108/JRIT-02-2019-0024

Dyson, B., Howley, D., & Shen, Y. (2020). 'Being a team, working together, and being kind': Primary students' perspectives of cooperative learning's contribution to their social and emotional learning. *Physical Education and Sport Pedagogy*, 1–18.

Dyson, B., Howley, D., & Wright, P. M. (2021). A scoping review critically examining research connecting social and emotional learning with three model-based practices in physical education: Have we been doing this all along? *European Physical Education Review, 27*(1), 76–95. https://doi .org/10.1177/1356336X20923710

Dyson, B., Wright, P. M., Amis, J., Ferry, H., & Vardaman, J. M. (2011). The Production, communication, and contestation of physical education policy: The cases of Mississippi and Tennessee. *Policy Futures in Education, 9*(3), 367–380.

Dyson, B. P., Linehan, N. R., & Hastie, P. A. (2010). The ecology of cooperative learning in elementary physical education classes. *Journal of Teaching in Physical Education, 29*(2), 113–130.

Garcia, E., & Weiss, E. (2016). Making whole-child education the norm: How research and policy initiatives can make social and emotional skills a focal point of children's education. *Economic Policy Institute*. https://eric.ed.gov/?id=ED568889

Goodyear, V. A. (2017). Sustained professional development on cooperative learning: Impact on six teachers' practices and students' learning. *Research Quarterly for Exercise and Sport, 88*(1), 83–94.

Goudas, M., & Magotsiou, E. (2009). The effects of a cooperative physical education program on students' social skills. *Journal of Applied Sport Psychology, 21*(3), 356–364. https://doi.org /10.1080/10413200903026058

Grenier, M., & Yeaton, P. (2012). The cooperative learning model as an inclusive pedagogical practice in physical education. *Cooperative Learning in Physical Education. A Research-based Approach*, 119–135.

Grenier, M., & Yeaton, P. (2019). Social thinking skills and cooperative learning for students with autism. *Journal of Physical Education, Recreation & Dance, 90*(3), 18–21.

Humphrey, N. (2013). Conclusion. In Social and Emotional Learning: A Critical Appraisal (pp. 134–146). *SAGE Publications Ltd*. https://doi.org/10.4135/9781446288603

Jacobs, J., & Wright, P. (2014). Social and emotional learning policies and physical education. *Strategies, 27*(6), 42–44. https://doi.org/10.1080/08924562.2014.960292

Johnson, D. W., and Johnson, R. T. (1989). *Cooperation and competition: Theory and research. Edina*, MN: Interaction Book.

Johnson, D. W., & Johnson, R. T. (2009). An educational psychology success story: Social interdependence theory and cooperative learning. *Educational Researcher, 38*(5), 365–379.

Jones, S. M., & Bouffard, S. M. (2012). Social and emotional learning in schools: From programs to strategies. *Social Policy Report, 26*(4), 1–33.

Jones, S. M., & Doolittle, E. J. (2017). Social and emotional learning: Introducing the issue. *The Future of Children, 27*(1), 3–11.

Jones, S. M., Barnes, S. P., Bailey, R., & Doolittle, E. J. (2017). Promoting social and emotional competencies in elementary school. *The Future of Children, 27*(1), 49–72.

Kagan, S. (1992). *Cooperative learning (2nd ed.)*. San Juan Capistrano, CA: Kagan Cooperative Learning.

Kirk, D. (2013). Educational value and models-based practice in physical education. *Educational Philosophy and Theory, 45*(9), 973–986. doi: 10.1080/00131857.2013.785352

Klavina, A., Jerlinder, K., Kristén, L., Hammar, L., & Soulie, T. (2014). Cooperative oriented learning in inclusive physical education. *European Journal of Special Needs Education, 29*(2), 119–134.

Kolb, D. A. (1984). *Experiential Learning: Experience as the Source of Learning and Development*. Prentice Hall.

Lund, J. (1992). Assessment and accountability in secondary physical education. *Quest, 44*(3), 352–360.

Martin, A. J., Collie, R. J., & Frydenberg, E. (2017). Social and Emotional Learning: Lessons Learned and Opportunities Going Forward. In E. Frydenberg, A. J. Martin, & R. J. Collie (Eds.), *Social and Emotional Learning in Australia and the Asia-Pacific: Perspectives, Programs and Approaches* (pp. 459–471). Springer. https://doi.org/10.1007/978-981-10-3394-0_24

Ministry of Education (2007), *The New Zealand Curriculum, Learning Media*, Wellington.

Noddings, N. (2005). Caring in education. *The Encyclopedia of Informal Education*, 935250-1.

Noddings, N. (2007). Caring as relation and virtue in teaching. *Working virtue: Virtue ethics and contemporary moral problems*, 41–60.

Perkins, D. (1999). The many faces of constructivism. *Educational Leadership, 57*(3), 6–11.

Polvi, S., & Telama, R. (2000). The use of cooperative learning as a social enhancer in physical education. *Scandinavian Journal of Educational Research, 44*(1), 105–115. https://doi .org/10.1080/713696660

Raver, C. C. (2002). Emotions matter: Making the case for the role of young children's emotional development for early school readiness. *Social Policy Report, 16*(3), 3–20. https://doi .org/10.1002/j.2379-3988.2002.tb00041.x

Rovegno, I., & Dolly, J. P. (2006). 3.4 Constructivist perspectives on learning. *Handbook of Physical Education*, 242.

Sánchez-Hernández, N., Martos-García, D., Soler, S., & Flintoff, A. (2018). Challenging gender relations in PE through cooperative learning and critical reflection. *Sport, Education and Society, 23*(8), 812–823. https://doi.org/10.1080/135733 22.2018.1487836

Sapon-Shevin, M. (2010). *Because we can change the world: A practical guide to building cooperative, inclusive classroom communities*. Corwin Press.

SHAPE America. (2013). National Standards for K-12 Physical Education for the Society of Health and Physical Educators (SHAPE America). SHAPE America 1900 Association Drive, Reston, VA 20191. www.shapeamerica.org

Siedentop, D., Hastie, P. A., & Van der Mars, H. (2011). *Complete guide to sport education (Second)*. Human Kinetics.

Slavin, R. E. (1996). Research on cooperative learning and achievement: What we know, what we need to know. *Contemporary educational psychology, 21*(1), 43–69.

Slavin, R. E. (2010). Co-operative learning: What makes group-work work? *The nature of learning: Using research to inspire practice*, 161–178.

Tousignant, M., & Siedentop, D. (1983). A qualitative analysis of task structures in required secondary physical education classes. *Journal of Teaching in Physical Education, 3*(1), 47–57.

Yoder, L. J. (1993). Cooperative learning and dance education. *Journal of Physical Education, Recreation & Dance, 64*(5), 47–56. https://doi.org/10.1080/07303084.1993.10609977

Zhai, F., Raver, C. C., & Jones, S. M. (2015). Social and emotional learning services and child outcomes in Third Grade: Evidence from a cohort of head start participants. *Children and Youth Services Review, 56*, 42–51. https://doi.org/10.1016/j .childyouth.2015.06.016

SECTION 3

Social and Emotional Learning in Specialized Programs and Contexts

CHAPTER 10

Social and Emotional Development through Preschool Education

Fernando Santos
Lauriece L. Zittel

CHAPTER SUMMARY

Social and emotional learning (SEL) have been conceptualized as crucial for children across the developmental spectrum. Preschool education represents an important setting to foster SEL, create opportunities for physical activity, and enable school readiness. Thus, a reflection centered on how to foster SEL is needed to guide education professionals toward deliberately providing high-quality developmental experiences for young children through physical activity. Such an approach may help children flourish and reach their full potential throughout childhood and later in life. In this chapter, insights about SEL through physical activity will be provided including practical and theoretical implications that may be useful for preschool educators and other key stakeholders.

Social and Emotional Development through Preschool Education

Social and emotional development in young children are critically important to overall child development (National Scientific Council on the Developing Child [NSCDC], 2004). Physical, preacademic, and social and emotional skills should all be areas of focus for effective early childhood programming in an effort to prepare preschool-age children (3–5 years of age) for the transition to kindergarten and early elementary grades (National Association for the Education of Young Children, 2009). However, with the demand for school-readiness focused on student achievement, early programming has placed a heavy emphasis on academics with social and emotional skills receiving far less attention (Burford, 2019). This narrow vision of school readiness and, therefore, development has raised concerns within the research and teaching communities. As Ang (2014) stated, "preschool education is, arguably, one of the most intensively debated topics in many societies. Public debates in various countries reveal the contentious nature of the subject, particularly for the local community and society" (p. 185).

In a time when the "whole child" perspective has become a priority for educational services around the globe (Formosinho & Figueiredo, 2014; Jenkins et al., 2018), there are cultural trends that, in some cases, also equate child development with becoming a "competitive learner."

In other words, transmitting the curriculum and showing expected behaviors align with the competitive nature of contemporary society where grades, school attainment, and tangible outcomes are prioritized (Bakken, Brown, & Downing, 2017). This perspective, however, neglects the importance of the skill-building nature of development in which deliberate efforts focused on enhancing SEL are needed. The individualist objectives and profit-driven nature of capitalist-centered market driven societies may undermine social and emotional learning (SEL) and negatively impact individuals' well-being and mental health (Butler, 2019). The impact of some SEL skills such as empathy, impulse control, and respect for others can be intangible in the sense that there might not be an immediate effect on school success (i.e., grades). During the preschool years, SEL outcomes represent stepping-stones for a successful developmental path where the child learns a range of skills in a process-focused environment that may later lead to other outcomes such as school success (Walker & Weidenbenner, 2019).

Considering the complexity and challenges encountered in contemporary society (e.g., highly competitive, increased use of technology, lack of social skills), there is a need to refine priorities and approaches within preschool education (Moreno, Nagasawa, & Schwartz, 2018). Researchers (Bakken et al., 2017; Johansson, et al., 2011) have raised awareness about the importance of developing SEL skills beginning early in childhood and creating well-structured programs that satisfy emergent developmental needs. More specifically, teaching Generation Z (Gen Z) children who increasingly rely on technology and media interactions, which results in less play time and interpersonal development, pose very important challenges (Hampton & Keys, 2016; Seemiller, & Grace, 2016). In reflecting on Gen Z, Gould, Nalepa, & Mignano (2019) explain that "...because of the amount of time they spend on technology, they are thought to have shorter attention spans, the need for frequent feedback, and a lack of independence" (p. 105). To counter these challenges, purposefully teaching SEL skills within an early childhood curriculum will help lay the foundation for healthy development beginning at an early age.

One of the key challenges for contemporary society is to develop carefully designed programs and curricula to help young children thrive. The decline of social and emotional skills and quality relationships with peers and supportive adults (Eccles, 2004; Thomson et al., 2018) should prompt reflection about the need to design developmentally appropriate activities and experiences. When discussing curricula for young children, we should have in mind that although child-directed play is critically important in the preschool years, teacher-facilitated learning environments are necessary. Concerning this notion, we must remember that (a) young children learn differently from older children and adolescents, (b) preschool teachers can carefully design experiences to foster positive, developmental outcomes, (c) reflection and awareness are key to enabling meaningful learning, and (d) the inclusion of child-directed play is crucial. Specifically, well designed experiences and activities enable social and emotional development, physical development, and cognitive development as these different domains of development are interrelated (Wright, Zittel, Gipson, & Williams, 2019).

Furthermore, interaction, experience, and reflection are key strategies for preschool teachers to help children learn more about themselves and others. For example, a preschool teacher might challenge children to work in pairs to find a magic box in the gym and place several obstacles that require the children to climb, jump, and crawl in order to find the box. After each pair finds a box, the preschool teacher might ask them to talk about the experience and reflect on how they felt working together. This provides an opportunity to discuss skills like respect for each other and helping your classmates. This activity may also set up another session in which children explore, in small groups, pictures that had been placed inside the box. Pictures of children helping each other or displaying various emotions (e.g., children laughing together, a child looking sad) gives a teacher the opportunity to ask leading questions and see how well the children understand their behaviors and emotions as well as those of others.

Ultimately, upon entering kindergarten, children are expected to regulate their behavior, control impulses, follow adult directions, take turns, and establish friendships with peers (Marotz & Allen, 2016; National Scientific Council on the Developing Child, 2004). In order for children to develop these skills, social and emotional development has to be a critical part of school readiness (Brown, 2013). Developmentally appropriate practices in early childhood programs can emphasize social and emotional development during movement and play to reinforce self-regulation and social competence while promoting language development and cognitive skills (NAEYC, 2009). Such a pedagogical approach requires a student-centered outlook toward the teaching and learning process in which children's developmental needs are prioritized in the preschool teacher's planning and implementation (Sousa, Loizou, & Fochi, 2019). It is also important to engage family members and program staff beyond teachers in creating an appropriate environment for preschool children to develop holistically.

Young children, who are at a sensitive developmental stage, need guidance to understand more about themselves and others while engaging in learning experiences. Discussions around what children need to learn and how they learn have dominated debates around child development (Sousa, Loizou, & Fochi, 2019). The Collaborative for Academic and Social and Emotional Learning (CASEL's) framework (2019) has been used as part of an evidence-based curriculum that may help children flourish. CASEL (2019) focuses on five core competencies that have deemed crucial for children's development: (a) self-awareness, (b) self-management, (c) social awareness, (d) relationship skills, and (e) responsible decision making. These five core competencies promoted by CASEL (2019) align with pedagogical models and approaches previously discussed in this book (e.g., Hellison, 2011; see Chapter 7) and can translate into developmentally appropriate skills for preschoolers such as sharing, turn-taking, empathy, following directions, respecting rights of peers, participation, task persistence, self-regulation, and independent problem-solving. CASEL has been used as a framework to help preschool teachers achieve objectives set for students' affective domain. As discussed in Chapter 3, a) motivation, (b) emotional responses, (c) self-concept, and (d) resilience may be considered crucial features of preschool programming, which can be integrated in physical activity (PA). Thus, students' affective engagement and development in and through PA may be accomplished through facilitative teaching practices focused on teaching SEL skills and by creating appropriate preschool environments.

Best Practices in Early Childhood Education

A more traditional perspective toward teaching and learning in early education supports teacher-centered approaches that position children as empty vessels to be filled rather than independent social actors responsible for their own SEL (Samuelsson & Carlsson, 2008). Several researchers across disciplines have acknowledged the need for empowerment and to gradually help children become more responsible for themselves and others (Power, Rhys, Taylor, & Waldron, 2019; Hellison, 2011). According to more student-centered, empowerment-based pedagogical approaches, children are seen as "a person—an individual in his/her own right" (Samuelsson & Carlsson, 2008, p. 624).

Developmentally appropriate practices in early childhood programming conducive to SEL require an explicit focus on children's needs, interests, and developmental readiness (Loizou, & Charalambous, 2017). Participatory pedagogy is one approach that has been utilized in preschool education (Formosinho & Figueiredo, 2014) and focuses on several pedagogical principles, including (a) learning occurs by *feeling* and interacting with others; (b) experience is key to fostering meaningful learning and, therefore, *doing* is paramount; (c) providing a sense of *belonging* through positive support and meaningful relationships; and (d) *reflecting* and creating meaning are central as children's narratives constitute a means for learning. A key pedagogical assumption is that children are independent social actors and are responsible for their own learning experiences as the preschool teacher facilitates opportunities based on their interests and needs. Such an approach connects with the tenets of social constructivism whereas preschool teachers "view planning as a day-to-day activity, shaped by the interests and needs of learners, and they evaluate students based upon the process as much as the product" (Mills, 2007, p. 101). For example, preschool teachers, according to this pedagogical approach, may prompt children to select activities and tasks, share decisions about the curriculum, and reflect on the meanings and significance of their learning experiences. We should keep in mind that ideally, preschool teachers plan activities with children. For example, at the beginning of the school year, teachers may leave a bulletin board empty and ask the children how they want to make it their own. Through discussion and idea sharing, the children come up with a handprint-footprint display. For the next several days, the teacher would schedule class time for the children to choose paint, crayons, markers, etc., to make their prints and facilitate the print making. Each child would then have the chance to select where on the board to place their prints.

As explained in Chapter 3, involving students in pedagogical decision making is one way that teachers can foster higher levels of engagement and share their power. This project may include experiential learning opportunities for children to explore a variety of themes such as emotions. These themes may lead children to a vast array of activities (e.g., working in pairs in a motor circuit holding hands to understand the meaning of empathy) and learning outcomes (e.g., SEL, motor skill development). Several pedagogical approaches have influenced the way we look at child development and provide insight on how we should look forward in terms of research and practice (Formosinho & Figueiredo, 2014). Developmental theorists (e.g., Bronfenbrenner, 2005) have acknowledged the role played by macro (e.g., policy) and micro (e.g., family, education services) systems (Hastie & Siedentop, 1999; Theokas et al., 2005) and the need to create environments that position children as active participants in their social worlds. However, practice is often characterized by a more traditional pedagogical approach. This type of approach tends to focus on remediating problems rather than actively developing children SEL (Damon, 2004). Putting children's needs first and fostering social and emotional development based on their developmental stage and social competence is crucial for program design and delivery as well as future childhood outcomes. In order to develop children as active agents of their own learning, it is crucial to move toward holistic, child-centered pedagogies.

Children's play, PA, and social interactions with peers and caring adults have been considered key factors for high-quality, early educational programming (Edwards, 2017). Throughout recent decades, PA has been utilized to support a range of outcomes (e.g., personal and social skill development, motor development, sport skill development, childhood obesity prevention) and across an array of settings, including preschool education (Reimers et al., 2019). The type of play a child engages in at home or in a childcare/preschool setting could change as the goal of the task(s) changes. Children may be quite content to build a block structure or ride a tricycle by themselves if they prefer solitary play. Those same tasks could be accomplished while in proximity to another child resulting in no interaction, i.e., merely parallel play with the same objects or toys (Brownell, Zerwas, Balaraman, 2020).

Once the task changes to become more focused on sharing a common goal (e.g., a cooperative task), children will need to interact with peers in more meaningful ways. If block building turns into creating a village with houses and roads with peers, children will be required to exchange and share blocks and cars as needed. When tricycle riding turns into a race, children will have natural opportunities to interact and

Figure 10.1 Playground.

© united photo studio/Shutterstock.

work together. As children mature socially and emotionally, cooperative play emerges as a means to interact with other children and accomplish movement and play tasks together or in small groups. In the early childhood years, specifically preschool-age, children's play may vary from solitary play, parallel play to cooperative play (see **Figure 10.1**) across a variety of settings and tasks (Brownell, Zerwas, Balaraman, 2020).

Peer play requires young children to consider others' feelings in order to negotiate situations that require mutually beneficial outcomes (Eggum-Wilken et al., 2014). Two children digging in a playground sandbox with pails and tools may share and exchange those toys as agreed upon. This interaction may not go so well if one of the two children is not inclined to "give up" the blue shovel for the green rake. Interactions requiring levels of sharing and cooperation are stepping-stones to relationship-building skills necessary for success in social life.

Developmentally appropriate early childhood classroom programming should incorporate daily movement and play opportunities to intentionally enhance the physical development of preschool-age children (NAEYC, 2009; see **Figure 10.2**). Large

Figure 10.2 Classroom areas.

© FatCamera/E+/Getty Images.

motor indoor classroom activities and outdoor play experiences can also provide preschool teachers with the opportunity to explicitly teach SEL competencies through PA. Quality SEL programming already practiced within a preschool curriculum can be reinforced and enhanced during designated daily movement, play, and PA (Durlak, Weissberg, Dymnicki, Taylor, & Schellinger, 2011). Quality SEL programming includes competencies such as self-awareness, self-management, and social awareness (Collaborative for Academic, Social, and Emotional Learning [CASEL], 2013; 2019).

The value of SEL in providing a framework for preschool teachers to help young children develop a range of competencies and positive behaviors has been recognized (National Association of State Boards of Education, 2013). Concurrently, the fact that physical education provides multiple, teachable moments, and developmental opportunities has prompted researchers, teachers, and policy makers to strengthen the connection between SEL and PA within physical education and out-of-school time programming (Jacobs & Wright, 2014). Teaching SEL skills is appropriate content to be integrated across age- and grade-levels, including early childhood (NAEYC, 2009). Understanding what is developmentally appropriate for each level is critical to shaping and maintaining a supportive learning climate. Finally, selecting evidence-based curriculum and classroom strategies focused on enhancing the emotional intelligence of preschool-age children can help them learn to manage their emotions and prepare them for their kindergarten experience.

Early childhood PA programming that intentionally incorporates and integrates quality SEL into daily routines can provide children with opportunities to practice the competencies outlined in the CASEL (2019) framework. Within each core competency, there are specific SEL skills that parents/guardians and classroom instructors can reinforce through activities and discussions (CASEL, 2017). In the following paragraphs, we present two examples of evidence-based programs for promoting SEL in early childhood settings, specifically into physical education environments.

Second Step Early Learning Curriculum in an evidence-based, developmentally appropriate program for prekindergarten classrooms. The curriculum is commercially available by the Committee for Children (Committee for Children, 2011; see https://www.secondstep.org/) and is focused on SEL skills such as identifying emotions, perspective taking, and empathy as well as executive functioning skills

involving attention and memory (Upshur, Heyman & Wenz-Gross, 2017). Due to the fact that these SEL skills need to be adapted to children's developmental stage and taught gradually, The *Second Step Early Learning Curriculum* model includes five major units with weekly themes and scripted daily activities. The five major units focus on: skills for learning, empathy, emotion management, friendship and problem-solving, and transition to kindergarten. Specific teaching strategies are included in this curriculum to reinforce skills, manage behavior, assist with attention, and encourage participation (Upshur, et al., 2017).

Home Links are a highlight of this curriculum. These are parent/guardian handouts that help explain what the children are learning and how these skills can be reinforced at home (see https://www.secondstep.org/early-learning-curriculum). The emphasis is placed on helping children develop SEL skills across life domains whereas teachers, parents/guardians, and school directors are considered key to creating a school culture that values SEL skills. The *Second Step Early Learning Curriculum* model provides an evidence-based foundation to help children from kindergarten to middle school learn SEL skills. A kit is provided to teachers, parents/guardians, and school directors that includes the five units described previously, sample activities, and education modules. There are also additional modules that focus on bullying prevention, child protection, safe (i.e., preventive measures to avoid abuse), and mindfulness activities. The kit, as stated, provides learning opportunities for teachers, parents/guardians, and school directors learn more about SEL skills and comprehend the program's guiding principles. Continual support is also provided to monitor the implementation process through webinars and discussion forums. Thus, *Second Step Early Learning Curriculum* model is comprehensive, available online, requires little teacher-training, and is cost-effective.

The RULER approach (Brackett & Rivers, 2013) is an evidence-based strategy designed to integrate emotional intelligence into daily classroom practices. RULER is an acronym defining five skills of emotional intelligence: **R**ecognizing, **U**nderstanding, **L**abeling, **E**xpressing, and **R**egulating emotions (Nathanson, et al., 2016). Putting these five skills into practice within preschool classrooms creates an opportunity for teachers to enhance the teaching and learning climate. For this to happen, teachers could help young children monitor their emotions gradually using a tool designed to implement the RULER skills (the mood meter). The mood meter is divided into two axes and four quadrants, which are used to help children identify type and intensity of emotion. The quadrants are color coded and are used to describe a type of emotion: red = mad; yellow = brave; blue = sad; green = calm. The vertical axis represents the *energy* a child feels (–5 to +5). Energy may be expressed as negative, –2 or –1, if a child is feeling scared or very tired. A positive energy, +4 or +5, may be reported if a child is feeling joyful or energized. The horizontal axis has the same –5 to +5 range but represents *pleasantness*.

Using the mood meter, children may express that they are feeling very unpleasant or mad that something has occurred. On the other hand, a child may say they are very happy about something and, therefore, feeling a +4 to +5 on the axis (Tominey, O'Bryon, Rivers, & Shapes, 2017). Older students would typically be able to use mood meter numbers and words to identify current emotions whereas younger children would typically identify just a color in the early stages (Nathan, et al., 2016). Considering children's developmental needs and that these are their first experiences managing emotions is crucial, so preschool teachers set clear and appropriate expectations. For example, a child on the playground may come running to a teacher crying and expressing that when they got off of their tricycle to pick a dandelion another classmate got on their tricycle and rode away. The teacher may say, "you sound frustrated and mad right now. Do you think you are feeling red?" To help the child transition to a more pleasant, calm emotion (green), the teacher could walk with the child over to the classmate and discuss the situation.

Implementing teachable moments such as the one referenced above is an opportunity to talk about turn-taking and sharing. After talking with both children, the teacher redirects them to a shared activity using a wagon to take turns pulling and riding. Making the activity more attractive, the teacher provides bubbles for the rider. Before the children take off on their new adventure, the teacher speaks with them about how they are feeling: "this seems like it will be really fun for both of you! How are you feeling now? Are you feeling more like yellow now?" Teachers trained to use the RULER approach, and the mood meter, learn how to discuss emotions with young children and use associated learning activities to correspond to the type and intensity of the child's emotion (Nathanson, et al., 2016). Collectively, a child's level of social and emotional competency will have a direct effect on their social interaction with peers. The CASEL (2019; 2013) foundation has established a guide for preschool and elementary school programs to help them identify effective, evidenced-based SEL programming for general education classrooms. In the next section, we provide sample activities and strategies that aim to develop SEL through PA and connect these examples with existing theory.

Core SEL Competencies and Associated Learning Activities

In this section, we will expand on how preschool teachers as well as other education professionals such as physical education teachers may foster the following SEL competencies: (a) self-awareness; (b) self-management; (c) social awareness; (d) relationships skills; (e) responsible decision making. As such, practical applications, specifically sample activities and strategies, will be provided.

Self-Awareness

Self-awareness is the ability of young children to identify accurately their own emotions and thoughts and try to understand what they mean (CASEL, 2019). If they are able to identify emotions such as frustration, fear, or anger and communicate how they are feeling, parents/guardians, providers, and teachers are better able to talk with them and assist them in working through those emotions before negative behaviors or consequences occur. For example, while on the playground, a child may appear frustrated that a peer took a ball away without asking. If a teacher can help the child identify the emotion (frustration), model a calming strategy (taking deep breaths), and then assist in talking through the situation, negative consequences may be avoided. This self-awareness competency is aligned with Hellison's (2011) conceptualization of *emotional regulation* and *respecting the rights of feelings of others* and is also a crucial life skill that can be applied in other life domains beyond PA and school. For example, preschool teachers may use teachable moments to explore emotions and ways they influence behavior choices and relationships with peers. Many teachers have class routines such as checking the weather, date, and time at the beginning of the session; check-ins on feelings and emotional states could be integrated into such routines. It is important to take time for children to express their emotions at their own pace and provide opportunities for all children.

Self-awareness could also be addressed explicitly as a goal for PA. This could include creating reflection opportunities throughout an activity and inviting children to provide their own narratives about how they felt while managing emotions such as frustration. Often at the end of the day, teachers create an opportunity for children to voice their opinions about how they felt throughout the different activities and what they accomplished. Preschool teachers can facilitate multiple opportunities for reflection and take time to listen to children's narratives. Concrete visual aids may help children self-assess and put their own experiences into perspective. For example, a teacher may create a "reflection blanket" for children to hold while they reflect after each activity and share their thoughts and feelings. In this area, the teacher may have a board with all SEL competencies (with illustrated figures that reflect desired behaviors) and the names of all of the children. The teacher may then engage children in a discussion about how they were able to develop SEL competencies and give a voice to all children. The use of verbal cues and visual aids could be considered help for children to communicate their feelings. We should have in mind that children are still developing language skills substantially at this developmental stage.

Using a strategy provided by Hellison (2011) for each lesson, children may, during an activity, go to the "reflection blanket" because they are feeling frustrated and need guidance. Based on the premises behind cooperative learning (see Chapter 9), the teacher may select a leader each day and give them the responsibility of helping peers who go to the "reflection blanket." Children may be frustrated because they cannot complete a motor task. The leader could then help children overcome this challenge and join them in a given task. The teacher serves as a facilitator who guides children through this SEL. Furthermore, preschool teachers might highlight their accomplishments and work with children to set SEL goals for the next sessions. Providing concrete guidelines and expectations is also crucial to helping children reflect and become more aware of their own behaviors. Krik and Jay (2018) remind us that "learning occurs across every moment of the day, not just in teacher-guided activities. When teachers enter child-guided activities, they can identify authentic moments in which they can model appropriate social and emotional response…" (p. 483).

Self-Management

One important aspect of self-management is a young child's ability to self-regulate and control impulses. This SEL competency can be difficult for young children if they are not self-aware. A child who is unable to identify and express emotions that negatively impact interactions with peers and teachers may become more impulsive and further lack self-control. Teaching children how to "use their words" or ask for help when they are feeling sad, lonely, or angry will give adults the opportunity to discuss what those emotions may mean and provide alternative outcomes. Preschool teachers could use Hellison's (2011) guidelines and develop deliberate efforts to create group discussions and reflection opportunities to explore key emotions and feelings derived from specific situations occurring in PA time (e.g., the preschool teacher might reflect with children at a specific moment in the session) and provide young children with a voice to express themselves (e.g., the teacher might prompt reflection about specific events and ask students to share).

Preschool teachers could be aware that children, due to their level of emotional and cognitive development, might engage more in these reflection moments if there are appropriate visual aids and instruction strategies. Keeping records and empowering children for these reflective moments may be key for them to grasp the nature of their experiences and understand their own emotions and feelings. For children who are hesitant to vocalize emotions, or do not know how, a designated space on the playground or classroom for *calming down*, *relaxing your body*, or *having alone time* may be helpful for self-management. Being aware of who enters the designated space and ensuring that children have the appropriate time to reflect is critical to the process. Such a space could be designated on the playground, in the classroom, and/or motor area to facilitate reflection in a variety of settings where PA occurs. Following-up with an authentic discussion about what prompted the child to be there is also critical. In some instances, this may be to validate an action or behavior and in other instances, it will be an opportunity to provide feedback on the action or behavior that occurred. For example, a child may be nominated to serve as the "leader of the day" and have the responsibility of being the line leader, opening the door in transitions, turning on lights after nap time, coming to the front of the room with the teacher to lead the morning greeting, and managing playtime.

In addition to the "leader of the day" role, children could be given other leadership opportunities that encourage them to exercise and model positive self-management. For example, a child may be responsible for helping manage playtime in each of the classroom's areas or in the gym and help other children share materials. If a child struggles in sharing materials, a designated peer could lead them to the "reflection blanket" and try to solve the issue with or without the help of the preschool teacher. Finally, as all children have diverse learning paces, preschool teachers could create teams of leaders and have two or three leaders of the day. This could help children who may struggle more in a leading role feel more comfortable with the support of others who may feel more comfortable in this position. All children could have the opportunity to develop their own SEL competencies and provide peer modeling for others in this regard. It is important that the preschool teacher provides constructive feedback and challenges the leaders to explore diverse tasks and roles.

Explicit efforts made by preschool teachers may provide opportunities to foster SEL outcomes and increase children's awareness about SEL. Thus, preschool teachers could create a board that clearly indicates the skills children should focus on, place it in the classroom, and acknowledge that these skills may change according to children's needs. Visual aids that include expected behaviors connected to each of the skills could also be used. For example, there might be a picture of a child helping another child complete a motor task. This board might also help children self-assess as each child may place a sticker if he/she is able to display that behavior throughout the PA session. Based on the number of stickers, this board might also be used to prompt reflection at the end of a PA session. Children could be awarded and award themselves with points after each positive behavior. While educators could strive to foster intrinsic motivation as children develop, the strategic use of extrinsic stimuli is appropriate for preschoolers who also benefit from concrete, tangible feedback toward desired behaviors (Pavão et al., 2018).

Social Awareness

Social awareness involves empathy and a young child's ability to understand and accept that peers may behave, think, feel, or express things differently than they do (CASEL, 2019). Teaching young children to respect the rights of others means they are able to "walk in someone else's shoes." A preschool-age child may be more likely to accept differences unconditionally before they are fully able to understand why the differences exist. Comprehending basic feelings and differences can be discussed with topics they experience and understand at an age-appropriate level. For example, a teacher may demonstrate *same and different* feelings by asking children to "stand if sirens hurt your ears or bother you and cross your arms if

they don't." If children can see this visual display of *difference* they begin to recognize that not everyone feels or thinks like they do.

Teachers could also model a respect for diversity by reading books, playing culturally diverse games, creating bulletin boards that show people who dress differently, or look different from most children in the class. This has been considered paramount in previous pedagogical approaches (Hellison, 2011). Fostering SEL should be considered a priority across content areas and activities. If teachers focus on SEL within PA as well as in other non-PA experiences, better outcomes could be attained. Discussing different family make-ups, holidays, or routines help children become aware of social differences. In addition, preschool teachers could use PA as a way to convey the notion that thinking about others matters and helps children succeed in a range of tasks and settings. Becoming responsible for others has been a cornerstone of cooperative learning and Teaching Personal and Social Responsibility (TPSR) whereas the value of learning with others is crucial. For example, children might have to do a motor circuit in pairs as one child is blindfolded and the other has the responsibility of leading through the different stations. This experience could be further explored and discussed in a debriefing at the end of the PA session and lead to an in-class assignment about empathy.

Relationships Skills

Relationship skills for young children will involve respecting others through action(s) and communication(s) and being able to interact effectively with others? Listening, taking turns, helping, and sharing with others may be difficult for preschool-age children because children are still discovering and learning how to connect with others and create meaningful relationships with peers. Demonstrating and role playing how to develop these skills could be helpful strategies for all adults interacting with young children. Developing positive communication skills like saying "please" and "thank you" will require frequent reminders. Modeling and role-playing polite communication while sharing toys or during mealtime could demonstrate and provide opportunities to practice appropriate methods for avoiding or resolving conflict. The same can be done throughout PA. "May I have a turn now?" instead of grabbing a toy, or "would you please pass me the carrots?" instead of reaching and bumping or spilling something will help young children see that they can have their requests honored without potentially creating conflict with peers.

If conflict does occur, relationship building will mean learning how to resolve those conflicts by saying "I am sorry." However, we could consider how teachers, but also community, influences values, norms, and social skill development. In some cases, there are discrepancies between the teachers' approach toward SEL and the child's family and community, which reflect different values, norms, and ways of showing respect (see Chapter 14 for a more detailed analysis of social justice issues including inclusive and culturally responsive pedagogy).

For young children, adults may need to model and role play conflict resolution. Furthermore, one strategy that may help preschool teachers is to use conflicts as learning opportunities and create an area within the classroom and/or gym designated the "peace bench" (Melo et al., 2020) where children may solve potential conflicts with or without the guidance of the teacher. Specifically, preschool teachers may use children's struggles to prompt reflection about a given SEL competency and listen to their narratives, which will help them overcome challenges and create meanings about their own experiences. In some cases, there is a tendency to eliminate inappropriate behaviors and avoid exposing children to challenges. However, these challenges are key for children to learn how to deal with frustration and regulate emotions. Carefully designed strategies may help children navigate through these challenges and attain SEL outcomes. An overprotective environment in preschools, and also at home for that matter, may ignore these teachable moments and learning opportunities. The "peace bench" may include a board with potential ways of solving conflicts and afterward cooperating again with others such as hugging, giving a handshake or a high five, talking, and playing together. These strategies and possibilities should be placed within a specific socio-cultural context. We should have in mind that fostering SEL has diverse nuances according to different socio-cultural contexts, which should prompt reflection in preschool teachers to understand how relationship skills could be developed for the diverse group of children in their classrooms.

Responsible Decision Making

Responsible decision making occurs when young children can make good decisions, that is, they have a good understanding of expectations, specifically desirable behaviors, and the positive or negative consequences that might accompany their different decisions and resultant behaviors. (CASEL,

2019). Making decisions flows from having choices. Teaching the difference between "good choices" and "not-so-good choices" is developmentally appropriate for most preschool-age children. One would anticipate that if a toddler wanted to get into the sandbox and a peer was in the way, the toddler would push or bump into their peer to make their way to a desired space. A preschool-age child would soon learn that pushing or bumping is not a good choice, but it is instead more appropriate and socially desirable to wait for a turn or find a different space in which to play. Creating scenarios to clearly demonstrate or model "responsible decision" versus "less responsible decision making" through actions or pictures is an effective strategy to intentionally teach young children these concepts.

In contemporary society, preschool teachers are expected to deliver a wide range of content in a short period of time and children are expected to acquire knowledge, skills, and desirable behaviors quickly. This reality may leave children, in some instances, without feedback or reflection for decisions and choices that they may have made during the day (Ungar, 2009). Children could be actively engaged in responsible decision making in and outside of PA and begin learning how to transfer those skills to multiple settings. For example, in a reflection at the end of a PA session, a preschool teacher could help children understand how their actions impacted others in the class. In addition to positive feedback, preschool teachers could explicitly communicate their messages with children (e.g., "be a good friend," "make good choices") and/or extending those messages within the classroom setting (e.g., "help someone finish a classroom clean-up task"). Additionally, teachers could take the opportunity at the end of the session to talk about how these skills could be used at home (e.g., "how can you help at home?" "who can tell us about an adult you know who is a leader?" "what makes them a good leader?"). Intentionally integrating these messages across the day can maximize the learning experiences while managing limited time.

SEL through Physical Activity: Potential Pathways

Early childhood educators have long understood that physical development is important, and they encourage physical activity for children under their care (Wright & Stork, 2013, p. 40). Relatedly, physical education and PA have been considered crucial platforms for pursuing a variety of outcomes related to cognitive function, motor-skill development, and SEL among preschool-aged children (Biddle, Ciaccioni, Thomas, & Vergeer, 2019; Lubans et al., 2016; Jacobs & Wright, 2014). Nevertheless, it should be noted that although PA has been considered crucial for preschool children's development, there is the need to understand how to use PA to foster SEL outcomes (Kirk & Jay, 2018). An important topic of discussion has been the notion that fostering SEL through PA is a complex endeavor that requires reflection and carefully designed programs and appropriate program delivery. We should have in mind that PA may not automatically lead to SEL outcomes (Ciotto & Gagnon, 2018). In this section, guidelines and challenges associated with developing PA-based programs that foster SEL are discussed.

Another issue that has been raised by researchers, policymakers, and preschool teachers is the lack of deliberate efforts while structuring PA which, in many cases, leaves SEL up to chance (Jacobs & Wright, 2014). In these cases, there is a false belief that any sort of PA automatically results in SEL outcomes such as social awareness, self-awareness, responsible decision making, self-management, and relationship skills (MacNamara, Collins, & Giblin, 2015). In fact, a parallel concern raised by many policymakers and researchers has to do with the lack of well-structured PA opportunities as other content areas still account for most of the planning conducted by preschool teachers (Stork & Sanders, 2008). Finally, there is a need to better define developmental PA goals for preschool children. SEL provides a solid evidence-based background for preschool teachers to use PA in a holistic way (CASEL, 2019). Based on the CASEL framework, preschool children need concrete expectations, guidance, and opportunities across developmental domains to develop cognitive, motor, and SEL-related skills. However, there is a need for explicit processes that increase and optimize developmental opportunities, contexts, and outcomes. Therefore, teachers and supervising adults play a crucial role in using PA to foster SEL outcomes. For example, a preschool teacher at the beginning of the session might let children choose two motor skills and two SEL competencies to work on.

One example of explicitly and deliberately addressing SEL in physical education could involve having each motor skill and SEL competency represented using pictures on a classroom bulletin board to provide visual aids. The teacher could then ask children to self-assess and voice their opinions about how they were able to work on the motor skills and SEL competencies they selected. In contrast, if the teacher does not set clear expectations about SEL competencies and does not facilitate opportunities for reflection, children are left with no guidance. Therefore, teachers and supervising adults should be able to deliberately encourage cooperative play and appropriate peer socialization by facilitating PA environments that provide children with the opportunity to extend their imagination and creativity. Vygotsky (1978) suggested scaffolding play environments so children play within their "zone of proximal development" while still problem-solving and interacting with peers. For example, if the skill objective for one activity center is balance, the teacher could place several different practice opportunities within the center. In addition to a traditional balance beam, there could be jump ropes or taped lines put down in a parallel fashion and in various widths for children to walk through. These types of play environments encourage children to practice self-regulation and self-control in order to accomplish the goals of their movement and play tasks (Walker & Venker Weidenbenner, 2019).

Monitoring and Evaluating SEL Instruction in Preschool Settings

A key aspect of fostering SEL is monitoring and evaluating children's developmental needs as observation and constant reflection are crucial for the preschool teacher (see Chapter 4 for further insights into assessment practices that align with SEL). It is important to remember that not all children have the same strengths and developmental pace (Geel et al., 2019; Smale-Jacobse, Meijer, Helms-Lorenz, & Maulana, 2019). It is crucial, while developing a range of skills, to strengthen the connection between SEL and differentiated instruction strategies. Based on this pedagogical principle, Melo et al. (2020) developed an observational tool to facilitate preschool teachers' efforts to implement differentiated instruction strategies. **Table 10.1** provides an overview of this observational tool and describes SEL skills that are developmentally appropriate for preschool-aged children (Gunter, Caldarella,

Table 10.1 Observational Tool for Evaluating SEL in Preschool Settings

Student Behavior	Operational Definition	Examples of Student Performance	Examples of Plans for Instruction
Participation	Child is following directions and participating in activities or tasks organized by the teacher.	■ The child makes efforts to actively participate in activities (e.g., poses questions, focuses on the goal). ■ The child is not keen to follow the teacher's directions.	■ Use individual conversations to engage the child. ■ Develop activities where participation will lead to high rates of success. ■ Integrate voices and choices in selecting activities that are appealing and that they agree to try. ■ Reinforce children's efforts to participate in all activities/sessions.
Engagement	Child seems to have a high level of interest and motivation for the task or educational activity, which could be evidenced by their level of effort, focus, and active contribution.	■ The child is enthusiastic about the session/activity. ■ The child never quits and tries his best to achieve the activity's goal. ■ The child quits after a few attempts.	■ Create activities that are challenging and where the child may struggle. ■ Provide positive feedback as the child improves his/her performance. ■ Provide constant support and recognize the challenges faced by the child but highlight his/her strengths.
Showing respect	Child is actively showing respect to others	■ The child includes and accepts others. The child pays attention to others. ■ The child does not follow rules and is verbally abusive toward other children	■ Set clear expectations. ■ Negotiate rules and consequences. ■ Provide positive feedback when the child demonstrates a positive behavior. ■ Provide strategies to manage conflicts such as the peace bench.
Cooperation	Child demonstrates the social skills needed to work effectively with others.	■ The child is able to work with others toward a common goal. ■ The child does not respect other children's roles and opinions.	■ Create activities that involve cooperation to succeed. ■ Create opportunities for the child to work with another colleague who usually does not interact with him/her to improve a motor skill.
Encouraging others	Child offers social support to others in proactive ways.	■ The child cares for a colleague who is struggling in a motor task. ■ The child expresses frustrations or impatience with others.	■ Create activities where the child depends on others to succeed. ■ Empower children for each other's performance and use teachable moments to reinforce this responsible behavior.
Helping others	Child takes on helping roles either voluntarily or when asked.	■ The child is willing to gather materials and assist others. ■ The child does not care about helping others and is not willing to take on any helping roles.	■ Provide roles and responsibilities that involve helping others (e.g., less skilled). ■ Value these roles and responsibilities and provide positive feedback for children's efforts.
Leadership	Child takes on a leadership role with regard to an educational task.	■ The child leads a team, or an activity. ■ The child struggles in voicing his/her opinion and lacks the necessary confidence to lead others.	■ Provide opportunities for the child to lead a team, an activity, and the entire practice. ■ Provide clear expectations about what a leader should do. ■ Work directly with the leader, and avoid providing feedback to the other children.

Expressing voice	Child makes suggestions, shares opinions, and/ or reflects in ways that express their personality and individuality.	■ The child shares his/her opinion. ■ The child provides his/her view on specific events/ situations. ■ The child does not share his/her opinion without arguing with others.	■ Create opportunities at the beginning and the end of the session for the child to voice his/her opinions. ■ Use individual conversations to get to know the child. ■ Create opportunities for choice time and/or self-directed practice.
Asking for help	Child seeks out assistance and asks for help from teacher, program leader, or peers.	■ The child seeks out help to lead his/her team. ■ The child does not seek help even when he/she is struggling in an activity.	■ Create awareness about the importance of seeking help from others. ■ Demonstrate how seeking help is useful.

Melo, M., Santos, F., Wright, P., Sá, C., & Saraiva, L. (2020). Strengthening the connection between differentiated instruction strategies and teaching personal and social responsibility: Challenges, strategies, and future pathways. *Journal of Physical Education, Recreation & Dance, 91*(5), 28–36. Reprinted by permission of the Society of Health and Physical Educators, www.shapeamerica.org

Korth, & Young, 2012; Murano, Sawyer, & Lipnevich, 2020; see Table 10.1).

The observational tool created by Melo et al. (2020) was based on the instrument developed by Escartí et al. (2015) for evaluating responsibility-based instruction and includes a range of behaviors (e.g., participation, expressing voice, asking for help) that are rated on a scale ranging from "absent," meaning the child struggles in displaying this responsible behavior through "very strong," meaning the child is able to display this responsible behavior consistently and well.

An operational definition of each behavior is also provided (e.g., participation; child is following directions and participating in activities or tasks organized by the teacher). In addition to identifying each child's behaviors, this observational tool may help preschool teachers reflect on pedagogical strategies and activities to foster SEL outcomes through PA (see 'examples of plans for instruction' section). For example, if a teacher notes that very few students have developed the skill of asking for help, he/she may design activities that introduce and allow students to practice that skill. While this is a whole group example, teachers can also tailor their interactions and feedback to individual students based on such observations to enhance differentiated instruction related to SEL development. Finally, the observational tool proposed by Melo et al. (2020) includes a section designated 'examples of student performance' that describes desired and undesired outcomes (e.g., participation; the child makes efforts to actively participate in activities, the child is not keen to follow the teacher's directions) and may help teachers assess each child's behaviors.

Challenges and Objectives for Integrating SEL in Preschool Settings

Within preschool education, there are many challenges to fostering SEL and creating high-quality developmental programs and experiences. Thus, preschool teachers may need to reflect on their typical strategies and understand how. They may not be compatible with SEL (Syslová, 2019). As such, the way we frame SEL, PA and related pedagogical models and frameworks such as TPSR (Hellison, 2011) may enable or constrain preschool teachers' training, their actual intervention efforts, potential SEL outcomes, and emergent subcultures. Considering previous notions about development and pedagogical approaches, teachers should be well trained in appropriate content and have the necessary tools and assistance to deliver instruction and foster SEL outcomes through PA. This means that teacher training should be constructed in a way that provides teachers with the knowledge, skills, and dispositions needed to teach SEL (Manning, Wong, Fleming, & Garvis, 2019). It is important to understand the effectiveness of teacher training programs based on teachers' behaviors and children's outcomes (Walk, Evers, Quante, & Hille, 2018). However, there are challenges to integrating frameworks such as SEL within teacher training programs across the world.

First, many teacher education programs still include few hours/modules focused on PA-based programs, which leave future preschool teachers and physical education teachers with insufficient knowledge and experiences to develop and sustain these type of interventions (Chow, Mckenzie, & Louie, 2015; Obeng, 2009). Second, teacher training programs could help preschool and physical education teachers integrate content areas and knowledge through a pedagogical approach that enables them to understand how to develop all domains concurrently (i.e., cognitive, emotional, motor, and social) and identify learning opportunities across the curriculum (Kain, Leyton, Soto-Sánchez, & Concha, 2018; Toussaint et al., 2019). SEL provides teachers with concrete guidelines to foster a holistic approach toward child development; however, it is necessary to equip preschool and physical education teachers with the knowledge base needed to use PA in a developmentally appropriate and safe way that also generates motor skill development. In some contexts, teacher education programs still deliver classes/modules whereas there are few connections between PA, SEL, and other content areas as preschool and physical education teachers are expected to "put the pieces together." As an alternative to this separation of content areas, SEL and PA materials could be introduced within professional development programs in order to help preschool and physical education teachers become better equipped to develop high-quality programs (Walk et al., 2018).

Second, experiential learning opportunities are crucial to help preschool and physical education teachers understand how (a) to use teachable moments to integrate SEL within PA and (b) create opportunities for skill development in PA in order to attain better SEL outcomes (Kolb & Kolb, 2005). There should be a commitment to using experiences to create reflexive routines that ultimately help teachers become autonomous learners and capable of seeking and creating professional development opportunities (Kim, Raza, & Seidman, 2019). According to Sheridan, Edwards, Marvin, and Knoche (2009):

> At the surface, professional development in early childhood programs refers to a number of experiences that promote education, training, and development opportunities for early childhood practitioners who do or will work with young children aged birth to 8 years and their families...Its ultimate, long-term goal is to facilitate the acquisition of specific learning and social-emotional competencies in young children and, in many cases, to promote important family-specific attitudes

or abilities to support children's learning and development. (p. 379).

Third, in order to change communities and embed SEL in real-world settings (e.g., preschools, childcare services), it could be necessary to establish a dialogue between teacher-training programs, education services, and evidence-based guidelines for preschool education. We should consider that professional socialization (Omdal, 2018) influences how preschool and physical education teachers apply course materials and transfer the perspectives constructed throughout teacher education to practice. Thus, teachers' conceptualizations and practices may change due to the lack of value given to SEL through PA and existence of a subculture centered on academic attainment. Engaging education services (i.e., institutions that offer education services for preschool-aged children) in teacher education is crucial to better prepare teachers for the challenges ahead and openly discuss issues that reflect the concrete reality of preschool.

Finally, preschool and physical education teachers could also be equipped with the necessary skill set to develop communities of practice focused on SEL implementation (Fleer, 2003) and influence stakeholders in their intervention contexts. In this sense, engaging other stakeholders within preschool settings in learning environments focused on SEL and PA is the last level of impact that teacher training programs might generate. Preschool and physical education teachers should be viewed as policy makers that may help make the case for explicit strategies to foster SEL outcomes through PA, influence organizational culture and priorities, and educate stakeholders about this theme. For this to happen, teacher training programs could create solid grounds for teachers to realize how to impact education services/institutions and instill a child-centered approach whereas SEL and PA are crucial pieces of the preschool curriculum.

Conclusions

Throughout recent decades, PA and SEL have received substantial attention from the research and teaching communities (Trost, Fees, & Dzewaltowski, 2008). However, the lack of value given to well-structured PA programs delivered by trained professionals has been identified as a problem (Kain et al., 2017). The combination of these factors may limit preschool teachers' efforts toward fostering SEL through PE and PA. In some cases, curricular guidelines are quite flexible and leave education services and preschool teachers to make complex decisions such as which is the best pedagogical approach/model to choose.

Therefore, as discussed throughout this book, participatory learning and assessment strategies need to be integrated systematically in PA but also across content areas (see Escartí, Llopis-Goig, & Wright, 2018). In order to develop such a philosophy and practices, TPSR, alongside other pedagogical models such as cooperative learning and adventure-based learning, may serve the purpose of conceptualizing a child-centered pedagogy where deliberate opportunities are created and teachable moments are used to optimize developmental outcomes. We do not intend to suggest that TPSR or any specific pedagogical approach is the only way of integrating SEL into preschool PA opportunities. Instead, we acknowledge that there are strategies from various pedagogical models and approaches that might be useful and represent child-centered pedagogies that may help foster SEL in PA. Those working in preschool settings could reflect on these various pedagogical models and approaches discussed elsewhere in this book that may be utilized to develop age-appropriate strategies and structures for young children.

A child-centered pedagogy and explicit curricular guidelines may further help preschool teachers design intentional experiences in PA and other content areas conducive to SEL outcomes. Additionally, the creation of an explicit, models-based, and differentiated curriculum that clearly addresses the skills and support that young children need could improve short and long-term benefits. As explained in Chapter 3, the rather vague and implicit ways in which PA and SEL are viewed in some cases may undermine the child's developmental experience.

Implementing SEL through PA is paramount for children's holistic development. While formal interventions may best be run by trained teachers in school settings, the carryover of strategies should occur on the playground, at home, and in the community. Consistent messages crossing such contexts and supported by a range of caring adult stakeholders will help children develop SEL competencies. The five CASEL core SEL competencies can give parents/guardians, childcare providers, and teachers a consistent framework and common language across settings (CASEL, 2013). Incorporating strategies like role-playing, modeling, and drawing pictures can carry over to a multitude of settings and SEL outcomes. Providing young children with the skills to identify their emotions, knowing the "triggers" that intensify those emotions, and communicating those emotions to adults who can encourage or help them is a functional life-skill that will enhance a child's emotional intelligence. Designing a preschool curriculum that explicitly includes strategies to foster SEL through PA may help preschool teachers deliberately create meaningful learning opportunities for young children. As we move forward and continually adjust to a child's changing needs, we should continue developing best practices for facilitating SEL development through PA, especially at the preschool level. Progress in this area requires research as well as practical strategies. Sharing such evidence, reflections, and lessons learned are important steps to broaden our perspectives toward teaching young children. This is the challenge for preschool teachers and researchers across the world who are committed to helping children flourish and to develop SEL competencies as part of their holistic development.

Questions for Discussion

1. Why is PA often viewed as a space whereas SEL occurs automatically?
2. How can preschool teachers and other education professionals use PA as a place to address SEL within preschool settings?
3. How would you describe the relationship between traditional programming in preschool settings and PA-based SEL programming?
4. What is the need that justifies an explicit SEL curriculum within preschool education settings?
5. How can teacher education and professional development programs help teachers deliberately use PA to increase SEL outcomes in preschool children?

References

Ang, L. (2014). Preschool or prep school? Rethinking the role of early years education. *Contemporary Issues in Early Childhood, 15*(2), 185–199. https://doi.org/10.2304/ciec.2014.15.2.185

Bakken, L., Brown, N., & Downing, B. (2017). Early childhood education: The long-term benefits. *Journal of Research in Childhood Education, 31*(2), 255–269. doi.org/10.1080/02568 543.2016.1273285

Biddle, S., Ciaccioni, S., Thomas, G., & Vergeer, I. (2019). Physical activity and mental health in children and adolescents: An updated review of reviews and an analysis of causality. *Psychology of Sport and Exercise, 42*, 146–155. doi.org /10.1016/j.psychsport.2018.08.011

Brackett, M. A., & Rivers, S. E. (2013). Transforming students' lives with social and emotional learning. In R. Pekrun & L. Linnenbrink-Garcia (Eds.), *International handbook of emotions in education* (pp. 368–388). New York, NY: Taylor and Francis.

Bronfenbrenner, U. (2005). *Making human beings human: Bioecological perspectives on human development*. Thousand Oaks, CA: Sage.

Brown, C. P. (2013). Reforming preschool to ready children for academic achievement: A case study of the impact of pre-K reform on the issue of school readiness. *Early Education and Development, 24*(4), 554–573. https://doi:10.1080/10409289 .2012.694352

Brownell, C., Zerwas, S., & Balaraman, G. (2002). Peers, cooperative play, and the development of empathy in children. *Behavioral and Brain Sciences, 25*, 28–30. https://doi: 10.1017 /S0140525X02300013

Butler, S. (2019). The impact of advanced capitalism on well-being: An evidence-informed model. *Human Arenas, 2*, 200–227. https://doi.org/10.1007/s42087-018-0034-6

Chow, B. C., Mckenzie, T. L., & Louie, L. (2015). Physical activity and its contexts during preschool classroom sessions. *Advances in Physical Education, 5*(3), 194–203. https://doi.org/10.4236 /ape.2015.53024

Ciotto, C., & Gagnon, A. (2018). Promoting social and emotional learning in physical education. *Journal of Physical Education, Recreation & Dance, 89*(4), 27–33. https://doi.org/10.1080/07 303084.2018.1430625

Collaborative for Academic, Social, and Emotional Learning. (2013). *Effective social and emotional learning programs: Preschool and elementary school edition*. https://casel.org/preschool-and -elementary-edition-casel-guide/

Collaborative for Academic, Social, and Emotional Learning. (2017). *Teaching Activities to Support the Core Competencies of SEL*. https://www.casel.org/wp-content/uploads/2017/08 /Sample-Teaching-Activities-to-Support-Core-Competencies -8-20-17.pdf

Collaborative for Academic, Social, and Emotional Learning. (2019). *What is social and emotional learning?* Retrieved from https://casel.org/what-is-sel/

Committee for Children (2002). Second step pre-K. Seattle, WA: Committee for Children.

Damon, W. (2004). What is positive youth development? *The Annals of the American Academy of Political and Social Science, 591*(1), 13–24. https://doi.org/10.1177/0002716203260092

Developmentally appropriate practice in early childhood programming serving children from birth through age 8: *Position statement*. (2009). National Association for the Education of Young Children.

Durlak, J., Weissberg, R. P., Dymnicki, A. B., Taylor, R. D., & Schellinger, K. B. (2011). The impact of enhancing students' social and emotional learning: A meta-analysis of school-based universal interventions. *Child Development, 82*(1), 405–432. https://doi.org/10.1111/j.1467-8624.2010.01564.x

Edwards, S. (2017). Play-based learning and intentional teaching: Forever different? *Australasian Journal of Early Childhood, 42*(2), 4–11. https://doi.org/10.23965/AJEC.42.2.01

Eggum-Wilkens, N. D., Fabes, R. A., Castle, S., Zhang, L. D., Hanish, L. D., & Martin, C. L. (2014). Playing with others: Head start children's peer play and relations with kindergarten school competence. *Early Childhood Research Quarterly, 29*(3), 345–356. https://doi.org/10.1016/j.ecresq.2014.04.008

Escartí, A., Llopis-Goig, R., & Wright, P. M. (2018). Assessing the implementation fidelity of a school-based teaching personal and social responsibility program in physical education and other subject areas. *Journal of Teaching in Physical Education, 37*(1), 12–23. https://doi.org/10.1123 /jtpe.2016-0200

Escartí, A., Wright, P., Pascual, C., & Gutiérrez, M. (2015). Tool for assessing responsibility-based education (TARE) 2.0: Instrument revisions, inter-rater reliability, and correlations between observed teaching strategies and student behavior. *Universal Journal of Psychology, 3*(2), 55–63. https://doi .org/10.13189/ujp.2015.030205

Fleer, M. (2003). Early childhood education as an evolving 'community of practice' or as lived 'social reproduction': Researching the 'taken-for-granted.' *Contemporary Issues in Early Childhood, 4*(1), 64–79. https://doi.org/10.2304/ciec .2003.4.1.7

Formosinho, J., & Figueiredo, I. (2014). Promoting equity in an early year's context: The role of participatory educational teams. *European Early Childhood Education Research Journal, 22*(3), 397–411. https://doi.org/10.1080/1350293X .2014.912902

Geel, M., Keuning, T., Frèrejean, J., Dolmans, D., Merriënboer, J., & Visscher, A. J. (2019). Capturing the complexity of differentiated instruction. *School Effectiveness and School Improvement, 30*(1), 51–67. https://doi.org/10.1080/09243453 .2018.1539013

Gould, D., Nalepa, J., & Mignano, M. (2019). Coaching generation Z athletes. *Journal of Applied Sport Psychology, 32*(1), 104–120. https://doi.org/10.1080/10413200.2019.1581856

Gunter, L., Caldarella, P., Korth, B. B., Young, K. R. (2012). Promoting social and emotional learning in preschool students: A study of strong start Pre-K. *Early Childhood Education Journal, 40*(1), 151–159. https://doi.org/10.1007 /s10643-012-0507-z

Hampton, D. C., & Keys, Y. (2016). Generation Z students: Will they change our nursing classrooms? *Journal of Nursing Education and Practice, 7*(4), 111–115. https://doi.org/10.5430 /jnep.v7n4p111

Hastie, P., & Siedentop, D. (1999). An ecological perspective on physical education. *European Physical Education Review, 5*(1), 9–30. https://doi.org/10.1177/1356336X990051002

Hellison, D. (2011). *Teaching personal and social responsibility through physical activity* (3rd ed.). Champaign, IL: Human Kinetics.

Jacobs, J., & Wright, P. (2014). Social and emotional learning policies and physical education. *Strategies, 27*(6), 42–44. https://doi.org/10.1080/08924562.2014.960292

Jenkins, J. M., Duncan, G. J., Auger, A., Bitler, M., Domina, T., & Burchinal, M. (2018). Boosting school readiness: Should preschool teachers target skills or the whole child? *Economics of Education Review, 65,* 107–125. https://doi.org/10.1016/j.econedurev.2018.05.001

Johansson, E., Brownlee, J., Cobb-Moore, C., Boulton-Lewis, G., Walker, S., & Ailwood, J. (2011). Practices for teaching moral values in the early years: A call for a pedagogy of participation. *Education, Citizenship and Social Justice, 6*(2), 109–124. https://doi.org/10.1177/1746197910397914

Kain, J., Leyton, B., Concha, F., Close, M., Soto-Sánchez, J., & Salazar, G. (2017). Preschool children's physical activity intensity during school time: Influence of school schedule. *Preventive Medicine Reports, 8,* 6–9. https://doi.org/10.1016/j.pmedr.2017.07.011

Kain, J., Leyton, B., Soto-Sánchez, J., & Concha, F. (2018). In preschool children, physical activity during school time can significantly increase by intensifying locomotor activities during physical education classes. *BMC Research Notes, 11*(438), 1–5. https://doi.org/10.1186/s13104-018-3536-x

Kim, S., Raza, M., & Seidman, E. (2019). Improving 21st-century teaching skills: The key to effective 21st-century learners *Research in Comparative and International Education, 14*(1), 99–117. https://doi.org/10.1177/1745499919829214

Kirk, G., & Jay, J. (2018). Supporting kindergarten children's social and emotional development: Examining the synergetic role of environments, play, and relationships. *Journal of Research in Childhood Education, 32*(4), 472–485. https://doi.org/10.1080/02568543.2018.1495671

Lerner, R., Almerigi, J. B., Theokas, C., & Lerner, J. (2005). Positive youth development: A view of the issues. *The Journal of Early Adolescence, 25*(1), 10–16. https://doi.org/10.1177/0272431604273211

Loizou, E., & Charalambous, N. (2017). Empowerment pedagogy. *Journal of Research in Childhood Education, 31*(3), 440–452. https://doi.org/10.1080/02568543.2017.1314396

Lubans, D., Richards, J., Hillman, C., Faulkner, G., Beauchamp, M., Nilsson, M., . . . Biddle, S. (2016). Physical activity for cognitive and mental health in youth: A systematic review of mechanisms. *Pediatrics, 138*(3), 1–13. https://doi.org/10.1542/peds.2016-1642

MacNamara, A., Collins, D., & Giblin, S. (2015). Just let them play? Deliberate preparation as the most appropriate foundation for lifelong physical activity. *Frontiers in Psychology, 6*(1548), 1–4. https://doi.org/10.3389/fpsyg.2015.01548

Manning, M., Wong, G., Fleming, C., & Garvis, S. (2019). Is teacher qualification associated with the quality of the early childhood education and care environment? A meta-analytic review. *Review of Educational Research, 89*(3), 370–415. https://doi.org/10.3102/0034654319837540

Marotz, L. R., & Allen, K. E. (2016). *Developmental profiles: Pre-birth through adolescence.* Boston, MA: Cengage Learning.

Melo, M., Santos, F., Wright, P. M., Sá, C., & Saraiva, L. (2020). Strengthening the connection between differentiated instruction strategies and teaching personal and social responsibility: Challenges, strategies, and future pathways. *Journal of Physical Education, Recreation & Dance, 91*(5), 28–36. https://doi.org/10.1080/07303084.2020.1734506

Miguel, J. (2018). *Transferência da responsabilidade pessoal e social através da educação física na educação pré-escolar [Transference of personal and social responsibility through physical education in preschool education]* (Masters in Preschool Education). School of Higher Education of Viana do Castelo, Viana do Castelo.

Mills, J. (2007). Constructivism in early childhood education. *Perspectives in Learning, 8*(2), 99–105.

Moreno, A. J., Nagasawa, M. K., & Schwartz, T. (2019). Social and emotional learning and early childhood education: Redundant terms? *Contemporary Issues in Early Childhood, 20*(3), 221–235. https://doi.org/10.1177/1463949118768040

Morse, L., & Allensworth, D. D. (2015). Placing students at the center: The whole school, whole community, whole child model. *The Journal of School Health, 85*(11), 785–794. https://doi.org/10.1111/josh.12313

Murano, D., Sawyer, J. E., Lipnevich, A. A. (2020). A meta-analytic review of preschool social and emotional learning interventions. *Review of Educational Research, 90*(2), 227–263. https://doi.org/10.3102/0034654320914743

Nathanson, L., Rivers, S. E., Flynn, L. M., & Brackett, M. A. (2016). Creating emotionally intelligent schools with RULER. *Emotion Review, 8*(4), 305–310.

National Association for the Education of Young Children (2009). Developmentally appropriate practice in early childhood programs serving children from birth to age 8 [Policy statement]. Retrieved from https://www.naeyc.org/sites/default/fils/globally-shared/downloads/PDFs/resources/position-statements/PSDAP.pdf

National Scientific Council on the Developing Child. (2004). *Children's emotional development is built into the architecture of their brains* (Working Paper No 2). Retrieved from https://developingchild.harvard.edu

Omdal, H. (2018). Creating teacher capacity in early childhood education and care institutions implementing an authoritative adult style. *Journal of Educational Change, 19,* 103–129. https://doi.org/10.1007/s10833-017-9315-y

Pavão, I., Santos, F., Wright, P. M., & Gonçalves, F. (2019). Implementing the teaching personal and social responsibility model within preschool education: Strengths, challenges and strategies. *Curriculum Studies in Health and Physical Education, 10*(1), 51–70. https://doi.org/10.1080/25742981.2018.1552499

Power, S., Rhys, M., Taylor, C., & Waldron, S. (2019). How child-centred education favours some learners more than others. *Review of Education, 7*(3), 570–592. https://doi.org/10.1002/rev3.3137

Samuelsson, I., & Carlsson, M. A. (2008). The playing learning child: Towards a pedagogy of early childhood. *Scandinavian Journal of Educational Research, 52*(6), 623–641. https://doi.org/10.1080/00313830802497265

Seemiller, C., & Grace, M. (2016). *Generation Z goes to college.* San Francisco, CA: Jossey-Bass.

Sheridan, S. M., Edwards, C. P., Marvin, C. A, & Knoche, L. L. (2009). Professional development in early childhood programs: Process issues and research needs. *Early Education and Development, 20*(3), 377–401. https://doi.org/10.1080/10409280802582795

Smale-Jacobse, A. E., Meijer, A., Helms-Lorenz, M., & Maulana, R. (2019). Differentiated instruction in secondary education: A systematic review of research evidence. *Frontiers in Psychology, 10*(2366). https://doi.org/10.3389/fpsyg.2019.02366

Sousa, J., Loizou, E., & Fochi, P. (2019). Participatory pedagogies: Instituting children's rights in day to day pedagogic development. *European Early Childhood Education Research Journal, 27*(3), 299–304. https://doi.org/10.1080/1350293X.2019.1608116

Stork, S., & Sanders, S. (2008). Physical education in early childhood. *The Elementary School Journal, 108*(3), 197–206. https://doi.org/10.1086/529102

Syslová, Z. (2019). The relation between reflection and the quality of a preschool teacher's education performance. *International Journal of Child Care and Education Policy, 13*(4), 1–21. https://doi.org/10.1186/s40723-019-0060-y

Theokas, C., Almerigi, J. B., Lerner, R. M., Dowling, E. M., Benson, P. L., Scales, P. C., & Eye, A. (2005). Conceptualizing and modeling individual and ecological asset components of thriving in early adolescence. *The Journal of Early Adolescence, 25*(1), 113–143. https://doi.org/10.1177/0272431604272460

Thomson, K. C., Oberle, E., Gadermann, A. M., Guhn, M., Rowcliffe, P., & Schonert-Reichl, K. A. (2018). Measuring social-emotional development in middle childhood: The middle years development instrument. *Journal of Applied Developmental Psychology, 55,* 107–118. https://doi.org/10.1016/j.appdev.2017.03.005

Tominey, S. L., O'Bryon, E. C., Rivers, S. E., & Shapses, S. (2017). Teaching emotional intelligence in early childhood. *Young Children, 72*(1) 6–14. Retrieved from https://www.naeyc.org/resources/pubs/yc/mar2017/teaching-emotional-intelligence

Toussaint, N., Streppel, M. T., Mul, S., Schreurs, A., Balledux, M., Drongelen, K., . . . Weijs, P. (2019). A preschool-based intervention for Early Childhood Education and Care (ECEC) teachers in promoting healthy eating and physical activity in toddlers: Study protocol of the cluster randomized controlled trial PreSchool@HealthyWeight. *BMC Public Health, 19*(278), 1–8. https://doi.org/10.1186/s12889-019-6611-x

Trost, S. G., Fees, B., & Dzewaltowski, D. (2008). Feasibility and efficacy of a "Move and Learn" physical activity curriculum in preschool children. *Journal of Physical Activity and Health, 5*(1), 88–103. https://doi.org/10.1123/jpah.5.1.88

Ungar, M. (2009). Overprotective parenting: Helping parents provide children the right amount of risk and responsibility. *American Journal of Family Therapy, 37*(3), 258–271. https://doi.org/10.1080/01926180802534247

Upshur, C. C., Heyman, M., & Wenz-Gross, M. (2017). Efficacy trial of the Second Step Early Learning (SSEL) curriculum: Preliminary outcomes. *Journal of Applied Developmental Psychology, 50,* 15–25. http://dx.doi.org/10.1016/j.appdev.2017.03.004

Vygotsky, L. S. (1978). Mind in society: The development of higher psychological processes. Cambridge, MA: Harvard University Press.

Walk, L., Evers, W. F., Quante, S., & Hille, K. (2018). Evaluation of a teacher training program to enhance executive functions in preschool children. *PLoS ONE, 13*(5), 1–20. https://doi.org/10.1371/journal.pone.0197454

Walker, G., & Weidenbenner, J. V. (2019). Social and emotional learning in the age of virtual play: Technology, empathy, and learning. *Journal of Research in Innovative Teaching & Learning.* https://doi.org/10.1108/JRIT-03-2019-0046

Wright, P. M., & Stork, S. (2013). Recommended practices for promoting physical activity in early childhood education settings. *Journal of Physical Education, Recreation & Dance, 84*(5), 40–43. https://doi.org/10.1080/07303084.2013.773830

CHAPTER 11

Social and Emotional Learning in Adapted Physical Education

Wesley J. Wilson
Justin A. Haegele
Alyssa M. Trad

CHAPTER SUMMARY

In this chapter, we discuss the social and emotional learning (SEL) of students with disabilities within the adapted physical education (APE) context. We cover our present understanding of SEL for those with disabilities by exploring special education literature and the limited work directly related to APE. We overview the crossovers between SEL and the inclusiveness of educational experiences and how to practically apply such concepts to APE services. Throughout this chapter, we also highlight the importance of SEL in bullying prevention, prosocial behaviors, and listening to voices of students with disabilities.

Social and Emotional Learning in Adapted Physical Education

This chapter focuses on the social and emotional learning (SEL) of students with disabilities, more generally in physical education (PE), and more specifically for those who receive specially designed PE (hereafter referred to as adapted physical education [APE]). Importantly, APE is guaranteed to eligible students through the *Individuals with Disabilities Education Improvement Act* (IDEIA; 2004). Over the course of this chapter, we discuss our current understanding of SEL for this special population while drawing heavily on special education literature due to the limited scholarship that expressly addresses APE. To this end, we seek to highlight salient crossovers between SEL in special education and practical applications to APE services. We rely on the framework proposed by CASEL (2020a,b) to discuss (a) SEL-aligned teacher instructional practices and (b) strategies to foster a classroom culture that values SEL. As we build this discussion, we acknowledge that the SEL of students with disabilities is contextually bound to their subjective experiences in PE and APE and that *feeling included* is foundational to social and emotional growth through these services (Spencer-Cavaliere & Watkinson, 2010). Thus, we explore challenges regarding student experiences that often preclude social and emotional development, provide three non-fiction narratives that have emerged through research with students with disabilities, and pose some introspective questions about SEL and inclusion in integrated PE. Finally, we offer some strategies to enhance SEL and inclusiveness within these APE contexts.

SEL for Students with Disabilities

In a general sense, SEL has been operationalized as the development of competencies related to understanding and managing emotions, thoughts, and behaviors, achieving of positive goals, demonstrating empathy for others, creating and maintaining positive relationships, and making responsible decisions in "equitable learning environments so that *all* students can thrive" (CASEL, 2020a; italics added). In short, SEL seeks to provide all students, regardless of background or educational need, with the fundamental skills required to manage themselves, their relationships, and their conduct within the social world (Norman & Jamieson, 2015). This conceptualization of SEL extends the importance of social and emotional development to a diverse range of students, including those with disabilities who receive special education services. To this end, SEL programming has demonstrated importance among such students in terms of bullying prevention, academic achievement, and prosocial behaviors (Espelage, Rose, & Polanin, 2015, 2016).

SEL Applications in Special Education

In special education, the significance of teaching SEL skills to students with disabilities is well documented (e.g., Espelage, Rose, & Polanin, 2015, 2016; Feuerborn & Tyre, 2009; Norman & Jamieson, 2015). Cavioni, Grazzani, & Ornaghi (2017) describe SEL as "a vehicle for the academic and social inclusion" and studies have explored SEL development among students with disabilities in a variety of contexts (p. 100). For example, Wiener & Tardif (2004) placed students with learning disabilities in different special education settings, ranging from integrated to self-contained classrooms. These researchers measured the students' social acceptance, number and quality of friendships, self-concept, loneliness, depression, social skills, and problem behaviors across the settings and found that students in more integrated settings had higher peer acceptance, better self-perceptions, and more satisfying relationships. They also had fewer problem behaviors and were less lonely. In another study, Probst (2017) examined the social awareness and self-awareness, two of the core competencies of CASEL's (2020b) framework, of a student with autism. The student selected three images of girls in swimsuits from Instagram and was asked: (a) who the target audience was for the image (i.e., social awareness), (b) what message they were trying to communicate with the image (i.e., social awareness), (c) how the image made the student feel (i.e., self-awareness), and (d) what was the student's interpretation of the image (i.e., self-awareness). This particular student had trouble effectively identifying specific emotions related to the images. The larger take-away from this study, however, may be the potential to use media literacy education in conjunction with SEL to better understand the social and emotional needs of students with disabilities. Collectively, research on SEL programming in special education contexts has explored a diverse range of social and emotional outcomes and has provided evidence of its effectiveness in such settings, prompting interest in its application within APE contexts.

SEL Applications in APE

While there is a developing body of literature related to SEL in special education, there is relatively little literature specific to students with disabilities who receive PE and/or APE services. Thus, we have expanded our discussion of SEL in APE to cover social and emotional development more broadly to include interrelated aspects such as *behavior management* as well as *personal and social responsibility*. We should note here that many teachers practice behavior management strategies that are reactive and negative to extinguish unwanted social behaviors among students, rather than proactively attempting to teach SEL skills (Loovis, 2017). While discussed in more detail in Chapter 3, we try to further this messaging to foster a fundamental shift from "managing" behaviors to "teaching" SEL-aligned behaviors. We admit that this shift has been challenging in APE. While a majority of APE teachers (93%) believe that it is essential to explicitly teach social skills to students, 60% feel untrained to do so (Samalot-Rivera & Porretta, 2009). When considering this along with the fact that *IDEIA*'s (2004) definition of PE does not specifically address outcomes related to the social and emotional domain, but rather focuses on motor learning and physical skill development, it is not surprising that teachers are less comfortable integrating SEL into their instruction (Wilson, Kelly, & Haegele, 2019).

While managing behavior is an important competency that many PE and APE teachers utilize, such an approach may undermine SEL if it is applied in a manner that is reactive and punitive (Lavay, French, & Henderson, 2016). Managing behavior by regulating its ensuing consequences (i.e., operant conditioning) is a common method that many PE and APE teachers use when teaching students with disabilities. While this approach includes a variety of reinforcement strategies, including positive and negative reinforcement, punishment, and extinction, positive reinforcement is considered best practice in APE (Loovis, 2017). For example, a teacher may incentivize a student with Down syndrome to participate in APE by playing a favorite song if the student practices "safe hands and feet" throughout the lesson. In this way, we hope the likelihood of this prosocial behavior will increase in the future (Cooper, Heron, & Heward, 2007). It is beyond the scope of this chapter to delve deeper into applied behavior analysis, but we wanted to highlight that such an approach, even when positive, tends to work in a reactive, rather than proactive, manner to shape future behavior.

Accordingly, teachers may consider employing the humanistic approach to modifying behaviors, which emphasizes development of self-concept, interpersonal relationships, and personal and social responsibility (Sherrill, 2004). Lavay and colleagues (2016) stress that intent of the humanistic approach is to "not merely redirect disruptive behaviors, but rather to change perceptions, create a sense of responsibility, and build character" (p. 106). The authors go on to describe teachers' responsibilities in using the humanistic approach as: (a) connecting with students through a safe environment in which all feel a sense of belonging; (b) understanding individual behaviors and feelings; (c) helping students understand their behaviors and feelings; (d) teaching personal and social responsibility; (e) encouraging participants to learn; and (f) helping students recognize that limits on behavior are to protect and not punish them. In this way, the humanistic approach emphasizes the importance of proactively creating an environment in which social and emotional skill development is possible (Sherrill, 2004).

One such humanistic approach that has emerged over the last 30 years is the teaching personal and social responsibility (TPSR) model (see Chapter 7). In alignment with SEL principles, Wright, White, and Gaebler-Spira (2004) explored an adapted martial arts program focused on developing personal and social responsibility among students with disabilities. This study was guided by the TPSR model and captured SEL-related behaviors such as self-control, participation, effort, decision making, leadership, and reflection. The participants, all children with cerebral palsy, experienced an *increased sense of ability*, in that they seemed empowered to try new martial arts techniques and to take on additional challenges. The program also seemed to evoke *positive feelings* including fun, excitement, and enjoyment among the participants. Furthermore, the *social interactions were positive* and were manifested through appropriate social behaviors such as improved listening to the teacher, being more aware of others, taking turns, respecting limits, and being more comfortable in group settings.

Similarly, a small but promising TPSR study demonstrated that integrated motor development programs can lead to increased socially acceptable behaviors among children with disabilities such as respecting others' rights, assuming responsibilities, and working autonomously (Monteiro, Pick, & Valentini, 2008). Extending this line of research, Menendez & Fernandez-Rio (2017) merged the Sport Education instructional model (see Chapter 8) with TPSR and found that students with disabilities seemed to thrive in their social environment as they reported feeling like *part of the team* and that they enjoyed their *friendships* and *cooperation* during integrated PE. The unique blend of Sport Education and TPSR may "be a powerful tool for including students with disabilities in PE" (Menendez & Fernandez-Rio, 2017, p. 508), since it appears that the participants with disabilities themselves *felt included* within this study, which is essential to inclusive education (Spencer-Cavaliere & Watkinson, 2010). This finding is notable given that integrated PE is generally problematized as being non-inclusive from the perspectives of those with disabilities (Haegele, 2019).

Collectively, these findings suggest that approaches such as TPSR are not only viable but can build SEL competencies among students with disabilities in APE contexts. Importantly, when attempting to improve personal and social skills through a model such as TPSR, teachers should consider their unique teaching situations and students so that they can modify the model accordingly (Coulson,

Irwin, & Wright, 2012). One point of consideration before the use of TPSR, or any other model, is the educational placement in which the students are learning (Wilson et al., 2019). Are they being educated in self-contained classrooms, solely with others with disabilities, or are they participating with classmates without disabilities in integrated PE? Or perhaps they are learning in yet another alternative placement option (Wilson, Haegele, & Kelly, 2020)? Thus, it becomes important to be cognizant of how their placements may influence their experiences with TPSR. Keep in mind, as we illustrated above, that building SEL among students with disabilities through TPSR programming appears possible in both self-contained settings (e.g., Wright et al., 2004) and integrated settings (e.g., Menendez & Fernandez-Rio, 2017; Monteiro et al., 2008). Next, we will step back and explore how SEL can address bullying, which is a threat to feelings of inclusion among students with disabilities.

SEL and Student Experiences with Bullying

Among the other documented benefits of SEL, is its utility in reducing bullying (Espelage et al., 2015, 2016). Bullying is defined as intentional and repetitive interpersonal aggression characterized by an imbalance of power between perpetrators and victims (Stough et al., 2016). It is estimated that 20–33% of youth experience bullying as either a victim or perpetrator (Chester et al., 2015; Lebrun-Harris et al., 2018). Youth with disabilities have been identified as being at particular risk of bullying victimization and perpetration (Haegele, Aigner, et al., 2020; Rose & Gage, 2017; Rose et al., 2015). This is largely attributed to them (a) being identified as "different" or "incapable" (Dane-Staples et al., 2013); (b) fitting the mold of those typically bullied, including being viewed as vulnerable and non-aggressive (Veenstra et al., 2007); and (c) struggling with communication, which can enhance the likelihood of bullying being a way to express or respond to others (Maiano et al., 2016). Highlighting this, an examination of a representative sample of American youth from the 2016 *National Survey of Children's Health* reported that bullying victimization was experienced by 52.36% of children and 60.28% of adolescents with developmental delays; bullying perpetration was carried out by 14.99% of

children and 13.69% of adolescents with developmental delays (Lebrun-Harris et al., 2018).

While the bullying of and among students with disabilities appears to be a widespread issue, a three-year project called Second Step-Student Success Through Prevention (SS-SSTP; Espelage et al., 2015, 2016) has been effective in reducing bullying and promoting prosocial and academic skill development. This project demonstrated a decrease in bullying perpetration among the students with disabilities in the treatment schools after 41 SEL lessons, which emphasized explicit instruction in empathy, communication skills, and emotional regulation (Espelage et al., 2015). Furthermore, SS-SSTP was found to increase positive behaviors toward a willingness to intervene when bullying occurs as well as an improvement in their academic grades compared with students with disabilities in the control schools (Espelage et al., 2016).

Of concern for this particular chapter, bullying instances appear to occur more commonly during less structured times of the school day, including PE classes where disability and differences appear more pronounced due to the physical and performative nature of the subject (Haegele, Zhu, et al., 2020; Migliaccio et al., 2017). As such, SEL may be immediately meaningful, in reducing instances of bullying, such as verbal, social-relational, and physical bullying, during PE and perhaps also decreasing the likelihood for bullying in other contexts throughout the school day. This is promising as integrated PE appears to be ripe with concerns, such as the bullying, discrimination, and student exclusion, which challenge SEL instruction and effective inclusion of students with disabilities (Haegele, Hodge, et al., 2020).

The Intersection of Integration, Inclusion, SEL, and APE Services

In schools today, most students with disabilities receive their education in integrated, general education settings with peers without disabilities (U.S. Department of Education, 2018). The term *integrated* is used purposefully here to signify an educational setting where all students, regardless of learning style or educational need, are educated in the same space (Haegele, 2019). Of importance, the term *integration* (a placement) should not be used interchangeably or conflated with *inclusion* (an educational philosophy), as placement in settings with peers without disabilities does not guarantee inclusive experiences for students with disabilities (Haegele, Hodge, et al., 2020; Spencer-Cavaliere & Watkinson, 2010). Nonetheless, the U.S. Department of Education (2018) reported that 63.1% of students with disabilities were educated in integrated settings at least 80% of the time in 2018, which is more than double the 30% educated in these settings in 1990. This shift is seen even more in PE, which is one of the first classes where students with disabilities are integrated with peers without disabilities (Alquarini & Gut, 2012). As such, physical educators should expect to be teaching, and implementing SEL curricula, for most students with disabilities in integrated settings.

Movement toward integrated educational contexts is largely underpinned by inclusive educational philosophies. According to the United Nations Educational, Scientific and Cultural Organization (UNESCO; 2005), inclusion is a social justice fulcrum that involves adopting a broad vision of *education for all* by addressing the needs of all learners, including those who are vulnerable to marginalization (e.g., students with disabilities). As such, an inclusive education requires that teachers provide content in ways that encourage diverse learning while taking the burden away from students to have to adapt their learning styles to understand content (Coates & Vickerman, 2008; Obrusnikova & Block, 2020). The hallmark of inclusive education is that students with a variety of learning needs and styles can successfully learn while enjoying a sense of belonging, acceptance, and value in their classes (Spencer-Cavaliere & Watkinson, 2010).

Importantly, we believe that *feeling included* is foundational to SEL for students with disabilities, as feelings associated with belonging, acceptance, and value underpin explicated competencies and potential outcomes associated with SEL, including social awareness and relationships (CASEL, 2020b; Newman & Dusenbury, 2015). However, although movement toward integrated education was largely influenced by inclusive educational philosophies, concerns exist about the discriminatory nature of integrated classes and whether education in these contexts contribute to feelings associated with belonging, acceptance, and value (Haegele, Hodge, et al., 2020). This may, in part, be influenced by instances where physical educators are unwilling to rethink the nature of activities in their classes and structure activities around competitive sports and games that communicate specific ideas about what abilities are desirable (Kirk, 2010; Petrie et al., 2018).

Instances in which PE teachers treat students with disabilities negatively are likely to reverberate into peer relationships, where teachers' actions toward those with disabilities are modeled for peers without disabilities, who in turn discriminate, bully, or socially isolate those with disabilities for being incapable or having non-ideal bodies (Fitzgerald & Kirk, 2009; Haegele & Zhu, 2017). These behaviors seem disqualifying of any opportunities to improve the social and emotional skills among students with disabilities as outlined by CASEL (2020b). For example, students with a disability would find it challenging to accurately assess their strengths and limitations while possessing a sense of confidence, which is one characteristic of self-awareness, if their PE experiences are marred by a devaluation of their bodies. Furthermore, we would suggest that students would struggle to learn prosocial behaviors and build and maintain friendships, indicative of social awareness and relationship skills, respectively, if they are bullied in PE.

We believe that these negative behaviors are largely underpinned by the belief that classes are *inclusive* simply because students with and without disabilities share the same physical space (Haegele, 2019), rather than focusing on engaging students in an environment in which everyone can achieve success and enjoy their experience. As such, research seeking to problematize integrated settings, and examine the inclusiveness of those experiences from the viewpoint of those with disabilities, is of the utmost importance (Block et al., 2020; Haegele, Hodge, et al., 2020). In the next section, we further explore student and teachers' perspectives on integrated PE and highlight differences in how teachers and the students with disabilities themselves perceive integrated and self-contained APE instructional environments.

Teachers and Students' Perspectives in Integrated and Self-Contained Classrooms

Most research examining inclusion and PE has been conducted from the perspectives of PE and APE teachers (Haegele et al., 2020; Tand & Watelian, 2016; Wilhelmsen & Soeresen, 2017), and provide largely favorable viewpoints toward teaching students with disabilities in integrated PE classes (Qi & Ha, 2012). Although physical educators tend to report embracing teaching students with disabilities, there are few teaching strategies that are evidence-based to support integrated PE (Haegele et al., 2015; Pocock & Miyahara, 2017). In addition, it can be argued that placing substantial value on the viewpoints of stakeholders when examining the appropriateness and benefit of integrated PE is misguided. That is, since the inclusiveness of an educational experience should be understood as a *subjective experience* associated with individual interpretations, feelings, beliefs, and perceptions (Haegele, Hodge et al., 2020; Spencer-Cavaliere & Watkinson, 2010; Stainback & Stainback, 1996), the most important perspective from which to understand inclusion is that of the individuals with disabilities. Framed in a different way, examining integrated PE from the viewpoints of stakeholders may be analogous to trusting restaurant reviews written by the restaurant's owner or soliciting reviews from actors about movies in which they starred.

When considering research that examines how students with disabilities themselves discuss PE, there is growing evidence that inappropriate practices are leading to negative experiences (Haegele, 2019). As alluded to earlier, students with a variety of disabilities have reported that instances of discrimination, bullying, and social isolation are commonplace in integrated PE classes (Coates & Vickerman, 2008; Fitzgerald, 2005; Haegele & Sutherland, 2015; Healy et al., 2013), which would seemingly preclude any SEL instruction. These findings conflict with the commonly presented benefits of integrated PE from advocates who often emphasize the importance of social benefits (e.g., Grenier, 2011). Perhaps most concerning is that students with disabilities tend to place the behaviors of their PE teachers at the center of their non-inclusive experiences (Bredahl, 2013; Haegele, Kirk, et al., 2020). That is, they tend to report that behaviors of teachers, perhaps unintentionally, create forms of exclusion during PE by highlighting students' inability, asking students with disabilities to take on unimportant roles within activities, or relegating students with disabilities to the sideline. These problems are further exacerbated as the way in which PE teachers treat students with disabilities are then reproduced by other students. These students may believe that, since teachers behave in a way that depicts students with disabilities as being incapable, they are, in fact, incapable.

While in contrast to perceptions of integrated settings and to research in special education (Wiener & Tardif, 2004), some evidence indicates that students with disabilities report generally positive feelings in self-contained APE classes (Blagrave, 2017; Pellerin et al., in press; Yessick et al., 2020). There is also growing empirical evidence that suggests SEL-related core competencies (CASEL, 2020b) are found in APE settings in which only students with disabilities are educated (i.e., self-contained classrooms). For example, Blagrave (2017) found that students with autism enjoyed their APE experience, especially their interactions with their APE teachers and paraeducators. The importance of friendships among students with disabilities has emerged as another prominent characteristic of self-contained APE (Pellerin et al., in press; Yessick et al., 2020). Nonetheless, it is clear that while students with disabilities are now more likely to be placed in integrated settings as a result of the "inclusion movement" (Heck & Block, 2020; Obrusnikova & Block, 2020), these practices may actually produce experiences that, in some ways, feel less inclusive than self-contained classrooms. In order to more clearly illustrate experiences in APE related to inclusion and SEL, we present first-person narratives from a person with a disability in the next section to help communicate some of these challenges further.

Reflective Narratives

As noted previously, the hallmark of inclusive education is that students with a variety of learning needs and styles can successfully learn while enjoying a sense of belonging, acceptance, and value in their classes (Spencer-Cavaliere & Watkinson, 2010; Stainback & Stainback, 1996). The voices of those with disabilities who are experiencing PE are, therefore, critical to understanding the inclusiveness of these experiences, and whether learning environments support the development of SEL competencies (Haegele, 2019). With that, we use this section to highlight the voice of a person with a disability and his reflections about PE to provide an opportunity for readers to think about how students with disabilities may experience the PE classroom, and consider how these reflections may be similar, or different, from those within the readers' classes. In so doing, we also connect this individual's experiences to our understanding of SEL, so that the relationship between integrated PE, inclusiveness, and social and emotional development is more apparent.

The following are non-fiction narratives that are borrowed from those presented by Haegele (2019) to help highlight the voices of individuals with disabilities in PE. The particular narratives included here were curated from interviews with one 24-year-old male, Toby, who is visually impaired. Toby was enrolled in integrated PE throughout his K–12 education and reflected upon his time in these classes and the inclusiveness of those experiences. After each of the three narratives is a brief set of reflective questions that can be used to help readers reflect upon the experiences and whether they may be present in their own classes. It is important to note that Toby's experiences are not intended to represent the experiences of all persons with disabilities in PE contexts, but rather to provide a snapshot of how one person with one specific disability (i.e., a visual impairment) reflects on his personal lived experiences.

Narrative #1: "Even though they [peers] thought they were helpful, they weren't"

The first narrative described Toby's experiences with peers during PE. Peer interaction is among the most commonly reported outcomes of integrating students with disabilities into general PE classes (Block & Obrusnikova, 2007) and is critical in developing SEL competencies related to social awareness and relationship skills (CASEL, 2020b). Therefore, Toby's reflections about his peer interactions may hold significant weight for his feelings about those classes. He explained:

> Most people that didn't know me tried to help me in a way that I look at now and think was probably inappropriate. They saw me as "the blind kid," even though I am a visual traveler and a visual learner, and I react and respond visually. For example, if we were playing basketball and I made a shot, they [peers] would say, "good job, buddy," and I'm like okay, "thanks, screw you." If I was in physical education and there was somebody who didn't know me, they would either be very indifferent toward my performance or very overtly trying to help me. My preference was indifference, mostly, because it didn't draw attention to the fact that I had just messed up, or that I was not as athletic as most of the people in my classes, which is definitely what I thought. I'm sure that they [peers] couldn't even express why they were reacting the way they were. I think that they just saw somebody struggling and they acted indifferently, or they tried to help overtly. I don't even think they understood. They were probably like, "Toby's

blind'" I'm sure they didn't even understand what my disability was, so I think it was probably mostly a misunderstanding. With that said, even though they thought they were helpful, they weren't. I didn't like it. It made me feel more incompetent than I already felt. Most of the time, if somebody started to help, I began to have a negative attitude toward that person. If you think about that happening as an adult, if you do something and someone says "oh, nice job buddy, let me help you with that," you'd be like "screw you." It's the same kind of feeling. I don't think that you can really understand something like this until you have an experience in which someone does it to you. (Haegele, 2019, p. 392).

In this narrative, Toby reflected on his experiences with his peers, and the ways in which his classmates reacted to him as a student with a visual impairment. According to Toby, he experienced challenging social interactions with his peers, particularly when the peers misunderstood the impact that attempts to help had on Toby's confidence and competence. Thus, Toby did not appear to be in a PE environment in which he could demonstrate competence or develop meaningful relationships with his peers, to the detriment of his SEL (Deci & Ryan, 2008; Richards, Ivy, Wright, & Jerris, 2019). These explicated concerns are consistent with those found in research with students with other disabilities (Bredahl, 2013; Fitzgerald, 2005) and appear to highlight a lack of perceived belonging, acceptance, and value that is associated with inclusive philosophies (Spencer-Cavaliere & Watkinson, 2010). Indeed, psychological safety and opportunities to belong are hallmarks of sport-based affective development (Perkins & Noam, 2007) that are often not typified in the PE experiences of those with disabilities (Haegele, 2019). Given Toby's reflections, we encourage readers to reflect on the following questions.

- Are the perspectives shared by Toby representative of what some students with disabilities may feel in your school?
- Do these perspectives make it appear that integrated PE is inclusive?
- Is it the responsibility of the teacher to help and enhance these perspectives?
- What strategies can we use, as teachers, to enhance the SEL of students with these negative experiences regarding their skill development in self-awareness, social awareness, and relationship building (CASEL, 2020b)?

Narrative #2: "When I Got to Middle School, I Really Started to Hate PE"

The second narrative brings us to Toby's middle school experience, which he explained as being the most tumultuous time he had in PE. Toby recalled instances where he developed defense mechanisms, such as laughing off uncomfortable social interactions or becoming invisible, that he developed in order to avoid participation. Thus, this narrative highlights issues that challenged Toby's work toward the CASEL (2020b) competencies of building relationships and making responsible decisions. Toby reflected that:

> Middle school was when many cliques started to develop, and there was a lot of social stuff and hormones going on, so it was already a hard time. Then, going into physical education, an environment where there was limited structure, while having a disability made me one of the kids that were picked last when there was a team. One vivid memory I have was from 6th grade, when we went out to play kickball. We were playing, I was up to bat, the pitcher rolled the ball to me, I did this awkward movement where I stepped on the ball, and it rolled under me. Everybody laughed. I had a reputation for laughing along with them, but at the same time it was one of those experiences that I was like, come on Toby, what are you doing? This did not have a very positive impact on my self-esteem. As an adult, if I were in that situation, I would just not play. If I saw people playing kickball, I would find something else to do, or sit on the side. That is how I would react now, because I am just not going to put myself in a situation where that could happen again.
>
> When I was in middle school, I thought the solution was to be invisible. If a teacher had tried to accommodate the whole sport just for me, it would have been more embarrassing than just missing the ball. Currently, as a special education teacher, I have many opinions on what could have been done differently. I think that the gut reaction by people who don't understand disability is to either ignore it and not accommodate the student at all, or to explicitly make it known that an accommodation is being made. As the student, neither worked out for me. In one, I was lost, or not able to participate, and in the other, I felt exposed. I would

venture to say that when a teacher made an explicit accommodation to a sport, just for me, I hated it even more because if I was not able to demonstrate any level of competence even with the accommodation, I not only felt exposed, but I felt extra incompetent. There was a number of times, when I walked into a PE class and the first thing out of the teacher's mouth was something along the lines of, "okay guys, today we will be playing basketball, but to make it easier for everyone to participate we are going to change the rules." And there I am still incompetent. (Haegele, 2019, p. 392-393).

As with the first narrative, the absence of prerequisites for SEL such as psychological safety and opportunities to belong followed Toby to middle school, making it challenging for him to develop confidence as a mover and friendships with peers. Furthermore, Toby seemed to be denied a positive peer group culture, which would seek to facilitate sportspersonship and reduce perceptions of isolation and alienation (Perkins & Noam, 2007); instead, he felt compelled to laugh off embarrassment and withdraw from activity as a way to cope in PE. In other words, Toby was unable to negotiate these situations constructively in that he sought to remove himself from participation rather than risk asking for help within his social environment, which is characteristic of relationship competency (CASEL, 2020b).

He also voiced challenges that emerge when PE teachers make accommodations specifically for those with disabilities, which appear to highlight or "call out" inabilities to peers. These types of call-outs can have detrimental social impacts, such as communicating to peers that a person with a disability is incapable of engaging in PE activities (Fitzgerald & Kirk, 2009), which exposes a lack of social awareness on the part of students without disabilities who struggle taking the perspective of peers with disabilities (CASEL, 2020b). In addition, Toby implied that he lacked agency in decisions related to these accommodations, leaving him at the mercy of his teacher's discretion. This may have deprived Toby of an environment where he could be reasonably empowered to make personally and socially responsible choices regarding his participation and effort in PE, causing him to decline taking part in class, attempting new or difficult skills, and accepting challenges for improvement (Hellison, 2011; Richards et al., 2019). Given Toby's reflections about middle school PE, we encourage readers to reflect on the following questions:

- Are the perspectives shared by Toby representative of what some students with disabilities may feel in your school?
- Do these perspectives make it appear that middle school integrated PE is inclusive?
- Is it the responsibility of the teacher to help and enhance these perspectives?
- What strategies can we use, as teachers, to enhance the SEL of students with these negative experiences regarding their skill development in self-awareness, social awareness, and relationship building (CASEL, 2020b)?

Narrative #3: "I was probably always able to swim"

In this final narrative, Toby reflects on his experiences learning to swim in school and provides readers with a glimpse of his development of self-awareness and self-confidence (CASEL, 2020b). According to Toby, he grew up in a fortunate situation where his school had an Olympic-sized pool, which allowed for swimming instruction during PE. The following excerpt depicts Toby's experiences with two different swimming instructors who had divergent viewpoints toward his ability to swim. He reflected that:

> We were very fortunate in my school to have an Olympic-sized pool, so swimming was mandatory. In each class, there were two groups: beginners and advanced. In 6th and 7th grade, I was in the beginners' group and I just stayed there for two years. During that time, I was very wary of participating in anything. I can say confidently, I wouldn't take risks and was often anxious. For example, if they had people going off the diving board, I would be the last person to do it. Or, if they forgot me, if everyone else was doing it and they didn't ask me to, I wouldn't say anything. I wasn't scared of the diving board; I was scared of people watching me do something.
>
> During the first two weeks of 8th grade, I was still in the beginner group with a new instructor. She asked the group, "does anybody know how to tread water?," and I happened to know how. So, she asked me to demonstrate it, and I did. Then she demonstrated a few different things, and talked about different techniques, and I was able to do those as well. She then said, "you know

what, Toby, go over to the advanced group." At the time, I was like "wow, crazy. I'm going to the advanced group," but looking back I am confused. Was the line between the beginner group and advanced group being able to tread water? At the time, moving up to the advanced group was really important to me because that type of thing didn't happen a lot for me in physical activities.

> I think I was probably always able to swim, in a sense. When I say swim, I mean move forward in water. In 6th and 7th grade, it might not have looked very graceful, but I think that I was able to get somewhere. I think when we took our swim test, they recognized that the way I was swimming was not a real stroke, and that I probably needed more instruction, so I was left in the beginner group. But, because there were only two groups, and since this was an integrated environment, I was put with kids who wouldn't even put their face in the water. Therefore, I was certainly in the high end of the beginner group. Looking back, I moved to the advanced group within the first two weeks of instruction during 8th grade. Maybe I had the ability beforehand to work with the advanced group, but maybe the swim instructor didn't feel comfortable with that. Maybe I had been able to be in the advanced group for two years. I don't know. It seemed like a good decision too, because I wasn't even really on the low end of the advanced group. (Haegele, 2019, p. 393-394).

In the third narrative, Toby depicts his experiences about learning how to swim, and the way in which his swimming instructors' views influenced his perceptions of his skills. It is clear that his two swimming instructors had different opinions about his abilities, and that those perspectives then influenced Toby's self-concept and perceived ability to swim. Toby's second swimming instructor was a notable departure from his first, which was illustrated by the second's strength-based focus. This approach to promote social resiliency in sport-based settings targets developing and refining strengths to foster youth's ability to thrive in their social surroundings (Perkins & Noam, 2007). It seems that the latter instructor held "high expectations that emphasize strengths and assets" (p. 81) of Toby as she recognized his skills and advanced him to a more appropriate learning group, resulting in his increased confidence. This process was facilitated by this instructor who likely created an environment that allowed Toby to take positive risks such as demonstrating swimming skills in front of the class (Deci & Ryan, 2008; Richards et al., 2019). Collectively, this narrative highlights Toby's journey to becoming a more self-aware swimmer, that is, having a better sense of his strengths and limitations (CASEL, 2020b). Given Toby's third narrative, readers are encouraged to consider:

- Are the perspectives shared by Toby representative of what some students with disabilities may feel in your school during swimming or other activities?
- Do these perspectives make it appear that middle school integrated PE is inclusive?
- In what ways do the views of teachers influence the experiences of students with disabilities during PE activities, such as swimming?
- Is it the responsibility of the teacher to help and enhance these perspectives?
- What strategies can we use, as teachers, to enhance the SEL of students regarding their skill development in self-awareness (CASEL, 2020b)?

In summary, the above narratives provide an opportunity to reflect on how one person with a disability experienced PE in integrated contexts. Again, this neither represents every person with a disability nor does it represent persons with other disabilities. Rather, this is one opportunity to listen to the voice of one individual reflecting back on PE experiences, and to consider how those reflections may be similar, or different, from students in our schools. Furthermore, we should acknowledge that Toby's PE classes were not intentionally designed or taught to increase social and emotional skills. Such SEL requires a "caring, participatory, and equitable learning environment" (CASEL, 2020b) that was clearly not present in Toby's experiences. For this reason, it is imperative to listen to how persons with disabilities perceive the world in which they live, and activities within that world, so that more insight can be gained into how they experience different elements of life (Haegele & Sutherland, 2015). Gaining this understanding can perhaps lead to deeper consideration of teachers about how those with disabilities experience educational and pedagogical strategies, which may inspire strategies to enhance the inclusiveness of education and set a better stage for SEL instruction (Byrnes & Rickards, 2011; Coates, 2011). In addressing the misconceived perceptions of students without disabilities toward those with disabilities (Fitzgerald & Kirk, 2009; Haegele & Zhu, 2017), PE and APE teachers may

consider intentionally designing and implementing SEL instruction focused on social awareness. This instruction may help students without disabilities better understand the perspectives of their peers who live with disabilities and may increase the likelihood of inclusion.

We reason that such inclusion and SEL are connected. That is, how can we expect students with disabilities to demonstrate and develop skills in self-awareness, social awareness, relationship building, and self-management, which are among CASEL's (2020b) core competencies, if they do not *feel included* in their PE classrooms? As contended above in our problematization of integrated PE and exemplified in the nonfiction narratives, students with disabilities must *feel* a sense of belonging, acceptance, and value if PE is to be inclusive (Spencer-Cavaliere & Watkinson, 2010). Undeniably, these feelings of inclusion stem from and sustain an environment that satisfies basic human needs such as physical and psychological safety, relatedness, and confidence (Engler, 2014). Thus, as PE and APE teachers, we must strive to create a "safe, nurturing environment in which all feel a sense of belonging" (Lavay et al., 2016, p. 107).

Strategies for SEL Instruction for Students in APE

By design, readers may have found the reflective prompts following each of Toby's narratives challenging to address. They are, however, indicative of the challenges that many teachers face when seeking to integrate students with disabilities and address SEL. In this section, we overview several strategies and resources that we have curated from available literature in special education and APE that may help teachers better understand and enhance SEL and the inclusiveness of PE and APE for students like Toby. In our discussion of these strategies, we are intentional in connecting them to the CASEL (2020a,b) framework. These strategies are based on best practices and are generally research-informed. Nevertheless, readers should bear in mind that SEL in the field of APE is an underdeveloped area of exploration and that while these strategies are currently considered best practice, most of them have not undergone the rigorous process to become evidence-based relative to the APE context. When possible, we do provide relevant APE-specific research to support the following strategies.

1. **Set the stage for SEL instruction by being reflective about the inclusiveness of your classroom.** Even well-meaning teachers may unintentionally exclude or diminish the participation of students with disabilities in their PE classes. Review Toby's narratives above, reflect on the accompanying questions, and discuss the questions with colleagues and other school staff. Question whether inclusion is working for all of the students with disabilities in your classes (Haegele, 2019). How might you tell? What might you do to further enhance feelings of belonging, acceptance, and value among these students in PE and APE (Spencer-Cavaliere & Watkinson, 2010)? How might you integrate instruction related to self-awareness, self-management, social awareness, relationship skills, and responsible decision making (CASEL, 2020b) to improve feelings of inclusion? Discussing these questions is a first step in creating a class environment that is primed for SEL instruction.

2. **Integrate bully prevention SEL programming into your curriculum.** As bullying is a threat to inclusive education and SEL instruction, teachers may wish to consider using the research-based bullying prevention unit from Second Step (https://www.secondstep.org/bullying-prevention) that was discussed earlier in this chapter. This program has shown to be effective in increasing the SEL skills of middle school students with disabilities (Espelage et al., 2015, 2016) but has not been directly applied in APE contexts. Teachers may also find the Committee for Children's bullying prevention resources (https://www.cfchildren.org/resources/bullying-prevention-information/) helpful for teaching anti-bullying behavior to younger children. This website contains various resources that are child-friendly and addresses SEL skills such as empathy, compassion, and recognizing and refusing bullying through activities, videos, comics, and other media.

3. **Focus on proactive and positive behavior management.** In line with the larger focus in this text on making behavior management explicit and part of the instructional process (see Chapter 3), teachers should strive to be proactive, rather than reactive, in managing behavior (Loovis, 2017). In preparation to be proactive, the first steps are to exhaust any available resources that may shed light on a student's behavior. This includes reading any IEP documents or behavioral intervention plans and talking with the parents or guardians and other school staff (Lavay et al., 2016). This will help a teacher identify possible underlying causes for the student's behaviors and drive potential strategies that will increase those that are prosocial, preferably by using positive reinforcement.

We would encourage teachers to consider adopting the humanistic approach that emphasizes development of self-concept, relationships, and personal and social responsibility as a means to proactively and positively manage behavior in APE-related spaces, especially since it is a natural fit for SEL (Hellison, 2011). For example, a student with attention deficit hyperactivity disorder (ADHD) may struggle with waiting for their turn during a PE activity and grabs a piece of equipment from a classmate, thus demonstrating an issue related to self-management. One strategy that a teacher may use to address this behavior is to offer positive reinforcement to other students who are appropriately waiting for their turns. As another example, a student with autism may struggle with relationship skills and exhibit difficulty with their social interactions with peers. To encourage prosocial behavior, a teacher may rely on the use of visual aids such as social stories, which are brief, personalized stories that help a child understand what acceptable social behavior looks like in specific settings, such as PE (Gray, 2010). To further highlight how a humanistic orientation toward behavior management in APE and SEL are intertwined, we have adapted **Table 11.1** from Lavay et al. (2016) and have connected CASEL's (2020b) core competencies to their behavior management strategies for students with a variety of different disabilities. We should note that Table 11.1 is not an exhaustive list of typical behaviors or characteristics of students with different disabilities; instead, certain behaviors were selected to demonstrate the range of SEL skills that are associated with them.

4. **Consider the TPSR model.** As noted earlier, TPSR is recognized as a best-practice model for teaching SEL in PE (Hellison, 2011) and there is a growing body of research that supports the use of TPSR in APE settings (Menendez & Fernandez-Rio, 2017; Monteiro et al., 2008; Wright et al., 2004). Teachers using the TPSR model can design their curricula to include skill-building for students with disabilities in the areas of respect, participation and effort, self-direction, helping others, and the transfer

Table 11.1 Connecting the Humanistic Approach to Behavior Management and SEL

Disability	CASEL Core Competency	Exhibited Behavior	Teaching/behavior Management Strategy
ADHD	Self-management	Struggles to follow instructions	Assign peer buddy to model and provide cues
		Excessive talking	Use proximity control
		Does not stay on task	Have student state PE class rules
		Disruptive/aggressive behavior	Use a token economy
Autism	Self-management	Cannot attend to appropriate stimuli	Use self-modeling video or visual aids
			Remove extraneous stimuli from gymnasium
		Anger	Reward positive replacement behavior
		Disruptiveness	Ignore student's inappropriate behavior
	Relationship skills	Struggles with social interactions	Use social stories about appropriate behavior
		Struggles with verbal/ nonverbal communication	Use communication boards and technology
			Use verbal communication with sign language
Behavioral disorders	Self-management	Hyperactivity, impulsiveness	Use behavioral contracts
			Use praise to positively reinforce behavior
	Self-awareness	Low self-concept	Ensure perceptions of success during class
	Relationship skills	Poor interpersonal interactions	Identify best grouping/pairings for students
	Responsible decision making	Challenging authority	Apply firm and consistent discipline
ID	Self-management	Frustration/lack of motivation	Ensure success early and often
	Social awareness	Cannot understand social rules	Foster socialization through team building
	Relationship skills	Poor communication skills	Use assistive communication, peer tutors
SLD	Self-management	Emotional instability	Use relaxation techniques, yoga
		Impulsiveness	Use behavioral contracts
			Use praise to positively reinforce behavior
	Self-awareness	Low self-concept	Ensure perceptions of success during class
TBI	Self-management & Self-awareness	Denial of condition, coping problem	Address perceived inaccuracies with condition
			Work with school psychologist/counselor
		Depression	Design goal-directed activities for success
	Responsible decision making	Inappropriate social behavior	Demonstrate and praise appropriate behavior

SEL = social and emotional learning; CASEL = Collaborative for Academic, Social, and Emotional Learning; ADHD = attention deficit hyperactivity disorder; ID = intellectual disability; SLD = specific learning disabilities; TBI = traumatic brain injury
Data from Collaborative for Academic, Social, and Emotional Learning. (2020b). What is SEL? https://casel.org/what-is-sel/; and Lavay, B. W., French, R., & Henderson, H. L. (2016). *Positive behavior management in physical activity settings.* Champaign, IL: Human Kinetics.

of such skills to other settings (Hellison, 2011; Richards et al., 2019). To illustrate what TPSR for an individual student can look like, consider the following example. Debra is a 9-year-old student with an intellectual disability. She does not mind being in PE class most days but when the teacher asks her to participate in any activity that she struggles with, she becomes unmotivated and looks for ways to disengage, which often results in her poking at other students. Furthermore, if her teacher is not constantly giving her feedback, Debra is not sure if she is performing the skill correctly. Debra also sometimes forgets to put her group's equipment away when it is her turn to do so. Her teacher considers the following TPSR strategies to improve Debra's responsibility skills:

a. *Respect.* To help Debra demonstrate more respect during PE, the teacher meets individually with her and together they develop a short list of social expectations and consequences if she cannot keep her hands to herself. Before each class, the instructional aide reviews the list with her.

b. *Participation and effort.* The teacher understands that Debra's object control skills are not particularly good and that she struggles with activities that require her to throw, catch, or strike an object. Since she becomes frustrated when she perceives that she is unsuccessful, her teacher controls her success/failure ratio by ensuring that the activities are developmentally appropriate and setting realistic performance goals. If Debra perceives that she is learning and that learning is fun, she will be more likely to participate in activities and practice new skills.

c. *Self-direction.* Since Debra struggles with evaluating her performance when the teacher and instructional aide are assisting other students, working without supervision is challenging. Thus, the teacher builds embedded feedback into individual activities that will help her to understand if she is correctly performing the skill. For example, to help Debra evaluate her progress on the overhand throw, the teacher places a rubber polyspot in front of her opposite foot. Each time she throws the ball, she can look down and see if her opposite foot is on the polyspot (i.e., that she stepped in opposition). In this way, Debra can independently assess if she performed that part of the skill correctly and improve her self-direction.

d. *Helping others.* To help prompt Debra to appropriately collect and store her group's equipment when she is the "equipment leader," the teacher devises short, easy-to-remember skill cues: (1) got your equipment? (2) got your classmates' equipment? (3) missing any?, and (4) put away.

e. *Transfer.* At the conclusion of the lesson, the teacher checks for understanding by asking Debra to repeat the skill cues for responsibly returning equipment when she is at recess.

Generally, the social aspect of the TPSR model such as respect and helping others correspond to the social awareness and relationship skills competencies of the CASEL (2020b) model whereas TPSR's participation, effort, and self-direction connect with CASEL's self-awareness and self-management. Opportunities for responsible decision making can be connected to all TPSR levels, including transfer. Refer to Chapter 7 for more information on how to implement TPSR.

5. **Use a media literacy approach.** The National Association for Media Literacy Education (NAMLE, 2021) describes media literacy as the ability to "access, analyze, evaluate, create, and act using all forms of communication" so that one may critically think about how such media influences individuals. In applying concepts from media literacy education to our understanding of SEL in APE, we have adopted a conceptual framework established by NAMLE in 2007. The NAMLE (2007) framework supports educators in assisting students with critically evaluating any media they consume. Using key media literacy questions from Rogow and Scheibe (2007), we have adapted a conversational script to elicit critical media discussion about the PE experiences of students with disabilities and have connected these questions to CASEL's (2020b) competencies (see **Table 11.2**). A PE or APE teacher could use this script to gain insight into a student's understanding of skills such as self-awareness, social-awareness, or self-management by showing a picture, drawing, or video clip related to participation in PE.

For example, a teacher may find a picture of a student smiling and playing basketball with his friends during PE, show it to a student with a disability, and ask the key media literacy questions outlined in Table 11.2 to explore the student's SEL competencies. We should note here that this particular strategy may not be as useful for students who have limited expressive and receptive communication skills. Nonetheless, continuing with this example, the teacher may seek to gauge the student's level of self-awareness and ask, "what does this picture want you to think about?" The student may respond,

Table 11.2 Conversational Script About (A)PE, Based on CASEL Core Competencies and Media Literacy

CASEL Core Competencies	Media Literacy Key Questions
Self-awareness	What does this picture/video want you to think about PE? How does this picture/video make you feel about PE?
Self-management	What might you do or think in response to this picture/video about PE?
Social awareness	What ideas or values are being communicated in this picture/video about PE? How might a (this) person think about what happened in this picture/video? Who might be harmed by this message? Who might benefit?
Relationship skills	What does the person who took this picture/video want you to remember about PE? Can you trust this person to tell you the truth about PE?
Responsible decision making	What actions might you take in response to the message of this picture/video? Is this message good for you?

(A)PE = adapted and physical education; CASEL = Collaborative for Academic, Social, and Emotional Learning
Data from Collaborative for Academic, Social, and Emotional Learning. (2020b). What is SEL? https://casel.org/what-is-sel/; Probst, D. (2017). Social media literacy as an IEP intervention for social and emotional learning. *Journal of Media Literacy Education, 9*(2), 45-57; and Rogow, F., & Scheibe, C. (2007). *Key questions to ask when analyzing media messages.* Cherry Hill, NJ: National Association for Media Literacy Education.

"that student is having fun; I like playing basketball in PE." In this way, the student is expressing a level of self-awareness in recognizing her feelings toward PE. For another example, the teacher may show this student a video clip of a person in PE grabbing a hula-hoop away from a classmate and ask, "how might this classmate think about what happened in this video?" If the student responds to the effect, "that was mean; that student is sad," it would indicate a level of social awareness.

Concluding Thoughts

In this chapter, we sought to present an informed perspective of SEL in APE, drawing on and applying literature from both special education and APE. We relied on CASEL's (2020a,b) framework and contended that social and emotional development and feeling included in PE and APE must be mutually inclusive for students with disabilities. We emphasized the importance of listening to the voices of those with disabilities as we begin to understand their unique needs for SEL and how they experience success in these contexts. To this end, we shared Toby's story to give meaning to our conversation about the challenge related to integrated PE, which has manifested itself in discrimination, bullying, and exclusion. Consequently, SEL in the APE field is appearing to become increasingly relevant. In highlighting strategies to support SEL, we provided several for instructional practices (proactive and positive behavior management, TPSR, media literacy) and for creating a more inclusive classroom culture (critical reflection on one's inclusive practices and bully prevention).

As the union between SEL and APE gains additional traction over the next few years, we hope for the emergence of new innovative programs that specifically address the social and emotional needs of students with disabilities within the PE and APE contexts. To spur this innovation, the field of APE should come to terms with reported deficits in SEL training (Samalot-Rivera & Porretta, 2009; Wilson et al., 2019). While this discussion has implications for teacher education programs and professional development, such discourse is beyond the scope of this chapter. As it stands, there is little empirically driven SEL scholarship that explicitly examines social and emotional skill development for students with disabilities. Consequentially, there is even less research exploring APE specifically. While investigations into community-based adapted programs is certainly worthwhile, it is an imperfect transfer to the public school context with all of the unique social complexities that it entails (e.g., student placement concerns; IEP goals; district-, school-, and class-level priorities). In addition, of the research that does exist, almost none explicitly prioritizes the voices of students with disabilities about their experiences in SEL-related activities. As such, it appears that researchers in this area of inquiry have adopted a similar brand of research as many in PE/APE, which ignores the perspectives and lived experiences of the consumers (i.e., those with disabilities). Because of this, we can only hypothesize about the social or emotional benefits that those with disabilities gain from their engagement in these programs from an outsider's perspective, until the voices of those with disabilities are valued and listened to by the research community. Thus, we unfortunately have to conclude that it seems we have overlooked SEL as an element of APE in our research, which is problematic if our self-proclaimed efforts to include students with disabilities in integrated PE continue to trend as they have been.

Questions for Discussion

1. How would you describe the connection between inclusion and SEL in APE?
2. In your own teaching situation, what strategies can you use to "set the stage" for SEL instruction in APE?
3. How might you enhance the self-awareness of the students with disabilities you teach? What about the self-management, social awareness, relationship skills, and responsible decision making?
4. How could you assist all students in your classes to be more understanding of and helpful and supportive to those with any disabilities?

References

Alquarini, T., & Gut, D. (2012). Critical components of successful inclusion of students with severe disabilities: Literature review. *International Journal of Special Education, 27*(1), 42–59.

Blagrave, J. (2017). Experiences of children with autism spectrum disorders in adapted physical education. *European Journal of Adapted Physical Activity, 10*(1), 17–27.

Block, M. E., Haegele, J., Kelly, L, & Obrusnikova, I. (2020). Exploring future research in adapted physical education. *Research Quarterly for Exercise and Sport.* doi:10.1080/02701367.2020.1741500

Block, M. E., & Obrusnikova, I. (2007). Inclusion in physical education: A review of literature from 1995-2005. *Adapted Physical Activity Quarterly, 24*(2), 103–124. doi:10.1123/apaq.24.2.103

Bredahl, A-M. (2013). Sitting and watching the others being active: The experienced difficulties in physical education when having a disability. *Adapted Physical Activity Quarterly, 30*(1), 40–58.

Byrnes, L. J., & Rickards, F. W. (2011). Listening to the voices of students with disabilities: Can such voices inform practice? *The Australasian Journal of Special Education, 35*(1), 25–34. doi:10.1375/ajse.35.1.25

Cavioni, V., Grazzani, I., & Ornaghi, V. (2017). Social and emotional learning for children with learning disability: Implications for inclusion. *International Journal of Emotional Education, 9*(2), 100–109.

Chester, K. L., Callaghan, M., Cosma, A., Donnelly, P., Craig, W., Walsh, S., & Molcho, M. (2015). Cross-national time trends in bullying victimization in 33 countries among children aged 11, 13 and 15 from 2002 to 2010. *European Journal of Public Health, 25*(s2), 61–64. https://doi.org/10.1093/eurpub/ckv029

Coates, J. (2011). Physically fit or physically literate? How children with special educational needs understand physical education. *European Physical Education Review, 17*(2), 167–181. doi:10.1177/1356336X11413183

Coates, J., & Vickerman, P. (2008). Let the children have their say: Children with special education needs and their experiences in physical education – A review. *Support for Learning, 23*(4), 168–175. doi:10.1111/j.1467-9604.2008.00390.x

Collaborative for Academic, Social, and Emotional Learning [CASEL]. (2020a). Social and emotional learning. https://casel.org/

Collaborative for Academic, Social, and Emotional Learning [CASEL]. (2020b). What is SEL? https://casel.org/what-is-sel/

Cooper, J. O., Heron, T. E., & Heward, W. L. (2007). *Applied behavior analysis* (2nd ed.). Upper Saddle River, NJ: Pearson Education.

Coulson, C. L., Irwin, C. C., & Wright, P. M. (2012). Applying Hellison's responsibility model in a youth residential treatment facility: A practical inquiry project. *Agora for Physical Education and Sport, 14*, 38–54.

Dane-Staples, E., Lieberman, L. J., Ratcliff, J., & Rounds, K. (2013). Bullying experiences of individuals with visual impairments: The mitigating role of sport participation. *Journal of Sport Behavior, 36*(4), 365–386.

Deci, E. L., & Ryan, R. M. (2008). Self-determination theory: A macrotheory of human motivation, development, and health. *Canadian Psychology, 49*(3), 182–185.

Engler, B. (2014). *Personality theories: An introduction* (9th ed.). Belmont, CA: Wadsworth.

Espelage, D. L., Rose C. A., & Polanin, J. R. (2015). Social-emotional learning program to reduce bullying, fighting, and victimization among middle school students with disabilities. *Remedial & Special Education, 36*(5), 299–311.

Espelage, D. L., Rose, C. A., & Polanin, J. R. (2016). Social-emotional learning program to promote prosocial and academic skills among middle school students with disabilities. *Remedial and Special Education, 37*(6), 323–332.

Feuerborn, L., & Tyre, A. (2009). Practical social-emotional learning tools for students with specific learning disabilities in the United States of America. *The Journal of the International Association of Special Education, 10*(1), 21–25.

Fitzgerald, H. (2005). Still feeling like a space piece of luggage? Embodied experiences of (dis)ability in physical education and school sport. *Physical Education & Sport Pedagogy, 10*(1), 41–59. doi:10.1080/1740898042000334908

Fitzgerald, H., & Kirk, D. (2009). Physical education as a normalizing practice: Is there space for disability sport? In H. Fitzgerald & A. Stride (Eds.), *Disability & Youth Sport* (pp. 91–105). Routledge.

Gray, C. (2010). *The new social story book*. Arlington, TX: Future Horizons.

Grenier, M. A. (2011). Coteaching in physical education: A strategy for inclusive practice. *Adapted Physical Activity Quarterly, 28*(2), 95–112.

Haegele, J. A. (2019). Inclusion illusion: Questioning the inclusiveness of integrated physical education. *Quest, 71*(4), 387–397. doi:10.1080/00336297.2019.1602547

Haegele, J. A., Aigner, C., & Healy, S. (2020). Extracurricular activities and bullying among children and adolescents with disabilities. *Maternal and Child Health Journal, 24*, 310–318. https://doi.org/10.1007/s10995-019-02866-6

Haegele, J. A., Hodge, S. R., Zhu, X., Holland, S. K., & Wilson, W. J. (2020). Understanding the inclusiveness of integrated physical education from the perspectives of adults with visual impairments. *Adapted Physical Activity Quarterly, 37*(2), 141–159. doi:10.1123/apaq.2019-0094

Haegele, J. A., Kirk, T. N., Holland, S. K., & Zhu, X. (2020). 'The rest of the time I would just stand there and look stupid': Access in integrated physical education among adults with visual impairments. *Sport, Education and Society*. Epub ahead of print, doi:10.1080/13573322.2020.1805425

Haegele, J. A., Lee, J., & Porretta, D. L. (2015). Research trends in *Adapted Physical Activity Quarterly* from 2004 to 2013. *Adapted Physical Activity Quarterly, 32*(3), 187–205. doi:10.1123/APAQ.2014-0232

Haegele, J. A., & Sutherland, S. (2015). Perspectives of students with disabilities toward physical education: A qualitative inquiry review. *Quest, 67*(3), 255–273. doi:10.1080/00336297.2015.1050118

Haegele, J. A., Wilson, W. J., Zhu, X., Bueche, J. J., Brady, E., & Li, C. (2020). Barriers and facilitators to inclusion in integrated physical education: Adapted physical educators' perspectives. *European Physical Education Review*. https://doi.org/10.1177%2F1356336X20944429

Haegele, J. A., & Zhu, X. (2017). Experiences of individuals with visual impairments in integrated physical education: A retrospective study. *Research Quarterly for Exercise and Sport, 88*(4), 425–435.

Haegele, J. A., Zhu, X., & Holland, S. K. (2020). School-based bullying experiences as reflected by adults with visual impairments. *Psychology in the Schools, 57*(2), 296–309. https://doi.org/10.1002/pits.22314

Healy, S., Msetfi, R., & Gallagher, S. (2013). 'Happy and a bit nervous': The experiences of children with autism in physical education. *British Journal of Learning Disabilities, 41*(3), 222–228.

Heck, S., & Block, M. E. (2020). *Inclusive physical education around the world: Origins, cultures, and practices*. Routledge.

Hellison, D. (2011). *Teaching responsibility through physical activity*. Champaign, IL: Human Kinetics.

Individuals with Disabilities Education Improvement Act (IDEIA) of 2004, Pub. L. No. 108–446, 118 Stat. 2647, codified at 20 U.S.C. §§ 1400-1487 (West Supp. 2006).

Kirk, D. (2010). *Physical education futures*. Routledge.

Lavay, B. W., French, R., & Henderson, H. L. (2016). *Positive behavior management in physical activity settings*. Champaign, IL: Human Kinetics.

Lebrun-Harris, L. A., Sherman, L. J., Limber, S. P., Miller, B. D., & Edgerton, E. A. (2019). Bullying victimization and perpetration among U.S. children and adolescents: 2016 National survey of children's health. *Journal of Child and Family Studies, 28*, 2543–2557. https://doi.org/10.1007/s10826-018-1170-9

Loovis, E. M. (2017). Behavior management. In J. P. Winnick, & D. L. Porretta (Eds.), *Adapted physical education and sport, 6th ed.* (pp. 101–119). Champaign, IL: Human Kinetics.

Maiano, C., Aimé, A., Salvas, M.-C., Morin, A., & Normand, C. L. (2016). Prevalence and correlates of bullying perpetration and victimization among school-aged youth with intellectual disabilities: A systematic review. *Research in Developmental Disabilities, 49–50*, 181–195. https://doi.org/10.1016/j.ridd.2015.11.015.

Menendez, J. I., & Fernandez-Rio, J. (2017). Hybridising sport education and teaching for personal and social responsibility to include students with disabilities. *European Journal of Special Needs Education, 32*(4), 508–524.

Migliaccio, T., Raskauskas, J., & Schmidtlein, M. (2017). Mapping the landscapes of bullying. *Learning Environments Research, 20*, 365–382. https://doi.org/10.1007/s10984-017-9229-x

Monteiro, T. R., Pick, R. K., & Valentini, N. C. (2008). Responasabilidade social e personal de criancas participantes de um programa de intervencao motora inclusiva [Social and personal responsiveness of children participating in an inclusive motor intervention program]. *Temas Sobre Desenvolvimento, 16*, 202–214.

National Association for Media Literacy Education [NAMLE]. (2007). *Core principles of media literacy education in the United States*. https://namle.net/wp-content/uploads/2020/09/Namle-Core-Principles-of-MLE-in-the-United-States.pdf

National Association for Media Literacy Education [NAMLE]. (2021). *About-NAMLE*. https://namle.net/about/

Newman, J., & Dusenbury, L. (2015). Social and emotional learning (SEL): A framework for academic, social, and emotional success. In K. Bosworth (Ed.), *Prevention science in school settings* (pp. 287–306). New York, NY: Springer.

Norman, N., & Jamieson, J. R. (2015). Social and emotional learning and the work of itinerant teachers of the deaf and hard of hearing. *American Annals of the Deaf, 160*(3), 273–288.

Obrusnikova, I., & Block, M.E. (2020). Historical context and definition of inclusion. In J.A. Haegele, S.R. Hodge, & D.R. Shapiro (Eds.), *Routledge Handbook of Adapted Physical Education* (pp. 65–80). London, UK: Routledge.

Pellerin, S., Wilson, W. J., & Haegele, J. A. (in press). The experiences of students with disabilities in self-contained physical education. *Sport, Education and Society*.

Perkins, D. F., & Noam, G. G. (2007). Characteristics of sport-based youth development programs. *New Directions for Youth Development, 2007*(115), 75–84.

Petrie, K., Devcich, J., & Fitzgerald, H. (2018). Working towards inclusive physical education in a primary school: 'Some days I just don't get it right.' *Physical Education and Sport Pedagogy, 22*(4), 345–357.

Pocock, T., & Miyahara, M. (2018). Inclusion of students with disability in physical education: A qualitative meta-analysis. *International Journal of Inclusive Education, 22*(7), 751–766. doi:10.1080/13603116.2017.1412508

Probst, D. (2017). Social media literacy as an IEP intervention for social and emotional learning. *Journal of Media Literacy Education, 9*(2), 45–57.

Richards, K. A. R., Ivy, V. N., Wright, P. M., & Jerris, E. (2019). Combining the skill themes approach with teaching personal and social responsibility to teach social and emotional learning in elementary physical education. *Journal of Physical Education, Recreation & Dance, 90*(3), 36–44.

Rogow, F., & Scheibe, C. (2007). *Key questions to ask when analyzing media messages.* Cherry Hill, NJ: National Association for Media Literacy Education.

Rose, C. A., & Gage, N. A. (2017). Exploring the involvement of bullying among students with disabilities over time. *Exceptional Children, 83*(3), 298–314. https://doi.org/10.1177/0014402916667587

Rose, C. A., Simpson, C. G., & Moss, A. (2015). The bullying dynamic: Prevalence of involvement among a large-scale sample of middle and high school youth with and without disabilities. *Psychology in the Schools, 52*(5), 515–531. https://doi.org/10.1002/pits.21840

Qi, J., Ha, A. S. (2012). Inclusion in physical education: A review of literature. *International Journal of Disability, Development and Education, 59*(3), 257–281.

Samalot-Rivera, A., & Porretta, D. L. (2009). Perceptions and practices of adapted physical educators on the teaching of social skills. *Adapted Physical Activity Quarterly, 26*(2), 172–186.

Sherrill, C. (2004). *Adapted physical education, recreations, and sport: Cross disciplinary and lifespan* (6th ed.). St. Louis, MO: McGraw-Hill.

Spencer-Cavaliere, N., & Watkinson, E. J. (2010). Inclusion understood from the perspectives of children with disability. *Adapted Physical Activity Quarterly, 27*(4), 275–293. doi:10.1123/apaq.27.4.275

Stainback, W., & Stainback, S. (1996). Collaboration, support network and community construction. In S. Stainback & W. Stainback (Eds.), *Inclusion: A guide for educators* (pp. 223–232). Baltimore, MD: Paul H. Brookes Publishing Co.

Stough, C. O., Merianos, A., Nabors, L., & Peugh, J. (2016). Prevalence and predictors of bullying behavior among overweight and obese youth in a nationally representative sample. *Childhood Obesity, 12*(4), 263–271. https://doi.org/10.1089/chi.2015.0172

Tant, M., & Watelain, E. (2016). Forty years later, a systematic literature review on inclusion in physical education (1975–2015): A teacher perspective. *Educational Research Review, 19*, 1–17. doi:10.1016/j.edurev.2016.04.002

United Nations Educational, Scientific and Cultural Organization (UNESCO). (2005). *Guidelines for inclusion: Ensuring access to education for all.* Paris, France: Author.

U.S. Department of Education (2018) *The condition of education 2018: Children and youth with disabilities.* Washington, DC: Author.

Veenstra, R., Lindenberg, S., Zijlstra, B. J. H., De Winter, A. F., Verhulst, F. C., & Ormel, J. (2007). The dyadic nature of bullying and victimization: Testing a dual-perspective theory. *Child Development, 78*(6), 1843–1854. https://doi.org/10.1111/j.1467-8624.2007.01102.x.

Wiener, J., & Tardif, C. Y. (2004). Social and emotional functioning of children with learning disabilities: Does special education placement make a difference? *Learning Disabilities Research & Practice, 19*(1), 20–32.

Wilhelmsen, T., & Sørensen, M. (2017). Inclusion of children with disabilities in physical education: A systematic review of literature from 2009 to 2015. *Adapted Physical Activity Quarterly, 34*(3), 311–337. doi:10.1123/apaq.2016-0017.

Wilson, W. J., Haegele, J. A., & Kelly, L. E. (2020). Revisiting the narrative about least restrictive environment in physical education. *Quest, 72*(1), 19–32. https://doi.org/10.1080/00336297.2019.1602063

Wilson, W. J., Kelly, L. E., & Haegele, J. A. (2019). Least restrictive environment decision making in physical education. *Journal of Teaching in Physical Education, 39*(4), 536–544. https://doi.org/10.1123/jtpe.2019-0161

Wright, P. M., White, K., & Gaebler-Spira, D. (2004). Exploring the relevance of the personal and social responsibility model in adapted physical activity: A collective case study. *Journal of Teaching in Physical Education, 23*(1), 71–87.

Yessick, A. B., Haegele, J. A., Zhu, X., & Bobzien, J. (2020). Exploring the experiences of children with ASD in self-contained physical education: A modified scrapbooking study. *Advances in Neurodevelopmental Disorders, 4*, 51–58.

CHAPTER 12

Integrating Social and Emotional Learning into Whole School Approaches

Collin A. Webster

CHAPTER SUMMARY

A "whole school" approach to promoting physical activity among children and adolescents is commonly conceptualized using the comprehensive school physical activity program (CSPAP) framework, which encompasses (a) physical education, (b) physical activity during school, (c) physical activity before and after school, (d) staff involvement, and (e) family and community engagement. This chapter presents a perspective that situates students' social and emotional learning (SEL) within the context of the CSPAP framework and considers the potential contribution of physical activity opportunities before, during, and after school to the affective learning goals of physical education.

Background and Perspective

In 2013, the National Academies Press published a 488-page report titled "Educating the Student Body: Taking Physical Education and Physical Activity to School" (Institute of Medicine [IOM], 2013). A 14-member ad hoc committee of the IOM (now called the National Academy of Medicine) prepared the report, in which they reviewed the status of physical education and physical activity in schools; assessed the impact of physical education and physical activity on the physical, cognitive/brain, and psychosocial health and development of children and adolescents; and recommended approaches to increase the influence of physical education and physical activity programming before, during, and after school. The committee concluded that "regular physical activity promotes growth and development and has multiple benefits for physical, mental, and psychological health that undoubtedly contribute to learning" (p. 97). The evidence supporting the mental and psychological health benefits of physical activity for children and adolescents, and the social and emotional learning (SEL) outcomes tied to these benefits, is central to this chapter in considering prospective directions for school programming and is the focus of the following section of the chapter.

In spite of the many benefits attributed to physical activity, the IOM (2013) committee also concluded that no more than half of school-age youth were meeting the U.S. guideline of at least 60 minutes of mostly vigorous or moderate physical activity each day. The committee further determined that most school-related policies to support physical education and physical activity were weak and this limits the translation of policy to practice. For example, the report includes findings from the Shape of the Nation Report (National Association for Sport and Physical Education [NASPE] and the American Heart Association [AHA], 2012), which showed that even though most states mandated school physical education, ultimately, 48–69% of students did not attend physical education classes in an average week. This is due to flexible policies that allow for numerous loopholes such as exemptions, waivers, and substitutions for physical education. Additional evidence included results from research in which state laws with specific time requirements for physical education were associated with the allocation of more physical education minutes in elementary and middle schools (Perna et al., 2012), while both state- and school district-level policies were associated with elementary schools providing the nationally recommended 150 minutes of physical education (Slater et al., 2012).

Whole-of-School Approach and the Comprehensive School Physical Activity Program Framework

Combined with their expressed need for a more robust policy environment to support physical education and physical activity in schools, the committee recommended that schools adopt a "whole-of-school" approach to physical education and physical activity promotion (IOM, 2013, p. 30). They defined a whole-of-school approach as when "all of a school's components and resources operate in a coordinated and dynamic manner to provide access, encouragement, and programs that enable all students to engage in vigorous- or moderate-intensity physical activity 60 minutes or more each day" (p. 30). The prevailing conceptual example of a whole-of-school approach is the comprehensive school physical activity program (CSPAP)

framework (Centers for Disease Control and Prevention [CDC], 2019), which the CDC adopted as the national framework for physical education and physical activity in schools. The framework encompasses five components: (a) physical education, (b) physical activity during school, (c) physical activity before and after school, (d) staff involvement, and (e) family and community engagement (**Figure 12.1**). According to the CDC (2019), "the goal of a CSPAP is to increase physical activity opportunities before, during, and after school and to increase students' overall physical activity and health" (p. 2).

Within the CSPAP framework, physical education is designed to serve as the primary educational pathway through which students learn the knowledge and skills needed to pursue a lifetime of physical activity (CDC, 2019). Physical activity during school includes opportunities for students to be physically active outside of physical education, but still during regular school hours. Examples of such opportunities include classroom-based physical activity, recess, and "drop-in" physical activity programs where students can use school facilities to be active during lunch or free periods (Castelli & Ward, 2012; CDC, 2019). A wide variety of opportunities represent the physical activity before and after school component of the framework. For instance, schools might offer physical activity clubs, intramural sports programs, or active transportation programs (Beighle & Moore, 2012; CDC, 2019). The staff involvement and family and community engagement components focus on the idea that promoting physical activity should be a collective effort of all teachers, administrators, family members, and other members of the school community at large. Through these components, students and their families might participate in physical activity opportunities together and schools can coordinate with other local organizations to maximize physical activity promotion (Cipriani, Richardson, & Roberts, 2012; CDC, 2019; Heidorn & Centeio, 2012).

Realizing the Full Potential of a CSPAP

In order to consider the potential contributions of a CSPAP to students' SEL, the history of the CSPAP framework and its application in research to date warrant careful consideration. A task force of four physical education professors, including Aaron Beighle, Eloise Elliott, Thom McKenzie, and Amelia Mays Woods, guided the development of the CSPAP framework, (National Association for Sport and Physical

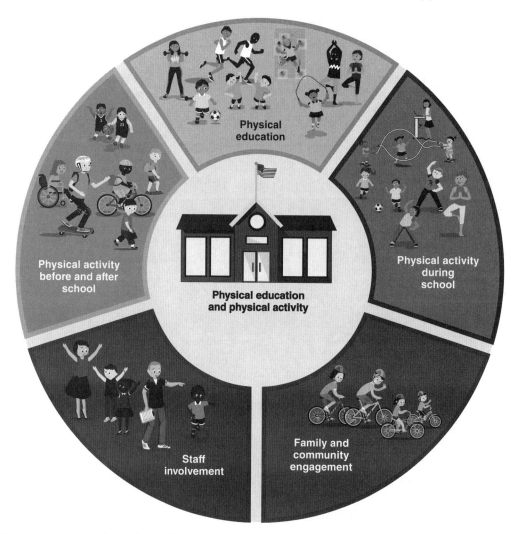

Figure 12.1 Comprehensive school physical activity program (CSPAP) framework.

Centers for Disease Control and Prevention. (2019). *Increasing physical education and physical activity: A framework for schools.* Centers for Disease Control and Prevention, US Department of Health and Human Services. www.cdc.gove/healthyschools/PEandPA

Education [NASPE[1]], 2008). Given its strong foundation within the field of physical education, the 2008 CSPAP position statement, along with early graphic representations of the framework, gave a special nod to physical education as the cornerstone component of a CSPAP: "quality physical education is at the core of a CSPAP because of its role in helping students gain the knowledge and skills to become proficient movers and participants in a lifetime of physical activity" (NASPE, 2008). Such knowledge and skills are reflected in the U.S. national standards for K–12 physical education, which include a focus on students' SEL in Standards 4 and 5 (**Table 12.1**; SHAPE America, 2014). In tandem with the 2008 CSPAP position statement, the IOM (2013) also viewed physical education's role in a whole-of-school approach as uniquely tied to the

educational goals of school-related physical activity programming: "physical activity programs are neither equivalent to nor a substitute for physical education, and both can contribute meaningfully to the development of healthy, active children … The former are behavioral programs, whereas the latter are instructional programs" (p. 265). Thus, early advocacy from national organizations expressed a clear stance regarding the instructional role of physical education in a CSPAP to support students' healthy and active development, which includes SEL.

In many ways, the application of the CSPAP framework in research has reflected the distinct purposes of physical education and physical activity programs, as proposed by NASPE (2008) and the IOM (2013). Researchers investigating physical activity opportunities beyond physical education tend to focus their attention on the effects these opportunities have on the physical activity behavior of children and adolescents (Beighle et al., 2020; Dauenhauer et al., 2020). There has also been considerable interest in

[1]NASPE was a member-based organization of the American Alliance for Health and Physical Education (AAHPERD) until 2014 when AAHPERD became the Society of Health and Physical Educators (SHAPE) America.

Table 12.1 U.S. National Standards for K–12 Physical Education

Standard	Descriptor
Standard 1	The physically literate individual demonstrates competency in a variety of motor skills and movement patterns.
Standard 2	The physically literate individual applies knowledge of concepts, principles, strategies, and tactics related to movement and performance.
Standard 3	The physically literate individual demonstrates the knowledge and skills to achieve and maintain a health-enhancing level of physical activity and fitness.
Standard 4	The physically literate individual exhibits responsible personal and social behavior that respects self and others.
Standard 5	The physically literate individual recognizes the value of physical activity for health, enjoyment, challenge, self-expression and/or social interaction.

the effects of nonphysical, education-based physical activity opportunities, particularly within general education classroom settings, on students' cognition and academic achievement related to classroom subjects, such as math and reading (e.g., Masini et al., 2020; Mavilidi et al., 2020). Seldom encountered, however, are studies in which researchers examined the effects of such physical activity opportunities on students' acquisition of knowledge and skills, including social and emotional skills, needed to become proficient movers and participate in a lifetime of physical activity. Yet, the CDC (2013) and SHAPE America (2015) offered a nuanced perspective about the roles that different CSPAP components might play. Although maintaining that physical education is the foundation of a CSPAP and distinct from other components in the framework, these organizations specified program goals emphasizing the potential of all physical activity opportunities to support the educational aims of physical education. For instance, in its updated position statement, SHAPE America (2015) lists the following as one of five goals of a CSPAP: "coordinate among the CSPAP components to maximize understanding, application and practice of the knowledge and skills learned in physical education, so that all students will be physically educated and motivated to pursue a lifetime of physical activity" (p. 3).

Consistent with this perspective, Webster and colleagues (2020) created an illustrative supplement for current CSPAP graphics (**Figure 12.2**) to clarify the full scale of a CSPAP's educational potential. In the supplement, dotted arrows connect the physical activity during school and physical activity before and after school components of a CSPAP to physical education. These arrows signify that it is important to consider possible links between physical activity opportunities beyond physical education and "education *for* physical activity" (i.e., targeted learning goals of physical education, including SEL outcomes). The arrows are bidirectional because physical education can also support students' physical activity experiences and learning (e.g., academics, SEL) in other school-related contexts, such as general education classrooms or before/after school programs (i.e., "education *through* physical activity"). The solid arrows signify that when CSPAPs do incorporate physical activity opportunities beyond physical education before, during and/or after school, staff involvement and family and community engagement are necessary components to support implementation.

Recognizing the potential influence of physical activity opportunities across all CSPAP components on learning outcomes in physical education fundamentally changes the way both researchers and practitioners might approach their work in relation to CSPAPs. Researchers who have sought to know how best to evoke positive changes in students' physical activity behavior might also strive to learn what types of physical activity experiences best leverage students' knowledge and skills, including SEL skills, in line with physical education standards and grade-level outcomes. Likewise, teachers and teacher educators might reconsider the ways they advocate for and engage with CSPAPs, shifting from conceptions that separate the focus of physical education from the focus of other components to new understandings that encourage planning and implementation of initiatives that use CSPAPs to extend physical education. This chapter is based on the idea that a CSPAP can be used to enhance and accelerate what students learn in physical

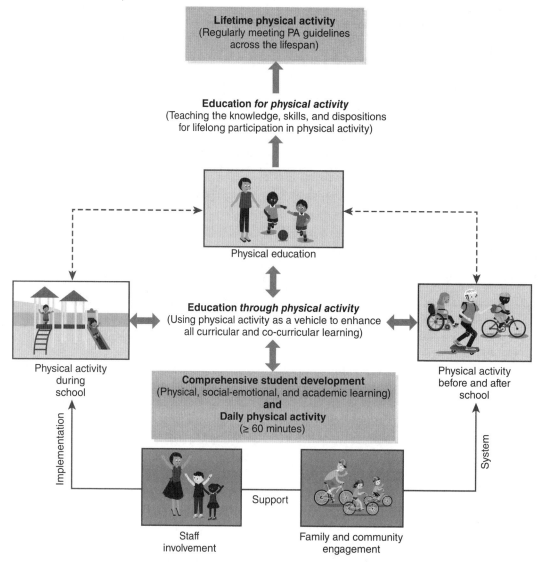

Figure 12.2 The potential of a CSPAP to support physical education learning.

Reproduced from Webster, C. A., Rink, J. E., Carson, R. L., Moon, J., & Gaudreault, K. (2020). The CSPAP model: A proposed illustrative supplement to help move the needle on youth physical activity. *Kinesiology Review, 9*(2), 112–121.

education, including physical, cognitive, and social and emotional skills that align with SHAPE America's national standards for K–12 learners (SHAPE America, 2014; Figure 12.2). From this perspective, all CSPAP components are not only connected through physical activity experiences but also with physical education. Taking this view is an important first step toward realizing a broader vision of a CSPAP's place and functions within the school environment.

Research on Physical Activity Promotion and SEL

SEL is connected to the larger realm of psychosocial and mental health (Payton et al., 2000). A sizeable body of research literature documents a wide range of

psychological and mental health benefits associated with physical activity in children and adolescents. The IOM (2013) report lists the following psychosocial correlates of physical activity: self-efficacy, self-concept, self-worth, social behaviors, proschool attitudes, motivation and goal orientation, relatedness, friendships, task orientation, team building, bullying, and racial prejudice. Identified mental health outcomes include reduced depression, anxiety, confusion, anger, tension, stress, anxiety sensitivity, psychological distress, emotional disturbance, negative affect, and emotional barriers, as well as improved mood and increased positive expectations, general well-being, satisfaction with personal appearance, life satisfaction, self-worth, and quality of life. Associations between these variables and physical activity demonstrate that when individuals participate in more physical activity, they also enjoy more psychosocial and mental health benefits.

The scope and diversity of psychosocial and mental health variables reviewed in the IOM (2013) report are indicative of the extensive canvas needed to capture the multidimensional nature of SEL. Research specifically focused on SEL further demonstrates the vast breadth of the construct, as evidenced in reviews of the literature (e.g., Durlak et al., 2011; Humphrey et al., 2011; Sklad et al., 2012). Authors of these reviews have used combinations or variants of the following terms to search for relevant studies of SEL: social, emotional, socioemotional, affect, interpersonal, positive youth development, coping, self-esteem, prosocial, self-awareness, self-management, self-control, responsibility, relationship, mindfulness, assertiveness, valuing diversity, perspective taking, self-talk, identifying emotions, problem-solving, self-regulation, resilience, emotion expression, challenging behavior, problem behavior, conflict resolution, decision making, inhibitory control, cooperation, prosocial, internalizing, externalizing, and on-task. The multidimensionality of SEL makes conducting a focused review challenging. Even though most authors in this book have adopted the Collaborative for Academic, Social, and Emotional Learning (CASEL) framework (see www.casel.org) to conceptualize the idea of SEL, the competencies in this framework (i.e., self-awareness, self-management, social awareness, relationship skills, and responsible decision making) are similar to many of the those described in the previously mentioned search terms used in reviews of the literature.

Conceptual challenges notwithstanding, mounting evidence supports the idea that physical activity contributes meaningfully within the area of SEL. Based on a meta-analysis of 15 studies, Lubans and colleagues (2012) concluded that physical activity programs with a focus on outdoor adventure activities, sport and skill-based activities, or fitness activities, have the potential to positively impact the SEL of youth who were labeled "at risk." Preliminary evidence was found for such programs to positively influence a range of outcomes, such as self-worth, self-concept, self-esteem, resilience, perceptions of alienation, and self-control. Owen and colleagues (2016) meta-analyzed 38 studies and found positive associations between physical activity and indices of school engagement, including behavior (e.g., time-on-task), emotions (e.g., lesson enjoyment), and cognition (e.g., self-regulated learning). Activity breaks during academic classroom lessons were found to be the most effective type of intervention to improve school

engagement. Conversely, sedentary behavior appears to have a negative impact on certain SEL outcomes. Suchert and colleagues (2015) conducted a systematic review of 91 studies and found that screen time was positively associated with internalizing problems. There was also a positive association for hyperactivity/inattention and a negative association for psychological well-being and quality of life.

Overall, beyond the physical education context, there is a paucity of CSPAP-related research on effective physical activity programming for students' SEL. However, important lessons can be learned from the broader research literature on school-based SEL programs. Durlak et al. (2011) meta-analyzed 213 school-based SEL programs and found that teachers and other school staff were able to successfully deliver such programs. This demonstrates that it is possible to design programs so that they can become part of routine practice in schools. Additionally, Durlak et al. (2011) found that SEL programs were successful across a variety of contexts, including at the elementary, middle, and high- school levels and in urban, suburban, and rural schools. SEL programs may not only benefit SEL but may also help to improve students' academics. After meta-analyzing 40 studies, Corcoran et al. (2018) found that SEL programs had positive effects on students' reading, math, and science performance. Moreover, programs that included a physical activity component had the largest effect on reading and math. These results are particularly important for dispelling perceptions that efforts to promote SEL and/or physical activity might compete with the academic curriculum. This concern has frequently been raised with respect to school-based physical activity programming (e.g., Michael et al., 2019).

There are several important considerations for future research related to physical activity and SEL in children and adolescents. One consideration is the kind of evidence needed to formulate firm conclusions about the effects of school-related physical activity on students' SEL. Many of the existing studies of physical activity and SEL are limited in terms of their research design, measurements, or lack of follow-up, and effect sizes tend to be small to moderate (Biddle & Asare, 2011; Lees & Hopkins, 2013; Lubans et al., 2012; Poitras et al., 2016), suggesting the magnitude of change among students may not be large. To address these limitations, researchers should conduct studies using rigorous experimental designs, valid measures, and follow-up protocols to determine both the short- and long-term impact of physical activity opportunities on SEL outcomes. Furthermore, increases in intervention effectiveness may be observed if physical activity opportunities are designed to specifically integrate with SEL. One way to do this would be to link physical activity experiences with the SAFE principles recommended for SEL programs (Hemphill et al., 2016). SAFE is an acronym that stands for sequenced (i.e., use step-by-step instruction), active (i.e., use participatory and engaging forms of learning), focused (i.e., spend sufficient time on developing skills), and explicit (i.e., have clear learning goals). SEL programs using all four of the SAFE principles have had positive effects on more outcomes than programs not using all four of these principles (Durlak et al., 2011).

Another consideration is the type of information that should be included in research articles describing studies of physical activity and SEL. It can be difficult to interpret the results of studies in which authors report limited details about the physical activity opportunities they investigated. Physical activity can vary in many ways, such as in its frequency, intensity, duration, type, location of occurrence, developmental appropriateness, learning focus (e.g., whether or not the physical activity was purposely integrated with social and emotional skills) and resource utilization (e.g., instructional support, equipment, and facility needs). There is some evidence to suggest that different kinds of physical activity opportunities may lead to different results with respect to students' SEL. Wu and colleagues (2017) conducted a systematic review of 31 studies and found that a higher frequency of physical activity was associated with better quality of life among children and adolescents. However, authors of research studies often do not include much detail when describing school-related physical activity programs or interventions. This makes it difficult to understand what kinds of physical activity opportunities are most beneficial to students' SEL or under what conditions such opportunities are most likely to succeed in terms of both implementation and outcomes. It also limits the ability of other researchers to replicate studies as a way to strengthen the evidence base in support of promising intervention approaches. Perhaps most importantly, providing insufficient details in research reports creates barriers to the effective translation of research into best practice recommendations that teachers, teacher educators, and other end users can use to guide their professional practices.

As stated earlier, the central premise of this chapter is that extended opportunities for physical activity beyond physical education, specifically as framed within a CSPAP, can align with the focus of the physical education curriculum. Therefore, a key consideration for future research is the extent to which physical activity opportunities before, during, and after school can synergistically support SEL outcomes that bolster students' performance in physical education. Specifically, what opportunities might different CSPAP components present to reinforce or increase students' learning in line with SHAPE America's (2014) National Standards 4 and 5, which focus on responsible decision making and values related to physical activity? Additionally, how can physical activity opportunities before, during, and after school be linked with existing SEL initiatives for students to further leverage achievement related to Standards 4 and 5? As SEL is a priority that cuts across the school curriculum, addressing these questions in research will enable those who design and implement CSPAPs to optimize the interdisciplinary impact of such programs on students' learning and development.

Overall, research into physical activity and SEL is an exciting and promising area of inquiry. Substantial research exists on a broad scale to clearly demonstrate positive associations between physical activity and psychosocial/mental health benefits for children and adolescents. This research has laid the groundwork to assert with cautious optimism that promoting youth physical activity has the potential to positively impact students' SEL in ways that leverage the work of all P–12 educators. There are also numerous examples of research that focuses on the specific contribution of particular CSPAP components, such as physical education and after-school programs, on certain social and emotional competencies of youth (e.g., Baptista et al., 2020; Pozo et al., 2018). Yet, the extant research is sparse regarding how CSPAPs and SEL, particularly multicomponent and coordinated approaches to youth physical activity promotion can support affective goals of physical education. Furthermore, not unlike most scientific inquiry focused on school-based physical activity interventions, investigations of school-related physical activity opportunities used to support SEL outcomes too often lack scientific rigor and the rich description needed to make confident claims about what works best and why. Addressing these limitations in future research will help to develop a more mature and elucidated knowledge base that can inform and improve educational policy and best practice recommendations for school professionals.

Integrating SEL into CSPAPs

This section of the chapter is devoted to considerations for integrating SEL experiences into CSPAP components beyond physical education in ways that directly support Standards 4 and 5 of SHAPE America's National Standards for K–12 learners (SHAPE America, 2014). The following subsections present these considerations, first in terms of curriculum alignment and then from the perspective of other curriculum design concepts. Finally, these considerations are applied in two examples of using CSPAPs to support Standards 4 and 5, respectively.

Curriculum Alignment Considerations

As illustrated throughout this book, affective learning outcomes in physical education closely align with the SEL competencies identified in the CASEL framework. Chapter 2 provided an overview of two taxonomies that are helpful in organizing curriculum approaches for addressing SEL. The first of these taxonomies is Hellison's (2011) Teaching Personal and Social Responsibility (TPSR) model, which is most closely tied to the focus of Standard 4. This model includes five levels: (a) Respecting the Rights and Feelings of Others, (b) Participating and Effort, (c) Self-Direction, (d) Helping Others and Leadership, and (e) Outside the Gym (see **Table 12.2**).

The second taxonomy is Krathwhol, Bloom, and Masia's (1973) framework of affective responses to class content, which primarily aligns with Standard 5. Five levels are also included in Krathwohl et al.'s (1973) framework: (a) Receiving, (b) Responding, (c) Valuing, (d) Organization, and (e) Value Complex (or Characterization) (**Table 12.3**). As with Hellison's (2011) model, higher levels of Krathwohl et al.'s (1973) framework represent higher levels of

affective response. A close examination of Hellison's (2011) and Krathwohl et al.'s (1973) taxonomies reveals consistent and overlapping perspectives of affective learning. The lower levels of both taxonomies generally focus on attitudinal and behavioral development that reflect a growing acceptance of and commitment to established class rules, behavioral expectations, and social norms. Affective qualities found within the middle levels of both taxonomies signify increasing internalization of the values and skills needed for achievement and growth in relation to self and class context. Higher levels of each taxonomy are associated with transfer of class-based learning to the broader sphere of one's life.

In Chapters 1-3, Richards and Wright articulate the alignment between the SEL competencies outlined in the CASEL framework and both of the above-mentioned affective learning taxonomies. In Chapter 1, the authors provide an overview of the relationship between SEL skills and Krathwohl et al.'s (1973) affective learning taxonomy, stating that "even though students' affective responses are internal processes rooted in attitude and emotion, they strongly contribute to and are often reflected in their behaviors." In Chapter 2, Richards and Wright draw from the work of Gordon et al. (2016) to identify specific links between the CASEL competencies, TPSR levels, and the affective responses from Krathwohl et al.'s (1973) taxonomy. With respect to TPSR, they link self-awareness to levels 1, 2, and 3, self-management to level 3, social awareness to levels 1, 4, and 5, relationship skills to level 4, and responsible decision making to levels 2 and 5. They also suggest that three CASEL competencies—self-awareness,

Table 12.2 Hellison's (2011) Taxonomy of Personal and Social Responsibility

Level	Affective Qualities
Level 1: Respecting the Rights and Feelings of Others	Using self-control, not interfering with others' learning, honoring the right to peaceful conflict resolution, and honoring the right for everyone to be included
Level 2: Participation and Effort	Being self-motivated and exploring effort
Level 3: Self-Direction	Maintaining on-task independence and setting appropriate goals
Level 4: Helping Others and Leadership	Showing care, compassion, sensitivity, and responsiveness
Level 5: Outside of the Gym	Using personal and social responsibility outside of physical education class in other physical activity contexts

Modified from Hellison, D. (2011). *Teaching personal and social responsibility through physical activity* (3rd ed.). Champaign, IL: Human Kinetics.

Table 12.3 Krathwohl, Bloom, and Masia's (1973) Taxonomy of Affective Responses to Class Content

Level	Affective Qualities
Lower Level Responses	
Level 1: Receiving	Being willing to tolerate the class environment/content (e.g., paying attention to the teacher, staying on task)
Level 2: Responding	Making a small commitment to the class content, but reacting more than acting (e.g., answering questions, following directions)
Higher Level Responses	
Level 3: Valuing	Taking agency as a learner of the content; acting more than reacting (e.g., engaging in effortful learning, assuming leadership roles)
Level 4: Organization	Rearranging personal value system to accommodate and prioritize value for class content (e.g., developing a personal plan related to the content)
Level 5: Value Complex (Characterization)	Consistently acting in accordance with the new value system (e.g., willfully and regularly engage in the content outside of class)

Data from Krathwohl, D. R., Bloom, B. S., and Masia, B. B. (1973). *Taxonomy of educational objectives, the classification of educational goals. Handbook II: Affective domain.* New York: David McKay Co, Inc.

self-management, and responsible decision making—are closely linked to Krathwohl et al.'s (1973) overall framework of affective responses. In Chapter 3, Richards and Wright reiterate the connectedness between SEL skills and the affective learning domain, drawing from the results of a recent systematic review (Teraoka et al., 2020) to assert that teaching practices known to support students' SEL also support students' positive affective responses.

For the purposes of this chapter, the five CASEL competencies are arranged hierarchically to correspond with the different levels of each affective learning taxonomy (**Table 12.4**). This arrangement is intended to illustrate that, similar to Hellison's (2011) model and Krathwohl et al.'s (1973) framework, it may be possible to organize CASEL competencies to generally move from a focus on understanding oneself (e.g., recognizing one's own emotions, thoughts, and values) to applying that understanding in relation to personally and socially responsible decisions (e.g., successfully regulating one's emotions, thoughts, and behaviors; empathizing with others; maintaining healthy relationships; making constructive choices). From this perspective, self-awareness is viewed as foundational to all other social and emotional skills, while responsible decision making is viewed as the culmination and assimilation of the competencies in the CASEL framework. Hierarchically conceptualizing the CASEL competencies may help teachers, curriculum specialists, teacher educators, and researchers

plan learning progressions for students with more targeted and manageable goals and outcomes. However, as Richards and Wright clearly demonstrate, it is important to recognize that there are likely numerous areas of overlap and intersection across the five CASEL competencies, and learning experiences will often capture and promote more than one of these competencies.

The alignment of SHAPE America's national standards (SHAPE America, 2014) with affective learning taxonomies and CASEL competencies can guide curriculum decisions about how to integrate SEL into each CSPAP component in ways that promote the educational goals of physical education. Returning to Table 12.4, end-users (i.e., those responsible for CSPAP implementation) who wish to adopt, adapt, or design physical activity experiences for students would first familiarize themselves with the relevant physical education standards, then decide which standard to focus on, and finally identify the appropriate tier of the matrix, based on an understanding of learners' development (i.e., what level of personal/social responsibility, affective response, and corresponding social and emotional skills are best suited to learners' current abilities). The Grade Level Outcomes for K–12 Physical Education (SHAPE America, 2014) is an excellent resource that provides more detailed information about expectations for developmentally appropriate learning tasks aligned with each standard for students at different grade levels.

Table 12.4 Alignment Matrix for Affective-based Physical Education Standards, Affective Learning Taxonomies, CASEL Competencies, and CSPAP Integration

	SHAPE America National Standard 4: *Exhibit responsible personal and social behavior that respects self and others* (primarily aligned with Hellison's, 2011 taxonomy)	SHAPE America National Standard 5: *Recognize the value of physical activity for health, enjoyment, challenge, self-expression and/or social interaction* (primarily aligned with Krathwohl et al.'s, 1973 taxonomy	SEL (aligned with the CASEL framework)	Overall Focus for CSPAP Integration
Tier 1	Respecting the Rights and Feelings of Others	Receiving	Self-Awareness	Learning to understand oneself in relation to physical activity and appreciate individual differences and needs in physical activity contexts
Tier 2	Participation and Effort	Responding	Self-Management	Learning to contextualize one's personal interests and goals within physical activity contexts
Tier 3	Self-Direction	Valuing	Social Awareness	Learning to pursue one's own physical activity goals, as well as recognize connections between physical activity pursuits of self and peers
Tier 4	Helping Others and Leadership	Organization	Relationship Skills	Learning to prioritize one's physical activity goals and develop mutual supports for physical activity pursuits of self and peers
Tier 5	Outside the Gym	Value Complex (characterization)	Responsible Decision Making	Learning to promote physical activity in community-based settings

Other Curriculum Design Considerations

In addition to clarifying areas of alignment between standards, learning taxonomies, and the CASEL framework, there are other aspects of curriculum design that merit consideration when the goal is to leverage physical education learning using all CSPAP components. Ornstein and Hunkins (2004) identify several interrelated dimensions of curriculum design. First, curricula are organized both horizontally and vertically. *Horizontal organization* is the side-by-side arrangement of curriculum elements. In the context

of a CSPAP, this would involve using multiple CSPAP components to reinforce students' learning of social and emotional skills at each tier of the matrix in Table 12.4. *Vertical organization* is the longitudinal and hierarchical arrangement of curricular elements, such that physical activity experiences across CSPAP components would continue but change over time to facilitate students' progression from lower to higher tiers of the matrix.

Curricula are also organized by scope and sequence (Ornstein & Hunkins, 2004). The *scope* is the range and depth of the curriculum content—in this case, all of the content reflected in the matrix—while the *sequence* is the order in which the content is introduced. Sequencing is related to the vertical organization dimension of the curriculum; subject matter should be sequenced to promote continual and cumulative learning. Also related to a curriculum's vertical organization is the concept of *continuity*, which has to do with revisiting targeted skills at multiple points in a progression (Ornstein & Hunkins, 2004). Thus, as students move from lower to higher tiers of the matrix in Table 12.4, they recurrently engage in physical activity opportunities that enable them to refine and apply the SEL skills they learned at earlier points in the progression.

Three other considerations related to curriculum design are the integration, articulation, and balance of the curriculum (Ornstein & Hunkins, 2004). *Integration* is the tying together of all areas of the curriculum into a unified whole. Its function is to capitalize on horizontal relationships in the curriculum to create holistic learning experiences. In a CSPAP, all physical activity opportunities at a given tier of the matrix in Table 12.4 would be designed in a coordinated manner in an effort to blend learning experiences and highlight unifying foci for SEL. *Articulation* is the linking of curriculum content both vertically and horizontally. Content is sequenced in the vertical dimension, while also overlapping with other curricular areas in the horizontal dimension, to broaden and deepen learners' understanding of concepts and skills that are recurring and related. Articulation is particularly pertinent within a CSPAP when planning classroom-based physical activity experiences that can support students' affective learning in physical education. This would involve identifying and capitalizing on links between the content of the matrix in Table 12.4 and the academic subject matter being taught in the classroom. Finally, *balance* is the assignment of equal weight to different educational priorities reflected in the curriculum. A balanced curriculum would ensure that all school professionals (e.g., teachers, principals, district officials) give SHAPE America's (2014) Standards 4 and 5, as well as other areas of focus in physical education, the same support (e.g., curriculum time, instructional resources) as other school priorities.

Examples of CSPAP Integration

The following are hypothetical examples of how the above-mentioned CSPAP integration considerations might be used to support SHAPE America's (2014) Standards 4 and 5. An example is provided for each tier of the matrix in Table 12.4 to illustrate how the

overall learning focus of the tier might be addressed first in physical education and then across other CSPAP components. For further guidance, readers are encouraged to also review resources mentioned earlier in this chapter, including the SAFE principles for SEL and the Grade-Level Outcomes for K–12 Physical Education (SHAPE America, 2014), as well as established guidelines for appropriate instructional practices for physical education (available from shapeamerica.org). These complementary resources should be given careful attention to optimize students' learning-focused physical activity experiences across a CSPAP.

Tier 1 Integration

In their early elementary years, a key focus of students' physical education lessons is learning to follow rules in both individual- and group-based physical activities. This focus underpins successful progression within Tier 1 of the matrix in Table 12.4, as students need to understand how their personal actions, and the actions of others, affect activity experiences and outcomes. The primary targeted CASEL competency at this tier is self-awareness, which can be viewed from a hierarchical perspective as a prerequisite for the other social and emotional skills in the framework. However, social awareness is closely tied to one's development of self-awareness, and participation in group-based activities at this early stage in a physical education program can engender in students an initial understanding of individual differences within physical activity contexts.

Learning experiences during other parts of the school day, and before and after school, support students' growing self-awareness and appreciation for individual differences with respect to physical activity participation. Classroom teachers, recess supervisors, before and after school program staff, and family members use physical activity to reinforce the rules pertinent to their respective settings. While it is inappropriate to use physical activity as punishment (see appropriate instructional practices for physical education available from shapeamerica.org), physical activity is used as a reward when students follow rules. Games students already know from physical education are modified for different settings to strengthen the horizontal organization of the integrated physical education content.

Tier 2 Integration

As students transition into their upper elementary years, class activities in physical education increasingly focus on exploring deeper connections between self and activity participation, consistent with Tier 2 of the matrix in Table 12.4. Students are given more responsibility for the selection, organization, and management of class activities. This promotes a greater sense of ownership and personal investment in relation to the learning experience, strengthening students' self-awareness while also beginning to develop their self-management skills. To help students further contextualize their personal interests and goals within physical activity contexts, the teacher frequently asks students to identify why they prefer some activities over others and to consider how these preferences relate to students' outside-of-class lives.

Horizontal organization at this level of learning involves giving students multiple opportunities before, during, and/or after school to practice making choices about physical activity options and sharing responsibility for the successful orchestration of activity experiences. Activities are given names and themes that associate with other life contexts to bolster students' perceived links between their physical activity participation and personal interests/goals. For articulation purposes, teachers also connect students' physical activity interests with other parts of the academic curriculum. Additionally, students are encouraged to reflect on the qualities of different activities they find most enjoyable. At home, for instance, parents might prompt students to keep a physical activity journal. Continuity with Tier 1 learning is achieved by maintaining a strong focus on playing by the rules across the CSPAP components, although students are given opportunities to modify rules as a way to reinforce feelings of ownership and personal investment in physical activity experiences.

Tier 3 Integration

While it is not uncommon for some students to begin engaging in Tier 3 learning during their elementary school years, many students are not ready to do so until they reach middle or high school. The focus in physical education at Tier 3 is twofold: first, to help students more clearly define their physical activity goals and develop strategies for pursuing these goals; and second, to help students understand how their own physical activity goals relate to those of their peers. These areas of focus continue to reinforce students' self-awareness and self-management skills and begin to emphasize social awareness as the primary targeted competency within the CASEL framework. The teacher helps students to outline physical activity plans and experiment with different approaches to achieving short-term goals. Working with partners or small groups that share similar physical activity interests and goals aids students in building support networks for progress monitoring and goal achievement.

Across other CSPAP components, physical activity opportunities are designed to assist students in reaching their goals. Students keep logs of their activities, discuss their progress, and give each other suggestions and encouragement. From a curriculum integration perspective, teachers, before and after school program staff, and other CSPAP implementers work together to plan and provide learning experiences that reinforce students' understanding of optimum pathways to goal achievement, appreciation for each other's needs in relation to goal pursuits, and the application of goal-setting skills to multiple contexts and situations.

Tier 4 Integration

Students at Tier 4 move from constructing and assimilating personal physical activity profiles to prioritizing physical activity in their lives. The physical education teacher designs challenges, which students must negotiate in their planning and implementation of goal-aligned physical activity experiences. Challenges might come in the form of hypothetical scenarios in which students have developed an injury, have a scheduling conflict, or are facing another unforeseen obstacle to physical activity participation. Much of the work performed at Tier 4 is group-based so students continue to advance in their understanding and ability with respect to building mutual support for one another. Learning experiences build on students' developing social awareness and emphasize relationship skills.

The theme of overcoming barriers to reaching physical activity goals extends beyond physical education to other CPSAP components through learning experiences in the classroom, in extracurricular activities, and in the home environment that require students to be resourceful in order to support their own, and their peers', successes. Integration across the school curriculum focuses on learning to apply problem-solving skills and relational skills learned through physical activity planning to a wide range of academic and social challenges encountered at school and at home. Students also continue to refine the skills they developed at Tier 3 by logging their physical activity engagement, developing longer-term goals and plans, and expanding their support networks for goal achievement.

Tier 5 Integration

The Tier 4 focus of developing support for physical activity pursuits, particularly in the face of obstacles, continues at Tier 5 with expanded application opportunities and increased emphasis on community-based challenges. In physical education, students work together to identify and address barriers to physical activity participation in their community. They build upon their understanding of the supports needed to sustain their own and their peers' physical activity with larger-scale assignments that require community engagement. The teacher uses established relationships with community partners to create a service learning platform for students. Class time is reserved for students to meet with community partners to draft physical activity promotion plans that support a range of settings and environments (e.g., preschools, parks, neighborhoods, company workplaces, assisted living facilities). Overall, Tier 5 learning experiences allow students to assimilate the social and emotional skills they have already developed in ways that demonstrate responsible decision making.

Service-learning is a theme across other CSPAP components, which helps to equalize the importance of physical education learning experiences within the school curriculum to achieve curricular balance. Students' physical activity promotion work is tied to service learning projects that incorporate knowledge and skills across multiple school subjects. For instance, a project that focuses on creating healthier communities might connect physical activity promotion to academic content from social studies (e.g., policy perspectives), science (e.g., environmental perspectives), and economics (e.g., financial perspectives). The aim of schoolwide service learning projects is to socialize students into active citizenship while also reinforcing, through interdisciplinary connections and realworld applications, students' internalized values for the knowledge and skills they are learning in school.

Example Activities for Preservice Preparation Programs

Physical education teacher education (PETE) programs might consider having teacher candidates participate in field experiences that focus on supporting SHAPE America's (2014) Standards 4 and 5 through physical activity promotion in multiple CSPAP components. Teacher candidates would work in groups

and use the alignment matrix from Table 12.4 of this chapter, along with the physical education grade-level outcomes for K–12 students (SHAPE America, 2014), recommended appropriate instructional practices for physical education instruction, and SAFE principles for SEL to plan and implement activities in elementary and secondary schools and other community settings. Methods courses and practicums provide existing platforms to embed these kinds of learning experiences for teacher candidates. The use of service learning principles to guide candidates' engagement with schools and communities would help to prepare candidates to adopt and use these principles when they transition into their professional work as teachers.

Courses designed for other preservice school professionals (e.g., preservice elementary and secondary school teacher candidates, preservice school administrators) might be designed in tandem with, or even integrated with, learning experiences for physical education majors. The primary focus of coursework for elementary and secondary teacher candidates would be on the integration of SHAPE America's (2014) Standards 4 and 5 with other academic content in the school curriculum and on physically active strategies to support integrated learning. Coursework for preservice school administrators would mainly focus on knowledge and skills needed to support CSPAPs, and particularly activity experiences that align with students' SEL, as a school leader. The same resources used to support physical education majors' planning and implementation of CSPAPs (e.g., alignment matrix in Table 12.4, grade-level outcomes in K–12 physical education), and the use of field experiences framed with service-learning principles, are relevant to the successful learning of all future school professionals.

Summary and Conclusion

This chapter foregrounds the potential of a CSPAP to support students' SEL, specifically in line with SHAPE America's Standards 4 and 5 for K–12 physical education (SHAPE America, 2014) and the CASEL framework. Early focuses of physical activity research, which centered on the obesity epidemic as a public health issue, have grown to encompass broader impacts of physical activity participation (Fox, 2000). It is clear that the importance of physical activity for children and adolescents extends well beyond physical health and reaches multiple dimensions of mental and psychosocial health (IOM, 2013). In line with the CSPAP integration suggestions provided in this chapter, researchers and practitioners are encouraged to explore possible applications of established affective learning taxonomies, curriculum design principles, and best practice recommendations for physical education within the various components of the CSPAP framework to strengthen students' physical education learning. This work will enhance the broader aim of better elucidating connections between SEL and all facets of the school-community system, as outlined in current conceptual models (see the Whole School, Whole Community, Whole Child [WSCC] Model as an example; Lewallen, Hunt, Potts-Datema, Zaza, & Giles, 2015), and will allow such models to evolve toward reflecting the many ways students' SEL can be supported.

Questions for Discussion

1. What is meant by a "whole-of-school approach" and what is a CSPAP?
2. Why is it important to consider how CSPAP components outside of physical education might contribute to targeted outcomes in physical education?
3. What claims can be made about physical activity, psychosocial/mental health, and SEL in children and adolescents based on the related research?
4. What similarities exist across Hellison's (2011) TPSR model, Krathwohl, Bloom, and Masia's (1973) framework, and the CASEL framework for SEL?
5. How would the curriculum design concept of continuity be applied to supporting elementary students' ability to accept feedback from others? (Use the matrix in Table 12.4, the SHAPE America, 2014 grade-level outcomes, and the SAFE principles for SEL as a guide.)

References

Baptista, C., Corte-Real, N., Regueiras, L., Seo, G., Hemphill, M., Pereira, A., Dias, C., Martinek, T., & Fonseca, A. (2020). Teaching personal and social responsibility after school: A systematic review. *Cuadernos de Psicología del Deporte, 20*(2), 1–25.

Beighle, A., Erwin, H., Webster, C. A., & Webster, M. A. (2020). Physical activity during school. In R. L. Carson & C. A. Webster (Eds.), *Comprehensive school physical activity programs: Putting research into evidence-based practice* (pp. 99–110). Champaign, IL: Human Kinetics.

Beighle, A., & Moore, M. (2012). Physical activity before and after school. *Journal of Physical Education, Recreation & Dance, 83*(6), 25–28.

Biddle, S. J. H., & Asare, M. (2011). Physical activity and mental health in children and adolescents: A review of reviews. *British Journal of Sports Medicine, 45*(11), 886–895.

Castelli, D. M., & Ward, K. (2012). Physical activity during the school day. *Journal of Physical Education, Recreation & Dance, 83*(6), 20–29.

Centers for Disease Control and Prevention. (2013). *Comprehensive school physical activity programs: A guide for schools.* Centers for Disease Control and Prevention, US Department of Health and Human Services.

Centers for Disease Control and Prevention. (2019). *Increasing physical education and physical activity: A framework for schools.* Centers for Disease Control and Prevention, US Department of Health and Human Services.

Cipriani, K., Richardson, C., & Roberts, G. (2012). Family and community involvement and the comprehensive school physical activity program. *Journal of Physical Education, Recreation & Dance, 83*(7), 20–26.

Corcoran, R. P., Cheung, A. C. K., Kim, E., & Xie, C. (2018). Effective universal school-based social and emotional learning programs for improving academic achievement: A systematic review and meta-analysis of 50 years of research. *Educational Research Review, 25*, 56–72.

Dauenhauer, B., Stellino, M. B., Webster, C. A., & Steinfurth, C. (2020). Physical activity programs before and after school. In R. L. Carson & C. A. Webster (Eds.), *Comprehensive school physical activity programs: Putting research into evidence-based practice* (pp. 111–126). Champaign, IL: Human Kinetics.

Durlak, J. A., Weissberg, R. P., Dymnicki, A. B., Taylor, R. D., & Schellinger, K. B. (2011). The impact of enhancing students' social and emotional learning: A meta-analysis of school-based universal interventions. *Child Development, 82*(1), 405–432.

Fox, K. (2000). Physical activity and mental health promotion: The natural partnership. *Journal of Public Mental Health, 2*(1), 4–12.

Gordon, B., Jacobs, J. M., & Wright, P. M. (2016). Social and emotional learning through a teaching personal and social responsibility based after-school program for disengaged middle school boys. *Journal of Teaching in Physical Education, 35*(4), 358–369.

Heidorn, B., & Centeio, E. (2012). The director of physical activity and staff involvement. *Journal of Physical Education, Recreation & Dance, 83*(7), 13–26.

Hellison, D. (2011). *Teaching personal and social responsibility through physical activity* (3rd ed.). Champaign, IL: Human Kinetics.

Hemphill, M. A., & Richards, K. A. R. (2015). "Without the academic part, it wouldn't be squash": Youth development in an urban squash program. *Journal of Teaching in Physical Education, 35*(3), 263–276.

Humphrey, N., Kalambouka, A., Wigelsworth, M., Lendrum, A., Deighton, J., & Wolpert, M. (2011). Measures of social and emotional skills for children and young people: A systematic review. *Educational and Psychological Measurement, 71*(4), 617–637.

Institute of Medicine. (2013). *Educating the student body: Taking physical activity and physical education to school*. The National Academies.

Krathwohl, D. R., Bloom, B. S., & Masia, B. B. (1973). *Taxonomy of educational objectives, the classification of educational goals. Handbook II: Affective domain*. New York: David McKay Co, Inc.

Lawson, G. M., McKenzie, M. E., Becker, K. D., Selby, L., & Hoover, S. A. (2019). The core components of evidence-based social emotional learning programs. *Prevention Science, 20*, 457–467.

Lees, C., & Hopkins, J. (2013). Effect of aerobic exercise on cognition, academic achievement, and psychosocial function in children: A systematic review of randomized control trials. *Preventing Chronic Disease, 10*, E174.

Lewallen, T. C., Hunt, H., Potts-Datema, W., Zaza, S., & Giles, W. (2015). The Whole School, Whole Community, Whole Child Model: A new approach for improving educational attainment and healthy development for students. *Journal of School Health, 85*(11), 729–739.

Lubans, D. R., Plotnikoff, R. C., & Lubans, N. J. (2012). A systematic review of the impact of physical activity programmes on social and emotional well-being in at-risk youth. *Child and Adolescent Mental Health, 17*(1), 2–13.

Masini, A., Marini, S., Gori, D., Leoni, E., Rochira, A., & Dallolio, L. (2020). Evaluation of school-based interventions of active breaks in primary schools: A systematic review and meta-analysis. *Journal of Science and Medicine in Sport, 23*(4), 377–384.

Mavilidi, M. F., Drew, R., Morgan, P. J., Lubans, D. R., Schmidt, M., & Riley, N. (2020). Effects of different types of physical activity breaks on children's on-task behaviour, academic achievement, and cognition. *Acta Paediatrica: Nurturing the Child, 109*(1), 158–165.

Michael, R. D., Webster, C. A., Egan, C. A., Nilges, L., Brian, A., Johnson, R. L., & Carson, R. L. (2019). Facilitators and barriers to movement integration in elementary classrooms: A systematic review. *Research Quarterly for Exercise and Sport, 90*(2), 151–162.

National Association for Sport and Physical Education. (2008). *Comprehensive school physical activity programs* [position statement]. Reston, VA: American Alliance for Health, Physical Education, Recreation and Dance.

National Association for Sport and Physical Education, & American Heart Association. (2012). *Shape of the nation report: Status of physical education in the USA*. Reston, VA: American Alliance for Health, Physical Education, Recreation and Dance.

Ornstein, A. C., & Hunkins, F. P. (2004). *Curriculum: Foundations, principles, and issues* (4th ed.). Boston, MA: Pearson Education.

Owen, K. B., Parker, P. D., Van Zanden, B., MacMillan, F., Astell-Burt, T., & Lonsdale, C. (2016). Physical activity and school engagement in youth: A systematic review and meta-analysis. *Educational Psychologist, 51*(2), 129–145.

Payton, J. W., Wardlaw, D. M., Graczyk, P. A., Bloodworth, M. R., Tompsett, C. J., & Weissberg, R. P. Social and emotional learning: A framework for promoting mental health and reducing risk behavior in children and youth. *Journal of School Health, 70*(5), 179–185.

Perna, F. M., Oh, A., Chriqui, J. F., Mâsse, L. C., Atienza, A. A., Nebeling, L., Agurs-Collins, T., Moser, R. P., & Dodd, K. W. (2012). The association of state law to physical education time allocation in US public schools. *American Journal of Public Health, 102*(8), 1594–1599.

Poitras, V. J., Gray, C. E., Borghese, M. M., Carson, V., Chaput, J.-P., Janssen, I., Katzmarzyk, P. T., Pate, R. R., Connor Gorber, S., Kho, M. E., Sampson, M., & Tremblay, M. S. (2016). Systematic review of the relationships between objectively measured physical activity and health indicators in school-aged children and youth. *Applied Physiology, Nutrition, and Metabolism, 41*(6), S197–S239.

Pozo, P., Grao-Cruces, A., & Pérez-Ordáz, R. (2018). Teaching personal and social-responsibility model-based programmes in physical education: A systematic review. *European Physical Education Review, 24*(1), 56–75.

Sklad, M., Diekstra, R., de Ritter, M., Ben, J., & Gravesteijn, C. (2012). Effectiveness of school-based social, emotional, and behavioral programs: Do they enhance students' development in the area of skill, behavior, and adjustment? *Psychology in the Schools, 49*(9), 892–909.

Slater, S. J., Nicholson, L., Chriqui, J., Turner, L., & Chaloupka, F. (2012). The impact of state laws and district policies on physical education and recess practices in a nationally representative sample of US public elementary schools. *Archives of Pediatrics & Adolescent Medicine, 166*(4), 311–316.

Society of Health and Physical Educators America. (2014). *National standards and grade-level outcomes for K-12 physical education*. Reston, VA: SHAPE America.

Society of Health and Physical Educators America. (2015). *Comprehensive school physical activity programs: Helping all students log 60 minutes of physical activity each day* [position statement]. Reston, VA: SHAPE America.

Suchert, V., Hanewinkel, R., & Isensee, B. (2015). Sedentary behavior and indicators of mental health in school-aged children and adolescents: A systematic review. *Preventive Medicine, 76*, 48–57.

Taylor, R. D., Oberle, E., Durlak, J. A., & Weissberg, R. P. (2017). Promoting youth positive development through school-based social and emotional learning interventions: A meta-analysis of follow-up effects. *Child Development, 88*(4), 1156–1171.

Teraoka, E., Ferreira, H. J., Kirk, D., & Bardid, F. (2020). Affective learning in physical education: A systematic review. *Journal of Teaching in Physical Education*. https://doi.org/10.1123/jtpe.2019-0164

Webster, C. A., Rink, J. E., Carson, R. L., Moon, J., & Gaudreault, K. (2020). The CSPAP model: A proposed illustrative supplement to help move the needle on youth physical activity. *Kinesiology Review, 9*(2), 112–121.

Wu, X. Y., Han, L. H., Zhang, J. H., Luo, S., Hu, J. W., & Sun, K. (2017). The influence of physical activity, sedentary behavior on health-related quality of life among the general population of children and adolescents: A systematic review. *PLoS ONE, 12*(11), e0187668.

Case Examples of Social and Emotional Learning with Marginalized Communities

CHAPTER 13

Sport-Based Youth Development and its Relationship to the Social and Emotional Development of Youth

Tom Martinek
Michael A. Hemphill

CHAPTER SUMMARY

Addressing the role that sport-based youth development (SBYD) plays in promoting social and emotional health in youngsters is the main feature of this chapter. Our purpose is to illustrate how social and emotional learning (SEL) is supported by the unique features included in SBYD programming. The essential elements of Positive Youth Development (PYD) and its historical role in serving children are provided. An understanding of how SEL is fostered through SBYD experiences is offered. Specific sport programs are profiled. These SBYD programs operate in different contexts and show how the various approaches are used to enhance the social and emotional qualities of youth.

Introduction

As captured in other chapters throughout this book, youth's social and emotional health has been a vital focal point for youth programming and schooling. The period of adolescent growth requires extra support in order for youth to learn and develop in a positive way. This support is more important than ever as we are faced with formidable social problems in our schools and communities. These problems must be acknowledged when creating programs that address the social and emotional qualities of youngsters. Hellison (2011) identifies three causes of social problems. One is immediate causes such as guns and violence in schools. These causes are the ones we all too often read about in the newspaper and social media. The second is root causes such as poverty, racism, inadequate health care, lack of parent education, and lack of opportunity. The third is intermediate causes including a need for skills in and a disposition toward social competence, problem-solving, autonomy, and a sense of purpose for pursuing future possibilities. According to Hellison (2011), there is little that program directors can do to change the root and immediate causes of problems. However, they can focus and perhaps attenuate the intermediate causes of problematic behavior. As discussed in more detail in Chapter 2, however, the implication is that youth programs must be intentionally formed so that various qualities of social and emotional growth can occur. Consequently, program directors must take care in structuring the features of their program to foster both positive and sustainable growth.

Our purpose for this chapter is to describe how SBYD programming can play an important role in promoting social and emotional growth in children and youth. The qualities of SBYD programs provide the necessary support for holistic development in youth (Coakley, 2016; Fraser-Thomas et al., 2005). These qualities have their roots in the principles that have guided past positive youth development (PYD) initiatives (Coakley, 2016). In this chapter, we explore the historical beginnings and growth of PYD and how specific programs, guided by these principles, have been essential in PYD and producing positive program outcomes. We describe how PYD values have informed various SBYD programs, which strive to nurture the social and emotional development of youth. Specific programs are profiled to illustrate the various contexts and frameworks that define each of their characters and mission.

Genesis of PYD

Early in the 20th century, American society assumed an increased sense of responsibility for the care of its young people, including a reach into education and schools, and delaying entry into the workforce (Hirsch, 2005). Families who historically had nurtured the development of their children were also supported (Catalano et al., 2008). Boys Clubs (later Boys and Girls Clubs), YMCAs/YWCAs, and 4H organizations were cornerstones for the delivery of youth support services in the community. As the century progressed, changes in the function of the family unit resulted in changes in the conceptualization of schools and community practices. This provided further support for the family in its mission to raise and educate children.

By the middle of the 20th century, juvenile crime and concerns about youth were surfacing. This was a challenge for families, schools, and the communities at large and led to federal funding that was made available to address these issues (Bumpass & Lu, 2000). Juvenile problems continued to accelerate during the 1960s, as did national rates of poverty, divorce, unintended pregnancy, family mobility, and single-parent households (Catalano et al., 2008; Bumpass & Lu, 2000). As a response to this shifting social landscape, intervention programs were formed to support families and youth. The aim of these programs was to reduce juvenile crime and to elevate the character of youth (Hirsch, 2009). Unfortunately, youth crime continued to rise. This resulted in the development of more and varied intervention and treatment responses. Research on the effectiveness of these programs have been studied extensively as they have been related to substance abuse, conduct disorders, delinquent and antisocial behavior, low academic performance, and teenage pregnancy (e.g., Agee, 1979; Clarke & Cornish, 1978; Cooper et al., 1983; De Leon & Zieggenfuss, 1986; Friedman, & Beschnes, 1985; Gold & Mann, 1984). By looking at the specific outcomes, it was possible to determine what programs needed to do to improve the efficacy of the interventions. At the same time, it brought attention to studying what efforts could best be applied to *prevention* approaches in youth programming. That is, rather than considering the problems that youth already experienced, effort was directed toward preventing those problems from arising in the first place.

In the 1990s, prevention approaches began to replace the more reactive treatment strategies (Halpern, 2006). Consideration for the conditions of youth's lives (e.g., families, schools, communities, neighborhood, peer connections) also became central features of youth programming. These conditions were now considered vital parts of the individual's life that determined their sense of capability and optimism (Seligman, 2018). During early implementation years, many prevention programs tended to target a single problem (Aspen Institute, 2018). These programs tended to only identify problems and not the root causes or potential solutions to the problems plaguing youth. This singular and deficit-oriented approach made it difficult to understand what specific changes could be made to the complexity of youth's lives in schools, community programs, perhaps families, and maybe, just maybe, neighborhoods.

Exploration into the cause of delinquency continued well into the 1990s. Scholars turned to Cloward and Ohlin's (1960) *opportunity theory*, which suggested that the lack of options to become successful was a key factor in creating delinquency in youth. Things such as employment opportunities, training programs, and neighborhood centers began to be included in larger prevention initiatives. By the turn of the 21st century, more positive or strength-based approaches to prevention were put in place (Witt & Caldwell, 2018). Rather than trying to keep youth from engaging in risky behaviors, youth development programs now focused on helping them develop into happy and healthy adults. This was an important shift in the approaches taken in intervention programs. Rather than focusing programs on the deficits of youth and communities, it became important to view the assets (i.e., strengths) that youth brought to the program (Pittman & Fleming, 1991). These strengths were to be nurtured through program experiences where opportunity to explore and learn about one's capacity to contribute were realized. An important point here is that the strength-based approach in PYD also set the stage for creating programs that were school based (e.g., SEL). The application of principles of PYD for enhancing social and emotional behavior in schools seemed both logical and necessary.

PYD Programming

Creating intentional programming requires an understanding of basic developmental processes as well as the type of activities that help youth engage and thrive. By taking a developmental approach in program planning, youth will be better prepared to make a successful transition from childhood to adulthood (Bundick et al., 2010; Witt, 2018). Although various researchers and other professionals have not agreed on a single definition of PYD, there have been several initiatives that have tried to come up with profiles of quality PYD programs. One of the first major efforts to do this was funded by the Dewitt Wallace Reader's Digest Fund (Dewitt Wallace Reader's Digest Fund, 1995). This project was a four-year evaluation of programs across the United States with the purpose of identifying the qualities of effective youth programs. A more recent study by the National Research Council and Institute of Medicine (NRCIM, 2004) also searched for the qualities that defined effective youth programs. Together, these studies (Dewitt Wallace Readers Digest Fund, 1995; NRCIM, 2004) led to a list of qualities that characterize quality PYD programming (see **Table 13.1**). These qualities have served as the guideposts for program development and delivery.

Table 13.1 Program Qualities to Promote PYD

- Physical and psychological safety
- Structure that is developmentally appropriate
- Supportive relationships
- Opportunities to belong and to be valued
- Positive social norms
- Support for efficacy and mattering
- Opportunities for skill building and mastery
- Integration of family, school, and community efforts
- Opportunities to make a contribution to one's community

Witt, P. A. & Caldwell, L. L. (2018). *Youth development principles and practices in out-of-school time settings* (2nd ed.). Champaign, IL: Sagamore-Venture.

Most importantly; however, their presence in the program enhance the likelihood that participating youth will gain the necessary values for social and emotional aptitudes for life.

It is important to note that the ultimate outcomes of effective programming come about from a complex collection of factors that intersect with program experiences. Borrowing from Bronfenbrenner's (1979) bioecological theory, outside factors come into play (e.g., gang involvement, lack of family support, poor-quality schooling). The physical and psychological characteristics of youth are also considered as any program must take into account the dynamic interplay of these factors alongside the goals and experiences of the program (Coakley, 2016; Witt & Caldwell, 2018). In fact, Hellison (2011) suggests that any program and its outcomes may be only a small, intermediate piece of the puzzle. This highlights the importance of taking a holistic approach in programming to alleviate the social and emotional challenges of youth. This is especially significant when the focal points of a program are related to social and psychological aspects of the participating youth. Holistic approaches can uphold the premise that confident and caring youths, who are positively connected to others and have character and integrity, will more than likely grow up to be adults who contribute to and support their families, themselves, and their communities (Lerner, 2006).

Lerner, Lerner, Bowers, and Goldhof, (2015) proposed a model that takes into account the various contexts where PYD programs are conducted. The centerpiece of this model is a set of five Cs that are outcomes that youth achieve in programs whose goals address various individual and context conditions (e.g., low self-esteem, toxic neighborhood). In many situations, the context variables and program goals may be reciprocal over time. That is, goals may be modified according to the nature of the context (e.g., resources available, program space) and the program may actually modify the context by improving the conditions in which the program operates. These five Cs are: competence, confidence, connection, character, caring/compassion, and contribution. A sixth C, contribution, has also been added when the other five Cs have been attained (see **Table 13.2**).

Another model that has emerged from the *America Promise* initiative is the Developmental Assets Model (Anderson, 2008; 2006). Similar to Lerner and colleagues' (2015) Five Cs model, this framework includes 20 *internal* asset-based outcomes that are desired products of youth programming—deemed necessary for youth to thrive socially and emotionally—to ensure successful transition to adulthood (Scales et al., 2000). These assets are grouped into four categories: making a commitment to learning, developing positive values, developing social competencies, and creating a positive identity. In addition, the Developmental Assets model includes 20 *external* assets that support the social and emotional health development of youth by nurturing internal assets. They also become important allies in effective PYD program delivery and are grouped into four areas: (a) support from family, neighborhood, schools, and other adults, (b) actions that empower youth, (c) establishment of boundaries and expectations, and (d) provision of opportunities for constructive use of time.

Table 13.2 The Six Cs

Competence: A positive view of one's capability in areas of social, academic, cognitive, health, and vocational aspects of life.

Confidence: A sense of capability and mastery of challenges. Self-efficacy is present (believe that success can be experienced).

Connection: Connotes an ability to establish positive relationships with others and community institutions, including family, school, teachers, and peers.

Character: Indicates a respect for societal, institutional, and cultural rules and expectations.

Caring/Compassion: Shows that a person can be sympathetic and empathic toward others.

Contribution: Refers to being involved as an active person in decision making in various services, organizations, and community.

Data from Witt, P. A., & Caldwell, L. L. (2018). *Youth development principles and practices in out-of-school time settings*. Champaign, IL: Sagamore-Venture.

Taken together, the six Cs and 40-asset models cover a wide range of support factors that can be applied in a PYD program. The success of directors to include these in their programs requires a strong commitment to develop the experiences and support systems necessary for total enhancement of social and psychological growth.

Sport-Based Youth Development and Social and Emotional Learning

Sports have come to occupy a privileged place in American culture. Interest in sports is ubiquitous; it spans age, social class, religion, and gender (Martinek & Hellison, 2016). Many have advocated for the inclusion of sport programs in communities and schools for the sole purpose of enhancing the moral and social development of children and youth. Unfortunately, replication of the "winning-is-everything," elitist, spectator-driven, commercialized orientation of the professional sport model has become the status quo in many sport programs in our communities and, in particular, our schools (Hellison, 2011). While some rule modifications have been implemented to make adult sports more appropriate for youth participants (e.g., lower baskets for youth children's basketball game play), the value of winning over participation, fair play, and personal and social development continue to be avoided by coaches, teachers, and parents. While many adults have the best intentions of promoting certain life skills through sport, they often fall prey to the dark side of traditional sport forms (Hellison, 2011).

Recently, program directors, coaches, teachers, and administrators have addressed the issue of competitive youth sport by forming initiatives that help to reeducate coaches and their approaches to working with young sport participants. These SBYD initiatives are bolstered by the societal concerns about youth and their role in community building (McLaughlin, 2000). Fostering life skills of social responsibility, moral judgment and behavior are seen as qualities that help define a more positive community. The principles of PYD become important guideposts for SBYD as they ensure the vitality of program delivery.

As we examine the impact of PYD programs on youth, we often find that sports play a central role. Spurred by the research that has shown sport and physical activity as an ideal context for promoting life skills (Camiré et al., 2011; Danish et al., 2004; Gordon et al., 2016), SBYD has flourished in schools and community programs. Skills such as persistence, conflict resolution, emotional regulation, and leadership have been some of the life skills identified by these studies. There are several reasons for why sport has become a central avenue for youth development. First, sport and physical activity offer highly interactive experiences for youth. This is especially true when team play or group activity are central to the learning experiences (Coakley, 2017; Cote & Vierimaa, 2014, Hirsch, 2005). Because of the highly dynamic nature of sport, "teachable moments" occur often and provide opportunities to respond to and reflect on the moment. For example, seeing a student who helps another fallen student off the floor during a basketball game offers a great opportunity to acknowledge and underscore the importance of helping others—both in the game and in life itself. Second, many youth enjoy engaging in sport and being physically active. Consequently, movement experiences become natural attractors of youth—they become the proverbial "hooks" for getting youth to engage in a values-based experience (Coakley, 2016). Of course, maintaining sustained participation in sport or physical activity is dependent on how well PYD principles are applied during program delivery.

The third reason is that sport engagement often becomes a moral experience. Part of this character of sport has come from the Christian and moral values that were applied to earlier youth programming (Albrecht & Strand, 2010). The roots of this belief originate from 19th century "muscular Christians" who embraced the idea that there was a connection between the physical and spiritual dimensions of human beings (Coakley, 2017). From this perspective, skill acquisition and fitness have moral significance. Finally, sport is a huge part of the American culture. It is part of our way of life as "we live sport" through what we see, do, and experience in our lives. The implication here is that a values-based sport culture creates an alternative view of sport within youth programming.

The very nature of a SBYD-driven experience offers the potential for enhancing the social and emotional qualities of youth. In essence, teaching and coaching social and emotional skills connects well with the central spirit of SBYD approaches (Gordon et al., 2016). That is, sports and other physical activities provide ample opportunities to help enhance the foundational skills of SEL (Kahn et al., 2019). Studies that have examined this relationship have found values-based sport programming to have a strong alignment with SEL competencies (Durlak et al., 2010; Gordon et al., 2016), although the strength of

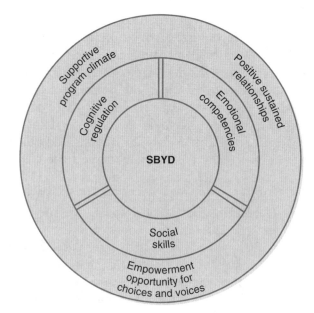

Figure 13.1 SBYD and SEL.

© Jones & Bartlett Learning.

this relationship is dependent on the level of fidelity with which programs are implemented. This has particular relevance for the models-based practices described in Section 2 of this book (Curtner-Smith et al., 2008; Kirk, 2013). SEL has been identified by the Collaborative for Academic, Social, and Emotional Learning (CASEL) to include such attributes as social awareness, positive decision making, and self-management CASEL, 2014; Gordon, et. al., 2016). Kahn, Bailey, and Jones (2019) have grouped the various SEL competencies (see Chapters 1 and 2 for more information on the competencies) into three inter-related categories: *Cognitive Regulation, Emotional Competencies, and Social Skills*. In **Figure 13.1**, we see how these SEL skills are reflective of those that are products of SBYD programming.

Cognitive Regulation and SBYD

Youth approach various learning tasks with pre-conceived ideas of how they will engage with and experience them. The level of engagement is largely influenced by self-perceptions of ability and optimism for success—both of which are central to SEL enhancement. Acquiring these attributes requires a set of skills that involve problem solving, motivation, an "I can" attitude, and the ability to concentrate (Martinek, 1996; Ryan & Deci, 2000). Gaining these skills requires the use of goal setting, provision of choices, and acceptance of failure in various learning situations. The structuring of sport experiences captures the character of process-oriented tasks that allow the learner to focus on those parts that can be addressed with repetitive attempts (Camiré et al., 2011; Gould & Carson, 2008). Guided goal setting is a part of this process. The goal is to enhance flexibility in the thought processing that goes into experiences that offer challenge and require decision making. This also involves the ability to concentrate and adapt to tasks that offer challenge. Choices of how to best execute a skill, choose an activity to engage in, or decide on how to lead a group of peers captures some of the ways in which careful thought and decision making can be facilitated (see Chapter 3 for more detail on decision making opportunities in a physical activity lesson). Clearly, SBYD programs widen the opportunities for success through choice-laden experiences. This lessens the impulse to quit and heightens commitment to keep trying. These skills can be transferred and applied in the school, neighborhood, and family settings (Turnnidge et al., 2014).

Emotional Competencies and SBYD

Emotional competencies are a set of skills and understandings that help youth recognize and regulate their emotions (CASEL, 2014). That is, being aware of one's emotions, having the capability to handle and express one's emotions in a positive way, position the individual to succeed in various life contexts (i.e., school, home, neighborhood). Cultivating this set of skills requires opportunity to engage in leadership where helping others becomes a main goal of the learning experience. From this emerges sympathy, empathy, and perspective-taking that allow youth to manage their own emotions and cope with different situations in constructive ways (Martinek et al., 2004). These skills form the foundation for positive social interactions and are critical in building relationships with peers and adults. Opportunities to lead and help others become part of the program agenda. Reaching out to support and teach someone else, or to coach a team, fosters the drive to support and care for others. This is a critical quality in that it pushes youth from the need to fulfill self-interests and toward actions that are beneficial to others (Noddings, 2003). This quality exists at the core of SBYD individual and team sports.

Social Skills and SBYD

One of the important outcomes of SBYD programs is the fostering of positive social skills among youth (Hemphill and Martinek, 2019; Holt, 2016; Fraser-Thomas et al., 2005). Conflict and indifference toward others are too often found in the classrooms

and neighborhoods. SBYD programs can help youth to more accurately interpret the behavior of others. This set of skills includes interacting positively with peers and adults and effectively navigating contentious social situations. Emphasizing respect for one another, dealing with conflict in a peaceful way, and resisting the impulse to fight back are important features of all programs. Gaining emotional competencies becomes an important factor in social and interpersonal skills building. Youth can be helped to realize that using these skills effectively is important when contributing to a team or group. Resolving disagreements and coexisting peacefully are critical to the broader health of a school or community.

Bringing the Components Together

All three of these elements interact with character, beliefs, and mindset. Character relates to ways of thinking and habits that support youth closely working effectively with peers, family, and community members. Core ethical values such as trusting, empathy, and caring for others are gained and understood in a way that support positive relationships with others. Integrity, honesty, and compassion form the foundation of character development. The mindsets and beliefs about themselves, others, and their circumstances—such as self-knowledge, motivation, and purpose—influence how youth interpret and react to the things that happen to them during program experiences. From the perspective of SEL, these skills and beliefs lead to success in schooling, community-based events, relationships, and citizenship (Kahn et al., 2019). Given the dynamic nature of sport and physical activity, it would seem that sport and physical activity offer the ideal context for nurturing these skills (Aspen Institute, 2018; Camiré & Kendellen, 2016; Coakley, 2017; Holt et al., 2011).

It is also important to note that the progression of skill development will vary according to age and past experience. Jones, Farrington, Jagers, Brackett, & Kahn, (2019) believe that the environment from which children and youth grow and play often changes. This creates varying demands on them. The chance to be successful, therefore, is dependent on how social and emotional skills are more or less operating in different phases of development. For example, being able to regulate emotions becomes an important prerequisite to successfully interacting with others. Positive communication skills such as "code switching" or controlling negative impulses, or making positive choices (adaptive distancing—avoiding negative influences) all come into play as youth engage in life experiences. Clearly, these experiences will intersect with the values they acquire from childhood to adulthood.

SBYD Programs

As we call upon sport and physical activity to be important in the fostering SEL competencies, program leaders must be able successfully integrate social, cognitive, and emotional skill building. There are many SBYD programs that serve youth. Each of them has their own way of forming learning experience—usually guided by a particular framework or model. All of them, however, use the sport experience to address a certain set of life skills that can help to augment SEL. Program settings also vary with some connected to school programming (i.e., before, during, and after-school), and some are community based (e.g., Boys and Girls Clubs, Recreation Centers, YMCAs). Each program offers its best practice for holistic development of youth. Many of these programs have been going for years and have a long history of successfully supporting SEL competency integration. **Table 13.3** highlights a select group of SBYD programs. Each operates within a specific context and provides a specific set of experiences that seek to build SEL competencies while accounting for the specific circumstances of youth participants. In describing each of these, we provide

a brief rationale for program creation, description of the mission and what happens during the program, and some of the outcomes that are born from various data sources.

Project Coach

Located in Holyoke and Springfield, Massachusetts, Project Coach is an after-school program designed to teach high-school age youth from underserved neighborhoods to be sport coaches (Intrator & Siegel, 2008). The program is part of a Parks and Recreation initiative and runs at a middle school facility. The "coaches" teach elementary-age neighborhood children. Initially funded by a private donor, the program has focused on promoting the enrichment of children's school behavior and academic performance and also improves the health of a high-needs community. The basic tenet of the program is to explicitly connect certain life skills (called supercognitives in the program) to the sport experience provided by the coaches. At the same time, coaches also absorb the values of coaching and leading others—creating a sense of purpose and vision of future opportunity. Guided by the collective input of other community partners (e.g., school principals, Parks and Recreation center directors), Intrator and Siegel (2008) identified attributes that would be the desired outcomes gained from program experiences, which include (a) the ability to work with a

Table 13.3 SBYD Programs that Teach Life Skills

Program	Best Practices to Promote SEL	Source
Project Coach	Leadership opportunities that serve to teach life skills to younger inner-city kids, community engagement, empowerment	Intrator & Siegel, 2008
Project Leadership	Empowerment, opportunities to teach others life skills, involvement, self-evaluation, reflection	Gordon et al., 2016
Harlem RBI	Opportunity to coach and teach baseball and life skills to inner-city youth, community engagement, mentoring	Berlin et al., 2007
First Tee	Learn golf skills, emphasis on core life skills, reflection, goal setting, self-pacing, self-evaluation, progression of skill development ensured, positive adult-youth relationship established	Weiss et al., 2015
Girls Just Wanna Have Fun	Participate in a variety of physical activities, each focused on life skill (e.g., goal setting, responsibility, empowerment, working with others, communication)	Bean et al., 2014

Data from Bean, C. N., Forneris, T., & Halsall, T. (2014). Girls just wanna have fun: A process evaluation of a female youth-driven physical activity-based life skills program. *SpringerPlus, 3*(1), 401–415; Berlin, R. A., Dworkin, A., Eames, N., Menconi, A., & Perkins, D. F. (2007). Examples of sport-based youth development programs. *New Directions for Youth Development, 115,* 85–106; Gordon, B., Jacobs, J. M., & Wright, P. M. (2016). Social and emotional learning through a teaching personal and social responsibility based after-school program for disengaged middle school boys. *Journal of Teaching in Physical Education, 35*(4), 358–369; Intrator, S. M., & Siegel, D. (2008). Project coach: Youth development and academic achievement through sport. *Journal of Physical Education, Recreation, and Dance. 79*(7), 17–23; and Weiss, M. R., Bolter, N. D., & Kipp, L. E. (2015). Evaluation of The First Tee in promoting positive youth development: Group comparisons and longitudinal trends. *Research Quarterly for Exercise and Sport, 83*(3), 271–283.

team, (b) time management and punctuality, (c) the ability to manage and avoid conflict, (d) resilience, (e) tolerance, (f) self-discipline, (g) self-direction, (h) industriousness, (i) communication, (j) problem solving and resolution, (k) integrity, and (l) competitiveness. These qualities transcend various domains and are very similar to those identified in SEL skill development (Kahn et al., 2019)—especially those connected to cognitive regulation. The program was based on the *theory of change* concept that if coaches/teachers develop supercognitives such self-discipline, they could thrive in a variety of settings (Intrator & Siegel, 2008; Izzo et al., 2004). Achieving the broad range of outcomes was determined, in part, by a quantitative measure (i.e., Developmental Asset Profile; Search Institute, 2005) and the Youth Experience Survey (Larson et al., 2005). Documentation of staff discussions, focus groups, and one-on-one interviews of coaches and children have also served to determine the fidelity of Project Coach (Intrator & Siegel, 2008). Asset development for success in school, community endeavors, and employment were found to be bottom line outcomes, which included the acquisition leadership skills, improved goal setting, and community engagement.

Project Leadership

The idea of getting youth to interpret and control emotions, build positive relationships, develop strong social skills, become a goal setter, and make healthy choices are outcomes sought in Project Leadership (Gordon et al., 2016). Project Leadership runs twice a week at a middle school located near a university. The participants are 11- to 14 year-old boys, who are perceived to be disengaged with their school and are determined to be at risk for dropping out of school. This program looks directly at how a values-based model for leadership development connects to SEL competency acquisition. The program grew out of a partnership between a university and a nearby public middle school. The purpose of this program was to teach life skills (e.g., respect, effort, self-direction, leadership) through sport activities and for the students to apply these skills to their school and community. Both university students and a professor worked with referred youth from communities affected by poverty. The university coaches (i.e., students) were trained in delivering values-based learning experiences. Another feature of this program, the close contact with teachers, principal, and counselor(s), was maintained during the program. The teaching personal and social

responsibility (TPSR) model (Hellison, 2011) formed the basis for the training and program. As discussed more in Chapter 7, the TPSR model focuses on five main goals: (a) respect for one another, (b) participation and effort, (c) self-direction, (d) helping and leading others, and (e) applying values learned in the program outside of the gym. Each of these goals was intentionally tied to SEL elements. For example, respect was aligned with self-awareness and social-awareness and participation was connected to positive decision making. Evaluation was conducted through interviews and field notes that became the prime data sources. Three outcomes emerged from the data. One was that the approaches and strategies were interfaced well with SEL qualities such as improved self-management, social awareness, and positive decision making. Also, school personnel felt the program supported the SEL of the students in the classroom. Finally, the actual presence of SEL behaviors (i.e., self-awareness, social awareness, self-management, relational skills).

Harlem RBI (Runs Batted In)

In Harlem, New York, Harlem RBI, a non-profit SBYD program, was created where baseball and softball are offered to inner city youth (Berlin et al., 2007). Initially, the program only offered mentoring, a newsletter, and a youth summer camp. Realizing that the complex needs of the youth were not being addressed, an expansion of the program took place. Baseball and softball were added for the purpose of attracting "and holding" more youth participants. Sport teams were formed so the efforts to enhance social and academic development could be fortified.

The program teams emphasize physical activity and an awareness of healthy habits and social skills such as teamwork and communication that ultimately lead youth to make better life choices. All of the youth came from underserved neighborhoods. Consequently, they have had little opportunity to acquire the essential skills to be successful and have consistent positive relationships with adults and peers. The intent of the program is to have youth recognize their responsibility in achieving personal goals and in attaining connection to their team and community.

Many of the SEL elements form the foundation of the program's mission (i.e., emotional competencies, social skills, cognitive regulation). Harlem RBI runs the entire school year and is "grouped base" so that it offers support among peers. A low adult-to-youth ratio fosters connections between youth and caring role models. Staff and volunteers receive extensive training to ensure high-quality programming. An important aspect of the program is that high expectations are held for the participants. These expectations are varied according to each of the participant's needs and their life circumstances.

Evaluation of the program is an ongoing process involving surveys, focus groups, and other forms of data collection. Improved academic scores (e.g., reading, math) were indicated over a single year of program operation. The social and emotional indicators were also identified with improvement in ability to praise others, focus on self-improvement, and apply problem-solving skills when challenged. Formulating long-term goals is a mainstay of the program that will rely on various approaches (e.g., follow-up, longitudinal evaluation) to assess.

First Tee

In 1997, a partnership among the LPGA, the Masters Tournament, the PGA of America, the PGA TOUR, and the USGA initiated a program to get more kids involved with Golf. First Tee started as a way to bring an affordable junior golf program to communities that did not have access to golf facilities, especially in economically disadvantaged areas. For over 20 years, the First Tee program has provided the teaching of golf skills to youth and also long-term life skills (www.firsttee.org; Weiss et al., 2015.). The program has been implemented in schools, community youth serving centers, and on golf courses.

First Tee has an international presence in five countries such as Africa, South Korea Japan, Canada, and Mexico (Weiss et. al., 2015). Life-enhancing learning is the hallmark of this program. Nine core values guide the golf experiences of First Tee: (a) honesty, (b) integrity, (c) sportspersonship, (d) respect, (e) confidence, (f) responsibility, (g) perseverance, (h) courtesy, and (i) judgment. The program has been sponsored by the World Golf Foundation and over 20 other organizations, and coaches are provided values-based training on how SEL competencies can be integrated into golf lessons. The program is offered to a wide range of ages (5 to 18 years) and cuts across various economic levels. There is a special school program that has provided great support for enhancing the social and psychological qualities of students. Inservice training and equipment are offered as a support for teachers who are seeking to implement First Tee. Widening the future pathways of participating youth has been an important outgrowth of the program. Many of the past participants have come back to be coaches—indicating

the wraparound nature of the program (www.firsttee.org: Weiss et al., 2015). Community leadership has taken place from past participants through volunteerism and through financial support for programs. Schools have also indicated that the program has caused a decrease in referrals of misbehavior and improved academic performance. Engagement in school activities has also been a positive byproduct of program participation (Weiss et al., 2015).

Girls Just Wanna Have Fun (GJWHF)

The "Girls Just Wanna Have Fun" (GJWHF) program (Bean et al., 2014) was created in response to low participation in programs at local Boys and Girls Clubs in a community in Eastern Ontario, Canada. Only 19% of the total participants at the clubs were represented by girls. Something had to be done to attract girls. A partnership between university faculty and local Boys and Girls Club staff was formed. Together, they implemented a physical activity program for girls, 11 to 14 years old, which was values-based with three main goals related to (a) providing girls with opportunities to be physically active, (b) facilitating life-skills development, and (c) enabling opportunities for youth to have a voice. The values that were taught came from two frameworks. Specifically, the program draws on Hellison's (2011) TPSR model as well as Danish's (2012) Sport United to Promote Education and Recreation (SUPER) approach. The SUPER program focuses on goal setting, working with others, and confidence building. The values from both of these models interfaced with the principles of PYD and closely support the qualities of SEL. The GJWHF program is year-long and includes a variety of sport activities. Within each activity, life skills (i.e., communication, teamwork, responsibility, empowerment, goal setting, seeking help, confidence, and leadership) are integrated. Choices are given to the participants, such as selecting an activity with which to engage, choosing a life skill on which to focus, and having opportunities to lead younger youth in the Boys and Girls Club. Peer relationships were also enhanced through group meetings, which included discussions about the challenges and successes not only occurring in the club but also in their own lives. Personal reflection became a significant part of this experience.

Evaluation was accomplished through a mixed-methods approach. Semi-structured interviews, questionnaires, and personal logs were main data sources. The data showed that the GJWHF program provided trusting relationships and a caring environment. Many of the girls felt the integration of life skills and that there was a physical and psychological safe environment in which to participate. This helped them to be themselves. The integration of life skills was a big factor in their perception of pursuing future goals, ability to control emotional urges, and to be a leader in their school and community.

Conclusions

SBYD programs have been inspired by the PYD movement to provide positive experiences to youth via sport participation that help them develop assets that can be used in their current lives and in their future (Fraser-Thomas et al., 2005; Holt, 2016; Turnbridge et al., 2014, Weiss, 2016). As the research in this area has grown, it is clear that SBYD programs can help youth develop social and emotional learning skills across the five domains of SEL defined by CASEL (2014), which include responsible decision making, relationship skills, social awareness, self-awareness, and self-management. Holt and colleagues (2016) suggest that coaches, parents, peers, and other leaders establish a climate that enables youth to have

experiences that promote social and emotional learning. These programs are also distinguished by a clear focus on teaching life skills through sports and promoting the transfer of life skills beyond the specific sport context. When implemented effectively, SBYD outcomes were found across several domains of learning related to positive personal, social, and physical development.

In this chapter, we have provided an overview of the historical development of SBYD and provided examples of exemplary programs. These programs promote SEL and suggest that SBYD has something to offer to the SEL movement. SBYD programs often have unique features, but scholars are building consensus around a working definition of SBYD. This definition suggests that SBYD can include all forms of organized and adult-supervised physical activity that is provided to school-aged children of both genders and for members of different ethnic and cultural groups. These programs aim to teach different life skills to youth that can be generalized to other settings and offers value to both the individual and to the community. Physical development is a unique aspect of SBYD that distinguishes it from PYD (Holt, Deal, & Smyth, 2016).

Questions for Discussion

1. In using SBYD programming to enhance the qualities of SEL, what kind of considerations would need to be made when applying the programs to different age groups (i.e., elementary, middle, secondary school age)?
2. In this chapter, we discussed how SBYD programming can take place in a variety of contexts. A common focus for these programs is how they fostered on qualities that connected to SEL. In order to see how these programs have a direct impact on the school and home settings, what types of "follow-ups" would best serve this purpose?
3. After reading this chapter, describe three important "take-aways" that impressed you the most. Why?
4. The CASEL model for SEL identifies five areas of student learning outcomes. Discuss how each of these areas were achieved in SBYD programs that are featured in the chapter. Are there any of the five elements that are more or less prominent in SBYD programs?
5. Are there particular social and emotional skills that you believe are important to foster in SBYD programs?

References

Agee, V. L. (1979). *Treatment of the violent incorrigible adolescent.* Lexington, MA: Lexington Heath Books.

Albrecht, J., & Strand, B. (2010). A review of organized youth sport in the United States. *Youth First: The Journal of Youth Sports, 5*(1), 16–20.

Anderson, L. (2008). The 40 developmental assets of inclusion. *Voice,* Winter, 3031.

Aspen Institute (2018). *State of play: 2018 trends and developments.* Washington, DC: The Aspen Institute.

Bean, C. N., Forneris, T., & Halsall, T. (2014). Girls just wanna have fun: A process evaluation of a female youth-driven physical activity-based life skills program. *SpringerPlus, 3*(1), 401–415.

Berlin, R. A., Dworkin, A., Eames, N., Menconi, A., & Perkins, D. F. (2007). Examples of sport-based youth development programs. *New Directions for Youth Development, 007*(115), 85–106.

Bronfenbrenner, U. (1979). *The ecology of human development: Experiments by nature and design.* Cambridge, MA: Harvard University Press.

Bumpass, L., & Lu, H.-H. (2000). Trends in cohabitation and implications for children's family contexts in the United States. *Population Studies, 54*(1), 29–41.

Bundick, M. J., Yeager, D. S., King, P. E., & Damon, W. (2010). Thriving across the life span. In W. F. Overton & R. M. Lerner (Eds.), *The handbook of life-span development, Vol. 1. Cognition, biology, and methods* (pp. 882–923). New York, NY: Wiley.

Camiré, M., & Kendellen, K. (2016). Coaching for positive youth development in high school sport. In N. L. Holt (Ed.), *Positive Youth Development through Sport* (pp. 126–136).

Camiré, M., Forneris, T., Trudel, P., & Bernard, D. (2011). Strategies for helping coaches facilitate positive youth development through sport. *Journal of Sport Psychology in Action, 2*(2), 92–99.

CASEL. (2020). What is social emotional learning. Accessed 5/04/20 from https://casel.squarespace.com/social-and-emotional -learning

Catalano, R. F., Hawkins, D. J., & Toumbourou, J. W. (2008). *Positive youth development in the United States: History, efficacy, and links to moral and character education.* New York, NY: Routledge.

Clarke, R. V., & Cornish, D. B. (1977). The effectiveness of residential treatment for delinquents. *Journal of Child Psychology and Psychiatry, 1,* 143–159.

Cloward, R. A. & Ohlin, L. E. (1960). *Delinquency and opportunity: A study of delinquent gangs.* New York, NY: Free Press.

Coakley, J. (2010). The "logic" of specialization: Using children for adult purposes. *Journal of Physical Education, Recreation & Dance, 81*(8), 16–25.

Coakley, J. (2016). Positive youth development through sport: Myths, beliefs, and realities. In N. Holt's (Ed.) *Positive Youth Development Though Sport,* (pp. 21–33). New York, NY: Routledge.

Coakley, J. (2017). *Sport and society: Issues and controversies.* New York, NY: McGraw-Hill Education.

Côté, J., & Vierimaa, M. (2014). The developmental model of sport participation: 15 years after its first conceptualization. *Science & Sports, 29,* S63–S69.

Cooper, J. R., Altman, F., Brown, B. S., & Czechowicz, D. (Eds.). (1983). *Research on the treatment of narcotic addiction: Treatment research monograph series.* Rockville, MD: National Institute on Drug Abuse.

Curtner-Smith, M. D., Hastie, P. A., & Kinchin, G. D. (2008). Influence of occupational socialization on beginning teachers' interpretation and delivery of sport education. *Sport, Education and Society, 13*(1), 97 117.

Danish, S. J., Forneris, T., Hodge, K., & Heke, I. (2004). Enhancing youth development through sport. *World Leisure Journal, 46*(3), 38–49.

De Leon, G., & Ziegenfuss, J. T. (Eds.). (1986). *Therapeutic communities for addictions: Readings in theory, research, and practice.* Springfield, IL: Charles C. Thomas.

DeWitt-Wallace Reader's Digest Fund (1995). *Strengthening the youth work profession.* New York: Author.

Durlak, J. A., Weissberg, R. P., & Pachan, M. (2010). A meta-analysis of after-school programs that seek to promote personal and social skills in children and adolescents. *American Journal of Community Psychology, 45*(3–4), 294–309.

Fraser-Thomas, J. L., Côté, J., & Deakin, J. (2005). Youth sports programs: An avenue to foster positive youth development. *Physical Education and Sport Pedagogy, 10*(1), 19–40.

Friedman, A., & Beschnes, G. (1985). *Treatment services for adolescent substance abusers.* Rockville, MD: US Department of Health and Human Serves.

Gold, M., & Mann, D. W. (1984). *Expelled to a friendlier place: A study of effective alternative schools.* Ann Arbor, MI: University of Michigan Press.

Gordon, B., Jacobs, J. M., & Wright, P. M. (2016). Social and emotional learning through a teaching personal and social responsibility based after-school program for disengaged middle school boys. *Journal of Teaching in Physical Education, 35*(4), 358–369.

Halpern, R. (2006). After-school matters in Chicago: Apprenticeship as a model for youth programming. *Youth & Society, 38*(2), 203–235.

Hellison, D. (2011). *Teaching responsibility through physical activity.* Champaign, IL: Human Kinetics.

Hemphill, M., & Martinek, T. (2019). Using simple interactions to improve pedagogy in a cross-aged leadership program. *Journal of Teaching Physical Education, 39*(1), 126–130.

Hirsch, B. J. (2005). *A place to call home: After-school programs for urban youth.* Washington, DC: American Psychological Association.

Hirsch, E. D. (2009). *The making of Americans: Democracy and our schools.* New Haven, CT: Yale University Press.

Holt, N. (2016). *Positive youth development through sport.* NY, New York: Routledge.

Holt, N. L., Kingsley, B. C., Tink, L. N., & Scherer, J. (2011). Benefits and challenges associated with sport participation by children and parents from low-income families. *Psychology of Sport and Exercise, 12*(5), 490–499.

Holt, N. L., Deal, C. J., & Smyth, C. L. (2016). Future directions for positive youth development through sports. In N. L. Holt (Ed.). *Positive youth development through physical activity* (pp. 229–240). NY, New York: Routledge.

Holt, N. L., Neely, K. C., Slater, L. G., Camiré, M., Côté, J., Fraser-Thomas, J., MacDonald, D., & Strachan, L. (2017). A grounded theory of positive youth development through sport based on results from a qualitative meta-study. *International Review of Sport and Exercise Psychology, 10*(1), 1–49.

Intrator, S. M., & Siegel, D. (2008). Project coach: Youth development and academic achievement through sport. *Journal of Physical Education, Recreation & Dance. 79*(7), 17–24.

Izzo, C. V., Connell, J.P., Gambone, M. A., and Bradshaw, C. P. (2004). Understanding and improving youth development initiatives through evaluation. In S. F. Hamilton and M.A. Hamilton (Eds.) *The youth development handbook—Coming of age in American communities* (301–326). Thousand Oaks, CA: Sage Publications.

Jones, S., Farrington, C., Jagers, R., Bracket, M., & Kahn, J. (2019). *A research agenda for the next generation.* Washington, DC: The Aspen Institute National Commission of Social Emotional, and Academic Development.

Kahn, J., Bailey, R., & Jones, S. (2019). *Coaching social & emotional skills in youth sports.* Washington, DC: The Aspen Institute.

Kirk, D. (2013). Educational value and models-based practice in physical education. *Educational Philosophy and Theory, 45*(9), 973–986.

Larson, R., Jarrett, R., & Hanson, D. (2005). *The YES survey instrument.* Unpublished manuscript. Retrieved from http.// web.aces.uiuc.edu/youdev/yesinstrument.htm.

Lerner, R. (2006). Developmental science, developmental systems, and contemporary theories of human development. In W. Damon and R.M. Lerner (Eds.) *Handbook of Child Psychology* (pp. 1–17), New York: Wiley.

Lerner, R. M., Lerner, J. V., Bowers, E. P., & Geldhof, G. J. (2015). Positive youth development and relational-developmental-systems. In W. F. Overton, P. C. M. Molenaar, & R. M. Lerner

(Eds.), *Handbook of Child Psychology and Developmental Science: Theory and Method* (p. 607–651). New York, NY: Wiley.

Martinek, T. J. (1996). Fostering hope in youth: A model for explaining learned helplessness in physical activity. *Quest, 48*(3), 409–421.

Martinek, T., & Hellison, D. (2016). Learning responsibility through sport and physical activity. In D. Holt (Ed.) *Positive youth development through physical activity* (pp. 180–190). New York, NY: Routledge.

Martinek, T., Schilling, T., & Hellison, D. (2006). The development of compassionate and caring leadership among adolescents. *Physical Education and Sport Pedagogy, 11*(2), 141–157.

McLaughlin, M.W. (2000). *Community counts: How youth organizations matter for youth development.* Washington, DC: Public Education Network.

National Research Council and Institute of Medicine (2002). *Community programs to promote youth development.* Washington, DC: The National Academies Press.

Noddings, N. (2003). *Caring: A feminine approach to ethics and moral education.* Berkeley, CA: University of California Press.

Pittman, K. J., & Fleming, W. E. (1991). *A new vision: Promoting youth development.* Written transcript of live testimony given before the House Select Committee on Children, Youth, and Families. Washington, DC: Center for Youth Development and Policy Research.

Ryan, R. M., & Deci, E. L. (2000). Self-determination theory and the facilitation of intrinsic motivation, social development, and well-being. *American Psychologist, 55*(1), 68–78.

Scales, P. C., Benson, P. L., Leffert, N., & Blyth, D. A. (2000). Contributions of developmental assets to the prediction of thriving among adolescents. *Applied Developmental Science, 4*(1), 27–46.

Search Institute (2005). *Developmental assets profile.* Minneapolis, MN: Search Institute.

Seligman, M. (2018) *The hope circuit.* New York, NY: The Hatchet Book Group.

Turnnidge, J., Côté, J., & Hancock, D. J. (2014). Positive youth development from sport to life: Explicit or implicit transfer. *Quest, 66*(2), 203–217.

Weiss, M. R., Bolter, N. D., & Kipp, L. E. (2015). Evaluation of *The First Tee* in promoting positive youth development: Group comparisons and longitudinal trends. *Research Quarterly for Exercise and Sport, 87*(3), 271–283.

Witt, P. A. (2018). Why and how youth services were developed. In P. A. Witt & L. L. Caldwell (Eds.), *Youth development principles and practices in out-of-school time settings* (pp.107–122) Champaign, IL: Sagamore-Venture.

Witt, P. A. & Caldwell, L. L. (2018). *Youth development principles and practices in out-of-school time settings.* Champaign, IL: Sagamore-Venture.

CHAPTER 14

Social Justice and SEL: Case Examples of Promising Practices

James D. Ressler

Brian Culp

Dillon Landi

Jeffrey Bainbridge

CHAPTER SUMMARY

Physical education is well positioned to integrate Social and Emotional Learning (SEL) into its teaching and learning practices. In addition, there is a pressing need to integrate social justice education (SJE) principles into physical education. This chapter presents specific examples of physical education experiences prioritizes SEL approaches that are hybridized with components of SJE. We examine four different cases of SEL and how to integrate SJE into those examples. As such, we argue that the SJE and SEL combined approach gives students and teachers the opportunity to examine and challenge inequitable conditions in physical education. To do so, we use Hackman's (2005) components for SJE as an understanding of SJE as both a goal and a process (Bell, 1997). Descriptions of these interactions in physical education (PE) are critiqued with realistic application of PE engagement and with suggestions for immediate, improved instruction.

Background and Overview

Thus far in this book, our colleagues have provided a detailed history and numerous examples of social and emotional learning (SEL) in physical education (PE). Indeed, one way to conceptualize SEL is to consider it an "umbrella term for the many different kinds of prevention programs that draw from public health, mental health, and juvenile justice" (Desai et al., 2014). The important word in the above definition is *prevention*. Different approaches to SEL have emerged since the 1990s in response to children's vulnerability to social and psychological problems (Hoffmann, 2009). Given this, schools were identified as one such place where we can work with youth to *prevent* the harmful effects of social and mental issues and improve academic achievement. Thus, it comes as no surprise that the subject of PE is considered "well positioned" to integrate SEL into our practices.

On the face of it, there is a lot of synergy between SEL and PE. Some have suggested that the Collaborative for Academic, Social, and Emotional Learning's (CASEL, 2019) five core competencies (i.e., self-awareness, self-management, social awareness, relationship skills, and decision making) could be a pared down composition of affective understanding in PE (Ciotto & Gagnon, 2018). This is because well-designed SEL programs have been shown to be associated with positive emotional, behavioral, social, and even academic outcomes (Durlak et al., 2011). Not to mention, SEL approaches generally work better in integrated and relational contexts (Jones et al., 2008).

Upon further reflection; however, we also wonder if our inclination toward SEL is due to the similar underlying philosophies that SEL and PE share. In other words, perhaps the common synergy between SEL and PE is based on their shared philosophical orientations. This is not to say that all PE philosophical orientations align with SEL (for example, public health approaches do not), but many education-based PE approaches do. Take the Teaching for Personal and Social Responsibility (TPSR) model (see Chapter 7; Hellison, 2011) as an example. The TPSR model is underpinned by the value that "physical development must take place side by side with emotional, social, and cognitive development" (Hellison, 2011, p. 18). Another example is the Sport Education model (see Chapter 8; Siedentop et al., 2011), which works to provide a PE experience that "will nurture healthy physical, psychological, and emotional development in children and youth" (p. 10). The way in which these models, along with several others discussed in this text and described elsewhere, focus on psychological, emotional, and social development align well with a SEL framework. Given their shared philosophical orientation, we argue that PE and SEL may also share similar limitations, or weaknesses.

Pedagogical models, like TPSR and Sport Education, have been considered one way to advance teaching in PE (Kirk, 2010). In other words, models-based practices have worked to shift PE from a multiactivity approach where students rarely learn in short units toward more in-depth learning experiences (Casey, 2014). In our opinion, SEL has many similar features to models-based practices. For example, SEL has non-negotiable principles that are integrated through a unit of instruction (Metzler, 2011) and is also underpinned by theories of learning and broader psychology. Yet, all models come with limitations. In PE, many pedagogical models, with few exceptions, have a major limitation in their ability to address issues of equity (Landi et al., 2016). Thus, Casey and Macphail (2018) argued that models should be hybridized (or combined) in order to address limitations that they may have individually.

Like models-based practices, SEL has also been criticized for its inability to address issues of equity (see, for example Kirshner, 2015). This led CASEL's

Vice President of Research, Robert Jagers and colleagues (2018) to develop a framework that encouraged teachers and researchers to hybridize (Jagers used the term integrate) other approaches such as culturally relevant pedagogy, equity content, and identity theory into the CASEL framework. Therefore, because of the similar philosophical orientation between PE and SEL, they also share similar limitations. Thus, it is not appropriate for SEL to completely replace PE's affective domain (as previously discussed), but there is promise in hybridizing SEL with PE models, *and* a socially just framework. In this chapter, we explain why social justice is needed in PE. We then outline Hackman's (2005) five essential components to social justice that could be hybridized into SEL. After outlining the components, we provide case examples of what this hybridization looks like in practice. The chapter concludes with some reflective questions and further readings.

Why Is Social Justice Important in PE?

There are a litany of social justice issues that persist in current communities that are wide ranging, diverse, and impactful for the quality of life for many individuals. Reflecting on this decade, one could point to the Black Lives Matter movement, the Me Too movement, Brexit, children being locked in cages at the United States/Mexican border, the "gig" economy, increase in gun violence, increase in suicide attempts and deaths by suicide, the largest wealth gap since the great depression, and health crises (e.g., COVID-19, others) as indicators of inequity. Under these concerns, educators more broadly have called for social justice, equity, and dismantling systems founded in white supremacy to be treated as issues to address as core requirements in schools. Moreover, there are scholars within physical education making similar claims and calls (Clark, 2019; Culp, 2016; Harrison & Clark, 2016; Hodge, 2014; Kirk, 2010; Walton-Fisette et al., 2019). Particular to this book, we aim to add to these calls by examining how a lens focusing on building equity in schools and fighting for social justice can be integrated into SEL practices.

Bell (1997) offers a description of social justice as a *goal* and a *process* that presents a clear, viable, and sustainable vision for equity. The *goal* of social justice is full and equitable participation of people from all social identity groups in a society that is mutually shaped to meet their needs (p. 34). As health and physical educators, this seems pretty straightforward. We want all persons (regardless of demographics, background, social class, etc.) to be able to fully participate in health and physical activity settings. As such, we cannot imagine anybody in our field not agreeing with social justice from this standpoint.

According to Bell (1997); however, attaining the goal of social justice is also a *process*. By process, Bell means that social justice aims to be democratic, participatory, inclusive, respectful of human diversity, and collaborative. This idea of social justice as a process is important because it means that it is: (a) continuous and never-ending, (b) requires multiple people and relationships, and (c) emphasizes agency and identity as a collective concern. Thus, social justice is a *process* that works toward a fair distribution of resources between people because this helps to sustain physical and psychological safety. By creating an environment that works toward the goal of social justice, individuals then have the ability to reach their full potential (Bell, 1997).

The *process* side of things, in our opinion, is where things get a bit "sticky" (Ahmed, 2010). Even though there may be acceptance and understanding on the *goal*, it is the *process* that people do not agree on. Like PE more broadly, SEL takes the view of focusing on the individual, whereas the social justice approach balances individual needs with the social needs. Thus, from a social justice perspective, if the goal is to provide a *process* that allows individuals to meet their full potential, the environment has to be set up in a way that allows this to occur. In other words, a social justice approach recognizes that agency is heavily influenced by environment, resources, and the different relationships that people enter into. As such, by focusing on social justice as a *process*, it highlights those relational and environmental needs in order to help all students, regardless of their background.

Research suggests that children who are exposed to prejudice and racism are socialized to embrace and accept it, even when they might not understand the feelings that go along with these ideas (Banaji & Greenwald, 2013). Thus, emphasizing social justice as a *goal* and *process* in physical education is timely and may provide different opportunities for youth to cultivate prosocial behaviors. Considering social justice education as a goal and process (Bell, 1997), one part of this process is to connect content to students' lived experiences so what we teach has meaning. By bringing students' lived experiences into the fold, teachers can challenge students to be informed, critically think, recognize inequalities, and see different perspectives in the hopes of helping to solve problems in their own communities.

It is important to note that teachers do not decide or teach content as either "right" or "wrong." A major misconception of social justice education is that it

works to indoctrinate youth into a certain political viewpoint (Bell, 1997). This is not the *process*. Rather, appropriate social justice education promotes critical thinking by engaging with topics that are uncomfortable to discuss. Indeed, this may cause students to be defensive; however, it is through this discomfort that students can challenge their own, and other classmates, preconceived ideas in order for them to grow (Hackman, 2005). Through this *process* of engaging with difficult concepts, students are challenged to think beyond their own needs with the *goal* of transforming environments to make them more inclusive (and this may look different based on the setting). Thus, the goal is not to "change" one's opinion; rather, it is to provide students with the opportunity to understand and sympathize with other perspectives in order to come to a common place of mutual respect.

In order to address inequities and social justices, we should consider the different frameworks that align to these ideals. While the scope of this chapter does not allow for an in-depth discussion of all frameworks, we want the reader to know that there are multiple approaches to social justice. Each of these approaches has the same *goal*, but the way they achieve that goal is different. Therefore, each social justice framework has a different *process*. In this chapter, we chose to draw on Hackman's (2005) concept and process of social justice. We do not claim this is the "best" or "correct" approach. We do claim; however, that this approach helps us frame teaching and learning in socially just ways. In the next section, we claim that Hackman's (2005) principles of social justice could be understood as a camera by which we examine the teaching and learning process of SEL in PE.

Using a Social Justice Camera: Principles of Social Justice Education

In this section, we are concerned with the *process* of social justice. To do so, we draw on Heather Hackman's five essential components of social justice (Hackman, 2005). We use Hackman's essential components as a sort of camera, or lens, by which to analyze our own teaching process. By using a social justice camera, it helps teachers to examine systems of power and oppression; and importantly, figure out ways for teachers to address those issues in class. The five components (or lenses) that make up our social justice camera are: (a) content mastery, (b) tools for critical analysis, (c) tools for social change, (d) tools for personal reflection, and (e) multicultural group dynamics.

Content Mastery

According to Hackman (2005), the first component to social justice is a deep mastery of content. Content mastery is foundational because if students are going to critically think about content, they first must understand the content. Yet, a deep understanding of content is not merely memorizing facts. Rather, it is understanding something from multiple perspectives. Let's take, as an example, the game of lacrosse as content in physical education. A portion of content mastery for lacrosse would require students to know and be able to perform skills. Such mastery would also include understanding the rules of the games as well as offensive and defensive tactics. Yet, mastery also includes the things that are often omitted in physical education. This includes the rituals and cultural norms of lacrosse, its Indigenous roots, and psychological and sociological factors that influence lacrosse participation.

What we are arguing for here is in line with previous scholars in physical education (Kirk, 2010). Good pedagogical practice means that any content that is taught must be done so through multiple lenses (e.g., biomechanical, sociological, psychological) and in enough depth (not breadth) so the student has a deep understanding of content. By having a deep understanding, students understand the content from a micro perspective (individual games), meso perspective (leagues and regional influences), and macro perspectives (demography and other historical processes). By understanding content in deep and meaningful ways, students have a foundation from which to critically think about content in relation to their own lives and communities. In order to critically think about these ideas, Hackman also offers tools for critical analysis.

Tools for Critical Analysis

Hackman's (2005) second component (lens) of social justice is having tools to critically analyze situations. As Hackman (2005) notes, "the mere possession of information does not necessarily translate into wisdom or deep knowledge" (p. 105). Rather, whenever students receive information, they should be encouraged to critically analyze this information. Critically analyzing information starts with considering the knowledge from multiple perspectives (e.g., psychological, sociological, biomedical). In addition to using multiple perspectives, critical thinking encourages students to move beyond their *own* interpretation or perspective and consider how others may perceive this same information. In other words, whenever a

student receives information, they should consider: do my classmates, teachers, or community members feel the same about this as I do? Another question a young person might ask is, how does power affect this situation? For example, who has access to physical activity based on gender, social class, ethnicity, race, and other factors; and why? Lastly, if youth do see an issue after analyzing a situation, they should be given the opportunity to create an alternative solution where access is equitable.

Thus, Hackman offers us four ways to critically think about information: (a) use multiple perspectives (e.g., psychological, sociological, biomedical), (b) consider how others perceive the information (e.g. mother, friend, senior citizen), (c) think about power relations (e.g., who has privilege in this setting and who doesn't?), and (d) consider what alternatives could exist (e.g., how can I change this to make it better?). Let's try and use these four tools in an applicable situation: the SHAPE America Standards (2014). According to the introduction of the SHAPE America (2014) national standards, the authors claimed, "in general, girls are less physically active than boys, and as they age, that trend continues or worsens" (p. 7). Indeed, this statement is true, but the way that it is delivered is ahistorical. In other words, from a public health perspective, it is true that young women and girls are less physically active than boys.

Rather than "accept" the information without critically analyzing it, let's use Hackman's tools. For example, we need to consider that sociologists have found that young women and girls are socialized into activities that require less physical activity (using multiple perspectives). Not to mention, young women and girls may perceive this statement differently from how it is written. In fact, many young women have argued that they want to be physically active but are not given the same opportunities as men (Cahn, 1994) (how others perceive this information). When we consider the unequal ways in which men's sports are funded at increasingly higher levels than women's sports (power relations), is it fair to state that young girls are less physically active? In fact, what would physical activity levels for girls look like if we did provide additional funding, socialized them into sports, and placed girls' interests at the heart of recreation programs (consider alternatives)?

The above example provides an illustration of how we can think critically about information. Instead of reinforcing the idea that young women and girls are not physically active; by drawing on the different tools, it paints a more complex picture of the statement. In so doing, different factors are highlighted that would normally be neglected and potentially reproduce an environment in which girls receive fewer opportunities. As such, critical thinking is not only important because it provides opportunities for students to think deeply about information but it also allows the student to consider different perspectives during this thought process. Thus, the statement in SHAPE America's (2014) national standards document can be questioned and deconstructed when we engage in critical thinking and consider the statement from multiple vantage points. It is not just important to critique things; however, because we also need to change things for the future.

Tools for Action and Social Change

It is not enough to just "teach about" social inequity through critical analysis. Indeed, if we just talk about "how bad it is," but then do nothing, we are part of the problem! In fact, upon learning about the litany of injustices through critical analysis, many students may leave the class feeling guilty, defeated, or even hopeless (Hackman, 2005). That is why Hackman (2005) argues that we need to work toward taking action and promoting social change. In this spirit, whenever teachers use critical tools for analysis, they should also promote ideas or activities to *shift* the environment and change the inequalities that are identified. As argued in Chapter 3, an approach of empowerment (i.e., sharing responsibility with students, promoting student transfer of learning) to teaching SEL in physical education is not common practice but research indicates it should be promoted as an important part of best practice.

In New Zealand, the physical education curriculum (Ministry of Education, 2007) requires students to do service-learning projects where they work to help their communities. In doing so, students engage in health promotion activities that are "reimagined, not as individualistic, but as an opportunity for young people to forward social justice aims, and to advocate and campaign for more equitable schools and communities" (Fitzpatrick, 2018, p. 6). In other words, students are posed with particular problems within their communities and use the above analysis tools to get at the heart of the problem from different angles. After the students deliberate this problem together, they then develop local solutions to the problem to enhance problem solving in their communities. Thus, physical education in New Zealand is not bound to a single gymnasium or classroom but rather extends into the lived experiences and communities of the youth who engage with it (Fitzpatrick, 2013).

Tools for Personal Reflection

Self-reflection is an integral part of progressing as a human being. When it comes to social justice education, both teachers and students need to reflect on their experiences. Unique to social justice education, however, is that reflection needs to be taught in relation to *power*, control, and authority. Power is a natural part of our world. Yet, if we are trying to be more inclusive, we want to distribute power more equally (Hackman, 2005). In schools, those dynamics are present between the teacher and students—as well as among students. Indeed, complete equity is never truly attainable (Hackman, 2005) and this is why social justice education is always *process* toward a *goal*. Yet, by reflecting on our own context and situation, it helps teachers and students to recognize their own role around power in relation to others.

In physical education, certain people have more power than others. For example, the teacher can exercise significant power in a classroom by virtue of them assigning grades to students. Students also have the ability to exercise power in different ways. For example, higher skilled students have the ability to control gameplay and who participates in activities. More popular students can exercise power on less popular students. Students with greater knowledge in a game can use that knowledge to outwit their classmates. Thus, it is important to embed activities that force students to reflect on this power. This can be done by asking questions such as, "how can you use your higher skills to help others?" "In what ways can your popularity be used to shift the climate of the class from exclusive to inclusive?" and "how can your knowledge of a game be used to socialize others into school culture?" By creating opportunities for students (and teachers) to reflect on the power they have, how that power can be a force for good, and what they can do to help others; reflection becomes a part of the social change process.

Multicultural Group Dynamics

The last component of Hackman's (2005) social justice education is being aware of the dynamic nature of relationships that surface when diverse people come together. In other words, the people who make up a class can influence the engagement and interactions of the class. For example, Landi (2019) has shown that the presence of queer people of color have the ability to shift the way masculinity is understood in PE. Others, such as Blackshear (2020) and Simon (2018), have argued that having a Black teacher shapes the way content is taught and often results in more culturally relevant practice. Given that it has been shown that student-centered (Fitzpatrick, 2013) and student-activist (Oliver & Kirk, 2015) approaches are effective forms of teaching in PE, it is even more important for educators to consider the group dynamics of their gymnasium.

In addition to paying attention to the class dynamics, there are additional things that teachers should consider. For example, just because someone from a minority group is not in the class doesn't mean the teacher should not teach about that particular group. For example, just because there may not be a person of color in a classroom does not mean the teacher should not teach about race/ethnicity. To that end, just because there is a minority in a particular class (say a person who identifies as LGBTQ+) does not mean they are the "expert" and represent all beliefs that fall in the LGBTQ+ rainbow. Taken together, it is important to remember that (a) teaching these issues is just as important (some would argue more) to students from privileged backgrounds and (b) we do not create environments where minority students feel they have to speak on behalf of all members of the communities to which they belong. Thus, activities should feel uncomfortable, but as long as the teacher lays down ground rules in advance, a mutual level of respect can be attained.

Our Social Justice Camera: Case Studies of Integrating SJE into SEL and PE

Now that we have outlined the five different components—we want you to consider them as different lenses to a "social justice camera." As noted previously, neither SEL nor models-based practice have an inherent focus on social justice issues. Thus, by looking at SEL practices through our "social justice camera," we can critically analyze an activity and alter it by using one of the above lenses to enrich and enhance students' learning. Below, we provide different examples of how teachers integrate SEL practices into PE. We also provide four different levels of focus to give additional perspective of the scope and relevance of SEL and SJE in PE spaces. Thus, we start at the program level by showing an example of a PE Leaders program. In this example, we examine how a youth-centered leaders program that already addresses SEL components can integrate social justice. We then take a case from a "course" level. At this level, we examine how a class created by a teacher to address SEL could benefit from social justice principles. After the course level, we then use the case of two specific teachers. In this example, both teachers attended an SEL workshop but they had vastly different applications of what they learned. As such, we highlight the differences between how a teacher may use an SEL-only approach and compare it with how a teacher may conduct an SEL and SJE hybrid approach. In our last case, we look at a specific activity that is used in SEL physical education (Minefield!). We examine how the game does not address issues of equity and diversity and then adapt the game using SJE principles. At each level, we argue that SJE hybridized with SEL has the potential to bolster learning, make learning meaningful, and address critical thinking skills.

Case Example #1: Physical Education Leaders Program

School PE programs offer a venue to present teaching and learning opportunities with a wide range of outcomes including SEL. Some of these SEL outcomes include cultivating leadership through providing opportunities in local communities and initiating programs (Gould & Voelker, 2012). As a regularly addressed SEL theme in a PE program, leadership can elevate the meaning and purpose of a curriculum and connect it to the lived experiences of the youth. The context in which leadership is represented in PE could include multiple activities, interactions among students and with teachers, and of course, practical applications for in-school and out-of-school environments.

An example that highlights SEL themes in action, in a PE environment, is the Physical Education Leaders (PEL) program at West Aurora High School (West) in Aurora, Illinois. West is a large, suburban/urban school with an enrollment of 3,500 students. The PEL program at West is an elective course for students in grades 10–12 that emphasizes leadership skills through a range of engagement patterns that are not available in traditional PE curricular course offerings. The program requires an admission process that includes a teacher recommendation, personal statement, and interview. The PEL program at West begins with an introductory, 18-week course (i.e., PEL Seminar) that shares time between classroom discussion and academic foundations for leadership in the program at West (MacGregor, 2007). To do this, we set up learning activities through small-group discussions, peer facilitations, advocacy projects, formative quizzes, and practice sessions on effective teaching and learning in PE environments.

The most popular role in PEL is serving as a co-teacher with one of the 18 full-time PE teachers at West. A key function of the course is to demonstrate responsibility with and for other students in the PE classes. Upon completion of the PEL Seminar, each leader is partnered with a teacher for the next academic term to assume some managerial and instructional duties as negotiated with the teacher. The direct experiences of each student may differ based on their comfort and readiness, as well as the effort of the PE teacher to integrate the support into daily instruction. The teacher's comfort with shifting from teaching to facilitation in their environment may also affect how involved the PEL student is in planned activities. Example tasks that a PEL youth may be asked to perform include leading warm-up routines, demonstrating new skills, creating and administering informal assessments, and integrating SEL principles across all instructional tasks.

At its core, the PEL program aims for the deliberate teaching and learning of leadership principles through the PE program. One such common practice is naming leadership concepts (e.g., honesty, integrity, advocacy, community service) and guiding discussions in a one-sided, direct instruction-type format. In practice, youth leaders at West are expected to support and develop activities in their assigned classes that often resemble traditional physical activities and games. While the opportunity exists to challenge the status quo, it is less likely for action and revision to gain traction in one-off classes or in isolation with one of the many PE staff at West. The current practice among the PEL program and its youth leaders often centers on the practical application of leadership skills and efforts to transfer them beyond the contained, class level of each PE setting at West.

When examining the PEL program through our social justice camera, we are flooded with potential innovation for action and social change. While current practice may identify "issues" or "problems" in the school such as truancy, academic achievement, and appreciation of diversity, a more active switch to explore alternative possibilities could energize small groups of students to advance the quality of unjust circumstances to benefit everyone. While the venue may be founded in PE because of a recognized need for more attention to personal and social interactions, the good work of PEL "leaders" could be noticed everywhere! In the example below, we chose to integrate two of Hackman's (2005) principles: (a) personal reflection and (b) multicultural dynamics.

Students are reminded regularly, but not always explicitly, that leadership is viewed as a skill to be practiced and used as a common theme in all activities. One could envision a committed, driven physical educator to teach in pursuit of social justice, and call and challenge the conditions as they exist for everyone. Such a teacher would personally reflect (perhaps using critical tools) on their own positioning in the classroom. In other words, as a teacher—they may consider the power they wield and how that structures what happens in PE. By recognizing this power dynamic, and looking to change it, the teacher may shift to more of a facilitation role than direct teaching. In so doing, the dynamics of the class change because balance of power is shifted to youth PEL leaders. As such, teachers look beyond their own perspective of power, insulation, and protection; but rather, excite their students through empowerment and changing the dynamics of the class.

As a PEL leader co-teaches with their assigned PE instructor during a co-ed team sport lesson, conversations and proper action could be more quickly implemented when issues of power, skillfulness, confidence, knowledge, and body image are present. Personal reflection may become easier for students because it is run by peers—rather than an adult who comes from a different culture. Thus, social justice education becomes a priority for effective teaching and learning in PE (and everywhere else) because it includes a commitment to continuous and formative checks of youth-driven implementation.

Lastly, we suggest taking another step in the process and goal of SJE. Borrowing a strategy from experiential educator Laurie Frank (2013), we call upon a regular exercise of naming themes or concepts as well as issues or barriers as they exist or emerge around the learning environment and beyond. Frank (2013) uses the structure of what each construct *looks like, feels like, and sounds like* as a way to refine conversation using more descriptive personal experiences, explaining lived truths, and sharing both realistic and metaphorical examples that hold meaning among individuals and groups in the given community (classroom). Such an approach provides a guided way to examine the embodied personal reflection of social justice in our schools.

In this first case, we related components of SEL to the PE Leaders program. Yet, upon using our social justice camera—we "zoomed" in using two lenses. First, the dynamics of the integrated discussion and physical activity participation can promote/hinder engagement patterns that can produce or reproduce particular power relations. By placing youth PEL in charge, the class dynamics shift to being student-centered and could potentially increase engagement and comfort with reflections. Such a change in classroom dynamics places students in new roles (i.e., co-teacher) but in a familiar environment (i.e., physical education class). Thus, the leadership of the youth can lead to deeper personal and group reflection that is connected to the lived experiences of the community. While each youth PEL may be trained on the technical rules, rituals, and expectations of their particular class, these technicalities become less obvious as they build meaningful relationships and purposefully address the sociocultural issues present based on contextual factors, curricular choices, student identity and interest, and satisfaction.

Case Example #2: A Class in Mindfulness (with a Twist)

In this case, we examine how tools for personal reflection can be used in yoga and guided meditations for students in a high school physical education unit. In this example, the students involved in this class come from privileged backgrounds. We argue that it is not enough to sympathize with others (or feel badly for others' misfortunes), but it is important for all students—but especially privileged students—to empathize with others (or try to put themselves in someone else's shoes to *understand* a different perspective). Such an approach, of empathy, can help students personally reflect and recognize the good (and not so good) practices they follow in their daily lives (Hackman 2005).

If we are trying to cultivate a community of empathy, accurate self-awareness is crucial. Without an accurate knowledge of oneself, we diminish our ability to be accurately aware of others and our ability to understand our own role in movements of social change. Therefore, tools for personal reflection have great importance in awakening the consciousness of our youth—and we examine its potential in a unit of instruction that focuses on mindfulness.

Mindfulness refers to a subtle process of awareness that occurs in the present. It is presymbolic, mirror-thought, nonconceptual, nonjudgmental, and nonegoistic (Hanh 1998; Mahathera, 2008). The benefits of physical fitness on our mental well-being have been well established. Yet, not as much focus has been placed on developing mindfulness with physical education. Mindfulness is a moment-by-moment awareness, of thought, feelings, bodily sensations, as well as the surrounding environment through a gentle lens neither occupied by thoughts of yesterday nor by thoughts of tomorrow. One could argue that such a practiced and dedicated self-reflection can generate the levels of self-awareness required for persons to be able to empathize with others (Hackman 2005). It may also help to mitigate some of the factors mentioned earlier (e.g., gendered curricular offerings, preference for other content areas, student groupings funneled to activity "types"). As more research around the usefulness of yoga in schools is conducted, a growing number of studies have argued that simple implementation of yoga into PE yields an increased sense of well-being in students (Grant, 2017; Knothe & Flores Marti, 2018).

With recent studies supporting positive results of mindfulness activities in schools, we aim to offer insight into how the concept can be integrated to enhance SEL practices in PE. In conjunction with schoolwide plans for academic and social supports, mindfulness and yoga practices in school settings can strengthen PE programs and may continue to facilitate the reduction in the levels of depression, anger, fatigue, and anxiety in the student body (Grant, 2017). Below, we provide an example of a current program where mindfulness is prioritized, naming specific learning experiences, formal and informal outcomes, and next steps for improved pedagogical practices inclusive of SJE components and a clear look through the social justice camera.

Michelle is a high school physical educator in Sycamore, Illinois, and has applied recent research to her own teaching practices. She created a PE class called Mind and Body Fitness (MBF). One of Michelle's essential practices with her students is to initiate a process of self-reflection working to create an environment of nonjudgmental mindfulness through all activities and practices. In structuring her course and communicating expectations to her students, she often begins with the practice of bringing about mindfulness through one's breathing. Whether practicing yoga, moving through high-intensity interval training (HIIT), Pilates, Step, ZUMBA, breathing is a common thread that cultivates a sense of mindfulness. The main principle for Michelle in Yoga and Pilates is breathwork and meditation, but she continues to apply these concepts throughout MBF. For example, Michelle regularly reminds and encourages her students to listen to the story their breath is telling them; a short, quick breathing pattern may tell them that they are fatigued or stressed—or a deep, long, smooth breath may tell them that in this moment, they are calm and focused.

As you can see, Michelle's approach requires the youth to focus on "breathing" and listen to the stories that their bodies are telling them. Such an understanding of self is essential before entering into social justice work. Further into meditation, Michelle begins to teach guided practices and then we make our way into some chanting and humming meditations. Again, the chanting and humming take some coaching to teach at first, but once the practices are felt, the students are hooked, even the students who in the beginning believed that Michelle may be overtly eccentric. It works on a physical, mental, and emotional level and draws mindfulness on an individual level. The students begin to feel a relief in their body systems, higher levels of focus and attention, clearer thoughts, and more empowerment in their bodies.

Once Michelle reinforces the mindfulness component, she then adds SJE components via her club, Chita Girls. The mission of the club is to improve oneself and to apply learned skills in the club to improve the community. Recognizing the vast gender inequity that exists, she has created a democratic space for her female students to share content outside of the dominant narrative, to reflect and analyze collectively, and to become agents of change. As students shared and analyzed their own experiences with gender bias and sexism and through the sharing of nondominant sources like the documentary *Girl Rising* (2013), they were more aware of not only their oppression in school space but also their privilege. In fact, in realizing their own privileged position, they were inspired to develop an annual fundraiser *Yoga for the Girls*—a large yoga class that helps educate girls internationally through the International Rescue Committee (IRC). The IRC works in more than 40 countries, including the United States, to provide food, shelter, healthcare, education, and empowerment to refugees and displaced and marginalized people. Main aspects of the approach of the IRC are education and gender equality.

While Michelle's incorporation of aspects of SJE is a targeted, gendered approach, she uses the potential of reflecting on oneself to create empowered agents of social change in her school. Thus, the combination of breathwork, meditation, and tools for personal reflection led these particular students into social change. It is the commitment to consistent self-reflection that makes the *individual* a site for *social* change and transformation (Hackman, 2005). The range of engagement in their physical education programs has helped students to recognize inequities across populations in education and how it has been used as a tool for female oppression in some international contexts.

Michelle's facilitation of MBF incorporated multiple components for SJE and offers a snapshot of how self-reflection in conjunction with SEL practices through meditation and breathwork can support subsequent efforts to address and bring about social change. Self-reflection practices shared previously also serve as an example of how SJE can be implemented outside of the classroom with clubs,

teams, and other interest groups. Thus, social justice work is not bound to the classroom (or gym) but rather expands into our communities, families, and other worldly connections. Thus, by drawing on SJE frameworks—the focus shifts from *only* the individual to a balance between the individual and social issues.

Case Example #3: Kyle and Randy

Hackman (2005) notes that an element for effective teaching for social justice involves teachers who are student-centered and aware of how group dynamics and student identities are constructed in the learning environment. At the core of a supportive classroom is a teacher who is authentic and able to prioritize relationships while focusing on the quality of their connections with youth (Williford & Pianta, 2020). These teachers use culturally responsive practices in environments that support, honor, and acknowledge the cultural assets, contributions, and needs of all students. Furthermore, effective teachers for equality collaborate with students to build community and work to improve through reflection (Guide to Schoolwide SEL, 2020).

Creating a climate where all students can succeed is not a simple undertaking. Numerous sociocultural, historical, and political issues impact the promotion of equity in schools and how students are positioned in society. Simmons (2019) notes that educators often shy away from "transformative pedagogies" because they are fearful that they will be accused of "politicization" or feel ill-equipped and uncomfortable in addressing topics related to injustice and inequity that affect students' lives. In addressing these fears, she believes that teachers should work to understand themselves, while recognizing that their power, privilege, and identity is impactful for the work that they do and the students with whom they work (Simmons, 2019). To underscore this point, a comparison of two physical education teachers who have different approaches to configuring their classes through the lens of SEL and equity is provided here.

"Kyle" and "Randy" were mid-career physical education teachers who work in a suburb 30 minutes outside of Atlanta, GA. Over the past seven years, they have seen the community of the middle school they work in change from predominately white, upper-middle class students, to one that is ethnically and racially diverse. Their school population reflected the changing demographics of the community. The composition of the student body is 34% Caucasian, 31% African American, 27% Hispanic, 4% two or more races, and

3% nonspecific. Kyle and Randy both believed that all students can achieve success in physical education. When they first began teaching, they were exposed to literature discussing the opportunity gaps or ways in which ethnicity, socioeconomic status, race, English proficiency, availability of community resources, familial situations, or other factors contribute to or perpetuate lower educational aspirations, achievement, and attainment for certain groups of students (da Silva et al., 2007). Many of the issues that Kyle and Randy encountered while teaching were related to communication and disruptive behavior. It was not uncommon for them to address students talking out of turn, teasing one another, or questioning lesson choices.

After attending a session on SEL and cultural diversity at a conference, Kyle decided to address these issues by focusing on how he can create a better, more engaging physical education experience. Kyle noticed that many of his students enjoy hip-hop, so he decided to let students create their own playlists of songs to be used during each class warm-up period. Noticing that the gym walls only had a few banners of fitness award winners, he installed motivational posters and painted quotes from famous champion athletes in different parts of the gym. Expecting that his students may become frustrated with learning new sport activities that were taught in class, Kyle incorporated basketball and soccer, two sports that students liked and were less frustrated with into each unit. A few months later, Kyle modified the school's field day to promote a more international focus, assigning each student a country that they would represent as they participate. Students were asked to dress up in the color of the flag of the countries they were representing for the event.

Randy, after attending the same conference session on SEL and cultural diversity, actively worked to find other professionals who could shed light on this topic. After some reflection, he came to believe that schools play a role in reproducing inequity and reinforcing power dynamics that privilege some groups over others. Randy spent time studying his own cultural points of view and how his point of view and biases could shape his teaching and perceptions of students. With the assistance of community members, Randy began to immerse himself in students' cultural ways of knowing and committed to learning the routines and communities that their students are from. Shortly thereafter, he uncovered SEL ideas that incorporated mindfulness, emotional literacy, and collaboration into instruction.

After noticing that the gymnasium walls were relatively empty, Randy asked his students for mindset quotes to post on the walls and took the time to hang posters that represented the backgrounds of students in the school. Much like Kyle, Randy noticed his students enjoyed hip-hop, but instead of merely letting them create a playlist, he asked students to take the role of developing verses that would help in remembering cues and rules for a particular unit in which they were working. One student chose a motivational quote from the wall and was asked to explain how they thought this exemplified the goals of a daily lesson. Using Socratic questioning and process praise, Randy challenged students to find similarities between the sports that they like and ones that they did not enjoy. After involving students in a series of lessons in which they created new games, the invented games were showcased at the end of the school year during the day historically reserved for field day. Pictures of the event were posted on several bulletin boards in the school and would be used to market the event next year.

On the surface, both Kyle and Randy incorporated methods of instruction that respected the learners they taught and their success in physical education. However, there were distinct differences in how they went about this process. Kyle, while concerned about his students, viewed them through a deficit lens and had not realized that his students were not problems that needed to be fixed. Including hip-hop into the warm-up routine of classes, while thoughtful, did not sustain students' cultures and was a surface-level addition without substance. Kyle's desire to change the physical environment involved no real reflection on how quotes and posters could impact a student's feeling of belonging, nor did it include student perspective for constructing the environment. When thinking of activities to teach, Kyle decided against raising learning expectations for fear of students becoming frustrated. Finally, in modifying the field day to incorporate more of an international focus, Kyle organized another surface-level engagement, with no discussion on why they dressed up in the color of the flag of the country they were representing and its relevance to the field day.

Randy, on the other hand, was concerned about the students he taught and engaged in practices that were critically conscious. He sought knowledge outside of what was presented to him at a conference and reflected on what ramifications this information would have for his teaching and students' learning. Additionally, Randy enlisted the support of professionals in the community to learn more about his students' communities. In developing respect for his students' culture, Randy saw an opportunity for engagement in incorporating hip-hop verses and motivational quotes as ways to add substance and meaning in the gym. As part of a continuous routine of sharing knowledge, Randy asked students what from their interpretations were related to their current lives and the lessons outlined for the week. Finally, Randy challenged students by involving them in a process of constructing new activities that they were able to showcase in a culminating event. Students' memories of the field day were captured through pictures that would be used by Randy to market future field day events.

To truly meet the needs of all students, we must recognize the difference between "being" and "doing." Addressing social justice in the context of SEL is challenging. It requires a commitment to moving from status quo thinking to actions that encourage transformative change and acknowledging that we come to terms with realities about our society that are hard to face. As information is still emerging on how SEL program implementation looks with respect to PE, it is important to remember that strategies are diverse and should be tailored to the individual needs of the class. Johnson and Wiener (2017) have identified some promising SEL practices, including a strong and intentionally integrated curriculum, as key factors contributing to student success. Research has also demonstrated that successful SEL educators are cognizant of the "languages and practices" of SEL and use them consistently, even during times where it is perceived that students have less structure (e.g., lunchroom, recess). As the use of SEL in physical education evolves, it is important to remember that educators who are effective facilitators of SEL have an intentional and sustained focus toward improving outcomes for all children—and this includes integrating principles of social justice.

In this case, we compared two teachers who are both well-meaning and intentioned. Yet, one teacher truly embodied some of Hackman's (2005) concepts. In particular, Randy used the multicultural group dynamics as a positive—shifting the culture of the class from seeing students as in need of intervention, to seeing them as agents of change and capable.

Furthermore, the students showed a much deeper understanding of content knowledge by being able to compare and contrast different activities—and how they relate to their everyday experiences. Lastly, Randy shifted education from "thinking" to "doing" in that the students created alternative paths for class—and conceptualized a new form of physical education that was inclusive and responsive to the community's shifting demographics and values.

Case Example #4: Minefield!

Most physical educators are familiar with the game Minefield in which the gym floor is covered with numerous objects and equipment (e.g., cones, bean bags, poly spots). The game starts with students in pairs on one side of the gym. In each pair, one student is blindfolded but their partner can see everything (i.e., no blindfold). The purpose of the game is for the nonblindfolded person to provide verbal instructions to their blindfolded partner to navigate through the "minefield." The goal is to reach the other side of the gym without hitting an object.

Indeed, the game of Minefield is a classic example of an SEL-informed activity because it is meant to promote relationship skills and social awareness—two core competencies (CASEL, 2019). Yet, as you can see, this game promotes a particular form of social awareness and relationship skills, but it ignores broader social inequities that exist in society. As such, power relations and equity are left out of the game. When we put on our social justice camera; however, we can imagine new ways to enact the game. Specifically, in this case study, we use our social justice camera to examine Minefield with three components: (a) personal reflection, (b) critical analysis, and (c) social change. In so doing, we adapted the activity into the case study below.

In social justice Minefield, the gym floor will be divided into three equal sizes (see **Figure 14.1**). The teacher will set-up the class by placing a different number of items in each section of the gym.

Students will still be in pairs on one side of the gym—one person with a blindfold, the other without a blindfold. The students who can see still have to

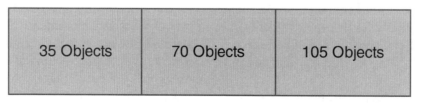

Figure 14.1 Minefield activity setup.

provide verbal instructions to their partner so they make it to the other side. This time, not only are they not allowed to hit an object, but they are also not allowed to leave their section of the gym. It is assumed that groups with fewer objects in their space will finish faster than pairs with more obstacles. When the students complete the activity, they will reflect in pairs on the following questions: (a) What were things you did well that helped you to succeed? (b) What were things you could have improved on? (c) Why do you think some pairs finished faster than others?

After the students reflect on the prompts, the teacher will lead a class discussion on each question. In the discussion, the teacher will field answers about the positive approaches that each pair took and how it helped them (i.e., self-awareness). Then, the teacher will solicit answers about how each pair could have communicated more effectively, collaborated, or prepared for the activity (i.e., relationship skills). Lastly, the teacher will ask why some students had a more difficult time completing the activity than others (i.e., social awareness with critical analysis). At this point, the teacher should not bring up anything around social inequities (yet!). After discussing the "uneven playing field" discussion, the teacher will ask the class to develop solutions (e.g., change rules, objects, space) to make the game more equitable (i.e., social action and change). Allow the students to enact those strategies during one last run through of the activity using the student-developed adaptations.

After the students do a second run of the activity, have them get back into their pairs. Give them the following prompt: in the original game, some of your classmates had more barriers than others to completing the activity. Can you think of people in your life who have more or fewer obstacles than you when trying to achieve goals? What are the reasons why some people have different obstacles? After students reflect, the teacher will lead a class discussion around how certain groups of people (e.g., gender, age, ability, race, sexuality, low socioeconomic status) have different obstacles than others (i.e., social awareness/critical analysis).

Finally, the teacher will ask students to reflect on their pairs using the following prompt: in our game, we made changes to the court, the objects, and rules to "even the playing field." Thinking about the obstacles you came up with from your lives and people you know, what are things that we can do, our government can do, or our society can do to even the playing field for all people? After discussing in pairs, lead a class discussion around these ideas and how it is important to reflect on the different situations that we all face. This is not to say that you do not have obstacles, but it is important to recognize that some folks have more obstacles than others.

In this second activity, we integrated three of Hackman's (2005) components of social justice into the original Minefield game. First, by splitting the gym into three different scenarios (i.e., low, medium, and high barriers), we provided a tool for critical analysis. That is, we created a situation that exaggerates inequity in order to allow students to critically analyze how this inequity occurs. We then provided students with time to discuss in pairs, and as a class, to discuss their personal struggles, group struggles, and overall inequities. In prompting students with probing questions, and providing them with time to think about these questions, the activity provides a tool for personal reflection. Importantly, this reflection includes the individual, the group, and the community more broadly. Finally, we asked the students to change the rules/ parameters/equipment of the game in order to make it more equitable. By handing this responsibility over to students, the activity provided a tool to create social action and change in order to create a more equitable space. By linking all of this to broader social issues, it increases the type of social awareness (SEL component) in which youth can participate. As such, a socially just infused activity can augment the personal, group, and societal SEL learning aims.

Summary

We began this chapter by arguing that SEL and PE have a lot of synergies. As such, it is understandable that many physical educators are developing ways to integrate SEL into PE practices. We also claimed, however, that because of these similarities, both SEL and PE often have similar limitations. For example, both SEL and PE tend to focus on individuals and in so doing, often do not address larger social justice issues in our society. Given this, we argue that any use of SEL in PE should also consider hybridizing to be an explicit focus on SJE.

SJE can be understood as both a *goal* and a *process*. The *goal* of social justice education is full and equitable participation in health and physical activity among diverse groups of people. This worthy goal, we believe, aligns with many other physical educators in the field. Yet, there are many different *processes* that can be used to attain this goal. Specific to this chapter, we argued that using a social justice camera that is underpinned by Hackman's (2005) components is one *process* that helps us to achieve the goal of social justice education, while also staying true to CASEL's framework for SEL.

The social justice camera we describe has five lenses: (a) content mastery, (b) critical analysis, (c) social action and change, (d) personal reflection, and (e) multicultural group dynamics. These lenses can be used to examine SEL activities and alter them to address equity and diversity issues in physical education. By using a social justice camera in relation to SEL, we can develop programs, create new courses, affect teacher practice, and even just modify activities to address equity and diversity. Given the synergies between SEL and PE, using a social justice camera will round out the limitations discussed earlier and help teachers align their practices with the broader equitable aims of education.

In order to make the social justice camera "come to life," we applied these lenses to four different case studies. Throughout these cases, we argue that the social justice camera can be integrated at different levels (e.g., program, class, activity, teacher) and in different settings (K–12, after school, etc.). Social justice is indeed a goal—and as this chapter shows—and a process. While the process may be different, one such process is to use the social justice camera in your own lives, lessons, and communities. Therefore, we argue to further enhance the value of health and well-being, social interaction, and self-expression in PE settings—we should pause and check (and even double check) the lenses that we bring and use in our communities.

Questions for Discussion

1. What are the limitations of SEL and many models-based practices in PE?
2. How can a social justice education approach address the above limitations?
3. What are the five components of SJE?
4. What is the purpose of the social justice camera?

Homework Challenge

1. Go to a previous chapter that had an SEL activity. Use the social justice lens to adapt the activity so it addresses issues of equity and diversity.
2. Examine a previous lesson plan/lesson activity you created for a class/assignment. Use the social justice lens to adapt the lesson/activity to address issues of equity and diversity.
3. Choose any PE instructional model (e.g., sport education, TGfU, etc.). Use the social justice camera to adapt the model to address issues of equity and diversity.

Further Reading

Butler, J. I. (2016). *Playing fair: Using student-invented games to prevent bullying, teach democracy, and promote social justice.* Champaign, IL: Human Kinetics.

Flory, S. B., Tischler, A., & Sanders, S. (2014). *Sociocultural issues in physical education: Case studies for teachers.* Lanham, MD: Roman & Littlefield.

Robinson, D. B., & Randall, L. (2016). *Social justice in physical education: Critical reflections and pedagogies for change.* Toronto, Canada: Canadian Scholars Press.

References

Ahmed, S. (2010). Happy objects. In M. Gregg & G. J. Seigworth (Eds.), *The affect theory reader* (pp. 29–51). Durham: Duke University Press.

Banaji, M. R. & Greenwald, G. (2013). Blindspot: Hidden biases of good people. [Kindle iPad version]. Retrieved from https://www.amazon.com/Blindspot-Hidden-Biases-Good -Peopleebook/dp/B004J4WJUC/ref=sr_1_1?keywords =Blindspot%3A+Hidden+biases+of+good+people&qid =1610738474&s=books&sr=1-1

Bell, L. A. (1997). Theoretical foundations for social justice education. In M. Adams, L. Bell, & P. Griffin (Eds.), *Teaching for diversity and social justice: A sourcebook* (pp. 3–15). New York: Routledge.

Blackshear, T. B. (2020). #SHAPEsoWHITE., *Physical Education and Sport Pedagogy, 25*(3), 240–258.

Cahn, S. (1994). *Coming on strong: Gender and sexuality in twentieth-century women's sport.* Cambridge, Massachusetts: Harvard University Press.

Casey, A. (2014). Models-based practice: Great white hope or white elephant? *Physical Education and Sport Pedagogy, 19*(1), 18–34. https://doi.org/10.1080/17408989.2012.726977

Casey, A., & MacPhail, A. (2018). Adopting a models-based approach to teaching physical education. *Physical Education and Sport Pedagogy, 23*(3), 294–310.

Ciotto, C. M., & Gagnon, A. G. (2018). Promoting social and emotional learning in physical education. *Journal of Physical Education, Recreation & Dance, 89*(4), 27–33. https://doi.org /10.1080/07303084.2018.1430625

Clark, L. (2019). The way they care: An ethnography of social justice physical education teacher education. *The Teacher Educator, 54*(2), 145–170.

Collaborative for Academic, Social, and Emotional Learning. (2019). *What is social and emotional learning?* Retrieved May 22, 2020. https://casel.org/what-is-sel/

Culp, B. (2016). Social justice and the future of higher education kinesiology. *Quest, 68*(3), 271–283. doi:10.1080/00336297.2016.1180308

da Silva, C.D., Huguley, J., Kakli, Z. & Rao, R. (Eds.). (2007). *The opportunity gap: Achievement and inequality in education,* Harvard Education Publishing Group: Cambridge, MA.

Desai, P., Karahalios, V., Persuad, S., & Reker, K. (2014). A social justice perspective on social-emotional learning. *Communiqué, 43*(1), 14–16.

Durlak, J. A. (2011). The importance of implementation for research, practice, and policy. *Child Trends Research Brief.* Retrieved April 9, 2020. www.childtrends.org/wp-content/uploads/2013/05/2011-34DurlakImportanceofImplementation.pdf

Durlak, J. A., Weissberg, R. P., Dymnicki, A. B., Taylor, R. D., & Schellinger, K. B. (2011). The impact of enhancing students' social and emotional learning: A meta-analysis of school-based universal interventions. *Child Development, 82*(1), 405–432. https://doi.org/10.1111/j.1467-8624.2010.01564.x

Fitzpatrick, K. (2013). *Critical pedagogy, physical education and urban schooling.* New York, NY: Peter Lang.

Fitzpatrick, K. (2018). Sexuality education in New Zealand: A policy for social justice? *Sex Education, 18*(5), 1–9. https://doi.org/10.1080/14681811.2018.1446824

Frank, L. (2013). *Journey toward the caring classroom: Using adventure to create community* (2nd ed.). Oklahoma City, OK: Wood 'N' Barnes.

Gould, D., & Voelker, D. K. (2012). Enhancing youth leadership through sport and physical education. *Journal of Physical Education, Recreation & Dance, 83*(8), 38–41.

Grant, S., Hamilton, L. S., Wrabel, S. L., Gomez, C. J., Whitaker, A., Leschitz, J. T., Unlu, F., Chavez-Herrerias, E. R., Baker, G., Barrett, M., Harris, M., & Ramos, A. (2017). Social and emotional learning interventions. *Rand Corporation.* 240–254.

Guide to Schoolwide SEL (2020). *Collaborative for Academic, Social, and Emotional Learning (CASEL).* Retrieved May 3, 2020. https://schoolguide.casel.org/

Hackman, H. W. (2005). Five essential components for social justice education. *Equity and Excellence in Education, 38*(2), 103–109. https://doi.org/10.1080/10665680590935034

Hanh, T.N. (1998). The heart of the Buddha's teaching: Transforming suffering into peace, joy, and liberation. New York: Broadway Books.

Harrison, L. Jr., & Clark, L. (2016). Contemporary issues of social justice: A focus on race and physical education in the United States. *Research Quarterly for Exercise & Sport, 87*(3), 230–241. doi:10.1080/02701367.2016.1199166

Hellison, D. (2011). *Teaching personal and social responsibility through physical activity* (3rd ed.). Champaign, IL: Human Kinetics.

Hodge, S. R. (2014). Ideological repositioning: Race, social justice, and promise. *Quest, 66*(2), 169–180. doi:10.1080/00336297.2014.898545

Hoffmann, D. M. (2009). Reflecting on social emotional learning: A critical perspective on trends in the United States. *Review of Educational Research, 79*(2), 533–556. https://doi.org/10.3102/0034654308325184

Jagers, R. J., Rivas-Drake, D., & Borowski, T. (2018). *Equity & social and emotional learning: A cultural analysis.* Retrieved from https://measuringsel.casel.org/wp-content/uploads/2018/11/Frameworks-Equity.pdf

Johnson, H. & Wiener, R. (2017), *This time, with feeling: Integrating social and emotional development and college- and career-readiness standards,* The Aspen Institute, Washington, DC, March. Retrieved from: https://assets.aspeninstitute.org/content/uploads/2017/05/ThisTimeWithFeeling.pdf

Jones, S., Brown, J., & Aber, J. (2008). Classroom settings as targets of intervention and research. In *Toward positive youth development: Transforming schools and community programs* (pp. 58–77). New York, NY: Oxford University Press.

Kirk, D. (2010). *Physical education futures.* London, UK: Routledge.

Kirshner, B. (2015). *Youth Activism in an Era of Education Inequality.* New York, NY: New York University Press.

Knothe, M., and Flores Martí, I. (2018). Mindfulness in physical education. *Journal of Physical Education, Recreation & Dance. 89*(8), 35–40.

Landi, D., Fitzpatrick, K., & McGlashan, H. (2016). Models based practices in physical education: A sociocritical reflection. *Journal of Teaching in Physical Education, 35*(4), 400–411.

Landi, D. (2019). Queer men, affect, and physical education. *Qualitative Research in Sport, Exercise and Health, 11*(2), 168–187. https://doi.org/10.1080/2159676X.2018.1504230

Lu, C., Francis, N. & Kentel, J. (2007). *Mindfulness: A new dimension in physical education.* History & Future Directions of Research on Teaching and Teacher Education in Physical Education Conference. Pittsburgh, PA, USA.

MacGregor, M. (2007). *Everyday Leadership.* Minneapolis, MN: Free Spirit.

Mahathera, H. G. (2008). Mindfulness. Retrieved August 24, 2020, from http://www.budsas. org/ebud/mfneng/mind13.html

Metzler, M. W. (2011). *Instructional models in physical education* (3rd ed.). Scottsdale, AZ: Holcomb Hathaway.

Ministry of Education (2007). *The New Zealand Curriculum.* Wellington, New Zealand: Learning Media Limited.

Oliver, K. L., & Kirk, D. (2015). *Girls, Gender and Physical Education: An Activist Approach.* Abingdon: Routledge.

Siedentop, D., Hastie, P. A., & van der Mars, H. (2011). *Complete guide to sport education* (2nd ed.). Champaign: Human Kinetics.

SHAPE America. (2014). *National standards & grade level outcomes for K-12 physical education.* Champaign: Human Kinetics.

Simmons, D. (2019). *Why we can't afford whitewashed social-emotional learning.* ASCD Educational Update. Retrieved February 9, 2020 from: http://www.ascd.org/publications/newsletters/education_update/apr19/vol61/num04/Why_We_Can't_Afford_Whitewashed_Social-Emotional_Learning.aspx.

Simon, M. (2018). "Playing the game" and "finding my way": Ethnic minority female PE teachers' counter-stories. In S. Dagkas, L. Azzarito, & K. Hylton (Eds.). *'Race,' youth sport, physical activity, and health: Global perspectives.* London, UK: Routledge.

Walton-Fisette, J. L., Sutherland, S., & Hill, J. (Eds.). (2019). *Teaching about social justice issues in physical education.* Charlotte, NC: Information Age Publishing.

Williford A.P., Pianta, R.C. (2020). Banking time: A dyadic intervention to improve teacher-student relationships. In A. Rashly, A. Pohl & S. Christenson (Eds). *Student Engagement.* Springer International: Switzerland, 239–250.

CHAPTER 15

Case Examples of Promising Practices in Outside-of-School Settings

Jennifer M. Jacobs
Karisa L. Kuipers
Zachary Wahl-Alexander
Alicia L. Richards

CHAPTER SUMMARY

This chapter provides case examples of four out of the school programs using sport for social change including, (a) a community-based urban soccer league; (b) a sport-based leadership program for incarcerated youth; (c) an afterschool girls boxing body empowerment club; and (d) a university-based summer program teaching academics, nutrition, and physical activity to youth in communities affected by poverty. Each program's connection to greater social justice issues is overviewed with an emphasis on how sport and social and emotional learning (SEL) can empower youth to be agents of change. Program design, unique features, and linkages to SEL are presented.

Introduction

Thus far, the chapters in this book have overviewed social and emotional learning (SEL), described relevant pedagogical models, and discussed general contexts for using SEL. While Chapter 14 provided case examples of SEL practice within school-based physical education, this chapter focuses on aspects of out-of-school time (OST) programs that integrate SEL and sport to achieve greater social change. Specifically, we provide snapshots of four SEL programs including, (a) a community-based urban soccer league addressing the academic achievement gap; (b) a sport-based leadership program for incarcerated youth addressing racial inequities; (c) an afterschool girls boxing body empowerment club addressing gender issues; and (d) a university-based summer program teaching academics, nutrition, and physical activity to youth from communities affected by poverty. Each program's description includes its connection to a greater social equity issue. Together, these case examples demonstrate how to design and structure programs to give youth the tools to be change agents in their own lives and in their communities.

Social and Emotional Learning in Out-of-School Environments

In the mid-1990s, SEL programming gained widespread attention within schools as a response to addressing the "missing piece" in the American educational system (Collaborative for Academic, Social, and Emotional Learning [CASEL], 2020). Integrating SEL during school time has many benefits including the opportunity to connect SEL competencies with greater school initiatives, as well as work with a large, captive audience of students (Elbertson et al., 2010; see Chapter 2 for more on the role of SEL in physical education). The out-of-school environment has been proposed as a critically important context for fostering positive youth development and SEL in ways that may not be feasible within the confines of an academic setting (Taylor et al., 2017).

For instance, OST programs offer the value of not being bound by specific school standards, curricular demands, or predetermined student outcomes (e.g., standardized testing, achievement scores, etc.; Hurd & Deutsch, 2017). Consequently, this allows for flexibility in adapting program aims, content, and format based on individual youth needs and interests. Furthermore, OST programs have the benefit of being suitable in a variety of environments such as through community-based organizations, afterschool programs, and summer camps. These settings allow for cross-age interaction and relationship-building, engagement with community-based entities, and hands-on learning outside of the school walls (Karcher, 2008). OST programs also play a critical role in keeping students connected to a physically and psychologically safe space outside of school hours, which is particularly important for youth from unstable or volatile home environments (Payton et al., 2000). Finally, the out-of-school environment allows for a variety of adults to be involved as program leaders including teachers, coaches, and parents (Hurd & Deutsch, 2017). This provides the opportunity for youth to connect with multiple positive figures, increasing the likelihood of establishing meaningful, positive relationships that can help lead to the acquisition of SEL competencies (Rhodes, 2004).

With all of these structural features in place, OST programs with a specific SEL focus have linked to numerous positive youth outcomes such as fostering a sense of belonging, promoting positive pro-social norms, and increased efficacy and perceived mattering (Hurd & Deutsch, 2017). A meta-analysis of 68 afterschool programs also revealed that SEL programs can increase positive attitudes toward school, foster academic achievement, and reduce risky behaviors (Durlak et al., 2010). Although far less research has been conducted on programs within OST settings (e.g., afterschool programs, community-based programs, summer camps, youth residential facilities), some recent studies have proposed a link between sport and psychosocial outcomes such as leadership, school engagement, and self-control (Anderson-Butcher et al., 2013; Wahl-Alexander et al., 2019; Wright et al., 2020).

Using Sport for Social Change

In recent years, the venture of using sport as a tool for fostering positive social change has been applied within a variety of contexts. Internationally, sport has been identified as an important lever that can promote political, developmental, or restorative efforts (Kidd, 2008). Global sport for social change programs have focused on advocating for social issues such as women's rights, sexual health and wellness, postwar reconciliation, and many other equity problems (Dyck, 2011; Lindsey & Banda, 2001; Willis, 2000). At a local level, youth sport programs have explored how to connect aims to psychosocial outcomes, teaching youth how to develop important life skills for them to achieve success within their schools, homes, and social circles (Holt et al., 2017). However, in some cases, sport programs have expanded their aims beyond fostering individual outcomes and also considered the potential for sport to have greater social impact through education, empowerment, and social justice (Jacobs et al., 2016; Whitley et al., 2016; Wright et al., 2016). In this way, sport becomes the vehicle for addressing a social equity issue, and youth are challenged to consider how they can develop the tools to become change agents within their communities.

With the wide range of potential individual and collective youth benefits for SEL programming in OST settings, there is a need to explore how these programs can be designed and implemented within the context of broader societal issues. In some cases, OST programs are faced with the challenges of adapting to organizational norms or overcoming contextual barriers, while others need to be diligent in tailoring programming for youth from specific backgrounds. In the following sections, we present case examples of four OST programs using sport for social change including (a) a community-based urban soccer league; (b) a sport-based leadership program for incarcerated youth; (c) an afterschool girls boxing body empowerment club; and (d) a university-based summer program teaching academics, nutrition, and physical activity to youth in communities affected by poverty. A variety of social and emotional skills will be addressed in the ensuing descriptions, with an emphasis on leadership, positive decision making, and relational skills, as they most aligned with the program aims. We offer insights to students, practitioners, and researchers alike who not only envision using sport as a launching pad for students to develop important social and emotional skills but also to address pressing social issues and give students the tools to be change agents for themselves and others.

The P.L.A.Y.S. Soccer Program

This program has taught [my son] discipline and it has been an incentive towards getting good grades in school. – (Parent of 4th grader, translated from Spanish)

Overarching Societal Issue

The academic achievement gap is a pervasive problem in many parts of the United States, with some of the most severe patterns among students from under-served urban areas (Haycock, 2001; Ladson-Billings, 2006). Common indicators of an achievement gap include pervasive disparities among academic performance (e.g., grades, standardized test scores), disciplinary referrals (e.g., detentions, suspensions, expulsions), and graduation rates among students from different socioeconomic or racial backgrounds. The achievement gap has been correlated with a variety of negative long-term youth outcomes including decreased opportunities for career success, reduced access to higher education, and an overall lower quality of life (Leach & Williams, 2007). In many ways, the achievement gap perpetuates the structural inequities in our society. While addressing these systemic issues in society and our educational system can be daunting, effort is needed at all levels. Relevant to the focus of this text, some studies have proposed strategies around closing the achievement gap that include providing students with access to physical activity (Basch, 2011) and quality SEL programming (Zins et al., 2007).

Program Setting

P.L.A.Y.S. (Participate, Learn, Achieve, Youth Soccer) is a youth outreach program overseen by the Chicago Fire Foundation, an organization affiliated with The Chicago Fire major league soccer (MLS) team. The program aims are not only to teach soccer skills to elementary students but also to enhance their academic performance and development of key SEL competencies such as self-awareness, positive decision making, and relationship building. Since the program's inception in 2013, their soccer leagues have served more than 700 youth across 30 Chicago public schools, with exponential growth each year that the program has been in existence.

P.L.A.Y.S. serves youth in a Chicago community where more than 40% of students do not graduate from high school and nearly 77% of students come from families who qualify for free and reduced meals through school, a common indicator of low socio-economic status (Chicago Public Schools report card report, 2019). The school district also has a significant amount of English Language Learning (ELL) students (18%) and many schools have ethnically homogeneous populations where over 90% of students come from either an African American or Hispanic background. Several schools in the district are located within neighborhoods with high incidences of gang violence, crime, and unemployment. With all of these factors in mind, the P.L.A.Y.S. program sought to create a community-based sport program that would holistically address some of the social and equity challenges youth experience in this district.

Program Development

The Chicago Fire Foundation partners with schools in the district that have a demonstrated commitment to schoolwide initiatives that target students' educational, emotional, and social needs. Upon invitation, schools are asked to select two teachers to serve as the coaches for the P.L.A.Y.S. program and in return they are given all supplies, equipment, necessary training, and compensation for the 10-week season. Most schools do not have access to soccer fields and utilize grassy areas, parking lots, or gymnasia, organized with cones and portable goals. Coaches do not need any specific experience or training with soccer or SEL to qualify. However, as coaches are recruited from a pool of licensed, practicing elementary school teachers, most have a working knowledge of SEL as it applies in the classroom setting. Before the season begins, coaches participate in an initial training covering the program logistics and the SEL-based curriculum. Along with the training, coaches are given lesson plans for all soccer practices that include directions for soccer drills and games, as well as a specific SEL theme that is to be introduced, integrated, and practiced throughout each practice session. Video resources are also made available to coaches who have less experience. In effect, to improve fidelity to program goals, coaches are expected to provide weekly attendance reports and documentation that lessons are being covered as outlined by the manual.

Program Structure

The P.L.A.Y.S. program is free for students and they are provided with team uniforms, a school-sponsored snack for each meeting, and transportation to all games. All coaches are supplied with team equipment including goals, balls, practice jerseys, and cones. The program includes two practices a week that are held directly before or after school, weekly soccer games against other schools in the league, and an end-of-season tournament at a large indoor sport facility utilized by The Chicago Fire MLS players. A culminating celebration where all teams are invited to attend an MLS game is also included as part of the experience. Third through fifth graders are eligible to participate on the teams and most rosters range from 15–25 female and male students. Based on the students' language needs, many practices are run bilingually, and coaches encourage students to speak about SEL concepts in their native Spanish language.

A typical practice includes both an SEL competency and soccer skill focus. Soccer skills center around core components of the game including dribbling, passing, scoring, and defense. The SEL skill is derived from one of the overarching five competencies (CASEL, 2019), and is broken down into subthemes. For example, relationship skills include communicating, being patient, and encouraging others. At each practice, the skill is introduced through an illustration of a story describing a student having a problem at school or home that can be solved using the SEL competency. For instance, students might be asked to solve the challenge of a friend who consistently forgets to bring their completed math homework to school. Students then discuss different solutions to the problem and make connections on how the SEL competency (e.g., following rules or showing self-discipline) can help with the issue related to soccer, school, or home life. The discussion is followed by soccer drills and games with ongoing encouragement and feedback on the SEL competency, and the conclusion of the practice includes another discussion debriefing on how SEL was used at practice. Students are also assigned SEL homework that involves applying the SEL lessons in school, home, and community settings.

Unique Program Feature: The SEL Workbook

Research has highlighted the importance of integrating students' various life systems into programming to maximize impact on youth using life skills learned from the program setting (Jacobs et al., 2017). Many programs are successful in achieving a safe space that facilitates psychosocial growth; however, youth are tasked with leaving those settings and adjusting to different sets of norms, expectations, and ways of behaving that may not match the program setting (Martinek & Lee, 2012). In a response to these findings, P.L.A.Y.S. attempts to account for setting differences by involving school and family systems in their programming through a variety of tactics.

One way the P.L.A.Y.S. program works to engage individuals from students' different life systems is through their program workbook, which is an interactive booklet that contains a collection of weekly activities given to every student. The workbook was developed by the P.L.A.Y.S. program administration in consultation with their evaluation partners who are university faculty specializing in sport-based youth development research. This resource was created with several objectives in mind. First, it operates as a communication tool between coaches and players' families to keep them informed on program updates and the SEL content. Next, it offers concrete ways to engage students in SEL competency practice outside of the program, which is a well-documented challenge in sport-based youth development programs (Jacobs & Wright, 2017). Finally, it provides formative feedback to coaches on what SEL competencies students learn and apply as a result of being in the program. This provides coaches with important information on how lessons are being received and informs how they present future material.

The workbook begins with an opening message from a member of the Chicago Fire MLS team who is associated with the program. Lessons are then organized by week (10 weeks in total) with specific challenges and opportunities for youth to gain "stamps" from their coaches for successfully meeting their weekly achievements. Each week focuses on one SEL skill (e.g., goal setting, self-control, responsibility, communication) and includes corresponding activities (word searches, crossword puzzles, drawings, case-based problems). For example, the focus of week three is self-control defined as, "the ability to control your actions, feelings, and emotions in a positive way to help you perform better." A corresponding challenge asks students to match cases where someone shows self-control with good choices, and prompts students to propose a better behavior when an instance where students do not demonstrate self-control is shown.

Each section concludes with an end-of-week, open-discussion section asking how the weekly SEL competency can be demonstrated in their lives. Prompting questions include "what do you feel when you start losing control of your emotions?" and "what helps you keep control of your emotions?" Some weeks include parental involvement (e.g., "show your parents your game schedule and have them circle which games they can attend"), while other lessons target school integration (e.g., "set a classroom goal and map out the steps you'll take to get there) or team participation (e.g., "share how you feel when you lose a game with another member of your team"). Week 10 represents a culmination of all SEL competencies and challenges students to think about their growth across

the season as a whole and consider what they still need to work on to be a better student, friend, and family member. See **Figure 15.1** for a sample lesson.

The benefits from this type of the workbook feature are extensive. First, it establishes the importance of the relationship between soccer skills and SEL content. Often, programs may place psychosocial growth as a secondary aim behind the sport content, but the legitimacy and significance of SEL is emphasized through the workbook and integrated consistently throughout all lessons during the season. Furthermore, the structure of a SEL workbook provides a tangible product for students to track their progress across a season. This could enhance feelings of empowerment or increased intrinsic and extrinsic motivation for learning SEL skills. It also provides the opportunity to harness family support and buy-in to the team experience. This is especially important for youth from marginalized backgrounds or backgrounds where language barriers or cultural differences may alienate family members (Jacobs et al., 2017).

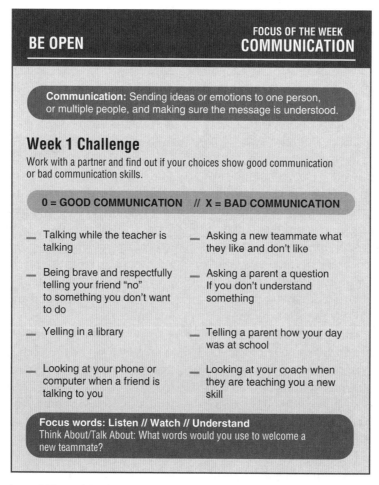

Figure 15.1 Sample page from SEL workbook.

Indications of Effectiveness

The P.L.A.Y.S. program has received several prestigious recognitions for their work of using soccer to give urban youth a better chance at academic achievement and future success. In 2016, they were awarded the Sport Team of the Year Award by Beyond Sport, a "global organization that promotes, develops and supports the use of sport to create positive social change across the world" (Beyondsport.org, 2019). They were also recognized by the Robert Wood Johnson Foundation Team of the Year Award, in 2015, and honored with the 2019 ESPN Sports Humanitarian Team of the Year Award. Beyond the accolades, subsequent research has been published on the program's impact and found that the program reflects many best practices inherent to sport-based youth development literature. For example, one study conducted with P.L.A.Y.S. coaches and students indicated that students demonstrated improvements in certain life skills (e.g., sportsmanship, classroom behavior, positive decision making) that could be extended into the school setting (Wright et al., 2020). Another comprehensive program evaluation provided early indications from parent, coach, and student perspectives that youth experienced various short-term impacts from the program including helping them make good decisions, staying calm, doing their best in school, and getting along with teachers and students (Wright et al., under review). Taken altogether, the P.L.A.Y.S. program illustrates a strong application of a sports-based SEL program that attempts to close the achievement gap for Chicago public school students using a novel, community-based tool of engaging students through soccer.

Project FLEX: A Fitness Leadership Program for Incarcerated Male Youth

Ninety-nine percent of the job is about relationships. Depending on how you hold and mold that child returns the outcome you are going to get. It's a positive cycle - the more involved you are, the more you'll see positive outcomes, which makes you want to be more involved with them. (Juvenile detention center, Activity director)

Overarching Societal Issue

It has been widely cited that the United States spends billions of dollars per year to incarcerate their citizens at a higher rate than any other country in the world. Notably, the incarceration rates of people of color are staggering. While African American, Hispanic, and Native American people make up 30% of our country's population, they account for over 60% of our prison population (Prison Policy Initiative, 2020). With comparable racial disparities among incarcerated youth, it is clear that stark inequities exist for people of color within the criminal justice system. The work of Dr. Rosie Meek has explored how sport can be used as an important tool for helping prisoners engage in education, develop positive behaviors, and decrease their chances for reoffending (2013).

Program Setting

Project Fitness Leadership Experience (FLEX) was established within a medium security, all male, juvenile detention center situated on a 100-acre plot of land near Chicago, Illinois. While this facility's grounds are expansive, they are littered with dilapidated, abandoned buildings intermixed with antiquated housing facilities, a school built in the 1990s, a recently constructed visitor center, and various recreational spaces (e.g., gymnasium, all-purpose recreation room, outdoor track, soccer field, garden, pond). The capacity of the facility is approximately 300 youth; however, it typically operates with an average daily population of 100.

Among those incarcerated, the youth range in age from 14–20 years old (average age, 18.6 years) and are predominantly African American (76%), followed by Hispanic (12%), Caucasian (9%), and biracial (3%). Accordingly, these racial statistics are representative of the greater population of imprisoned youth in the United States, where African American youth are five times as likely to be incarcerated compared with their Caucasian peers (Annie E. Casey Foundation, 2013). Similar patterns exist for Hispanic and American Indian youth, which presents the case that youth of color are being institutionalized at alarmingly disproportionate rates. As this is the most secure juvenile detention center in the state, individuals have committed serious crimes varying from theft to homicide, most often related to involvement in gang violence. Average sentence time is about eight months, with more than half of youth returning to the facility after repeated offenses or parole violations. For more serious crimes, youth are transferred to adult facilities before their 21st birthday. The facility employs approximately 300 staff including security guards, school counselors, leisure time activity specialists (LTAs), medical staff, educational specialists, and administrators.

Due to statewide mandates, various educational and recreational opportunities are afforded for individuals at the facility. Educational opportunities include mandatory daily classes required for students who have not graduated from high school, as well as optional vocational training, drug-treatment programs, tutoring, mentoring, and faith-based programs. Spearheaded by the LTAs and facilitated by outside volunteers, the facility offers recreational opportunities for youth to engage in a variety of activities (e.g., drum circle, prayer groups, dog training, meditation, rap circles), with most programs offered once a week.

Although the facility provides youth with supplementary programming that complements what is state-mandated, all programs are voluntary, and youth may not elect to or not be permitted to take full advantage. For example, while national juvenile justice guidelines stipulate that incarcerated youth are entitled to 60 minutes of daily physical activity, researchers postulate that 75% of juvenile offenders spend more than 14 hours confined by leg or hand restraints, (Jenson et al., 2001). This results in decreased physical health outcomes and subsequently creates an influx of idle time where youth are confined to their living spaces and tempted to participate in antisocial behaviors.

Program Development

The idea for Project FLEX was introduced in the spring of 2018 when two university faculty members contacted detention center administration with the intent of creating a program where youth could be physically active and develop life skills linked to SEL competencies. After several months of stakeholder meetings, site visits, pursuing Institutional Review Board permission to conduct research, and creating a memorandum of understanding between the university and the facility, Project FLEX was launched in the fall of 2018.

Project FLEX is a physical activity-based mentoring program that uses sport and fitness as vehicles for fostering positive, developmental qualities such as leadership, resiliency, and responsibility. The three primary objectives of this program are to (a) develop a sense of personal and social responsibility, (b) improve overall health-related fitness markers (e.g., cardiovascular endurance, muscle strength, muscle endurance, body composition), and (c) transfer these physical and psychosocial skills into their daily lives.

Youth are invited to participate in the program based on maintaining high behavioral ratings that are deemed necessary by the facility to be eligible for outside programs. When they express interest, youth are put on one of two program rosters that meet twice a week for 80 minutes. Rosters are divided based on housing assignments, which assures that youth who have conflicting gang affiliations and a track record of physical violence are not put in the same physical space. Based on staff ratios, approximately 15 youth are allowed to attend each session. Daily attendance ranges from four to 15 youth based on individuals not wanting to participate or being deemed ineligible due to behavioral infractions. Consistent attendance in this program, or any other program offered through the facility, awards youth with reduced sentence time, based on the belief that they are committing to rehabilitation and the betterment of themselves.

Program sessions are facilitated by university faculty and graduate teaching assistants from the kinesiology, physical education, and sport management programs. In order to be prepared for teaching in a nontraditional environment, graduate assistants participate in a variety of training exercises. First, they completed a month-long immersion phase at the facility, where they attended other existing programs to acclimate to the facility culture, rules, and norms (Jacobs et al., 2019). During this time, they were assigned a series of readings centered around best practices relevant to the program setting (e.g., teaching gang-affiliated youth, building relationships in OST programs, navigating biases in the criminal justice system) and completed written reflections on how to integrate these strategies into their work. After an immersion phase, the graduate assistants and faculty supervisors co-create teaching content that the graduate students then delivered once the program started. As an ongoing developmental tool, the graduate assistants participate in spontaneous voice memos, recording candid thoughts and reflections verbally immediately before and after each teaching session. This method allows for a practical and time-sensitive way for the graduate students to capture reflections and questions that arise during the program. Faculty supervisors then listen to the voice memos and they use them both as a debriefing tool to provide formative feedback and for a research data collection method to understand experiences of graduate students teaching in the unique setting.

In addition to graduate assistants, two facility LTAs are also present and mainly serve as participants in the activity or necessary authority when disciplinary situations escalate. Notably, these staff members dress in athletic clothes and do not carry restraining equipment as security officers do. The decision to exclude correctional staff from the program setting was intentional based on the goal of creating a psychologically safe space where youth did not feel as if they were under surveillance (Peterson-Badali & Koegl, 2002). During the program, instructors employ the teaching personal and social responsibility (TPSR) model, a pedagogical framework designed to foster life skills through sport with the eventual goal of transferring those skills outside of the sport context (Hellison, 2010; see Chapter 7 in this book). The instructor's main approach through this model is to intentionally foster relationships with youth while helping prepare them for life outside of the program and a larger juvenile detention center. Each program session is structured similarly, focusing on a specific SEL skill that is integrated throughout the lesson content (see **Table 15.1**).

Program Structure

A typical Project FLEX lesson begins with a team-building activity designed to establish a sense of community and set the tone that youth are transitioning out of their rigid, supervised routine into a social, positive setting. This is followed by an awareness talk where the instructor introduces a life skill (e.g., self-awareness, conflict resolution, sharing emotions) for the day and illustrates it through the sharing of an anecdote from their life that either positively or negatively demonstrates their use with it. For example, on a day where the skill, "self-control" is highlighted, a graduate instructor might illustrate a story from their life about getting a speeding ticket while driving with friends because they prioritized immediate gratification over safety and law. The technique of sharing personal stories was employed in the current setting for the purpose of establishing

credibility and facilitating connection/relatedness in a setting that has significant relational barriers (Shank, 2006).

After the awareness talk, youth participate in a thirty-minute responsibility-based sport or fitness activity with the goal of engaging in high levels of moderate to vigorous physical activity. During this time, youth are challenged to practice and apply the SEL competency within the activity for the day. For example, if a dispute erupts following a bad call or a youth displays overt frustration with a teammate, the instructor will pause gameplay, prompt the youth to dialogue about behavioral options, and then come to a consensus on a resolution. Subsequently, facilitating a concentrated debrief (e.g., 1–2 minutes) avails the opportunity for the group to assess the situation, identify the teachable behavior that can resolve the situation, and then efficiently return to game play. At the end of the lesson, a more extensive debrief can take place where youth are asked to extrapolate the experience beyond the sport setting (e.g., give examples of behaviors that frustrate them in life), share stories of how these behaviors were handled in the past, and consider more appropriate ways of managing situations moving forward. Each lesson concludes with a teambuilding activity designed to end on a positive and interactive note, while simultaneously reintegrating the daily SEL competency.

Unique Program Features
Exposure to College

Over time, it was observed that some youth in Project FLEX became curious about college life and career options postincarceration. Unfortunately, many youth are unfamiliar with the college and career exploration process and most have never set foot on a college campus. Research on the impact of college readiness for high school youth from disadvantaged backgrounds has found that students who attend campus visits and receive information about college support services are one and a half times more likely to attend college (Tillery, 2013). With this in mind and following the example set by other programs that integrate college and career readiness into sport-based programs (Walsh et al., 2012), Project FLEX expanded to include two subsequent offerings.

The FLEX CREW (College Readiness Exposure Week) invites selected leaders from Project FLEX to participate in a comprehensive leadership retreat while experiencing a "day in the life" of a university student. This includes a full day, offsite visit that

Table 15.1 Project FLEX Lesson Structure

Time	Activity
10 minutes	Relationship/Team-building Activity
10 minutes	Awareness Talk (life skill introduced)
40 minutes	Responsibility-based Physical Activity Component
10 minutes	Debrief, Reflection, and Self-Assessment
10 minutes	Relationship/Team-building Activity

incorporates a campus tour, attendance in a college class, touring a residence hall, eating at a dining hall, and meeting with academic advisors, all while emphasizing life skills learned during Project FLEX (e.g., asking stakeholders questions, introducing themselves, interacting with peers). Prior to the retreat, youth participate in weekly orientation sessions practicing tangible skills that translate to their campus visit, with activities including role playing, case studies, discussions, and written prompts. Each session is centered around one main SEL competency (e.g., relationship skills, social awareness, decision making). For example, youth learn how to appropriately introduce themselves to different members of the community with whom they may interact (e.g., college student, professor, potential boss) and are coached on strategies that can optimize their time with academic advisors, peers, and college coaches.

Individual Training

Another need that arose from Project FLEX programming was a more deliberate effort to connect with youth outside of a large group setting with a space for goal setting and discussions about their futures. As a result, the "Swole Patrol" was established to offer one-on-one personal training and mentoring to selected Project FLEX youth. The participants are nominated by facility staff to enter into the program based on consistent attendance and a show of interest in advanced fitness. They then interview and self-select their own certified personal trainer from a pool of graduate student instructors to participate in biweekly, 90-minute fitness mentoring sessions for eight consecutive weeks with options to "renew" at the end of the process. Each session focuses on fitness, nutrition, mindfulness, and self-management, and emphasizes how exercise can be done in any setting, regardless of limited space or equipment. The overall objectives of Swole Patrol are to (a) provide youth with a caring adult figure in a one-on-one environment, (b) effectively manage stress and control impulses, (c) set and learn how to achieve fitness and nutritional goals, and (d) encourage youth to transfer skills postincarceration.

Swole Patrol sessions begin with an introductory conversation focused on developing rapport (see **Table 15.2**). During each meeting, trainers choose one core SEL competency to integrate into daily content (e.g., self-control) as well as introduce SMART goal setting and collaboratively come up with short-term

Table 15.2 Swole Patrol Lesson Structure

Time	Activity
5 minutes	Relationship Building & Warm-up
10 minutes	Knowledge Session (SEL competency integration and nutrition)
60 minutes	High-Intensity Physical Activity Session
5 minutes	Cool Down and Debrief
10 minutes	Transfer of SEL Competency and Fitness Skills, Homework Assignment

and long-term goals related to fitness, nutrition, or other areas (e.g., career, behavior, family). Youth then engage in prolonged bouts of moderate to vigorous physical activity and high-intensity interval training, dedicated predominantly to full body movements (e.g., due to safety restrictions on equipment in a detention center). A five-minute cool down immediately follows, with discussions centered around feasibility of performing specific exercises on their own, in their personal rooms. Finally, every session concludes with another knowledge component addressing how youth can utilize what they learned within their everyday life both while incarcerated and upon release. Youth are then given homework assignments to complete before their next session, including exercising, tracking workouts on their own, and using stress-reducing techniques that they learned (see **Figure 15.2**).

Indications of Effectiveness

While Project FLEX is still a newly developed program, it provides a snapshot of how to use available resources at a local level (i.e., fitness and sports) to guide a small group of incarcerated young men. Specifically, the program demonstrates how a sport and SEL program can help individuals become resilient and empowered in the face of systematic inequities, racial marginalization, and previous poor choices. It also accesses a highly understudied population and provides insight into how to engage university students in a unique setting in a way that fosters mutual growth for both the students and the youth. Emerging research on the project is examining the fitness markers and psychosocial outcomes of individuals from the program as well as attempting to capture longitudinal results of program members who are now released from incarceration.

Project Flex

Name: _____

Stress Management Worksheet

Directions: For the next week, record any stressful events that happen to you and fill out each column.

Stressful event: What happened?	Rate your stress level 1 (totally relaxed) to 10 (most stressed possible)	What were 3 things you felt in your body or mind in this moment?	How did you react/ handle it?
		1. 2. 3.	
		1. 2. 3.	
		1. 2. 3.	
		1. 2. 3.	

Project FLEX: Positive Self-Talk

Self-talk is supportive statements said to oneself (either out loud or in head) during tough times

Verbal examples – *try saying*	Mental examples – *try thinking*
• I got this	• I can handle this
• I'm good	• Everything will be ok
• It doesn't phase me	• I am cool and calm always

<u>My positive self-talk statements</u>

Verbal:

Mental:

<u>My goals related to managing stress</u>

For this week:

For the future:

Figure 15.2 Sample mental skills worksheets from Project FLEX.

She Hits Hard: An Afterschool Boxing Program for Middle School Girls

So, my mom made me try out boxing club, and I actually really liked it. When I started, I was in seventh grade, and now I feel like I have a second family. But even though people come in and out of the boxing club, I still feel safe here. (Lily, 2-year club member)

Overarching Societal Issue

Participation in sport has been widely linked with a variety of positive self-perceptions, including increased confidence, self-efficacy, and motivation (Magyar & Feltz, 2003). While these represent important outcomes for youth from any background, these qualities are particularly important for girls, who have been underrepresented and marginalized in the sports world due to the longstanding history of inequity issues (Coakley & Pike, 2001). Developing confidence and a healthy body image are critically important for young girls, as adolescence represents a time when females with unhealthy body perceptions are vulnerable to developing eating disorders or engaging in antisocial behavior (Leon et al., 1993). Fortunately, youth sport programs have been identified as one protective factor for overcoming negative self-perceptions, especially when those sport programs are aligned with opportunities for developing life skills (Holt et al., 2017).

Program Setting

"She Hits Hard," is an afterschool body empowerment boxing program for middle school girls. It was designed by a faculty member from Northern Illinois University in collaboration with the middle school's administration (e.g., principal, school counselor) to support the schoolwide initiative of student engagement, which is measured through students' participation in afterschool activities. Specifically, school administrators described a subgroup of female students who were identified as not having strong connections to the school community or their peers. Evidence of this included lack of participation in extracurricular clubs or sports and frequent visits to the school counselor to address issues of bullying and confidence, often stemming from issues associated with body dissatisfaction. Prior research has

demonstrated the impact of sport participation on building body satisfaction (Dorak, 2011), increasing global self-confidence (Stein et al., 2007), and providing a positive psychosocial setting for students (Holt & Neely, 2011). Therefore, the purpose of the program was to meet the needs of these female students through a novel sport program (i.e., boxing) focused on ways to increase their overall confidence and body satisfaction. Specifically, the "She Hits Hard" program operated with the primary aims of (a) building meaningful relationships and (b) teaching students important life skills that they can apply outside of the program (e.g., leadership, self-awareness, etc.). The instructional approach is guided by the TPSR model (Hellison, 2011). Within this framework, specific strategies help promote life-skill development, including fostering social interaction, leadership, and giving choices (Escarti et al., 2015; see Chapter 7 in this book for further reading).

Program Development

"She Hits Hard" meets weekly at a middle school in a university town in the Midwest. The demographics of the school are 40% Caucasian, 26% Hispanic, 25% African American, 5% Asian, and 4% two or more races, which is reflected in the program demographics. Female students in 6th, 7th, and 8th grades are invited to the club based on referrals from their school counselor. This was done to limit the program size, as smaller groups can be more conducive to establishing relational bonds and fostering a psychologically safe space (Rhodes et al., 2002). Over time, students in the program were given permission to invite other female friends to join in order to empower students as leaders and decision makers.

The program meets twice per week for 75 minutes in a minimally used classroom in the school where program equipment such as boxing gloves, boxing instructor pads, a boxing bag and stand, and art supplies are stored. The daily attendance has historically been inconsistent, ranging from five to 15 students. Over time, the disparity in attendance was due to students joining additional afterschool clubs or sports that met on one of the same days as the boxing program. While this made program planning difficult at times, it was deemed a success because students felt confident and connected enough to be involved in other school programs.

The coaches in the program are university graduate students studying kinesiology and physical education and were trained by the faculty supervisor and graduate student program director to implement the TPSR model. During this process, they completed background readings from Hellison's (2011) book accompanied by weekly written reflections that included a self-assessment of their teaching performance, along with questions they have about the teaching model. This process served the dual purpose of promoting interactions between the program directors and graduate students and providing a rich data source for research. Program coaches also participated in postprogram debrief discussions on TPSR integration and challenges associated with program students. Additionally, monthly planning meetings are scheduled for the coaches to plan curriculum and assign leadership for each session. In addition to TPSR model training, the coaches also received basic boxing training from the faculty director, who had been practicing the sport for five years. While none of the graduate students had prior boxing experience, basic knowledge and training was deemed sufficient since the primary emphasis of the program was to develop confidence rather than boxing competency.

Program Structure

In the "She Hits Hard" program, lessons follow a structured format based on recommendations for TPSR model integration (Hellison, 2011; see **Table 15.3** for a summary of components and time

spent on each component). Aspects of the session format are integrated with SEL skills as prior research has demonstrated the combination of these frameworks as effective within sport-based afterschool programs (Gordon et al., 2016). Sessions begin with relational time where coaches connect with individual students about life outside of the program while the students eat a school-provided snack in the cafeteria. The time in the cafeteria provides students with the opportunity to practice social awareness and relationship skills as they interact with coaches and their peers. Then, after transitioning to the classroom, the program commences with an awareness talk where the coaches present the life skill focus for the day (e.g., "communication"). The students discuss the definition of the word with a specific emphasis on what it looks like and sounds like in the program setting. For example, when discussing communication, students communicate that evidence of good communication includes making eye contact, not talking when others are talking, and using respectful language. The awareness talk encourages students to practice self-awareness, set their focus for the program session, and practice relationship skills as they listen to the input of their peers.

Following the awareness talk, the session transitions into the physical activity portion, which comprises the bulk of program time. This includes

Table 15.3 "She Hits Hard" Program Components with Connections to SEL Competencies

Lesson Component	Description	Primary SEL Competencies	Time
Relational Time	Students and coaches build meaningful relationships through one-on-one conversations before the program begins.	Social awareness; Relationship skills	10–15 mins.
Awareness Talk	A brief coach-led talk occurs to define the daily life skill focus and prompt students to consider how to implement it during the program.	Self-awareness; Relationship skills	5–10 mins.
Physical Activity	The fitness activities and sport skill development are integrated with the life skill practice.	Self-management; Social awareness; Responsible decision making	25–35 mins.
Body Image Activity	Intentional body image activities occur to provide students with reflection time and body empowerment strategies.	Self-awareness; Social awareness	5–15 mins.
Group Meeting	The group gathers for a discussion to evaluate the effectiveness of the program session in terms of the sport skill and the life skill.	Self-awareness; Social awareness	5–10 mins.
Reflection Time	Coaches help students to engage in reflection on how to transfer the life skill to other settings like school, home, and the community.	Responsible decision making	5–10 mins.

a structured warmup, strength exercises, and boxing skill development, all of which are intentionally integrated with the life skill practice. For example, one student may serve as the fitness leader to a select warmup stretches and exercises. She then demonstrates, leads, and provides feedback to the larger group. In addition to the physical component in the warmup, there is a dual focus of encouraging teammates, which is important for communication skills and encourages social awareness.

During boxing skill development, one coach reviews the technique for "stance," punches "one" (jab) and "two" (cross) and defensive moves "bob" and "parry" while students follow along. In order to further foster relationship skills and responsible decision making, program coaches assign students coaches to call out combinations of the moves and then provide feedback using the "sandwich" approach. This includes a positive point (i.e., a specific area of strength demonstrated), a negative point (i.e., an area to improve), and a second positive point (i.e., general motivational encouragement). Students with consistent attendance who show progress are invited to learn more advanced moves (e.g., additional punches, defensive blocks) and those students who have inconsistent attendance or progress slower can spend extra time with coaches reviewing the initial moves. The ability to address different skill progressions and offer tailored feedback is possible based on the program's small coach-to-student ratio (i.e., one to three). Finally, the physical activity portion of the lesson often concludes with a game such as "Rousey Says," modeled after the "Simon Says" imitation game,

with reference to the well-known, successful female boxer, Ronda Rousey. In this game, students are given an opportunity to practice self-management and responsible decision making by self-identifying when they make a mistake to transition from a participant to encourager role.

Unique Program Feature: Body Image Application

After the physical activity portion, the lesson focuses on a brief activity targeting specific body image discussions. While this is distinct from the boxing content, best practices dictate that body supportive content is consistent throughout the entirety of the program, such as through asking the students about a healthy snack they prepared during relational time and reminding students during the introduction of new boxing content that their bodies are capable and strong. Aside from integration throughout the lesson, coaches devote program-specific time to facilitating a discussion of students' body questions or incorporating different problem-solving activities or role-playing scenarios (see examples of body image activities in Fuerniss & Jacobs, 2020). As an example, a "Body Image Question Box" was adopted to invite anonymous student questions about their bodies, sexuality, gender, or any topic that promoted exploration in a respectful way. Example questions might include: "how can we take toxic people out of our lives without feeling guilty about it?," and "how come some days we like our bodies and other days we think we are fat?" (See **Figure 15.3**). Early on in

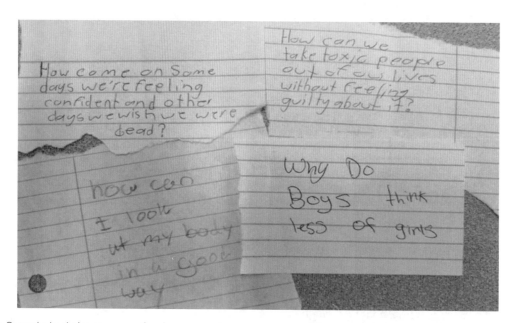

Figure 15.3 Sample body image question box prompts.

the creation of the program, these conversations were primarily facilitated by coaches and students tended to be reserved in contributing. Over time; however, the group dynamics shifted to being more comfortable and open, with students running the discussion by soliciting input or leading role-play scenarios.

The program concludes with a brief group meeting conducted by the coaches to evaluate the session with regards to the life skill focus. Similar to the body image activity, this component of the program allows for self- and social awareness. The coaches utilize the following prompt, "think about your communication during the peer coaching activity today. Rate how well you did by giving a thumbs up, a thumbs sideways, or a thumbs down. Is anyone willing to explain your rating?" The coaches also seek input from students about the boxing and body image activities and what they might like to focus on in upcoming program meetings. The final group meeting time during the program focuses on transfer and how the life skill practiced that day can be applied to other settings. While a best practice of any sport-based youth development program, discussing transfer in a way that prompts action beyond discussion can be challenging. In an effort to promote accountability and immediacy, the transfer discussions are framed as "homework" (e.g., "how can you use today's life skill before the next program meeting?"). During the transfer talk, the coaches ask for examples of what it could look like to practice or think about the life skill at school with friends and at home with family. During the next session, they are given an opportunity to report what they did.

Often, students were prompted to reflect on how using the assigned life skill could relate to their body perceptions such as through practicing affirmations, making healthy choices, or supporting fellow classmates when being made fun of. In these discussions, it was also acknowledged that sometimes successful application of a life skills does not equate to an observable behavior. For example, thinking, "I am thankful for how my body functions to meet my daily needs" would be strong evidence of transfer from the program despite the fact that it does not include a behavior change. The program takes an active role in encouraging changed mindsets and perceptions, common challenges for those who struggle with body image issues, as important progress in the path toward self-acceptance and empowerment.

Indications of Effectiveness

Sport programs subscribing to a youth development framework have a longstanding history of using the power of sport to foster important personal life skills

(e.g., self-awareness, responsible decision making, etc.). Less often, programs incorporate a social justice approach aimed at addressing the needs of a specific population with the intention to impact the greater social environment. The "She Hits Hard" program, while small in reach, exemplifies how a program can be tailored to timely (i.e., adolescence), targeted (i.e., females) equity issues (i.e., sport participation, body image). Additionally, the program offers a novel way to foster body empowerment both through teaching the nontraditional youth sport of boxing and through incorporating body image exercises (e.g., the question box, role playing, affirmations; Fuerniss & Jacobs, 2020).

The Illinois Physical Activity and Life Skills Wellness Program

The camp encourages healthy eating and physical activity, and it shows physical activity not as a punishment, like it's something fun. It's something fun that you should be involved in and be engaged in. (Camp counselor)

Overarching Societal Issue

Income inequality and access to out-of-school enrichment programs for children are not new issues. Children from low socioeconomic backgrounds have been shown to be at risk for numerous health (e.g., obesity, malnourishment) and academic (e.g., reading and math skills) losses, especially during the summer months when school resources are not available (Campbell et al., 2019; Von Hippel et al., 2007). Among the many existing potential solutions to address these equity issues, one strategy is to consider how OST programs can be intentionally designed and delivered to not only include children from impoverished backgrounds but also to further meet their needs in a customized and holistic setting.

Program Setting

The Sport Fitness Program (SFP), one of the longest-running summer youth sport programs in the United States, has served children in the greater Champaign, IL, area through a multiweek summer sport experience since the 1950s. Past SFP goals have focused on developing fitness behaviors, learning motor skills, and fostering an appreciation for lifetime physical activity participation. However, two structural components have contributed to declining enrollments over the past decade: (a) a fee-based structure and (b) the narrow focus on sport and physical activity programming. The fee-based structure has limited the SFP's reach to those who can afford it, resulting in a relatively homogeneous population that limits access to youth who live in local neighborhoods affected by poverty. Beyond the restrictions of the fee-based structure, the SFP's emphasis on sports prevented it from having wider appeal to the community, particularly those families interested in other forms of summer learning.

It became clear that, while physical activity was an important component of the design, it would need to expand to include other foci to meet youth needs. This has included overhauling program aims to expand beyond physical activity to incorporate an SEL component along with nutrition education and academic enrichment. With such changes made to its original structure and mission, the SFP has since rebranded itself as the Illinois Physical Activity and Life Skills (iPALS) Wellness Program. The Program now features a specific framework targeted toward helping youth develop healthy lifestyles, exhibit positive prosocial behavior, and prepare for their academic and professional futures. The explicit SEL framework used for the Program is adapted from the Teaching Personal and Social Responsibility (TPSR; Hellison, 2011) model and will be described following a broader framing of the Program.

Program Development

The primary objectives of the iPALS Wellness Program are to improve physical activity, academic, and SEL outcomes for students; provide opportunities for enrichment activities in a safe and healthy environment; and strengthen connections between the University and community to better serve and support students facing the greatest challenges over the summer months. The Program serves approximately 150 elementary school-aged youth (i.e., first through fifth graders) who are divided into groups of approximately 25 based on their grade level. The majority of youth come from underrepresented ethnic minority backgrounds and are eligible for the school free and reduced lunch (FRL) program. Running throughout the month of June, iPALS is scheduled from 8:00 AM to 3:00 PM Monday through Friday for four weeks. One of the three targeted elementary schools that has the largest enrollment of youth from communities affected by poverty in the area houses the Program. The school provides indoor gymnasium and classroom space, sufficient outdoor space in the grass and empty parking lots, is adjacent to a large community

park, and is walking distance from a branch of the local community library.

The Program receives broad scope oversight and guidance from two faculty members within the Department of Kinesiology and Community Health at the University of Illinois at Urbana-Champaign who serve in an advisory capacity. A program director carries out the day-to-day operations of iPALS and implements the aforementioned conceptual framework. A staff of approximately 15 university students from relevant programs and majors (e.g., physical education, elementary education, nutrition) are hired to serve in the following capacities: (a) group leaders who oversee and travel with one group of children throughout the duration of iPALS, (b) station activity leaders who plan and deliver developmentally appropriate instruction related to physical activity, academics, and nutrition; and (c) conflict management staff who work proactively to build a positive culture throughout iPALS in ways that align with the TPSR model while providing support when behavioral problems arise.

Program Structure

The daily schedule includes breakfast and a morning meeting followed by six activity stations of 45 minutes each, with a lunch break after the third rotation. Throughout the course of the day, each group participates in four physical activity stations, one academic enrichment station, and one nutrition education station. At the end of the day, each group leader hosts an afternoon meeting to reflect on the day and plan for the next day. This rotation schedule is used throughout the duration of iPALS, with the focus of academic enrichment and nutrition education lessons changing every few days and physical activities after 10 days to allow for a progression of skill development over time (see **Figure 15.4**).

Unique Program Feature: Holistic Full-Day Curriculum

Reflective of larger movements related to SEL in education (Collaborative for Academic, Social, and Emotional Learning [CASEL], 2019), SEL is a central component of the iPALS Wellness Program design with the focus on helping students understand the importance of and develop life skills related to taking responsibility for themselves and their surrounding communities. This is particularly important among youth from communities affected by poverty who often have outside-of-school experiences (e.g., violence, food insecurity) that influence their behavior in school. The TPSR model guides the implementation

	SESSION 1: WEEKS 1 AND 2 (6/1/20 – 6/12/20) ROTATION SCHEDULE 2020 iPALS Wellness Program					
7:45 to 8:00 AM	PARTICIPANT DROP-OFF AND CHECK-IN (BUS CIRCLE/SCHOOL FOYER)					
8:00 to 8:15AM	BREAKFAST/GROUP AND TPSR TIME (AT FIRST STATION LOCATION)					
8:25 to 9:10 AM	TEAM	ACTIVITY	LOCATION	TEAM	ACTIVITY	LOCATION
	1	Badminton	Gym 1	4	Tchoukball	Gym 2
	2	Nutrition	Classroom 1	5	Academic Enrich.	Classroom 2
	3	Lacrosse	Field 1	6	Cooperative Games	Field 2
9:20 to 10:05 AM	TEAM	ACTIVITY	LOCATION	TEAM	ACTIVITY	LOCATION
	1	Nutrition	Classroom 1	4	Academic Enrich.	Classroom 2
	2	Lacrosse	Field 1	5	Cooperative Games	Field 2
	3	Tchoukball	Gym 2	6	Badminton	Gym 1
10:15 to 11:00AM	TEAM	ACTIVITY	LOCATION	TEAM	ACTIVITY	LOCATION
	1	Lacrosse	Field 1	4	Cooperative Games	Field 2
	2	Tchoukball	Gym 2	5	Badminton	Gym 1
	3	Academic Enrich.	Classroom 2	6	Nutrition	Classroom 1
11:15 to 11:55AM	LUNCH (CAFETERIA)					
12:05 to 12:50 PM	TEAM	ACTIVITY	LOCATION	TEAM	ACTIVITY	LOCATION
	1	Tchoukball	Gym 2	4	Badminton	Gym 1
	2	Academic Enrich.	Classroom 2	5	Nutrition	Classroom 1
	3	Cooperative Games	Field 2	6	Lacrosse	Field 1
1:00 to 1:45 PM	TEAM	ACTIVITY	LOCATION	TEAM	ACTIVITY	LOCATION
	1	Academic Enrich.	Classroom 2	4	Nutrition	Classroom 1
	2	Cooperative Games	Field 2	5	Lacrosse	Field 1
	3	Badminton	Gym 1	6	Tchoukball	Gym 2
1:55 to 2:40 PM	TEAM	ACTIVITY	LOCATION	TEAM	ACTIVITY	LOCATION
	1	Cooperative Games	Field 2	4	Lacrosse	Field 1
	2	Badminton	Gym 1	5	Tchoukball	Gym 2
	3	Nutrition	Classroom 1	6	Academic Enrich.	Classroom 2
2:45 to 3:00 PM	GROUP AND TPSR TIME (AT LAST STATION LOCATION)					
3:00 to 3:15 PM	PARTICIPANT CHECK-OUT AND PICK-UP (SCHOOL FOYER/BUS CIRCLE)					

Figure 15.4 iPALS example rotating schedule.

of SEL in the Program by providing the structural framework for Program organization (Hellison, 2011). First, iPALS adopts the TPSR interpretation of SEL goals focused on (a) respect, (b) participation and effort, (c) self-direction, (d) leadership and helping others, and (e) transfer. Each of the four weeks of the Program is framed by one of these different goals. In the later weeks of the Program, intentional connections are also made back to previous week's goals to reinforce and scaffold learning. The transfer goal is addressed on a daily basis and in relation to the identified goal for the week.

In addition to the goals, TPSR offers a flexible guiding structure that can be adapted to meet contextual demands inherent to a particular program and includes (a) relationship time, (b) an awareness talk, (c) lesson focus, (d) group time, and (e) reflection time (Hellison, 2011). Throughout iPALS, these lesson components are incorporated into the daily schedule through (a) morning activities and framing through SEL, (b) content stations with SEL integration, and (c) afternoon activities and debriefing discussions. Influenced by the restorative youth sport model (Hemphill et al., 2018), relationship development and conflict management focuses on creating positive culture and addresses conflict with the goal of group restitution.

Morning Activities and Framing Through SEL

The first TPSR lesson component, relationship time is intentionally built into the Program as youth arrive in the morning, pick up their breakfast, find their group and greet their group leader, and speak informally. The second component of TPSR, the awareness talk, follows as the group leader identifies and introduces a focus goal based on the week (e.g., effort in week one), and children discuss their understanding of the goal. Having one goal selected for the entire week allows the group leader to scaffold learning and encourage deeper thinking about each goal, aligned behaviors, and applications in other settings (i.e., transfer).

Content Stations with SEL Integration

The third phase of the TPSR lesson format is the lesson focus (Hellison, 2011), as the youth learn the content associated with each station while also addressing the responsibility focus of the day. At iPALS, each station activity leader (i.e., physical activity, academic enrichment, nutrition education) intentionally weaves the goal for the week into their lesson content. This continuous reinforcement provides youth with regular opportunities to practice developing social and emotional skills linked to the TPSR model (e.g., positive decision making, relationship skills, etc.). Station leaders work intentionally to weave discussions of transfer into their lesson content with a particular emphasis during the introduction and conclusion of each station. Similar to SEL, the station content foci on physical activity, academic enrichment, and nutrition education were selected to reflect the interests and needs of community stakeholders in the greater Champaign, IL, area. This is particularly the case in reference to the underrepresented youth from communities affected by poverty who are the target population for the Program.

With reference to *physical activity*, children from communities affected by poverty are at a higher risk for developing sedentary lifestyles that contribute to the incidence of preventable health-related diseases. Accordingly, iPALS provides youth with more than the recommended 60 minutes of physical activity each day, while equipping them with the knowledge, skills, and dispositions that support independent, leisure-time physical activity. Physical activity is provided in a developmentally appropriate manner focused on (a) enjoyment for movement, (b) basic motor competencies required for future physical activity, (c) an understanding of the importance of movement for health and well-being, and (d) encouragement to continue physical activity outside of the Program. A diverse selection of physical activities and sports are intentionally selected, with examples including badminton, cooperative games, dance, lacrosse, and tchoukball. As physical activity content is introduced, station leaders intentionally link content to the TPSR goal for the week in order to reinforce connections to SEL. During a dance unit in week three of the Program (e.g., self-direction), for example, the instructor may provide youth with a list of dance steps accompanied by visual images or video clips so they can self-teach the dance and then demonstrate competence by performing for classmates.

The *academic enrichment* component of iPALS acknowledges that children from communities affected by poverty often experience opportunity and achievement gaps that are compounded through disengagement with academic learning over the summer. Sometimes referred to as the "summer slide," this phenomenon relates to youth from more affluent families remaining engaged in learning over the summer while their peers from communities affected by poverty disengage to a greater degree (Smith, 2012). To reduce this gap, academic lessons are designed to help students integrate more seamlessly back into the next school year. Content consists of a combination of academic subject areas (e.g., language arts, mathematics, science) and is aligned with grade-level benchmarks. For example, in a language arts lesson, children learned about and wrote their own haiku poem, then shared with their group over hot chocolate during a "Poetry Café." Meanwhile, a science lesson provided information on chemical reactions, illustrated through each child making their own slime. Similar to the physical activity component, SEL competencies are addressed alongside academic content, as would be the case in a science lesson where students learn the importance of taking personal responsibility for maintenance of laboratory equipment used during a session. Discussions of transfer during this session tend to focus on the application of SEL competencies for the upcoming school year.

Engaging students in *nutrition education* helps to address the fact that youth from communities affected by poverty may experience food insecurity over the summer as they do not have the same consistent access to meals through the FRL lunch program. Accordingly, healthy meals are provided for breakfast and lunch on all days of the Program. The nutrition education component also acknowledges that families from communities affected by poverty may not have the same knowledge of or access to healthy foods by helping students understand and make healthy food choices (Casey et al., 2001). Specific nutrition lessons are based on the United States Department of Agriculture (USDA) MyPlate curriculum for children and provide hands-on experiences in basic food preparation and cooking skills to promote the safe handling of food. As part of this process, students have the experience of preparing and then consuming their own food from raw ingredients. SEL integration is consistent throughout the nutrition education lessons as youth discuss the connections between nutrition activities and responsible decision making. For example, during a lesson related to food preparation, students could be engaged in a discussion about the importance of washing food before preparing it to avoid transmitting diseases or pesticides. Discussions of transfer focus on using SEL competencies in their home environments and as a way to positively influence their eating habits and those of other family members.

Afternoon Activities and Debriefing Discussions

At the end of each day, the groups have 15 minutes for an afternoon meeting and debriefing session. This presents space to integrate the final two TPSR lesson components related to group time and reflection time. Group leaders facilitate conversations related to the SEL competencies used throughout the day and youth are encouraged to provide examples of how they and others worked toward the specific TPSR goal. Transfer is specifically addressed during this part of the Program and students are encouraged to think holistically about how the SEL competencies they have discussed influence and can be used in other aspects of their lives. In addition to group discussion and reflection, youth are provided with time to think about their own learning and growth relative to SEL competencies (e.g., self-awareness, social awareness, relationship skills). Sometimes this reflection is private, but at other times, youth are invited to share their reflections verbally or by writing or drawing in a journal. At the end of the afternoon meeting, youth board the busses to head home and Program staff stay on site for a brief afternoon and debriefing meeting. In line with recommendations for teaching SEL and TPSR more specifically (Hellison, 2011), Program staff are encouraged to reflect and share thoughts about the Program, including ideas for improvement and change.

Relationship Building and Conflict Management

In addition to framing the Program scheduling through TPSR and intentionally integrating SEL competencies with station content, iPALS seeks to promote a positive, student-centered learning culture that facilitates the development of positive peer relationships while helping to reduce conflict. Staff training and development initiatives adopt Hellison's (2011) vision for a humanistic learning environment in which youth's needs and interests are prioritized and they are treated like contributing members of the Program community. Intentional efforts are made to develop student-centered learning contexts that allow youth to feel a sense of autonomy, competence, and relatedness (Deci & Ryan, 1985) and in which they are provided with voices and choices relative to the activities in which they participate (Hellison, 2011). Above all else, the goal is to help the children develop a sense of belonging and feelings of physical and emotional security in the Program. These features help to increase Program morale and community, thereby reducing instances of conflict.

While developing a positive culture may help to reduce interpersonal conflict, the children in the Program come from communities affected by poverty and many struggle with various factors (e.g., violence, fluid family structures). These experiences can be traumatic and lead the youth to act out in negative ways. Rather than taking a punitive approach to managing negative behavior, Program staff seek to adopt a stance influenced by the restorative youth sport model (Hemphill et al., 2018) that views conflict as a naturally occurring part of human interaction and a learning experience. Rather than merely punishing negative behavior, iPALS leaders seek to identify SEL-related learning experiences that can frame the conflict resolution process. For example, if a child becomes angry and kicks a basketball across the gymnasium, conversations focus on how the behavior negatively affected others and relates to the need for self-control when we become angry. When conflicts involve multiple students, such as teasing or physical altercations, conflict management strategies focus on teaching conflict resolution and communication skills as the youth seek to understand one another's perspective and develop feelings of closure and restitution. The results of conflict management processes typically involve consequences for all parties, which may include punishments such as being removed from the Program due to a serious offense. These consequences are, however, the result of a greater effort to restore feelings that may have been hurt as a result of the conflict.

Indications of Program Effectiveness

As mentioned previously, the iPALS program started in 2018 after overhauling one of the longest-standing summer programs in the country, which had been in existence since 1951. This program represents one way that established projects can rebrand to align with important social issues, such as increasing accessibility of summer engagement opportunities for impoverished families. In 2019, the iPALS program gained increased recognition through receiving a grant from the Illinois State Board of Education to expand their programming for more families from underserved backgrounds. Ongoing evaluation research seeks to examine the impact of the summer program on various youth outcomes including fitness markers, academic achievement, and psychosocial development.

Conclusion and Final Thoughts

The four case examples presented in this chapter are OST SEL programs that are unique in their own right but have a variety of common characteristics. To begin, each case example illustrates how programs can use sport and SEL principles to connect to larger social justice and equity issues. Like many SEL-based programs, program aims were designed around helping individuals develop skills to become positive leaders, good communicators, and effective decision makers. However, these programs extended beyond the typical focus on the individual personal behavior choices by cultivating critical awareness and creating change agents to address broader equity issues in society. Programs with this clear intention provide the opportunity to foster critical thinking and self-reflective skills that can lead youth to greater opportunities for promoting action and solutions within their communities.

Strategies for integrating SEL content with program context were also introduced in the cases. Many of these approaches arose out of the needs of the specific population or the priorities of the partner organizations. One important tactic when implementing an OST SEL program is to conduct a needs analysis with a variety of different stakeholders. This might look like connecting program aims with current organizational initiatives, such as the boxing program addressing the need for engaging disconnected girls from after-school programs, or the prison program providing an opportunity for the young men to engage in the only physical activity they can. Programs with an SEL focus should consider building a program with a partnership mindset, working with organizations to adopt consistent aims and language.

Finally, each of the programs presented demonstrated innovative and tangible ways to promote youth transferring SEL skills to their various life contexts. When devising program content, it is important to address all aspects of children's physical and social environments, especially when working with youth from marginalized communities.

For example, the iPALS Wellness program was situated in a community where educational attainment and success was a struggle. Therefore, the program evolved overtime to involve a more targeted approach to enhancing educational outcomes through fun, play-based activities. In the prison program, discussions of life skills were centered around how ideas could be applied at home and in their communities upon their release, with a special emphasis on how to build relationships with positive role models in their community.

When encouraging youth to develop and adopt behaviors outside the program setting, it is critical to be aware of environmental barriers that might impact their ability to make healthy choices. For example, it has previously been cited as a programmatic challenge that the culture of sports programs does not always reflect that of the outside world (Lee & Martinek, 2010). For instance, the norms of self-expression, reflection, support, and camaraderie that have been established in a sport program might be in stark contrast to the realities some youth face in their home lives. Therefore, program staff should work to integrate school, family, and community entities through promoting open lines of communication and creating shared expectations of the program. This intentionality might make it easier for youth to develop consistent behaviors and establish new habits when they have the support of multiple systems (Hurd & Deutsch, 2017).

Several recommendations for practice can be generalized from the previous case examples. Designing programs with a core relationship-building component is critical for building an effective program culture. Whether it was building relationships among peers or between coaches/adults and players, this represents an important aspect of sport-based youth programs. The soccer program demonstrated how teams can come together and encourage one another to be successful both in soccer and in life. Elements of the boxing and iPALS Wellness programs highlighted the importance of relational time through the TPSR model (Hellison, 2011) and illustrated how building rapport can be achieved during program downtime. Along with relationship-building, each program demonstrated how SEL competencies were integrated within sport and physical activity content (e.g., soccer, boxing, games), rather than presented separately. Practitioners should consider maximizing on the authentic experiences that arise through sport, look for opportunities to highlight teachable moments

such as winning, losing, conflict, achievements, etc. Finally, it appears that quality implementation of programming is strongly related to the makeup of the leadership team. The programs presented cases of coaches and teachers intentionally trained to address holistic student development, with an emphasis on understanding and meeting the needs of the unique program environments. Therefore, program leaders are encouraged to intentionally recruit quality staff through available resources (e.g., universities, social justice-related careers) and provide training tailored to the specific population with whom they will be working.

Altogether, although the program descriptions provided valuable insights on design and implementation, it is important to acknowledge some of the universal challenges inherent to the OST setting. For example, outside of schools, it can be difficult to measure program impact. According to Hurd and Deutsch (2017), since attendance isn't mandatory in OST programs, that can make it challenging to accurately assess if youth are receiving positive benefits, or if these benefits are due to the program or some other factor in their life. Since programs are voluntary, it may be that personal characteristics of the students are what led them to the program in the first place. This can be especially challenging when staff turns over frequently, as is often a struggle in many community-based programs that rely on volunteers. While not explicitly stated, another challenge to be mindful of is how sport-based SEL programs may end up replicating the very social issues they seek to remedy. These types of programs may require access to transportation, equipment, and, in some cases, additional participation costs, which may alienate or restrict youth from certain backgrounds to participate. Program staff should be mindful of how to recruit students from a variety of backgrounds, develop programs to be as inclusive and accommodating, and when possible, provide support for families that have financial restrictions.

Sport programs adopting an SEL approach not only have a unique opportunity to foster psychosocial skills that youth can use in their own lives but also address broader social inequities that both challenge norms and contribute to community change initiatives. Program leaders interested in fostering SEL are encouraged to consider greater impacts beyond "the individual" and expand program missions to explore ways to develop youth empowerment and capacity for change.

Questions for Discussion

1. What are some advantages to running SEL programs outside of the traditional school day setting? What are some challenges in this context?

2. In what ways can OST SEL programs consider expanding program aims to address social justice and equity related issues?

3. Identify three commonalities related to program structure, design, or curriculum across the four program cases presented.

4. Design an OST sport program for a particular population that connects with a specific social-justice issue. Then, describe how you would integrate each of the five SEL competencies into program content.

References

Anderson-Butcher, D., Iachini, A., Riley, A., Wade-Mdivanian, R., Davis, J., & Amorose, A. J. (2013). Exploring the impact of a summer sport-based youth development program. *Evaluation and Program Planning, 37*, 64–69.

Annie E. Casey Foundation (2013). Youth Incarceration in the United States Infographic. Retrieved on 12 May 2020 at https://nicic.gov/youth-incarceration-united-states-infographic

Basch, C. E. (2011). Healthier students are better learners: A missing link in school reforms to close the achievement gap. *Journal of School Health, 81*(10), 593–598.

"Beyond Sport" Vision and Mission. Retrieved on 13 May 2020 at http://www.beyondsport.org/

Campbell, L. O., Sutter, C. C., & Lambie, G. W. (2019). An investigation of the summer learning effect on fourth grade students' reading scores. *Reading Psychology, 40*(5), 465–490.

"CASEL" Collaborative for Academic, Social, and Emotional Learning (2019). *SEL History.* Retrieved on 10 April 2020 at https://casel.org/history/

Casey, P. H., Szeto, K., Lensing, S., Bogle, M., & Weber, J. (2001). Children in food-insufficient, low-income families: Prevalence, health, and nutrition status. *Archives of Pediatrics & Adolescent Medicine, 155*(4), 508–514.

Coakley, J., & Pike, E. (2001). *Sports in Society.* Boston: McGraw-Hill.

Collaborative for Academic, Social, and Emotional Learning. (2019). *What is social and emotional learning?* Retrieved on 15 April 2020 at https://casel.org/what-is-sel/

Deci, E. L., & Ryan, R. M. (1985). *Intrinsic motivation and self-determination in human behavior.* Plenum.

Dorak, F. (2011). Self-esteem and body image of Turkish adolescent girls. *Social Behavior and Personality, 39*(4), 553–561.

Durlak, J. A., Weissberg, R. P., & Pachan, M. (2010). A meta-analysis of after-school programs that seek to promote personal and social skills in children and adolescents. *American Journal of Community Psychology, 45*(3–4), 294–309.

Dyck, C. B. (2011). Football and post-war reintegration: Exploring the role of sport in DDR processes in Sierra Leone. *Third World Quarterly, 32*(3), 395–415.

Elbertson, N. A., Brackett, M. A., & Weissberg, R. P. (2010). School-based social and emotional learning (SEL) programming: Current perspectives. In *Second International Handbook of Educational Change* (pp. 1017–1032). Springer, Dordrecht.

Escartí, A., Wright, P. M., Pascual, C., & Gutiérrez, M. (2015). Tool for Assessing Responsibility-based Education (TARE) 2.0: Instrument revisions, inter-rater reliability, and correlations between observed teaching strategies and student behaviors. *Universal Journal of Psychology, 3*(2), 55–63.

Fuerniss, K., & Jacobs, J. M. (2020). We are strong: Strategies for fostering body empowerment in a boxing program for middle school girls. *Journal of Sport Psychology in Action, 11*(1), 45–56.

Gordon, B., Jacobs, J. M., & Wright, P. M. (2016). Social and emotional learning through a teaching personal and social responsibility based after-school program for disengaged middle-school boys. *Journal of Teaching in Physical Education, 35*(4), 358–369.

Haycock, K. (2001). Closing the achievement gap. *Educational Leadership, 58*(6), 6–11.

Hellison, D. (2011). *Teaching personal and social responsibility through physical activity* (3rd ed.). Champaign, IL: Human Kinetics.

Hemphill, M. A., Janke, E. M., Gordon, B., & Farrar, H. (2018). Restorative youth sports: An applied model for resolving conflicts and building positive relationships. *Journal of Youth Development, 13*(3), 76–96. https://doi.org/10.5195/JYD.2018.603

Holt, N. L., & Neely, K. C. (2011). Positive youth development through sport: A review. *Revista iberoamericana de psicología del ejercicio y el deporte, 6*(2), 299–316.

Holt, N. L., Neely, K. C., Slater, L. G., Camiré, M., Côté, J., Fraser-Thomas, J., MacDonald, D., Strachan, L., & Tamminen, K. A. (2017). A grounded theory of positive youth development through sport based on results from a qualitative meta-study. *International Review of Sport and Exercise Psychology, 10*(1), 1–49.

Hurd, N., & Deutsch, N. (2017). SEL-focused after-school programs. *The Future of Children, 27*(1), 95–115.

Jacobs, J. M., Castañeda, A., & Castañeda, R. (2016). Sport-based youth and community development: Beyond the ball in Chicago. *Journal of Physical Education, Recreation & Dance, 87*(5), 18–22.

Jacobs, J. M., Lawson, M., Ivy, V. N., & Richards, K. A. R. (2017). Enhancing the transfer of life skills from sport-based youth development programs to school, family, and community settings. *Journal of Amateur Sport, 3*(3), 20–43.

Jacobs, J. M., Wahl-Alexander, Z., & Mack, T. (2019). Strategies for gaining access to deliver sport programs with highly vulnerable youth. *Journal of Youth Development, 14*(1), 155–164.

Jacobs, J. M., & Wright, P. M. (2017). Transfer of life skills in sport-based youth development programs: A conceptual framework bridging learning to application. *Quest, 70*(1), 81–99.

Jenson, J. M., Potter, C. C., & Howard, M. O. (2001). American juvenile justice: Recent trends and issues in youth offending. *Social Policy & Administration, 35*(1), 48–68.

Karcher, M. J. (2008). The cross-age mentoring program: A developmental intervention for promoting students' connectedness across grade levels. *Professional School Counseling, 12*(2), 2156759X0801200208.

Kidd, B. (2008). A new social movement: Sport for development and peace. *Sport in Society, 11*(4), 370–380.

Ladson-Billings, G. (2006). From the achievement gap to the education debt: Understanding achievement in U.S. schools. *Educational Researcher, 35*(7), 3–12.

Leach, M. T., & Williams, S. A. (2007). The impact of the academic achievement gap on the African American family: A social inequality perspective. *Journal of Human Behavior in the Social Environment, 15*(2–3), 39–59.

Leon, G. R., Fulkerson, J. A., Perry, C. L., & Cudeck, R. (1993). Personality and behavioral vulnerabilities associated with risk status for eating disorders in adolescent girls. *Journal of Abnormal Psychology, 102*(3), 438–444.

Lindsey, I., & Banda, D. (2011). Sport and the fight against HIV/AIDS in Zambia: A 'partnership approach'? *International Review for the Sociology of Sport, 46*(1), 90–107.

Magyar, T. M., & Feltz, D. L. (2003). The influence of dispositional and situational tendencies on adolescent girls' sport confidence sources. *Psychology of Sport and Exercise, 4*(2), 175–190.

Martinek, T., & Lee, O. (2012). From community gyms to classrooms: A framework for values-transfer in schools. *Journal of Physical Education, Recreation & Dance, 83*(1), 33–51.

Meek, R. (2013). *Sport in prison: Exploring the role of physical activity in correctional settings*. New York: Routledge.

Peterson-Badali, M., & Koegl, C. J. (2002). Juveniles' experiences of incarceration: The role of correctional staff in peer violence. *Journal of Criminal Justice, 30*(1), 41–49.

Prison Policy Initiative (2020). *"United States Profile."* Retrieved on 13 May 2020 at https://www.prisonpolicy.org/profiles/US.html

Rhodes, J. E. (2004). The critical ingredient: Caring youth-staff relationships in after-school settings. *New Directions for Youth Development, 2004*(101), 145–161.

Rhodes, J. E., Grossman, J. B., & Roffman, J. (2002). The rhetoric and reality of youth mentoring. *New Directions for Youth Development, 2002*(93), 9–20.

Shank, M. J. (2006). Teacher storytelling: A means for creating and learning within a collaborative space. *Teaching and Teacher Education, 22*(6), 711–721.

Smith, L. (2012). Slowing the summer slide. *Educational Leadership, 69*(4), 60–63.

Stein, C., Fisher, L., Berkey, C., & Colditz, G. (2007). Adolescent physical activity and perceived competence: Does change in activity level impact self-perception? *Journal of Adolescent Health, 40*(5), 462.e1–462.e8.

Taylor, R. D., Oberle, E., Durlak, J. A., & Weissberg, R. P. (2017). Promoting positive youth development through school-based social and emotional learning interventions: A meta-analysis of follow-up effects. *Child Development, 88*(4), 1156–1171.

Tillery, C. Y. (2013). *The Summative Impact of College Access Interventions: A Program Evaluation of GEAR UP North Carolina*. Appalachian State University.

Von Hippel, P. T., Powell, B., Downey, D. B., & Rowland, N. J. (2007). The effect of school on overweight in childhood: Gain in body mass index during the school year and during summer vacation. *American Journal of Public Health, 97*(4), 696–702.

Wahl-Alexander, Z., Jacobs, J. M., & Mack, T. (2019). Lessons learned from the field: Teaching in high-risk physical education environments. *Journal of Physical Education, Recreation & Dance, 90*(5), 8–15.

Walsh, D., Veri, M. J., & Scobie, D. (2012). Impact of the Kinesiology Career Club: A TPSR-base possible futures program for youth in underserved communities. *Ágora para la Educación Fisica y el Deporte, 14*(2), 213–229.

Whitley, M. A., Hayden, L. A., & Gould, D. (2016). Growing up in the Kayamandi Township: II. Sport as a setting for the development and transfer of desirable competencies. *International Journal of Sport and Exercise Psychology, 14*(4), 305–322.

Willis, O. (2000). Sport and development: The significance of Mathare Youth Sports Association. *Canadian Journal of Development Studies, 21*(3), 825–849.

Wright, P. M., Howell, S., Jacobs, J., & McLoughlin, G. (2020). Implementation and perceived benefits of an after-school soccer program designed to promote social and emotional learning. *Journal of Amateur Sport, 6*(1), 125–145.

Wright, P. M., Howell, S., Jacobs, J. M., Yavitz, J., Mangino, M. (under review). Parent, coach, and player feedback on the implementation and short-term feedback of an urban community-based soccer program.

Wright, P. M., Jacobs, J. M., Ressler, J. D., & Jung, J. (2016). Teaching for transformative educational experience in a sport for development program. *Sport, Education and Society, 21*(4), 531–548.

Zins, J. E., Bloodworth, M. R., Weissberg, R. P., & Walberg, H. J. (2007). The scientific base linking social and emotional learning to school success. *Journal of Educational and Psychological Consultation, 17*(2–3), 191–210.

SECTION 5

Concluding Thoughts

CHAPTER 16

Concluding Thoughts and Future Directions for Social and Emotional Learning in Physical Education

Paul M. Wright
K. Andrew R. Richards

CHAPTER SUMMARY

This concluding chapter reflects back on the major themes raised throughout the book. It considers the relevance of social and emotional learning (SEL) in physical education in light of current challenges, such as the COVID-19 pandemic, and civil unrest in relation to social justice issues, such as systemic racism. Key insights, common themes, and lingering questions are identified from each of the book sections. Overarching lessons learned and implications for research, policy, and practice that transcend the sections are then discussed.

Concluding Thoughts and Future Directions for Social and Emotional Learning in Physical Education

We began this book project with the hope of providing a much-needed resource to support the integration of social and emotional learning (SEL) with physical education in school and community settings. The project has been a rich experience for us, prompting reflection and challenging us to think more deeply about the importance of bringing these two content areas together in intentional ways. Much of our own learning in the process has resulted from working with the incredible group of authors who have contributed to the various chapters. They have exceeded our expectations in delivering thoughtful, compelling, and practical messages that explore various aspects of SEL in PE. These contributors have also identified relevant resources for future reading and posed questions for further reflection. We feel, however, that it is important to take advantage of the opportunity to consider the contents of this book as a whole. While much of the text is complementary, some of the chapters offer contrasting view points and we note some gaps in what the book addresses as a whole. Our aim in this final chapter is to take a broader view and offer some final reflections on the insights, themes, questions raised, as well as next steps for this line of work.

We must note that, in the time we spent preparing this book for publication, our world has faced substantial, unanticipated, and unprecedented challenges. In terms of public health, the COVID-19 pandemic has had an impact the likes of which have not been seen in a century. In the midst of this global public health crisis, the need for social distancing has impacted every sector of society, including education. The delivery of physical education and sport programs in schools and communities was brought to a standstill and/or moved into virtual spaces through synchronous or asynchronous instruction. At a time when access to traditional educational and physical activity spaces has been limited, the social and emotional needs of youth have never been higher. We applaud teachers, coaches, and youth workers who have been committed and innovative in navigating this challenging time. They have been creative in staying connected virtually and providing digital resources. When possible, they have come together physically with modifications to space, equipment, and activities to accommodate social distancing restrictions. These changes have highlighted for many that the social and emotional aspects of physical education and sport are the most sorely missed when they are reduced or taken away.

In addition to the COVID-19 pandemic, during our work on this project, social unrest in the United States reached a boiling point after the killing of George Floyd in May of 2020. Mr. Floyd's death as a result of excessive violence on the part of police was tragic, yet all too familiar. This unjustified killing of a person of color was one of several that have sparked outrage, protest, and civil unrest that have continued into the fall of 2020 as we worked to finalize this book for submission. Making political commentary is beyond our scope, but the challenges of our time only accentuate the importance of addressing social, emotional, and mental health for all of our citizens. Fear, isolation, depression, anxiety, frustration, and trauma stemming from systemic racism and other forms of inequity challenge the health and well-being of many children and adolescents. Addressing their social, emotional, and mental health are more vital now than ever.

Teachers, coaches, and youth workers have the opportunity to create safe spaces, promote respect for diversity, teach problem-solving and conflict resolution skills, and engage students in meaningful conversations about what it means to not only take responsibility for one's self but also for others in our society. We hope it has been made clear in this book that all of these topics can be addressed in meaningful ways through physical activity programming. Therefore, we share the concepts and strategies contained in this book not as an academic exercise, but with the sincere hope that they be put to use in schools and communities to help youth endure the challenges they cannot avoid. Physical activity programs that integrate SEL can help students feel engaged, empowered, and confident as learners. Such experiences can not only help them thrive as individuals but also to become leaders and change agents who contribute positively to the world. From our perspective, these are among the highest aims of education and we humbly applaud the caring teachers, coaches, and youth workers who make it part of their mission.

Key Themes across Book Sections

Approaching the structure of the book, we created four sections that organized the content around common themes. The first section provided an introduction to and background on SEL in education generally as well as specifically in physical education curriculum, instruction, and assessment. The second section addressed pedagogical models common in physical education that align well with SEL. Third, SEL was examined in specialized programs and contexts including preschool education, adapted PE, and whole school applications. Finally, section four examined case examples of SEL in physical activity spaces and with marginalized communities. In the paragraphs that follow, we review the chapters within each section and highlight key takeaways messages. Connections across chapters and sections are also made as we attempt to illustrate the interconnectedness of topics that frame our understanding of SEL in physical education and physical activity contexts.

Section One: What Is SEL?

In the first section of this book, we introduced the notion of SEL and its intersection with physical education curriculum, teaching practice, and assessment strategies. In Chapter 1, we framed SEL and positioned it within the context of the U.S. educational system and policy shifts. For example, moving out of the *No Child Left Behind* era and into the *Every Student Succeed Act* era, which creates more space for a holistic focus that includes nonacademic skills and learning outcomes. The Collaborative for Academic, Social and Emotional Learning (CASEL; 2019) was offered as one of several leading frameworks. Whether educators adopt that particular model or another related one, we strongly encourage approaches that can define and articulate intended SEL learning objectives and outcomes. Without this, it is challenging to plan for, deliver, and assess SEL instruction in an effective and coordinated manner. In Chapter 9, Dyson and colleagues highlighted the SEL framework promoted by Jones and Boufford (2012) in relation to cooperative learning, and Martinek and Hemphill make use of positive youth development (Coakley, 2016) as a framework in Chapter 13. These examples illustrate the fundamental point that if one has not articulated what SEL skills and competencies they intend to foster, it is unlikely that they can be explicit and focused in their delivery. Readers are encouraged to think critically and review a range of frameworks and strategies that can inform their practice.

In Chapter 2, we illustrated the strong connections between SEL and the physical-education curriculum. While these natural linkages have long existed and great potential exists to integrate SEL into the physical-education curriculum, there is a need to be deliberate in planning the curriculum to explicitly integrate SEL objectives and align them with national, state, and local standards. Without this intentionality, SEL outcomes may not be met as it cannot be expected that sport, PE, and physical activity settings will naturally build character and prosocial behavior. Furthermore, while SEL can be integrated seamlessly within the K–12 curriculum, the concepts and strategies promoted throughout this book can also be adapted and implemented in other physical activity settings (e.g., afterschool, summer camp, juvenile detention, preschool).

As we point out in Chapter 3, implementing SEL effectively may require a reexamination of typical teaching practice. For example, rather than viewing management tasks as a necessary precursor to effective instruction, we encourage teachers to involve students in these tasks as authentic opportunities to take on responsible roles and apply SEL skills. For example, procedures for distributing and collecting equipment can be empowering opportunities for youth to practice leadership and helping others when designed accordingly. Similarly, we hope teachers will reflect on their approach to behavior management and make sure it is integrated with a more comprehensive approach to promoting SEL. This point is reinforced by Santos and Zittel in Chapter 10 as well as Wilson and colleagues in Chapter 11, both of whom question the applicability of teacher-centered strategies in favor of those that position behavior management as an educational opportunity and space for students to learn. Furthermore, a comprehensive approach to SEL involves the integration of explicit and empowering SEL teaching strategies. While the SAFE guidelines promoted by CASEL (2019) represent best practice for SEL in general, our model presented in Figure 3.1 is informed by practice and research in the field of PE. Another key feature of Chapter 3 was the use of the Spectrum of Teaching Styles (Mosston & Ashworth, 2017) to dissect teaching decisions and practices that can be integrated with or intentionally selected to promote SEL. Many of these styles re-emerge in subsequent chapters (e.g., reciprocal teaching is a prototypical style that appears in Chapter 4 as peer assessment, Chapter 7 as student leadership, and Chapter 9 in cooperative learning activities).

Our introductory section concluded with a discussion of assessment in Chapter 4, which we wrote with Jenna Starck. This chapter reviews best practices relative to assessment and illustrates how these can be readily integrated with teaching practice to provide authentic and performance-based learning experiences. Much work has been done in recent years to develop best practice in physical education assessment as scholars have called for a move toward assessment literacy (DinanThompson & Penney, 2015). Authentic and performance-based practices, for example, tend to integrate cognitive, affective, and psychomotor development. Therefore, as indicated in the chapter, it becomes quite natural to highlight and integrate SEL into assessment *for* learning experiences (Hay, 2006). In this chapter, we argue that SEL skills, like any skill worth teaching, should be assessed directly. Examples are provided of assessment activities and rubrics tailored to assess and give feedback on SEL development. Unfortunately, assessment of affective outcomes (e.g., enjoyment and motivation) and related personal and social skills have often been neglected in PE. While we refute many of the excuses and assumptions underlying this trend, we do acknowledge that there are legitimate questions about this topic. While much of the focus in this book has been on observable behaviors (e.g., cooperation with peers), SEL skills are often tied to affective responses (e.g., attitudes, values, and feelings). To what extent can/should teachers assess these? What influence do cultural norms and values have on aspects of the student's affective response (e.g., motivation)? Regarding behaviors, if the teacher has a different cultural perspective that frames their understanding of SEL, is it fair for them to impose that on their students (e.g., in certain cultures, eye contact is expected in conversations but in others, avoiding eye contact is a sign of respect)? As our understanding of SEL practice in physical education develops, we should be cognizant of such issues and committed to being inclusive, equitable, and culturally responsive. Across the book, these issues are addressed most directly in Chapter 14 by Ressler and his co-authors.

Section Two: What Are Some Ways to Teach SEL?

The second section of this book highlighted several pedagogical models aligned with SEL integration in PE. Each of these models is well-established in its own right and all have substantial research and practice to support them. We invited authors to write about models with strong and obvious connections to SEL (Dyson et al., 2020); however, we do admit that not all prominent models were represented. In the end, we hope that we have presented enough variety and depth to help readers extrapolate and find ways to be more intentional and explicit with SEL integration as they implement a wide range of practices. In the case of those models that we did highlight, in each chapter, authors described the model, reviewed supporting literature and research, and provided concrete examples of how it can be integrated with explicit SEL learning objectives.

In Chapter 5, Parker and colleagues highlighted the skill themes approach (Graham et al., 2020), which is especially relevant in elementary school settings and has been shown to integrate effectively with SEL (Richards et al., 2019). While many of the subsequent models are widely applied in secondary settings after students have already developed a wide range of movement skills, this approach targets students who are still learning the fundamental movement patterns needed to be skilled movers.

Likewise, this chapter sheds light on ways that early movement experiences and a developmental focus can help students acquire SEL skills. Similar to teaching physical skills, it recommended that SEL competencies be taught in a progression and using critical elements to define successful performance for students (Richards, Ivy, et al., 2019). The developmental focus in this chapter resonates with later chapters on preschool settings (Chapter 10) and adapted physical education (Chapter 11).

Sutherland and her co-authors describe the adventure-based learning (ABL) model (Sutherland & Legge, 2016) in Chapter 6. The challenges and adventure initiatives they present to prompt experiential learning are well-established in practice and have always had a key focus on SEL. This is reflected in the research on the model as well as the practical examples provided by the authors. For example, the focus on effective processing and debriefing that has always characterized ABL serves as a prime example of how to be focused and explicit in addressing self-awareness, social awareness, and relationship skills. Moreover, this is one of the models that has always emphasized the notion of relevance and transfer of such skills outside of the physical education or physical activity setting by emphasizing questions such as "what?" "so what?" and "now what?"

Walsh provides an overview of Hellison's (2011) Teaching Personal and Social Responsibility (TPSR) model in Chapter 7. Among the established models in this field, TPSR has perhaps the longest-standing history and most direct connection to SEL (Dyson et al., 2020). Decades before SEL was a major focus of the curriculum in physical education or general education, Hellison (1973, 1978) developed this model with the express aim of helping students develop personal and social skills that would help them in all aspects of life. Framed as personal and social responsibility goals, many of the skills promoted in this model map naturally to the leading SEL models (e.g., CASEL, 2019; Jones & Bouffard, 2012). Hellison's (1978; 2011) approach was to use physical activity as a vehicle to achieve these aims and; therefore, the strategies, structures, and concepts from the TPSR model lend themselves naturally to SEL integration. A major component of SEL-related instruction, from Hellison's (2011) point of view, is the notion of transfer, which is positioned as the ultimate goal of TPSR.

The influence of TPSR on the fields of physical education and physical activity is evident in many subsequent chapters featuring case examples of SEL in practice and draw from the model (e.g., Chapters 10, 11, 13, and 15). Because this model is so relevant to the development of SEL in physical education and is so well developed, many of the research and evaluation tools associated with this model are proving useful in promoting SEL more broadly. As elaborated in Chapter 4, tools such as the Personal and Social Responsibility Questionnaire (PSRQ; Li et al., 2008), which assesses self-reported personal and social skills, the Tools for Assessing Responsibility-based Education (TARE 2.0; Escarti et al., 2015), and the Transfer of Responsibility Questionnaire (Wright et al., 2019) have been developed with reference to TPSR but have utility in evaluating SEL across physical education and physical activity environments. These instruments and others that assess positive youth experiences (e.g., Youth Experience Survey 2.0; Hansen & Larson, 2005) may prove useful in evaluating SEL outcomes, supporting teacher development, and promoting best practice.

Sport Education (Siedentop et al., 2004) is another well-established and research model in the physical education field. As explained by Hastie and colleagues in Chapter 8, this model is student-centered and rife with opportunities to engage students in roles and activities that require and, therefore, develop SEL skills. The team affiliation and positive interdependence offered through Sport Education provide important avenues for personal and social development as students learn to rely on and support one another toward the pursuit of common goals. While many of the other models presented in this book downplay competition or offer alternatives to it, Sport Education embraces competition as a natural part of the sport experience that mirrors larger society and provides opportunities for learning. These authors illustrate that constructive competition, if managed appropriately, can provide rich opportunities for SEL development. As competitive sport is such a prominent feature in secondary physical education (Ferry & McCaughtry, 2013), teachers' ability to align sport units with SEL using this model offers widespread practical value.

The last model presented in this section is Cooperative Learning (Chapter 9; Dyson & Casey, 2012). This chapter, by Dyson and colleagues, is unique in that it takes a pedagogical model developed in general education and applies it to PE. Decades of research on both sides have shown that Cooperative Learning (CL) structures can support student learning of subject-specific content (e.g., mathematics, psychomotor skills) simultaneously with communication, cooperation, and problem-solving skills (Dyson et al., 2004). In fact, CL practice highlights the value of accentuating the social and active nature of learning. When students are put at the center of the learning activity and challenged to work together, opportunities for SEL abound, which makes this a particularly appealing model, particularly for physical educators who want to emphasize the social aspects of SEL.

Section Three: Where Else Can SEL Be Addressed?

Section three highlighted the integration of SEL in specialized physical activity programs and contexts beyond traditional PE. In Chapter 10, Santos and Zittel addressed the application of SEL content in preschool settings. In early childhood education, play and movement tend to be more integrated into the educational experience rather than being presented as separate topics or subjects (S. M. Kirk et al., 2014). Unfortunately, these aspects of overall development are sometimes assumed or neglected. Santos and Zittel highlight ways that movement and play can not only be integrated but intentionally combined with SEL development. The examples and insights make it hard to imagine how physical or SEL development could be fully addressed during early childhood education without being taught together. As is stands;, however, physical education teacher education programs rarely provide preschool experiences and early childhood education programs rarely provide much development related to PE. Accordingly, while the opportunity to promote SEL through the physical in preschool settings, availability of best practices and professional development may be limiting factors. Challenging some of the points in Chapter 8 on Sport Education, Santos and Zittel critique the emphasis on efficiency and competition in our educational system and how those underlying values can act as barriers to the development of student- or child-centered learning. These values, they argue, contribute to larger numbers of students in classes and a greater emphasis is placed on achievement outcomes to define academic success.

In Chapter 11, Wilson and his co-authors address SEL in adapted PE. They discuss best practices in adapted PE, such as creating an inclusive environment, and highlight through vignettes the often neglected perspective of individuals with disabilities in the design and development of physical education learning experiences. While acknowledging that research and practice related to SEL in adapted physical education is limited, they highlight several strategies that may lead to greater integration in the future. The authors also highlight the ways in which learning environments that do not actively promote inclusion can promote negative experiences for all students in PE. Such environments can promote bullying behaviors, which may also be more likely in physical education given the physical nature of the content and required social interaction (O'Connor & Graber, 2014). While this is the only place that bullying is addressed in the book, we recommend that readers seek to develop all programs in ways that promote positive social interaction and support students' feelings of physical and emotional safety. Helping students practice and learn SEL competencies has much to offer in this respect and is an important consideration for research and practice.

In Chapter 12, the final chapter in the third section of the book, Webster introduces the notion of whole school approaches to physical activity that capitalize upon but are not limited to PE. Such approaches have become a major focus in the field as a lever for increasing physical activity and wellness throughout the school environment. However, as Webster makes clear, this approach and the promotion of SEL are not mutually exclusive. In fact, SEL integration is likely to foster more positive and motivating physical activity experiences for students whether they take place in PE, intramural sport, extramural sport, afterschool programs, or in other school-adjacent settings. In fact, a commitment to SEL integration could serve as a theme that adds coherence across physical activity experiences in a school. Taking a whole school approach also fosters greater alignment between SEL in physical education and physical activity opportunities and those promoted at the school level. As discussed in Chapter 2, many schools have whole school initiatives that promote SEL and character development (e.g., Covey, 1989). Syncing up with these initiatives and whole-school approaches can help demonstrate greater legitimacy for physical education (Richards & Gordon, 2017).

Section Four: What Does SEL Look Like in Practice?

The final major section in the book provides case examples of SEL promotion and integration through physical activity in marginalized communities. As noted previously, we recognize that social inequities and injustices are woven into the fabric of our society. Countless students are negatively impacted by such patterns not through their own actions, but

because of their gender, the language they speak, the color of their skin, or the zip code in which they were born. Even the actions of children and youth are often shaped by the choices, resources, support, and examples provided by adults and caregivers around whom they grew up. All children and youth, regardless of the social circumstances of the conditions into which they were born, have the right to be included, respected, and educated.

In the fields of physical education and sport, many programs have been designed specifically to meet the needs of underserved youth from marginalized communities. While we applaud much of the good work done with this intent, it is important to note that such programs must be careful not to fall into the trap of promoting whiteness (i.e., the cultural values, norms, and expectations of the historically privileged Caucasian community in the United States; Azzarito & Simon, 2017). Too often, well-meaning White people enter communities affected by poverty and impose their own cultural frame on the communities they are seeking to serve. Programs should; therefore, be careful not to take the stance of trying to "help" or "save" those less fortunate. This type of deficit-based thinking and the "savior complex" that often comes with it are not the foundation for truly empowering and culturally responsive pedagogy (Shiver et al., 2020).

In Chapter 13, Martinek and Hemphill shine a light on the field of positive youth development (Coakley, 2016) and the associated subfield of sport-based youth development (Holt, 2008). They highlight several real-world programs that have been designed and implemented using various program models to promote positive development and teach life skills through sport, focusing primarily on youth from marginalized backgrounds. The featured programs take place outside of the regular school curriculum but often build off strong school-community partnerships. In this way, they highlight the importance of reaching youth where they are and reinforcing positive messages and life lessons across programs. While the term SEL may be more commonly associated with the formal school curriculum, the descriptions of these cases make a clear case that personal and social development can be addressed in out-of-school spaces as well, including those built around physical activity.

In Chapter 14, Jim Ressler and his co-authors tackle issues of social justice and equity head on. They present a framework that can help educators and youth workers think about doing work that is culturally responsive. They make it clear that social justice is not just a goal but a process. To provide a concrete framework for the process of social justice education, they present Hackman's (2005) five components, which include (a) content mastery, (b) tools for critical analysis, (c) tools for social change, (d) tools for personal reflection, and (e) multicultural group dynamics. Through a series of case examples, they illustrate different ways these can be addressed by practitioners and at different school levels. Topics raised in this chapter are extremely relevant in light of current social tensions around race, gender, and LGBTQ+ status, to name a few. We take a firm stance in noting that, for SEL integration to be meaningful and authentic, students who are typically marginalized or disconnected must be made to feel supported and included. At the same time, their peers have the right and need to be educated about issues such as implicit bias so they can be more informed about, better friends with, and stronger advocates for one another. When SEL integration is used to shine a light on such issues and further critical reflection, it exemplifies the empowering approach described in Chapter 3.

Finally, in Chapter 15, Jacobs and colleagues note promising practices outside of school settings focused on populations of students who are negatively impacted by some form of social inequity. The case examples illustrate how programs can be designed intentionally not only to serve youth from marginalized backgrounds, but to explicitly address pertinent social issues such as gender equity, poverty, the academic achievement gap, and the overrepresentation of young men of color in the juvenile justice system. These case examples, as several from the other chapters, give glimpses of ways to highlight SEL not only for content mastery and individual development but also as a lever to promote cultural awareness, critical thinking, and positive social change. If students are to go forth and make a positive difference in their communities and larger social spheres, they must be equipped with the understanding and skills needed to navigate and communicate through difference. That development can be advanced through physical activity environments that foster SEL.

Lessons Learned and Implications for the Future

In this final section, we identify some broad topics that we feel merit further exploration in relation to SEL but did not fit neatly into any one single section of the book. These are organized under the following categories: professional socialization, advocacy, and research.

Professional Socialization

Drawing upon the occupational socialization theory (Richards et al., 2019; Templin & Schempp, 1989), recent studies (e.g., Richards & Gordon, 2017; Wright et al., in press) indicate that teachers' practices related to SEL are influenced by their own formative experiences with sport and physical education (i.e., acculturation) and their practical experiences in schools and on the job (i.e., organizational socialization). Unfortunately, it appears that practicing teachers report limited knowledge or skill coming from their university-based teacher education programs (i.e., professional socialization). This may reflect a history of neglecting the affective domain in such programs and in the broader field of physical education (Wright et al., in press). It may also reflect the relatively recent intensification of the focus on SEL in the field along with a great deal of ambiguity about what SEL is and how it should be implemented (Dyson et al., 2020; Wright et al., in press; Wright et al., 2020).

As explained in our framing of this book, we believe resources and practical strategies are needed to support the integration of SEL in PE. While it has been alluded to in several chapters, we reiterate here just how important teacher education programming is if we want to see widespread change in practice. If teacher education programs are not intentional, explicit, and clear in the ways they introduce SEL integration, we are likely to see an expansion of "buzzwords" and "lip service" without significant improvement in the substance of practice. Recent research has explored how preservice teachers learn to use the TPSR model to integrate and promote SEL (Richards et al., 2020; Shiver et al., 2020). This work provides important initial insight into the challenges that preservice teachers face as they grapple with incongruence between their ideas of physical education (i.e., sport-based) and expectations around SEL integration. Students need time and support from instructors as they navigate changes in their personal understandings, or subjective theories (Grotjahn, 1991), of PE, which highlights the importance of protracted and in-depth field experiences (Richards et al., 2020).

Advocacy

Related to our last point about professional socialization, we acknowledge that another topic not fully addressed in this book has been advocacy. Based on the recent literature, topics at professional conferences, and Society of Health and Physical Educators (SHAPE) America's endorsement of this very book, there is no doubt that SEL in physical education has become a "hot topic." However, for full, serious, and sustained implementation to occur, stakeholders must be willing to advocate for its importance (Jacobs & Wright, 2014). In the introductory section, we discussed how outdated and narrow views of what constitutes physical education might obscure the place of SEL. For example, if stakeholders assume the primary (or sole) purpose of physical education is to keep students physically active, they might view management tasks and assessment as cutting into their activity time. However, if these same stakeholders understand the full breadth of the national standards and the policy support for SEL, they can readily justify a more balanced focus. At different times, teachers, administrators, parents, and even students need to be challenged on their assumptions about the aims of physical education and the place of SEL within it. While SHAPE America is promoting this topic and providing resources, these ideas and materials need to be championed in schools, community, and in the policy sector. Unfortunately, CASEL (2019) has not devoted much attention to the promotion of SEL in PE. They, however, do provide a very effective model for how to promote SEL generally in terms of policy and practice (see www.casel.org).

Research

The final topic we address in this section is research. Throughout this book, we have based our analysis and recommendations upon what is known about SEL in the academic literature. In each chapter on models-based practice, for example, the relevant research literature was presented and discussed in relation to the use of the model. While there is no shortage of physical education and sport pedagogy research connecting to SEL, the body of research making direct and explicit use of SEL as a framework and/or to define outcomes is in a nascent stage (Dyson et al., 2020). Based on the clear relevance and growing interest, we encourage researchers to continue building a comprehensive line of research on SEL in physical education that can inform theory, practice, teacher education, and advocacy efforts. As Dyson and his colleagues pointed out in Chapter 9, much of the literature on SEL in general education is quantitative. We encourage researchers in this field to use a range of methods so that context, implementation, and multiple perspectives (e.g., teachers and

students) are represented. Recent studies, for example, have demonstrated the effectiveness of combining systematic observation with qualitative methods (i.e., interviews and focus groups) to describe and interpret SEL implementation in physical education settings (Richards & Gordon, 2017; Wright et al., in press; Wright & Irwin, 2018), particularly as a way of documenting the fidelity of SEL integration. Especially as researchers and practitioners strive to promote empowerment and transfer of learning with SEL, we encourage them to make use of existing frameworks and methods that have proven useful in related work on sport-based youth development and physical education (Jacobs & Wright, 2018; Wright et al., 2019).

Conclusions and Final Thoughts

As we conclude this chapter and book, we return to the broad focus we used to open Chapter 1. We believe the highest aims of education involve providing students with knowledge, skills, and experiences that will help them succeed in life and contribute to society. In the history of American schools, PE, as well as the values, attitudes, and skills associated with SEL, have often been neglected or marginalized because they have been perceived to be nonacademic. However, current educational trends indicate that there is more appreciation for the role physical education and SEL play in a well-rounded education. While this is true of both content areas, we are especially energized by the synergies that are possible when they are brought together. Due to their dynamic, emotional, and interactive nature, PE, play, and sport provide ideal contexts to develop SEL. Intentional SEL integration enables physical educators to effectively address all aspects of their subject matter (i.e., cognitive, affective, and psychomotor learning), often simultaneously. Beyond this, effective SEL integration can impart lessons that transfer to other settings for the good of individuals and communities.

In terms of policy, research, and practice, there is a strong foundation for integrating SEL with physical education in school and community settings. However, to realize the full potential of this synergy, continued effort is required on all of these fronts as well as through teacher education and advocacy. Regarding advocacy, all stakeholders have a role to play in advocating for the unique role physical activity programming can and should play in promoting SEL. The more students, parents, community partners, educational administrators, and researchers understand and promote this topic, the faster best practice will be developed and implemented. The importance of integrating SEL with physical education was clear to us when we began this book project. These beliefs have grown stronger as we have learned from and been inspired by our contributing authors. Concurrently, the importance and urgency of this topic has been underscored by the challenges of the COVID-19 pandemic and unrest stemming from social injustice and inequity in the United States. In short, we find ourselves in a moment where the opportunity AND the need to promote SEL have reached a crescendo. We must take up this challenge and capitalize on this moment. This book celebrates the solid foundation and superb work done thus far to leverage the power of physical education to promote SEL. Hopefully, it will also serve as a resource that supports innovation and the continued development of best practice by you and others.

Questions for Discussion

1. What elements of the SEL and the associated curricular, instructional, and assessment implications discussed throughout the book resonated most with you?
2. Which of the pedagogical models discussed in this book do you find the most helpful for integrating SEL? Explain your answer, citing evidence from the book.
3. What role do we have as physical educators in addressing social injustices in our schools and communities? How does SEL fit into this process?
4. Provide at least two takeaway messages from the book that you plan to use in your own instruction in the future.
5. After working through the entire book, how do you view the role of SEL in the physical education curriculum? Explain.

References

Azzarito, L., & Simon, M. (2017). Interrogating Whiteness in physical education teacher education: Preparing prospective teachers to become educators of culturally relevant pedagogy and social justice. In *Teacher socialization in physical education: New perspectives* (pp. 176–193). Routledge.

Coakley, J. (2016). Positive youth development through sport: Myths, beliefs, and realities. In N. Holt (Ed.), *Positive Youth Development Though Sport* (pp. 21–33). Routledge.

Collaborative for Academic, Social, and Emotional Learning. (2019). *What is social and emotional learning?* https://casel.org/what-is-sel/

Covey, S. R. (1989). *The 7 habits of highly effective people: Powerful lessons in personal change.* Freer Press.

DinanThompson, M., & Penney, D. (2015). Assessment literacy in primary physical education. *European Physical Education Review, 21*(4), 485–503.

Dyson, B., & Casey, A. (Eds.). (2012). *Cooperative learning in physical education.* Taylor & Francis.

Dyson, B., Griffin, L. L., & Hastie, P. (2004). Sport education, tactical games, and cooperative learning: Theoretical and pedagogical considerations. *Quest, 56*(2), 226–240.

Dyson, B., Howley, D., & Wright, P. M. (2021). A scoping review critically examining research connecting social and emotional learning with three model-based practices in physical education: Have we been doing this all along? *European Physical Education Review, 27*(1), 76–95. https://doi.org/10.1177/1356336X20923710

Escarti, A., Wright, P. M., Pascual, C., & Gutiérrez, M. (2015). Tool for Assessing Responsibility-based Education (TARE) 2.0: Instrument revisions, inter-rater reliability, and correlations between observed teaching strategies and student behaviors. *Universal Journal of Psychology, 3*(2), 55–63.

Ferry, M., & McCaughtry, N. (2013). Secondary physical educators and sport content: A love affair. *Journal of Teaching in Physical Education, 32*(4), 375–393.

Graham, G., Holt/Hale, S. A., Parker, M., Hall, T., & Patton, K. (2020). *Children moving: A reflective approach to teaching physicla education* (10th ed.). McGraw Hill.

Grotjahn, R. (1991). The research programme subjective theories: A new approach in second language research. *Studies in Second Language Acquisition, 13*(2), 187–214.

Hackman, H. W. (2005). Five essential components for social justice education. *Equity and Excellence in Education, 38*(2), 103–109. https://doi.org/10.1080/10665680590935034

Hansen, D. M., & Larson, R. (2005). *The youth experience survey 2.0: Instrument revisions and validity testing.* The University of Illinois.

Hay, P. (2006). Assessment for learning in physical education. In D. Kirk, D. Macdonald, & M. O'Sullivan (Eds.), *The Handbook of Physical Education* (pp. 326–346). Sage Publications.

Hellison, D. (1973). *Humanistic physical education.* Prentice-Hall.

Hellison, D. (1978). *Beyond balls and bats: Alienated (and other) youth in the gym.* American Alliance for Health, Physical Education, and Recreation.Washington, D.C.

Hellison, Don. (2011). *Teaching personal and social responsibility through physical activity* (3rd ed.). Human Kinetics.

Holt, N. L. (Ed.). (2008). *Positive youth development through sport.* Routledge.

Jacobs, J., & Wright, P. (2014). Social and emotional learning policies and physical education. *Strategies, 27*(6), 42–44.

Jacobs, J. M., & Wright, P. M. (2018). Transfer of life skills in sport-based youth development programs: A conceptual framework bridging learning to application. *Quest, 70*(1), 81–99.

Jones, S. M., & Bouffard, S. M. (2012). Social and emotional learning in schools: From programs to strategies and commentaries. *School Policy Report, 26*(4), 1–33.

Kirk, S. M., Vizcarra, C. R., Looney, E. C., & Kirk, E. P. (2014). Using Physical activity to teach academic content: A study of the effects on literacy in head start preschoolers. *Early Childhood Education Journal, 42*(3), 181–189. https://doi.org/10.1007/s10643-013-0596-3

Li, W., Wright, P. M., Rukavina, P. B., & Pickering, M. (2008). Measuring students' perceptions of personal and social responsibility and the relationship to intrinsic motivation in urban physical education. *Journal of Teaching in Physical Education, 27*(2), 167–178.

Mosston, M., & Ashworth, S. (2017). *Teaching physical education* (1st online). Spectrum of Teaching Styles. https://spectrumofteachingstyles.org/

O'Connor, J. A., & Graber, K. C. (2014). Sixth-grade physical education: An acculturation of bullying and fear. *Research Quarterly for Exercise and Sport, 85*(3), 398–408. https://doi.org/10.1080/02701367.2014.930403

Richards, K. A. R., & Gordon, B. (2017). Socialisation and learning to teach using the teaching personal and social responsibility approach. *Asia-Pacific Journal of Health, Sport and Physical Education, 8*(1), 19–38.

Richards, K. A. R., Ivy, V. N., Wright, P. M., & Jerris, E. (2019). Combining the skill themes approach with teaching personal and social responsibility to teach social and emotional learning in elementary physical education. *Journal of Physical Education, Recreation & Dance, 90*(3), 35–44.

Richards, K. A. R., Jacobs, J. M., Ivy, V. N., & Lawson, M. A. (2020). Preservice teachers perspectives and experiences teaching personal and social responsibility. *Physical Education & Sport Pedagogy, 25*(2), 188–200.

Richards, K. A. R., Pennington, C. G., & Sinelnikov, O. A. (2018). Teacher socialization in physical education: A scoping review of literature. *Kinesiology Review, 8*(2), 86–99.

Shiver, V. N., Richards, K. A. R., & Hemphill, M. A. (2020). Preservice teachers' learning to implement culturally relevant physical education with the teaching personal and social responsibility model. *Physical Education & Sport Pedagogy, 25*(3), 303–315.

Siedentop, D., Hastie, P. A., & van der Mars, H. (2004). *Complete guide to sport education*. Human Kinetics.

Sutherland, S., & Legge, M. (2016). The possibilities of "doing" outdoor and/or adventure education in physical education/teacher education. *Journal of Teaching in Physical Education, 35*(4), 299–312.

Templin, T. J., & Schempp, P. G. (1989). *Socialization into physical education: Learning to teach* (T. J. Templin & P. G. Schempp, Eds.). Benchmark Press.

Wright, P. M., Gordon, B., & Gray, S. (2020). Social and emotional learning in the physical education curriculum. In *Oxford Research Encyclopedia of Education*. Oxford University Press. doi: https://doi.org/10.1093/acrefore/9780190264093.013.1061

Wright, P. M., Gray, S. & Richards, K. A. R. (2020). Understanding the interpretation and implementation of social and emotional learning in physical education. *The Curriculum Journal*. Online first at http://dx.doi.org/10.1002/curj.85

Wright, P. M., & Irwin, C. (2018). Using systematic observation to assess teacher effectiveness in promoting personally and socially responsible behavior in physical education. *Measurement in Physical Education and Exercise Science, 22*(3), 250–262.

Wright, P. M., Richards, K. A. R., Jacobs, J. M., & Hemphill, M. A. (2019). Measuring perceived transfer of responsibility learning from physical education: Initial validation of the Transfer of Responsibility Questionnaire. *Journal of Teaching in Physical Education, 38*(4), 316–327. https://doi.org/10.1123/jtpe.2018-0246

Index

Note: Page numbers followed by *f* or *t* represent figures or tables respectively.